PIGEONS AND DOVES
OF THE WORLD

PUBLICATION No. 663

STANDARD BOOK NUMBER 56500663 0

PIGEONS AND DOVES
OF THE WORLD

SECOND EDITION

By DEREK GOODWIN

Illustrations by
ROBERT GILLMOR

BRITISH MUSEUM (NATURAL HISTORY)

Comstock Publishing Associates, a division of
Cornell University Press | Ithaca and London

First published 1977 by Cornell University Press.

International Standard Book Number 0–8014–1100–9

Library of Congress Catalog Card Number 76–55484

Printed and bound in Great Britain

CONTENTS

COLOURED PLATES

INTRODUCTION

THE pigeons are a large and successful family of birds. Typically they are arboreal, living, or at least nesting, roosting and taking cover in trees. They have, however, produced cliff-dwelling and ground-dwelling forms also. Indeed, from the tropics to the cold temperate regions there are few areas that are not inhabited by some kind of pigeon. The beautiful and strikingly-patterned Snow Pigeon breeds and roosts about the snow-line of the high Tibetan mountain ranges; the sombre little Black-winged Dove dwells dangerously among the hook-leaved Puyas of the bleak Peruvian plateaux; the shining green, white-tailed Nicobar Pigeon wanders from islet to islet across tropic seas and in cities the world over, from Perth to Moscow, Feral Pigeons bring a welcome touch of life and beauty.

Pigeons vary in size from the Diamond Dove, the Mauve-spotted Dove, and the Dwarf Fruit Dove, all of which are about the size of a Skylark, to the crowned pigeons of New Guinea which are as large as a smallish hen Turkey. Some are among the most vividly coloured birds in the world, others clad in dull and cryptic plumage. Most often, however, they are tastefully dressed in soft pastel browns, greys and pinks set off with bright touches of colour. Their tails and wings may be long or short; some have crested heads or protuberant ceres. Yet, in spite of their variety, they are in many aspects of appearance and behaviour a rather homogeneous family. I think that of them all only the Tooth-billed Pigeon, the Pheasant Pigeon and the crowned pigeons might not be instantly recognised as pigeons by any ordinarily observant person who was familiar with the domesticated species. I have often noticed, when watching pigeons in public zoos, how even such exotic forms as the green pigeons or the Plumed Pigeon are at once recognised as being 'some kind of pigeon' by almost every lay visitor.

On anatomical grounds the pigeons are placed in the same order as the sandgrouse. They have, so far as I know, no behavioural features in which they resemble sandgrouse more than other birds, since it is now known that some other birds drink as pigeons do and sandgrouse have been said to. The movements of those sandgrouse which I have seen drinking have been intermediate between those of pigeons and the 'sip, lift and swallow' of most other birds. From what I have seen of sandgrouse, both in the wild and in captivity, I think that their anatomical similarities to pigeons may be due to convergent evolution. Like some pigeons sandgrouse are seed-eaters which fly long distances in fast sustained flight. But in all other aspects of their behaviour they give the impression of being nearer to the plovers.

It appears at first rather surprising that the pigeons are so successful. They are, as a general rule, highly edible, and therefore much sought after by predators, man included. They are relatively defence-less as although they can give a good cuff with the carpal joint of the wing most of them have no means of quickly doing serious damage. They can indeed (as has been too often pointed out in proof of their alleged aggressiveness) peck an unresisting enemy to death if they are shut up in a cage with it and given plenty of time, but such things do not occur in freedom. They lay small clutches of only one or two eggs from which hatch helpless nestlings. Their bills are rather weak (the few exceptions will be mentioned later) and, in general, they can only feed on seeds, fruits, or other objects small enough for them to swallow whole.

Pigeons appear, for example, to be 'out-pointed' in many ways by the parrots. The parrot family are also mostly seed and fruit eaters, also mostly strong fliers, also mainly arboreal with some ground-living forms, but with strong and formidable bills to deal with food or foe. However, pigeons not only thrive successfully in all parrot-inhabited lands but they also have a more extensive distribution than parrots. It is, therefore, evident that they are biologically at least the equals of parrots and most other birds. They appear to owe their success to being physically and psychologically 'tough' in spite of their delicate, fragile appearance and their timidity. In response to heavy predation on their eggs and nestlings most of them have developed short incubation and fledging periods. Their small broods are quickly reared if all goes well and, if all goes ill the eggs and young are, to a large extent, expendable. Provided food is plentiful the parents soon nest again when a brood of young or clutch of eggs are destroyed. Hence nest predation must be very heavy indeed before it has an appreciably adverse effect on any species. Also, although as individuals pigeons often given the impression of being rather stupid when compared to passerine birds or parrots, many species have proved remarkably adaptable. Compare, for example,

KEY TO PLATE 1

Some pigeons, drawn to scale, to show diversity within the family

(1) Pink-necked Green Pigeon, *Treron vernans*; (2) Many-coloured Fruit Dove, *Ptilinopus perousii*; (3) Marche's Fruit Dove, *Ptlinopus marchei;* (4) Cloven-feathered Dove, *Drepanoptila holosericea;* (5) Reinwardt's Long-tailed Pigeon, *Reinwardtoena reinwardtsi;* (6) White-bellied Plumed Pigeon, *Petrophassa plumifera;* (7) Mauve-spotted Ground Dove, *Uropelia campestris;* (8) Purple Quail Dove, *Geotrygon saphirina;* (9) Pheasant Pigeon, *Otidiphaps nobilis* (Aru Islands form); (10) White-collared Pigeon, *Columba albitorques*.

(Note: None of the very large crowned pigeons, *Goura*, is shown here because, apart from difficulties of scale, very many coloured plates and photographs of them exist elsewhere)

Plate 1

how the Wood Pigeon exploits human tolerance and charity in London with its fear of man in agricultural areas where it also thrives in spite of continual and intensive persecution.

The fact that pigeons – of both sexes – produce crop-milk to feed their young in the early stages has often been suggested as one reason for their success. It is argued that because of this they do not, like other seed-eaters, have to turn to an insect diet when seeking food for their young. This would be a more plausible argument if all other seed-eating birds fed their young on insects. In fact many species of passerine birds rear their young on seeds, usually half ripe ones, and seed-eating parrots regurgitate special food for their young. Moreover, pigeons appear to need a more generous diet when they are actually rearing young. The Rock Pigeon, and its domestic descendants often take quantities of small snails and other invertebrate life at this period. Many species of pigeons when breeding in captivity will, when they have young, eagerly take such foods as crumbled-up cheese or bread and milk, which they eat little of or entirely refuse at other times.

No doubt the production of crop-milk has been one factor in the success of the pigeons in their struggle for survival, but it is only one of several ways in which seed-eating birds have solved the problem of how to feed their young. Their quick reproductive rate, efficient escaping behaviour, hardiness and (bar

FIG. 1: Outline sketches, for size comparison, of (top left to bottom right) Wood Pigeon (Length 433 mm, wing from carpal joint 252 mm, tail 139 mm, tarsus 32 mm, bill from forehead feathers 24 mm); Feral Pigeon (l. 356 mm, w. 233 mm, t. 107 mm, tar. 39 mm, b. 18.5 mm.); Barbary Dove (l. 267 mm, w. 155 mm, t. 79 mm, tar. 22 mm, b. 16 mm,); Diamond Dove (l. 214 mm, w. 96.5 mm, t. 99 mm, tar. 17 mm, b. 13 mm).

accidents) longevity have, I think, contributed more to the success of the pigeons than their production of crop-milk.

The layman interested in these birds is often puzzled as to the distinction between pigeons and doves. Ornithologically there is none. The word 'pigeon' is of Norman-French, the word 'dove' of Anglo-Saxon origin. In common speech, in Britain, the word 'pigeon' is usually applied to the larger species such as the Wood Pigeon and 'dove' to the smaller ones such as the Barbary Dove. But the names given to the different species by ornithologists have not followed popular usage in this matter. The Stock Dove is a typical member of the group thought of as 'pigeon' by the layman and even the ancestor of our domestic pigeons, *the* pigeon in common parlance, is often, but in my opinion regrettably, called Rock *Dove* by ornithologists.

In this book I have tried to give facts, so far as known, about all living or recently extinct species of pigeons. The first part of the book discusses such matters as behaviour, coloration, etc., in reference to all pigeons. Such subjects are, therefore, only dealt with in descriptive terms under the species' headings. In the species section groups and species believed to be most closely related to each other are placed together so far as this is possible within the confines of linear arrangement. Some unrelated groups have had to be adjacent: the brown fruit doves following the Tooth-billed Pigeon, for example. For each group, such as the mountain pigeons or the turtle doves, its general characteristics and the relationships and status of the forms comprising it are discussed first. Under the heading for each species is given a description together with a black and white drawing (except where the bird closely resembles in shape and markings some other species that is illustrated) and a synopsis of what is known about it.

The drawings, by Robert Gillmor, are from sketches that he or I have done from living birds or from photographs, where this was possible. For many species, however, such material was not available and Mr Gillmor had to base his drawings on sketches I had done from museum specimens. Lists of measurements are apt to be misleading. I have, therefore, described size in reference to four well-known pigeons, the Wood Pigeon, Feral Pigeon, Barbary Dove and Diamond Dove. Outline sketches of these and the measurements of the individual specimens from which the sketches were made are given here. I have given field characters only for species that I have seen in the wild state or where I have been able to obtain information from observers who have done so.

The references given fall into two main categories which are not always mutually exclusive. There are those where part or all of the information given is derived from one or a few sources only or where some piece of information seems questionable as being possibly based on an isolated or misinterpreted observation. Secondly, with species for whom the information given is from personal observations or is widely disseminated in regional bird books or other literature, as is the case, for example, with the Collared Dove, then the references given are to papers that appear to me to be particularly worth the reader's while to consult. The context and remarks in the text should make clear the type of reference.

In the dendrograms to show relationships members of the same superspecies are connected by one dotted line; very distinct and geographically separated races of the same species are connected with two dotted lines. Parallel lines between the 'stem' of a species or group and its 'branch' indicate that its derivation is uncertain but is thought to be, most probably, from this branch.

The distribution maps indicate the approximate geographical areas inhabited by each species. It is, of course, to be understood that any species is only likely to be found in suitable habitat within the given range. For recently exterminated or reduced species their former ranges are given on the maps and the present situation, so far as known, in the text. I have used the word India in a geographical sense for the Indian subcontinent of (politically) India and Pakistan.

I have little doubt that, like others, I also have overlooked some published information that should have been included here. Also that not everyone will agree with my ideas on the relationship of species and groups or my interpretations of certain behaviour patterns. For the first I apologise unreservedly and shall be glad to have such omissions pointed out. As regards the second, I shall always welcome any comments or constructive criticisms and reply to them as best I can. It must, further, be emphasised that one purpose of this book is to indicate what is *not* known. I hope it will thereby encourage those of my readers who have the opportunity to study some little-known species. If they observe it carefully they will be sure to learn new and interesting facts about its behaviour or ecology. In so-doing they will not only contribute significantly to our knowledge of pigeons (provided they published their results) but they will I am sure, have got a great deal of enjoyment out of their pigeon-watching.

ACKNOWLEDGEMENTS

While preparing this book I have received much help and encouragement from my friends and colleagues in the Bird Room of the British Museum (Natural History) and from many ornithologists elsewhere who have given me valuable information. I am most grateful to them and also to the administrators of the Chapman Memorial Fund for a grant which enabled me to visit the American Museum of Natural History and to work on the pigeon collection there.

NOMENCLATURE: GENERA, SPECIES, SUB-SPECIES, VARIETIES AND BREEDS

Here I shall try to define such scientific and popular terms as are likely to concern the average person interested in pigeons. Also to define the sense in which certain terms, which might otherwise be slightly ambiguous, are used in this book. Those wishing to delve at all deeply into avian taxonomy will, however, need to consult one of the many works dealing more specifically with that subject.

All pigeons belong to the order of birds known as Columbiformes. This order includes the extinct Dodo and Solitaire, which were large flightless pigeons, and also the sandgrouse, a group of birds resembling the pigeons in some anatomical features. The sandgrouse also resemble pigeons in some behavourial characters but these are all ones which both families share with many other birds. I think that the sandgrouse are not so near to pigeons as they are generally believed to be but are more closely related to the plovers.

Most authorities place all the pigeons together in the family Columbidae and this, I think, is the best treatment. Some, however, give separate family rank to the Pheasant Pigeon (putting it in the family Otidiphapidae), the crowned pigeons (Gouridae), and the Tooth-billed Pigeon (Didunculidae). Some even place the fruit pigeons in a family of their own, Treronidae. It is preferable, in my opinion, to treat all the above only as subfamilies, thus Otidiphapinae, Gourinae, Didunculinae and Treroninae. In the case of the fruit pigeons it is doubtful if they differ sufficiently from the majority of pigeons to justify even sub-family rank.

Below the sub-family the term 'tribe' is sometimes used to embrace numbers of closely related genera. However, the only term that need much concern the non-taxonomist is the genus (plural genera). A genus is a group of species that are closely related to each other and all of whose members appear to be more closely akin to other species within the same genus than they are to any species of other genera, for example, the turtle doves genus *Streptopelia* or the green pigeons genus *Treron*. As would be expected authorities sometimes differ in their conception of what constitutes a genus, some (the 'lumpers') preferring to recognise large genera and others (the 'splitters') to put in the same genus only very close relatives. Most recent workers on pigeon taxonomy, including myself, have favoured the former course. Naturally, for Nature has no regard for man's convenience, there are some individual species that are intermediate between those in one genus and those in another. The 'lumper' can usually assign them to that genus with which they have most in common, but the 'splitter', whose genera are separated on smaller differences, is forced, if consistent, to give each such species a genus of its own. Such proliferation of monotypic genera based on small differences tends, I think, to mislead rather than help the student.

The categories of sub-genus, species-group and species sub-group are (sometimes) used to denote (in that order) degrees of relationship within a genera. They are not, however, involved in the scientific nomenclature. Below them comes the superspecies, but this is better discussed after dealing with the species category.

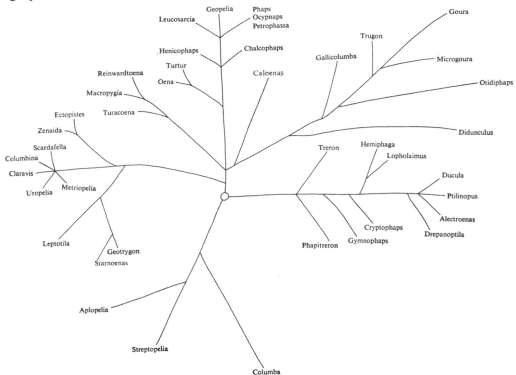

FIG. D.1: Presumed relationships of pigeon genera.

The species is the basic category of classification in the sense that the species concept is more closely related to observable facts than most others. The term species has been variously defined and most definitions have been objected to by someone on some grounds, good or otherwise. So far as pigeons (and other birds) are concerned one might, I think, say that a species consists of a number (usually a very large number) of individuals all of which show more resemblances to each other than to other species, interbreed freely with each other, and do not normally breed with members of another species. Our five British pigeons, the Wood Pigeon, Stock Dove, Rock Pigeon, Turtle Dove and Collared Dove are, obviously, 'good' species. In scientific nomenclature the species name, *not* capitalised, follows the generic name. Thus *Columba leuconota* (the Snow Pigeon), or *Ptilinopus victor* (the Orange Dove), and so on.

In different parts of its range a species of pigeon, like man, may show geographical variation. For example, the Rock Pigeons of peninsular India differ from those of Europe in being darker and having no white on the lower back, those of the Nile Valley are very small and pale in colour. Such differing populations are termed races or subspecies. They are given a third scientific name (tri-nomial) which in the case of the nominate form is a repetition of the specific name. Thus the European Rock Pigeon is *Columba livia livia* (usually written *Columba l. livia*), the Rock Pigeon of peninsular India is *Columba livia intermedia* and so on.

The form of the species that was first described and named in a book or other publication is usually called the nominate form. Sometimes it is called the typical form because the first specimen so described is known as the 'type' of the species. Typical form or typical race can be, however, misleading terms since they may wrongly suggest that the form first described is, somehow, more typical (using the word in its everyday sense) of its species than other forms that happened to be discovered and described later.

Unless they are separated by natural barriers, such as the sea or areas of country unsuitable for the species to inhabit, subspecies intergrade with each other, and many individuals, – indeed all of them in some areas – will be intermediate in character. Also, of course, some subspecies are more distinct than others. Many of them have been named because of very small average differences by over-zealous taxonomists. Under the species headings in this book I have in most cases described and named only the more distinct of such geographical races. By doing this it is possible to give a general idea of what the species looks like and the degree of difference that it shows in different parts of its range. On the other hand, to describe all the many races that have been named on very slight differences of size and colour would have confused rather than clarified the position for the average reader and would have taken up too much space. Any subspecies that has not been described here is very similar indeed to one or other of those that have been.

Geographic races may in time come to differ so much from their parent stock that they evolve into new species. Usually, perhaps always, such speciation can take place only if they are isolated from other populations. This may come about in many ways. Some members of a species may invade an island whither others of their kind do not follow. A species may disappear from large areas of its range through alteration of the habitat, leaving isolated populations separated by areas of country no longer suitable for it. If, after such a period of isolation, something happens to cause the two populations to come together again they may now have become so different that they will no longer interbreed. They have, in fact, each become separate species.

They may, however, interbreed when they meet again but if the resultant offspring are for any reason less viable than the 'pure' members of both populations then selection will favour any characters that tend to prevent mating between the two stocks. Such characters as a tendency to prefer different types of country when breeding, which would tend to 're-isolate' the two stocks even though they were in the same geographical area; or the development of different colour patterns which, by 'imprinting' would discourage pairing between the two might, for example, be 'seized on' and developed by natural selection in such circumstances. In this way definite specific status may be achieved only after a period during which there has been some interbreeding between the reunited 'species in the making'.

Where two similar forms that have clearly derived from a common ancestor now occupy different geographical areas and appear too distinct to be treated as races of one species they are commonly given specific rank but within the same superspecies. A superspecies is, as its name suggests, a form whose geographical representatives have evolved to the point where they are best considered as species rather than races. Perhaps it would be more correct to say that they have evolved to a point between the category of race and that of species but, in scientific nomenclature, are considered best treated as species and given specific names. Occasionally the term 'semi-species' is used for such members of a superspecies but there is as yet no particular designation for them in the scientific (latin) terms. Sometimes the geographical representatives of a form have diverged considerably. In such cases they are not usually classed as members of a superspecies even although this is, or at any rate was, their relationship. I have in this book used the term 'geographical representatives' to indicate the status of all such forms.

Naturally there is sometimes doubt as to whether the geographical representatives of any form should be considered as species within a superspecies or as races of one species. This cannot always be decided solely on the amount of visible difference between its members.

For example, some of the races of the African Green Pigeon (*Treron calva*) differ more in appearance from one another than do such related species as the Green-spotted Wood Dove and the Blue-spotted Wood Dove (*Turtur chalcospilos* and *T. afer*). In these cases there can be little doubt as to the correctness of this treatment, the most different forms of the African Green Pigeons are connected by intermediate ones in the intervening parts of Africa; the Green-spotted and Blue-spotted Doves live in the same general areas (although typically in rather different habitats) without interbreeding. In many cases too little is known about the behaviour of the species concerned to permit a proper evaluation of its behavioural characters. I think it is usually preferable to give 'borderline' cases specific rank (within a superspecies) and I have done so in this book. The most important thing, however, is to recognise these borderline cases for what they are. Provided this is done and their relationship made as clear as present knowledge permits their classification as races or species is of secondary, and largely academic, importance. For this reason all such 'doubtful' species (and some others whose close affinities are also of special interest) are dealt with in the introduction to the group to which they belong where the taxonomy and relationships within each group are discussed.

Where two closely related species whose ranges overlap or adjoin are very similar in appearance they are often termed sibling species. Needless to say there are differences of opinion as to what degree of resemblance must be shown before this term should be used.

Just as the term 'race' is commonly misused by people, especially politicians, who talk about the 'human race' when they mean the human species *Homo sapiens* in all its diverse races, so the term 'variety' is often wrongly used instead of 'species' or 'race'. Properly speaking the term variety should be used only for those aberrant individuals that differ markedly from the norm of their species or race, such as white Blackbirds or pink Wood Pigeons. In a wild state such varieties are usually less viable than normal birds and soon die or are killed. Should they survive and breed their aberrant characters usually prove recessive and thus their young do not outwardly resemble them.

By preserving and breeding from such chance varieties man has produced the many breeds of domesticated pigeons (and other domestic animals). The term 'breed' indicates a well-established domesticated variety that has been 'fixed' by artificial selection to the extent that it 'breeds true' and produces offspring of the same appearance as itself. In pigeons the degree to which different breeds 'breed true' varies considerably. Some of the older breeds, whose 'standard of excellence' has not been greatly altered over the centuries, reproduce their like with a fidelity approaching that normally seen in wild species. In some of the more recent breeds or some which have been much 'out-crossed' in order to obtain new colours or to obtain an altered (so-called) standard of excellence the reverse is true.

Throughout this book the terms 'group(s)' and 'form(s)' are used in a general sense as convenient. Their meaning in any particular case will be clear from the context.

ADAPTIVE RADIATION AND SOME ADAPTIVE CHARACTERS

The differences found within the pigeons as a result of speciation and adaptation to different environments have been broadly indicated in the introduction. I propose here to discuss more fully the adaptive radiation shown within this family, its geographic distribution and some structural characters that appear to be correlated with such adaptations.

Forms that roost, perch and nest on trees or shrubs but obtain some or all of their food on the ground are found in all the main geographical regions where pigeons exist. They include a great many species that vary much in size, proportions and ecology. Some of them are short-winged, long-legged forms that spend most of their time on the ground but these are absent from the northern temperate regions. This is, most probably, because in these regions pigeons usually have to migrate, or at least to travel long distances on the wing when local bad weather cuts off food supplies.

Some pigeons have become adapted to roosting and nesting in caves, cliffs, rock holes and similar places. This has enabled them to establish themselves in relatively tree-less areas. Most of the species that do this are ground feeders. Typically they inhabit rather barren, open country or mountainous districts. I think it more likely that the cliff and cave dwellers have evolved from arboreal forms than *vice versa*. It has been suggested that the conspicuous whiteness or near-whiteness of pigeons' eggs indicates that the pigeons were originally hole or cave-nesting forms some of whom have, relatively recently, taken to building open nests in trees and bushes. However, pigeons do not often leave their eggs uncovered unless the incubating parent has been forced to flee. As, like other birds that lay conspicuous eggs, they usually 'sit tight' until an approaching predator is close to the nest (some species making an exception for man in areas where they have been persecuted by him) there would be little chance of the predator failing to see and obtain the eggs whatever their colour. In such a situation it may even be advantageous that it should as, if the eggs were left after a predator had tried unsuccessfully to catch one of the parents, it might succeed in catching the other (which would not immediately desert even if its mate had done so as a result of its fright) on its return visit. Similar factors may be responsible for the conspicuously coloured (white or cream) eggs laid by many pheasants; birds which no one has suggested to be derived from hole nesters. No large rock-dwelling species occurred in the Americas prior to the introduction of the Domestic Pigeon *Columba livia*, although some small South American forms nest and probably shelter in rock cavities.

Superficially partridge-like, ground dwelling forms which, nevertheless, usually nest above ground level are found in the Americas, the Philippines and Celebes, Australasia and some Pacific Islands. New Guinea and nearby islands have three large pigeons (*Trugon*, *Otidiphaps* and *Microgoura*) and one very large (*Goura*) pigeon that are mainly terrestrial. It may be significant that these occur in an area where the only gamebirds of comparable size are the megapodes. The majority of 'partridge-like' pigeons are woodland birds that keep in or near the cover of trees or bushes. In Australia, however, some pigeons have become adapted to living and even nesting on the ground in relatively open country. Most, like their woodland counterparts, have rather rounded wings and they tend to keep near to the potential cover of rocks or scrub (although often or usually nesting on more or less open ground) but one, the Flock Pigeon, flies far and high on its large wings and appears to fill a similar ecological niche to that of some of the sandgrouse in Africa and Asia. That Australasia (like some islands elsewhere) has several pigeons that *normally* nest on the ground may be connected with the relative paucity of predatory mammals and the lack of any placental carnivores prior to the introduction of the Dog and Fox by Man.

Pigeons that are highly arboreal and obtain all (or almost all) their food from the branches occur widely in the tropics and sub-tropics but are particularly abundant in Indonesia and Australasia. Most typical of these forms are the fruit pigeons (*Ducula*, *Ptilinopus*, *Treron* and allied genera) of the old world tropics and sub-tropics but they include also some of the *Columba* species. These tree-living pigeons are mostly strong flyers with relatively large or pointed wings but a few island and montane forms have rather short, rounded wings and may fly only short distances. Such arboreal forms, cannot, of course, exist in regions where trees and shrubs are in fruit for only limited periods and even buds and flowers, which some fruit pigeons eat as a stop-gap when fruit and berries are not available, are not produced in winter. The abundance of forest-dwelling arboreal pigeons in the Austro-Malayan sub-region is probably, as was long ago suggested by Wallace (1865), correlated with the absence of monkeys from this area, these mammals being serious predators on the eggs and young of any birds that build relatively unconcealed open nests in the branches.

Differences in relative size and shape of the bill are, without much doubt, usually correlated with differences of food or feeding methods although too little is known about most species at present to be able to explain all such differences. Bills that are relatively stout and hooked and others relatively thin and slightly hooked at the tip occur in both tree-feeding and ground-feeding forms. Among the latter slender bills are characteristic of some species known to feed largely on small seeds and are, presumably, the most efficacious for picking up such small objects.

A few species of fruit pigeons have greatly enlarged ceres. No other wild pigeon shows this feature except the Nicobar Pigeon, *Caloenas nicobarica*, in which it is developed to a much lesser degree. As varieties of *Columba livia* with greatly enlarged ceres have been produced under domestication it is probable that the lack of such a feature in any wild ground-feeding species is due to their feeding habits. An enlarged cere would, probably, be much in the way when its owner was picking seeds from among short vegetation or scratching in the substrate with its bill. The Nicobar Pigeon may seem to be the exception that tests the rule but its enlarged cere is relatively smaller and apparently harder than those of the large-cered fruit pigeons and its bill is rather long even for a ground-feeding form.

Long tails in which the (sometimes pointed) central two or four feathers exceed the others in length have evolved independently in several species. Such tails are, therefore, possessed by some species whose closest relatives have short and square or only slightly round-ended tails. In some cases, as with the Passenger Pigeon and the Masked Dove *Oena capensis* this type of tail and the correlated relatively long wings appear to be adaptations to flying far and fast either on regular migrations or wanderings in search of food or water. In others, such as some of the green pigeons, the function of the long pointed tail is unclear.

Many forms have a markedly attenuated outer primary. Most (but not all) of these are species that live in forest or at any rate, thick scrub or woodland. Some keep on or near the ground, others mainly to the canopy. It has been suggested, probably correctly, that an attenuated outer primary is an adaptation to facilitate quick changes of direction or speed in flight. We find, however, many closely related forms, living in similar habitats, some of which have attenuated outer primaries and others not. Also the Old World Barred Ground Dove *Geopelia striata* has an attenuated first primary while the Inca and Scaly Doves *Scardafella*, which appear to fill a similar ecological niche in the Americas, have not whereas the case is reversed with the American genus *Leptotila* and its ecological counterpart in Africa

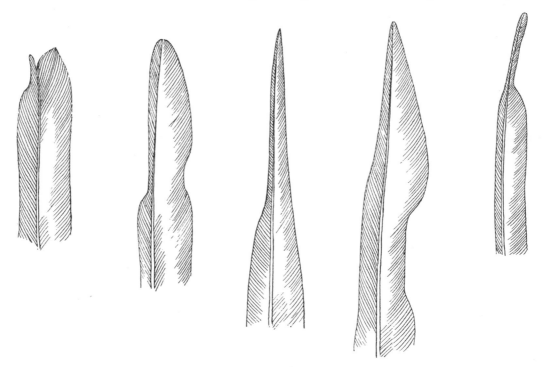

FIG. 2: Modified primary wing feathers: Left to right – Second from outermost primary of Cloven-feathered Dove; same of Bronze-winged Ground Dove; third from outermost primary of Crested Pigeon; same of Yellow-legged Green Pigeon; outermost primary of Pink-necked Fruit Dove.

the Lemon Dove *Aplopelia*. These apparent contradictions will, no doubt, be explicable when sufficient is known of the species involved. The peculiar 'scooped-out' indentations and other modifications of one or more primary feathers which some species have may function as sound producers or as mechanical aids to certain types of flight (or both) but in most cases their function is as yet unknown.

REFERENCE

WALLACE, A. R. 1865. On the Pigeons of the Malay Archipelago. *Ibis*, New Series, **1**: 365–400.

COLORATION OF PLUMAGE AND SOFT PARTS

Descriptions of the individual species are given elsewhere in this book but it seems worth-while also to discuss the coloration of pigeons in general. More particularly since many of the rules or tendencies we find in the pigeons apply equally to other groups of birds. For example, because they are usually more preyed upon by avian predators, such as hawks and falcons, smaller species of pigeons tend to be more cryptic in colour than the larger species.   Forms long isolated on islands or, in some cases, in montane forests, often show a partial or complete loss of bright markings.   This is, presumably, because one of the functions of such markings is to ensure species recognition and once the birds are isolated from close relatives the advantages of such markings may not compensate for their disadvantages in making the bird more conspicuous.

In every species of pigeon whose behaviour is known (and this is true for all other birds also) all bright or conspicuously contrasting areas of plumage serve a social function.   Either they are exhibited by special movements in hostile or sexual displays as in the case of the neck markings of the Wood Pigeon or the iridescent wing spots of the Common Bronzewing, or else they are shown automatically when the bird spreads its wings or tail.

The terms 'display plumage' and 'signal markings' have been – and often are – used for both the types of conspicuous markings above detailed.   Where possible I shall restrict the former term to those plumage areas which are 'deliberately' displayed by specific movements by a threatening or courting bird and use the latter for markings which are automatically displayed by movements used in taking wing or before alighting.   The same feathers may however function both as 'display' plumage' and as 'signal markings' even when the two terms are used in this precise sense.   For example, the strikingly white and dark patterned outer tail feathers of the Turtle Dove and the Diamond Dove are shown automatically when the bird spreads its tail as it rises from the ground.   They then serve to attract the attention of other individuals, alert them to possible danger and sometimes to stimulate them to follow the rising individual.   They are also used in self-assertive or courtship display: as by the Turtle Dove in its display flight and by the Diamond Dove in its bowing display.

In a few species of pigeons the sexes are alike in colour.   In very many in which the sexes are usually described as being alike, the females are a little duller than the males.   Generally their greys are somewhat browner or less bluish than those of their mates, their browns less reddish and more olivaceous;   irid-escent display plumage on their necks or wings less brilliant and the reds, pinks or yellows of their legs or orbital skin less pure and bright in colour.   In some species, however, the sexes show striking differences in colour.

The main trends in these sexually dimorphic or more properly speaking sexually dichromatic species are as follows.   Firstly;   conspicuous markings or patches of colour on the head, neck, breast or belly of the male are absent or only faintly suggested in the female.   This is so in several species of fruit doves, in the Pink-breasted and Orange-breasted Green Pigeons, in Delegorgue's Pigeon, in several ground doves of the genus *Gallicolumba*, in the extinct Passenger Pigeon, the Masked Dove, the Tam-bourine Dove, the Flock Pigeon and the Brown-backed Emerald Dove.   Secondly, there may be a large area of plumage quite differently coloured in the two sexes.   This is found in the Orange Dove and the Golden Dove, whose males are respectively brilliant orange and golden-green and the females dark green;   in some green pigeons in which the males have the wing-coverts and mantle dark purple, these areas being green like the rest of the plumage in the females;   in the Ruddy Quail Dove in which the male is purplish chestnut and the female olive brown, and the three species of *Claravis*, in which the males are blue-grey and the females brown.

These two types of sexual dichromatism may be combined as in the Passenger Pigeon whose male had a blue-grey head and upper parts and rufous-orange breast, these areas in the female being respectively brownish-grey and pale drab.   A different and less usual form of dichromatism is shown in some of the cuckoo doves (*Macropygia*) where the male has a plain brown and the female a barred brown plumage, but neither sex is at all bright or conspicuous.

Thus in most of the very markedly sexually dichromatic pigeons, the sexes differ in colour of head, neck or breast.   These are just the parts of the body that are presented in all 'close-range' displays.   The head itself is the focal point of all attacks and of most sexual advances.   The use made of the bright patch on the lower breast or belly in many fruit doves (*Ptilinopus*) appears to be unknown.   I think, however, that one may infer its probable function from behaviour of better known species.   In these, when the pair or two birds in process of pairing, are together on a potential or actual nest site, either male or female may show a tendency to attack its mate.   The latter will then lower its head and push

2—P & D

KEY TO PLATE 2

Examples of sexual differences in coloration.

Males left, females right.

(1) Masked Doves, *Oena capensis*;   (2) Golden Doves, *Ptilinopus luteovirens*;   (3) Purple-breasted Ground Doves, *Claravis mondetoura*;   (4) Laughing Doves, *Streptopelia senegalensis*.

PLATE 2

it under the aggressor's body. When it does this the head is usually pushed under the partner's body in just the area that is marked by a bright patch in so many species of *Ptilinopus*. Perhaps in these fruit doves such aggression and the need to inhibit it may have been of more importance and hence have resulted in the evolution of a bright signal marking on the lower breast.

In general, very marked differences in appearance between the sexes of birds are correlated with the male being able (if lucky) to mate with more than one female, either taking no care of his mate's eggs or young or, at least, not being of vital importance to their survival. This is not the case with pigeons since in all species whose parental behaviour is known, and this includes several of the highly dichromatic ones, the male takes a full share of parental duties. Both sexes incubate and brood for about the same number of *daylight* hours, both produce crop milk and feed the young. Hence the death of the father is just as disastrous as that of the mother so far as the eggs and young are concerned.

In some other sexually dichromatic birds only the female incubates and here it is usually thought that in so doing she is more vulnerable to predation and thus natural selection (through more bright females being caught on the nest) may have kept the females from developing conspicuous plumage or caused them to develop a more cryptic one. In those species, such as the Masked Dove, where the male's bright markings are confined to his face and breast it is possible that he is not much more conspicuous to predators than the female when he is crouching still in fear on the nest. The case is very different, however, with such species as the Blue Ground Dove and the Orange Dove. Here it is impossible that *both* sexes should be *equally* inconspicuous or otherwise in any one environment and it is pretty certain that in fact the male must be much more easily seen than his mate.

In spite of this I think it is possible that in such cases predator pressure may function to make the female less conspicuous. Some predator that hunts by sight and attacks such a species when it is feeding might, for example, tend to hunt mostly during the middle hours of the day. Alternatively, some predator which finds nests by spotting the sitting parent, might be more active during the early morning and evening than in the mid-day hours. Either of the above circumstances would mean that, during nesting time, the female was subjected to heavier selection for concealing plumage than the male.

Since such sexual dichromatism has evolved it must presumably confer some advantage in spite of monogamy and shared parental duties. Too little has been recorded of the ecology and behaviour of most of the species concerned to allow more than speculation as to why a much more marked degree of sexual dimorphism than is usual in pigeons may be of use to them. However, I feel speculation is justifiable in order to stimulate interest and suggest possible lines of study to readers who are able to observe any of the species concerned. At least three of such species, the extinct Passenger Pigeon, the Flock Pigeon and the Masked Dove are nomadic or migratory in habits. In these species a great number of individuals invade and breed in a limited area that temporarily supplies an abundance of food. Under such conditions there may well be more intense selection for any character that would aid more speedy and efficient pair formation than would otherwise obtain. An increased degree of sexual differentiation and appropriate responses to it would come into this category.

In view of the importance of the head and the extent to which it and the regions adjacent to it exhibit sexual dimorphism it seems at first anomalous that there are a few species in which, although large areas of the plumage differ in colour, the heads of male and female are alike. The most extreme examples of this are the Orange Dove and the Golden Dove, whose orange or golden-green males and dark green females both have heads of almost the same shade of olive-yellow. The answer lies no doubt, in the fact that large areas of plumage differently coloured in the two sexes would permit sexual recognition at a distance, whereas differently marked heads or breast serve the same function at closer quarters. There would, obviously, be less likelihood of selection for both forms of sexual dichromatism in the same species.

The juvenile plumage of most pigeons differs from that of the adults. Usually the ground colour is duller and the majority of the cover feathers have a dark subterminal band and a light edging. This pale edge may vary from pale buff or greyish white to dark rusty brown, and the width and degree of demarcation of the subterminal band may also vary greatly. In some species the feathers may have two, or more light, or rust brown, bars and the same number of dark bars. In the fruit doves (*Ptilinopus*) the blue fruit doves (*Alectroenas*) and some of the green pigeons (*Treron*), the pale feather edges are yellow (from pale lemon to deep buttercup) in colour.

In some species, which will be discussed shortly, the juvenile dress does not differ from that of the adult except that the colours, especially greys, are a little less bright and pure in tone and purple or mauve-pink is replaced by rusty-brown or rusty-orange. Where the adults show a type of sexual dimorphism involving the possession by the male of colours not shown by the female and which would appear to make him much more conspicuous than her, no *comparable* difference is shown in the juvenile plumage. This situation is found, for example, in the Masked Dove (*Oena capensis*), the Blue Ground Dove (*Claravis pretiosa*), and the Orange Dove (*Ptilinopus victor*). Where, however, the sexual dimorphism involves only the male's possessing brighter shades of similar colours, as in the Rock Pigeon (*Columba livia*), or these, together with markings that do not render him much more conspicuous, as in the Common Bronzewing (*Phaps chalcoptera*), a comparable degree of sexual dimorphism is shown in the first plumage.

The colour patterns found in the juvenile plumages of pigeons bear a close resemblance to those found in the juveniles of many passerines, waders and owls. They may be wholly or partly explicable in terms of the physiological processes involved. At any rate in the owls the juvenile plumage is not more cryptic than that of the adults. However, it does seem to me probable that the juvenile plumage of pigeons is of some protective value from predators which hunt by sight. This is suggested by the fact that where the young differ very little from the adults the latter are either large in size like the Red-knobbed Imperial Pigeon (*Ducula rubricera*), hole nesters like the Rock Pigeon (*Columba livia*), or species in which the adult plumage is highly cryptic like the Bare-eyed Ground Dove (*Metriopelia ceciliae*), and the Scaly Dove (*Scardafella squammata*).

The Scaly Dove is a particularly interesting case since the appearance of the juvenile is very similar to that of two other small, long-tailed doves, the Diamond Dove (*Geopelia cuneata*) and the Masked Dove. In detail the markings are quite different, however, juvenile Masked and Diamond Doves having dark subterminal bands and (large) buffy tips to their feathers, quite unlike the pattern of the adults, whereas in the Scaly Dove both adults and young have feathers with a pale subterminal area and a dark edging. In most pigeons the young begin to moult within a week or two of leaving the nest and are in complete adult plumage (from the point of view of appearance), when two to four months old. Hence any protective function of the juvenile dress could operate only for a short period. It is, however, likely that predation by birds of prey is heaviest at, and immediately after, fledging.

At least in many species of *Columba* and *Streptopelia* the juvenile plumage does not in any way inhibit attack by adults of the same species. Indeed adult Wood Pigeons (*Columba palumbus*), and Feral Pigeons often attack trespassing juveniles, even prematurely fledged nestlings, with extreme ferocity; probably because they are not inhibited at all by fear as they usually are, to some degree, when attacking other adults.

Signal markings on wings and tail that are displayed automatically when wings or tail are spread are present in the juvenile dress although sometimes they are less bright or less extensive than in the adult. The Nicobar Pigeon (*Caloenas nicobarica*) is, however, an exception to this rule, the juvenile having a dull blackish tail while that of the adult is pure white, in striking contrast to its otherwise dark plumage. This species inhabits only small islands, has a very wide range and is known to wander or migrate between islands. If the white tail tends to elicit a following reaction in flight then it is possible that there may have been selective pressures against its possession by inexperienced juveniles.

When I first studied juvenile plumages I hoped to determine whether they indicated phylogenetic relationship and if so to what extent. Some undoubted affinities such as that of the Masked Dove (*Oena capensis*) with the *Turtur* species and *Alectroenas* with *Ptilinopus* are certainly emphasised by the much greater similarity between the juvenile, as compared with adult plumages. Similarly, the Diamond Dove (*Geopelia cuneata*) has an adult plumage very distinct from that of its congeners, the Barred Ground Dove (*G. striata*), and the Bar-shouldered Dove (*G. humeralis*), but the juvenile plumages of all three are extremely alike, even to the possession of curious dark markings on the scapulars suggestive of those possessed by some of the American doves in the genus *Columbina*.

On the other hand, the quail doves, *Geotrygon linearis*, and *G. frenata*, have a reddish brown strongly barred juvenile plumage very like that of the emerald doves (*Chalcophaps*) and cuckoo doves (*Macropygia*), and differing considerably from that of a much more closely related quail dove (*Geotrygon lawrencii*) in which the juvenile plumage has only narrow and obscure dark subterminal bands and narrow pale terminals. Also the juvenile of the Black Bronzewing (*Henicophaps albifrons*) resembles the adult (except for being a little duller) although its relationships to the *Chalcophaps* species with their barred juveniles can hardly be doubted. The Black Bronzewing is, however, nearly twice as large as the emerald doves and has, for a pigeon, a quite remarkably large, strong, heavy bill, two factors which may make it much less liable to predation. It is also pertinent to this question that some of the domesticated colour varieties of *Columba livia* have a juvenile pattern unlike that of wild, or wild-coloured, specimens but rather similar to the juvenile plumages of those unrelated wild species whose adult coloration is somewhat like that of the colour varieties in question.

It is evident that similarities or differences in the juvenile plumages must be used with caution when assessing affinities. Very close similarities in details of juvenile plumages, often indicate close relationship between the species possessing them but dis-similarity does not necessarily indicate otherwise.

The soft part colours of juvenile pigeons also differ from those of the adults. Their irides are usually dull grey or brown and only gradually acquire the adult brilliance. To give a typical example: the adult Barbary Dove has irides of a deep and brilliant red. Those of the nestling are at first a neutral grey tinge and as the bird matures gradually change through light brown, yellowish brown and orange to the red adult colour. The bare orbital skin, where present and brightly coloured in the adult, is also at first some dull tint in the juvenile. The same is true of legs and feet although these tend to be darker as well as duller than the adult colour and in some species the (usually) red, pink or purple adult foot colour may be acquired early, sometimes even before leaving the nest. There may be both sexual and individual variation here. For example some young male Stock Doves (*Columba oenas*) have quite pink legs and feet at about three weeks of age whereas those of female young of this age are always dusky.

So far as I know, or the point has been recorded, the bill coloration of young pigeons of all species is very similar. It consists of a white or pale tip with a very dark area immediately behind it and dull base. The significance of this coloration is discussed in the chapter on parental care. In white or pale colour varieties of either domesticated or wild species the bills of the nestlings do not, of course, show the characteristic natural colour pattern. As with the other soft parts the bills of the young only gradually attain their adult coloration. In most species they lose the nestling's bill colours within two or three weeks, becoming a nearly uniform dull grey, black or brownish which, in turn gradually changes to the adult colour where this is of a brighter hue.

Because of this gradual change in the soft part colours no attempt has been made to give eye, bill or foot colours of juveniles under the species headings. To do so would, except in a few cases where the course of the change could be described fully, be more misleading than helpful. For example, if two forms in which the colours and colour change of the young birds eyes are identical were described from data based on a three-week old juvenile of one and a five-week old of the other this could suggest specific differences where only age differences existed. The soft part colours of pigeons, especially those of the iris and orbital skin, usually become dull or paler when the bird is in poor health.

PLUMAGE SEQUENCES

Newly hatched young pigeons are clad in coarse hair-like down. The amount of down varies slightly between species but is usually sufficiently sparse for the bare skin to show through plainly. Usually it is yellow or golden in colour but varies from pale straw to rusty buff in different species. In 'dilute' colour varieties the nestling down is very short and sparse so that the newly hatched squab looks almost naked.

The nestling down is replaced by the juvenile plumage, to the top of which it adheres for some little time. The juvenile plumage is usually defined as 'the first set of true feathers'. Some qualification or at least description is, however, necessary to explain the differences that may be seen in some species if a fledgling juvenile is compared with one that has been flying for a week or two. Many of the first

KEY TO PLATE 3

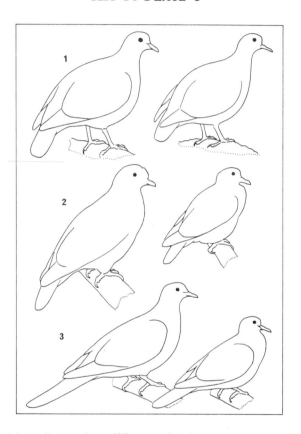

Adults and juveniles to show differences in plumage and soft part colours
(1) Emerald Doves, *Chalcophaps indica* (females);   (2) Seychelles Blue Pigeons, *Alectroenas pulcherrima*;   (3) African Collared Doves, *Streptopelia roseogrisea*.

PLATE 3

cover feathers grown by the young bird while still in the nest tend to be, as compared with adult feathers, rather loose and/or woolly in texture and to show the juvenile markings very clearly. However, by the time the young bird fledges more cover feathers have grown or are now growing, apparently from tracts that have not already produced feathers. These 'latecomers' to the juvenile plumage are usually intermediate in texture and colour between the first juvenile feathers and the adult dress although nearer to the former in most cases. In most species they do not radically change the general colour pattern although they do make some difference in general appearance. This is particularly the case in such forms as some of the fruit doves *Ptilinopus* where the nestling is feathered while still very small, in proportion to the adult, fledges at this size and grows a great many more feathers as its size increases in the ensuing few weeks.

In the green pigeons of the genus *Treron* the young of many, perhaps all, species are very small at fledging time (in relation to adult size); the cover feathers on neck, breast, rump and underparts are very loose and woolly in texture and appear to be largely, if not entirely, replaced at or shortly after fledging time by similarly coloured or very slightly brighter feathers of a rather stronger texture. This apparent replacement of many of the juvenile's first cover feathers has taken place before the feathers have grown around the base of the bill and hence presumably, while it is still being fed by its parents. Thus the feathering of the flying juvenile cannot be termed 'juvenile plumage' in a strict sense since it is a combination of juvenile and sub-adult dress. However, it has been used previously for young green pigeons in this 'mixed' plumage and it is convenient and reasonable to do so since this plumage consists partly of true juvenile feathers and is worn at the same time as the juvenile plumage of other species.

In most pigeons the adult plumage is assumed at the post-juvenile moult, fully coloured adult feathers replacing the shed juvenile feathers. The speed and age at which this moult takes place varies with the species, the condition of the individual and, in some cases, the time of year. In temperate regions the moult may be temporarily halted, especially in the case of the wing quills, during the winter months. The post-juvenile moult is complete and involves the wing and tail quills as well as the cover feathers.

In a few species, particularly in some of the imperial pigeons, the bird moults from the juvenile into a sub-adult plumage which may differ considerably in colour from the adult plumage although it is usually very similar in pattern and texture. It is not known whether or to what extent such species breed while still in sub-adult dress. Besides the normal succession of plumages, feathers intermediate in character between two plumages may be produced to replace any that are lost through accidental injury. Whitman (1919) has shown that in the Diamond Dove feathers showing progressive degrees of intermediacy between the colour patterns of juvenile and adult wing coverts (which in this species differ greatly) can be produced by successive plucking of feathers.

Once the adult plumage is assumed there are, so far as is known, no pigeon species in which it is ever replaced by a different type of plumage. Deformed, unpigmented or otherwise abnormal feathers may, however, be produced at any moult as a result of defective metabolism due to sickness, injury or unsuitable diet. One of the commonest manifestations of this is the induced melanism sometimes seen in captive pigeons (and other birds). The normally coloured feathers, when moulted, are replaced by ones that show varying degrees of increased melanin pigmentation and may be entirely black. A combination of unsuitable feeding, often with foods with a high oil content, together with fairly close confinement appear usually to be causative or contributory factors (Goodwin, 1957). Sometimes, however, black feathers are produced by birds in apparently good health in large aviaries. In at least one group of pigeons, the crowned pigeons or gouras, black feathers may partially replace the normal plumage in wild specimens that appear otherwise perfectly normal.

REFERENCES

Goodwin, D. 1957. Temporary melanism in a Spotted Dove. *Bull. B.O.C.*, 77 : 3–5.
Whitman, C. O. 1919. *Orthogenetic Evolution of Pigeons*. Posthumous works of C. O. Whitman. Vol. 3. Carnegie Inst. Washington.

CLUTCH SIZE AND EGG COLOUR

All species of pigeons lay one or two white or (more rarely) cream or buff eggs to a clutch.   At least this is the case with all the many species whose nests have been found in a wild state or which have bred in captivity.   Clutches of three or four eggs have been recorded now and again for European species and three or four eggs are sometimes found in the nests of feral or domestic *Columba livia*.   I think, however, that in such cases, the apparently large clutch is due to two hens laying in the same nest.   In Domestic Pigeons, Barbary Doves and captive Diamond Doves *Geopelia cuneata* this can be artificially induced in various ways.   One of these, the destruction of the nest very shortly before the female is due to lay, may well happen occasionally in the wild and cause a female to 'play the cuckoo' and lay in another's nest.   Also the presence of a predator on or near it may at times prevent a wild pigeon from laying in her own nest.

The Purple Wood Pigeon *Columba punicea* and some of the American species of *Columba* have been recorded as laying sometimes one and sometimes two eggs per clutch.   The African Green Pigeon *Treron calva* seems on present evidence to lay one egg clutches in some parts of its range and two egg clutches elsewhere.

One egg per clutch is laid by most fruit pigeons ; by some species of *Columba* which are either largely tree feeders, large in size or island dwellers (or show a combination of two or more of these attributes) ; by large ground-feeding forms such as *Trugon*, *Otidiphaps* and *Goura* (and one or two quail doves) ; by the colonially nesting Passenger and Nicobar Pigeons.

Thus the pigeons that lay one egg are either predominantly fruit eaters, large in size or colonial nesters. It seems likely that one egg clutches are an adaptation to a relatively un-nutritious diet which affects the quantity or quality of parental crop milk or to intense selection pressure for quick growth and early fledging of the young.   In the smaller fruit doves it is probable that both these factors have operated.

Typically pigeons' eggs are white, sometimes with a creamy tinge and sometimes, when fresh, with a faint pinkish tinge in certain lights due to the contents showing through to a very slight extent.   Buff or cream coloured eggs are laid by some species of both old and new world quail doves *Gallicolumba* and *Geotrygon* and by the African spot-wings *Turtur* and *Oena*.   All these tend to nest rather low down and, although many species with similar nesting habits lay white eggs, it is possible that the buff coloration of the eggs serves to protect them. Although I do not think the white shells of most pigeons' eggs are liabilities in a biological sense (see section on adaptive radiation) it may be that the situation is different for the buff egg laying forms.   If, for example, they are more liable to be flushed from their nests by predators that are *not* likely to be able to catch the incubating adult on a return visit then there might in their case have been selection for less conspicuous eggs.

FEEDING HABITS

In their feeding habits pigeons can be divided into three main categories; those that normally seek their food above ground in trees, shrubs or vines ; those that seek food both in trees and on the ground and those which normally seek food only on the ground.   The first group are, naturally, found mainly in the tropics and sub-tropics.   They include all the fruit pigeons (green pigeons, imperial pigeons, fruit doves and their relatives) and, probably, some of the more arboreal species of typical pigeons of the genus *Columba*, the mountain pigeons *Gymnophaps* and the long-tailed pigeons *Reinwardtoena*.   All these live on such foods as fruits, buds, flowers and young leaves taken from the branches.   One of them at least, the White-crowned Pigeon, is known to eat snails as well as berries and it is likely that many of the others also supplement their diet with invertebrates at times even though there appear to be no records of their so-doing.   They do not, normally, go to the ground for food, although some are known to do so to obtain 'grit', salt-impregnated earth or other mineral matter, and some take fruits of low growing plants that they must obtain on or very near ground level.

Most fruit pigeons, *Treron* excepted, probably all of them, have a broad gut and void intact the stones of the fruit they have eaten. They thus, unlike seed-eating pigeons, serve to distribute and perpetuate their food plants. Correlated with arboreal feeding are usually the ability to cling, hang and clamber among slender branches, a large distensible gape so that large fruits can be swallowed whole and plumage which is often green with bright but disruptive patches of colour.

Pigeons that feed both in trees and on the ground are numerous, probably many species so far recorded only as tree feeders or only as ground feeders will be found to come into this second category when more is known about them. Our Wood Pigeon (*Columba palumbus*) is an example of a species which feeds freely both in trees and on the ground. This group grades into the third category, of ground feeders, many of which, like some of the turtle doves (*Streptopelia* sp.) may sometimes feed on berries or seeds in trees.

So far as is known, no ground-feeding pigeons scratch for food with their feet but only shift the substrate, if it is loose and friable, with a sideways flicking movement of the bill, or, in a few species such as the Galapagos Dove, a pecking, hoe-like movement towards the bird, similar to that of many game-birds, may be used. However, Gifford (1925) who kept one of the quail-like *Gallicolumba* species, *G. rubescens*, found that it uses its feet when feeding. It has an apparently innate habit of jumping up to sieze the head of a plant whose seeds it wishes to eat, pulling it down and then holding the stem under one foot as it picks the seeds from the ear. Also, if it gets a fibre or thread tangled round its feet it does not panic, as do other doves in this situation, but quietly inspects its toes and then tries to pull the thread off with its bill. These unusual behaviour patterns were observed in captive birds. It would be most interesting to learn if such behaviour is adapted to any special danger the bird runs of getting its feet entangled in any of the natural vegetation of the Marquesas Islands. Neither of these behaviour patterns were, apparently, shown by Philippine Bleeding Heart Pigeons *G. luzonica*, which Gifford kept at the same time.

Some of the Australasian bronzewings have very hard bills (for pigeons) with the upper mandible nearly opposed to the lower, forming a more pointed bill than in most other pigeons where the upper mandible overlaps the lower more at the tip. I have seen an individual of one of these species, *Petrophassa plumifera*, in captivity, hammer at a peanut with its closed bill and break it up in this way, much as a game-bird would do. Probably this action is common to the other bronzewings that have similar bills. Some of the fruit pigeons of the genus *Treron* apparently sometimes use their hooked bills to tear pieces off large fruits. I have found pieces of fig in the crops of specimens that were shot in the wild. Usually, however, pigeons swallow their food whole, whether it is fruit, seeds or invertebrate animals. They cannot bite, chew, or de-husk their food in the way that some other birds – such as finches and parrots – are able to. They can detach suitably sized morsels from fairly soft growing (and thus firmly attached) leaves or shoots by closing the bill on them and then tugging. The same method is used when taking seeds of grass or other plants from the ear.

If one watches a Feral Pigeon feeding in this manner it will be seen that if the seed is not detached when the bird pulls at it the pull is followed by a violent shake of the head while the bill still grips the seed. This combination of movements is very effective for the purpose although the shake appears to be a purely innate reaction to a 'foreign body' (in this case the seed-head of the plant) touching or nearly touching the bird's head. These same innate movements are also used when trying to feed from a large lump of bread or other artificial food and can be quite effective if the bread is soft and easily breakable. As can often be seen by anyone who observes Feral Pigeons in towns, these birds are quite unable to feed successfully from large pieces of really hard or frozen bread.

Many, and very probably all, of the tree feeding pigeons such as the Wood Pigeon and the green pigeons also use a peculiar twisting movement of the head if a fruit or nut they have seized is at all hard to pluck and this twisting wrench is very effective in plucking fruits or acorns if they are nearly ripe. Tame Wood Pigeons, if they are used to being offered all sorts of tit-bits from the hand, often try to pluck their owner's finger nails in this manner.

Some species of pigeon take a good deal of animal food in the form of various small invertebrates. The more quiescent of these, such as small snails, gorged ticks and pupae do not require any more 'catching' than seeds.   Some pigeons will, however, take quite active invertebrates; many African species take winged termites readily when the latter are swarming.   The only species for which any special behaviour adapted for the catching of live prey has been recorded is the extinct Passenger Pigeon.   Whitman (1919) who bred this species in captivity described how, when they had young in the nest, his Passenger Pigeons searched diligently for earthworms and used a stereotyped, very quick movement to seize the head end of the worm and drag it from its burrow.   As is described in the section on parental care adult pigeons adapt their diet, where possible, to the needs of their young.

How pigeons recognise their food and how they (sometimes) learn to eat new and often rather unnatural foods is an interesting and as yet far from solved problem.   As they feed chiefly on seeds or fruits swallowed whole there seems little possibility of taste, in any way similar to our own, giving them information. They do, however, appear to be able to correlate the pleasant or unpleasant after effects of foods taken with the (? remembered) appearance of the food in question.   For example, when I kept Barbary Doves at liberty I noticed repeatedly that inexperienced individuals would freely eat the berries of the mountain ash.   These evidently disagreed violently with them as some time after making such a meal the dove would be violently sick and vomit up the contents of both stomach and crop; after which it never ate mountain ash berries again.   I was, incidently, surprised that the mountain ash berries harmed the Barbary Doves in this way since they are eaten with apparent impunity by Wood Pigeons.   The elder and bryony berries that the Barbary Doves also ate had no unpleasant after effects.   Conversely a pigeon that has, with some reluctance, accepted peanuts for the first time will, after digestion has taken place although not usually before, become extremely eager for them and prefer them to most other foods.

When old enough to be able to feed themselves, young pigeons of seed-eating species peck at all sorts of small objects or patterns that contrast to some degree with the substrate.   If moveable these are picked up, held a moment in the tip of the bill and dropped again.   If some edible seeds are found the bird will eat them.   The first grain eaten will, however, usually be picked up, dropped and picked up again many times before it is actually swallowed.   The second will be swallowed with less hesitation and the third, at any rate if the young pigeon is really hungry, with no hesitation at all.   Young Wood Pigeons, and no doubt other species that feed much on young foliage, will also tear pieces from any young growing leaves, at first discard and then swallow them in a similar manner.   A young captive-bred African Green Pigeon pecked at every little protuberance or inequality of its perches, obviously an adaptation to finding fruits and buds.

If other pigeons are present when the young one first starts to feed itself its behaviour is somewhat different.   It shows excited interest as soon as it sees another pigeon pick up food.   The young one goes to it, looks eagerly when it pecks again and often tries, without success, to take the foot item from the other's bill tip at the moment it is picked up.   This may be repeated several times but soon realisation comes and the young pigeon starts to eat, usually with much less hesitation over the first grain than it would have shown if 'learning to feed' alone.   In many species the young pigeon normally follows its parents, or one of them, to their feeding grounds and starts to feed itself in their company.   None of the hesitation shown by young pigeons at this age is due to insufficient maturation of the feeding movements.   In a natural state, for example, young Feral or Rock Pigeons do not feed themselves until they are strong on the wing.   They can, however, as every pigeon keeper knows, be taught to feed themselves long before they can fly by placing a supply of corn beside the nest so that they constantly see their parents eating.

Adult pigeons confronted with some food new to them behave in the same manner as described above for young birds except that they usually tend to be a bit 'quicker on the uptake'.   The seed-eating pigeons, or at least such of them as have been studied in this connection, always 'learn' more quickly to take new foods if these are small in size.   For example Feral and Domestic Pigeons will, on encountering them for the first time, start to eat such seeds as wheat, millet, rice or canary seed more quickly than they will larger seeds such as maize, tic beans or peanuts.   This bears no relation to their choice when experienced. It is difficult to see the utility of this behaviour.   It can hardly be to guard against the ingestion of unsuitable foods since once it has 'convinced itself' of the edibility of some new food and swallowed the first morsel the pigeon will always continue to eat.   Thus it will – if there is enough available – consume as great a total bulk of small seeds as it would of large.   Where unnatural foods that do not resemble natural foods in form, such as bread, are concerned the example of other pigeons that have already learnt to take them usually plays an even greater role. Here there is, apparently, no innate recognition of the food itself as 'something potentially edible' and it may be ignored even by starving individuals unless they see other pigeons eating it.

It is difficult to ascertain to what extent, if any, pigeons have any innate recognition of 'likely' feeding places. In some (perhaps all) ground feeding species there is certainly a tendency to alight on the ground and search there when hungry. In the case of *Columba livia* (probably also in other species) young captive individuals that have never been fed at ground level will descend to the floor and search there if left without food till hungry. In many species of pigeons, at any rate those that feed in the open on the ground or in the canopy of fruiting trees, hungry individuals are strongly attracted by the sight of others of their own species (and, to a lesser extent, by related species) already feeding, fly to and alight near them. In any area there are likely to be many experienced adults that know the district and its food sources. Such experienced individuals may recognise sources of food through learning and memory where there can be no possibility of innate recognition. This is the case with the many Feral Pigeons (and other birds) in towns which immediately recognise the human 'intention movements' of distributing food to them or will crowd around one particular human being, by whom they have often been fed, even though he or she is surrounded by other people and making no move to proffer food. In other cases artificial sources of food may share certain features with natural ones and in such cases innate recognition may play a part. For example; a newly sown field or a freshly cut stubble has certain similarities to naturally bare or relatively bare ground and species, such as the Stock Dove, that feed on seeding weeds or wind-blown seeds may have an innate tendency to seek food in such places.

It seems pertinent here to refer again to the behaviour described for young and old pigeons when in process of 'learning' new food objects. This picking up a morsel, holding it a moment in the bill tip, dropping it and picking it up again has often been described as 'testing' the food. It is possible that, in some cases, the bird is able to make some 'judgement' as to how far texture, shape and weight approach or differ from items already known to be edible. The behaviour does not, however, give rise to immediate rejection or acceptance of the object as would be expected if some effective 'testing' were involved, also, as we have seen with the Barbary Doves that ate mountain ash berries, it does not always prevent the bird consuming harmful objects. In fact this 'testing' behaviour seems to be merely intention movements of picking up and swallowing. It is shown whenever the bird is 'undecided' whether to eat, regardless of whether the food objects so treated are new or well-known to the individual and habitually consumed by it. Thus when, through satiety, a pigeon finishes eating from a superabundant supply of food it will, usually, pick up, 'test' and drop again without finally swallowing before leaving the food supply or ceasing to show any interest in it.

REFERENCES

MURTON, R. K. 1964. The feeding habits of the Wood Pigeon *Columba palumbus*, Stock Dove *C. oenas* and Turtle Dove *Streptopelia turtur*. *Ibis* **106**: 174–188.

WHITMAN, C. O. 1919 *The Behaviour of Pigeons.* Posthumous works of C. O. Whitman. Vol. 3. Carnegie Inst. Washington.

DRINKING, BATHING, SUNNING, PREENING AND COMFORT MOVEMENTS

Most pigeons drink regularly at least once and usually more often each day. It has been suggested that some of the fruit-eating species do not do so and it is possible that they may, at any rate for considerable periods, obtain enough moisture from their food. It has been claimed that the dry-country, seed-eating African Collared Dove can go for months without water but proof is lacking and it is known that in many places this species is an avid drinker. Most seed-eating pigeons of arid country regularly visit the nearest supply of surface water and have often been of use to man by indicating its whereabouts to him. Domestic and Feral Pigeons usually drink after they have finished feeding although if water is available on the feeding ground they may drink before they have filled their crops and then continue food-seeking. The available evidence suggests that most wild species behave similarly. At least one arid country species, however, the Crested Pigeon, comes to drink before feeding. In many species of *Columba* and *Streptopelia* and in the Diamond Dove, parents with young old enough to take food as well as crop milk invariably drink before feeding them. If a number of breeding Domestic Pigeons are kept without water for half an hour or so after being fed they show obvious distress and make no attempt to feed their young. As soon as water is given them each bird at once drinks deeply and immediately flies to its young and feeds them. Probably most or even all species behave in this way.

Pigeons drink by inserting the bill and sucking up a continuous draught of liquid. Immediately after the bird lifts its head and slightly expands its gape, presumably taking a deep breath just as we do after drinking deeply. Sometimes a second or third but shorter drink follows the first. The only species that has been observed to drink differently is the Tooth-billed Pigeon *Didunculus*. Sandgrouse are said to drink in the same manner although the few that I have watched did not. In any case many other birds drink in 'pigeon' manner either regularly or as an alternative to the more usual method in which the drinking bird appears to scoop up water and raise it's head after each mouthful as if using gravity to get the water down its throat. Drinking by continuous sucking appears to be an adaptation to enable liquid to be taken as quickly as possible. It is commonly, but not exclusively, used by species inhabiting arid country although their need for haste is, I imagine, primarily due to their being often in danger when they visit water. In arid regions birds of prey and, in some areas, primitive men, regularly try to catch birds coming to drink at isolated sources of water. Nowadays sportsmen with shotguns often make havoc among pigeons and sandgrouse under these conditions. The depth to which the bill is inserted into the water may vary in different species but in some, and perhaps in all, it seems to depend chiefly on the relative thirst of the pigeon and the cleanness or otherwise of the water. At least in some *Columba* species a very thirsty bird may plunge half its head beneath the surface whereas if not very thirsty and drinking from scummy water it will first clear some of the scum with the same side to side flicking movement of the bill as is used when searching for seeds in friable soil and then insert only the end of its bill to drink. Pigeons normally drink from the bank, from a bough hanging into water or similar perch. Rock and Domestic Pigeons and the Flock Pigeon *Phaps histrionica* sometimes alight on the water to drink. The former species only does so, so far as I am aware, when it is either unable to reach the water from the bank or, for some reason, fears to alight there. Many other pigeons have been observed settling on water at times but it is not certain that they always do so in attempts to drink. I have four times seen a Wood Pigeon (at different times and in different places so almost certainly not the same individual) alight on a sheet of water. In each case the bird appeared 'astonished' at finding itself afloat and quickly flew out. I had the impression that some 'trick of light' (reflection in the water?) may have given it the impression that it was alighting on some solid object, certainly it made no attempt to drink and there were places where it could safely have alighted to drink nearby.

Many pigeons, including species in the genera *Columba*, *Streptopelia*, *Zenaida*, *Treron* and *Ducula*, have very similar or identical rain-bathing postures which are probably shared with most if not all other species. These consist of leaning over to one side, often lying partly on one wing and raising the other so that the rain can fall on its under surface and on the flanks. At high intensity the bird may lean over so that the 'raised' wing is near the horizontal and the bird almost completely on its side. At the same time the plumage generally is more or less fluffed out so that rain can penetrate the feathers. When a pigeon which is not in a mood to bathe is caught in the rain it adopts an upright posture with neck contracted and feathers sleeked down to allow the rain to run off as freely as possible and minimise its effects.

Some (possibly all) pigeons that rain bathe also bathe when they have access to some shallow pool or other suitable water in a place where they feel secure and at ease. The pigeon wades into the water, fluffs out its feathers, makes one or two pecking or side to side movements of its bill in the water then may remain still for a few moments, often with one wing lifted as when rain bathing. This period of standing or lying in the water is followed by a violent ducking of the head and neck and beating the wings (only partly opened) in water. The two forms of behaviour may be repeated until finally the bird steps or flies out, stands up and violently flaps its wings, then settles in some safe and preferably sunny place to dry and preen.   When so doing it often partly spreads one wing and even if no such sun-bathing takes place stands or squats with wings slightly opened so that the primaries are a little spread.   It is possible that some pigeons do not practice any form of water bathing.   This appears to be sowith the Diamond Dove.   None of my Diamond Doves ever, to my knowledge, showed any signs of bathing.   Nicolai (1962) had the same experience with a much larger number of individuals but found that his were fond of resting on damp earth or grass in hot weather and considered this to be a vestigial 'relic' of the bathing behaviour now lost in this species.

Nearly all pigeons whose behaviour in this respect is known are fond of sunning themselves.   The wing-lifting movement shown in rain bathing is used also when sunning; at lower intensity the pigeon lies slightly on one side with one wing partly spread and the tail spread on the same side.   In very high intensity sun bathing, which I have only seen indulged in momentarily by some *Streptopelia* species, the bird fully spreads both wings and tail.   Sun-bathing with the above postures is followed by standing or squatting in the sun with the feathers, especially on the rump, somewhat raised and, usually, by preening.   One species, the Spectacled Ground Dove, *Metriopelia ceciliae*, dust bathes (Nicolai, 1962) and it is quite likely that some related species may also.   Often, however, the fondness of some pigeons, such as the Turtle Dove and the Diamond Dove, for lying on the ground to sun themselves has led to incorrect records of dust bathing by pigeons that do not practice it.

Preening behaviour of pigeons is generally similar to that of other birds.   I have, however, not seen use made of the preen gland which would appear to be non-functional or at least not to function in connection with preening.   The powder down which permeates the plumage of pigeons, appears to function in lieu of preen oil to aid in waterproofing of the feathers.   Pigeons try to remove any irritant matter or foreign body from the eye by repeated blinking of the nictitating membrane and by turning the head and rubbing the eye on the shoulder.   The head and bill are cleaned by scratching with the foot which is brought up directly, not over the wing as in sandgrouse and many other birds.

Stretching and similar movements are often termed 'comfort movements' but they may well have important physiological functions also.   Most noticeable in pigeons (and occurring also in other birds) are a series of movements in which the folded wings are held vertically upwards and are apparently 'stretched', at the same time as the head and tail are lowered and one in which one leg is stretched backwards and at the same time the wing on the same side is extended backward towards or over the leg being stretched and the tail spread.   Standing up and wing flapping is shown most often as a drying movement in many species but in some of the ground-dwelling forms it is more frequent and seems, like the similar and possibly homologous wing-flapping of game birds, likely to be an adaptation to keep the flight muscles in an efficient condition in birds which fly comparatively seldom but may *need* to do so at any moment.

Ruffling and shaking in which all the feathers of the body are erected, the folded wings held a little away from the body and both wings and body vigorously shaken is frequent, especially after preening.   A lateral shaking or wagging of the tail is often shown, after preening or ruffling.   The movement is very like that of ducks but only one or a few side to side movements of the tail are performed at any one time.   A sudden lowering of the tail and then bringing it back to its former position, which is shown by many species, appears, at least in *Columba livia*, to be sometimes a comfort movement that functions to reposition the tail in relation to the folded wings and sometimes a very low intensity flight-intention movement.

'Aiming' movements in which the head is thrust or thrown forward are usally flight-intention movements and are correlated with a slight crouch in readiness for the take-off.   They differ in detail in different forms and may be incorporated in displays.   Captive birds, especially flying breeds of Domestic Pigeon, when strongly motivated to fly will stand in a crouched posture with feathers sleeked down, hold the partly folded wings slightly away from the body and move them in the same rhythm as in flight for several seconds or even minutes at a time.   Head shaking is discussed elsewhere owing to its significance in social contexts.

When roosting or dozing pigeons do not tuck the head behind the wing but draw it close into the body.   At such times the feathers are often fluffed out, particularly if the bird is cold or unwell.   In some species, at any rate some that commonly roost on ledges or large boughs, resting individuals often stand on one leg with the other drawn up into the feathers. When resting by day pigeons adopt the same posture as when roosting although they may also squat or lie down as they do when sunning or after bathing. Even in species, such as the Rock Pigeon, which usually rest on one leg sick individuals never do so. Shivering of the body and wings occurs if the bird is very cold and sometimes when it, apparently, feels psychologically ill at ease.

REFERENCES

MILLER, J. W. & L. S. 1958. Synopsis of behaviour traits of the Ring-neck Dove. *Animal Behaviour* **6**: 3–8.
NICOLAI, J. 1962. Uber Regen-, Sonnen- und Staubbaden bei Tauben (Columbidae). *Journ. f. Orn.* **103**: 125–139.
SIMMONS, K. E. L. 1964. Feather maintenance, in Landsborough Thomson, A. *A New Dictionary of Birds*, pp. 278–286. London.

VOICE AND OTHER SOUND SIGNALS

Compared with passerine birds pigeons have a rather limited range of vocalisations. This is, at any rate, the case with those species (by no means the majority) which have been well studied and all of whose calls are known. Most pigeons utter both 'cooing' calls, that usually involve inspiration and some degree of inflation of the neck and sharper or harsher 'non-cooing' calls that are not usually accompanied by any swelling of the neck. The whistling calls of the green pigeons *Treron* sp. seem to be equivalent to and are possibly homologous with the cooing calls of other forms. In attempting to give some idea of the sound of those species whose cooing I have heard I have used the following: "ŏŏ" sounds like the shortened 'oo' as in 'look' or 'book'; 'ōō' as a long 'oo' as in 'boot' or 'coot'.

In many species of typical pigeons, *Columba*, and turtle doves, *Streptopelia*, the vocalisations of adults can be divided into four or perhaps five 'basic' calls. To a large extent this is true of some species in other genera and will, I think, prove valid as a general concept. These four basic calls I have termed the advertising coo, the display coo, the distress call and the excitement cry and these terms are used, where applicable, in the species section of this book.

The advertising coo has also been called the perch coo and the song. The latter is a fairly appropriate term since it is, broadly speaking, functionally equivalent to the songs of many passerines. Perch coo can, however, be misleading as the advertising coo may be given from the nest as well as when perched away from it. The advertising coo is, usually, a characteristic utterance of a territory-holding male and has been sometimes referred to as the territorial call on that account. It may, however, be uttered by birds well away from their territory or not yet holding any. I have heard it from Turtle Doves on migration and from Wood Pigeons at a communal roost.

The advertising coo appears, in most species, to be confined to birds that are either in some phase of the breeding cycle or at least coming into reproductive condition. It is uttered in a wide variety of situations which seem to have as a common factor that the calling bird is being prevented from performing some other (usually reproductive) activity by some cause which does not arouse overt fear or aggression. The typical situations in which the advertising call is given are by an unpaired male who is in breeding condition and holding territory, by a male whose mate is incubating, or is out of sight for any other reason. In some species territory-holding males appear habitually to answer their neighbours' advertising coos. I think it is more likely that, as has been suggested for passerines (Andrew, 1961), this is due to some impulse to answer a particular call in kind than to aggressive feeling. So far as I know once two birds begin hostilities the advertising coo is never uttered, even 'between rounds', although as soon as the loser flees the winner may (and usually does) utter this call. The loser, if he has re-entered his own territory or is at a safe distance may at once 'answer back'; one then has the impression of mutual challenging. I think, however, that in this situation also the advertising coo is a response to the *absence* of the other bird and consequent 'enforced' cessation of activity and not an expression of aggressiveness. The function of the advertising coo appears to be to advertise the presence of a male (or, exceptionally, a female) in breeding condition to potential mates. Also, perhaps, in some species to maintain contact between members of a pair.

The nest call is usually similar to the advertising coo and in many species does not differ at all from it in sound, at least to human ears. The situations in which the nest call is uttered are discussed in the chapter on social behaviour.

The display coo accompanies the bowing display or its homologue. Compared with the advertising coo or the nest call it is (except in those cases where it does not differ from the advertising coo) less loud, often indistinct and more prone to variation. In some species, such as the Stock Dove, *Columba oenas*, the display coo is very faint and only audible, to human ears, within a few yards. There appears to have been less selection for specific distinctness and audibility in the display coo than in the advertising coo. This is understandable as the latter functions 'at long range' whereas the former is always an accompaniment of the bowing display which is only given when two birds are close together and visible to each other. The display coo probably serves to enhance the general effect of the bowing display and may play a part in species recognition although I think it is likely to be usually of less importance for this than the colour patterns of the plumage, eyes and bill exhibited.

The display coo is often called the bow coo by American ornithologists. This term, although descriptive and clear when applied to such forms as the Rock Pigeon *Columba livia* or Diamond Dove *Geopelia cuneata*, can mislead because in some forms, such as the Mourning Dove *Zenaida macroura*, no actual bowing movement occurs in the homologue of the bowing display.

The distress call is a grunting, panting or gasping sound that could perhaps be written 'oorh!' or 'eerh!'. It is very similar in all pigeons whose voices are known to me, allowing for differences linked with size; it is usually deepest in larger species and higher pitched, almost a whistle, in the very small ones. In extreme fear it may be heightened in pitch and lengthened almost to a scream.

The distress call often functions as a warning note. It is given at the sight of a flying bird of prey, if the latter is too far distant to elicit more definite evasive action. It may also be given at the sight of other predators, including man and is often given by pigeons when handled. It is, however, also given in situations where the bird shows no signs of fear and its feelings seem rather to be of annoyance, discomfort or indecision. Adults usually give it when they see their young handled. I have often heard captive Barbary and Red-eyed Doves, *Streptopelia* 'risoria' and *S. semitorquata*, utter the distress call from their roosting perches at dawn on rather cold mornings. Here it seemed to be an expression of discomfort or of conflict (? causing psychological discomfort) between the impulse to fly down to feed and reluctance to leave the perch.

Some species of *Columba* give what sounds like an intense version of this call immediately after copulation. Here it seems equivalent to the excitement cry of other species. When used after copulation it is, I think, an expression of conflict or aggressive feeling rather than of pleasure as has been suggested.

The excitement cry is an emphatic and usually 'non-cooing' call. It may intergrade with the distress call but, at any rate in the *Streptopelia* species, is usually quite distinct from it. It is uttered in many social contexts and can, apparently, express either aggressive or sexual excitement but seems linked rather with the intensity than the specificity of the (presumed) emotion felt. It may function as a threat note but is also often used in apparent greeting between members of a pair.

Under normal circumstances female pigeons coo less loudly and less often than males and they do not use the display coo unless they are of a species which also uses this in hostile contexts. Unpaired females in reproductive condition will often use the advertising coo as freely as a male. Under some circumstances they may also perform the bowing display and utter the display coo. Females use the distress call and the excitement cry as freely as males.

Nestling pigeons utter only the puffing and bill-snapping used in the defensive threat display (q.v.) and a sibilant squeaking call. This latter is used as an expression of almost any apparent excitement although its most typical use is when begging to be fed. As in the case with young birds of some quite unrelated groups such as the grebes and the estrildines, young pigeons use the same calls and movements when begging an adult to feed them as they do when they are fiercely attacked by an adult. The only difference is that when begging for food the young one reaches up eagerly, trying to insert its bill into the adult's mouth whereas when 'begging for mercy' it turns its head away from the adult and cowers or flees. The squeaking call probably functions to help elicit parental feeding but it seems of no value in appeasing aggressive adults.

I have the impression that as soon as a young pigeon is capable of feeling the same (apparent) specific emotional moods as the adult it will 'try' to utter the adult calls. In the Speckled Pigeon, Rock Pigeon and Barbary Dove (probably also in other species) this may occur as soon as or even a little before the bird is able to fly. At first it can only squeak in the same rhythm as the adult's coos and its voice gradually 'breaks' over a period. Even after it has begun to coo and cry in the adult manner (although not as yet with the proper adult sound and intonation) the young pigeon will still use the infantile squeaking when begging or if it is attacked by another pigeon and does not dare to fight back.

The loud wing claps which often accompany display flights or wing clapping displays appear to be functionally equivalent to self assertive calls. Some species make distinctive whistling or creaking sounds with the wings when in normal flight, these may serve to help maintain contact between individuals in flight. Sometimes one or more primaries are especially modified for the production of such flight sounds.

REFERENCE

ANDREW, R. J. 1961. The displays given by passerines in courtship and reproductive fighting; a review. *Ibis* **103**:: 315–348 and 549–579.

DISPLAY AND SOCIAL BEHAVIOUR

I propose in this chapter to discuss in general terms the displays of pigeons ; and some behaviour-patterns that they show in various encounters with others of their species. This is in order to avoid pointless repetition in the sections on individual species and to make clear the terminology used.

How far one should extend the term 'display' when dealing with behaviour-patterns shown in agonistic situations is a moot point. Where movements and postures are directed towards another individual and exhibit striking plumage areas, as does the bowing display, it is clearly right to use the term. On the other hand one can hardly consider such undirected gestures as head-shaking to be 'displays'. But some actions, such as nodding or nest-calling, fall between the above extremes. So long as we recognise them and know their significance it does not much matter how we mentally classify them. In the species section of this book, however, nodding is described under the 'display' heading for convenience's sake. It is now the latest fashion to discard such terms as displacement activity and use instead 'irrelevant activity'. In spite of some theoretical justification for this I have used the term displacement preening here for the ritualised preening movements used by pigeons. The term has been so widely used for this and homologous behaviour of other birds that I feel it would be misleading to discard it here.

The Defensive-threat Display

In this the displaying pigeon erects its plumage, spreads its tail and lifts one or both wings. This display is given when the bird is simultaneously activated by conflicting impulses to attack and to escape and is commonly shown at highest intensity towards potential nest predators. A very great number of vertebrates have homologous and similar displays. As Darwin wrote when discussing such defensive displays in his *Expression of the Emotion in Man and Animals* (Darwin, 1872) : 'These appendages (i.e. fur, feathers and fins) are erected under the excitement of anger or terror ; more especially when these emotions are combined . . . the action serves to make the animal appear larger or more frightful'.

The components of this display are easily analysed. The erection of the feathers indicates a conflict situation in which the greater the conflict, or the greater the intensity of the conflicting impulses, the greater the erection of the plumage. The drawn-in position of the head and its orientation towards the alarming object are preparations for attack or active defense. The lifting of the far wing serves to help the bird keep its balance if it strikes out with the nearer wing. It seems often caused, however, by the impulse to flee. Should this tendency increase both wings will be lifted. Then a slight increase of the frightening stimuli will usually cause the bird to 'lose its nerve' and leap into the air with a quick downward stroke of its wings.

FIG. 3: Pigeon in defensive-threat display.

From the time they are about half-feathered nestling pigeons react to the appearance of a frightening object with a very similar display. They rear themselves up, erect the feathers, especially on the neck, inflate and deflate their necks (though not to the same degree as an adult when cooing), snap their bills, and may peck or strike at the intruder. Young able – or nearly able – to fly, will flee from the nest under such circumstances, although they may give this display if they are cornered in a cage or in a nest-cavity. Because under such conditions adults would flee, an exactly similar display to that of the young is seldom shown by them. Under certain circumstances they may, however, behave exactly as do nestlings. When I was training some Red-eyed Doves to roost in the shelter of their aviary it was necessary to put them therein each night. To avoid handling them I endeavoured to do this by lifting each under the breast so that it perched on the hand and allowed itself to be carried. They were nervous and would sometimes panic and fly wildly into the darkness, but usually it was possible to carry the bird in this manner. Often in such cases, however, it showed its fear in 'infantile' manner by erecting its feathers, inflating and deflating its neck with quick gasping puffs and snapping its bill. An adult Stock Dove with an injured wing was brought to me. Although unbroken one wing seemed incapable of movement, and presumably any attempt to move it caused pain. If I approached when it was on the ground the bird would run quickly away, but if on a perch it performed the 'nestling's' defensive display. It did this also when carried on the hand, particularly if lifted close to my face. This behaviour lasted only a few days. As soon as the wing began to heal it ceased to behave thus but would flutter down off its perch if approached and would no longer permit itself to be lifted on the hand.

The difference in motivation between the defensive-threat display of free, uninjured adults and that of nestlings (or of adults under such conditions as described above) seems to be that in the first the birds' aggressive impulses are conflicting with the impulse to flee. In the second it is incapable of escaping either through physical incapacity or through *fear* of something else (e.g. taking wing in the dark, the pain of using an injured wing) conflicting with fear of the object. The factor common to both cases is the inhibition of a very strong tendency to flee. The similarity in the movements and behaviour shown, suggest that this situation arouses a similar emotional mood in the bird whether the inhibiting factor is an overt force or its own aggressive tendencies.

In some pigeons raising of the wings may be used in actively aggressive as well as in defensive contexts. Here, however, it is not usually accompanied by any marked erection of the body plumage. In such species the raising of both wings may indicate a tendency to fly at rather than from the adversary and so be connected with attacking rather than escaping impulses. This seems to be the case with some, perhaps all, of the American ground doves. Some pigeons have large black or chestnut areas on the underwing which appear to function as display plumage of a threatening character when the wing is raised and also, perhaps, to enhance their fearsomeness in the eyes of some potential nest-predators.

The Bowing Display

This display is common to many species of pigeons. It is primarily a sexual display and is shown at fullest intensity by a male towards females to whom he is strongly sexually attracted. In many species, however, it is also used in threatening or defensive contexts. It appears always to be self-assertive in character but also indicates that the displaying bird is inhibited from attacking, even if only momentarily.

FIG. 4 *Top row:* Position at climax of the bow, or its equivalent, in the bowing display of (left to right) Plumed Pigeon, Blue Crowned Pigeon, Mourning Dove and Luzon Bleeding-heart.
Bottom row: The bow of the Stock Dove (right to left) (note: the bird does not (normally) move forward while bowing)

When giving its bowing display a pigeon usually faces the object of its attentions, lowers its head, at the same time exhibiting display plumage frontally and often uttering a characteristic cooing call. At the lowest point of the bow the bird's bill may be at about right angles to the ground, as with the Barbary Dove and the Rock Pigeon, pointing slightly upward as in the Bar-shouldered Dove, or at any angle between these extremes. In all species that have display plumage on the neck, as have the turtle doves and most of the typical pigeons, there is marked inflation of the neck and/or erection of neck feathers. The Australian bronzewings on the other hand show no marked inflation of the neck or erection of its feathers but partly open their wings and present them frontally so that the brilliant display plumage, which in their case is on the wings and not on the neck, flashes into view. Contraction of the pupil and consequent dilation of the (usually) brightly-coloured iris accompanies the bowing display of most species. To appreciate the bowing display fully it must be seen as the pigeon displayed at would see it – from in front and from 'pigeon's eye-level'. Then even the black bill, white cere and orange eyes, set against a shining globe of vivid green and purple that a Rock Pigeon (or a Domestic Pigeon of the wild colour) presents, is striking and almost awe-inspiring. In some species the bowing display, or rather the homologous behaviour pattern, does not involve actual head lowering movements.

Although the bowing displays of different species are now of a stereotyped nature most of their components seem to have been derived from locomotory or intention movements. The crouching posture assumed at the culmination of each bow probably originated in a preparatory movement for jumping or flying at or onto the other bird. In such species as the Bar-shouldered Dove the posture adopted makes this fairly obvious. In others the position of the head destroys this impression and perhaps indicates a more complete ritualisation of this part of the display. Some inflation of the neck usually seems to be a necessary concomitant of cooing and, together with the erection of the neck feathers, often also serves to exhibit the display plumage. We have seen, however (when discussing the defensive-threat display), that neck inflation and erection of plumage is shown by young, and sometimes also adult pigeons, when the impulse to escape is thwarted. It seems possible therefore, that these elements of the bowing display originated in, and may perhaps still indicate in some species or under some circumstances, a conflict situation in which sexual or aggressive impulses are inhibiting and/or being held in check by an impulse to flee.

Spreading of the tail occurs during the bowing display of many species. In the geopelias and the Wonga Pigeon the chief display plumage is on the tail, which is exhibited as an erect fan at the culmination of the bow. In others, such as the Wood Pigeon, the tail is spread during its upward movement but usually closes again before it is fully erect. Spreading and erection of the tail, which are often combined, appear likely to have originated from movements used when alighting or checking in flight. Many species of pigeons (and other birds) usually throw up the tail when they alight. In the Wood Pigeon this movement, even in 'everyday life' has evolved to the point where it is no longer a simple balancing movement but appears to have a psychological rather than physical significance. Instead of throwing up the tail at the moment of alighting the Wood Pigeon does so a few seconds afterwards. This it appears to do when sufficiently at ease to have 'decided', at least for the moment, to remain where it is. If it is frightened or sexually excited at the moment of alighting the Wood Pigeon may remain perched for a considerable time without making any tail movement. In the bowing display of this species raising of the tail is correlated with cessation of forward movement in the displaying bird. Thus the movement still retains something of what may have been, in an evolutionary sense, its original significance.

Spreading of the tail seems connected with a tendency to flee from or at least avoid closer contact with the object. This is fairly clearly indicated in the Rock Pigeon. In this species the spreading of the tail in no way enhances the display's optical effect but is usually shown when the bird moves towards or is very close to the object of its display. It seems likely that tail spreading originated in an impulse to escape. Possibly a tendency to escape may still be felt by the bird when it raises or spreads its tail in display. If so it is, however, very unlikely, in my opinion, that such a tendency to escape is accompanied by feelings anything like those evoked by a predator. The feelings accompanying such escaping tendencies as are shown in sexual display are probably more akin to those of ours which we call by such names as 'diffidence', 'shyness' and so forth, than they are to true fear.

A high lifting of the feet, often with a 'marking time' effect accompanies the bowing display of many species.   These are intention-movements of mounting as can be clearly seen when, as sometimes happens, a male giving the bowing display carries straight over to copulation without interposing the usual 'billing' ceremony.

The Display Flight.

It is probable that most pigeons have a display flight although so far it has only been described in detail for a relatively small number of species.   As in other birds the display flight involves movements that make the displaying bird very conspicuous and often also make it appear larger than it does in normal flight.   In display flight a pigeon usually spreads its wings widely, beats them rather slowly through a wider arc than usual and often makes a loud clapping noise when so doing.   This is followed by, or alternates with, gliding forward and/or downward with the wings, and usually the tail also, outspread.

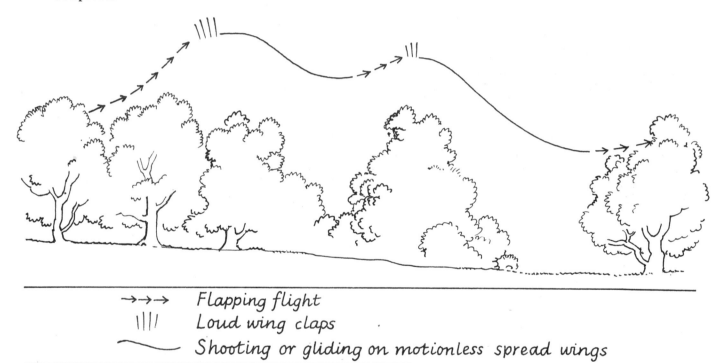

→→→   Flapping flight
\|\|\| Loud wing claps
⌒⌒   Shooting or gliding on motionless spread wings

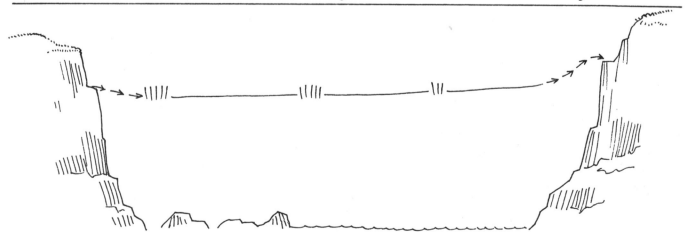

FIG. 5: Diagrammatic sketch of display flight of Wood Pigeon (top) and Rock Pigeon (bottom).

In many species such as the Wood Pigeon and the Crested Pigeon and many, probably all, of the turtle doves, the displaying individual first flies upwards and the display flight thus normally takes place *above* any others of the species who may be perched in the neighbourhood. This form of display flight is often correlated with conspicuous light and dark or black and white markings on the *underside* of the tail. In species, such as the Rock Pigeon, where the display flight is usually at, or even below, eye-level of neighbouring birds (the displaying Rock Pigeon usually flies straight out from the cliff or slightly downward) there are no conspicuous markings on the underside of the tail.

Full intensity display flight is only used by birds in reproductive condition. In Feral and non-monstrous Domestic Pigeons (*Columba livia*) a sexually active male commonly performs the display flight in the following situations :

(1) When he notices another pigeon on the wing.
(2) When he sees his mate or another pigeon in display flight nearby.
(3) When about to alight at or near his home after having been away foraging, or after having been taken away by man and thus forced to fly back.
(4) When flying in company with his mate (possibly then also as a response to some of the other stimuli listed above).
(5) Immediately after copulation (in about 40 per cent of cases only).

The female uses the display flight in the first situation only if she is unpaired and in reproductive condition and then less often and less emphatically than a male in similar plight. Under all other circumstances listed above she may use the display flight if her mate first initiates this behaviour. I have never seen a paired female, in company with her mate, begin to clap and glide unless he first did so. So far as I have seen the stimuli that elicit display flights from other species, at least in some *Columba* and *Streptopelia* species, are similar situations to (1), (2) and (3) listed above. Males of some *Streptopelia* species will, if isolated, perform display flights even without any stimulus from conspecifics.

The function of the display flight is to advertise the presence of a bird in reproductive condition. Unpaired females are strongly attracted to a display flying male. So, at least in *Columba livia*, are lost individuals, a fact that has long been known to unscrupulous pigeon-keepers, who make use of unpaired males for stray-catching. Since such lost birds are usually repelled or frightened by the subsequent sexual advances of the male they have followed, it is probable that his apparent attraction for them is due to his making reciprocal efforts to maintain contact with them in flight, which other pigeons do not do. It sometimes seems, however, that in pigeons as in man, lost or bewildered individuals have a tendency to follow any of their species who shows a self-assured and determined manner. Such behaviour would be useful to them since it would ensure that, sooner or later, they would be led to sources of food and water.

The mood of the display flying bird seems self-assertive and sexual rather than positively aggressive, but there are indications that thwarted or sublimated aggressiveness may at times by involved. The use of the display flight (sometimes) after copulation suggests this, as many birds show aggressive or escaping movements at such times. In the early spring of 1955 workmen were repairing a tower in South Kensington where many Feral Pigeons had their breeding and roosting territories. Again and again pairs, single birds, or small parties would fly over to try to return to their homes but be forced to retire for fear of the men. Almost always the pigeons went into display flight as, or immediately after, they turned back from their objective. Two wild Rock Pigeons that I flushed (separately) from hatching eggs in South Uist went into a low intensity form of display flight as soon as they were about fifty yards away from me. In these cases the wings, although passing through as wide an arc, as normally did not smite the air with such vigour and no audible clapping resulted. Such low intensity versions of the display flight are often shown by a young Domestic Pigeon, if the group with which it is flying splits up and it is undecided for a few moments which birds to follow.

It thus seems likely that those elements of the display flight which actually slow down forward movement – the wide, slower wing beats, spreading tail, gliding instead of beating the wings – originate in a conflict between tendencies to move away from and to remain in or return to a certain area. Although in its perfect form the display flight appears now to be quite ritualized it is nevertheless still shown, at least in its low intensity forms, as a response to such stimuli. The vigorous smiting of the wings shown in the normal display flight seems due to self-assertive or perhaps aggressive, impulses being super-imposed on the (presumably) more primitive 'slowing down' of the flying movements.

The causation of the display flight and mood of the bird performing it appear to be similar in other species to those suggested above for *C. livia*. In those which defend a larger territory such as the Collared Dove, the display flying bird more often carries over into attacking behaviour. In these species it is possible that the mood of the bird in display flight is more overtly aggressive than seems to be the case with *C. livia*. I think however, that the fundamental mood is self-assertive and only changes to aggression as a result of further stimuli (such as recognising the bird whose appearance elicited the display flight to be a stranger). Even the *Streptopelia* species will display-fly at times over 'neutral' ground, as the Wood Pigeon and Stock Dove, as well as *C. livia*, frequently do. Some species have wing clapping displays in which the male flies a few feet into the air towards the female, claps his wings loudly and alights beside her. Such displays seem to represent a 'condensed' version of the display flight and to be similarly motivated. Probably they will be found to be far more widespread than present records indicate.

The Wing-lifting Display.

When sexually excited pigeons tend to hold the wings with the primaries slightly spread and often to hold the folded wings partly open, especially at the moment of alighting. Some, such as the Stock Dove, have developed this into a more or less ritualised display in which the folded wings are lifted and held in about the same horizontal plane as the back. This serves to show the black wing markings. If we are looking down on it from above the sudden increase of conspicuousness of a Rock Pigeon or Stock Dove when it displays in this way is quite startling even to the human observer.

The wing-lifting display is given in response to the approach from above and (usually) behind by a bird of the same species. It doubtless originated as a flight-intention movement but now serves to display the wing markings and inform the bird at whom it is directed that the displaying bird is a conspecific in breeding condition.

This display is homologous with the relatively slight wing opening that other species show in similar circumstances. This is shown by the fact that when given at low intensity it does not differ appreciably from the latter and, on the other hand, some species that do not usually lift their wings into the horizontal plane may do so when, apparently, at a very high level of excitement.

Parading and Jumping.

When sexually excited pigeons walk with a rather high-stepping gait and exaggerated emphasis of movement. In *Columba* the head tends to be held high, in *Streptopelia* and *Geopelia* to be lowered. The wings are often somewhat lowered and primaries spread a little. At one time I called this 'strutting', but this suggests a jerkiness of movement such as is shown by some game-birds, and which is very different from the rather graceful deliberation of pigeons. Heinroth's term 'parademarsch', which I venture to anglicize as 'parading' seems therefore a much better one to use. Erection of the feathers of the lower back and rump is also usual under these circumstances. The movements above described may be due to tension caused by conflicting tendencies to approach and flee from the other bird. They serve, usually in conjunction with other more definite behaviour patterns, to indicate sexual readiness. Jumping towards or away from the other bird is also characteristic of most pigeons when in a state of sexual or aggressive excitement.

Nodding.

A downward stroke of the head, at the lowest point of which the bill is at an angle of about 85 to 90 degrees to the horizontal, is given by the Rock, Feral and Domestic Pigeons (*Columba livia*), under the following circumstances: (1) by both members of a pair when at the nest-site or when coming together again after a short parting, (2) by a female in response to sexual, self-assertive, or aggressive behaviour from a male with whom she is eager to pair, (3) by a bird alone (normally only if its mate is within sight) on the nest-site, (4) by a bird threatening (usually defensively) another. In all these instances it is interspersed with various self-assertive, aggressive or sexual behaviour patterns.

Thus the nodding is shown in what at first seem different situations. When given by a sexually aroused female in response to the sometimes rather rough advances of a male, it gives the impression of being a submissive display. When given by a nest-calling bird, that tilts its head to eye its mate whilst so-doing, it suggests an eager beckoning. When given by a defending or threatening bird its hostile character is at once obvious. If one tries to analyse the precise difference between 'friendly' and 'hostile' nodding the most one can say is that in the latter the movement tends to be swifter and more forceful, but also more often incomplete. Yet few pigeon-keepers, seeing a bird nod, are ever in doubt as to whether the gesture is directed at mate or foe – an interesting example of the superiority of man's perception to his rational analytical faculties.

Nodding in some form is probably common to all pigeons. I will here confine myself to discuss its occurrence in a few in which I have closely observed it on many occasions. In the Wood Pigeon, the Stock Dove and the Speckled Pigeon the movement is nearly the same as in *C. livia*. In the Barbary Dove the movement is slight. Even when on the nest this species usually only moves its head forward and downward through a small arc. In sexual and aggressive encounters away from the nest the movement is even less definite and so interspersed with the 'aiming' flight-intention movements as to be difficult to separate from them. In the Red-eyed Dove the nod, although similar to that of the Barbary, is more emphatic and quite easily recognisable.

These species all use the nodding in the same situations as does the Domestic Pigeon. In the Wood Pigeon and the *Streptopelia* species it may sometimes seem to be the accompaniment of active rather than defensive aggressiveness. The nodding of an attacking bird is, however, shown in intervals between attacks, when it is, for the moment, only 'holding its ground'. This in fact appears to be the basic 'meaning' of the movement. It always signifies the bird's intention of holding its ground and refusing to be driven from it. Probably the mood of the nodding bird is very different in the different situations but it always embodies a determination to remain in spite of the opposition.

I was for some time unable to decide whether this movement was a ritualised intention-movement of pecking, or of nest building. The frequent occurrence of actual pecking of the prospective mate by courted Wood Pigeons and Stock Doves and the very obvious aggressiveness in the quick 'spiteful' nods of Rock and Speckled Pigeons when angry suggested the former. On the other hand the most intense form of the nodding movement in all these species suggested the movement used when adding material to the nest. I became convinced that the latter explanation was correct when I first saw the nodding of the Bar-shouldered Dove (*Geopelia humeralis*). In this species the nod culminates in the typical movement of a pigeon fixing a twig into its nest. The Bar-shouldered Dove nods in threat, when away from any possible nest-site, even more freely than the others mentioned, although otherwise nodding under like circumstances. It is indeed bizarre to see the bird, with empty bill, continually lowering its head and making the typical 'shuddering' movement as if fixing an imaginary twig in an imaginary nest. The male Wood Pigeon when inviting the female to join him on the nest-site sometimes makes deep nods that culminate in a slight 'twig-fixing' movement.

It seems probable that the nod has been derived from the nest-building movement. It may have originally been used only at the nest-site and in such form might be 'translated' as the equivalent of saying 'Here I intend to nest', this 'statement' being either hostile or inviting according to circumstances. Its extension to hostile and sexual encounters away from the nest-site is explicable if during such the bird is always, to some extent, in the same mood as one calling on or defending its nest-site. Since in pigeons fighting and sexual behaviour are usually linked with possession of territory, this seems highly likely. It could perhaps be suggested that instead of having evolved from a completed building movement the nodding is the original movement – of displacement or redirected pecking – shown when the impulse to attack is inhibited by fear or sexual attraction and that the complete building movements have been developed out of it by natural selection. This second theory seems less likely, but by no means impossible.

Displacement-preening or Ritual-preening.

In its usual form this is a movement in which a pigeon turns its head, thrusts its bill between body and scapulars, quickly withdraws it and brings its head back, to face forward again. It is probably common to most if not all species, at any rate it is found in all those whose behaviour has been described in any detail. Displacement-preening may in some (? perhaps all) species also be directed at the sides of the breast. In the Rock Pigeon and its domestic and feral descendants, this usually indicates a lower intensity of arousal than 'behind-the-wing' displacement-preening.

So far as I have seen, displacement-preening in other species appears to occur in the same situations as it does in Rock and Domestic Pigeons (*Columba livia*). In these it is given by the male when he is sexually aroused but unable to copulate or commence the pre-copulatory billing *either* because the female is not yet giving the appropriate response or because of his own incapacity. That the same movement is shown in these apparently different situations suggests that it is used whenever an impulse to bill or copulate is being frustrated but no other positive conflicting tendencies, such as to flee or to attack, are present. This act appears to provide auto-erotic stimulation as well as serving as a signal to the mate.

The female does not usually displacement-preen so much as the male. This seems to be because she reacts to sexual unreadiness on her mate's part by more intense soliciting of billing or coition, by 'switching over' to caressing him, or (if the male crouches and invites her) by mounting him instead. She will, however, displacement-preen freely if thwarted in her sexual desire and unable to find outlet in the above mentioned alternatives. Thus a female 'paired' to a human being will displacement-preen as much as, or more than, a male normally does.

It is not always possible to draw an absolute line between the displacement-preening behind the wing, and real preening in this area. If a pigeon that is engaged in preening is very slightly sexually aroused by the arrival or sexual behaviour of another, it will preen behind its wing. It then uses normal preening movements – not the stereotyped displacement form. Nevertheless its subsequent behaviour towards the other bird usually indicates that they were sexual impulses – at low intensity – that caused it suddenly to pay attention to this area.

The function of this displacement-preening is to indicate the bird's sexual and peaceable intentions and to arouse a similar mood in the partner.

Nest-calling.

When a pigeon seeking a nest site has discovered what appears to it to be a suitable place, it adopts a crouching posture with tail and rump somewhat raised, lowers its head and calls repeatedly. At the same time the bird nods (see 'Nodding') and makes movements with its wings or tail.

In some (probably all) species of *Columba* and *Streptopelia* these wing movements consist of a sharp spasmodic twitching of the folded wings. The *geopelias* use a more rapid, almost fluttering movement of the nearly closed wings, and the Common Bronzewing a rather slow movement of the partially opened wings. These wing movements appear to derive from and to be homologous with the wing movements made by the fledged young when begging for food. In both cases the tempo of the wing movement is similar to those used in flight. Usually the nest-calling bird only moves the wing nearer to its mate if the latter is to one side of it. If the mate is approaching from more or less directly in front then both wings are usually moved simultaneously. The derivation of the wing movements and, indeed, the whole demeanour of the nest-calling bird, suggests that they are appeasing or conciliatory in character. However, like nodding (q.v.) the wing movements are, in some species, also used in defensive fighting when the bird intends to 'hold its ground'. The tail movements used when nest-calling by some species seem in all respects equivalent to the wing movements of others. In some cases wing and tail movements used when nest-calling serve to exhibit display plumage, as in the case of many green pigeons (*Treron*) where the up and down tail movements display the long chestnut under tail-coverts.

Both sexes nest-call, but most commonly the male does so more often and at a higher intensity than the female.   This is simply because he usually takes the lead in seeking a nest-site or in returning to one already selected.   Exceptionally lone pigeons that are in full reproductive condition may nest-call, but usually this behaviour is only shown when the mate, or a prospective mate, is nearby.   The opinion to the contrary held by some laboratory workers has undoubtedly been due to the tame Barbary Doves or Domestic Pigeons with which they were experimenting, reacting sexually to *them*.   This can be very clearly seen in species, such as the Wood Pigeon, in which the coo uttered when nest-calling differs from the usual advertising-coo.   When alone on his nest site a male Wood Pigeon usually stands in normal posture giving the advertising coo – the well-known 'tak-too-coos, taffy-tak!.   When the female perches near and shows interest he crouches in the nest-calling posture and utters his two-syllabled nest coo.

When the female approaches the nest-calling male she often shows signs of fear and hesitation, and when she finally makes a little run or hop (according to species) right up to him she may show some aggression and peck him quite roughly about the head, and if not she caresses his head.   In most species she behaves at this moment very like a displaying male, a further indication that the nest-calling of the male is of an appeasing nature and so tends to arouse self-confidence in the partner.   The male may, especially if the female is being rough, push his head under her breast (very much as a nestling pigeon does when brooded by the parent), but he does not retaliate although a little later the rôles may be reversed, and of course, the female may, in some cases, take the initiative in nest-calling.   Although shown most intensely in the case of newly paired or pairing birds at a newly discovered nest-site, nest-calling precedes every nesting and, to some extent, occurs during the nest building period.   The amount of it shown is, however, very much less in the case of well established pairs starting a second (or third, fourth or fifth) brood.

The function of nest-calling is to indicate to the mate the selected nest site 'for her (or his) approval'.   Also, probably, the caressing and calling on the site together play an important part in forming a bond between the two birds.   In Domestic and Feral Pigeons (and I think the same is true of wild species) this behaviour seems to play a much greater part in forging a strong emotional bond between a newly formed pair than does the billing and copulation which have usually preceded it.

Caressing or Allo-preening.

The caressing or preening of another individual, now usually called 'allo-preening' by behaviour students, is indulged in by many, perhaps all, species of pigeons.   It appears to have both psychological and 'utilitarian' significance.   Before discussing these we must consider what the caressing (or allo-preening) pigeon does and under what circumstances it does it.

The caressing consists of a gentle-looking nibbling movement of the bill, which is thrust into and moves about among, the partner's feathers apparently in contact with the skin.   Frequently the bird will seize some small object in its bill tip and either swallow it or (less often) cast it away.   The rump, back, wings and breast of the partner may be treated very briefly in this manner, but in general the caressing bird confines its attentions to the other 's head and nape.   At least ninety-nine per cent of all caressing is where the bird cannot reach with its own bill.   In some species of *Columba* and *Streptopelia* these are approximately (but not exactly) the areas above, and on the upper periphery of, the display plumage on the neck, and the caressing bird often begins by plunging its bill into the display plumage and then working upwards.   Although usually gentle it may be rather rough on occasions, and distinct though they are in their typical forms, it is difficult, even on the observation level, to say where aggressive pecking ends and caressing begins, or *vice versa*.

Mutual caressing by members of the pair occurs on the nest site, particularly by the female in the early stages when she joins the male on his selected site.   It may occur before or after copulation, in such case usually initiated by the hen when more eager for coition than her mate.   It occurs very frequently and in prolonged 'sessions' between birds that are paired but whose nesting is delayed because they are not yet in full reproductive condition.   Whichever bird is more forward sexually usually does a major share of the caressing.   In the Barbary Dove and Domestic Pigeon (probably also in other species) both sexes, but more often the male, may caress their young, particularly when these are fully fledged and beginning to fly about.   Juvenile birds, even when still in the nest, may caress each other   Owing to the amount of caressing indulged in being so much correlated with sexual readiness, or lack of it, it could be misleading to try to draw specific distinctions.

I think there can be no doubt that one function of caressing, on the physical level, is the removal of ectoparasites, and perhaps also other foreign bodies, from the mate's head. It is often shown when sexual tendencies are thwarted, owing either to the bird or (more often) its mate not being ready to copulate. At other times, as with a newly mated pair on a nest-site, it seems likely that it is aggressive, rather than sexual, impulses that are checked and find an outlet in caressing. Although caressing is shown in situations where aggressive or sexual impulses are inhibited, I do not think it likely that the bird caressing its mate or young is usually in the same mood as one about to attack or copulate. On the contrary, it appears rather to be in a mood of affectionate tenderness in which overt sexual and aggressive tendencies have been sublimated. As has been mentioned, the caressing partner may, however, be quite rough on occasions. In juvenile pigeons one often sees aggressive behaviour 'switch over' into caressing.

Normally, in pigeons, caressing only takes place between mates, or other birds that have an apparently affectionate social bond between them. The bird actually being caressed often moves its head about as if trying to avoid the other's attentions. This is particularly the case with young birds caressed by their parents. The evidence suggests that in all situations in which caressing occurs, the caressing bird would have become angry and shown aggression had there not been a bond of affection between it and the recipient of its caresses.

Billing.

This aspect of pigeon behaviour is familiar to all, at least in name, owing to the frequent use of the term 'billing and cooing' to describe rather different, if in some ways homologous, behaviour in men and women. Actually, the phrase should be the other way round as, in pigeons, the bowing display with its accompanying cooing usually takes place before, not after billing.

Billing, in its fullest form, consists of the male offering his open bill to the female, usually after ritualised displacement-preening. She then inserts her bill into his mouth and is fed by him much as a fledged young bird would be. More commonly, even in species such as the Rock Pigeon in which actual feeding of the female may occur during billing, the male does not disgorge food. He does, however, usually make regurgitating movements, as may the female also, while their bills are together. In many species billing is reduced to a momentary insertion of the female's bill or even to a brief 'fencing' or touching of bills.

Billing usually occurs as part of the copulation ceremony and is followed by the female crouching with her shoulders slightly raised to invite the male to mount her. As with the courtship-feeding of other birds, such as finches and parrots, billing seems to indicate and facilitiate the dominance of the male over the female.

Driving.

This is a pigeon fancier's term, which being brief and descriptive can be recommended to ornithologists, for the behaviour shown by a male pigeon when he wishes his mate to move away from (usually) the proximity of other male pigeons. The object of driving has, however, sometimes been misinterpreted owing to its being studied in the rather crowded conditions in which domestic Pigeons are commonly kept, or in small aviaries or cages in research institutes.

Driving occurs regularly in Domestic Pigeons, kept in flocks, from about a week or more before laying until the first egg has been laid. It can also be seen among wild or feral populations of *C. livia* wherever numbers of breeding birds are gathered at some common feeding ground. In its more intense forms, as seen in the pigeon loft or in some town square it is familiar to all. The driving male follows his mate everywhere, often literally 'treading on her tail'. He pecks, usually in a gentle, inhibited manner but often quite fiercely at her head. If she takes wing he flies closely behind and above her. If she goes to the nest (captive birds) the male stops driving.

Many pigeon-keepers suppose that the male is trying to force the female to go to the nest site but this is seldom, if ever, the case under natural conditions or even in the conditions under which Feral Pigeons live in towns.

Driving does not take place, even with young pigeons or pairs using a new nest-site, if there are not others of their species nearby. Of course a male pigeon that is reacting socially to man will often begin to drive his mate when a human being approaches them closely. The male's behaviour when driving shows a variable intermixture of aggressive and sexual elements. If the female goes to a distance of about thirty yards or more from other pigeons, he usually stops driving. If she flies on to a ledge or roof where there are no others he almost always stops. If the female approaches other pigeons or they approach her the male begins to drive by getting between his mate and the others, thus forcing her to move away from them. Occasionally driving pairs are seen on the ground at a greater distance from others of their species, and one may often see males driving in flight when no others are anywhere near. The first is often due to the female having ventured into a place where the male is afraid or ill at ease. Sometimes it seems to be due to the male's not having realised that the pair are now alone, if the female stops for any reason the male will look around and (apparently on seeing they are now alone together) cease to drive. That the same explanation is true for the male driving in flight is suggested by the number of times when I have seen a pair fly up from some crowded feeding ground and the male, who was at first driving hard in flight, swing out beside or in front of his mate as they got well away from others in the air, usually going into display flight as he did so.

The usually gentle nature of the pecks delivered show that the male's aggressiveness is inhibited but his aggressive impulses often 'get the better of him' and he may fairly run after the harried female, pecking hard at her head. Driving is a form of redirected aggression and appears to be usually motivated by sexual jealousy involving anger aroused by a sexual rival. A male pigeon usually drives very fiercely and pecks the female hard if she approaches a male of whom he is much afraid. Then the element of redirected aggression is very obvious to the observer.

During the driving period – or most of it, the female is sexually receptive. Should her mate be killed or removed she will usually pair again at once with any male that offers. If her own mate is sexually inactive she may desert him and, even when she does not, will allow another male to tread her.

It is, I think, evident that the function of driving, is to remove the female from the immediate neighbourhood of possible sexual rivals. It prevents the female from being fertilized by other males and gives the pair opportunity to copulate undisturbed. That in a relatively crowded pigeon-loft or aviary the male does not stop driving unless his mate goes to the nest is doubtless because under these conditions his next-box is the only place where the male feels sufficiently secure from interference to be at ease with his mate at this stage of the nesting cycle.

Driving in other species appears to have the same causation and function as in *C. livia*. In species that hold larger territories and which do not feed much in company during the breeding season, it is, naturally, much less in evidence. The behaviour of such colonially-nesting species as the white imperial pigeons and the Nicobar Pigeon in this connection would be of great interest but has not been recorded. Most of the people who visit their breeding grounds do so in the rôle of predator rather than that of observer.

In the vast majority of cases driving is caused by the presence of another male. A cock pigeon may, however, try to drive his mate away from any place where he feels frightened, but not sufficiently so to flee without her. Thus the male of a pair of Diamond Doves, that I kept in a small room, repeatedly drove his hapless mate when slightly frightened by my presence, unable to comprehend that she could no more 'get away' than he could. Similarly, I have seen a cock Domestic Pigeon drive a tame female Rock Pigeon, with whom he was paired, from strange gardens and roofs where she (lacking the Domestic Pigeon's inhibition against alighting in strange places) had settled.

Interference with Copulation.

In Domestic and Feral Pigeons copulating pairs are frequently interfered with by others. This behaviour has also been observed in many other species in captivity. To what extent, if any, it occurs in such species under natural conditions is uncertain. Pairs of Wood Pigeons, for example, habitually copulate on the same perches (in London often a modern concrete street-lamp standard) at about the same time day after day. I have never seen a neighbouring Wood Pigeon interfere.

In Domestic and Feral Pigeons attacks on copulating pairs are usually made only by males in full sexual condition. The interfering bird runs or flies straight at the mating pair, dislodges the mounted male, then at once begins to peck the female's head. If the female remains crouching, he may mount and copulate with her, but this does not often occur. When the female rises the male usually desists from his attack, and often begins the bowing display. Rarely he may chase the female a short distance, pecking at her head. If several males interfere simultaneously (as often happens in such places as Trafalgar Square where large numbers of male birds are present) some or all of them will often chase the female for some moments after, pecking her head as they do so. Thus throughout the period that his attention is focused on her, the behaviour of the interfering male towards the female is identical with that of a very aggressive driving male towards his own mate. Interference with copulation seems to be part of the same behaviour-complex as driving. As we have seen the latter functions to prevent the female being fertilized by a male other than her own mate and is elicited by the presence of a potential sexual rival in her vicinity. Since such driving is shown more intensely according to the degree of sexual interest which other birds show his mate, it is reasonable to suppose that the highest possible stimulus for it would be the sight of another male actually mounting her. In such a situation it is obvious that only an instantaneous reaction could remedy matters. A male who paused to make sure that it was his mate and not another female who was involved could never interfere in time to prevent insemination. Hence, it is not surprising to find that selection has favoured those males that showed an instantaneous response to the sight of any others of their kind copulating. That this is the true explanation is suggested by the behaviour of the interfering male towards the female, his apparent 'indignation', his ferocious attempt to drive her quickly away, and his desisting as soon as he realises that she is not his mate. The continued driving that may occur if more than one male interferes seems due to the fact that in such circumstances each is for some moments too occupied in trying to get her away from the others to recognise her.

Head Shaking.

This consists of a sudden, quick shaking or jerking of the head. The movement appears chiefly lateral, but at times seems to involve a rotary movement also. This last is most noticeable when the head-shaking is performed more slowly than usual.

This movement is shown immediately after drinking or as a response to physical irritation of the head, especially the mouth. Gently prodding or tickling the head of a pigeon (if it is sufficiently tame not to be frightened by one's close proximity) with a grass stem will at once elicit this reaction. The use of the movement under these circumstances is clearly to remove drops of water or other foreign objects adhering to the head or bill. It is very similar to, and possibly homologous with the head-shaking movements that many water-birds – grebes, gulls, guillemots, etc., – invariably show after feeding, drinking or preening.

In many species this movement is also made under what at first appear to be quite different circumstances. When a pigeon coos at another the latter will head-shake if it is not aroused to overt sexual, aggressive or fleeing behaviour. It is evidently the sound that elicits this response, not the display which usually accompanies it. Under the same conditions to those mentioned above tame pigeons will head-shake if their owner 'coos' at them. I have seen two Speckled Pigeons (a male and female) head-shake when another, completely hidden from their sight, gave the advertising coo.

Since the head-shaking of a pigeon that is displayed to by another may be followed by, or interspersed with, movements of avoidance or withdrawal, one is tempted to regard it as an appeasing or submissive display. I have, however, seen nothing to suggest that it serves any such function. It seems rather that a pigeon when not in sexual or self-assertive mood, finds the cooing displeasing; that it acts as the psychological equivalent of a physical irritant and that the bird thus reacts to either stimulus with the same movement. On what may be (but I think is not) a higher plane of behaviour, we see the same phenomena in Man. Most of the gestures of disgust, contempt or repudiation used by *Homo sapiens*, of varying races, are essentially identical with those used on the purely physical level to rid the mouth or body of irritating or distasteful substances.

I think head-shaking is used in the above sense by all pigeons and have seen it in a great many species. *Columba livia* uses it far less freely than other species known to me. Indeed, whereas I have seen this gesture hundreds of times from all other species of pigeons I have kept I have seen it very seldom in Rock, Feral or Domestic Pigeons. Perhaps because this gregarious species seldom feels 'irritated' by the sound of another cooing.

The following incident seems worth giving as showing how the head-shaking response will be inhibited by any positive sexual feelings towards the cooing bird. A pair of Wonga Pigeons in a zoo had been separated and placed in aviaries a few yards apart. The hen was desperate to rejoin her mate. She alternately ran up and down the wire trying to get to him or perched on a ledge and there uttered her advertising coo. A cock Turtle Dove in the same aviary, who was inhibited from cooing or displaying by an aggressive pair of Red-eyed Doves, frequently showed a strong sexual response to the Wonga Pigeon when she stood still calling on the ledge. He would cautiously approach her, obviously torn between fear (probably because of her much greater size) and desire to copulate with her, and begin to make the intention-movements of mounting. During the hour or so that I watched he made several such attempts, but since, when he was near her, any movement of the Wonga Pigeon caused him to flee a little from her, he never got any further. The Wonga Pigeon showed no reaction at all towards him. The Turtle Dove's tentative approaches alternated with periods when he apparently lost interest and sat lumpishly on the far end of the ledge. When thus sitting he shook his head at each repeated fluting coo of the Wonga's call. During the periods when approaching her, however, he never head-shook in response to her cooing.

Sociability and Flocking.

Many pigeons, probably most, are more or less gregarious and often or commonly fly, feed, rest or roost in company. The term 'flock' when applied to birds usually implies some degree of cohesion or unison of action among its members. A party of Rock Pigeons that set out together from their roosting cliff, fly together to their feeding grounds, alight and seek for food together, fly up together and move to a new feeding ground, etc., can, therefore, rightly be termed a flock. Conversely a number of Turtle Doves seeking food together in some field or stackyard to which they have flown singly or in pairs and from which they will similarly depart are better considered as a mere aggregation than as a flock. Often, however, the position is less clear as every intermediate degree of social cohesion, or lack of it, between the two extremes given above may obtain in gatherings of pigeons. For example, a feeding or pre-roosting flock of Wood Pigeons may consist partly of birds that came in smaller flocks which have not maintained their identity once their members joined the larger group, partly of birds that came singly or in pairs. If the gathering is frightened some may fly off in large groups, while others scatter singly or in twos or threes.

As with other birds the tendency to form more or less cohesive flocks is particularly characteristic of forms that fly over open country or over the sea in their everyday life. On the other hand forms that inhabit forest, do not fly far in their everyday life (even though they may do so when migrating or dispersing) and feed much on the ground, seldom tend to gather together in large numbers. Forms that are primarily dwellers in woodland or forest (or were before man altered their environments) and which fly distances over the canopy in search of food supplies, such as fruiting trees, may form quite cohesive flocks when thus engaged. Even species that are not very gregarious at other times usually travel in flocks when migrating.

Sociability tends to be strongest when roosting, when flying for some distance (especially over unfamiliar country or sea), and when resting, preening, bathing or sunning. Species which are highly territorial and maintain large territories when breeding may have recognised 'loafing' and feeding places where not only juvenile and non-breeding individuals but even, at times, breeding pairs gather together without any serious friction. Possibly in some species the tendency to gregariousness when feeding or nesting is equally strong but it is difficult to be sure as in most colonial nesters the food source or nesting area chosen could be and certainly often is the major factor bringing the birds together. In *Columba livia*, and probably also in other species, the need for 'companionship' as indicated by the degree of readiness or eagerness shown to join or follow others is usually strongest in lost or immature individuals.

The above facts suggest that a pigeon feels most in need of company when it is bewildered or slightly afraid and it is then particularly ready to follow any member of its own species. Its behaviour in such situations is suggestive of that of the fledged young which, at least in some species, closely follow a parent for the first few days after they become strong on the wing. In all probability the motivation underlying the following behaviour is similar in both cases.

Flocking, using this term in the widest sense, may have many functions. It probably facilitates the discovery and maximum utilisation of food supplies that are plentiful but scattered in distribution; it enables young or inexperienced individuals to benefit from the initiative or knowledge of local food or water supplies possessed by older or more experienced birds. It enables many individuals to meet and may thus facilitate pairing between unrelated individuals. Also, I think, it may act as a significant check on predation. Two heads may or may not always be better than one but a hundred eyes are certainly more likely to spot an approaching predator than two are. Even allowing for the fact that in some instances, especially where man is concerned, large numbers may attract predators that would have overlooked a few individuals, it is probably true that a pigeon in a flock not only 'feels' safer but actually is safer from most forms of predation.

Species recognition.
Some (most probably all) pigeons either do not recognise their own species instinctively, or else, as is now known to be the case with some other birds, innate species recognition can be obliterated or suppressed by conditioning in early life. They appear to learn the characteristics of their species from their parents and, to a lesser extent, from their nest mates (if any) and from other members of the species whom they associate with early in life. This learning, or, perhaps, one might better call it realisation, appears to take place mainly during the periods shortly before and after fledging and while they are still dependent on their parents. This learning of a creature's own species, when restricted to a definite early period, has been termed 'imprinting'. Under natural conditions it ensures that the young bird will learn to recognise and respond to its own kind. If, however, through human interference a young pigeon is reared by foster parents of another species it will usually later show sexual and social responses towards that species. Pigeons that have been taken from the nest and reared by hand may become imprinted on human beings and show social and sexual reactions to them in preference to their own kind. Such a definite and permanent preference for human beings usually only comes about if the hand-reared bird has been much in human company after as well as during its nestling period. With Barbary Doves experiments have shown that young taken between seven and nine days old, when the fear responses are beginning to develop, are not only more likely to become imprinted on a human fosterer than young taken later when the fear responses are more fully developed but also than nestlings taken when younger (Klinghammer and Hess, 1964). The same will, probably, be true of other species. It is, presumably, due to young doves taken when fear responses are present but have not developed enough to prevent altogether the acceptance of a substitute parent, feeling more intense emotional arousal and this somehow leading to more complete fixation on the new parent.

In a natural state the young pigeon will, of course, continue to associate with birds of its own species and this certainly reinforces the early imprinting on the parents. Under unnatural conditions in captivity or semi-captivity the young pigeon may identify itself with such associates, instead of with the species which stood *in loco parentis* to it, especially when it has been reared by a human being. For example, a male Wood Pigeon that was reared by its own parents until about ten days and then by hand later showed social responses only to Domestic Pigeons, which had been frequently in its sight while it was being hand-reared and with which it associated when old enough to fly. A male Turtle Dove similarly treated showed social reactions towards both its own species and Domestic Pigeons; at first its sexual preferences were for the latter but it eventually paired and bred successfully with a female of its own kind. On the other hand Domestic Pigeons that have not been fostered by a human but have been much handled and talked to by their owner may show responses to humans as well as to their own species.

In Domestic and Feral Pigeons where differently coloured birds of the same species associate, individuals usually show a strong sexual preference for birds of the same colour as their parents irrespective of their own coloration. This preference may, however, be modified in later life as a result of pairing with a mate of another colour, even although the original pairing was due to the unavailability of a mate of the preferred colour. One worker (Warriner, 1960) found that with his Domestic Pigeons only males showed this preference for a sexual partner of the parent's coloration. This, however, is not always the case; I have known female Rock and Domestic Pigeons show very clear preference for mates of their foster parents' colour.

From the above facts it is easy to see how the development of different coloration could function as an isolating mechanism to reduce or prevent interbreeding between related forms in areas where they overlap. We find several instances where closely related sympatric species differ strikingly in head colours although otherwise rather similar in colour pattern. For example, the White-crowned Pigeon *Columba leucocephala* and the Red-necked Pigeon *C. squamosa* of the West Indies and several of the fruit doves of the genus *Ptilinopus*.

REFERENCES

GOODWIN, D. 1958. The existence and causation of colour preferences in the pairing of feral and domestic pigeons. *Bull. Brit. Orn. Cl.* **78**: 136–139.
WARRINER, C. C. 1960. Early experience in mate selection among pigeons. University Microfilms, Inc., Ann. Arbor, Mich., U.S.A.
KLINGHAMMER, E. & HESS, H. E. 1964 Imprinting in an Altricial Bird: The Blond Ring Dove. *Science* **146**: 265–266.

PAIR-FORMATION AND THE RELATIONSHIP OF THE PAIR

Pair-formation in pigeons has been chiefly studied in *Columba livia*, usually domestic birds kept under conditions of fairly close confinement. For this reason many have had the impression that pair-formation starts with the male nest-calling and the female being attracted by this. Actually, in free-flying *C. livia*, the female usually first becomes interested in the male through seeing him giving his display flight or through his flying to her and directing the bowing display at her. If she is sexually aroused she responds to the bowing-display by nodding and parading. Soon the male begins to displacement-preen behind his wing and to offer his open beak. The female responds. They bill, copulate and indulge in post-copulatory display. It is not, usually, till after this that the male either goes to his nest-site and nest-calls, or, if he has no nest-site, the pair go seeking one together, the male usually taking the lead.

Depending on individual circumstances pair-formation may proceed quickly or slowly in Feral and free-living Domestic Pigeons. Sometimes a pair of young birds, often a brother and sister from the same nest, are sexually attracted to each other and may indulge in low intensity, and often rather abortive sexual behaviour on and off for months before they really pair. On the other hand, a pair may be firmly formed in a few minutes if an unmated cock and an unmated hen in full breeding condition come together and are mutually attracted.

If captive pigeons have been kept unpaired until they are at a very high pitch of reproductive condition and then put together they may respond to each other so intensely that parts of the normal 'courtship' are omitted. Thus the female may crouch and invite coition the moment the male starts to display and before he attempts to initiate the pre-copulatory billing. Exceptionally, the male may omit display or displacement-preening and if his nest-site is at hand respond to the female's appearance by intense nest-calling. The above remarks hold good for the domestic Barbary Dove also.

Pair-formation in wild pigeons probably takes place in an essentially similar manner. At least this appears to be the case with the Wood Pigeon, Stock Dove and Turtle Dove. In the Stock Dove there is some evidence (Delmée, 1954) that the female will often refuse to accept a male who does not possess a nest-site. No doubt in this species, as in most hole-nesting birds, selection strongly favours those females who are willing to desert a male without a good nest-site when a male with one is available. The pairing for life which is usual in Feral and Domestic Pigeons and the Barbary Dove is probably largely due to their being sedentary (or caged), constantly together and almost constantly in reproductive condition. It probably does not occur in wild species that migrate or wander after breeding.

In such species, however, birds may often pair again with the mate of the previous year through their both returning to the same breeding territory. When this happens with the Wood Pigeon, the two appear at once to recognise and accept one another as soon as they meet again. No doubt the same is true with other species.

Observers have differed in their opinions as to the nature of the relationship between cock and hen of a pigeon pair, some concluding that the male dominated the female, and others denying it. To me it seems that these differences stem largely from different interpretations of such words as 'dominance', 'submission' and so forth. The male cannot and does not 'compel the female to submit . . . ' as has been claimed, although when the birds are closely confined the observer may get this impression if the male bird is more forward in reproductive condition. A stronger bird may cause a weaker one to 'want' to flee and even kill it if it is unable to do so, but cannot compel its *co-operation* in any activity that it does not 'want' to participate in. On the other hand, the female is subject to the male in the sense that she frequently submits to attack from him without resistance and/or shows signs of a tendency to flee from him.

When the pair are on the nest-site together, the female often utters notes intermediate between the advertisement-coo and the alarm note, though less loud than either. She may do this, crouching and lowering her head, when pecked by the male. Often she will push her lowered head under the male's breast as she does so. This behaviour is also shown by the nest-calling male, particularly when the female caresses him roughly. One reason for its effectiveness in inhibiting aggression is because it conceals the head, always the focal point of an attack. Tame females often give these notes and behave in this way when handled on the nest by their owner. It is difficult to interpret this other than as of an appeasing or submissive nature.

Particularly significant is the fact that a female pigeon 'desperate to pair' will respond sexually to an aggressive attack by a male even if he shows no definitely sexual behaviour towards her. For example, a captive Speckled Pigeon repeatedly drove from his nest-box a female who wished to pair with him. His hostility slowly lessened over a period of about seven weeks, after which he accepted her and they began to build and copulate. Throughout this period the female had entered the male's box at every opportunity, nodding and wing-twitching towards him whenever he came in view. She never attempted to fight back when he attacked and drove her off, but on *every* occasion that this happened she at once flew and attacked one of the three other Speckled Pigeons (all males in non-reproductive condition) in the same enclosure. Redirected aggression of this nature occurs in most vertebrates. It is, of course, particularly common in man, in whom, however, its true nature is often disguised by its being underwrit by religious, moral or political sanctions.

As soon as he had accepted her the male Speckled Pigeon – backed up by his mate – became so aggressive towards the others that they had to be removed at once. After the pair had copulated the male was never seen to show any aggression towards the female nor she to show overt fear of him. I had them under observation for two successful (young fully reared) nesting cycles, and a part of a third.

REFERENCES

DELMÉE, E. 1954. Douze Années d'observations sur le comportment du Pigeon Colombin. *Le Gerfaut* **44**: 193–259.
GOODWIN, D. 1956. The significance of some behaviour patterns of pigeons. *Bird Study* **3**: 25–37.
—— 1963. Nodding, driving and caressing in pigeons. *Ibis* **105**: 263–266.
HEINROTH, O. & K. 1949. Verhaltensweisen der Felsentaube (Haustaube) *Columba livia livia. Zeitschr. f. Tierpsychol.* **6**: 153–201.
WHITMAN, C. O. 1919. *The Behaviour of Pigeons.* Posthumous works of C. O. Whitman. Vol. 3. Carnegie Inst. Washington.

NESTING AND PARENTAL CARE

The nesting places chosen by pigeons vary both from species to species and according to the environment and opportunities of the individual pairs. However, these differences are often less than one might expect and some general principles can be stated here in order to save repetition under the species' headings.

Those species of pigeons which nest in trees or shrubs normally choose sites which offer some horizontal or nearly horizontal support. Most species also choose, where possible, a place that is well screened by vegetation. If the site offers some support on one or more sides as well as from below, so much the better. Thus typical sites are, for example: (1) On a horizontal or near horizontal fork near the periphery of some tree or shrub. (2) On a large horizontal bough that has smaller, upward-growing shoots on either side of the part selected. (3) On a nearly horizontal part of some large leaf or frond of some tropical fern or other plant. (4) On the old or deserted nest of any bird that builds a flat or shallow-cupped nest in trees or shrubs. Pigeons do not deliberately push material down into nearly vertical forks as do such birds as jays, indeed, I have only once known a pair (of Wood Pigeons) to succeed in building in a fork, or rather two forks, of about 45 degrees. A pigeon's nest in such a situation will usually be found on examination to have been built on the foundation made by some passerine species.

Availability, or otherwise, of 'ideal' sites and the abundance or otherwise of nest predators may locally influence the types of nesting places chosen. For example, in the English countryside it is unusual for Wood Pigeons to nest in deciduous trees while these are still bare. In London they commonly do so. Like many other arboreal birds most of the tree-living pigeons tend to nest fairly low down in shrubs or creepers rather than high up, even when allowance is made for the fact that nests in such low situations are much more easily found by human beings than are those high in the tree tops. This is probably because such low nests are less liable to be found by predatory birds or such arboreal mammals as monkeys and martens.

Given the tendency, which most branch nesting species have, to choose a nest site which gives a firm support and is screened by vegetation, therefore in shade, it is easy to see how some forms, or rather their ancestors, took to nesting in holes or caves. A shallow hollow in a tree trunk or a ledge near the mouth of a cave would supply much the same stimuli as the more usual site. Indeed many normally branch nesting species, such as the Wood Pigeon, quite often nest in such situations, especially in towns. Once a species had, either through choice or necessity begun to nest habitually in such places there would probably be strong selection in favour of those pairs that nested in deeper holes or further inside the cave. Thus any initial inhibitions against entering such cavities would be overcome in the course of evolution. Probably most of the species that have gone furthest in this way, such as the Rock Pigeon, have done so in the course of adapting themselves to a comparatively tree-less environment.

Holes in trees or cliffs usually offer a greater degree of safety from predation than sites among the branches. This may be somewhat offset, however, by the greater chance of one of the parents being killed as well should a predator find the nest hole. For example: female Stock Doves are often caught and killed in their nesting holes by Tawny Owls and martens. Holes in steep cliffs and, to an even greater extent, ledges in caves, offer a relatively high degree of safety from predators. Really good sites of this nature tend to be limited in numbers. This is why the species that use them, whether of pigeons or other birds, tend to nest colonially. Colonial nesting implies the ability to be psychologically capable of 'making do' with a very small nesting territory thus enabling the species to take the fullest possible advantage of safe breeding places. Where man has entered the scene as a predator on birds the situation is, of course, now very different, and colonial nesting is highly detrimental to any species showing it to a strong degree. However inaccessible the Rock Pigeon's nest may be on some high ledge in the gloom of a sea cave or hundreds of feet below ground in some desert pot-hole modern man can, and does, wait with his gun at the cave entrance to shoot the departing or returning adults. The Passenger Pigeon has already been exterminated by him and, as his numbers increase, it is likely that other colonially nesting pigeons will share the same fate.

A few terrestrial species, such as some of the Australian bronzewings, always nest on the ground and some other species quite often do so. Here again the situations chosen are usually suggestive of those of typical branch nesting forms except that cover is represented by surrounding grass and herbage and the ground itself serves as support. Most of the species that quite often nest on the ground are, as would be expected, ones which spend much of their time feeding and resting there. At least one of them, however, the beautiful White-throated Pigeon, is otherwise arboreal in its habits.

The nests of pigeons are usually small for the size of the birds and with only a slight central depression in which the eggs lie. Typically they are built of small twigs, thin roots, or the dead stems of grasses or other plants. The Stock Dove and some other species sometimes take dead leaves as nesting material. Pigeons nesting where they have a solid support, such as in a hole, on a ledge or on the ground, may use little or no nesting material. This applies more especially to such thoroughgoing ground-nesters as the plumed pigeons.

In many species of *Columba* and *Streptopelia* the amount of nesting material brought by the cock, and hence the ultimate size of the nest, depends on the following variable factors : (1) the length of time between the selection of the nest site and the laying of the first egg; (2) the time needed to find food, and hence the amount of time that the hen can spend building and the cock finding material; (3) the availability of suitable material. For these reasons the nests of captive pairs, provided they have been given unlimited suitable material, are usually larger than wild nests of the same species. These factors probably operate in the same way for most other species. Statements as to the size, bulk, or slightness of the nest of any species which are based on the finding of only a few nests may, therefore, indicate the circumstances of individual pairs rather than specific characters.

Both sexes, at least in the Rock Pigeon, the Wood Pigeon, andthe Barbary Dove may bring a few pieces of material to the nest-site shortly after it has been selected. I have seen a male Wood Pigeon carrying twigs to a half-built nest when no female was in the vicinity. As a general rule, however, the male pigeon searches for material and carries it back to the nest-site where the female does the building. The usual rôle of the sexes may be reversed or the male may build with material he brings but, in my experience, both happen rather rarely. Serious nest building is initiated by the female squatting at the selected nest-site. The male reacts to this by seeking for suitable material and carrying it back to her. In many species the male usually walks or jumps onto his mate's back and presents the twig to her over her shoulder or head. A nest-building session usually lasts until the female tires of sitting and building and leaves the nest site, unless she or the male is put to flight by some predator. With pigeons, as with gulls and some other birds, nest building seems not completely emancipated from its possible origin as a displacement activity. If, during incubation, the female is reluctant to quit the nest when the male comes to take his turn he may react by going off and collecting a twig for the nest. With Domestic Pigeons this often happens if the male comes to take over at the moment eggs are actually hatching, when the female is often reluctant to leave them.

Species which feed on the ground seek nesting material there. The arboreal species break off dead or dying twigs of trees and shrubs. Species which, like the Wood Pigeon, feed freely both in trees and on the ground, seek nesting material in either situation. The male picks up any twig or stem that, apparently, looks suitable to him and shakes or jerks his head while holding it one or more times before rejecting it or carrying it off. Twigs or stems of a tough 'wiry' nature are usually preferred. If therefore, the male comes upon pieces of wire of suitable size they supply a 'supra-normal' stimulus to him and he takes them eagerly. Hence in towns where quantities of discarded wire can be found on waste ground pigeons' nests are quite often built partly and sometimes entirely of pieces of discarded wire.

In many species (but not all) whose laying times are known the first egg is laid in the evening. The female usually sits on the nest for some time before laying; often she may spend most of the day on the nest, quietly resting when not arranging material brought by her mate. Once an egg has been laid it is seldom left uncovered unless the incubating parent is forced to flee from the nest. Domestic Pigeons and captive wild ones that are fed in limited quantities at certain times will, however, learn to leave the nest for a few minutes at feeding time if the alternative is to go hungry. Similarly, the hen of a pair of wild Collared Doves, who had nested in an apple tree in a fowl run, would leave her nest in order to get a share of grain when the chickens were fed. In captivity at any rate male pigeons usually roost well away from their sitting mates even though they may have roosted close to the nest before the first egg was laid.

The same behaviour is usually shown by Wood Pigeons in a wild state and is probably very widespread and not an artifact of captivity.   In some species, however, both male and female of captive pairs may roost together side by side on the nest, particularly when they have hatching eggs or small young.   This has not been recorded in the wild but very few detailed observations have been made of the roosting habits of most wild pigeons during the breeding season.

In all species for which incubation and brooding periods are known the male takes over about mid-morning and the female returns about one to three hours before dusk. Sometimes, at least in captivity, the female may also take over for an hour or two around mid-day.   Either sex may go on to the nest 'out of turn' if it sees the eggs uncovered or if it sees its mate away from the nest.   Both sexes normally incubate for about the same number of daylight hours and the female all night also.

Pigeons usually feed their young within an hour or two of hatching.   This at least is the case with the species I have kept and bred in captivity and it is probably true for others also.   The parent takes the squab's soft bill, with its swollen boat-shaped under mandible, into his, or her, own mouth and regurgitates pigeons' milk.   In a series of careful experiments on the Barbary Dove (Klinghammer and Hess 1964), it was found that the feeding of the newly-hatched nestlings is innate and performed in a normal and perfect manner by inexperienced parents of even this long domesticated form.

FIG. 6: Head of young nestling to show characteristic colour pattern of the bill.

The bills of adult pigeons vary in colour from black to white but they show strongly demarcated contrasts of colour in only a very few species.   Newly-hatched nestlings of all species that I have seen (or have seen descriptions of) have, however, a very similarly coloured bill with a very pale tip, then a blackish band.   This striking colour pattern doubtless serves to reinforce the parent's instinct to take the nestling's bill into its own and makes it easier for it to see what it is doing when the nest is in a gloomy situation, as pigeons' nests often are.   The nestling, when its bill is taken by the parent pushes further until it reaches the parents' mouth.   The latter then disgorges pigeons' milk to feed it.   When the young are fairly small, two are often fed at the same time (in those species which normally have a brood of two) although later they grow too big, and usually push and thrust too vigorously when being fed, for the parent to cope with more than one at a time.

For the first few days the young are fed only on pigeons' milk.   Then, at about the third or fourth day in the case of the Barbary Dove and at about the fourth or fifth in Domestic Pigeons, they also get morsels of any soft foods and any small seeds that the adults have eaten.   By the time they are half-fledged they are getting whatever their parents have eaten but with the addition, usually, of a little pigeons' milk. This seems to come about not through the deliberate giving or withholding of various items by the parent but as a simple result of the feeding processes.

When a pigeon feeds very young nestlings it is gentle or restrained in all its movements.   Its crop is then largely congested with pigeons' milk and such of this as is ready to feed lies above what other food there may be in the crop. After each regurgitating movement it swallows back any food left in its throat by the nestling before regurgitating again. As the youngster grows and becomes more vigorous so the parent regurgitates more violently, bringing up more of its crop contents, but still at once swallowing back any food that the young one does not take. Thus, without any special attention on the parent's part, the nestling is able to take those foods which are of a suitable size or consistency for it and to reject larger items without their being wasted.

The parents do, however, try to adjust their diet according to the needs of their young. Many species, when feeding young, search for and eagerly eat such animal food as caterpillars, termites and other small invertebrates, and consume large quantities of mineral matter. This behaviour is obviously related to the need for proteins and minerals of the rapidly growing young. Also during the short period when their young can take from them only small seeds (and crop-milk) the parents of seed-eating species (of medium size) will eagerly take small seeds such as millet, canary-seed, or linseed in preference to larger seeds such as maize, peas and peanuts. This can easily be observed in Domestic Pigeons, unless they are ravenously hungry and have to compete with others for a limited ration, in which case the need to fill their crops quickly while they can may make them take the largest seeds first.

When feeding young that are more than a few days old a parent pigeon usually disengages its bill, pauses and then offers its open mouth again several times during each feeding session. This behaviour seems motivated by the need for a momentary respite on the parent's part but it functions so as to allow both young equal opportunities of feeding. There does not, however, appear to be any deliberate attempt on the part of the parent to see that the young get fair shares. If one young one is, for any reason, much weaker and less vigorous than the other, it may fare very badly. At the age (about four to eight days in most species) when the young are normally getting a considerable amount of pigeons' milk but also other food, the former – for reasons stated above – is fed first. Hence, if one of two squabs is much more vigorous than the other it will always succeed in being first into the parental mouth until its hunger is satisfied. As a result it will get all the pigeons' milk from its parents and the weaker squab will get only other food. This state of affairs quickly leads to the death of the weaker from malnutrition.

Pigeons, like passerine birds, learn to recognise their young as individuals about fledging time. Domestic Pigeons and Barbary Doves will, for example, accept any young one placed with their own nestlings if it is about the same age and appearance. Indeed, they will usually accept it even if its appearance is appreciably different. In such cases they undoubtedly *see* the difference as can be deduced from the puzzled and somewhat alarmed way in which they stare at the new arrival. But, unless they desert the nest altogether (and I have never known this to happen) they offer no violence to the strange squab and subsequently feed and care for it without distinction. The situation is very different if fully feathered fledglings are given to a pair with young of the same age, in which case they are seldom adopted and are usually attacked. A very few male Domestic Pigeons will adopt any young, apparently from an excess of parental instincts rather than a failure to distinguish individuals, but the majority will not.

A cock Barbary Dove once showed me very clearly how he evidently learnt to recognise his young as individuals only after they had left the nest. When the eggs of this pair of Barbary Doves were chipping, I had placed under them two chipping Turtle Dove's eggs. These hatched at the same time and were reared together with the young Barbaries. I supplemented the food given by the parent Barbaries in order that none of the young should suffer from the crop-milk being divided among four instead of two. All four young throve but the two Turtle Doves naturally developed much more rapidly than the young Barbaries. They left the nest when about twelve days old. The parent Barbary Doves continued to feed the flying young Turtle Doves as well as their own offspring, when, however, the latter left the nest their father fiercely attacked them. When I put them back on the nest he left them in peace but as soon as they left it he again attacked them and I had to remove them from his aviary. Apparently having learnt to recognise two flying young (in this case the two Turtle Doves) as his own he was not mentally equipped to accept any further fledglings away from the nest as his offspring.

The above occurrence also demonstrated the fact that, unlike some fish, pigeons do not become specifically imprinted on their first brood of young and afterwards refuse to show parental behaviour to the young of later broods if they differ in appearance from those of the first. The Barbary Doves which reared the young Turtle Doves had previously reared several broods of their own species and subsequently reared many more.

Once the stage has been reached at which the young are individually recognised by the parent, the latter's parental impulses have reference to its own young as individuals. A male pigeon whose flying young have become separated will feed to one part of the food he has collected and then go and give the rest to the other. If they have separated since he last visited them he will search for the second young one in order to feed it. Very often, in such circumstances, the first young one is still begging eagerly for more food when its father leaves it. It is therefore obvious that, at this stage of the breeding cycle, the parent does not just blindly respond to appropriate stimuli but understands that it has two young, each of which need feeding.

Many, probably most species of pigeons, attack the young of the first brood (if they are still in the nesting territory) and drive them away when the second brood hatches. In the Rock Pigeon, and its feral and domestic descendants, it is the female who, usually, does this; the male being rather tolerant of his grown-up young. In Speckled Pigeons, however, at any rate in my captive specimens, the male birds violently attacked their offspring in these circumstances. Feral Pigeons nesting in sites so dark that they cannot see their young at all will often (probably always) tolerate the first brood young near the nest after the next brood hatches. This shows pretty conclusively that, at any rate in this species, it is the *sight* of the newly-hatched nestlings which 'sparks off' the change from tolerance to violent hostility towards the young of the previous brood.

REFERENCE

KLINGHAMMER, E. & HESS, E. H. 1964. Parental feeding in Ring Doves (*Streptopelia roseogrisea*): Innate or Learned? *Zeitschr. f. Tierps.* **21**: 338–347.

ESCAPE AND SOME OTHER ANTI-PREDATOR BEHAVIOUR

Many characters, such as cryptic coloration and short fledging periods, function to protect the species concerned from predators. Here I shall discuss only the behaviour shown by pigeons when they or their young or eggs are immediately threatened by a predator. Most of what is known of such behaviour is from relatively few species. Nevertheless it seems worth describing in general terms to enable comparisons to be made and because it is highly likely that the anti-predator behaviour patterns of any pigeon would be shown in similar form by related species.

FIG. 7: Typical posture of pigeon 'freezing' in alarm at sight of a predator below (left) and above (right).

The following represent 'typical' consecutive responses to the approach of a predator; sleeking down the plumage, eying the danger and usually uttering the distress call; 'freezing' motionless in either an erect or crouched posture; taking wing and fleeing and then, if pursued by a hawk or falcon, trying to avoid being seized by dodging and swerving and to outfly it or to get into cover. Freezing in an erect posture occurs particularly in tree perching forms and in reference to man or other predators seen on the ground below.

Pigeons normally become alarmed and look for danger if they see or hear others of their kind fly up in sudden fear or utter alarm notes. At night they will, at least in many cases, fly blindly from their roosting places if they hear another bird take wing in panic close to them or the wild flapping of a struggling bird seized by a predator. By day, however, pigeons do not usually flee until they themselves see the cause of the alarm. One can easily have the contrary impression through incomplete or imprecise observation. If, however, one is watching, for example, a large flock of Wood Pigeons, some feeding on the ground and some sitting around in the trees and observes, from one's hidden vantage point, what happens when a man approaches them, one sees that their fleeing in panic is progressive not instantaneous. Even after most of the birds have taken wing some individuals may, and usually do, remain, alert and peering about but not taking wing until they also see the oncoming human. When I climbed into a great fissure in a Hebridean cliff, where many Rock Pigeons were resting and others incubating and brooding young, the sound of the fleeing individuals alerted many others still out of sight. Each of these walked out from its niche peering nervously but, in spite of seeing others taking wing, no individual actually flew until it saw me. Such situations as the above differ, of course, from those involving audible stimuli, such as gunshots, which are perceived by all individuals in a given area at the same moment. The erect alarm posture probably indicates a tendency to draw away from the alarming object. Pigeons approached from above, as when one is walking high above cliff ledges or above the trees of a hanging wood do not usually show it, at least not to anything like the same degree, even though they hold their heads well up.

Individual experience and consequent conditioning may influence the distance at which any particular pigeons take flight from an approaching danger but the extent to which alarmed birds freeze motionless before flying away appears largely a specific character correlated with the environment. Forms whose plumage is cryptic or disruptive in their usual surroundings rely much more on freezing than do those with conspicuous plumage. Individuals in cover will allow a closer approach before they fly, no doubt because under such circumstances they feel less afraid than they would in the open. It is commonly seen that when a motor backfires loudly in town Feral Pigeons on the ground nearby all fly up in alarm while many of those perched on ledges or in niches equally near freeze with sleeked plumage but do not take wing.

Domestic and Feral Pigeons, when chased by a falcon, fly at great speed and dodge or swerve 'at the last moment' in response to the falcon's attempts to seize them. They will, if they get the opportunity, dive headlong into any cave, hole, or other available shelter. Descriptions of the behaviour of wild Rock Pigeons show that these reactions are the normal ones for the species although I have not myself seen pure wild Rock Pigeons escaping from falcons except once and all too briefly, the two birds vanishing out of sight behind a headland almost as soon as I saw them.

Wood Pigeons attacked from above by a Peregrine Falcon when flying high scattered in all directions, the individuals diving down at great speed into the cover of the trees below (Geyr von Schweppenburg, 1952; R. Spencer, pers. comm.). When I have seen falcons (and sometimes harmless waders) swoop down at or into flocks of Domestic Pigeons the latter have always scattered in a similar manner. Wild Rock Pigeons have, however, been seen to pack closely as do flocked Starlings, and manoeuvre in unison when attacked by falcons. It would be interesting to know whether this is an escaping behaviour pattern which has been lost in their domestic descendents or whether, which I think more likely, its use depends on some particular features of the attack that elicits it. In some other birds packing into a dense flock is a common and apparently successful method of dealing with attacks by birds of prey which are usually unwilling or unable to seize an individual from such a flock. When attacked by hawks or falcons in open country Wood Pigeons try to escape by rising above their pursuer (Curry-Lindahl, in litt.).

Little is known of the interactions between pigeons and such mammals as prey on them. Town-living Feral Pigeons and Laughing Doves *Streptopelia senegalensis*, when stalked by a Domestic Cat, often wait till it is nearly on them before escaping by a quick, almost vertical, upward flight. It would be interesting to know whether the distance at which they fly up in this situation is innate or the result of experience. Cats in London seem to have little luck with healthy Feral Pigeons but they more often catch Wood Pigeons, I think this difference is because the Wood Pigeon more often feeds in small gardens where there is a dense cat population (probably averaging at least one per garden) and where plants or other cover enable the cat to lie in wait or approach unseen. Domestic Pigeons will often desert their loft if a cat or dog enters it, especially if they have difficulty in getting out quickly when this happens.

As with other birds, some (probably all) pigeons tend to fear any place where they have been badly frightened. When catching Feral Pigeons to ring them I have repeatedly noticed that if a bird can be grasped without any violent movement on my part and without allowing it to struggle, flap or lose feathers, the others feeding with it show little or no alarm. A combination of a noticeably violent movement on my part, flapping and loss of feathers (and their consequent sudden appearance around) by the caught pigeon causes considerable alarm. In such a situation the birds will not usually approach again to nearer than about two yards to the 'danger spot'. In such cases, where, of course, the pigeons were used to being fed by people, the fear thus caused was clearly linked with the exact location of the frightening happenings. If I moved to another seat a couple of dozen yards away and offered more food the same birds would come to me without hesitation although still fearing to approach the food left at my previous catching place. Although useless against man such behaviour would be highly adaptive in reference to most ground predators. It is worth remarking here that these reactions do not indicate that the birds do not or are not able to discriminate between individual human beings as there is ample evidence that they can and do make such discriminations both in reference to hostile and to food-providing individuals.

The fear which pigeons show of gunshots and other sudden, very loud and unexpected sounds seems (like the similar fear-responses of human beings to the same stimuli) independent of experience and due to the 'shock' to the nervous system caused by such extreme stimuli. These responses may be shown to some natural sounds such as very loud and close claps of thunder which will cause Wood Pigeons to fly wildly off trees they are resting in just as they would in response to being shot at and missed. Although it seems very unlikely that such fear responses to sudden very loud sounds could have originally have had a function *per se* they may well have 'pre-adapted' the birds to conditions where the man with the gun is a serious predator. Where pigeons are much persecuted by sportsmen some of the escape behaviour shown towards him seems specifically adapted to such predation. For example Wood Pigeons, where often shot at, will not fly over a man (unless very high) but will jink or swerve aside as they come within or near gun-range. Where they are not shot at they show no such behaviour and will freely fly towards and over a man if he happens to be in their line of flight.

Mobbing of predatory birds seems not usually to occur in pigeons but there are eye-witness accounts of numbers of Collared Doves swooping repeatedly at a Kestrel in flight, although not actually striking it and the Hon. Miriam Rothschild saw a group of Feral Pigeons repeatedly swoop at a Kestrel (pers. comm.). I have seen, at different times, a Turtle Dove and a Barbary Dove attack a Magpie that came near their nests and Hofstetter (1952) records similar behaviour from the Collared Dove towards Magpies. The defensive threat behaviour that may be shown towards humans is discussed under in the chapter on display. I have, however, had a Speckled Pigeon behave towards me in a manner suggestive of the swooping attacks on Kestrels above described. This bird was a male that was rather timid and invariably left his nest when closely approached. When there were young in the nest and I went to look at them, he would fly quickly and repeatedly at me, uttering loud distress calls or excitement cries (which in this species do not differ in sound) and pass between my face and the nest. This he did even when there was only about a foot of space to manoeuvre in; the bird did not appear to try to clout me with his wings and certainly never pecked me. I had the impression that this behaviour was a form of distraction display rather than an attack as, when attacking a human being, birds unless completely unafraid, attack the back of the head rather than the more frightening face. This Speckled Pigeon never attempted to strike or peck me from behind, as he could easily have done, but deliberately and repeatedly passed in front of my face, between it and his young.

Distraction display from birds flushed from the nest is common in pigeons of many species. In the more extreme forms the bird flutters or falls to the ground and flops about as if crippled, progressing largely on its wings (wrist joints) before finally taking wing, at first in hesitant and apparently impeded flight.   This may be followed by perching or standing on the ground with violently flapping wings in much the same manner as a nestling pigeon 'exercising' in the days prior to fledging.   Often only this violent wing flapping is shown. A less intense form of distraction display consists of dropping nearly to ground level and then flying low in slow and impeded flight for some distance.   Any degree of inter-gradation between the above and fleeing in normal flight may occur.   In terms of motivation distraction display is probably usually due, or at least mainly due, to intense conflict between the impulse to escape and to remain with the eggs or young.   This is no doubt why it is most often shown by birds with hatching eggs or newly hatched young.   At such times the parental impulses are very strong.   There is, however, reason to suspect that extreme terror may at times result in unco-ordinated movements and that the more intense forms of distraction display may result from the fact that the bird has 'stayed till the last minute' on the nest and so is in a state of great fear when it leaves.   Out of thirty-two adult Wood Pigeons which I caught and ringed, away from any nests they may have had, three when released fluttered to the ground and there indulged in very intense 'distraction display', such as I have never seen from this species when flushed from the nest, flapping about in an unco-ordinated manner for some moments before recovering and flying away.   Here there could hardly be any question of an impulse other than that to escape and the behaviour shown would seem to have been due to partial loss of motor control as a result of extreme fear.   Similar behaviour has been observed from some tropical boobies when suddenly alarmed.   The caution which pigeons often, especially in arid regions, show when coming to drink (see pp. 181 and 186, and Cade 1965), serves as a partial defence against attacks by birds of prey.   It is not known to what extent, if any, such behaviour is innate.

REFERENCES

CADE, T. J.   1965.   Relations between raptors and columbiform birds at a desert water hole.   *Wilson Bull.* **77**: 340–345.
GEYR VON SCHWEPPENBURG, H. F.   1952.   Vorteile der Zuggeselligkeit.   *Die Vogelwarte* **16**: 116–119.
HOFFSTETTER, F. B.   1952.   Das Verhalten einer Türkentauben-population.   *Journ. f. Orn.* **93**: 295–312.

THE TYPICAL PIGEONS

The pigeons that are put in the genus *Columba* include all those species that most people would regard as 'typical pigeons', such as the Rock Pigeon, the Stock Dove and the Wood Pigeon.   The birds of this genus are small–medium to large–medium sized pigeons with fairly short legs, medium to long wings and square-ended or rounded tails.   They vary much in colour, from silver with black wing-tips through every shade of brown or grey to black.   Most of them have well-developed display plumage on the neck but in some species this is absent.

Typically they are strong fliers which perch, rest and roost in trees or cliffs.   Some are ground feeders, others feed partly or (so far is known) entirely in trees or shrubs.   Some of the American species appear to fill, or partly fill, the 'fruit pigeon niche', in the New World.

They are found in nearly all parts of the world where pigeons exist at all.   It is not, however, certain whether all the *Columba* species are more closely related to each other than they are to other pigeons. Biochemical studies of the blood antigens of some species have suggested that the New World species of *Columba* may be no very close relatives of the Old World species in spite of their similarity to them in appearance and structure.   Some details of their sexual behaviour also suggest that they may be more closely related to the American ground doves than to Old World species of *Columba*.   Much further study will be needed, however, before the above hypothesis can be regarded as more than possible.   If it should prove true then the similarity in appearance and plumage patterns between the American and Old World species will be a striking instance of convergence.

The relationship of the Old World *Columba* species is less questionable.   Particularly is this the case within the species group whose two extreme types – the Wood Pigeon and the Rock Pigeon – show the greatest morphological and adaptive divergence.   This happens to be the group whose behaviour has been studied in most detail owing to some of them occurring in Europe and others often being imported as aviary birds.

The typical pigeons of the old world can be divided into four species-groups (Goodwin, 1959). The largest and most familiar group are the wood pigeons and rock pigeons of Eurasia and Africa. Our familiar Wood Pigeon (*Columba palumbus*) has given rise to two, possibly three, derivatives on the Canaries and Madeira and is represented in Africa by the African Wood Pigeon *C. unicincta*. The stock doves form a link between the wood pigeons and the rock pigeons. The Somali Stock Dove *C. oliviae* and the Yellow-eyed Stock Dove *C. eversmanni*, together form a superspecies. The former occurs only in a very limited area as does the White-collared Pigeon *C. albitorques* which is probably rather more closely related to the Rock Pigeon *C. livia*, and the Speckled Pigeon *C. guinea*, than to the stock doves. The Speckled Pigeon is probably fairly closely related to the Rock Pigeon in spite of their rather superficial differences in appearance (Goodwin, 1956). It may indeed be its geographical representative although they have certainly diverged too greatly to be treated as members of a superspecies even if their ranges did not now show a slight and probably secondary overlap.

These hole or ledge nesting and cliff-haunting African pigeons replace one another geographically except in two small areas. The Speckled Pigeon slightly overlaps the range of the Rock Pigeon and completely overlaps that of the White-collared Pigeon. In the former area the two species show ecological divergence, the Rock Pigeon alone haunting cliffs and the Speckled Pigeon breeding in palm trees (Harwin, 1963). In Ethiopia, however, both the Speckled and White-collared Pigeons occur together and appear to have very similar ecological requirements (Pitwell and Goodwin, 1964). At the moment both species are numerous in Ethiopia so possibly their requirements do differ or else, in spite of their apparent abundance, they are being kept down by predation below the numerical level at which competition between them would occur. On the other hand we may be witnessing a phase in a process of interspecific competition which will end in the replacement of the White-collared Pigeon by the Speckled Pigeon even in the former's present restricted range.

The Rock Pigeon *C. livia*, and the Eastern Rock Pigeon *C. rupestris*, are extremely similar in appearance, ecology and behaviour. Over most of their respective ranges they are completely allopatric but they overlap in some parts of Central Asia and Afghanistan (Vaurie, 1961). Whether the two actually breed at the same altitudes seems a little uncertain from present evidence but they are evidently in at least potential contact during the breeding season. The Rock Pigeon and Eastern Rock Pigeon seem therefore on present evidence best considered as sibling species.

The Snow Pigeon, *C. leuconota* is probably closely related to the rock pigeons although it differs strikingly in appearance and voice. Its range overlaps those of both *rupestris* and *livia* and it often associates with them although it normally breeds and roosts at higher altitudes. In view of the striking differences in head and neck coloration between the Snow Pigeon and the Eastern Rock Pigeon which have, presumably, been evolved largely as isolating mechanisms, it is surprising that the two rock pigeons should themselves show so little difference from each other and yet not be known to have hybridised where they overlap.

The Laurel Pigeon *C. junioniae*, is usually considered to be derived from the first colonisation of the Canary Islands by the Wood Pigeon *C. palumbus*. This is quite possible but its appearance and what is known of its behaviour do not give any certain indication of this and it might be an offshoot from primitive palearctic *Columba* stock prior to its subsequent speciation. When dividing up the typical pigeons it seems best therefore to consider the Laurel Pigeon as a monotypic group.

The third group consists of a number of pigeons which inhabit the Indo-Malayan and Ethiopian regions. The African Olive pigeons form a closely related group of allopatric forms. I formerly treated them as races of a single species, *C. arquatrix*, but now think it is preferable to treat them here as members of a superspecies for the following reasons. The differences in appearance between them, especially in the coloration of head and bill are, in most cases, as great as those one finds between some related sympatric species. The undoubted specific distinctness of the closely related White-naped pigeon *C. albinucha*, whose range now overlaps with that of *Columba arquatrix* but which undoubtedly evolved from an isolate of *arquatrix* or *proto-arquatrix* stock also suggests that the present-day geographical representatives of *arquatrix* might behave as good species if they came together. A further argument for treating them as members of a superspecies is that by so doing the available information on each can be un-ambiguously attached to the form concerned.

The Speckled Wood Pigeon *C. hodgsonii*, of the Himalayas is clearly the Asiatic representative of the African olive pigeons and a member of the same superspecies. These are mainly pigeons of high altitude forest although some forms may occur at low altitudes or visit lowland forest for feeding purposes. The related White-naped Pigeon (see above) inhabits forest at lower altitudes but its feeding grounds overlap those of *arquatrix*.

The Ashy Wood Pigeon *C. pulchricollis*, the Nilgiri Wood Pigeon *C. elphinstonii* and the Ceylon Wood Pigeon *C. torringtoni*, together form a superspecies whose members show considerable divergence in colour but little in plumage pattern. They also are birds of hill forest and probably allied to the olive pigeons to whom they show some resemblance in colour pattern also. The Purple Wood Pigeon *C. punicea*, of Assam and parts of south-east Asia, the Andaman Wood Pigeon *C. palumboides* and the Silver Pigeon *C. argentina* of islands in the Java sea and adjacent areas appear to be most nearly related to the above group and may, especially in the case of the Purple and Silver Pigeons, be geographic representatives in spite of their diverseness of colour and size. The Silver Pigeon shows a striking resemblance to the Pied Imperial Pigeon *Ducula bicolor*. It differs, however, in details of plumage pattern and I think its resemblance to *D. bicolor* is due to convergence not affinity. It, like the African Wood Pigeon and the Snow Pigeon, is another *Columba* species which lacks specialised display plumage on the neck, a point compatible with its presumed relationship to the Purple Wood Pigeon which shows what appears to be a regressional stage of this display plumage. The plumage coloration of the Andaman Wood Pigeon suggests that it may form a link between this and the next group.

The last group of old world pigeons are a number of dark coloured and richly iridescent arboreal species that are found in the East Indian, Australasian and Pacific regions, chiefly on islands and archipelagoes. They are all closely related but there are three cases of overlap in distribution without apparent interbreeding. The Black Wood Pigeon *C. janthina*, and the White-throated Pigeon *C. vitiensis*, are allopatric and seem best considered members of a superspecies to which the Australian White-headed Pigeon *leucomela*, an obvious derivative of *vitiensis* stock, also belongs. The range of the Black Wood Pigeon overlaps that of the Silver-banded Black Pigeon *C. jouyi* of Riu Kiu and Borodino Islands and that of the now extinct Bonin Island Pigeon *C. versicolor*. These two forms almost certainly represent the earliest (successful) invasions by *janthina* or 'proto-janthina' of the islands they inhabit. Probably the silver crescent mark of the Silver-banded Black Pigeon functioned or was developed as an isolating mechanism in reference to *C. janthina*.

The Yellow-legged Pigeon *C. pallidiceps* appears to be a derivative of *vitiensis* stock. It now overlaps the latter on some of the Solomon Islands (Mayr, 1934) but it alone is found on New Britain, where it probably originated. Stresemann (1939) suggests that all these forms probably originated in New Guinea and spread from there into their present ranges. The Yellow-legged Pigeon and the form of White-throated Pigeon with which it is partly sympatric are much alike in general coloration but differ strikingly in the colour of the head, which is silver grey in the former and dark purple with a white throat in the latter and in the feet which are yellow in *pallidiceps* and red in *vitiensis*. It would be interesting to know if the difference in leg colour plays any part as an isolating mechanism. Rather surprisingly it is not correlated with any difference in bill colour which is mainly red in both species. In other related and sympatric forms of *Columba* species, such as the Olive Pigeon and the White-naped Pigeon, in which one has yellow and one red legs there is a correlated difference in bill colour.

The subgenus *Turturoena* is a group of three small, dark and richly iridescent pigeons *C. delegorguei*, *C. iriditorques* and *C. malherbii* which together form a superspecies. Their plumage structure and what little is known of their behaviour suggests that they are rightly included in *Columba*. The relationships of the Pink Pigeon are unclear. It was put in a separate genus, *Nesoenas* by Salvadori (1893) because of its more rounded wings and rufous tail. In coloration this pigeon does not closely resemble any other but its colour pattern shows some resemblance to those of many *Columba* species and it seems likely to represent a rather divergent offshoot of *Columba* stock. I have therefore thought best to include this species in *Columba*, giving *Nesoenas* only subgeneric rank.

The American *Columba* species fall into two main groups. The Red-necked Pigeon *C. squamosa* and the White-crowned Pigeon *C. leucocephala* occur on islands of the Carribean region. They overlap over part of their range but there show different habitat preferences. They are closely related, and have nearly identical plumage patterns but strikingly different head and neck coloration which doubtless functions or has functioned as an isolating mechanism. The Scaled Pigeon *C. speciosa*, which replaces them in Central and South America appears to be fairly closely related to the Red-necked and White-crowned Pigeons and in some respects its plumage characters are intermediate between them and the Picazuro Pigeon of central and south-eastern S. America. This species although largely a woodland bird feeds much on the ground. It forms a superspecies together with the Bare-eyed Pigeon of the arid Caribbean coast of northern South America. The Spotted Pigeon *Columba maculosa*, largely overlaps the range of the Picazuro Pigeon to which it is closely related. Like the rock pigeons of the Old World to which it shows convergence in wing and tail proportions, it has become adapted to feeding on the ground in open and often rather arid country. It is, however, a tree breeder (so far as known). It is indeed, rather surprising that none of the larger American Pigeons are hole and cliff nesters as are many of the typical pigeons of the Old World. The Spotted Pigeon lacks display plumage on the neck, this, as in other *Columba* species, is almost certainly a recent evolutionary loss not a primitive condition.

The Band-tailed Pigeon *C. fasciata* of North and South America forms a superspecies together with the Jamaican Band-tailed Pigeon *C. caribaea* and the Chilian Pigeon *C. araucana*. Johnston (1962) considers that the band-tailed pigeons are more closely related to the Old World Wood Pigeon *C. palumbus* and its relatives than to other American species. His reasons were that the band-tails, alone among the American *Columba* species, have a trailing fringe on the inner web of the outermost primary as has the Wood Pigeon and, to some extent, other Old World species. I do not agree with this opinion. The trailing fringe to the first primary seems a character of doubtful value in assessing relationships. It is

Fig. D.2: Presumed relationships within the genus *Columba*. Owing to the number of species in this genus most groups are arranged in alphabetical order and members of the same superspecies are not indicated as such except in the case of *Columba goodsoni* and *C. nigrirostris*. In this and subsequent dendrograms parallel lines between the 'stem' of a species or group and its 'branch' indicate that its derivation is uncertain but thought to be, most probably, from this branch.

more or less correlated with the general texture of the plumage and may be present in one species and absent in a related one where plumage texture differs. The colour pattern of the band-tails, especially as regards their display plumage, seems to me to have far more in common with other American species such as the Picazuro, Red-necked and Scaled Pigeons than with the Wood Pigeon to which the (differently positioned) white on the neck of the Band-tailed and Chilian Pigeons gives them only a superficial resemblance.

The Rufous Pigeon *C. cayennensis*, is intermediate in some respects between the *fasciata* superspecies and the superspecies which consists of the Red-billed Pigeon *C. flavirostris* of Mexico and Central America, Salvin's Pigeon *C. oenops* of Peru and the Plain Pigeon *C. inornata* of Cuba and Jamaica. It has a much more extensive range than either but overlaps the Red-billed Pigeon in Central America. In the area of overlap it is paler, especially on the rump and tail, than in most of its range and thus more strongly differentiated from the Red-billed Pigeon in colour.

The other group of American *Columba* species are those of the subgenus *Oenoenas*. They are a very distinct group of small purplish or dull brown pigeons with no striking markings, rounded tails and small bills. They comprise a superspecies consisting of Goodson's Pigeon *C. goodsoni* and the Short-billed Pigeon *C. nigrirostris* which replace one another in geographically, and the Plumbeous Pigeon *C. plumbea* and the Ruddy Pigeon *C. subvinacea*. These two latter appear to be sympatric over most of their considerable ranges. If this were not so they would be considered, in appearance, forms of one species since they differ only in minor details of colour and bill size. Presumably vocal, behavioural and ecological differences between them exist but they do not appear to have been studied and recorded.

Although the *Oenoenas* group differ rather markedly I think it best to include them in *Columba*. The display plumage on their necks appears to represent a degeneration of the type found in other American pigeons such as *C. corensis*. They almost certainly represent a fairly early offshoot from the other American *Columba*. Their sombre concolorous dress, with lack of signal markings and obsolescent display plumage, presumably evolved as a consequence of increased predator pressure consequent on small size and/or increased reliance on vocal differences as isolating mechanisms.

The putative additional species in this group *C. chiriquensis* is known only from the unique type and from descriptions would appear to be a rather aberrant specimen of *C. subvinacea* or, possibly, a hybrid.

REFERENCES

SALVADORI, T. 1893. *Catalogue of Birds* in the British Museum, Vol. 21.
GOODWIN, D. 1956. Observations on the voice and some displays of certain pigeons. *Avic. Mag.* **62**: 17–33 and 62–70.
—— 1959. Taxonomy of the genus *Columba*. *Bull. Brit. Mus.* (*Nat. Hist.*) *Zool.* Vol. 6: No. 1.
JOHNSTON, R. F. 1962. Taxonomy of Pigeons. *Condor* **64**: 69–74.
STRESEMANN, E. 1939. Die Vögel von Celebes. *Journ. f. Orn.* **87**: 300–424 (351).

ROCK PIGEON *Columba livia*

Columba domestica. β *livia* Gmelin, Syst. Nat., 1. Pt. 2, 1789, p. 769

This species is *the* pigeon since it is the ancestor of all our domestic pigeons and of the feral pigeons which are found in large towns almost throughout the world. I propose here to deal first with the wild forms of the species and then with those aspects of its domestic and feral descendants that are of interest to the ornithologist and bird-watcher rather than the pigeon fancier.

DESCRIPTION: About the size of the average Feral Pigeon but more compact in shape than most town ferals. Broader across the shoulders (looking heart-shaped in body when seen from above), more muscular and with a shorter tail than many feral pigeons have. Bill more slender and with a smaller cere than most feral and domestic forms.

General coloration bluish grey, darkest on the head and rump and palest on the wing-coverts. Two conspicuous black bars across the folded wing. Black subterminal band across tail and white outer edge to basal half of the two outer-most tail feathers. Underwing and lower back white, the latter sharply demarcated from the dark grey of the lower rump. Neck and upper breast iridescent green and purple, the individual feathers of this display plumage are bifurcated. Irides orange, red-orange or golden-orange. Orbital skin blue-grey matching the surrounding feathers. Bill blackish, cere powdery white. Legs and feet red or purplish red.

The female is slightly duller grey and has less iridescence on the neck. In many females from Shetland and the Hebrides the iridescent feathers are confined to the sides of the neck. The juvenile is duller with dull eyes and feet. Juvenile males have some iridescence on the sides of the neck only. Females usually show little or no iridescence in the juvenile plumage.

The above description applies to the nominate race *Columba l. livia*, which is found in the Faeroes, Shetland and Hebridian Islands, Scotland, Ireland, the Iberian Peninsula, N.W. Africa and the northern shores of the Mediterranean. The Rock Pigeons of extreme northern India, Syria and northern Palestine are very similar. Those of Cyrenaica and Libya are smaller and of a somewhat paler blue-grey colour with brighter iridescence on the neck. The Rock Pigeons of Arabia and north Africa (Egypt excepted) south of the Sahara are also small but have no white on the rump. In parts of the Middle East and northern India grey-rumped and white-rumped Rock Pigeons intergrade. There has been much disagreement as to how many races to recognise in these areas and what names should be used for them so it seems best here to describe the geographic variations without applying names. The Rock Pigeons of Peninsular India and Ceylon *C. livia intermedia* are darker blue-grey with no white on the lower back. A very small, pale, but grey-rumped form, *C. livia schimperi*, lives in the Nile Valley, and an even paler one, *C. livia daklae*, in the Dakla and Kharga oases west of the Nile. The darkest Rock Pigeons of all are found in tropical West Africa. This very dark race, *C. livia gymnocyclus*, has a white lower back like the other western forms from further north, and an extensive area of *red* orbital skin.

In all the above races, however, the black wing bars across the grey wing are present and conspicuous and the females and juveniles show differences comparable to those found in the nominate form. In the Azores, Madeira, and the Cape Verde Islands 'chequered' and 'velvet' Rock Pigeons, many with a considerable amount of chestnut suffusion ('bronze' of pigeon fanciers) form a large percentage of the population. They have been named *C. livia atlantis*, but probably derived from feral domestic pigeons.

FIELD CHARACTERS: In Europe and coastal North Africa the only bluish-grey pigeon with white underwing coverts and lower back. Elsewhere the much more conspicuous black wing bars on a very bluish-grey ground distinguish it from either stock dove. Some Feral Pigeons not separable in field.

DISTRIBUTION AND HABITAT: The Faeroes, Shetland and Orkney Islands, the Hebrides, Ireland and Scotland. Countries bordering the Mediterranean Sea, eastern Europe and western Asia, Arabia, India and Ceylon, Transcaspia and Turkestan and Africa, north of the Equator. Possibly also parts of Mongolia and northern China, but the populations here may be feral birds (q.v.). Requires cliffs, gorges or potholes with caves, hollows or sheltered ledges for nesting and roosting and open country for feeding purposes. In some places (e.g. parts of India) genuine wild birds breed and roost in or on buildings. It seems likely that the Rock Pigeon evolved in arid or semi-arid and nearly treeless regions and that it spread into many of the areas it now occupies subesquent to man's agricultural and sylvicidal activities creating suitable feeding grounds for it. It is significant that it became extinct on St. Kilda, where it was once numerous, subsequent to the depopulation of that island. Usually resident but some evidence suggests local migration, especially in northern and Saharan parts of its range. Said to be a regular passage migrant on Fair Isle (Davis, 1963).

FEEDING AND GENERAL HABITS: Primarily a seed-eater, taking seeds of many kinds, especially, when available, those of vetches and cultivated grains. Also takes small snails and other molluscs, Camel ticks (probably found gorged and quiescent on ground when it is searching for spilled grain) and some berries. Feeds on ground that is more or less bare or covered only with short or scattered vegetation. In Scotland and the nearby islands it feeds chiefly, if not entirely, on arable land or land that has been closely grazed by sheep or other domestic mammals. Walks and runs about quickly when feeding. Flight swift and usually low over land or water. Usually alights only on cliffs, buildings or the ground but in some places perches regularly on trees. Apparently no records of wild Rock Pigeons feeding in trees although Feral Pigeons sometimes do so.

Commonly in pairs or small parties but quite frequently in large flocks and at all times considerable numbers may aggregate on good feeding grounds. Flocks or parties tend to fly in fairly close order especially when crossing considerable areas of open or semi-desert country. When flying along a cliff or hillside usually keeps close in and follows the contours. These are, doubtless, adaptations to minimise predation by falcons. When attacked by a falcon flocks sometimes 'close ranks' and manoeuvre in concert. When a flock is scattered or when a single bird is attacked the pursued individual tries to reach the shelter of some hole or crevice. When walking about or standing after having moved and especially when pausing in its walk to investigate something often lowers its tail and then brings it back to normal position, possibly a vestigial flight checking movement.

NESTING: Nests on sheltered ledges or in holes. Often far back in a cave or deep down in a pothole or well. Appears to prefer a site in semi-darkness, as its domestic descendants have been proved to do. In caves not liable to predation by man, otter or other mammals, some pairs may nest on the cave floor if all suitable ledges and niches are already occupied. Nests in holes in trees have been recorded in Asia (e.g., Ludlow and Kinnear, 1934). In buildings sites chosen are the obvious substitutes for the natural cave and ledge sites. Has been recorded nesting at all time of the year. In Shetland and the Hebrides the first broods often fledge in May. Probably, as with other pigeons, much depends upon the local food supplies. Sometimes the presence of adult pairs at their nest sites has been, with doubtful wisdom, taken as proof of breeding. Two white eggs. Incubation period 17–18 days.

VOICE: The advertising coo is a moaning 'ōōrh' or oh-ōō-ōōr' subject to some variation. It is used in the same form when nest calling. Tame specimens when breeding will also give this coo when waiting for their owner to feed them. The display coo is a rather hurried-sounding 'Ōō-rŏŏ-cŏŏ t'cōō'. In the intense sexual form of the bowing display (q.v.) this phrase becomes blurred and its final syllable emphasised and longer drawn. The distress call is a gasping grunted 'ŏŏrh' or 'ĕĕrh'. Long-drawn, loud, panting forms of it are given by timid domestic or captive individuals defending their nest against an intruding hand. Intermediate forms between the distress call and the advertising coo are used by the female towards her mate in appeasing contexts and, more rarely, vice versa.

There appears to be no true excitement cry, but a low fretful murmuring sound, only audible at very close quarters, is often uttered, usually when the bird giving it appears perturbed or angry. This may be a vestigial form of excitement cry.

DISPLAYS: The bowing display has three distinct, but intergrading forms. These might be conveniently termed the sexual, self-assertive, and defensive. These terms are arbitary and must not be deemed exclusive; self-assertiveness is certainly present in the 'sexual' and 'defensive' forms of the display and a state of sexual activity is a pre-requisite for the self assertive form.

In the sexual version the male flies up into the air towards the female, claps his wings, alights near her and runs, or leaps into the air, clapping his wings as he does so, towards her, cooing loudly as he comes up to her with inflated neck and feathers of neck, rump, lower back and belly erected. On reaching her he lifts his head high but with bill still pointed somewhat downwards. Spreading (and re-closing) and depressing of the tail accompanies this bowing display, most often – but not always – correlated with the upward movement of the head. Then the male turns in a quick circle, bowing low and cooing, then again lifts his head and turns away. Quick nodding movements are shown during momentary pauses in the display. The male may run round the female displaying and is particularly likely to run in front of and then around her if she walks on away from him. The male gives this form of the bowing display to known females, to strange individuals of either sex and, but more rarely, to other males known to him. Exceptionally the female, at least in domestic forms, may give this display to her mate immediately after both have been involved in agressive behaviour with neighbours. Very similar posturing is also used by the female when joining her nest-calling mate on the nest site.

In the self-assertive form the bird turns round and round, cooing with lowered head but shows little or no lifting of the head – except in intervals – or spreading of the tail. This display may 'die away' or lead on into the sexual form, into fighting or advertising cooing. It is given by the male when in reproductive condition on alighting in or near his territory or in some other familiar place where he feels self-assured or when (in such an area) he sees another pigeon – particularly a stranger or a known rival male – approaching. A male returning home (after having been away some time) or re-visiting a former home may display in this manner on alighting even if no other pigeons are in sight. This is the only situation in which I have seen this display given by a bird completely alone.

The defensive form of this display consists merely in lowering the head and uttering the self-assertive 'ŏŏ-rŏŏ-cŏŏ-t'cōō'. Normally the bird doing this faces the enemy, but may turn partly from it. This display is shown as a prelude to attack or in defiance, and is not restricted to birds in breeding condition.

The female seldom uses the self-assertive and defensive forms of the bowing display except when at her own roosting or nesting site. In the self-assertive version she seldom moves round in a complete circle, as the male usually does, but makes a partial turn and then back again through the same arc.

The display flight is in a more or less horizontal plane. The bird flies outwards from the cliff or building with loudly clapping wings, then glides with tail somewhat spread and wings lifted well above the horizontal plane.

Copulation is usually preceded by billing. Immediately afterwards both sexes usually walk a few steps with lifted head, erected neck and rump feathers and slightly spread tail and wings. This commonly is followed by the male taking wing in a display flight in which the female follows him. Sometimes the male may adopt the female soliciting posture immediately after dismounting and, if he does so, the female may mount him and perform all the movements of a copulating male. The male may (rarely) give the bowing display immediately after dismounting.

Nodding occurs in both hostile and inviting situations. At the lowest point of the nod the bird's bill is usually at about or near right angles to the substrate. Displacement preening may be directed at the sides of the breast as well as behind the wing. Driving of female by male frequent and persistent in appropriate situations.

OTHER NAMES: Rock Dove, Blue Rock, Wild Pigeon.

REFERENCES

BANNERMAN, D. A. 1936. *Birds of the Atlantic Islands*, Vol. 1. London.
DAVIS, P. 1963. The Birds of Fair Isle. Pt. 2. *Fair Isle Observatory Bulletin*. S.36.
LUDLOW, F. & KINNEAR, N. B. 1934. A Contribution to the Ornithology of Chinese Turkestan. *Ibis* 4, 13th Series, p. 95.
MACGILLIVRAY, W. 1837. *A History of British Birds*. Vol. 1, pp. 268–286.
NIETHAMMER, G. 1955. Zur Vogelwelt des Ennedi-Gebirges (Französich Aequatorial-Afrika). *Bon. Zool. Beitr.* 6: 29–80.

FERAL PIGEON *Columba livia*

The Feral Pigeons of our towns (and of towns throughout most of the world) are often ignored by ornithological writers who consider that because they are not native wild birds they are unworthy of notice. This has always seemed to me a silly and unrealistic attitude. That, like the townspeople who feed them, they are results of man's interference with nature, sheltered from some predators and fed on artificial food may, and indeed does, make them less aesthetically pleasing than their wild forbears but it does not make them less worthy of interest.

Feral Pigeons are derived from domestic pigeons that have strayed, become lost, or been abandoned by their owners. In most old towns the original stock probably stemmed largely if not entirely, from the old-time Dovecote Pigeons. In newer towns, at any rate in Britain, lost or strayed Homing Pigeons have been the main progenitors. The more 'highly bred' and artificial Fancy Pigeons seldom live long or breed successfully in a feral state. Nondescript domestic pigeons, pigeons of flying breeds (but not their fancy derivatives) and very 'badly bred' (i.e. less monstrous) fancy pigeons have also contributed in some, usually relatively small, degree to the feral population. This is, of course, a generalisation which is true for the vast majority of feral pigeons throughout the world but may not hold good for any particular area or even for a micro-population in one part of a large town.

DESCRIPTION: Feral Pigeons must be familiar to almost everyone. Typically they are similar to wild Rock Pigeons in general shape but often have proportionally narrower bodies, longer tails, broader bills and larger ceres.

They vary much both individually and locally in these respects, probably in most cases according to their ancestry. For example, the majority of the Feral Pigeons of inner London which, although heterogeneous, probably stem largely from the old type Dovecote Pigeon, are smaller and have finer bills and smaller ceres than those in Richmond, only about ten miles away. These latter have obviously derived mostly from lost or strayed Racing Homer Pigeons.

In briefly describing the colours most prevalent in Feral Pigeons, which are also usually the colours found most commonly in Domestic Pigeons, such as Racing Homers, which are not (usually) especially bred for colour or pattern, I use the terms most commonly used by pigeon fanciers in England. The 'red' found in the bars and wing-spots of red chequers and mealies is a reddish brown, varying in tone but usually more or less tinged with purple. This is the colour known to pigeon geneticists as 'dominant red' or 'ash red'. The recessive red – a colour rather rare in Feral Pigeons – gives a bird almost wholly of a chocolate or rufous colour without markings and without the pale whitish primaries and tail usual (but not invariable) in dominant reds.

Blue. The natural colour of the Rock Pigeon. General plumage blue-grey, usually pale blue-grey on wings and sometimes also on underparts. Two conspicuous black bars across the wing, and a broad black bar at end of tail. Rump usually white or pale grey, but often same grey as rest of plumage. Neck and upper breast iridescent green and purple. A very common colour among Feral and Homing Pigeons.

Blue Chequer. As in blue, but the wing bars wider and the rest of the wing feathers with black markings (chequering), giving a spotted effect. In dark blue chequers only a small grey mark may be left on each feather, and the closed wing appears very dark. In such birds the grey of the rest of the plumage is also darker, and the black spotting may extend to rump and flanks. The commonest colour among Feral and Homing Pigeons in Britain.

Velvet. As dark blue chequer, but wing-coverts entirely black. All the 'blue' colours may show a chestnut or rusty tinge on the black portions of the plumage, and may show a good deal of minor variation in shade of grey, type of chequering, amount and colour of neck gloss, and so on.

Mealy. As in blue, but ground colour silvery or creamy grey, neck and breast usually tinged brown and with green and purple gloss, often rich chestnut-brown, head may be brown, or mealy-white in contrast to brown neck. Two brown bars across the wing, no tail bar.

Red-chequers and *Reds* have the same colours as mealies, but pattern (except for absence of tail bar) as in Blue Chequers and Velvets. The 'red' colours are usually rather infrequent in Feral Pigeons, except where these have been derived largely from Homing Pigeons, in which this colour is frequent.

Grizzle. A pattern difficult to describe, in which all the feathers are curiously streaked and intermixed with white. Grizzles vary from the 'light print' which is predominantly white with dark-tipped primaries, and some dark feathers in its head and neck, through various shades of grizzled grey (with darker wing bars), and the same in the 'red' colours. In juvenile plumage grizzles are usually much paler than they will be after moulting.

Black. The deep solid black found in some fancy Pigeons is rare in feral birds but specimens of a uniform slaty-black are not uncommon.

Pieds. Any of the colours mentioned may be pied, that is marked with white, the underparts, rump, primaries and head being the parts most often affected. Such birds are common among Feral Pigeons in English towns. Gay-pieds, birds with more white than coloured plumage, are rarer. Pure white birds – other than first generation escapes – are uncommon, although gay-pieds coloured only on tail and scapulars are much less so.

Some other colours occur rarely (in feral populations). Most of the colour varieties described are subject to some variation. Thus blues may be 'smoky', a dull dark grey ground colour on wing coverts; 'silver blue', of a bright pale silvery hue; 'plummy' with pinkish eye-rims, a peculiar dulling of the plumage and much non-iridescent wine-red colour on the upper breast; or 'pencilled' with slight black marks along the vanes of the wing-coverts. But it would have taken up too much space to describe fully such minor variants of each colour phase.

DISTRIBUTION AND HABITAT: Cosmopolitan, owing their presence to introduction by man. Found in the tropics and north of the Arctic Circle as well as in temperate regions.

In some areas inhabit caves and cliffs and feed in open country like the wild Rock Pigeons. Also breed and roost in old buildings, barns, on ledges under bridges and similar places in open agricultural country. Most abundant, however, in towns, particularly in the central areas of large cities such as London and New York. Here the sites chosen for roosting and nesting are the nearest edificarian equivalents to the caves, holes and sheltered cliff ledges used by wild Rock Pigeons. In parts of Australia nest in hollows in gum trees *Eucalyptus* sp. growing along creek beds in fairly open country.

FEEDING AND GENERAL HABITS: As Rock Pigeon where not relying directly on food given or spilled by Man. In some towns all or part of the pigeon population may fly out into the surrounding country to feed, returning to roost and nest on the buildings. The same individuals may feed both inside the town and in the surrounding fields.

Feral Pigeons living in large towns often, and in England usually, feed inside the town itself. Some natural food is obtained from exposed earth or grass plots in parks and gardens but the greater part consists, as a rule, of bread or other artificial food which is given to them by the public, or obtained by scavenging. Large numbers congregate in parks and squares where they are regularly fed. Others seek food in the roads, railway stations, dockyards, and so forth. Grain spilled from horses' nose-bags once constituted an important food source, but owing to the decline in horse-traffic is now a negligible one in most places. Bread is usually the staple food, since being cheaper it is given in greater quantity than any other, but grain, pulse, peanuts, or cheese are always taken in preference except by individuals that have not learnt that these substances are edible. Cooked meat, fat, bacon-rind, apple, potato, chocolate and other sweetmeats are also eaten, at least by some individuals. The need for lime, especially by breeding birds, prompts them to eat the mortar from buildings. This they can do only where it is already sufficiently loose and crumbled for their weak bills to detach pieces of suitable size. The idea that they are capable of harming sound buildings in this way is, of course, ludicrous.

Much of the food of 'town' Pigeons is deliberately given to them by Man. Thus the feelings of pity, friendliness, or compassion which they evoke in man (or woman) is of the utmost importance to them.

Even in country districts Feral Pigeons are largely dependent, albeit indirectly, on man, since most of their feeding grounds are produced by his activities.

Individual pigeons that are fed by people soon learn not only the human 'intention movements' of food giving, but also to recognise individual men and women who have on two or three occasions singled them out for generous treatment. A Feral Pigeon will often recognise such a person even among scores of other people and will approach him (or her) hopefully even if he makes no signs of food giving. Such mutual recognition tends to be gratifying to the person and hence rewarding to the pigeon and often plays an important part in the survival of hook-billed or injured Feral Pigeons.

Feral Pigeons show a strong tendency to roost in company. This tendency is, however, often over-weighed by individual preference or chance of circumstances. In a town where Feral Pigeons are abundant any good roosting site, such as a high wind-sheltered and overhung ledge, which is large enough is almost sure to be a communal roost. On the other hand pairs and individuals that have discovered a good roosting site where there is only room for one or two, often use it throughout the year.

Much time is spent idling, preening or sun-bathing in company, especially in the early morning on sunny but cold days. The sites chosen for this are, if available, wind-sheltered ledges which catch the morning sun and are backed by a wall or cliff-face which forms a 'sun-trap'.

NESTING: As Rock Pigeon, but the ledges and holes are more often in or on buildings than cliffs, sometimes in holes or recesses of trees. Feral Pigeons are often unable to get a nest to 'stay put' on a flat or slightly downward sloping ledge, such as wild Rock Pigeons (at least in the Hebrides) often nest on. Probably this is due to the materials (dead heather-stems chiefly) available to the wild birds holding more firmly together than the plane twigs and odd straws used perforce by London Feral Pigeons. May nest (in Britain) at all times of year if food available. Most pairs, however, stop breeding with the onset of the main stage of the moult in late August or September. Some start breeding again as soon as the moult is finished in October or November, others do not lay again until late winter or early spring.

VOICE: As Rock Pigeon.

DISPLAY: Ditto.

OTHER NAMES: Common Pigeon, Town Pigeon, Park Pigeon, Field Pigeon, Rock, Blue Rock, Link, Skinnum.

REFERENCES

GOMPERTZ, T. 1957. Some Observations on the Feral Pigeon in London. *Bird Study* **4**: 2–13.
GOODWIN, D. 1954. Notes on Feral Pigeons. *Avicult. Mag.* **60**: 190–213.
—— 1960. Comparative ecology of pigeons in Inner London. *Brit. Birds* **53**: 201–212.

EASTERN ROCK PIGEON   *Columba rupestris*

Columba Oenas δ *rupestris*. Pallas, Zoogr. Rosso-Asiat. 1, 1811, p. 560.

DESCRIPTION: Very similar to that of the nominate form of the Rock Pigeon (q.v.) but a paler grey, not quite such extensive black wing bars and white central area to the tail feathers, forming a white band across the spread tail. Iridescence on the neck tending to be less intense. Usually there is some non-iridescent wine-red colour on the breast just below the glossy area. This may, however, occur in Rock Pigeons and is common in Feral and Domestic Pigeons. The populations from the western parts of the species' range, *C. rupestris turkestanica*, are slightly paler grey and often nearly white on the belly.

FIELD CHARACTERS: White tail band distinguishes it from Rock Pigeon. Smaller size, pale bluish grey colour and two (not three) black wing bars from Snow Pigeon.

DISTRIBUTION AND HABITAT: Central and eastern Asia to North China and Korea west to Semerel-chensk, Zaissan and the Russian Altai south through Turkestan and western Tibet to Gilgit and southern slopes of the Himalayas. Inhabits open country and/or cultivated areas where suitable rock formations or buildings are available for nesting and roosting. In some places frequents towns.

FEEDING AND GENERAL HABITS: Apparently as Rock Pigeon (q.v.). Where not persecuted by him, shows little or no fear of man (Schäfer, 1938) and nests freely in inhabited buildings. Often feeds in company with Rock Pigeons (*C. livia*) or Snow Pigeons (*C. leuconota*) where the species' ranges overlap (e.g., Paludan, 1959). In Ulan Bator, the Mongolian capital, it nests and feeds together with Feral Pigeons but appears not to interbreed with them (Grummt, pers. comm.).

NESTING: As Rock Pigeon; on sheltered ledges of caves or buildings, holes or niches in coastal or inland cliffs, rocks or buildings. In north-eastern Tibet breeds in summer, most young fledging in September, the warmest month (Schäfer, 1938) but elsewhere breeding season more prolonged; sometimes beginning in March or even February (Mecklenburtsev, 1951). In Ulan Bator Grummt (1960) saw many recently fledged juveniles as early as mid May and there is a juvenile about four to five weeks old in the British Museum that was taken at Amur Bay on 19th May.

VOICE: Hartert (1920) and Grummt (1961) describe the voice as, respectively, exactly like and similar to that of the Rock Pigeon, *C. livia*, Ali (1949), however, describes 'its call' as 'a high pitched, quick repeated rolling gut-gut-gut-gut'. It would be interesting to know if, as the above suggests, there is geographical variation in the voice of *C. rupestris*.

DISPLAY: I can find nothing recorded but this very lack suggests the probability that its displays are similar to those of *C. livia*. If they differed appreciably one would expect this to have been noticed and recorded.

OTHER NAMES: Eastern Rock Dove; Bar-tailed Rock Pigeon; White-tailed Rock Pigeon; Blue Hill Pigeon.

REFERENCES

ALI, S. 1949. *Indian Hill Birds*, p. 173. Oxford.
GRUMMT, W. 1961. Ornithologische Beobachtungen in der Mongolei. *Beiträge zur Vogelkunde* 7: 349–360 (354–355).
MEKLENBURTSEV, R. N. 1951. In Dementiev, G. P. and Gladkov, N. A. (eds), Pitisy Sovietskogo Souiza, Moscow, Sovietskaya Nauka, Vol. 2, pp. 14–19.
PALUDAN, K. 1959. On the Birds of Afghanistan. *Vidensk. Medd. Dansk Naturhist. For.* 122: 110–111.
SCHÄFER, E. 1938. Ornithologische Ergebnisse zweier Forschungsreisen nach Tibet. *Journ. f. Orn.* 86: Sonderheft pp. 102–104.

SNOW PIGEON

Columba leuconota

Columba leuconota Vigors, Proc. Comm. Zool. Soc. London, Pt. 1, 1831, p. 23.

DESCRIPTION: About the size of the average Feral Pigeon. Slightly larger and with, proportionately, slightly longer wings and tail than a wild (European) Rock Pigeon. Mantle, scapulars and lesser wing-coverts light greyish brown; rest of wing pale slate grey crossed with three blackish-brown bars, sometimes with a trace of a fourth. Outer webs of primaries and tips of primaries and secondaries blackish. Lower rump, upper tail-coverts and tail black, the latter with a broad crescentic band of white. Head dark slate grey. Neck, underparts, lower back and upper part of the rump white. Snow Pigeons from the eastern part of the species range *C. leuconota gradaria* are a little larger than the nominate form from the western Himalayas and have the grey and brown parts of their plumage slightly paler. Irides yellow or greenish yellow. Feet and legs bright red or pinkish red. Bill black.

The juvenile is duller and browner with pale edgings to the grey and brown feathers and has the white areas suffused with greyish buff; dark eyes and feet.

FIELD CHARACTERS: White neck and breast contrasting with blackish head diagnostic.

DISTRIBUTION AND HABITAT: The Himalayas from western Afghanistan eastwards, mountains of Tibet, extreme north-western Burma and western China, and south-western Turkestan. Inhabits high rugged mountains, normally above 9,000 feet but comes down as low as about 5,000 feet in winter. Normally found in areas of high precipitation and absent from dry mountain-steppe regions.

FEEDING AND GENERAL HABITS: Feeds on the ground; seeds, cultivated grain, small bulbs and other vegetable matter have been recorded from the crops of shot specimens. Where available feeds much in cultivated fields, often in company with Eastern Rock Pigeons. In summer commonly seen in single pairs but in winter often in flocks of hundreds or even thousands of individuals. When feeding runs about actively. Has a strong buoyant flight.

Schäfer (1938) who observed this species in Eastern Tibet found that there, in winter, the Snow Pigeons performed an impressive vertical migration twice daily between their roosting places in the high snow-clad mountains and their feeding grounds in the arable fields in the inhabited valleys.

NESTING: Nests in caves and crevices in cliffs, often nests in colonies. Two eggs laid. Incubation period (in captivity) 17–19 days.

VOICE: Both the advertising coo and the nest call would appear, from Newman's descriptions, to be a hiccough-like note repeated twice, followed by a note like 'kuck-kuck' and then the hiccough sound again. The hiccough note by itself is used with the bowing display and also as a threatening or self-assertive coo and thus appears equivalent of the 'ōō-rŏŏ-cŏŏ-t'k-cōō' of the Rock Pigeon.

DISPLAY: In the bowing display (Newmann, 1911), the head is bobbed down and the hinder part of the body and tail jerked upwards. The tail is not, however, spread. When very excited the male may hop towards the female, slightly spreading and depressing his tail as he does so.

The species evidently has a display flight in which the wings are widely spread and clapped. Further details would be of interest. Schäfer (1930) says a high-pitched whistling sound is heard during the display flight but does not indicate whether this is vocal or instrumental.

ALTERNATIVE NAMES: White-bellied Pigeon, Tibetan Dove.

REFERENCES

NEWMAN, T. H. 1911. The Snow Pigeon. *Avicult Mag.* Third Series. **2**: 173–178.
SCHÄFER, E. 1938. Ornithologische Ergebnisse zweier Forschungsreisen nach Tibet. *Journ. f. Orn.*, supplement, May, 1938.

SPECKLED PIGEON   *Columba guinea*

Columba guinea Linnaeus, Syst. Nat., ed. 10, 1, 1758, p. 163.

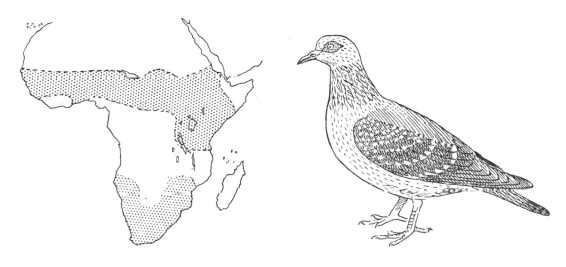

DESCRIPTION: About the same size as an average or fairly large Feral Pigeon but with rather closer plumage and proportionately longer bill which give it a rather more slender appearance. Mantle and wing-coverts a dark, rich reddish purple (which may bleach to light chestnut brown in worn plumage), outer wing-coverts bluish grey. White triangular-shaped marks on the tip of most of the wing-coverts form a profuse white spotting over the closed wing. Primaries and secondaries dusky slate. Tail blackish with pale grey central bar and white edges to the two outermost feathers. A broad collar of bifurcated feathers encircles the neck. These are chestnut at the base and tipped with silvery green and/or silvery pink. Rest of plumage light bluish grey, almost silver on the rump. A narrow white 'eyebrow' divides the red orbital skin from the grey of the crown. Irides yellow, whitish yellow or golden with an orange, red or purplish outer ring. Feet and legs salmon, flesh-pink or reddish. Orbital skin purplish red, red or purple. Bill slate or blackish with powdery white cere. The juvenile is much duller with ill-defined wing spots, dull unbifurcated neck feathers and (at first) dull greyish feet and orbital skin. The above description is of the tropical African form *C. g. guinea*. The form found in South Africa (*Columba guinea phaenota*) is slightly smaller and has denser feathering and a proportionately smaller bill, which give it a more compact and plump appearance. It also differs in colour, being much darker on the grey parts of the plumage and with smaller white spots on the wings.

FIELD CHARACTERS: Combination of large size, grey or silver-grey head, lower back, rump and under-parts and chestnut or purple shoulders distinguish it from other African pigeons. At a distance in flight wings look dark in contrast to silver grey back and rump (in nominate form).

DISTRIBUTION AND HABITAT: Africa from Senegal east to Eritrea south to the northern territories of Ghana in the west and the Iringa district of Tanganyika in the east. The darker southern form is found in South Africa north to Angola and Southern Rodesia. Inhabits open country, cultivated regions and open woodland, avoids forest. Usually in areas where there are either *Borassus* palms or else cliffs, rocky outcrops or buildings which it uses for roosting and nesting. In some places abundant in towns and villages. Where it overlaps with the Rock Pigeon, *Columba livia*, it appears not to make use of cliffs and caves as it does elsewhere (Harwin, 1963). In southern Africa also often nests and roosts in sea caves.

FEEDING AND GENERAL HABITS: Mainly, perhaps entirely, a ground feeder. Feeds largely on seeds, including cultivated grains. Fond of groundnuts when these are available on or near the surface after harvesting. In south-west Africa feeds largely on the fruits of *Tribulus terrestris* (Hoesch and Niethammer, 1940). Usually in pairs, small parties or singly but large numbers may aggregate at good feeding grounds. Sometimes forms large and cohesive flocks when not breeding, this flocking habit appearing to be more common in South Africa than in the northern parts of its range; another feature in which the southern form seems to show more convergence towards the Rock Pigeon than does the tropical form.
Flight direct and fairly fast with strong wing beats. Walks and runs nimbly on the ground.

NESTING: Nests in cavities at the base of the leaves of Borassus palms, in holes in trees and in holes or on sheltered ledges of cliffs or buildings. In southern Africa often on ledges in sea caves. In parts of Uganda it regularly nests, in darkness, in mine shafts and mine adits (Pitman, *in litt.*). Two white eggs. In captivity, in England, eggs hatched in 15-16 days; young fledged at 20–23 days.

VOICE: The advertising coo, in its high intensity form, is unmistakeable but difficult to transliterate. It could, perhaps, be written as 'Wōōrh wōōrh wŏŏ-wŏŏ-wŏŏ-wŏŏ' or Ōōrh-ōōrh-hŏŏ,hŏŏ-hŏŏ-ŏŏ' the opening notes usually faint, slow and muffled and the succeeding ones increasing in loudness, speed and emphasis. At a lower intensity the 'Ōōrh-ōōrh' notes are uttered more slowly and they are then hardly distinguishable from the homologous notes of the Rock Pigeon.
The display coo is a deep, emphatic 'Ŏŏrŏŏ-cōō' or Ŏŏr-ŏŏ-cōō-ōō' commonly repeated twice or more in succession and subject to some variation of tone and emphasis. Often a soft, short 'ŏŏ' is audible before the main phrase. The last syllables of the display coo tend to be more lengthened and emphasised in sexual than in purely threatening contexts.
The distress call resembles that of the Rock Pigeon but averages perhaps, a little louder. It seems sometimes, like the excitement cry of turtle doves, to be used as an expression of any intense emotion. Thus it is given immediately after copulation and also (sometimes) when attacking other birds.

DISPLAY: The bowing display is very similar to that of the Rock Pigeon (q.v.) but the tail is not often spread so fully or depressed to the same extent and the head, when lowered, is held only slightly below the horizontal not at right angles to the substrate. At the close of each cooing phrase, as it lifts its head, the bird makes quick, jerking movements to either side. Immediately after lifting its head the displaying bird often turns half around and may make a complete circle like a Rock Pigeon although more often it turns back through the same arc. In the self-assertive and defensive versions of this display the Speckled Pigeon faces its potential adversary and does not turn round, nor does it spread the tail much, if at all. The display flight apparently consists of wing clapping followed by gliding on outspread wings but most accounts of it are not very detailed. Mr. Donnelly, who has kept this species and observed it in the wild in Southern Rhodesia, described to me (*in litt.*) a display flight he saw in which a bird flew from a ledge on the side of a kopje, with clapping wings, at an angle of about 15 degrees for about 30 yards, then turned and glided back to its ledge in a half circle.

Copulation, at least that of captive pairs, is similar to the Wood Pigeon's.

Nodding, as in the Rock Pigeon, but the head is commonly at an angle of about 45 degrees from the substrate at the lowest point of the nod, not at about right angles to it.

OTHER NAMES: Triangular-spotted Pigeon; African Rock Pigeon; Red-eyed Pigeon; Guinea Pigeon; Hackled Pigeon.

REFERENCES

BANNERMAN, D. A. 1931. *The Birds of Tropical West Africa* **2**: 320–321.
—— 1951. *The Birds of Tropical West Africa* **8**: 238–239.
GOODWIN, D. 1956. Observations on the voice and some displays of certain pigeons. *Avicult. Mag.* **62**: 17–33 and 62–70.
HARWIN, R. M. 1963. Thoughts on a five weeks study in Northern Nigeria. *Bokmakerie* **15**: 2 : 10–12.
HOESCH, W. & NIETHAMMER, G. 1940. Die Vogelwelt Deutsch – Sudwestafrias. *Journ. f. Orn.* **88**: Sonderheft, pp. 101–102.
McLACHLAN, G. R. & LIVERSIDGE, R. 1957. *Roberts Birds of South Africa;* revised ed., p. 166. Cape Town.
PITWELL, L. R. & GOODWIN, D. 1964. Some observations on pigeons in Addis Ababa. *Bull. Brit. Orn. Club* **84**: 41–45.

WHITE-COLLARED PIGEON   *Columba albitorques*

Columba albitorques. Rüppell, Neue Wirbelth; Vög, 1837, p. 63, pl. 22.

DESCRIPTION: About the size of a rather small Feral Pigeon. General colour dark slate grey, bluest on the rump. Primary coverts largely white forming a white patch concealed when the wing is folded but conspicuous when it is spread. Some black chequering on the wing-coverts and an ill-defined grey central band across the blackish tail. Striking pure white collar across back of nape from ear to ear, the feathers behind the white band are acuminate and with shining, silvery tips. Bill black or dark grey with powdery white cere. Legs and feet red or pinkish. Irides very dark red or purplish red. (See pl. 1)

FIELD CHARACTERS: Dark bluish grey pigeon, appearing almost uniform in colour at a distance, with conspicuous white wing patch in flight. Wings make a characteristic whistling or creaking sound in flight at all times (Pitwell *in litt.*). At close quarters the white collar is diagnostic.

DISTRIBUTION AND HABITAT: Highlands of central and eastern Ethiopia and Eritrea. Inhabits rocky mountainous regions and high plateaux where suitable cliffs, rocks or buildings are available. Feeds much in cultivated fields.

FEEDING AND GENERAL HABITS: Feeds on the ground, largely on seeds, including cultivated grains when available. In Addis Ababa it fills the rôle taken elsewhere by the Feral Pigeon and takes bread and other artificial foods as well as spilled grain (Pitwell and Goodwin, 1964). Flight swift when going any distance. Can fly vertically up the face of a cliff or building or hover in front of a ledge or niche where it wishes to alight. Walks and runs nimbly on the ground. In Addis Ababa Pitwell found it usually in pairs or small parties although large numbers would aggregate, often in company with Speckled Pigeons, at good feeding grounds. Cheesman (1935) found that birds returning to their roosting places in the canyons and chasms that cut into the high plateau came in flocks of from 50 to 100. On reaching the edge of the ravine they would hurl themselves over 'dropping several hundreds of feet in an instant of time'. Usually perches on rocks, cliffs or buildings, much less often on trees.

NESTING: Nests in holes in cliffs, on sheltered ledges of caves and equivalent sites in or on buildings. In Addis Ababa freely enters buildings and nests inside them if permitted to do so. Usual pigeon nest. Two creamy white eggs. Incubation period (in captivity in Italy) 16 days, young fledge at 27–28 days (Taibel, 1954). Breeding season evidently prolonged, has been recorded nesting in all months.

VOICE: The advertising coo has been described by Taibel as 'Goo-hoo-ho' and by Pitwell as 'a long soft drawn-out cooing "Coo-oo".' The display coo (Taibel, 1954) is described as a very soft 'Hoo-ho, ho-hoo-ho, ho' only audible at very close quarters.

DISPLAY: Bowing display (Taibel, 1954) involves a deep bow and raising of the tail. The display flight consists of gliding followed by an upward swoop but not (*fide* Pitwell) accompanied by wing clapping. Billing precedes copulation.

OTHER NAMES: Abyssinian Rock Pigeon.

REFERENCES

CHEESMAN, R. E. 1935. On a collection of birds from north-western Abyssinia. Pt. 2. *Ibis* **5**: 13th Series, 297–329 (307).
PITWELL, L. R. & GOODWIN, D. 1964. Some observations on pigeons in Addis Ababa. *Bull. Brit. Orn. Club* **84**: 41–45.
SMITH, K. D. 1957. An annotated check list of the birds of Eritrea. *Ibis* **99**: 307–337.
TAIBEL, A. M. 1954. Notizie sulla riproduzione in cattivita del Colombo dal collare bianco (*Columba albitorques* Rüppell) *Rivista It. Orn.* 1954 (Seconda Serie), pp. 195–203.

STOCK DOVE   *Columba oenas*

Columba Oenas Linnaeus, Syst. Nat., Ed. 10, 1, 1758, p. 162.

DESCRIPTION: Rather smaller and more compact than the average Feral Pigeon with the wings proportionately slightly shorter although longer in proportion to the tail than a Wood Pigeon's. General coloration a slightly darker and bluer grey than the Wood Pigeon. Blackish tips to the secondaries and primaries that are conspicuous in flight. Two short black bars across the upper part of the folded wing, trace of a third bar often visible (always present beneath concealing tips of other feathers) and in a minority of males conspicuous. Upper breast mauve-pink, less extensively so than in Wood Pigeon. Patch of brilliant green and mauve-pink iridescence on sides of neck, often meeting across hind neck. Tail grey with blackish terminal band, ill-defined pale central band and white edgings to outermost feathers.

Irides very dark brown, looking quite black at a little distance but fading to pale yellow-brown when bird is ill or badly injured. Orbital skin blue-grey as surrounding feathers. Bill yellowish or dull white, pink at base with powdery white cere, looks flesh-pink at a little distance. Feet bright coral red.

The female is usually of a less clear and bluish grey than the male, often her feet and bill have a dusky suffusion. The young are duller and have rusty-fawn instead of mauve-pink on the breast, and dark legs and feet. The legs of young males (but not young females) may turn pink at about three weeks old though usually not until later.

FIELD CHARACTERS: At a distance, when settled, appears a darker and more uniform blue-grey than Wood Pigeon or most Feral Pigeons. In flight, especially at a distance, dorsal surfaces of wings show a paler central area which contrasts with the darker shoulder and blackish tip and trailing edge of wing. Normal flight swifter and with quicker wing beats than Wood Pigeon but not quite so fast as Rock or Feral Pigeon. Holds head, in flight, with bill pointing more downward than Rock or Feral Pigeons usually do thus giving somewhat different profile.

DISTRIBUTION AND HABITAT: Britain and western Europe, north to Finland and southern Scandinavia, south to Portugal and north-west Africa, east to Asia Minor and the 'forest islands' of the west Siberian steppe. Also northern Persia and parts of Turkestan. Many winter south of their breeding ranges, some south to northern Sinai and, occasionally in the Egyptian Delta. Probably originally a bird of forest edge and open woodlands and still occurs in such places. More usual, however, in open partly cultivated country and parkland.

FEEDING AND GENERAL BEHAVIOUR: Feeds almost entirely on the ground where, if at all hungry, it runs about quickly and nimbly as it seeks food. Eats seeds of many weeds and cultivated grains, small snails and other forms of invertebrate life. Also, but to a lesser extent than Wood Pigeon, young buds, shoots and leaves. Said to take berries and acorns but the writer has not seen it do so. It is certainly not capable of swallowing any but small acorns even if it wished to. I have once (only) seen Stock Doves feeding on ash flowers, taking them from the terminal branches in a Wood Pigeon-like manner. Driving of female by male as in the Rock Pigeon. Very aggressive and courageous in nest-site defence against rivals of its own species. Two pairs will not infrequently fight fiercely over a potential nest hole until all four birds are tottering with exhaustion and too weak (temporarily) to deal another peck or cuff.

NESTING: Often uses dead leaves of laurel and other trees as well as the more usual twigs, roots, etc., but frequently little or no nesting material used. Nests in holes in trees, in holes or on sheltered ledges of cliffs, old buildings or quarries, on old nests of other species, on the débris that often accumulates on 'witches broomsticks' in old lime trees. Less often in rabbit burrows or on the ground under thick bushes. Supposed records of the Stock Dove building on the branches of trees and bushes are probably due to its taking over deserted or old nests of Wood Pigeons. This is quite common in some areas. Two white eggs. Incubation period 16 days.

VOICE: Advertising coo a deep 'oo-er-oo' or 'coo-oo' usually uttered in a series; subject to some variation but always distinct from any notes of the Wood Pigeon and Rock Pigeon. This coo is also used when nest-calling. The display coo is a very faint, droning coo, interspersed with a double click which is, *apparently*, caused by snapping the mandibles together, but may be vocal. The display coo is too faint to be heard except at close quarters hence the frequent statement that the Stock Dove does not call during its bowing display.

DISPLAY: Bowing display like that of the Wood Pigeon, but often prefaced by walking towards female with depressed and partly spread tail. Display flight very similar to that of Rock Pigeon but usually less pronounced. The bird flies along in a horizontal or near-horizontal plane, every now and then beating its wings rather slowly through a wide arc and then gliding with them held somewhat above the horizontal. Copulation ceremony similar to that of Wood Pigeon but male usually performs the bowing display, once, immediately after dismounting. Nodding as in Wood Pigeon, but I have never seen it culminate in the twig-fixing movement.

OTHER NAMES: Stock Pigeon; Rock Dove; (locally in Britain).

REFERENCES

CAMPBELL, B. 1951. A colony of Stock Doves. *Bird Notes* **24**: 169–176.
DELMEE, E. 1954. Douze Années d'Observations sur le Comportement du Pigeon Colombin. *Le Gerfaut* **44**: 193–259.
MURTON, R. K., WESTWOOD, N. J. & ISAACSON, A. J. 1964. The feeding habits of the Wood Pigeon *Columba palumbus*, Stock Dove *C. oenas* and Turtle Dove *Streptopelia turtur*. *Ibis* **106**: 174–197.

YELLOW-EYED STOCK DOVE   *Columba eversmanni*

Columba eversmanni, Bonaparte, Compt. Rend. Acad. Sci. Paris, 43, 1836, p. 838.

DESCRIPTION: Slightly smaller and slimmer than Stock Dove (q.v.) but otherwise very like it. Coloration similar but differs in the head being mauve-pink like the breast; lower back and upper part of rump pale grey to white, contrasting with the darker grey of the lower rump and upper tail coverts. Underwing coverts pale grey or white in correlation with rump colour. Irides yellow or yellowish-brown; orbital skin pale yellow or cream-coloured. Bill yellowish, greenish yellow or green with a dark grey or brownish basal area. Differences of female and juvenile comparable with those of Stock Dove (q.v.).

DISTRIBUTION AND HABITAT: Turkestan from the Aral Sea to northern Afghanistan and east to Zaissan-nor. In winter south to northern India. Often and perhaps usually in open agricultural or rather barren country with or without trees.

FEEDING AND GENERAL HABITS: Known to feed largely on the ground and to take seeds, including cultivated grains. Also recorded feeding largely on mulberries when these were ripening in April (Whitehead, in Baker, 1913). Roosts colonially in trees in winter (Baker, 1913).

NESTING: Probably nests in holes anywhere, like Stock Dove. Meinertzhagen (1938) found it apparently breeding in holes in willow and mulberry trees, from which birds were flushed, and in ruined buildings. Elsewhere in northern Afghanistan it has been found nesting colonially in holes in clay cliffs bordering rivers (Paludan, 1959). The holes were in narrow layers of gravel and pebbles in the clay; the implication is that they were excavated by the pigeons themselves but this seems to me highly unlikely. Breeding season, in northern Afghanistan, probably in full swing in June, July and August. Young about four to six weeks old have been taken in August, September and early October.

VOICE: No information.

DISPLAY: No information.

OTHER NAMES: Eversmann's Stock Dove; Eversmann's Stock Pigeon; Eastern Stock Dove.

REFERENCES

BAKER, E. C. S. 1913. *Indian Pigeons and Doves.* pp. 150–151. London.
MEINERTZHAGEN, R. 1938. On the Birds of Northern Afghanistan, pt. 2. *Ibis* **2**: 14 Series, pp. 671–717 (708–709).
PALUDAN, K. 1959. On the Birds of Afghanistan. *Vidensk. Medd. Dansk Naturh. For.* **122**: 116.

SOMALI STOCK DOVE   *Columba oliviae*

Columba oliviae Stephenson Clarke, Bull, Brit. Orn. Cl., 38, 1918, p. 61.

DESCRIPTION: A little larger than a Barbary Dove. General colour a pale lavender grey, tinged with brown on the mantle and wings. Lower back and rump a darker and bluer grey. Wing quills tipped with blackish. Tail blackish with grey central band. Forehead, crown and nape mauve pink. Hindneck iridescent coppery brown shot with green. Irides yellowish. Orbital skin red or purplish red. Feet and legs pink. Bill black with powdery white cere. Some individuals show a few blackish flecks on the wings which are (in an evolutionary sense) the last remnants of the black wing bars such as are seen in *eversmanni*.

I have not seen a juvenile of this species. It probably differs *vis à vis* the adult, in much the same way as the juvenile Stock Dove (q.v.).

FIELD IDENTIFICATION: In flight looks pale grey with dark tip to tail. When perched the red orbital skin is conspicuous.

DISTRIBUTION AND HABITAT: Coastal hills south and east of Berbera, British Somaliland and northern Italian Somaliland. Inhabits barren sandstone hills and escarpments in the maritime desert or semi-desert regions. Mr. Myles North, to whom I am indebted for the information on ecology, nesting and voice of this species, found it in or near rocky ravines, usually at less than 1,000 feet above sea level but sometimes up to about 2,500 feet.

FEEDING AND GENERAL HABITS: Feeds chiefly, probably entirely, on the ground. Known to take seeds and berries. During the 1914–18 war large numbers gathered to feed on scattered (imported) cultivated grain at a camel depot established at Gubar (Archer and Godman, 1937). Flies extremely fast.

NESTING: Two nests were found by North, one at Galgalo (8° 00′N, 49° 00′E) at 2,500 feet and one at Eil (8° 00′N, 50° 00′E) at 400 feet. Both were of dried grass and placed in recesses in the roofs of caves that were situated on open hillsides not in main gorges. In each case the nest site was almost dark. The nest at Eil contained one egg, and the parent was flushed from the recess, on August 24. The one at Galgalo, found in May, contained an addled egg. At Galgalo the local Somalis reported finding a nest with an egg in late December and one with young in February.

VOICE: The only call heard by North was the display coo. This he describes as 'wuk-wuk-wuk-oh, wuk-ow, the wuks being short coos and the oh and ow deep growls'.

DISPLAY: No information.

OTHER NAMES: Somali Rock Pigeon.

REFERENCES

ARCHER, G. A. & GODMAN, E. M. 1937. *The Birds of British Somaliland and the Gulf of Aden.* Vol. 2. pp. 573–575.
NORTH, M. E. W. 1964. Letter dated 12th June, filed in Bird Room, British Museum (Nat. Hist.).

WOOD PIGEON   *Columba palumbus*

Columba palumbus Linnaeus, Syst. Nat. Ed. 10, 1, 1758, p. 163.

This is by far the most abundant wild pigeon in Britain and may be more numerous than the Feral Pigeon (q.v.) although never so 'thick on the ground' as the latter is in some towns. It maintains its numbers in spite of persecution. Probably this is due to the fact that, in most country districts, game-preserving interests keep down its natural enemies, and in towns and suburban areas it does little harm, gives pleasure to all who love to see and hear handsome, musical-voiced birds and so is allowed to breed unmolested. In some other parts of its range it has, on the contrary, proved very sensitive to shooting pressure.

DESCRIPTION: A little larger than the average Feral Pigeon and rather more heavily built, with proportionately shorter wings and legs, and longer tail. General coloration bluish grey, rather duller on the wings than elsewhere. Primaries blackish drab with pale edging. Breast a delicate mauvish pink shading to creamy on the belly and greyish on the flanks. A white mark along the wing edge that forms a band across it when the wing is open. A white patch on either side of the neck surrounded by an iridescent area glossed purple-pink and green, the feathers in front of the white area being iridescent green with a 'crimped' appearance. Tail grey with a broad blackish terminal band, a pale greyish white central band well defined on the underside of the tail, but less so on the upper side. Irides greenish white to pale golden, usually a pale lemon tint. Feet and legs dark reddish purple. Orbital skin grey. Bill golden, purplish-pink at base; cere powdery white. The juvenile is duller and paler, with pale fawn or rusty feather-edges, sometimes very apparent but usually only faintly indicated. The breast is rusty fawn and there is no white or iridescent colour on the neck. Little sexual difference in colour. Most males have, however, rather larger white neck patches and richer pink breasts than most females. The form found in Persia *C. palumbus iranica*, has a whitish or pale yellow bill; that of northern India, *C. palumbus casiotis*, has creamy buff instead of white patches on the sides of the neck; that of North Africa tends to be rather brighter in colour, and those of Madeira and the Azores *C. p. madarensis* and *C. p. azorica* are duller with smaller neck patches.

FIELD CHARACTERS: In flight white band across wing, when settled white neck patch (in adult) diagnostic. Proportionately longer tail than other European *Columba* species. Habit of usually raising and re-lowering tail a few seconds after alighting often enables sure identification at a considerable distance.

DISTRIBUTION AND HABITAT: Europe north to about 66°N, east to Persia and northern India. Eastern and central islands of the Azores, mountain forests on Madeira (now probably extinct there), and mountain forest regions of north-west Africa. Originally a bird of forest and/or forest edge the Wood Pigeon has adapted itself well, in many places, to man's alteration of the landscape. Now frequents not only woodlands but also open country interspersed with odd trees, high hedges or plantations, and suburban areas with trees. Common in some towns such as London and Baghdad, and occurs in some almost treeless areas of the Orkneys where it nests on the ground. Some populations migratory.

FEEDING AND GENERAL HABITS: Has a very varied diet including buds and young leaves of many trees and plants, seeds of grasses and other weeds, grain, acorns, beech nuts, berries and invertebrates such as caterpillars, small snails and even earthworms. In agricultural districts clover is often an important winter food (Murton *et al.*, 1963 and 1964). In towns and suburbs it readily eats bread and much other human food although individuals to whom such foods are new may at first refuse them even when very hungry. Feeds both in trees and on the ground. Can cling and clamber among slender branches and twigs with an astonishing facility in view of its weight and apparent clumsiness. Can – and often does – hang upside down to take acorns or berries when all the more easily reached ones have already been eaten.

Tail is raised and then lowered again after alighting. This is not done as with some other pigeons, at the moment of alighting, but a few seconds after. It appears to indicate that the bird is sufficiently at ease to have 'decided' to remain where it is, at least for the moment. If frightened or sexually excited at the moment of alighting it may remain perched for some time before it makes the tail-lifting movement. Driving of female by her mate less obvious than in the Rock or Feral Pigeons, but may occur if another male comes near to the hen when the pair are outside their own territory.

Usually roosts communally when not breeding, and pairs that have taken up breeding territory and males whose mates are incubating may also use these roosts. Prior to and during breeding small roosts may form in or near the breeding territory of a pair. Large roosts are often in conifers or, especially in London, on small, thickly wooded islands.

NESTING: Usual pigeon nest on tree, shrub or (in towns) on the ledge of a building. Rarely in hollow or on the ground. Very often in quite low situations in hedges or hawthorn bushes. Breeding may occur at any time, but from March to October (in London and Suburbia) and from April to October in country districts are the times when nests with eggs or young can normally be expected.   The peak of the breeding season is usually from June to mid-September.   Nest building by male not uncommon (*fide* Murton and Isaacson, 1962).   Two white eggs.   Incubation period 15½–17 days.

VOICE: Advertising coo a loud, musical 'cōo-cōo, cōocōo, cŏŏk' the phrase usually repeated from two to four times but almost always ending on the abrupt 'cŏŏk'.   To those who know it this cooing is well paraphrased by the familiar rendering 'tak too coos, taffy, tak', but the initial 'tak' or 'cook' is given very faintly (sometimes omitted) so that unless one is very close to the calling bird it always appears to begin 'too coos . . .'.   Some individual variation, I have heard one male whose advertising coo was 'cōo-cōo, cōo-cōo-cōo, cŏŏk', and another who called 'cŏŏ-cōo, cŏŏk'.   In Baghdad the advertising coo of the Wood Pigeon is normally a tri-syllabic phrase very like that of the Collared Dove (Harrison, 1955).   Possibly other geographical variations in voice exist which have not yet been recorded.   The advertising coo may be given from the nest-site but when nest calling with nodding and wing-twitching a two-syllabled phrase 'ŏŏ-ōōr' is given.   This varies much in intensity.   It can be loud, with a very strained intense tone, but is usually softer and less loud than the advertising coo.   Exceptionally the bird may utter this nest call when perched normally on a branch.

The display coo is deep intense-sounding 'cōo-cōo, cŭ-cŭ, cōo, cōo', or 'cōo, cu-cu-cu-cu, cōo', subject to much variation, sometimes surprisingly loud, sometimes rather quiet.   The hurried panting cŭ-cŭ sounds (? inspirations) between the longer 'coos' are softer and may sound much like panting laughter.

DISPLAY: In the bowing display the neck is inflated, the white and iridescent areas of the neck frame the head with its golden bill and pale eyes whose pupils contract to pinpoints during the display. The tail is raised and opened as it is lifted but usually closed again before it reaches its highest point at the culmination of the bow.   The tail raising does not take place when, as often happens, a Wood Pigeon tries to give the bowing display while walking after another that is moving away from it over the ground or along a large branch.   Display flight consists of towering up, clapping the wings loudly and then gliding down in a gentle arc with the wings held more or less horizontally, not half raised as in the Rock Pigeon and Stock Dove.   Usually each such flight consists of two or more such towerings, clappings and glides before the bird perches again.   At low intensity there is no audible wing-clap. Copulation is usually preceded by billing and immediately afterwards the male stands for a moment in a peculiar upright posture with neck feathers ruffled, as do the males of the Turtle Dove and Speckled Pigeon at this time.   Nodding (q.v.) occurs when nest-calling and in hostile situations.   In the former it may, at high intensity, culminate in a suggestion of the twig fixing movement.   Performs more or less formal hops or leaps towards or even away from other bird in many situations involving aggressive or sexual excitement.   Rarely male may leap into air and wing clap before attacking or displaying.   Distraction display frequent when flushed from hatching eggs or newly hatched young.   Usually bird drops nearly to ground and flies, at first with somewhat impeded flight, very low over the ground for 30 to 100 yards before rising.   Less often bird will flop and flutter wildly over the ground or low cover before taking wing.   I have seen identical behaviour from some (but not many) Wood Pigeons on being released after I had caught and ringed them.

OTHER NAMES: Ringdove;   Cushat;   Cushadoo;   Quest;   Ring Pigeon;   Stock Dove (by poets only).

REFERENCES

CRAMP, S.   1968.   Territorial and other behaviour of the Wood Pigeon.   *Bird Study* **5**: 55–66.

GOODWIN, D.   1955.   Notes on European wild pigeons.   *Avicult. Mag.* **61**: 54–85.

—— 1956.   Observations on the voice and some displays of certain pigeons.   *Avicult. Mag.* **62**: 17–33 and 62–70.

—— 1960.   Comparative ecology of pigeons in Inner London.   *British Birds* **53**: 201–212.

HARRISON, J. G.   1955.   The Call Note of Iraki Wood Pigeons.   *Bull. B.O.C.* **75**: 69–70.

MURTON, R. K.   1958.   The Breeding of Wood Pigeon populations.   *Bird Study* **5**: 157–183.

MURTON, R. K. & ISAACSON, A. J.   1962.   The functional basis of some behaviour in the Wood Pigeon *Columba palumbus*. *Ibis* **104**: 503–521.

MURTON, R. K., ISAACSON, A. J. & WESTWOOD, N. J.   1963.   The feeding ecology of the Wood Pigeon.   *British Birds* **56**: 345–375.

MURTON, R. K., WESTWOOD, N. J. & ISAACSON, A. J.   1964.   The feeding habits of the Wood Pigeon *Columba palumbus*, Stock Dove *C. oenas* and Turtle Dove *Streptopelia turtur*.   *Ibis* **106**: 174–188.

TROCAZ PIGEON   *Columba trocaz*

Columba trocaz Heineken, Edinburgh Journ Sci. (N.S.) 1, 1829, p. 230.

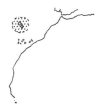

This species was probably derived from an early invasion of the Wood Pigeon into Madeira. Since, however, it has apparently not interbred with the later Wood Pigeon invasion it must be given specific rank (Goodwin, 1959).

DESCRIPTION: Somewhat larger than a Wood Pigeon, with rather longer legs, very long middle toe and more sloping forehead. In colour and markings can be described as a dark, dull version of Wood Pigeon, predominantly dark slate grey in colour with the white neck patches replaced by larger silver-grey patches meeting round the back of the neck and with no white on the wing. The throat and upper neck are grey and the pink of the breast duller and more orange in hue and more restricted in area than in the Wood Pigeon.

DISTRIBUTION AND HABITAT: Madeira. Inhabits the laurel forests and may now be nearing extinction owing to progressive de-forestation and shooting for food.

FEEDING AND GENERAL HABITS: Probably much as Wood Pigeon. Said (Godman, 1872) to feed on fruits of bay and til-trees picked up from the ground, and also to feed sometimes in the cultivated areas.

NESTING: Usual pigeon nest on sheltered cliff ledges or in tree or shrub. One white egg.

VOICE: The advertising coo of a captive male was 'coo-coo, coooo, cŏŏk' repeated several times. Similar to that of a Wood Pigeon in its abrupt ending and tone, though less loud. The display coo sounded like a muffled version of a Wood Pigeon's but on each occasion I witnessed the bowing display other birds and people nearby were making a lot of noise so that I could not hear the Trocaz Pigeon properly.

DISPLAY: Bowing display and nodding (of captive birds) as Wood Pigeon.

OTHER NAMES: Long-toed Pigeon.

REFERENCES
BANNERMAN, D. A. 1965. *Birds of the Atlantic Islands*. Vol. 2. London.
GODMAN, F. D. 1872. Notes on the Resident and Migratory Birds of Madeira and the Canaries. *Ibis*: Third Series, 210–224.
GOODWIN, D. 1959. Taxonomy of the genus *Columba*. *Bull Brit. Mus. (Nat. Hist.) Zool.* 6: 1: 1–23.

BOLL'S PIGEON   *Columba bollii*

Columba bollii Godman, Ibis. 1872. p. 217.

Another presumed derivative from Wood Pigeon stock this bird is often considered as a race of the Trocaz Pigeon. I consider, however, that it is better to give it specific rank (Goodwin, 1959).

DESCRIPTION: Much like Trocaz Pigeon but with a *small* coppery brown patch on either side of the neck instead of an extensive silver-grey area.

DISTRIBUTION AND HABITAT: Canary Islands. Inhabits the laurel forests at high altitudes. Recorded as also feeding at times in cultivated lands. Possibly now nearing extinction or actually extinct as its habitat is fast being destroyed.

FEEDING AND GENERAL HABITS: Probably much as Wood Pigeon. Recorded as feeding on fruit of *Persea indica*.

NESTING: Nests found in tree heath and laurel trees were about twenty feet from the ground and similar to Wood Pigeons' nests. One white egg. Breeding season (*fide* Koenig, 1890) prolonged, from January to September inclusive.

VOICE: Koenig (1890) describes the advertising coo as a short 'trŭ-trŭ-trŭ-trŭ-tru'. The display coo as 'trŭ-Trŭ-trŭ, trŭ-trŭ, trŭ-trŭ, trŭ' and an aggressive call (? or distress cry) as a grunting 'yur, yur'.

DISPLAY: Koenig (1890) describes a deep bow but does not say if tail is raised.

OTHER NAMES: Boll's Laurel Pigeon.

REFERENCES

GOODWIN, D. 1959. Taxonomy of the genus *Columba*. *Bull. Brit. Mus. (Nat. Hist.) Zool.* **6: 1**: 1–23.
KOENIG, A. 1890. Ornithologische Forschungsergebnisse einer Reise nach Madeira und den Canarischen Inseln. *Journ. f. Orn.* **38**: 257–488 (443–445).
MEADE-WALDO, E. G. 1889. Notes on some birds of the Canary Islands. *Ibis*, Sixth Series **1**: 6–9 and **4**: 4–5.

AFRICAN WOOD PIGEON   *Columba unicincta*

Columba unicincta Cassin, Proc. Acad. Nat. Sci. Phila, 1859 (1860), p. 143.

DESCRIPTION: About the size of the average Feral Pigeon but proportions nearer to a Wood Pigeon though rather more compact than the latter. Crown and hind neck silver grey. Rest of upperparts and wings blackish-slate with silver-grey edges to the feathers, these being rather broad on the mantle, back and rump feathers and narrowest on the outer wing coverts, secondaries and primaries. Tail dark slate with a broad greyish-white central band, this being less pronounced on the two central feathers. Breast vinous pink to salmon pink, shading to creamy white on the throat and belly. Irides orange or red.

Orbital skin dark red.   Feet and legs grey.   Bill grey with pale grey or whitish tip.   Female has pink on breast less bright and often suffused with grey.   Juvenile (to judge from a single specimen which has nearly completed its moult, and from descriptions) is strongly barred with dark subterminal bands and conspicuous buff and chestnut tips to the feathers like the young of many other rather dark-coloured species.

DISTRIBUTION AND HABITAT: Equatorial forest region of Africa; from Liberia south to Gaboon and eastward through the Congo to Uganda.   A forest dweller but often feeds in more open country adjacent to or near the forest edge.

FEEDING AND GENERAL HABITS: Fruits, berries, seeds and termites have been found in the crops of shot specimens.   Records of birds seen feeding all refer to feeding in trees, often in company with green pigeons.   Like many other pigeons it frequently perches on any large dead tree that towers above others nearby.

NESTING: In trees, only one or two nests have been found and these have been unreachable.

VOICE: What is probably the advertising coo has been described as 'a series of seven to twelve deep coos, delivered rather slowly' (Chapin, 1939).   A display flight, apparently identical to that of the Wood Pigeon, has also been recorded (Mackworth-Praed and Grant, 1951).

DISPLAY: No information.

OTHER NAMES: Grey Pigeon; Afep Pigeon; Congo Wood Pigeon.

REFERENCES

CHAPIN, J. P.   1939.   The Birds of the Belgian Congo.   Pt. 2.   *Bull. Amer. Mus. Nat. Hist.* Vol. LXXV: 168–169.
MACKWORTH-PRAED, C. W. & GRANT, C. H. B.   1951.   *African Handbook of Birds*, Series 1. **1**: 467.

LAUREL PIGEON   *Columba junioniae*

Columba junioniae Hartert, Nov. Zool. 23, 1916, p. 86.

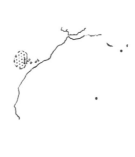

DESCRIPTION: About size of Wood Pigeon but wing rather shorter and more rounded. Forehead, face and throat darkish grey with trace of mauve or green iridescence. Hind crown, nape and neck predominantly iridescent green shading to iridescent reddish purple on the neck and upper mantle and wine red on lower breast and underparts. Back and wings dark greyish brown with narrow whitish edgings to outer webs of primaries. Lower back and rump dark bluish grey shading to lighter bluish grey on upper tail coverts and two central tail feathers. Outer tail feathers dark bluish grey with broad but ill-defined whitish terminal band. Underside of tail with the light and dark (here drab grey) areas rather more sharply demarcated. Irides orange, eyelids red (Koenig). Bill pale pink or pinkish white, wine-red at base. Legs and feet red. Sexes alike, but female averaging a little paler red-purple on neck and breast. Juvenile duller and browner, with rusty-brown fringes to wing coverts.

FIELD CHARACTERS: The broad whitish terminal band on the tail, which usually looks predominantly white at a little distance in flight, and the wine-red underparts are diagnostic.

DISTRIBUTION AND HABITAT: The Canary Islands of Palma and Gomera but now very rare or possibly extinct in the latter island. Inhabits scrub covered slopes, areas where there is a mixed growth of pines interspersed with laurel and other shrubs and (*fide* Koenig) laurel forest. May visit more open and cultivated areas for feeding purposes.

FEEDING AND GENERAL HABITS: Recorded feeding on fruits and berries, especially those of the til-tree and vinatigo, also taking cherries, barley, wheat and linseed in the cultivated regions. Feeds both in trees and on the ground. Meade-Waldo who observed it both in the wild and in captivity described it as having a 'soft, floppy flight' but other observers (Etchécoper, Cullen *et al.*) describe it as similar to that of the Wood Pigeon. Possibly the 'soft floppy flight' is used when travelling only a short distance and not alarmed? On the ground Meade-Waldo described it as 'marching along with a long swinging gait' but also able to run quickly like a partridge.

NESTING: The very few nests recorded seem all to have been in cavities or on ledges of rock or on a stump (on cliff side?). One creamy white egg. Eggs have been found in March and in May.

VOICE: The 'pairing call' (? display coo) has been described by Koenig as 'Kurūh, kurūh . . . kurúkědi-kūh . . . kūh . . . kūh'.

DISPLAY: Etchécopar implies that the display flight is like that of the Wood Pigeon. Koenig says that the male, when sexually excited, flies with widely spread tail from tree to tree.

REFERENCES

BANNERMAN, D. A. 1963. *Birds of the Atlantic Islands.* London.
CULLEN, J. M. 1952. Birds on Palma and Gomera. *Ibis* **94**: 68–84.
ETCHÉCOPAR, R. D. & HüE, F. 1964. *Les Oiseaux du Nord de l'Afrique.* Paris.
KOENIG, A. 1890. Ornithologische Forschungsersergebnisse einer Reise nach Madeira und den Canarischen Inseln. *Journ. f. Orn.* **191 & 192**: 257–488.
MEADE-WALDO, E. G. 1889. Notes on some birds of the Canary Islands. *Ibis*, Sixth Series **1**: 6–9 and **4**: 509–510.

OLIVE PIGEON   *Columba arquatrix*

Colomba (sic) *arquatrix* Temminck, in Knip, Les Pigeons, 1809, les Colombes, p. 11, pl. 5.

DESCRIPTION: About size of Wood Pigeon but tail a little shorter and shape more compact. Forehead and face dark, dull purple, throat paler, shading to silvery purple or bluish mauve on the breast and on the tips of the lanceolate feathers of the hind neck. Hind crown and nape silver grey. Mantle and inner wing dark purple shading to very dark bluish slate on outer wing converts and rump and blackish on primaries and tail. Lower breast and belly dark purple shading to dark bluish grey on flanks and under tail coverts. The upper mantle, inner and median wing coverts, purple areas of the under parts (not the silvery purple upper breast) are profusely spotted with small white spots, each feather having one or two such spots at the edge of its outer web or on both webs. Underwing dark slate. Irides dull pale greenish yellow, greenish grey or light brown. The extensive orbital skin, bill, legs and feet are yellow, usually a deep yellow or orange yellow but sometimes (in not very fit individuals?) a pale yellow or creamy yellow. Female usually a little less bright, the purple parts less bluish and the hind crown and nape not quite so pale and silvery. Juvenile duller, paler and more rufous with a freckled rather than spotted appearance. The feathers that have white spots in the adult have white fringes, often with a rusty area at the edge of the white. Those on parts that are purplish and unspotted in the adult have rufous or rusty buff fringes.

FIELD CHARACTERS: A large dark pigeon with yellow legs and bill.

DISTRIBUTION AND HABITAT: Eastern Africa from Ethiopia, Southern Sudan, Uganda and the eastern Belgian Congo to Angola and South Africa. Inhabits forest, usually at high elevations.

FEEDING AND GENERAL HABITS: Feeds on seeds, berries and fruits taken from the branches, possibly also from the ground. Olives, wild chestnuts, wild figs and fruits of *Trema* have been recorded. In parts of its range it makes daily altitudinal migrations, breeding and roosting in the mountain forest but descending to the lowland forest to feed (Van Someren, 1949; Verheyen, 1955). Flight swift and strong. When descending to lowland forest to feed often plunges downwards at an almost incredible speed; when ascending circles round on rising air currents when available. Commonly in pairs or small parties, often in large flocks and at all times numbers may aggregate at feeding trees. On or shortly after alighting often raises its tail rather like a Wood Pigeon does but the movement is slower and less pronounced.

NESTING: Usual pigeon nest in tree or shrub. Often, perhaps usually, the nest tree is on the edge of the forest, just outside its borders or on the edge of a clearing. One white egg. Incubation period, in captivity in England, 17 days (Collins, 1959). Both sexes incubate in the usual manner. Recorded breeding November to January in southern Sudan, June and July in Ruwenzori, March to November in Kenya, December and January in Nyasaland, January to April in Transvaal and November to February in the Cape.

VOICE: The advertising coo of a captive male, one of a pair, that I have observed at the London Zoo, is a very deep, muffled, throbbing 'Cŏō-cŏō! crŏŏ-crŏŏ, crŏŏ-crŏŏ, crŏŏ-crŏŏ . . .' the first two notes loudest the others more throbbing and 'dying away'. Both tone and cadence very suggestive of the advertising calls of the spot-winged doves, *Turtur* sp. and unlike the cooing of any other *Columba* species whose voice I know. When the bird coos it stands rather upright and all the mauve areas of neck and upper breast are swelled out and become sharply demarcated from the spotted areas around and below. What is, probably, the same call has also been described by Chapin (1939) as low and hoarse, with a tremor or quaver, so that it . . . may break into two or three syllables', by some later writers (? abstracting from Chapin) in very similar terms and by Verheyen (1955) as 'h'-ou . . . h'ou . . . hourouhourou'. Collins heard no audible coo from his captive birds during the bowing display although Verheyen implies that the advertising coo, or something very like it, is used in this display. Verheyen describes a call (? excitement cry), uttered during the display flight, as being like the bleating of a goat.

DISPLAY: Bowing display of a captive male (Collins, 1959) consisted of a series of deep bows with neck inflated, at commencement of each bow male stood up at full height. There was no appreciable movement of the tail. Verheyen describes the bowing display as incorporating a lowering movement of the tail ('la queue rabattue . . . ') but implies that all *Columba* species have the same or similar tail movements in their bowing display, which is incorrect. J. O. Harrison (pers comm.) saw a bowing display like that described by Collins, but with shallow bows, from the male and a rapid opening and shutting of the bill from both sexes of the London Zoo pair.

Verheyen describes two forms of display flight, one in which the male flies upward with loudly clapping wings for some yards and then glides in a circle and one in which after the clapping ascent he nose-dives downwards uttering the bleating call.

OTHER NAMES: Rameron Pigeon; Yellow-eyed Pigeon; Speckled Wood Pigeon.

REFERENCES

CHAPIN, G. P. 1939. The birds of the Belgian Congo. Pt. 2. *Bull. Amer. Mus. Nat. Hist.* Vol. LXXV: 170–172.
COLLINS, D. 1959. Breeding of the Rameron Pigeon. *Avicult. Mag.* **65**: 169–172.
MACKWORTH-PRAED, C. W. & GRANT, C. H. B. 1957. *African Handbook of Birds.* Series 1. **1**: 465–466.
McLACHLAN, G. R. & LIVERSIDGE, R. 1957. *Roberts Birds of South Africa,* revised ed. pp. 166–167. Cape Town.
VAN SOMEREN, V. G. L. & G. R. C. 1949. *The Birds of Bwamba,* pp. 24–25. Special supplement to the Uganda Journal, vol. 13. Kampala.
VERHEYEN, R. 1955. Le Pigeon Bleu (*Columba arquatrix* Temm.) du Ruwenzori. *Gerfaut* 1955: 127–145.

CAMEROON OLIVE PIGEON   *Columba sjöstedti*

Columba sjöstedti Reichenow, John. f. Orn., 46, 1898, p. 138.

DESCRIPTION: Like the previous species *C. arquatrix* (q.v.) but differs as follows. Entire head rather dark bluish grey, there is only a slight purplish pink tint on the lanceolate neck feathers, the silvery purple area on the upper breast is more restricted. The white spots on the underparts are larger and extend well up onto the breast so that the bird appears more boldly and profusely spotted. There is little or no bare orbital skin. The bill is yellowish horn, yellow or orange at the tip and red or dark red at the base. The legs and feet are dark purple with yellow claws. Female with duller grey head and purplish of upperbreast extending up into throat. Juvenile bears same relation to adult as in previous species.

DISTRIBUTION AND HABITAT: The highlands of Cameroon, above 6,000 feet, and Fernando Po Island. Inhabits forest.

FEEDING AND GENERAL HABITS: Probably very similar to *Columba arquatrix* with which it may be conspecific. Eisentraut encountered it in pairs and small parties, feeding on yellow berries.

VOICE: A deep "uur" irregularly repeated (Eisentraut). Possibly this was the alarm or distress call.

DISPLAY: No information.

OTHER NAMES: Sjostedt's Pigeon; Cameroon Rameron Pigeon.

REFERENCE

AMADON, D. 1953. Avian systematics and evolution in the Gulf of Guinea. *Bull. Amer. Mus. Nat. Hist.* Vol. 100. Art 3.
EISENTRAUT, M. (1956). Notizen über einige Vögel des Kamerungebirges. J. Orn. **97**: 294–295.

SÃO THOMÉ OLIVE PIGEON   *Columba thomensis*

Columba arquatrix var. *thomensis* Bocage, Jorn. Sci. Math. Phys. E. Nat., Acad. Real Sci. Lisboa, 12, 1888, p. 230, 232.

DESCRIPTION: This island representative of the olive pigeons shows features characteristic of island forms in its relatively softer plumage, longer tail and less distinct colour pattern. Head dark grey. Lanceolate feathers on hind neck less developed than in *C. arquatrix* and *C. sjöstedti*. Breast, sides of lower neck, mantle and wing coverts rusty purple or maroon shading to a very dark slate grey on rump and belly and greyish black on wing quills and tail. Wing coverts and lower breast speckled with white, the white spots much less sharply defined than in the mainland forms. Irides dull olive. Bill, legs and feet yellow. Female duller with only slight tinge of maroon on breast and wing coverts which are predominantly dark brownish grey but spotted as in male. I have not seen a juvenile of this species, it probably resembles those of other olive pigeons.

DISTRIBUTION AND HABITAT: São Thomé Island in the Gulf of Guinea, formerly also on Rollas Islet. Inhabits forest, chiefly, perhaps now only, the considerable areas of original forest still remaining round the Pico (6,600 feet) where it was quite numerous in 1949 in spite of human persecution (Snow, 1950).

FEEDING AND GENERAL HABITS: Little recorded. Three specimens collected by Snow had been feeding on the berries of a montane tree *Schefflera mannii*. Although much shot by the inhabitants it has, apparently, not yet learned much fear of man and will permit a close approach.

NESTING: Nothing apparently recorded. Presumably much as in *C. arquatrix*.

VOICE: Snow records 'a short, rolling "Crrrrrrrr" '.

DISPLAY: No information.

OTHER NAMES: Maroon Pigeon; São Thomé Maroon Pigeon; São Thomé Pigeon.

REFERENCES

BANNERMAN, D. A. 1931. The Maroon Pigeon of São Thomé. *Ibis* 1: Thirteenth Series, 652–654.
SNOW, D. W. 1950. *The birds of São Thomé and Principe in the Gulf of Guinea. Ibis* 92: 579–595

COMORO OLIVE PIGEON   *Columba pollenii*
Columba pollenii Schlegel, Nederl. Tijdschr. Dierk., 3, 1866, p. 87.

DESCRIPTION: This is the Comoro representative of *Columba arquatrix* with which it may be conspecific. About size of Wood Pigeon. Head, neck, breast and upper mantle dull reddish purple more or less suffused with grey (grey bases to most feathers) except for the display plumage on hind neck. This consists of slightly lanceolate feathers that have either purplish centres and white edges or a white streak on outer web only the whole forming a conspicuous dark-streaked white patch on back and sides of neck. Lower mantle, most of wings and upper tail coverts dark greyish brown, washed with bluish grey. Primaries and tail feathers brownish black. Underparts below the breast and underwing coverts dark bluish grey, often with some obsolescent whitish spots. Lower back and rump a lighter bluish grey than the underparts. The bluish grey feathers, especially those on the rump, fade to a brownish grey when old and worn. Irides yellowish brown, pale brown or yellow. Orbital skin, bill, legs and feet yellow. Female duller with little or no purplish red tinge on head and breast, and underparts browner. Juvenile like female but with tawny or reddish buff fringes to most cover feathers. As with all pigeons the juvenile's bill, feet and irides are at first dark and dull.

DISTRIBUTION AND HABITAT: The Comoro Islands. Inhabits evergreen forest; in most of the islands at fairly high elevation but on Mayotte, at least, also down to sea level (Benson, 1960).

FEEDING AND GENERAL HABITS: Known to take fruit, presumably from the branches but comes to the ground for grit and probably feeds there also.

NESTING: A nest found by Benson was 5 metres high near the top of a pollarded tree in evergreen forest. Usual pigeon nest. One white egg. Breeding season probably at least from August to November perhaps more prolonged.

VOICE: What is probably the advertising coo was considered by Benson to be identical with the same call of the mainland *C. arquatrix*. Benson also records a single note very deep and reminiscent of the 'moo' of an ox.

DISPLAY: No information.

OTHER NAMES: Comoro Pigeon; Comoro Wood Pigeon.

REFERENCE

BENSON, C. W. 1960. The Birds of the Comoro Islands. *Ibis* **103B**: 5–106 (46–47).

SPECKLED WOOD PIGEON   *Columba hodgsonii*
Columba hodgsonii Vigors, 1832, Proc. Comm. Zool. Soc. London, Pt. 2 : 16.

DESCRIPTION : About size of Feral Pigeon but with more sloping forehead.   General appearance very similar to the Olive Pigeon with which, and its relatives, it forms a superspecies.   Head silver grey. Breast and sides of neck pinkish silver with darker spots ; the individual feathers being silver with a broad dark purplish centre streak and dull silvery pink tip.   Feathers on hind neck lanceolate ; blackish or (these nearest mantle) dark purplish at base with silver grey tips.   Mantle and inner wing coverts dark reddish purple shading to dark bluish grey on outer wing coverts and rump and greyish black on wing quills and tail ; upper mantle with a few silver flecks and inner and median wing coverts spotted with small white spots.   Underparts below the breast dull dark reddish purple streaked with pinkish white ; the individual feathers being purplish with broad off-white fringes.   Ventral area and under tail coverts and underwing dark bluish grey   Irides white or greyish white.   Bill black or purplish black, usually more reddish or purplish at base.   Legs and feet yellowish black, dull green or greyish green with yellow claws. Female differs in having the silver areas light grey, the purplish red areas dark grey (but spotted or streaked in same manner as male) and the irides usually more tinged with grey or brown.   The juvenile is like the female but paler and browner, the lanceolate neck feathers not developed, the spotting less conspicuous and, especially in the young male, rufous fringes to many of the wing and mantle feathers.

DISTRIBUTION AND HABITAT : The Himalayan regions from Kashmir south and east to Burma and western China.   Inhabits temperate, sub-tropical and tropical forest from 5,500 to 13,000 feet ; but has been recorded at 15,200 feet (Ludlow, 1944).   Locally in cultivated areas near forest (Ludlow, 1937).

FEEDING AND GENERAL HABITS : Baker (1913) seems to be the source of such information as is available.   Feeds on berries, small fruits, acorns and, where available, cultivated grains.   Feeds both in the branches and on the ground.   Usually in pairs or small parties.   Flight swift and strong, clatters wings loudly when rising in alarm.

NESTING : Usual pigeon nest in tree or shrub.   One white egg.   In Nepal nests found in late May and June but breeding season probably extends at least further into summer than this.

VOICE : Baker (1913) records a call (? the advertising coo) that '. . . begins with a coughing jerked-out note, and then continues with a double rolling-note which might be syllablized as 'whock-whrroo-whrroo', the third note more prolonged than the second.   It is a very deep resonant note and can be heard at a great distance'.

DISPLAY : One observer mentions watching the species' display flight but does not describe it!

OTHER NAMES : Hodgson's Pigeon ; Jungle Pigeon.

REFERENCES

BAKER, E. C. S. 1913. *Indian Pigeons and Doves.* pp. 156–159. London.
LUDLOW, F. 1937. The Birds of Bhutan and adjacent territories of Sikkim and Tibet. *Ibis* **1** : Fourteenth Series, 467–504 (494).
—— 1944. The Birds of South-eastern Tibet. *Ibis* **86** : 348–389 (375).
RIPLEY, S. D. 1961. *A synopsis of the birds of India and Pakistan*, p. 161. Madras.

WHITE-NAPED PIGEON   *Columba albinucha*

Columba arquatrix albinucha Sassi Orn. Monatsb., 19, 1911, p. 68.

DESCRIPTION: Very similar to the Olive Pigeon *C. arquatrix* (q.v.) but a little smaller in size and differs in coloration as follows: No white spots on wing coverts and mantle. Display feathers of hind neck more tinged with green. Tail slate grey with broad, ill defined greyish-white terminal band. Hind crown and nape usually paler, sometimes white, sometimes pale grey. Irides buff or yellow with an outer ring of orange or orange-red. Orbital skin very narrow and yellowish. Bill blackish purple at base, red at tip. Legs and feet red or purplish red. Female probably with nape usually less white, more grey than in male. Juvenile mainly dark grey with rusty and/or white fringes to feathers of breast and belly and rusty brown fringes to those of the mantle.

FIELD CHARACTERS: Large, dark pigeon with whitish end to tail.

DISTRIBUTION AND HABITAT: Eastern Congo and western Uganda. Inhabits forest, usually at or below about 3,000 to 4,000 feet altitude. Rare in collections but is (Prigogine *in litt*.) common to the west of Lake Edward and near Kamituga and Kakanda, west of Rusisi Valley. Found also in woodland near Dikume, Rumpi Hills, West Cameroons where it is sympatric with *C. unicincta* but not with *C. sjöstedti* (Eisentraut 1968). May have a more extensive range than present records indicate.

FEEDING AND GENERAL HABITS: Little recorded except by the Van Somerens (1949) who observed and collected it in the Bwamba district of Uganda. Feeds, at any rate in part, on fruits and berries taken from the branches. Usually in pairs or small parties. Flight swift but rather quiet not clattering off when alarmed as does *C. arquatrix*. When mildly alarmed 'freezes' and is then difficult to see.

NESTING: No information.

VOICE: What is probably the advertising coo is described as 'a deep, rather quavering deliberate "tuu-uu" followed by three to four "tuu tu tu tu" in lessening volume or just a long quavering "tuuuu", not unlike the call of the Olive Pigeon'.

DISPLAY: No information.

REFERENCES

CHAPIN, J. P. 1939. The Birds of the Belgian Congo. Pt. 2. *Bull. Amer. Mus. Nat. Hist*, Vol. LXXV: 172–173.
EISENTRAUT, M. 1968. Beitrag zur Vogelfauna von Fernando Po und Westkamerun. *Bonner Zool. Beiträge* 1/2: 49–68.
VAN SOMEREN, V. G. L. & G. R. C. 1949. *The birds of Bwamba*. Special supplement to the Uganda Journal, vol. 13.

ASHY WOOD PIGEON   *Columba pulchricollis*

Columba pulchricollis 'Hogdson', Blyth, Journ. As. Soc. Bengal, 14, Pt. 2, 1845 (1846), p. 866.

DESCRIPTION: A little smaller than a smallish Feral Pigeon but considerably larger than a Barbary Dove. Head pale bluish grey shading to white on throat. Broad collar at back of neck and narrowing at sides of feathers with shining buff or cream tips and darker bases so that collar appears more or less spotted when bird's neck is stretched. Rest of neck and upper parts dark bluish grey glossed with green or (in some lights) purple on upper mantle, neck and upper breast. Lower breast lighter grey shading to pale greyish or buffish on ventral regions and buffish white on under tail coverts. Primaries and tail feathers greyish black. Irides pale yellow, greyish white or greenish white. Orbital skin grey. Bill greyish green or bluish green at tip, purplish or brownish at base. Legs and feet pinkish red or pinkish purple. Female slightly duller, breast often more or less suffused with brownish buff. Juvenile duller, with narrow rusty buff fringes to feathers of breast and underparts and to some wing coverts and with the red markings only obscurely indicated.

DISTRIBUTION AND HABITAT: Tibet, Nepal, Sikkim, Assam, Burma, Siam and Formosa. Inhabits forest, usually at high elevations from about 4,000 to 10,000 feet. Apparently either uncommon or easily overlooked throughout its range.

FEEDING AND GENERAL HABITS: Little data available. Said to feed on fruits, grain and seeds (Ali, 1962). Baker (1913) records shooting individuals that had eaten berries from a creeping terrestial plant, cardamom berries and small snails. He saw two others apparently gleaning rice on a stubble. He states that their flight, although powerful, is surprisingly silent; that when flushed they always fly downwards out of the tree and that they dodge expertly when flying amongst trees.

NESTING: Nests found by Osmaston and Baker (see Baker, 1913) were of usual pigeon type but with 'a sparse lining of feathers'. Most of these belonged to the pigeons themselves and I should have attributed them to moulting of the parents (pigeons' nests often contain a few moulted body feathers) but Baker states that a few feathers of other birds were included which, if correct, seems unusual. The four nests found by Osmaston and Baker each contained a single egg but Ali (1962) states that two white eggs are laid.

VOICE: Only Baker (1913) appears to have heard a call of this pigeon which he describes as 'a deep sonorous coo' very like that of a Wood Pigeon *C. palumbus* but 'more abrupt and less soft'.

DISPLAY: No information.

OTHER NAMES: Buff-collared Pigeon; Nepal Wood Pigeon.

REFERENCES

ALI, S. 1962. *The Birds of Sikkim*, p. 43. Oxford.

BAKER, E. C. S. 1913. *Indian Pigeons and Doves,*, pp. 172–175. London.

NILGIRI WOOD PIGEON   *Columba elphinstonii*

Columba elphinstonii Sykes, Proc. Comm. Zool. Soc. London, 2, 1832 (1833), p. 149.

DESCRIPTION: About size of smallish Feral Pigeon. Head pale silvery bluish grey shading to slightly darker bluish grey on neck and breast and a less pure slightly brownish grey on belly and under tail coverts. Feathers of hind neck black, tipped with white, forming a broad spotted half-collar. Hind neck, behind collar, iridescent green shading through iridescent purple to dark brownish purple on mantle. Back, inner wing coverts, scapulars and rump either predominantly brownish purple or black with brownish purple fringes to most feathers. Rest of upper parts including tail greyish black. Irides reddish brown, yellowish brown or yellow. Bill yellowish or whitish at tip, pink or pinkish red at base. Legs and feet pink or pinkish red, marked with white and with white nails.

Female slightly duller than male, purplish on upper parts usually less extensive and blue grey of head sometimes suffused with brown. Juvenile like adult but duller with display plumage on neck less developed and rusty fringes to wing coverts.

DISTRIBUTION AND HABITAT: The hill tracts of south-western India from southern Bombay State, western Madras, Mysore and Kerala. Inhabits both evergreen and moist deciduous forest from about 2,000 feet elevation.

FEEDING AND GENERAL HABITS: Has been recorded feeding on fruits, berries, buds and small snails. Feeds both in the branches and on the ground (Jerdon, 1863). Usually in pairs, small parties or singly. Flight similar to that of European Wood Pigeon (Baker, 1913).

NESTING: Usual pigeon nest in tree or shrub. One white egg. Has been recorded with eggs or young in March, April, May and June.

VOICE: Said by a correspondent of Baker (1913) to have 'soft, sweet notes' indistinguishable from those of the European Wood Pigeon. Such a description seems almost worthless but I can find no other.

DISPLAY: No information.

OTHER NAMES: Spotted-necked Pigeon.

REFERENCES

BAKER, E. C. S. 1913. *Indian Pigeons and Doves*, p. 164–167. London.

JERDON, T. C. 1863. *The Birds of India*. Vol. 2, pp. 465–467.

CEYLON WOOD PIGEON

Columba torringtoni

Columba torringtoni, "Layard" Bonaparte, Compt. Rend. Acad. Sci. PARIS 39, 1854, p. 1103.

DESCRIPTION: Very similar to the previous species but slightly smaller and darker. Rather smaller than a Feral Pigeon. Throat whitish; rest of head purplish grey becoming darker and slightly iridescent on hind crown and nape. Broad spotted half collar of black, white-tipped feathers on hind neck. Back and sides of neck (behind collar) iridescent purple, glossed green in some lights and shading to a duller but still slightly iridescent greyish purple on the breast. Underparts below the breast dull purplish grey or purplish. Under tail coverts greyish. Mantle, back and wings slaty black, primaries and tail less slaty and primaries especially may be brownish black when worn. Irides pink or light red; orbital skin dull pink. Bill dark grey at base, bluish grey at tip.

The female has little or no grey tinge on the head and breast. On her breast and lower part of hind neck the purple often shows a more or less coppery lustre. Juvenile duller and browner, dull grey with reddish fringes where purplish grey in adult, barred blackish and rust brown where purple in adult, with faint narrow rusty fringes to wing coverts and feathers of display plumage dull black, tipped with iridescent greenish grey.

DISTRIBUTION AND HABITAT: Ceylon. Inhabits both evergreen and moist deciduous forest in the hill zone. Normally at or above 3,000 feet but sometimes as low as 1,000 feet in the damp forests of the wet zone (Henry, 1955). Migrates or wanders locally in search of food.

FEEDING AND GENERAL HABITS: Known to feed largely on fruits and berries taken from the branches. Flight strong and fast but with rather leisurely wing beats. Usually wary of humans and keeps much to the canopy.

NESTING: Usual pigeon nest in tree or shrub. One white egg. Breeding season prolonged. Recorded from February to May and August to October.

VOICE: A deep owl-like 'hoo' is recorded by many writers. Since it is usually noted as 'the' call one would expect it to be the advertising coo but Henry (1955) states that it is used 'when courting' (i.e., is the display coo).

DISPLAY: No information.

REFERENCES

BAKER, E. C. S. 1913. *Indian Pigeons and Doves*, pp. 168–171.
HENRY, G. M. 1955. *A guide to the Birds of Ceylon*, pp. 248–249. Oxford.
WAIT, W. E. 1925. *Manual of the Birds of Ceylon*, pp. 307–308. Ceylon Journal of Science. Colombo.

PURPLE WOOD PIGEON   *Columba punicea*

Columba (Alsocomus) puniceus 'Tickell' Blyth, Journ. As. Soc. Bengal, 11, Pt. 1, 1842, p. 461.

DESCRIPTION: About the size of the average Feral Pigeon, but with proportionately rather shorter wings and longer tail and with more sloping forehead. Forehead, crown, and nape silver grey. Throat and neck coppery brown shading to a duller and more purplish brown on underparts. Bronze green and purplish pink iridescence on sides and back of neck. Mantle, back, upper part of rump and most of wing-coverts dark rich purplish chestnut, the individual feathers when new being dark chestnut red with broad iridescent purple fringes. Inner secondaries and greater wing-coverts dusky chestnut. Primary coverts, primaries and outer secondaries black. Lower part of rump greyish black, all feathers edged with iridescent green and purple. Upper and under tail-coverts blackish grey. Tail black. Irides yellow, yellow-brown, orange, or reddish. Eyelids red. Orbital skin purplish. Bill pale bluish, whitish or pale grey at tip, purplish at base. Legs and feet red or purplish red with pale yellowish or whitish claws. Female a little duller and with the grey parts of the head darker and usually suffused to a varying degree with brown or purple. Juvenile duller and paler with rusty fringes to feathers of the parts that are chestnut in the adult.

DISTRIBUTION AND HABITAT: South-east Asia from eastern Bengal, Assam, and Laos, south to the northern parts of the Malay Peninsula, Siam and Annam. Inhabits forest both in plains and foothills. Will feed in cultivated areas near to woodland and also cross open plains lying between areas of suitable habitat.

FEEDING AND GENERAL HABITS: Known to feed on fruits, berries and seeds; the latter including cultivated rice, millet and maize where available. Feeds both in trees and on the ground. Apparently usually seen in pairs or singly (? the latter breeding birds whose mates are on the nest), sometimes in small parties. May gather in large numbers to areas where bamboos have seeded and provided a super-abundant food supply. Flight said to be strong and swift. Gait on ground similar to but less clumsy than a Wood Pigeon (*Columba palumbus*).

NESTING: Usual pigeon nest in tree or bush. One white egg. Two egg clutches have been recorded, possibly in error. Most nests found have been in June or July.

VOICE: Apparently has at least one call that is monosyllabic but I can find no first hand or detailed description of it.

DISPLAY: No information.

OTHER NAMES: Red Wood Pigeon, Chestnut Pigeon, Purple Pigeon.

REFERENCES
BAKER, E. C. S. 1913. *Indian Pigeons and Doves*. London.
ROBINSON, H. C. & CHASEN, F. N. 1936. *The Birds of the Malay Peninsula* 3: 56–57. London.
SMYTHIES, B. E. 1953. *The Birds of Burma*. London.

SILVER PIGEON *Columba argentina*

Columba argentina? 'Temm', Bonaparte Consp. Av., 2, 1885, p. 36, in synonymy of *Myristicivora grisea* Bonaparte.

DESCRIPTION: About the size of a Wood Pigeon or large Feral Pigeon (but with proportionately longer tail than the latter) but with a sloping forehead (see sketch). Coloration is simple but striking, being a pale bluish grey fading to a very pale greyish cream in worn plumage, with black primaries and secondaries. Tail greyish white for basal half, rest black. Hind neck with faint greenish iridescence. Irides reddish brown, orange, orange-red, or yellowish. Orbital skin purplish brown. Bill pale green or yellowish green at tip, purplish or brownish at base. Feet and legs dull grey or blue grey blotched or tinged with red. Female a slightly darker and less silvery grey than male, but this is not noticeable unless birds in same state of plumage are compared. I have not seen the juvenile which is said to have sandy buff edges to the feathers of the upperparts and a sandy buff breast (Robinson and Chasen, 1936).

DISTRIBUTION AND HABITAT: Anamba Islands, Karimatu and North Natuna Islands, Bintang Islands in the Rhio Archipelago, Sumatra, Mentawi Islands, formerly Butong Island off Borneo. Present status in some areas very doubtful. Usually found on small islands often in company with the rather similarly coloured Pied Imperial Pigeon (*Ducula bicolor*).

FEEDING AND GENERAL HABITS: Little recorded. Said to associate with *Ducula bicolor* and to have similar habits. It seems probable, however, that in fact their feeding habits will be found to differ. The Silver Pigeon is said to be now a rare species although formerly common in some areas.

NESTING: Usual pigeon nest in tree or shrub. One white egg. Shelford, in Robinson and Chasen, 1936, who found this species and the Pied Imperial Pigeon both nesting in large numbers on Butong Island in 1890, noted that the Silver Pigeon's egg was somewhat larger and of a more chalky texture.

VOICE: No information.

DISPLAY: No information.

OTHER NAMES: Silvery Wood Pigeon, Grey Wood Pigeon.

REFERENCE

ROBINSON, H. C. & CHASEN, F. N. 1936. *The Birds of the Malay Peninsula* 3. London.

ANDAMAN WOOD PIGEON

Columba palumboides

Carpophaga palumboides anonymous = Hume, Stray Feathers, 1, 1873, p. 302.

DESCRIPTION: About the size of a Wood Pigeon (*Columba palumbus*) but rather more heavily built and with sloping forehead. Head and neck silver grey shading into medium grey, glossed with green on upper part of mantle and through light grey on breast to dark grey on flanks and under tail-coverts. Upper parts greyish black with a silvery blue 'bloom' in fresh plumage, and the mantle, back and rump feathers fringed with iridescent purple, amethyst and green. Irides yellow or orange, usually with darker orange or red outer ring which is not sharply defined. Feet and legs bright light red or pink, claws white. Bill greenish white or pale yellow at tip, purplish red at base. Orbital skin purplish red. Female has head and neck darker and less silvery than male. Juveniles predominantly brownish grey and brownish black with little or no iridescence.

DISTRIBUTION AND HABITAT: The Andaman and Nicobar Islands. Inhabits forests.

FEEDING AND GENERAL HABITS: Little recorded. Believed to feed largely on fruit and berries. Walnut-sized fruits have been found in the crops of shot specimens (Hume, 1874). Hume had a captive bird which in its 'mode of holding itself and its broad substantial body' reminded him of an Imperial Pigeon (*Ducula*) rather than a *Columba* species.

NESTING: No information.

VOICE: A 'deep cooing' is the only description I can find of the calls of this species.

DISPLAY: No information.

REFERENCES

ABDULALI, H. 1967. The Birds of the Nicobar Islands, with Notes on Andaman Birds. *J. Bombay Nat. Hist. Soc.* **64** (2): 139–190.

HUME, A. 1874. The Islands of the Bay of Bengal. *Stray Feathers* **2**: 53–54, 263–264 and 498.

BLACK WOOD PIGEON

Columba janthina

Columba janthina Temminck, Pl. Col., Livr. 86, 1830, pl. 503.

This dark but richly iridescent pigeon is a very close relative of the White-throated Pigeon (q.v.), the extinct Bonin Wood Pigeon and the Silver-banded Black Pigeon.

DESCRIPTION: About the size of a Wood Pigeon, with slightly rounded tail. Black in colour but with the exposed portions of most of the cover feathers vividly iridescent. This iridescence is mostly rich green on the neck, purple on head, mantle and rump and shows a lesser degree of mingled green, purple and bronze iridescence elsewhere. Only slight iridescence on wings and upper tail coverts, none on primaries and tail feathers. Irides brown. Feet and legs red. Bill greenish blue. The juvenile is duller with a rusty tinge (as in all pigeons) on the areas that will be iridescent purple in the adult.

The above description applies to the nominate form. The Black Wood Pigeon of the Bonin and Volcano Islands, *C. janthina nitens*, has a purplish brown head.

DISTRIBUTION AND HABITAT: The warm, sub-tropical islands of Japan, the Riu-kui, Bonin and Volcano Islands. Inhabits small wooded islands. Does not occur on the four main islands of Japan. Inhabits dense evergreen forest.

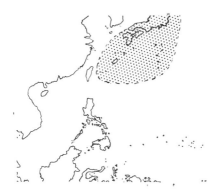

FEEDING AND GENERAL HABITS: Arboreal but feeds on the ground as well as from the branches. Feeds largely on *Camellia* seeds but probably takes other seeds, buds and fruits as well. Said to be solitary (Yamashina, 1961) but this might, perhaps, be based on observations of individuals whose mates were sitting. Flight direct with jerky wing beats (Yamashina) and in flight appears crow-like in movements as well as in colour (*fide* Austin and Kuroda, 1953). The Japanese name 'Karasu-bato' means 'Crow Pigeon'. Usually shows little fear of man and soon becomes exterminated where much shot at.

NESTING: Jahn (1942) implies that it nests in the branches but Yamashina (1961) states that it nests 'in holes of trees, sometimes on rocks'. Usual pigeon nest. One white egg. Breeding season apparently prolonged; from February to September in the Izu Islands (Austin and Kuroda) but elsewhere eggs and young have been found also in late autumn and winter.

VOICE: What is, probably, the advertising coo is a long-drawn deep cooing 'o͞o-wo͞o, o͞o-wo͞o' or 'Mo͞o-ŏŏ, mo͞o-ŏŏ' said to be suggestive of the lowing of a cow.

DISPLAY: No information.

OTHER NAMES: Black Pigeon, Japanese Wood Pigeon.

REFERENCES

AUSTIN, O. L. & KURODA, N. 1953. The Birds of Japan, their status and distribution. *Bull. Mus. Comp. Zool. Harvard* **109**: 4: 465–466.
JAHN, H. 1942. Zur Oekologie und Biologie der Vögel Japans. *Journ. f. Orn.* **90**: 7–301 (165–266).
YAMASHINA, Y. 1961. *Birds in Japan*, p. 164. Tokyo.

WHITE THROATED PIGEON   *Columba vitiensis*

Columba vitiensis Quoy and Gaimard, Voy. 'Astrolabe', Zool; 1, 1830, p. 246; Atlas, Ois, pl. 28.

DESCRIPTION: A large, heavily built pigeon about the size of a Wood Pigeon or a little smaller. Upperparts with feathers having slaty black bases and iridescent green or green and purple tips except for the wing and tail quills and outer secondaries which are entirely black. The general effect is that the mantle, back and rump appear predominantly shining green or green and purple and the wing coverts black beautifully laced with iridescence. Forehead, crown, neck and underparts deep chestnut with a vivid purple-pink gloss or slaty brown with purple and green gloss. Chin, throat and face below the eye pure white. Irides orange or red with buff or yellow inner ring. Feet and legs dull purplish-red. Orbital skin maroon or carmine red. Bill purplish red or red with yellowish, whitish yellow or horn coloured tip. Sexes alike or nearly so. The juvenile is similar to the adult but duller and with little or no iridescence to the underparts.

The above description is of *C. vitiensis halmaheira* which is the most beautiful form of this species and the one that inhabits the largest area, being found in Banggai, Sula Islands, Kei Islands, Moluccas, Western Papuan Islands, New Guinea, Louisiade Archipelago, D'Entrecasteaux Islands, Bismarck Archipelago and the Solomon Islands. *C. vitiensis leopoldi* from the New Hebrides is similar but less brilliantly iridescent and browner below. *C. vitiensis hypoenochroa* from New Caledonia, the Isle of

Pines and Loyalty Island is similar to *leopoldi* but often duller and greyer. *C. vitiensis griseogularis* from the Philippines, Sulu Archipelago and north Bornean Islands has a greyish throat and its underparts are usually predominantly grey. *C. vitiensis metallica* has a darkish grey throat and forehead, no purplish chestnut colouring and very intense iridescence on crown and hind neck. A similar form, *C. v. godmanae*, formerly inhabited Lord Howe Island (Hindwood, 1940). *C. v. vitiensis* from the Fiji Islands is lighter and much less richly iridescent with a grey rather than blackish ground colour, the lower breast and belly dull purplish brown and dull white throat. *C. vitiensis castanieceps* from Samoa is like *C. v. vitiensis* but is entirely greyish below and has a purplish chestnut forehead and crown. In the less brilliant forms of this species there tends to be a greater degree of sexual difference most females being appreciably duller than most males.

FIELD CHARACTERS: Large dark pigeon with pale throat and squarish-ended tail.

DISTRIBUTION AND HABITAT: Philippine Islands, Sulu Archipelago, north Bornean Islands, Lesser Sunda Islands, Banzzai, Sula Islands, Moluccas, Kei Islands, New Guinea and adjacent islands and archipelagoes. New Hebrides, New Caledonia, Isle of Pines, Loyalty Islands, Fiji and Samoa Islands. Inhabits woodland, on some islands in high-level mist forest, on others in lowland forest.

FEEDING AND GENERAL HABITS: Known to feed on fruits and berries. Probably takes seeds and other foods also. Newman's captive specimens thrived and bred successfully on a diet of grain, chiefly maize. Frequently associates in large or small flocks.

NESTING: Nests in trees, from 10 to 20 feet above ground and also on the ground in cover of vegetation. Breeding season probably prolonged. In England a captive pair nested throughout the year (Newman, 1912). One white egg laid. Incubation period, in captivity, 17–19 days. Young fledged at about 21 days and could then fly strongly (Newman, 1910 and 1912). Newman's captive birds were very peaceable. There was little fighting even when four males and two females were kept together. The adults did not attack the young of a former brood when the next brood hatched as most pigeons do in captivity and probably in the wild also.

VOICE: What is probably the advertising coo has been described by Mayr (1945) as 'a booming hoo-hoo' and by Warner (1949) as a 'loud hooting "coooo-OOO-OOOO".' Cain and Galbraith (1956) heard a 'deep soft cooing "kooroo" and "koo" ' in the eastern Solomons which the natives told them was this species.

The display coo, as uttered by Newman's captive males, was a 'single very deep note, followed by a second one as if he were drawing his breath'.

DISPLAY: The bowing display, as described by Newman, involves inflation of the neck and a slow bow without tail raising. On raising its head the displaying bird may make a jump up and down on the bough.

OTHER NAMES: Grey-throated Pigeon (the duller races).

REFERENCES

CAIN, A. J. & GALBRAITH, I. C. J. 1956. Field notes on the Birds of the eastern Solomon Islands. *Ibis* **98**: 100–134 (123–124).

HINDWOOD, K. A. 1940. *The Birds of Lord Howe Island.*

MAYR, E. 1945. *Birds of the southwest Pacific*, pp. 64–65. New York.

NEWMAN, T. H. 1910. Nesting of the White-throated Pigeon. *Avicult. Mag.* Third Series **1**: pp. 158–164 and 193–195.

—— 1912. The White-throated Pigeon. ibid. **4**: 110–115.

WARNER, D. W. 1949. The White-throated Pigeon nesting on the ground in New Caledonia. *Auk*: 66: 90–91.

WHITE-HEADED PIGEON

Columba leucomela

Columba leucomela Temminck, Tr. Linn. Sec. 13, p. 126 (1821).

DESCRIPTION: About the size of a Wood Pigeon. Back, wings and tail black with most feathers, except the large wing and tail quills, broadly fringed with iridescent purple or purple and green. Throat white. Head, neck and breast pale pinkish-buff shading to darker buff on the belly, and greyish on flanks and under tail coverts. The pinkish buff areas fade to white in old plumage. The female differs from the male in having the head (except for the white throat), neck and breast vinous grey to deep creamy buff suffused with grey. Irides yellowish, orange or orange-red. Bill pinkish-red with whitish cere and whitish or yellowish tip. Feet buff and pink or pinkish red with white claws. I have not seen a juvenile of this species or description of it. It probably much resembles the juvenile of the very closely related White-throated Pigeon (q.v.).

DISTRIBUTION AND HABITAT: Forested regions of eastern Australia. Inhabits chiefly coastal woodlands. Also frequently in more open country with trees, up to 40 miles from true forest (Frith, 1952).

FEEDING AND GENERAL HABITS: Feeds both in trees and on the ground on fruits, berries and seeds; those of the bangalow and cabbage-tree palms, camphor laurel and inkweed have been recorded. Probably also takes buds and young leaves. When feeding in trees will clamber about and hang upside down to feed when necessary. Commonly in pairs or small parties of up to twenty birds. Locally migratory or nomadic.

NESTING: Usual pigeon nest in tree or shrub. Commonly at no great height. One egg laid. Said to lay two occasionally but such records, if correct, may refer to isolated cases of two females laying in the same nest. Prefers to nest in a fairly dark part of the forest (*fide* Hyem, 1936).

VOICE: What is, probably, the advertising coo is described by Frith as 'a series of gruff, melancholy "Oom" notes' and by Hyem as a deep 'Oo-ooo' with the accent on the first syllable and the second somewhat drawn out and sometimes followed by a third and very low 'oo'.

DISPLAY: Hyem records a distraction display in which a bird flushed from the nest will fly about 30 yards and then perch and violently flap its wings.

OTHER NAMES: White-headed Fruit Pigeon.

REFERENCES

FRITH, H. J. 1952. Notes on the Pigeons of Richmond River, N.S.W. *Emu* **52**: 89–99.
HYEM, E. L. 1936. Notes on the Birds of Mernot, Barrington, New South Wales. *Emu* 36: 109–127.

BONIN WOOD PIGEON   *Columba versicolor*

Columba versicolor Kittlitz, Kupfertaf, Nature, Vog., 1, p. 5, pl. 5, fig. 2.

DESCRIPTION: Rather larger than but otherwise similar to the Black Wood Pigeon, *C. janthina*, but paler and more richly iridescent. Upperparts greyish black with brilliant iridescence except on wing and tail quills. This iridescence is predominantly bright amethyst, bright red-purple or golden-green (according to incidence of light) on crown, mantle, back and rump and golden-green on wing coverts. Face, neck and underparts grey, palest at back and sides of neck and brightly glossed with golden-green on the breast. Irides dark blue. Bill greenish yellow. Legs and feet dark red. The above description is of a single male specimen in the British Museum of Natural History. From Greenway's (1958) description it appears that the few other extant specimens are similar but, perhaps, a paler grey on the underparts.

DISTRIBUTION AND HABITAT: The Bonin Islands; recorded only from Nakondo Shima and Peel Island. Now extinct.

FEEDING AND GENERAL HABITS: No information.

NESTING: No information.

VOICE: No information.

DISPLAY: No information.

OTHER NAMES: Bonin Fruit Pigeon, Shining Pigeon.

SILVER-BANDED BLACK PIGEON   *Columba jouyi*

Janthoenas jouyi Stejneger, Am. Nat. 21, 1887, p. 538.

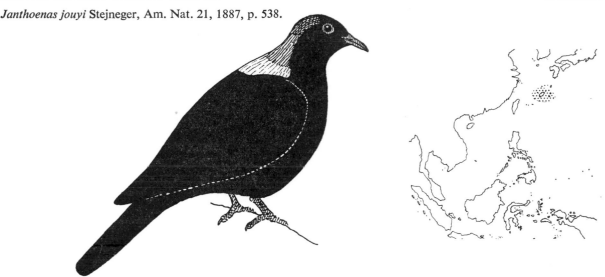

DESCRIPTION: About size of Wood Pigeon but with proportionately longer tail. Black with purple iridescence on sides and back of neck. A broad crescent-shaped silver band divides the green of the hind neck from the black of the mantle. Irides brown. Bill greenish blue with paler tip. Feet purplish.

I have only been able to examine three unsexed adult specimens and have not been able to find descriptions of sexual differences (if any) or the juvenile plumage.

DISTRIBUTION AND HABITAT: The Riu-Kiu Island and the Borodino Islands. Now apparently extinct on Okinawa and possibly elsewhere also.

FEEDING AND GENERAL HABITS: No information.

NESTING: No information.

VOICE: No information.

DISPLAY: No information.

OTHER NAMES: Riu-Kiu Black Wood Pigeon, Silver-crescented Pigeon.

REFERENCE

GREENWAY, J. C. 1958. *Extinct and vanishing birds of the World.* Cambridge, Mass., U.S.A.

YELLOW-LEGGED PIGEON   *Columba pallidiceps*

Ianthaenas pallidiceps Ramsay, Proc. Linn. Soc. New South Wales, 2. 1877, p. 248.

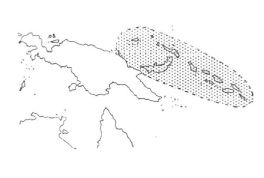

This magnificent bird is a very close relative of the White-throated Pigeon, with which it overlaps in some areas.

DESCRIPTION: About the same size as the White-throated Pigeon, or slightly larger. General colour black above and slaty black on the underparts on the basal areas of feathers but with the most intense and brilliant pink, purple and green iridescence on the feather edges. Entire head pale silvery-grey. Irides yellow and orange. Bill proportionately larger than, but similar in colour, to that of White-throated Pigeon. Feet and legs yellow. The female's head is a slightly duller silver-grey than the male's. The juvenile is like the adult but the head feathers (where silver in adult) are brownish black with broad buff tips and it has very little iridescence on the wing coverts and underparts.

DISTRIBUTION AND HABITAT: Bismarck Archipelago and the Solomon Islands. Inhabits forest.

FEEDING AND GENERAL HABITS: Little recorded. Often feeds on the ground (*fide* Mayr, 1945). Apparently a rather rare bird throughout its range.

NESTING: No information.

VOICE: No information.

DISPLAY: No information.

OTHER NAMES: Silver-headed Pigeon.

REFERENCE

MAYR, P. 1945. *Birds of the south-west Pacific*, p. 226. New York.

WHITE-CROWNED PIGEON   *Columba leucocephala*
Columba leucocephala Linnaeus, Syst. Nat. ed. 10. 1, 1758, p. 164.

DESCRIPTION: About the size of a small Feral Pigeon but more slightly built, with proportionally longer tail and sloping forehead. General plumage dark slate grey with a white cap, velvety purplish black nape patch and patch glossy green, black-edged feathers at sides of neck. Irides white or yellowish-white. Orbital skin white. Bill dark red or purplish, with whitish tip.

The female has the slate of the upperparts suffused with olive-brown and the cap brownish-white not snow-white. The juvenile is a dull slaty brown with pale fringes to most feathers, and a dull white forehead.

FIELD IDENTIFICATION: Entirely dark pigeon except for white or whitish grey cap. Looks black in flight.

DISTRIBUTION AND HABITAT: Islands off the Caribbean coast of Central America from Yucatan to north-western Panama; extreme southern Florida, Bahamas, Greater Antilles and Lesser Antilles, east and south to Antigua. A lowland species, migratory between islands and only found in low coastal areas of larger islands such as Cuba.

FEEDING AND GENERAL HABITS: Largely, if not entirely arboreal in its feeding. Recorded foods are various fruits and berries, cultivated grain (dari) taken from the plants, and snails. From Gosse's (1847) descriptions of the behaviour of a tame captive bird 'playing' with his finger it is evident that this species has similar fruit-plucking movements to those of the Wood Pigeon *C. palumbus* (q.v.). General movements, in captivity, much as Wood Pigeon, even more ponderous and awkward-looking on the ground. Does not throw up tail on or after alighting as many arboreal pigeons do. Flight swift; able to fly swiftly among branches and to alight suddenly with little or no fluttering. Highly gregarious, roosts communally.

NESTING: Usual pigeon nest in trees. Commonly nests in colonies. Some observers record one, others two eggs per clutch.

VOICE: The advertising coo is a very loud, deep and clear 'Cŏō-cŏŏ-cŏŏ-cŏō, Cŏŏ-cŏŏ-cŏō, Cŏō! and slight variants of the above phrasing. A shorter phrase that I think is the nest-call which I have only heard a few times, is 'Cŏō-crrŏŏ! Rather like a deep gruff version of the Barbary Dove's coo, but with the second note much shorter.

DISPLAY: Nodding as in European *Columba* species in form. A friend saw (once only) the bowing display of a captive male, which he described as like that of the Barbary Dove. Post copulatory display (seen only twice, from two males in captivity) in which male sleeks plumage and stretches neck towards mate, then jerks half round with a sudden movement and adopts typical crouched soliciting posture but with stretched-out neck. Wing shaking as in Picazuro Pigeon (q.v.) seen twice in apparent sexual frustration.

OTHER NAMES: Baldpate, White-headed Dove.

REFERENCES

BENT, A. C. 1932. Life Histories of North American Galliniaceous Birds. *U.S. Nat. Mus. Bull.* No. 162.
GOSSE, P. H. 1847. *The Birds of Jamaica.* London.
GUNDLACH, J. 1874. Neue Bieträge zur Ornithologie Cubas. *Journ. f. Orn.* 1874, p. 289.
WETMORE, A. & SWALES, B. H. 1931. The Birds of Haiti and the Dominican Republic. *U.S. Nat. Mus. Bull.* **155**: 184.
WETMORE, A. *Unpublished MSS. on Birds of Central America.*

RED-NECKED PIGEON   *Columba squamosa*

Columba squamosa Bonnaterre, Tabl. Encyc. Meth; orn., Pt. 1, 1792, p. 234.

DESCRIPTION: Dark slate grey. Head and breast dull wine-purple, display plumage on sides and back of neck iridescent wine-red with dark edges to feathers, on nape a patch of velvety dark purple feathers. Irides light red, orange or ringed yellow and red. Orbital skin orange, orange-pink, purplish pink with scattered yellow papillae, buff or bright red; there being much apparently geographical variation in colour of orbital skin (Voous, 1957). Bill red with yellowish grey or whitish tip. Feet red or dark red.

The female is slightly duller and browner on the back and the scapulars. The juvenile has the purple and wine red areas of the adult reddish brown, the grey areas brownish-slate with red-buff fringes to the feathers.

DISTRIBUTION AND HABITAT: Greater Antilles (except Jamaica); Lesser Antilles; Virgin Islands; Islands of Curaçao and Bonaire; Los Testigos Island. Usually in wooded country inland at higher altitudes and further from coast than the White-crowned Pigeon.

FEEDING AND GENERAL HABITS: Probably much as White-crowned Pigeon. Recorded taking various fruits and berries, also buds, succulent leaves and shoots and small snails. The seeds of some (probably all) of the fruits taken are digested.

NESTING: Usual pigeon nest in tree or shrub; in some localities believed to nest in holes and crevices in rocky cliffs. Clutch certainly at times of one egg only (Wetmore, 1927) but two egg clutches have been recorded by an observer in the last century.

VOICE: What is, presumably, the advertising coo, is described by Wetmore as a loud, strongly accented 'Who who hoo-oo-hoo', and by Voous (*in litt.*) as 'a very strong Rukuku'; possibly this refers to a different or local variant of the call. Wetmore also describes another call as a 'burring guttural hoo-o-o' given with throaty rattle.

DISPLAY: Wetmore describes a display flight in which the male glides on set wings, traversing a circular or elliptical course but tilting from side to side and changing direction slightly every few feet as it does so.

OTHER NAMES: Scaled Pigeon.

REFERENCES

VOOUS, K. H. 1957. The birds of Aruba, Curaçao and Bonaire. *Studies on the fauna of Curaçao and other Caribbean Islands* **7**: 152–153.
WETMORE, A. 1927. *Scientific Survey of Porto Rico and the Virgin Islands* **9**: 389–392.
WETMORE, A. & SWALES, B. H. 1931. The birds of Haiti and the Dominican Republic. *United States Nat. Mus. Bull.* No. 155, pp. 185–188.

SCALED PIGEON   *Columba speciosa*

Columba speciosa Gmelin, Syst. Nat., 1, Pt. 2, 1789, p. 783.

DESCRIPTION: Slightly smaller than the average Feral Pigeon; plump and compact in shape with sloping forehead. Head purplish brown or reddish brown. Feathers of neck blackish with white subterminal spots or patches and iridescent purple fringes; these change on the upper breast to feathers with a large golden brown, white tipped subterminal patch and on the hind neck to feathers with a coppery gold subterminal patch. Lower breast and belly whitish with dull brown-purple edges to feathers. Mantle, back, rump and wing coverts reddish purple (worn feathers chestnut brown). Primaries blackish with very narrow whitish fringe on outer webs. Tail black. Upper tail coverts dark purplish brown, under tail coverts white with narrow dark fringes. Irides purplish with blue outer ring, dark bluish or brown (one specimen). Orbital skin dark red. Bill bright red or crimson red with white or yellowish tip. Legs and feet purplish red.

Female lacks the purplish chestnut on mantle, back and wing coverts which are dull brown with slightly iridescent purplish fringes to some feathers. Her head, neck and underparts are slightly duller and paler than the male's. Juvenile female like adult but duller and paler, scaled pattern of neck feathers less developed and pale buffish fringes to feathers of wing coverts. Juvenile male similar but with upperparts, where purplish in adult, reddish brown with rusty buff feather fringes.

FIELD IDENTIFICATION: Dark pigeon with white under tail coverts, brown or purplish chestnut upperparts and *no bluish grey on rump* (or anywhere). At close quarters scaled or spotted pattern of neck and breast distinctive.

DISTRIBUTION AND HABITAT: Tropical central and South America from south-eastern Mexico to eastern Peru, eastern Bolivia, Venezuela and Trinidad, Brazil and Paraguay. Inhabits forest and wooded regions; feeds also in bushy areas.

FEEDING AND GENERAL HABITS: Little recorded. Known to feed on fruits and berries taken from the branches. In captivity will eat various grains and also maggots and chopped-up cheese. Usually singly or in pairs but sometimes in flocks. Flight swift and direct; flies high when crossing open areas (Skutch, 1964).

NESTING: Usual pigeon nest in tree or shrub. In Costa Rica Skutch (1964) found nests from February to May, and saw birds building in July, usually about 7 to 15 feet above ground. One white egg. Fledging period (one nest) 16–17 days. Two egg clutches have been recorded (*fide* Belcher and Smooker, 1936; Herklots, 1961), but evidence from captive specimens that (Naether, 1961) corroborates Skutch's findings of one egg clutches.

VOICE: Wetmore (MS) describes a 'whoo, whoo whoo, whoo, the first and last syllables rendered slowly the two between more quickly', a deeper toned 'groo-oo coo groo-groo' and a 'guttural roll', this last call being, apparently, uttered by the male only. Naether (1961) who bred this species never heard them utter any calls.

DISPLAY: No information.

OTHER NAMES: Scallop-necked Pigeon, Scale-necked Pigeon, Splendid Pigeon, Fair Pigeon, Red-backed Pigeon, Speckle-neck Pigeon, Dominick Pigeon.

REFERENCES

BELCHER, C. & SMOOKER, G. D. 1936. Birds of the Colony of Trinidad and Tobago. Pt. 3. *Ibis* **6**: Thirteenth Series, p. 1.
BOOSEY, E. J. 1962. *Foreign bird keeping*, pp. 349–351. London.
HERKLOTS, G. A. C. 1961. *The birds of Trinidad and Tobago*, p. 107. London.
NAETHER, C. 1961. Nesting of the Splendid Pigeon. *Avicult. Mag.* **67**: 136–138. Further Data relating to the breeding behaviour of the Splendid Pigeon. *Op. Cit.*: 165.
SKUTCH, A. F. 1964. Life Histories of Central American Pigeons. *Wilson Bull.* **76**: 211–247.
WETMORE, A. *Unpublished MSS. on birds of Central America.*

PICAZURO PIGEON   *Columba picazuro*

Columba picazuro Temminck, Pig. et. Gall., 1, 1813, pp. 111, 449.

DESCRIPTION: About the size of a largish Feral Pigeon and of similar proportions although slightly heavier in build. Head, nape and upper breast dull pinkish purple becoming somewhat paler on the lower breast and belly. Flanks, under and upper tail coverts and underwing dark bluish grey. Back and sides of neck and upper mantle with iridescent black edged feathers, giving a scale-like pattern. The individual feathers of the upper part of these areas have subterminal bands of silver or greenish-silver and black fringes, those lower down of pinkish coppery colour with less pronounced black fringes. Lower mantle, inner wing coverts, and inner secondaries dull brown with paler edges to the feathers. Outer parts of wing dark bluish grey with white fringes to the outer greater and median coverts, forming white lines on the closed wing and a whitish band across it when opened. Tail dark blue-grey with ill-defined black terminal band. Irides brownish orange to dull red, usually with very narrow grey inner ring. Orbital skin red overcast with powdery white. Bill dull reddish at base, powdered whitish on cere and with yellowish tip. Legs and feet dark red.

Female a little paler and duller, tinged grey on top of head and with the purple of the lower breast and underparts more or less (usually more) suffused or replaced by dull buffish. Juvenile like female but duller and paler and with the display plumage on back of neck much less developed.

DISTRIBUTION AND HABITAT: South America from north-eastern Brazil south through the Matto Grosso to Tucuman and Buenos Aires districts of Argentina. Inhabits both woodland and open country with trees or (when feeding on ground) within easy reach of trees. Often near human habitations.

FEEDING AND GENERAL HABITS: Feeds on seeds, buds, young leaves, berries, probably also some invertebrates. Feeds much on the ground but also in trees. Gait on the ground less agile than Rock Pigeon but more so than Wood Pigeon. Has been recorded as regularly visiting slaughtering grounds and gathering at skinned carcases of domestic animals, although unfortunately the observer did not ascertain what the pigeons so-doing were eating (Gibson, 1880). Commonly seen in pairs or small parties, in winter often in flocks of up to two hundred or more.

NESTING: Usual pigeon nest in tree or shrub. Normally one white egg but clutches of two have been recorded, possibly in error. Nesting recorded in November and December (Gibson, 1880).

VOICE: The advertising coo begins with a muffled, moaning sound that changes into a 'coo' and is followed by a clear, emphatic coo and then a series of three coos of which the middle one is strongly accented. The cooing phrase, but not the introductory long-drawn moaning note, is usually repeated from two to five times. Could be written 'Uuraaoo; Cōō! Cŏŏ-cōō-ōō'. The cooing notes have a very clear, sad, human-sounding tone suggestive of that of the Mourning Dove.

The nest call is a low-pitched growling 'Corr' or Oorr'. The display coo is a muffled 'Crōō-ŏŏ' or 'Crōōō' also quite lacking the beautiful sad tone of the advertising coo.

DISPLAY: In the bowing display the bird perches rather upright and gives a series of quick, bobbing bows of the head and neck but with little or no lowering of the body. The tail is not raised but may be slightly spread. After every two or three bows the bird partly opens its wings and vibrates them very rapidly with a loud, sharp, rustling sound. Sometimes, presumably when the display is given at lower intensity, the wing movements are omitted.

The bowing display is given with the displaying bird sideways on to, or even turned slightly away from its partner, a position which fully exhibits the expanded area of display plumage on nape and hind-neck. I have, however, only seen this display a few times from the males of two captive pairs and it is possible that it may sometimes be given frontally or in somewhat differing versions.

A male walking or running after a female in which he is sexually interested often flies up a yard or so into the air, claps his wings and drops down just behind or beside the female. The performance is very similar to that often shown by male Rock, Feral and Domestic Pigeons (*Columba livia*) except that only a single wing clap is given and the bird does not immediately give the bowing display after alighting.

The display flight (which I have not seen) is said (Wetmore, 1926) to be like that of the Domestic Pigeon. When approaching another with aggressive or sexual intent the Picazuro Pigeon often adopts a posture with lowered head and somewhat 'arched' back like that of the turtle doves in similar situations.

OTHER NAMES: Argentine Wood Pigeon, Scaly-necked Wood Pigeon, Brown Wood Pigeon.

REFERENCES

GIBSON, E. 1880. Ornithological Notes from the Neighbourhood of Cape San Antonio, Buenos Ayres. *Ibis* **4**: Fourth Series, 1–38.

STEINBACHER, J. 1962. Beitrage zur Kenntnis der Vögel von Paraguay. *Abhandlungen der Senckenbergischen Naturforschenden Gesellschaft* **501**: 1–106.

WETMORE, A. 1926. Observations on the birds of Argentina, Paraguay, Uruguay and Chile. *Bull. U.S. Nat. Mus.* No. 133.

BARE-EYED PIGEON *Columba corensis*

Columba (*corensis*) Jacquin, Beytr. Gesh. Vög., p. 31, 1784.

DESCRIPTION: About the size of a smallish Feral Pigeon. In shape and general appearance very similar to the Picazuro Pigeon to which it appears sufficiently closely related to consider them both members of a superspecies. Differs in its paler and more beautiful coloration and the extreme development of its orbital skin.   Head, neck and breast light mauvy-pink, tinged with bluish grey on top of head and shading to creamy white on chin, ventral regions and under tail coverts.   Display plumage on back of neck consists of broad-ended feathers that have silver or pinkish bronze black-edged terminal bands and very narrow pale brown fringes, the whole giving a scaled effect.   Mantle, wing coverts and inner secondaries have broad white edges that form a broad white line along the edge of the wing when closed and a band across it when opened.   Lower back, rump and upper tail coverts pale bluish grey.   Primaries and outer secondaries blackish with narrow white edges.   Central tail-feathers brownish grey, outer ones very pale brownish grey with obscure whitish tips.   Irides light brown, yellow-brown or orange-brown. Orbital skin highly developed; immediately adjacent to eye it is relatively smooth and bluish grey or pale blue. This part is surrounded by a broad ring of papillose or granulated skin of buffish brown or reddish brown colour.   Bill pale flesh colour or pinkish white.   Legs deep red.   Sexes apparently alike but only two females examined.   Juvenile pale and duller with only faint tusty-pink ringe where adult is mauve-pink. Display plumage on hind neck indicated by feathers with conspicuous pale subterminal bars.

DISTRIBUTION AND HABITAT: The arid coastal regions of southern Colombia and Venezuela and the adjacent islands of Aruba, Curaçao, Bonaire and Margarita.   Inhabits arid and semi-desert country with thorn scrub, cactus and acacia, but also mangroves and cultivated areas.

FEEDING AND GENERAL HABITS: Recorded feeding both on the ground and in trees or shrubs but, according to one recent observer (Voous, 1957), usually feeds above ground.   Eats seeds and fruits of various kinds;   Voous recorded peas of several kinds of leguminous trees, mesh apples (*Achras saputa*), fruits of *Melicocca bijuga* and ripening cultivated millet.   When taking the last the birds perched on the growing plants or on the stooks in the fields.   Very wild and timid owing to intense persecution by man.

NESTING: Usual pigeon nest in tree or shrub.   One white egg.   Appears to breed immediately after the rains.   On Curaçao and Bonaire Voous found nests with eggs or young in January, March and April, and noticed that the bird called and displayed most during wet weather.

VOICE: Described by Voous as a rather high-pitched and not very musical 'roo-oo-koo' with stress on the last syllable; by Hartert (1893) as 'a deep cooing, consisting of four sounds'.   Presumably both refer to the advertising coo.

DISPLAY: Voous says the display flight closely resembles that of the Wood Pigeon, *Columba palumbus*, but he says the same of the voice which would not, from his own description (see above) appear very close to that of *palumbus*.

OTHER NAMES: White-winged Pigeon.

REFERENCE

VOOUS, K. H. 1957. The Birds of Aruba, Curaçao and Bonaire. *Studies on the Fauna of Curaçao and other Caribbean Islands* 1: 153–155.

SPOTTED PIGEON   *Columba maculosa*

Columba maculosa Temminck, Pig. et Gall., 1, 1813, p. 113, 450.

DESCRIPTION: About the size of the average Feral Pigeon and very similar in proportions and general appearance, but with the bill proportionately shorter and, of course, without the large cere of some ferals. Head and underparts medium grey, more or less tinged with dull purplish pink except on flanks, under tail coverts and belly.   The forehead, crown, nape, hind neck and breast often predominantly dull purplish pink.   Mantle, wing coverts and secondaries dark dull brown, each feather tipped with a triangular creamy-white mark, giving a spotted effect.   Outer greater coverts bluish grey, the outermost are edged

white.   Primaries and secondaries greyish black with narrow whitish edgings.   Underwing pale grey.
Lower back, rump and upper tail coverts bluish grey, some feathers with paler tips.   Tail dark bluish
grey with ill-defined black terminal band.   Bill dark grey or blackish with powdery white cere.   Irides
grey, whitish grey or white.   Legs and feet dull red.   Sexes alike, female perhaps a little duller on head
and neck.   Juvenile much like adult but duller and with greyish drab head and breast.

The above description is of the nominate form, *C. m. maculosa*, of northern Argentina, Paraguay and
Uruguay.   The form found in southern Peru and western Bolivia, *C. maculosa albipennis*, is slightly
longer-billed with the spots on the wing coverts less sharply defined and with broad white edges to the
outer greater wing coverts forming a white stripe along the edge of the wing when closed and a conspicuous band across it when spread.

DISTRIBUTION: Southern South America in northern Argentina, Uruguay, Paraguay, Bolivia and
southern Peru in the temperate zone.   Inhabits arid or semi-arid and cultivated regions where some trees
are available for nesting and roosting.

FEEDING AND GENERAL HABITS: Feeds on the ground, largely on seeds, but has been said by at least
one observer to eat 'fruit and green stuff' also.   In feeding habits appears largely to parallel the rock
pigeons (*Columba livia* and *C. rupestris*) of the Old World, often or usually feeding in flocks and running
about with great agility when seeking food.

NESTING: Said to nest in trees and lay two eggs, but I can find no detailed or recent description of its
nesting habits.

VOICE: The advertising coo of a captive male of the race *albipennis* consisted of a few very low soft
coos followed by a very loud, harsh and guttural, almost explosive 'Ōō, ōō-ōō!' or 'crōō, crōō-ōōr!'
repeated two to four times.   The late Duke of Bedford, who kept the nominate form of this species at
full liberty described its advertising coo as 'a peculiar ... hoarse rhythmical corrw, cor, cor, coorrw, cor,
cor, coorw' and noted that the bird usually perched on the top of a bare tree to utter it. The display coo
he described as a 'short corw'.   The nest call of the male *albipennis* mentioned above, was a quiet 'ōō-a-ōō'
or 'ōō-a-rōō' very like the softer nest calls of a domestic or Feral Pigeon but with a harsh growling tone
running through it in spite of its quietness.

Wetmore has heard 'a harsh growling note' given by a wounded bird when he picked it up.   Probably
this is a very intense version of the distress call.

DISPLAY: The bowing display was described by the then Marquis of Tavistock (1914) as 'a deep quick
bow ... followed by a shiver of the wings'.   It would thus appear to have much in common with the
bowing display of *Columba picazuro*.   When nest-calling the male *albipennis* that I watched nodded and
twitched its wings in a manner very similar to that of *C. livia*.   The nods were perhaps a little slower and
less emphatic and the wing movement a little more 'shaky' than is usual in *livia*.

OTHER NAMES: American Spotted Pigeon; Spot-winged Pigeon; White-winged Pigeon (the race *albipennis* only).

REFERENCES

RUSSEL, MARQUIS OF TAVISTOCK 1914. Foreign Doves at Liberty. *Avicult. Mag.* **5**: Third Series, 123–132. .
WETMORE, A. 1926. Observations on the birds of Argentina, Paraguay, Uruguay and Chile. *Bull. U.S. Nat. Mus.*
     No. 133, pp. 185–186.

BAND-TAILED PIGEON   *Columba fasciata*

Columba fasciata Say, in Long's Exped. Rocky Mts.; Phila. ed., 2, 1823, p. 10, note.

DESCRIPTION: Rather smaller than the average Feral Pigeon, but a little heavier in build, being in shape and posture very similar to a Wood Pigeon, and if seen alone gives the impression of being the same size.   If, however, one sees a Wood Pigeon and a Band-tailed Pigeon in the same aviary the latter will be seen to be appreciably smaller.   Head, neck, breast and most of underparts light pinkish purple tinged with grey; the colour is rather darker and of a somewhat different tone to the mauve-pink on the Wood Pigeon or Stock Dove.   This colour shades to grey on the flanks and white on the ventral regions and under tail coverts.   A narrow white half-collar divides the mauve-pink of the head from the iridescent golden olive-green or bronzy olive-green hind neck.   Mantle and inner wing coverts and inner secondaries dull olivaceous grey.   Outer wing coverts bluish grey, narrowly edged white.   Lower back, rump, and upper tail coverts bluish grey.   Primaries blackish, very narrowly edged with whitish fawn.   Base of tail blue grey, then a blackish band across it not quite at centre, end half of tail pale creamy grey.   Irides pale yellow with mauve or pinkish outer ring.   Orbital skin (very narrow) reddish.   Bill yellow with black tip. Legs and feet deep yellow.

The female is duller especially on the neck and breast which are much less pink than in the male.   The juvenile is paler and duller with pale rusty fawn fringes to most of the body feathers and (at first) dark eyes, feet and bill.

The above description applies to the nominate form which is found in western North America.   The forms found in Lower California and Central America north of Costa Rica (*C. f. vioscae*, *C. f. letonai* and

C. f. parva) are very similar. The form from Costa Rica and western Panama, *C. f. crissalis*, is however considerably darker in colour and has reddish brown irides.

The forms found in South America, *C. f. albilinea* and *C. f. roraimae*, are very much darker, being predominantly dark purplish, very dark iridescent green and dark grey. The distribution of their plumage colours is similar except that *roraimae* has a certain amount of green gloss on its back and rump. Their bills are, however, entirely yellow, thus lacking the striking parti-coloured effect of the North American Band-tail's bill.

FIELD IDENTIFICATION: Largish pigeon with pale end to tail; white neck ring diagnostic when visible.

DISTRIBUTION AND HABITAT: Mountainous parts of western North America from Vancouver Island, south-west British Columbia, Montana and western North Dakota, south to southern Lower California, Central America and northern and western South America, south to northern Argentina in the states of Tucuman and Catamarca. Inhabits forest in temperate and subtropical mountain ranges and highlands. Particularly in areas where oaks are plentiful on wooded slopes or in canyons. Locally in cultivated areas in mountainous country.

FEEDING AND GENERAL HABITS: Feeds on seeds, berries, buds, young leaves and blossoms of a wide variety of trees and plants. When available acorns are usually taken in quantity. Like the European Wood Pigeon it feeds both in trees and on the ground and when feeding in trees can cling, clamber about and hang upside down with an agility which, in view of its bulk, surprises those who are unfamiliar with arboreal pigeons.

Commonly in parties of several individuals, often in large flocks when on migration or on the wintering grounds. Territorial when nesting but, as is usual with many territoral pigeons, several pairs commonly nest quite near each other in adjacent territories. Individuals tend to aggregate for feeding purposes even during the breeding season.

NESTING: Usual pigeon nest in tree or shrub. In North America (and probably elsewhere as well) the nest tree usually stands above a small precipice or slope and is adjacent to or very near a clearing. One white egg. Incubation period said to be 18 to 20 days. In northern coastal California peak nesting season is mid-June to mid-July with only one brood reared (Glover 1953).

VOICES: Peeters (1962) who made a detailed study of this species in the San Francisco Bay area records the following: What is evidently the advertising coo is described as 'whoo-hoo-whoo-hoo-whoo-h-oowhoo-roo-whoo-roo', with the pitch dropping sharply at the ends of the shorter syllables. The same coo would appear to be given when displaying to the female. Peeters notes that the coo is tonally weak and carries little more than fifty yards and that, to him, it sounded similar in quality to the cooing of other pigeons not owl-like as some observers have considered.

The excitement cry is variously described as 'chirping' 'peculiar wheezing' and 'like the creaking-door call of the Stellar Jay' – it is given by the male during the display flight. A captive male gave it 'whenever angry or excited'. A higher pitched version of this call was heard from a male flying in display flight from tree to tree during a temporary absence of his mate.

A grunting call has been heard from feeding birds of both sexes when approached closely by their companions and various soft or guttural cooing notes prior or during the change-over of an incubating pair. The distress call is a short, gasping sound as with other pigeons.

DISPLAY: In what appears to be the equivalent of the bowing display the Band-tailed Pigeon coos in an upright posture with inflated neck and tail depressed and fully spread. This is (? always) prefaced by the male adopting a horizontal posture, lowering his head and, with inflated neck, swinging his head slowly first to the left and then to the right.

Displacement-preening behind the wing occurs as in other pigeons, but copulation is not, or at least not usually, preceded by billing. Immediately after copulation the male stands with bill pointed upwards As compared with most Old World species of *Columba* most of the above movements are executed very slowly.

In display flight the male first glides horizontally or slightly downwards with neck extended and wings and tail fully spread.   He then swerves to right or left and glides in a circle, uttering the excitement cry. Towards the end of the display flight, after describing half or three-quarters of the circle, he beats his wings with rapid shallow beats.   During this only the primaries appear to move and speed is very slow.

The above descriptions of voice and display are taken from studies of the North American Band-tail (Swarth, 1904; Whitman, 1919; and Peeters, 1962).

It is probable that the behaviour and voice of the South and Central American populations of the species are similar or identical, but I can find no detailed information on them.

OTHER NAMES: White-collared Pigeon; Blue Pigeon.

REFERENCES

GLOVER, F. A.   1953.   A nesting study of the Band-tailed Pigeon in north-western California.   *Calif. Fish and Game* **39**: 397–407.
PEETERS, H. J.   1962.   Nuptial Behaviour of the Band-tailed Pigeon in the San Francisco Bay area.   *Condor* **64**: 445–470.
SWARTH, H. S.   1904.   Birds of the Huachuca Mountains, Arizona.   *Pac. Coast Avif.* **4**: 1–70.
WHITMAN, C. O.   1919.   Behaviour of Pigeons.   Posthumous works of Charles Otis Whitman.   *Carnegie Inst. Wash., Publ.* **257**: 257.   Vol. 3.

CHILEAN PIGEON   *Columba araucana*

Columba araucana Lesson, Voy. 'Coquille', Zool. 1, Livr. 4, 1827, Atlas, pl. 40; Livr. 6, 1830, p. 706.

DESCRIPTION: About the size of a Feral Pigeon. Very similar in shape and marking to the previous species with which and *Columba caribaea*, it forms a superspecies.   Head, neck, except for a narrow white half-collar on nape and a patch of iridescent golden green behind it, underparts, mantle and scapulars dark reddish purple.   Wing coverts and inner secondaries dull grey shading to lighter bluish grey on the outer wing coverts which, like the black primaries and outer secondaries have narrow whitish fringes. Lower back, rump, under tail coverts and axillaries dark bluish grey.   Tail bluish grey at base with broad blackish central band and lighter brownish grey end.   Irides orange with pink or yellow outer ring. Orbital skin purple.   Legs and feet bright red.   Bill black.

Female duller and more brownish than male with only a little reddish purple on the mantle.   Juvenile bears same relation to adult as that of *C. fasciata*.

DISTRIBUTION AND HABITAT: Central and southern Chile and the forested slopes of the Andes in Argentina from Neuquen to western Chubut.   Found in wooded country, both lowland and hills, particularly in areas where the tree *Araucaria araucana* grows, the fruits of which are a favoured food.

Formerly common in suitable areas, this species was nearly wiped out by Newcastle Disease in 1954 (see Behn, 1957).   By the Summer of 1955 only a few scattered individuals were known to be still alive.

FEEDING AND GENERAL HABITS: Little in detail apparently recorded. Probably very similar to the Band-tailed Pigeon (q.v.).

NESTING: Usual pigeon nest in tree or shrub. One white egg. Known to nest from December to March, sometimes as late as May.

VOICE: What is presumably the advertising coo has been described as 'a deep booming coo'.

DISPLAY: No information.

OTHER NAMES: Chilean Band-tail.

REFERENCES

BEHN, F. 1957. *Columba araucana* in Chile durch die Newcastle Krankheit dezemiert. *Journ. f. Orn.* **98**: 124.
GOODALL, J. D., JOHNSON, A. W. & PHILIPPS, R. A. 1946. *Las Aves de Chile.* Vol. 1. Buenos Aires.
LANE A. A. 1897. Field Notes on the Birds of Chile. *Ibis* **3**: Seventh Series, 297–317.

JAMAICAN BAND-TAILED PIGEON   *Columba caribaea*

Columba caribaea Jacquin, Beytr, Gesch. Vög., 1784, p. 30.

DESCRIPTION: General appearance like the Band-tailed Pigeon (q.v.) but with proportionately somewhat longer tail, no white neck ring and paler and more delicate colours. Head, neck, breast and underparts a delicate pale mauve-pink. Throat whitish. Golden-green and amethystine-pink iridescence on hind neck, these glossy feathers differ in appearance and texture from these of the continental band-tails and more resemble those seen in *Columba cayennensis* and some Old World *Columba* species. Upperparts bluish-grey, wing quills black with narrow pale fringes. Tail light grey with broad black central band. Under tail coverts whitish. Irides orange-red to vermilion, orbital skin purplish red. Legs and feet (*fide* Gosse, 1847) coral red. Bill black.

Female slightly duller and browner than male. Juvenile (1 only seen) brownish grey with rusty feather fringes on wing coverts, inner secondaries and scapulars. Head pinkish with rusty feather edges. Breast and underparts pale rutsy orange.

DISTRIBUTION AND HABITAT: Jamaica. Found chiefly in wooded areas inland from 1,000 to 2,000 feet above sea-level.

FEEDING AND GENERAL HABITS: Known to feed on fruits and berries. Probably much as Band-tail (q.v.). Grosse quotes others to the effect that this species usually perches near the middle of a tree, never on terminal branches.

NESTING: No information.

VOICE: A deep 'croo' recorded. Doubtless has other notes.

DISPLAY: No information.

OTHER-NAME: Ring-tailed Pigeon.

REFERENCES

GOSSE, P. H. 1847. *The birds of Jamaica.* London.
SCOTT, W. E. D. 1892. Observations on the birds of Jamaica. *Auk* **9**: 120–129

RUFOUS PIGEON   *Columba cayennensis*

Columba cayennensis Bonnaterre, Tabl. Enc. Méth., orn., 1, livr. 51, p. 234, 179.

DESCRIPTION: A little smaller than a Feral Pigeon with a proportionately smaller and more slender bill. Throat greyish white shading to grey on face and lower throat. Crown and nape iridescent green, bronze and/or pinkish-mauve, according to angle of light. Forehead, breast and neck dull pinkish purple shading to purplish chestnut on mantle and wing coverts and medium grey on flanks, belly and under tail coverts. Outermost greater wing coverts and secondaries dark drab grey. Primaries blackish grey or blackish drab with narrow pale fringes. Lower back, rump, upper tail-coverts and underwing dark bluish grey. Central tail feathers dark grey with ill-defined blackish central band and broad, ill-defined light drab terminal bar. Irides pinkish red, red, orange, or purplish red. Orbital skin red or dull red and narrow. Legs and feet purplish red.

The female is a little lighter and much duller than the male. She is drab brown where the male is purplish and brownish grey where he is dark grey except that she has a varying amount of purplish red suffusion on forehead, neck and upper breast. The juvenile female is like the adult but has pale edgings to most feathers, especially pronounced on the outermost greater wing coverts. The young male is similar but has rufous edges to the feathers of those parts which are purplish in the adult.

The above description is of the nominate form, *C. c. cayennensis*, from the Guianas and adjacent areas of northern South America. *C. cayennensis pallidicrissa* from Central America is slightly paler. The male has whitish belly and under tail coverts, medium blue grey rump and a pale drab tail that shades to only a slightly darker and greyer hue towards its base. *C. c. sylvestris*, from southern South America is similar to *cayennensis* but has the dark and light barring of the tail more clearly defined. Other races have been described, all of which closely resemble one or other of those described above.

DISTRIBUTION AND HABITAT: Central and South America from south eastern Mexico to eastern Peru, Brazil, Paraguay, Rio Grande do Sul and northern Argentina and the islands of Trinidad and Tobago. Inhabits savannas; open country with clumps of trees, shrubs or palms; open forest and semi-arid regions with some trees. Locally also in mangrove swamps.

FEEDING AND GENERAL HABITS: Little recorded. Feeds both in branches and on ground on seeds and berries. In some areas large flocks gather to feed on rice stubble (Young, 1928).

NESTING : Usual pigeon nest in tree or shrub. One white egg (Belcher & Snooker, 1936; Newman, 1910) is the normal clutch but a two egg clutch has been recorded.

VOICE : What are, possibly, different calls have been described as 'a soft stacatto co, co, co-ooo' (Young, 1928), 'ku-u, ruk-tu-ku-u' (B. & S.), 'woo-oo-oo woo-tit-woo woo-tit-woo' (Wetmore, MS) and a 'resonant and stirring' 'woo co-co-co-coo' (Skutch, 1964).

DISPLAY : In display flight males fly, raising their wings well above the horizontal then glide on stiffly spread wings which are sometimes held horizontally and sometimes at an upward angle (Wetmore, MS).

OTHER NAMES : Cayenne Pigeon ; Pale-vented Pigeon ; Blue Pigeon.

REFERENCES

BELCHER, C. & SMOOKER, G. D. 1936. Birds of the Colony of Trinidad and Tobago, Pt. 3. *Ibis* **6** : Thirteenth Series, 1–35.
DARLINGTON, P. R. 1931. Notes on the Birds of Rio Frio, Magdalena, Colombia. *Bull. Mus. Comp. Zool.* **71** : **6** : 349–421.
NEWMAN, T. H. 1910. Nesting of the White-throated Pigeon. *Avic. Mag.*, Third Series **1** : **5** : 193–195.
SKUTCH, A. F. 1964. Life Histories of Central American Pigeons. *Wilson Bull.* **76** : 211–247.
YOUNG, C. G. 1928. Ornithology of the Coastland of British Guiana. *Ibis* **4** : Twelfth Series, 748–781.
WETMORE, A. 1964. Manuscript for a book on the birds of Panama.

RED-BILLED PIGEON *Columba flavirostris*

Columba flavirostris Wagler, Isis von Oken, 1831, col. 519.

DESCRIPTION : Rather smaller than the average Feral Pigeon. Head, neck, breast and lesser wing coverts dull reddish purple shading to dark bluish grey on outer wing coverts, secondaries, flanks, belly, lower back, rump and under tail coverts and dull brownish grey on mantle and scapulars. Very narrow white fringes to outer greater coverts and outer secondaries. Primaries greyish black with narrow whitish fringes to outer webs. Tail dark slate grey at base shading to greyish black at end. Underwing light grey. Irides orange or reddish orange. Orbital skin dark red. Bill pinkish flesh, whitish or pale horn at end, basal half and cere red or deep pink. Legs and feet dark red.

Female has the purplish red areas paler and duller than the male. Juvenile very like female but purplish areas paler and more rusty-coloured ; young male brighter than young female.

The above description is of the nominate form, *C. f. flavirostris*, of Texas, eastern and southern Mexico, south to Salvador. The other races that have been described differ only in very minor points of size or amount of white edging on the wing feathers.   *C. f. madrensis* from the Tres Marias Islands off western Mexico, which is the most differentiated, is only slightly larger and has broader white edges to the greater wing coverts.

DISTRIBUTION AND HABITAT: The Lower Rio Grande Valley of Texas, Mexico and Central America south to Nicaragua and Costa Rico.   Inhabits woodland near water; also pasture land and other open areas with patches of woodland or clumps of trees.   Typically in semi-arid or arid country, with nearby water supplies.

FEEDING AND GENERAL HABITS: Recorded feeding on berries, small fruits and small acorns.   Mistletoe berries evidently a favourite food when available.   Dickey & Van Rossem (1932) record large numbers coming to the ground to feed on rock salt that had been dumped near some buildings at the edge of a stream.   Flight swift and strong, usually direct.

NESTING: Usual pigeon nest in tree or shrub.   One white egg.   In Costa Rica nests from March to August (Skutch, 1964).

VOICE: The advertising coo has been transcribed by Sutton (1951) as 'cooooooo! Up, cup-a-coo! Up, cup-a-coo! Up, cup-a-coo!' and by Skutch (1964) as a 'loud, deep-toned . . . "Wooo, C'c'coo, c'c'coo, c'c'coo" '. Skutch also describes a shorter 'long-drawn sonorous ascending note followed by three shorter notes – cooo cu cu coo'. Other observers describe cooing notes like those of the Domestic Pigeon but louder, and a clear short and high-pitched cooing.

DISPLAY: Distraction display in which bird drops from nest, flies low in fluttering flight and, if followed, alights and flaps wings in an unco-ordinated manner (Skutch, 1964).

OTHER NAME: Blue Pigeon.

REFERENCES

DENT, A. C.   1932.; Life Histories of North American gallinaceous Birds.   *U.S. Nat. Mus. Bull.* **162**.
BICKEY, D. R. & VAN ROSSEM, A. J.   1938.   The Birds of El Salvador.   *Publ. Field Mus. Nat. Hist. Zool.* Sᴛʀ. **23**: 185–187.
SKUTCH, A. F.   1964.   Life Histories of Central American Pigeons.   *Wilson Bull.* **76**: 211–247.
SUTTON, G. M.   1951.   *Mexican Birds.   First Impressions*, pp. 120–121.   University of Oklahoma Press.

SALVIN'S PIGEON   *Columba oenops*

Columba oenops Salvin, Nov. Zool. 2, 1895, p. 20.

DESCRIPTION: Closely related to the Red-billed Pigeon, *C. flavirostris*, with which it forms a superspecies.   In colour and colour-pattern like *C. flavirostris* (q. v.) but with the bill yellow or yellow with a blackish tip and with the entire mantle, inner wing coverts and scapulars purplish chestnut.   The female has the purplish chestnut on the mantle and scapulars more or less replaced by or intermixed with dull brown and is thus somewhat intermediate in colour between her mate and the male of *flavirostris*.

DISTRIBUTION AND HABITAT: The subtropical zone of the Upper Marañón Valley in northern Peru. Inhabits woodland but little precise data available.

FEEDING AND GENERAL HABITS: No information.

NESTING: No information.

VOICE: No information.

DISPLAY: No information.

PLAIN PIGEON   *Columba inornata*

Columba inornata Vigors, Zool. Journ. 3, 1827, p. 446.

DESCRIPTION: An island representative of the Red-billed and Salvin's Pigeons with which it forms a superspecies. About the size of a largish Feral Pigeon and rather similar in general shape but with longish, slender bill. Head, neck, breast and underparts dark purplish pink shading to bluish grey on the flanks and under tail coverts; a patch of the same colour on top central part of folded wing. Mantle, scapulars, inner wing-coverts (where not purplish) dull slate grey. Outer wing coverts bluish grey with broad white edgings to outer webs. Secondaries bluish grey shading to blackish grey on outer secondaries and primaries which are narrowly edged whitish on outer web. Irides greyish white or with a bluish and an orange ring. Orbital skin grey, purplish, or purplish pink. Bill dull black, greyish at base. Legs and feet dark red. Three races of this pigeon are currently recognised *C. i. inornata* from Cuba and Hispaniola and the Isle of Pines *C. i. exigua* from Jamaica, and *C. i. wetmorei* from Puerto Rico but they differ only very slightly.

DISTRIBUTION AND HABITAT: Cuba and the Isle of Pines, Hispaniola, Jamaica and Puerto Rico. Now rare in Jamaica and was long thought to be extinct on Puerto Rico (Bond, 1956) where it must, however, have continued to exist and has, since 1961, occurred in some numbers and been shot and sold for food (Leopold, 1963). Inhabits cultivated or open country with some trees, woodland, including pine woods, and rain forest.

FEEDING AND GENERAL HABITS: Little recorded. In Haiti Wetmore & Swales (1931) found it usually in parties of two to ten and rather tame. Probably feeds much as the Red-billed Pigeon (q.v.).

NESTING: Usual pigeon nest in tree or shrub. One white egg, sometimes two, *fide* Bond (1960).

VOICE: What is probably the advertising coo consists of a series of slow hooting coos, often prefaced by a guttural growling note. Wetmore transcribes it as 'kr-r-r-r-coo-whoo-hoo, coo-whoo-oo'. Bond as 'a hooting crooo-cruh-cruh repeated a number of times, sometimes preceded by a gutteral note'.

DISPLAY: No information.

OTHER NAME: Blue Pigeon.

REFERENCES

BOND, J. 1956. *Check-list of Birds of the West Indies.* Philadelphia.
—— 1960. *Birds of the West Indies.* London.
LEOPOLD, N. F. 1963. Check-list of the birds of Puerto Rico and the Virgin Islands. *Bull.* **168**: University of Puerto Rico Agricultural Experimental Station, p. 119.
WETMORE, A. & SWALES, B. H. 1931. The Birds of Haiti and the Dominican Republic. *U.S. Nat. Mus. Bull.* **155**: 188–190.

PLUMBEOUS PIGEON   *Columba plumbea*

Columba plumbea Vieillot, Nouv. Dict. Hist. Nat. 26, 1818, 358.

DESCRIPTION: About midway in size between a Barbary Dove and a Feral Pigeon, with medium-length wings and rather long and round-ended tail. Head, neck and underparts dark to medium grey, pinkish grey, greyish mauve or dull purplish. Throat paler, often nearly dull cream colour. Mantle, back, rump, wings and tail dark greyish brown, sepia or olive drab, in some races tinged with purple or sometimes predominantly dark brownish purple in colour. Faint paler bronzy spots may be present on hind neck formed by obsolescent display plumage, the feathers having faint pale bronzy subterminal bars on either side of the shaft and dark purplish edges. Bill black with reddish cere. Irides dark red. Orbital skin purplish red. Legs and feet red.

Female like male but usually with purple tinge on neck and breast less intense, and the obscure pale spotting on the hind neck more evident. Juvenile duller with little purple tinge and rusty fawn edges to feathers of breast and wing coverts (and to a lesser extent elsewhere). Many slightly differing geographical races have been described but the above description covers them all.

DISTRIBUTION AND HABITAT: South America in eastern Colombia, Ecuador, Peru, Bolivia, Brazil and the Guianas. Inhabits tropical and subtropical woodland.

FEEDING AND GENERAL HABITS: Known to feed on fruits and berries.

NESTING: No information.

VOICE: No information.

DISPLAY: No information.

RUDDY PIGEON   *Columba subvinacea*

Chloroenas subvinacea Lawrence, Ann. Lyc. Nat. Hist. N.Y., 9, 1868, p. 135.

DESCRIPTION: Very similar to the previous species (*C. plumbea*) from which it differs, visually, only as follows: It is smaller in size, being about as large as, or only slightly larger than, a Barbary Dove.   Its bill is proportionately smaller and shorter.   The underside and inner webs of its primary wing feathers show a reddish buff, chestnut or cinnamon tinge.   Its general coloration is usually of a warmer and more reddish tone.   This is most marked in the Costa Rican and Panamanian populations which are predominantly rich reddish purple or rufous on the upperparts.   The bill is black with a greyish cere or entirely black. Irides purplish red, pink or brownish; orbital skin dull red.   Legs and feet dull red or purplish red.

DISTRIBUTION AND HABITAT: Central and South America in Costa Rica and Panama, Colombia, Venezuela, northern Brazil, Ecuador, north-eastern Peru and eastern Bolivia.   Inhabits tropical and subtropical woodland.   In Costa Rica (*fide* Skutch, 1951) it is a bird of higher altitudes and is replaced in the lowlands by *Columba nigrirostris*.

FEEDING AND GENERAL HABITS: No information.

NESTING: No information.

VOICE: What is probably the advertising coo is described by Wetmore (MS) as a four syllabled 'Oh, whit mo gó' somewhat harsher and more strongly accented than the very similar cooing of *Columba nigrirostris*.   Described as 'melodious' and 'far-carrying' by Skutch (1951).

DISPLAY: No information.

REFERENCES

SKUTCH, A. F. 1951. Congeneric species of birds nesting together in Central America. *Condor* **53**: 3–15.
WETMORE, A. 1964. *Manuscript for a book on the birds of Panama.*

SHORT-BILLED PIGEON   *Columba nigrirostris*

Columba nigrirostris Sclater, Proc. Zool. Soc. London, 1859 (1860), p. 390.

DESCRIPTION: Very similar to the Ruddy Pigeon but a shade more heavily built and with a larger and stouter bill.   In spite of its name the bill averages longer than that of *C. subvinacea* but appears shorter because it is thicker.   Coloration of plumage essentially like that of the Ruddy Pigeon but mantle, back, rump and wing coverts are dark olive brown or dark purplish brown and hence darker than the very reddish nominate form of *C. subvinacea* which is geographically sympatric with it in Panama and Costa Rica.   Bill and cere black, reddish at gape.   Eyelids red.   Irides pink or vinous.   Legs and feet red. Sexes alike but female averaging a little paler and duller and with indications of obsolescent display plumage on hind neck (feathers with blackish centres and light purplish or bronze at sides), more noticeable than in most males.   Juvenile duller with narrow rusty fringes to feathers of upper parts and broad rust red fringes to feathers of head, neck and breast.

DISTRIBUTION AND HABITAT : Central America from south-eastern Mexico to eastern Panama. Inhabits lowland rain forest but sometimes found up to 5,000 feet above sea-level. Often comes into clearings (Skutch, 1964). In Costa Rica (*fide* Skutch, 1951) is a bird of low levels replaced by the allied *C. subvinacea* at higher altitudes.

FEEDING AND GENERAL HABITS : Known to feed on fruits and berries. Commonly found in high trees but often comes into low fruiting trees and shrubs to feed, and sometimes comes to the ground.

NESTING : The only egg apparently recorded was white and taken in June in Panama. Skutch (1964) found two nests, 25 and 100 feet above ground in dense vegetation and unreachable.

VOICE : Wetmore (MS) describes what is, probably, the advertising coo as a four or five syllabled call very similar to that of *C. subvinacea* but a little softer. The male (only ?) also utters a guttural 'groo-oo-oo'. Skutch (1951 and 1964) writes of 'melodious and far-carrying "ho, cu-cu-cóoo" or "oh, je t'adore"' like that of *subvinacea* but softer and more liquid.

DISPLAY : No information.

REFERENCES

KUTCH, A. F. 1951. Congeneric species of birds nesting together in Central America. *Condor* 53 : 3–15.
—— 1964. Life Histories of Central American Pigeons. *Wilson Bull.* 76: 211–247.
WETMORE, A. 1964. *Manuscript for a book on the Birds of Panama.*

GOODSON'S PIGEON   *Columba goodsoni*

Columba goodsoni Hartert, Bull. Brit. Orn. Club, 12, 1902.

DESCRIPTION : Very similar to the last species with which it forms a superspecies. Differs in having the crown, sides of head, throat and breast predominantly grey or purplish grey, and the rufous on the under wing brighter and more extensive.

DISTRIBUTION AND HABITAT : Western Colombia and western Ecuador in the tropical zone. Inhabits forest.

FEEDING AND GENERAL HABITS: No information.

NESTING: No information.

VOICE: No information.

DISPLAY: No information

DELEGORGUE'S PIGEON   *Columba delegorguei*

Columba Delegorguei Delegorgue, Voy, Afr. Austr., 2, 1847, p. 615.

DESCRIPTION: Slightly larger than a Barbary Dove but plumper in build with proportionately shorter tail. Face and forehead dark grey, crown with slight iridescence. Nape and neck with vivid iridescence, which appears predominantly pink, mauve or amethyst in most lights. Hind neck crossed by a white band or 'third moon' shaped patch of white. Mantle scapulars and wing coverts dark reddish purple or purplish brown. Rest of upperparts and underwing slaty black with narrow ill-defined grey tips to the tail feathers. Breast very dark mauve pink, many of the feathers often finely and obscurely speckled or vermiculated with dark grey. On lower breast and belly brownish finely speckled feathers become more numerous, belly usually appearing predominantly dull reddish brown. Flanks and under tail coverts predominantly dark grey. Irides dark brown, whitish, grey or yellow; possibly dark brown is usual and other colours may have been taken from dead or sick birds whose eyes had faded. Orbital skin pink or greyish pink. Bill bluish grey or dark grey with pale grey or pale horn-coloured tip. Legs and feet pink or red.

The female differs strikingly from the male. She has no white collar. Her crown and nape are bright coppery brown. Her mantle and wing coverts are blackish. Her underparts show no purple tinge but look generally dull grey or greyish tawny; the individual feathers being finely speckled and vermiculated with tawny buff on a slate grey ground. The juvenile male like adult, but crown and nape grey, less iridescence on neck and rufous fringes to wing coverts and feathers of underparts. I have not seen a juvenile female.

The above description is of nominate *C. d. delegorguei* from Natal and Zululand in South Africa. In *C. delegorguei sharpei* from Kenya and the Sudan the male has no reddish purple on the upperparts which are, where not iridescent or white, entirely slaty black. The iridescence on his neck and mantle looks predominantly green in most lights and his belly and flanks are predominantly slate grey. The female resembles the female of the nominate form but the iridescence on her hind neck is often, though not most usually, green rather than pink or amethyst. Some individual males of this form (and, perhaps the same is true of the southern form) have the white neck patch very much reduced, only a few feathers showing the white or partially white tips which produce this marking. Irides of males dark brown, reddish purple or pinkish grey; of females red, pink or orange.

Over much of eastern Africa the populations are intermediate between the above-described forms and the males show varying amounts of purplish red on the upperparts and either green or pink iridescence on nape. In these intermediate populations males with purplish mantle may show green iridescence on neck and 'black' males may have pink iridescence as well as *vice versa*.

DISTRIBUTION AND HABITAT: Eastern Africa from southern Sudan and Kenya to South Africa· Inhabits forest and thick woodland, usually in mountainous country.

FEEDING AND GENERAL HABITS: Feeds largely on berries and fruits taken from the branches. Females (but not males) have occasionally been seen on the ground (Sclater & Moreau, 1932); presumably in search of food or minerals necessary to them. Keeps much to cover in the canopy of tall trees but will cross open ground from one forested hill to another. Apparently subject to local movements but little detailed observation of its habits available.

NESTING: Usual pigeon nest in tree or shrub, usually about 15 to 20 feet high. Two white eggs. Recorded nesting December and March to June in Kenya and in November and April in South Africa.

VOICE: The advertising coo has been described by Moreau, observing in north-east Tanganyika, as starting with 'three emphatic coos', the second much lighter pitched than the other and ending with 'four to five rapid coos', all of low pitch and uttered diminuendo. What is probably but not certainly the same call of the South African form is described (McLachlan & Liversidge, 1957) as 'a descending series of 7 to 10 'du, du, du's' . . . the first three soft and higher pitched than the others.

DISPLAY: No information.

OTHER NAME: Bronze-naped Pigeon.

REFERENCES

MCLACHLAN, G. R. & LIVERSIDGE, R. 1957. *Roberts Birds of South Africa*, revised edtion, p. 167. Cape Town, S.A.
SCLATER, W. L. & MOREAU, R. E. 1932. Taxonomic and Field Notes on some birds of north-eastern Tanganyika Territory. Pt. 1. *Ibis* **2**: Thirteenth Series, 487–522.

BRONZE-NAPED PIGEON   *Columba iriditorques*

Columra (sic) *iriditorques* Cassin, Proc. Acad. Nat. Sci. Phila; 8, 1956, p. 254.

DESCRIPTION: Very similar to the previous species together with which and *C. malherbii* it forms a superspecies. About size of Barbary Dove but plumper and more compact in shape. Head bluish grey, palest on throat and with purplish pink or green iridescence on crown and nape. Hind neck and extreme upper part of mantle bright golden bronze with a pinkish or, in some lights, greenish gloss. Upperparts slaty black with some iridescence on mantle and scapulars. Central tail feathers broadly but obscurely tipped dark grey; outer tail feathers with varying but usually broad buff terminal bands and inner webs predominantly dark chestnut. Underside of tail dusky chestnut tipped buff. Breast and underparts dark mauve pink shading to chestnut on under tail coverts. Irides pink, red or pinkish grey or pink with brown or grey inner ring; pink or golden. Orbital skin red (this based on two specimens only). Bill bluish grey or grey usually with whitish tip and purplish, dark red or purplish black cere. Legs and feet pink, flesh pink or light red.

The female differs strikingly from the male although very like the female of Delagorgue's Pigeon. She has the face suffused with brown, crown and nape bright bronze brown but hind neck (where male is bronze) iridescent pink or green. Her breast and underparts appear generally buffy grey or dusky rufous the feathers being finely speckled and vermiculated with grey and tawny or grey and rufous. Her under tail coverts are chestnut. Her irides sometimes greenish yellow, otherwise as male. The juvenile resembles that of the previous species in relation to the adult. A supposed race *C. iriditorques incerta* was described from a captive specimen showing the abnormal increase of melanin common in badly kept captive doves.

DISTRIBUTION AND HABITAT: Western Africa from Sierra Leone eastward to the Cameroon, Gaboon, northern Angola and the Congo to the Semliki Valley and the forest along the eastern edge of Rutshuru Plain. Also in north-western Zambia (Benson 1959). Inhabits forest, both primary and second growth.

FEEDING AND GENERAL HABITS: Known to feed on small fruits and berries taken from the branches. 'Small black seeds' were found in the crop of one individual collected. In southern Cameroon the fruits of *Musanga* and *Haronga* are important foods (Bates, 1930).

NESTING: The only record appears to be of a nest found by Bates in an *Haronga* tree. He did not, apparently, see or take the eggs but collected the incubating bird.

VOICE: What is, probably, the advertising coo, is described by Chapin (1939) thus 'It begins . . . with two to four notes audible at no great distance, continues with four or five very loud coos of uniform tone, then suddenly lowers its voice and finishes with three to five notes a little louder than those at the start'. Most descriptions by others who have heard it appear to refer to the same call less completely heard or recorded in less detail. Heinrich's (1958) description, of a deep cooing in which a series of somewhat higher pitched coos are followed by a shorter series of deeper coos may, however, refer to some other call, perhaps the nest call.

DISPLAY: No information.

REFERENCES

BATES, G. L. 1930. *Handbook of the birds of West Africa*, pp. 8–9.
BENSON, C. W. 1959. *Turturoena iriditorques* in the Mwinilunga District, Northern Rhodesia. *Ibis* **101**: 240.
CHAPIN, I. P. 1938. The birds of the Belgian Congo **2**: 167. *Bull, Amer. Mus. Nat. Hist.* 75.
HEINRICH, G. 1958. Zur Verbreitung und Lebensweise der Vögel von Angola. *Journ. f. Orn.* **99**: 322–362 (325).

SÃO THOMÉ BRONZE-NAPED PIGEON   *Columba malherbii*

Columba malherbii J. & E. Verreaux, Rev. et Mag. Zool. (2), 3, 1851, p. 514.

DESCRIPTION: This species' English name is descriptively misleading but does at least emphasise the close relationship between it and *C. iriditorques*. Between Feral Pigeon and Barbary Dove in size. Throat and forehead pale grey, face and crown darker grey with some green and/or pink iridescence. Nape and hind neck iridescent purple-pink, pink or green according to angle of light. Rest of upperparts slaty black shading to dark slate grey on rump and tail.   Breast and underparts bluish grey, palest on belly.   Ventral regions and under tail coverts buff or reddish buff, more or less freckled with grey. Female has breast and underparts suffused and freckled with buff or reddish buff and outer tail feathers suffused with reddish buff or chestnut, especially on inner webs.   Irides pale grey, bill lead grey with pale tip.   Legs and feet bright red.   (I have been unable to find specimens with the soft part colours recorded. Those given are taken from existing literature and may well be based on only one or two specimens.) The juvenile is like the female but less iridescent and with broadly buff-tipped feathers on forehead and forecrown.

DISTRIBUTION AND HABITAT :   The islands of São Thomé, Principe and Annobon in the Gulf of Guinea. Inhabits forest.   Apparently rare (? or difficult to find) on São Thomé and Principe but common, or at any rate formerly common on Annobon (Bannerman, 1931).

FEEDING AND GENERAL HABITS :   No information.

NESTING :   No information.

VOICE :   Said to have a 'guttural note' that is tiresomely montonous (Fea, in Bannerman, 1931).

DISPLAY :   No information.

OTHER NAME :   São Thomé Grey Pigeon.

REFERENCE

BANNERMAN, D. A.   1931.   *The Birds of Tropical West Africa* **2** : 332–333.

PINK PIGEON   *Columba mayeri*

Columba mayeri 'March', Prévost. in Knip, Les Pigeons.   Ed. 2. 2. (1938–1843), 1843, p. 113, pl. 60.

DESCRIPTION: About size of Feral Pigeon with proportionately shorter and more rounded wings and long, slightly round-ended tail. Head, neck and underparts a soft, light pink shading to white on face and forehead, to creamy buff on belly and to brownish pink on upper mantle. Wings and a narrow band across mantle dark brown, the primaries narrowly edged with rufous buff on outer webs. Upper back dusky pink. Rump pale bluish grey shading to chestnut on upper tail coverts. Tail bright chestnut except the outermost pair of feathers which are usually pinkish grey more or less tinged with chestnut. In worn plumage the tips of the pink feathers fade to a creamy tinge. Irides yellow. Bill yellow shaded red towards base. Legs and feet red. Sexes nearly alike but female a little less bright and with rump more suffused with brown. I have not seen a juvenile of this species.

DISTRIBUTION AND HABITAT: Mauritius. Now rare and local, confined to the remote forests of the south-western Plateau (Rountree *et al.*, 1962).

FEEDING AND GENERAL HABITS: I can find little recorded. Meinertzhagen (1912) recorded only that 'They are very tame and confiding and do not seem to care for the high forest trees . . . they have a heavy flight, but never go very far'.

NESTING: No information.

VOICE: Display coo described as 'a rather hoarse, whispered crooning on a falling note' (Niven, 1964). Meinertzhagen (*op. cit.*) refers to 'mournful cooings' that 'express sadness'.

DISPLAY: Mrs. Niven (1964 and pers. comm.) saw a bowing display from the male of a pair watched on the ground. It 'bowed with its tail fanned out and down . . . behaved much as a Domestic Pigeon does; strutted after the female, inflated its throat, and bowed, but slowly and deeply'.

OTHER NAMES: Mauritius Pigeon; Pigeons des Mares; Chestnut-tailed Pigeon.

REFERENCES

MEINERTZHAGEN, R. 1912. On the birds of Mauritius. *Ibis* 6: Ninth Series, 82–108.
NIVEN, C. 1964. A field day on the Island of Mauritius. *Bokmakerie* 16: 6–7.
ROUNTREE, F. R. G., GUERIN, R., PELTE, S. & VINSON, J. 1952. Catalogue of the birds of Mauritius, p. 185. *The Mauritius Inst., Bull.*, 3 vol. 3. Pt. 3.

THE TURTLE DOVES

The pigeons in the genus *Streptopelia*, commonly called turtle doves, are familiar to the majority of people. They are, indeed, the birds that are most commonly, if unscientifically, thought of as 'doves' in contradistinction to 'pigeons'. They occur, often very abundantly, in the temperate and tropical regions of Europe, Asia and Africa, and some of them have been successfully introduced into the Pacific, Australasian and Nearctic regions. Also one of them, the Barbary Dove or Blond Ringdove, which is a domesticated variety of the African Collared Dove, *Streptopelia roseogrisea*, is kept as a cage bird almost throughout the world.

It is perhaps unfortunate that the generic name *Turtur* formerly used for this genus, and still used as the specific name for the bird to which the Romans originally gave it, the Turtle Dove *Streptopelia turtur*, must, owing to the exigencies of scientific nomenclature, now be used for the African wood doves. The reader should therefore remember that the older naturalists, including Darwin, used the genus *Turtur* for the turtle doves, not for the wood doves.

The turtle doves are trim, shapely pigeons, mostly about half the size of the average Feral or Domestic Pigeon, although some species are rather smaller or larger than this. They can be divided into four main groups of species. The first of these consists of the typical turtle doves which are characterised by having wing coverts and/or scapulars with dark centres and broad buff or chestnut fringes forming a brightly mottled or chequered pattern. To this group belong the Turtle Dove, *Streptopelia turtur*, the Eastern Turtle Dove *S. orientalis*, the Dusky Turtle Dove *S. lugens* and the Pink-bellied Turtle Dove *S. hypopyrrha*. All these forms are allopatric and replace one another geographically with the exception of the Eastern Turtle Dove and the Turtle Dove whose breeding ranges overlap in parts of Asia. There is evidence (Hartert, 1936) that the actual breeding areas of the two usually differ. This, however, appears not to be invariable and, at least in some parts of western Siberia, both may occur in the same habitat (Johansen, 1959) during the breeding season. Because of this it seems preferable not to treat them as members of a superspecies in spite of their close relationship.

The Dusky Turtle Dove and the Pink-bellied Turtle Dove inhabit high altitudes in, respectively, East Africa and Arabia, and West Africa. They may be conspecific but in view of their rather considerable differences and lack of information on their habits, calls and behaviour seem best treated as members of a superspecies. From their distribution it seems likely that they are most closely allied to the Turtle Dove in spite of the fact that in appearance the Pink-bellied Turtle Dove and the Arabian form of the Dusky Turtle Dove show slightly more resemblance to *S. orientalis* than they do to *S. turtur*.

The next group consists of the ring-necked turtle doves or ringdoves. In Eurasia these are represented by the Collared Dove, *S. decaocto*, the Javanese Collared Dove, *S. bitorquata* its geographical representative in the islands of south-east Asia and the very distinct Red Collared Dove, *S. tranquebarica*. In Africa there has been considerable speciation within this group and five 'good' species occur. The Eurasian Collared Dove is there represented by the African Collared Dove, *S. roseogrisea*; they have very differently sounding calls besides slighter morphological differences and therefore seem better treated as members of a superspecies than as conspecific. It is probable that the White-winged Collared Dove *S. reichenowi* is also closely related to and a geographical representative of *decaocto* and *roseogrisea* although it has certainly now evolved to the point of being a very distinct species.

The Mourning Collared Dove, *S. decipiens* also appears to be closely related to *decaocto* and *roseogrisea* and produces fertile hybrids with the domesticated form of the latter in captivity. In a wild state, however, its range overlaps that of the much smaller African Collared Dove and also those of the Red-eyed Dove, *S. semitorquata*, the Vinaceous Dove *S. vinacea* and the Ring-necked Dove, *S. capicola*. Although very similar in general plumage pattern and appearance these species all show small but constant morphological differences, a considerable degree of ecological separation and have differently sounding calls. It is probable that in this group the calls, particularly the advertising coo, function as important isolating mechanisms.

The Ring-necked Dove and the Vinaceous Dove are usually considered separate species although Grote (1927) treated them as conspecific and gave cogent reasons for so doing. The two are largely and perhaps entirely allopatric. I can find no certain records of both species occurring at the same place although Jackson (1938) states definitely that both occur together at Mubende, in Uganda, and the general distributions given for the two by Mackworth-Praed and Grant (1957) appear to indicate some overlap. Any actual overlap, however, would appear to be marginal at most and probably does not involve breeding birds.

In appearance the Vinaceous Dove differs from the Ring-necked Dove in being slightly smaller, brighter in colour and with an entirely pinkish head. The precise pattern of the black and white on the outermost tail feathers – often given as a diagnostic distinguishing character – is of doubtful value since occasional individuals of either form may approach the other in this feature. With the possible exception of this tail marking there are no significant differences of colour pattern between the two. The above differences to some extent parallel these between two other forms of the northern savannas, the Black-billed Wood Dove *Turtur abyssinicus* and the Yellow-bellied Green Pigeon *Treron waalia*, and their nearest relatives the Green-spotted Wood Dove, *T. chalcospilos* and the African Pigeon *T. calva*.

Grote (1927) claims that the form found in the eastern Congo near Lake Kivu *S. capicola dryas*, is intermediate between *vinacea* and *capicola*. I have seen no specimens from the type locality of this race (which some subsequent authors have considered unseparable from *S. c. tropica*) but some specimens from Unyoro, in western Uganda in the British Museum (Natural History) appear somewhat intermediate in their rather dark coloration, strong tinge of grey on the hind crown and amount of white on the outer-most tail feathers.   In general, however, they resemble *vinacea* more strongly than they do *capicola*.

On morphological characters and their distribution the evidence is in favour of treating the Vinaceous and Ring-necked Doves as conspecific.   However, most descriptions of their voices suggest that at least their respective advertising coos differ in sound.   Jackson says that they can be immediately identified by this voice difference and Harwin's (1963) observation confirms this.   This suggests, in view of the apparent importance of vocal differences as isolating mechanisms among the African ring-necked turtle doves, that *vinacea* and *capicola* may have reached specific level.   In view of this it seems preferable to treat them here as members of a superspecies rather than as races.   This decision has, admittedly, been reached largely from practical considerations because it will be less confusing for the reader to have the relevant information for each form under separate headings.   Particularly will this be so for anyone who is able to observe the two forms in field or aviary and wishes to compare his own observations with those already made by others.

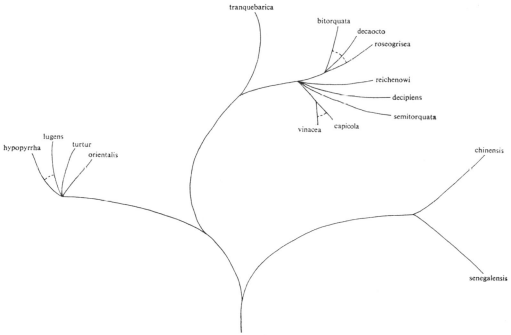

Fig. D.3:   Presumed relationships of species in the genus *Streptopelia*.   In this and subsequent dendrograms a single dotted line connects members of the same superspecies.

The Madagascar Turtle Dove, *S. picturata* of Madagascar and the islands of the Indian Ocean differs from other *Streptopelia* species in its heavier build and longer legs, both characteristics often evolved in island forms.   The bifurcated display plumage on its neck is much like that of the Spotted and Laughing Doves.   I think this resemblance is, however, due to convergence and that it is probably most nearly related to *S. turtur* and its allies, as is suggested by its rather long and pointed wings.   One would not expect to find such wings on an island species derived from a shorter-winged mainland form.

The Spotted Dove *S. chinensis* and the Laughing Dove, *S. senegalensis* stand rather apart from the rest.   They appear to lack any equivalent to the excitement cry which, in differing forms, is so character-istic an utterance of the other turtle doves.   They show some resemblance to the *Geopelia* species in their rather long tails and short wings but this is almost certainly due to convergence and not to any very close relationship.

The differences between the Chinese and Indian forms of the Spotted Dove are marked and are com-parable to those between such species as, for example, the Turtle Dove and Eastern Turtle Dove.   In the present case, however, intermediate forms connect the two and they must be treated as conspecific.

The turtle doves are primarily ground feeders although they rest, roost and perch in bushes and trees. Most of them are strong, fast flyers and some are highly migratory. They form a rather discrete group of pigeons. Apart from *Aplopelia* (q.v.) their nearest relatives seem likely to be the typical pigeons of the genus *Columba*.

REFERENCES

GROTE, H. 1927. Zur Kenntnis der Formenkreises *Streptopelia vinacea*. *Verh. Orn. Ges. Bay.* **17** : 205–206.
HARTERT, E. 1936. *Die Vögel der Paläarktischen Fauna, Ergänzungsband.* **5** : 458.
HARWIN, R. M. 1963. Thoughts on a five week stay in Northern Nigeria. *Bokmakerie* **15** : 10–12.
JACKSON, F. J. 1938. *The birds of Kenya Colony and the Uganda Protectorate.* **1** : 461–463.
JOHANSEN, H. 1959. Die Vogelfauna Westsibiriens : Pt. 3. *Journ. f. Orn.* **100** : 417–432.

TURTLE DOVE   *Streptopelia turtur*

Columba turtur Linnaeus, Syst. Nat., Ed. 10, 1, 1758, p. 164.

DESCRIPTION : Slightly smaller than a Barbary Dove and slightly lighter in build with proportionately longer and more pointed wings. Forehead pale bluish grey shading to medium blue-grey, sometimes suffused with drab, on nape and hind neck. Throat pinkish white, sides of face light pinkish grey. Lower throat and breast a delicate mauve-pink shading to pure white on belly and under tail coverts and pale grey on flanks. A patch of black, silver-tipped feathers on sides of neck which in life usually appear as more or less diagonal black and silver lines. Mantle light drab brown, often tinged grey and with ill-defined darker feather centres giving slight mottled appearance. Inner wing coverts and scapulars bright orange-buff spotted with black ; this effect due to individual feathers having black, drab-edged centres and broad orange-buff fringes. Outer wing coverts and underwing bluish grey. Primaries, outer secondaries and primary coverts dark dull grey or blackish grey. Lower back and rump drab, tinged blue-grey on median area and largely blue-grey at sides. Upper tail coverts and central tail feathers greyish drab. Outer tail feathers dark grey with broad white terminal bar, outermost pair with white outer webs also. Underside of tail black and white. Irides golden, deep golden yellow or light orange. Orbital skin dark reddish purple. Bill blackish, with purplish tinge, tip slightly paler. Legs and feet purplish red.

Female sometimes as bright as male but usually a little duller and paler. Grey of head and pink of breast often suffused with drab. Edges of wing coverts less clear and reddish. Juvenile duller and browner, generally light drab with buffish, reddish buff or rufous tips to most cover feathers. Markings of wing coverts obscure and those on side of neck absent or only slightly indicated by area of greyer, darker-based feathers. Blue grey of outer-wing coverts is, however, only a little less distinct than in adult. Juvenile male more reddish in hue than most juvenile females.

The above description is of the nominate form *S. t. turtur* which breeds in western Europe. Those breeding in north Africa average rather brighter in colour, chiefly due to rather broader orange-buff edges to the wing coverts. They are usually included under the same subspecific name *S. t. arenicola* as those breeding in Western Asia. This latter tends to be slightly smaller in size and paler in colour, at least so far as the populations breeding in Palestine and Persia are concerned. Those breeding in Yarkand and nearby regions of Turkestan are larger and richer in colour, the wing coverts broadly tipped a deep orange buff and the breast a deep mauve-pink and with the mantle orange-rufous rather than drab. Those breeding in the Ahaggar Massif of the Central Sahara and the oases of Fezzan and Tibesti, *S. turtur hoggara*, are very rich in colour, having very broad deep orange-buff (male) or golden-buff (female) fringes to the wing coverts and some sandy tips or suffusion on head, rump, and, in some females, breast also. This tendency is still more developed in the form *S. turtur isabellinus* which breeds in the Dakla Oases and, at least at times, also in the Nile Delta and the Fayum. In this the male is predominantly of a rich dark sandy orange shade above and on the crown and deep pink on the breast and the female a paler sandy buff hue and with her lighter pink breast often suffused with buff.

FIELD CHARACTERS: Buff to bright rufous, black-spotted wing coverts distinguish adult from all *Streptopelia* species except Eastern Turtle Dove which is larger and darker. Broad white edges to tail and small size from all *Columba* species. In flight white belly distinguishes from Collared Dove, when seen from below.

DISTRIBUTION AND HABITAT: Breeds in Europe, Madeira, the Canary Islands, Northern Africa, the Saharan oases, south-western Asia from the Kirghiz Steppes and Turkestan south to Iraq, Persia, Afghanistan, the Fayum and, possibly not regularly, in parts of the Nile Delta. Migrates through the Mediterranean regions, the near east and Arabia. Most, perhaps all, winter in northern Africa south of the Sahara but north of the Equator.

Inhabits country that gives a combination of trees, bushes or scrub for roosting and nesting and ground that is bare or covered with scattered, sparse or short vegetation for feeding purposes. Thus is found in open woodlands, cultivated or arable country with scrub, copses or tall hedges and, in England at least, especially in districts at the stage where agriculture is fighting a slowly losing battle against gravel extraction, building and other forms of 'progress' and woodlands have been destroyed but have re-burgeoned into scrub. In Central Asia also in very arid areas provided there is some cover and water available. In oases among date groves, in almond and apricot orchards. Locally in gardens also in Europe.

FEEDING AND GENERAL HABITS: Feeds mostly, if not entirely, on the ground. Takes seeds of weeds, especially Fumitory (*Fumaria*), cultivated grain when available, leaves of sainfoin and probably other leaves and buds to some extent, small snails and other invertebrates. Its distribution in England largely coincides with that of the Fumitory on whose seeds it largely feeds (Murton, 1964). Also takes fallen seeds of Scots Pine, and perhaps other trees, from ground in open woodland. I have flushed Turtle Doves from trees swarming with smooth green caterpillars and think they may have been eating them as when I offered these caterpillars to captive Turtle Doves they ate them eagerly. In Britain, and perhaps elsewhere, often comes into stackyards and about poultry runs to pick up scattered grains.

Flight swift and powerful but with a rather jerky appearance, the bird appearing to 'fight the air'. Walks and runs nimbly on ground. On migration often or usually in small, rather 'loose knit' flocks, at other times usually in pairs or singly but many will aggregate at a good feeding area which appears to be often discovered by watching and following others of their species.

NESTING: Usual pigeon nest in tree or shrub, usually from three to eight feet above ground but sometimes higher. In Turkestan often nests inside temporarily deserted houses (Grote, 1920). Often many pairs nest near each other, especially when a copse with many suitable nest sites is situated in otherwise rather open country that offers good food supplies or in orchards in oases. Two white eggs.

In Britain two broods probably usual (if both successful), the first started soon after arrival in early May. In Dahkla oases many nests with eggs in March (Meinertzhagen, 1930) and breeding in Tibesti oases in April (Guichard, 1955).

Incubation period 13–14 days. Young can fly at 11 to 12 days if fit. Distraction display in which bird perches near or walks with wildly beating wings or shows impeded flight common when flushed from hatching eggs or small young.

VOICE: The advertising coo is the purring 'Cōōrr-coōrr' or 'Tūrr-tūrr' from which the species' name derives. The nest call is a variant of this in which three coos, of which the middle one is shorter, are given at a time, 'Cōōrr-cŏŏr-cōōr'. Sometimes, however, this form is given also as an apparent alternative to the more usual advertising coo. The display coo is a hurried Crŏŏr(wa) crŏŏr(wa) crŏŏr(wa) in time with the rapid bobbing movements of the bowing display. The cooing of the female is hoarser and less musical as well as less loud than that of the male and less often uttered.

The excitement cry is a short, percussive or popping note suggestive of that made by the sudden withdrawal of a cork from a bottle. It is used less freely than but in similar situations to the homologous excitement cries of the Barbary and other ring-necked doves. The distress call is a panting gasp, rather higher pitched than in *Columba* species, in extreme terror as when a timid individual is roughly seized, it may be intensified almost to a scream.

DISPLAY: The bowing display consists of a series of rapid bobbing bows; at the culmination of each bow the bird's head and bill are at approximately right angles to the substrate. The erected display plumage of the neck forms a black and silver ruff on either side of head. In display flight towers up and then glides down with wings and tail outspread; sometimes may glide around high in the air for some time before re-alighting. Aggressive and parading postures as in Barbary Dove (q.v.). Copulation usually preceded by parading and displacement preening behind wing by male (or both) and 'billing' in which pair appear merely to 'fence' with their bills for a moment and female does not insert her bill into male's. Immediately after copulation male stands in a peculiar erect penguin-like posture with neck feathers erected and female 'parades' or turns round on perch in parading posture.

OTHER NAMES: European Turtle Dove; Common Turtle Dove; Isabelline Turtle Dove; (the desert forms).

REFERENCES

GROTE. H. 1920. Ornithologische Beobachtungen aus dem sudlichen Uralgebeit (Orenburg). *Journ. f. Orn.* **68**: 33–70.
GUICHARD, K. M. 1955. The birds of Fezzan and Tibesti. *Ibis* **97**: 393–424.
MEINERTZHAGEN, R. 1930. *Nicoll's Birds of Egypt* **2**: 508–509. London.
MURTON, R. K. *et al.* 1964. The feeding habits of the Woodpigeon *Columba palumbus*, Stock Dove *Columba oenas* and Turtle Dove *Streptopelia turtur*. *Ibis* **106**: 174–188.

DUSKY TURTLE DOVE   *Streptopelia lugens*

Columba lugens Rüppell, Neue Wirbelth., Vög., 1837, p. 64, pl. 22, F.2.

DESCRIPTION: About size of Barbary Dove. Proportions as Turtle Dove together with which, and *S. hypopyrrhus*, it forms a superspecies. Throat pale buff. Head, neck and underparts dark bluish grey with a lavender tinge, black patch on side of neck and an ill-defined pinkish tinged area on the lower breast. Mantle, back, some of the inner wing coverts, central area of rump and upper tail coverts very dark brownish grey, most of the feathers having lighter greyish or slightly rufescent fringes. Inner secondaries and inner greater coverts broadly edged with orange-buff or light chestnut on outer webs. Outer secondaries, primary coverts and primaries greyish black with narrow pale edges. Central tail feathers dark brownish grey; outer ones black broadly tipped pale grey. Irides brownish orange, orange or golden; orbital skin purple, purplish red or blue grey intermixed with purple. Bill black, purplish black or dark grey, usually with paler tip. Legs and feet dark purple, purplish red or brownish red. In life the plumage has a strong bluish sheen and the bird appears predominantly a deep greyish blue except for the bright orange-buff wing markings and the black neck patches

Sexes nearly alike but female tends to be a little paler and duller and sometimes has yellow irides. Juvenile much paler and browner, a general dark drab with pale rufous fringes to most feathers and the inner primaries, as well as the inner secondaries, broadly edged with rufous. The above description is of the African form *S. l. lugens*. The Arabian form *S. lugens bishaensis* is a little larger and duller in colour.

DISTRIBUTION AND HABITAT: Eastern Africa from the eastern Belgian Congo to Ethiopia and Nyasaland. Also Arabia, in the wooded mountains of the Yemen. Inhabits forests, woodlands, gardens and cultivated regions with clumps of trees, usually at high altitudes. Also in the bamboo and heather zones at high altitudes in Kenya. Sometimes in towns and villages provided there are plenty of trees or bushes.

FEEDING AND GENERAL HABITS: Feeds chiefly on the ground, both on the forest floor and in open spaces and including cultivated fields and gardens. Occasionally feeds perched on bushes or growing crops. Recorded taking weed seeds, cultivated grain and sunflower seed, bulbous roots, small molluscs, fallen berries and young leaves from aromatic shrubs. Usually in pairs, singly or in small parties but large flocks sometimes recorded. From descriptions, however, these flocks may have been merely aggregations at good feeding grounds.

NESTING: Usual pigeon nest in tree or shrub. Two white eggs. Incubation has been recorded as being by the female only, fed on the nest by the male (Van Someren, 1956). I think, however, that this must have been a case either of incorrect observation or else of abnormal behaviour on the part of the particular pair concerned. Breeding season probably prolonged. Has been recorded breeding most months between December and June inclusive (Mackworth-Praed and Grant, 1957).

VOICE: The advertising coo has been described as 'a monotonous deep koo-oor, koo-oor' (Curry-Lindahl, 1960); 'a deep slow bi-syllable note "cu-oor, cu-oor"' (Van Someren, 1956). Others describe it in similar terms. What may be a different call is described as ' . . .deep and harsh . . . usually of four syllables, the second larger and higher pitched than the others'. (Mackworth-Praed and Grant, 1957). Van Someren (*op. cit.*) also recorded a low purring alarm call when a bird brooding young saw a dog nearby.

DISPLAY: Display flight similar to that of Turtle Dove (q.v.) (Cheesman, 1935).

OTHER NAMES: Black Dove; Pink-breasted Dove.

REFERENCES

CHEESMAN, R. E. 1935. On a collection of Birds from North-western Abyssinia, pt. 2. *Ibis* 5: Thirteenth Series, 297–239.
CURRY-LINDAHL, K. 1960. *Ecological Studies on Mammals, Birds, Reptiles and Amphibians in the eastern Belgian Congo*.
    Pt. 2 (Report No. 1 of the Swedish Congo Expeditions 1951–2 and 1958–9), pp. 102–103.
MACKWORTH-PRAED, C. W. & GRANT, C. H. B. 1957. *The African Handbook of Birds*, Series 1 1: 470.
PITWELL, L. R. & GOODWIN, D. 1964. Some observations on pigeons in Addis Ababba. *Bull Brit. Orn. Ch.* 84: 41–45.
VAN SOMEREN, V. G. L. 1956. Days with birds. *Feldiana: Zoology* 38: 131–136. Chicago Nat. Hist. Mus.

PINK-BELLIED TURTLE DOVE   *Streptopelia hypopyrrha*

Turtur hypopyrrhus Reichenow, Orn. Monatsb; 18, 1910, p. 174

DESCRIPTION: In general appearance rather intermediate between *S. turtur* and *S. lugens* but probably more closely related to the latter with which it may be conspecific. About size of Barbary Dove or a little larger. Forehead, face and throat silver grey. Crown, nape, neck and breast bluish grey; black patch on side of neck as in *S. lugens*. Lower breast and belly dark salmon pink with a purplish tinge. Ventral regions, flanks, sides of rump, underwing and under tail coverts dark bluish grey. Mantle, back, rump and upper tail coverts dark greyish brown with faint reddish buff fringes. Inner wing coverts and inner secondaries blackish brown with tawny buff fringes, outer wing coverts with grey and buff or greyish fringes. Primaries and outer secondaries dark greyish brown with narrow pale fringes to outer webs. Irides with pink or orange inner ring and dark outer ring; orbital skin dark red. Bill black. Feet and legs purplish red.

I have not seen a female or juvenile of this species although one of the three male specimens examined retains a few juvenile feathers. Most probably the female and young differ from the adult male in the same degree and manner as in other turtle doves.

DISTRIBUTION AND HABITAT: Known, so far, only from the highlands near the source of the Benue river in Cameroon and the similarly high Bauchi plateau and Pankshin plateau in Nigeria. Inhabits wooded slopes and ravines (Bates, 1930) and in Pankshin is fairly common wherever there are trees growing along the banks of streams (McLelland, 1943).

FEEDING AND GENERAL HABITS: No information.

NESTING: Usual flimsy pigeon nest, often over water. Two white eggs. Nests with eggs or young have been found in September, October, November and March (Smith 1966, Woods 1967).

VOICE: What is probably the advertising coo is described by Bates as 'low heavy-toned cooing' and by McLelland as deep and reminiscent of that of the Wood Pigeon.

DISPLAY: No information.

OTHER NAMES: Adamawa Turtle Dove.

REFERENCES
BATES, G. L. 1930. *Handbook of the birds of West Africa*, p. 11. London.
McLELLAND, V. S. 1943. Letter in British Museum (Bird Room) files.
SMITH, V. W. 1966. Breeding records for the Plateau Province over 3,000 feet, 1957–1966. *Nigerian Orn. Soc. Bull.* 3, No. **12**: 81.
WOODS, P. J. E. 1967. Some notes on the birds of the Kigom Hills on the western edge of the Jos Plateau. *Nigerian Orn. Soc. Bull.*, 4, Nos **13–14**: 30.

EASTERN TURTLE DOVE   *Streptopelia orientalis*

Columba orientalis Latham, Ind. Orn., 2, 1790, p. 606.

DESCRIPTION: Very similar in general appearance to the Turtle Dove and with an almost identical colour pattern. Differs in being larger (most forms), rather more heavily built with more rounded, less pointed wings and darker (most forms) or more rufous in coloration.

Between Barbary Dove and Feral Pigeon in size. Markings similar to those of Turtle Dove (q.v.). Display plumage of neck tipped pale bluish grey not silver and tail tips light grey and less extensive than the white areas on *S. turtur*. Forehead bluish grey shading to brownish grey washed with rufous on nape and with pinkish on face. Throat pale buff shading to dull greyish pink on neck and breast, dull salmon pink or pinkish buff on belly, whitish on ventral regions and pale grey on under tail coverts. Hind neck dark grey with dull rufous-buff feather fringes, mantle similar but feather centres blackish. Wing coverts, scapulars and inner secondaries with the dark centres more extensive than Turtle Dove and edges rich orange-buff or light-chestnut on scapulars and innermost secondaries only, elsewhere the rufescent colour usually tinged with or largely replaced by bluish grey or the feather having a black centre, grey subterminal area and narrow pinkish fawn border. The general effect is to make the folded wings look darker and less distinctly marked than those of *S. turtur*. Primaries blackish with pale edges. Underwing and rump dark bluish grey. Upper tail coverts dark grey with pale grey tips. Central tail feathers dark blackish grey or brownish grey. Outer ones blackish with pale grey tips and web of outermost largely pale grey. Irides orange, orange-red, light red or golden; orbital skin dark purple or dark pinkish. Legs and feet purple, reddish purple or dark pink. Bill blackish, dull purplish or grey with paler horn-coloured tip and purplish or dark red at base and gape edges.

Female similar to male but usually duller on breast and neck which are brownish grey tinged with salmony-buff rather than greyish pink. Juvenile similar to that of Turtle Dove, but darker, generally drab greyish brown with conspicuous rufous-buff fringes to feathers of back, wings and breast.

The above description is of the nominate form *S. o. orientalis* from Siberia, China, Japan and Formosa. The forms breeding on the Riu Kiu Islands, *S. orientalis stimpsoni* and on Formosa, *S. orientalis ori* are very similar. The form breeding in Burma, Assam and Bengal *S. orientalis agricola* is a little smaller in size and more reddish in coloration. This tendency to reddish colour and smaller size is even more pronounced in the form breeding in peninsular India, *S. orientalis erythrocephala*. This form is about the size of a Barbary Dove. Its head and neck, except for the black and grey display plumage, are rich pinkish rufous, the broad edges to its wing coverts are deep orange rufous and its breast a deep rusty pink. The form breeding in the western Himalayas from Kashmir east to the central valley of Nepal, *S. orientalis meena* is only slightly smaller than the nominate form but paler and brighter in colour with broader, more golden-buff or light rufous fringes to its wing coverts; white belly and under tail coverts and greyish-white instead of grey tips to the tail feathers.

The above described forms intergrade and in many areas populations occur intermediate between two or more of those described above. Males only have been described, the sexual differences being comparable to those described for the nominate form.

DISTRIBUTION AND HABITAT: Asia from western Siberia east to Manchuria, Sakhalien Island and Japan south to southern India, Burma and the Indo-chinese countries. The populations breeding in the northern parts of the species' range or at high elevations are migratory, wintering south of their breeding areas.

Inhabits wooded regions, particularly light or open forest near to cultivated or open areas. Also in open regions with some trees or bushes, parks, large gardens and dense forest, the latter probably only when more open areas are within easy flying distance. Much more often in or near cultivated country than in areas unaffected by man's agricultural activities.

FEEDING AND GENERAL HABITS: Feeds on the ground, principally on seeds, including cultivated grains, especially rice, gleaned after the fields have been harvested. Usually in pairs or singly, sometimes in small flocks. Large numbers may gather on good feeding grounds, such as rice stubbles, but in such cases usually arrive and depart singly or in pairs. May form flocks when on migration (Ali, 1962). Flight swift and strong with wing beats appearing more jerky than those of Feral Pigeon.

NESTING: Usual pigeon nest in tree or shrub. Two white eggs. Where much persecuted by man usually nests in dense cover well away from its feeding grounds in the cultivation (e.g., Jahn, 1942). Breeding season restricted to late spring and summer in colder parts of its range but prolonged elsewhere.

VOICE: What appears from the contexts to be the advertising coo has been described (to list only the more divergent transcriptions) as a deep sounding 'Grugrúo-ho-ho' several times repeated and ending in a short 'Ho' (Jahn, 1942), 'a very deep and sonorous Coo-cooroo-coocoo' (La Touche, 1932), 'a hoarse, rather mournful 'Goor . . . gur-grugroo'' (Ali, 1962) and a 'repeated "Ze-ze-poh-poh"' (Yamashina, 1961). The advertising coo of a bird of the nominate form that I heard was a series of four coos 'cōo-cōo, cŏŏ-cŏŏ' the first two with an upward inflection, the second two downward inflected and lower in pitch. Probably there is a certain amount of geographical or individual variation in this call. Blewitt (in Baker, 1913) wrote of a captive pair 'when irritated they utter a peculiarly loud hissing kind of note'; probably this is the excitement cry.

DISPLAY: From descriptions of several of the above-listed authors it is evident that the display flight is similar to that of the Turtle Dove (q.v.). I have seen no sufficiently detailed descriptions of other displays.

OTHER NAMES: Rufous Turtle Dove; Mountain Turtle Dove; Japanese Turtle Dove.

REFERENCES

ALI, S. 1962. *The Birds of Sikkim*, pp. 44–45. Oxford.
BAKER, E. C. S. 1913. *Indian Pigeons and Doves*, pp. 194. London
JAHN, H. 1942. Zur Oekologie und Biologie der Vögel Japans. *Journ. f. Orn.* **90**: 1–301 (266–267).
LA TOUCHE, J. D. D. 1932. *A handbook of the birds of Eastern China* **2**: Pt. 3, 213–214. London.
SHÄFER, E. 1938. Ornithologische Ergebnisse zweier Forschungsreisen nach Tibet. *Journ. f. Orn.* **86**: Sonderheft, 99–100.
YAMASHINA, Y. 1961. *Birds in Japan*, p. 165. Tokyo.

JAVANESE COLLARED DOVE   *Streptopelia bitorquata*

Columba bitorquata Temminck, in Knip, Les Pigeons, 1810, les colombes, p. 86, pl. 40.

DESCRIPTION: About the size of a Barbary Dove or slightly larger and with, proportionately, slightly longer tail. Forehead pale grey shading to medium blue-grey on crown and nape. Broad black white-edged half collar on hind neck, the white edging being especially prominent at the front and sides. Rest of neck and upper mantle dark wine-pink, often with a rusty tinge. This shades to a slightly paler mauvish pink on breast to greyish on the flanks and white or greyish white on belly and under tail coverts. Back, inner wing coverts and inner secondaries and upper tail coverts drab brown. Rest of wing coverts dark blue-grey. Primary coverts, primaries and outer secondaries blackish. Rump dark blue grey, more or less suffused with drab brown. Central tail feathers drab brown, outer ones pale grey with basal third dark grey. Outer web of outermost tail feathers entirely pale grey. Underside of tail greyish white basal third black. Irides yellow, orange or orange-red. Bill blackish or dark grey, red at gape. Feet purplish red or pinkish red. Juvenile duller and paler with the wine-red replaced by dusky fawn and the neck markings indistinct and at sides of neck only.

The above description is of the nominate form, *S. b. bitorquata*, which inhabits Java, Bali, Lombok, Sumbawa, Flores, Solor and Timor. The form found in the Philippine Islands, Sulu Archipelago and (probably as a result of introduction) the Marianne Islands and North Borneo, *S. b. dussumieri* is generally duller and paler in colour. It has a pale pinkish grey head, the half collar is dark grey and greenish with only an indistinct greyish white edging in front and a more strongly rusty or coppery tinge on the hind neck below the collar. The outer web of its outer most tail feather is mainly white not whitish grey and its belly and under tail coverts creamy white. Its irides are often orange-brown or brownish red rather than pure orange-red or orange.

DISTRIBUTION AND HABITAT: Java, Bali, Lombok, Sumbawa, Flores, Solor, Timor, the Philippine Islands and Sulu Archipelago. Also Marianne Islands where probably introduced. Formerly (and possibly still in small numbers) in North Borneo, presumably as a result of introduction.

Frequents open country with trees, cultivated areas and the outskirts of villages.

FEEDING AND GENERAL HABITS: Little recorded in spite of its being a very common bird of inhabited areas in the Philippines and elsewhere. Feeds largely on seeds picked up from the ground. This species is probably most closely related to *S. decaocto* and may, perhaps, prove to be conspecific with it, although in colour it has more resemblance to the African species *S. semitorquata* and *S. decipiens*.

NESTING: Usual pigeon nest in a low tree, bush, or shrub. Two white eggs.

VOICE: What is, probably, the advertising coo has been described as a very clear 'tuk-m-m-m' repeated several times at moderate intervals (Ripley and Rabor, 1956).

DISPLAY: No information.

OTHER NAMES: Philippine Collared Dove; Java Turtle Dove; Java Ring Dove; Philippine Turtle Dove; Red-neck Ring Dove.

REFERENCE

RIPLEY, S. D. & RABOR, D. S. 1956. Birds from the Canlaon Volcano in the highlands of Negros Island in the Philippines. *Condor* **58**: 283–291.

COLLARED DOVE *Streptopelia decaocto*

Columba risoria L. var. *decaocto* Frivaldsky, K. magyar tudos Tarsasag Evkonyvi, 3, 1834–36 (1838), pt. 3, p. 183, pl. 8.

This species is remarkable for the way it has spread north-westwards across Europe in recent years.

Stresemann and Nowak (1958) and Fisher (1953) give detailed accounts of this spread up to the dates concerned, but the advance continues still to some extent. It now (1969) breeds regularly in Great Britain, and is widespread but local in distribution.

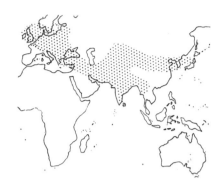

DESCRIPTION: A little larger than a Barbary Dove and with a proportionately longer tail than most (but not all) Barbaries have. Coloration, as in the African Collared Dove (q.v.) but slightly darker; under wing coverts usually light grey, though sometimes nearly white, and with the black on the outer tail feathers more extensive. This description applies to the nominate form, *S. d. decaocto*, of India, the Middle East, Europe, China and Korea. The form from Chinese Turkestan, *S. decaocto stoliczkae* is slightly larger and paler in colour; that from the Irrawaddy Valley of Burma, *S. decaocto xanthocyclus*, is darker and has bright yellow instead of whitish orbital skin.

FIELD IDENTIFICATION: Greyish fawn dove with longish, white-edged tail and dark primaries. Greyer coloration and different voice distinguishes it from Barbary Dove.

DISTRIBUTION AND HABITAT: India, the Middle East, south-west to southern Palestine, much of Europe, including Britain, the coastal regions of the Oman peninsula in eastern Arabia; Chinese Turkestan; northern, central and western China, Korea, and a small area of Japan. In India, Ceylon and Burma and elsewhere in Asia, inhabits arid country with trees or scrub usually near to cultivation. Elsewhere it is more dependent on man's activities being usually found only in or near towns, villages or cultivation. It is thought to have been originally introduced from India into northern China and Korea and perhaps also into the Middle East. It is known that the Japanese population was introduced from China. Its spread north-westward across Europe and, indeed, its survival during winter in these regions has been made possible only because of its reliance on man for food in winter.

FEEDING AND GENERAL HABITS: Feeds chiefly on seeds picked up from the ground but also takes breadcrumbs and other human food, other greenstuff, berries and, in Europe, cherries. Probably also takes some invertebrate animals. In Europe almost parasitic on man, relying largely on grain spilled about goods-yards or fed to poultry. Even in Turkestan, which it almost certainly inhabited prior to the arrival of agricultural man, it would appear now to be largely dependant on man for food in winter.

NESTING: Usual pigeon nest on tree, bush, or ledge of a building. Two white eggs. In Germany breeds from March to October. In India apparently at almost any time when food conditions are suitable. Incubation 14–16 days. Fledging period 15–17 days but young often return to nest after fledging. Distraction display frequent.

VOICE: Advertising coo a loud tri-syllabic 'kŏŏ-kōō-kŏŏk'. Nest call similar but often softer and with last syllable more drawn out. Display coo 'kōō-kōō-kŏŏ' the last note very short and much less loud. Subject to some individual variation. Excitement cry a long-drawn, rather nasal call, prone to some variation, difficult to describe but has been likened variously to a faint version of the Peacock's scream, mewing or snarling. A very intense version of this cry is uttered during the display flight.

DISPLAY: Exactly the same as the Barbary Dove except for the differences of the vocal accompaniments.

Display flight more frequent and spectacular however, the bird towering up with clapping wings and then gliding down, often in a spiral, with wings and tail outspread.

OTHER NAMES: Indian Ringdove; Collared Turtle Dove; Ringdove; Eastern Ringdove; Eurasian Ringdove.

REFERENCES

DYRCZ, A. 1956. On the biology and distribution of the Collared Dove, *Streptopelia decaocto* Friv. in Poland. *Zool. Poloniae*, Vol. 1, Fasc. 4.

FISHER, J. 1953. The Collared Turtle Dove in Europe. *British Birds* **46**: 153–181.

HOFFSTETTER, F. B. 1952. Das Verhalten einer Türkentauben-Population. *Journ. f. Orn.* **93**: 295–312.

—— 1954. Untersuchungen an einer Population der Türkentaube. *Journ. f. Orn.* **95**: 345–410.

STRESEMANN, E. & NOWAK, E. 1958. Die Ausbreitung der Türkentaube in Asien und Europa. *Journ. f. Orn.* **99**: 243–296.

BARBARY DOVE   *Streptopelia "risoria"*

Columba risoria Linnaeus, Syst. Nat., Ed. 10, 1, 1758, p. 165.

This bird is a long-domesticated form of the African Collared Dove *S. roseogrisa*. However, as it is usually, if incorrectly, given specific status under the name *risoria* and has, unlike its parent form, long been familiar to almost everyone interested in doves everywhere in the world and been the subject of large numbers of observations and experiments, there seems justification for treating it separately here.

DESCRIPTION: About half the size of the average Feral Pigeon, slightly larger than a Turtle Dove, and appreciably larger than a Mourning Dove. Wing and tail proportions usually as in the parental form but often with proportionately longer tail. It is possible, but unlikely, that this may be due to past hybridisation of domestic stock with *S. decaoto*. General coloration warm creamy buff shading to white or near white on chin, belly and under tail coverts. Some light grey along wing edge, primaries and primary coverts light drab grey. Near black and white patterning on undersides of tail feathers similar to wild form but dark areas sometimes less extensive. Black, white-edged half collar on neck. Irides ruby red, orbital skin pale greyish, feet purplish red, bill dark purplish black with silvery bloom. Juvenile paler and duller with faint pale fringes to most covert feathers, and dully greyish feet and irides that gradually change to the adult colour. In the case of the eyes, they become first yellowish and then orange during transitional stages. Exceptionally, the irides of adults may be orange.

A white variety with dark eyes, misleadingly called 'Java Dove' by bird dealers, is also common in domestication. Pink-eyed albinos and birds with 'silky' and otherwise abnormal feathering have been produced in laboratories in America and elsewhere but are, happily, not yet commonly distributed. The usual creamy buff colour must originally have arisen as a recessive mutation from the wild form. When Barbary Doves of the usual buff colour are crossed with any wild species of turtle dove the resultant hybrids usually show no trace of the pale creamy tint of the domestic parent although showing, in partial degree, its other characteristics. Thus the commonly-bred hybrid between the Barbary Dove and the Turtle Dove is, in colour, what one would expect if one had paired a wild African Collared Dove to a Turtle Dove. As is usual with pale or 'dilute' colour varieties the plumage of the Barbary Dove bleaches considerably if it is much exposed to sun and rain, the original warm brownish buff of the back and wing coverts becoming under such conditions almost white with – much of the time – a mottling of darker new feathers that have not yet weathered.

The sexes are, for all practical purposes, alike in colour. Actually males tend to be slightly paler, but this difference is of no value in sexing unless related birds in an identical state of plumage wear are being compared. (See Fig. 1.)

DISTRIBUTION AND HABIT: Domesticated. Often locally established in a feral or semi-feral condition but such colonies seldom prosper unless they are artificially fed and the wastage due to predation countered by liberation of young bred in captivity. A colony has however, existed for many years in the centre of Los Angeles, California, and the usually more delicate white variety was at one time said to be established in a wild state on the Pescadores Islands.

GENERAL BEHAVIOUR: When at liberty Barbary Doves show much greater activity than when caged. Flight, if over any distance, is swift but without giving the same impression of an impetuous fighting of the air as is the case with the Turtle Dove. More than any other domesticated bird the fear of large, strange or moving creatures seems to have been bred out of the Barbary Dove. Almost all individuals are naturally tame, never have any great fear of human beings, and can very easily be made absolutely hand-tame. The innate recognition and fear of birds of prey seems, however, to have been little if at all affected by domestication, and the hawk-escaping behaviour patterns are usually shown in perfect form when needed provided that the bird is in good health. One common response to the sudden near appearance of a hawk is to 'freeze', the bird still instinctively trusting to the protective coloration of the wild form in its natural setting although it itself is glaringly conspicuous against most English backgrounds.

NESTING: Usual pigeon nest, in any tray, bowl, open box or even on floor of cage. Two white eggs, first usually laid in evening and second in morning of next day but one. Incubation period about 14 days.

VOICE: The advertising coo is a mellow and, to my ears, extremely pleasing 'Kŏŏ, k'rrōō', or 'Kŏŏ, Kŏŏrōō', with an apparent inspiration afterwards, so that – particularly at close quarters – it often sounds more like 'Kŏŏ, k'rrōō(wa)'. The display coo and the nest call are closely similar, so much so that, allowing for individual variation, it does not seem to me to be possible to distinguish them.

The excitement cry is the well-known rather high-pitched jeering laugh that could be written as 'Heh-heh-heh'. I once had a male whose excitement cry was a single drawn-out note, very similar to that of the Collared Dove. A male that greets the appearance of its mate (or a stranger) with the excitement cry and then goes over into the bowing display often gives the most odd and comical sounding utterance intermediate between the excitement cry and the display coo during the transitional moments between the two forms of behaviour.

The cooing of the female is usually softer and with the trilling 'rr' sound perhaps rather more pronounced.

DISPLAY: In the bowing display the male bows deeply so that the bill is at approximately right angles to the ground at the lowest point of the bow. The black half collar is seen framing the lowered head when the displaying bird is viewed frontally. Nodding is rather ill-defined, usually only a slight downward movement of the head and bill and often so intermixed with the 'aiming' flight-intention movements as to be difficult to distinguish from them. Wing-twitching as in *Columba* species, is shown when nest-calling, but not (or not normally) by fighting individuals.

The display flight consists of towering up, clapping the wings, and then gliding downwards with wings and tail outspread, often in a half circle. In some individuals the instinct to perform this display seems to have died out through centuries of cage-breeding, and those individuals (a majority in my experience) that do use the display flight often do so in a much less spectacular and prolonged form than Turtle Doves or Collared Doves do, or, one suspects, their wild ancestors did.

OTHER NAMES: Blond Ringdove; Ringdove; Domestic Ringdove; Domestic Collared Dove; Fawn Dove; Java Dove.

REFERENCES

CRAIG, W. 1909. The Expressions of Emotion in the Pigeons. (1) The Blond Ring Dove (*Turtur risorius*). *Journ. Comp. Neurol. and Psychol.* **19**: 29–80.

GOODWIN, D. 1952. Observations on Barbary Doves kept at semi-liberty. *Avicult. Mag.* **58**: 205–219.

KLINGHAMMER, E. & HESS, E. H. 1964. Parental Feeding in Ring Doves (*Streptopelia roseogrisea*): Innate or Learned? *Zeitschr. f. Tierpsychol.* **21**: 338–347.

AFRICAN COLLARED DOVE *Streptopelia roseogrisea*

Columba roseogriseam Sundevall, Kongl. Sv. Vet. Akad. Hand. (n.s.) 2, No. 1, 1857, art. 3, p. 54.

DESCRIPTION: Slightly smaller than and similar in proportion to the shorter-tailed type of Barbary Dove. General coloration of upperparts a pale greyish fawn with pale blue-grey along the wing edge (outermost coverts and primary coverts). Two central tail feathers greyish drab, primaries nearly black when new but fading to dark greyish drab. Head, neck and breast pale mauve-pink shading to white on chin and belly. Under wing coverts white. Outer tail feathers grey tipped white above, near black tipped white below. Neck markings, soft parts, and differences of juvenile plumage similar to Barbary Dove, but irides a little darker red and orbital skin not quite so pale a grey. (See pl. 3)

The above description is of the nominate form *S. r. roseogrisea* which is found from east of Lake Chad through Darfur and the Sudan to western Ethiopia. The western form, *S. roseogrisea bornuensis*, tends to be slightly darker in colour and tinged with grey on the under wing coverts. The eastern form, *S. r. arabica*, from the coastal parts of Eritrea, northern Somaliland and Arabia is, as a rule, appreciably darker and with pale grey underwing coverts.

DISTRIBUTION AND HABITAT: Northern Africa, south of the Sahara, central and southern Arabia. Found in arid country with thorn scrub, acacia or other trees. Most abundant near wells or other sources of water, but sometimes found far away from any known surface water (Lynes, 1925).

FEEDING AND GENERAL HABITS: Recorded foods are seeds of grasses and other plants and cultivated grains. The latter picked up from where they have been spilled on tracks or roadways or about habitations or camp sites. Said (Lynes, 1925) to be able to go without water for considerable periods because it has been found far from water in arid country at times when there is no dew from which the bird could quench its thirst. This needs further investigation however, especially in view of its gathering round wells and very frequently drinking where it has the chance to do so. Probably as Bates (1927) suggested, it will be found that where apparently independent of water it is consuming berries with a high water content.

NESTING: Nests in trees or bushes often low down. Two white eggs. Nest of usual pigeon type. Recorded nesting January to June in the Sudan but probably breeds whenever food and water are easily available.

VOICE: Identical with that of its domesticated descendant, the Barbary Dove. This is the case at least, with the African populations. The possibility that the Arabian birds, which look more like the Eurasian Collared Dove, may also be closer to it in voice must be considered.

DISPLAY: As in the Barbary Dove but, probably, the display flight is given in more complete form than is usual with the domestic bird.

OTHER NAMES : Rose-grey Turtle dove ; Pink-headed Dove.

REFERENCES

BATES, G. L. 1927. Notes on some Birds of Cameroon the Lake Chad Region : Their Status and Breeding-times. *Ibis* Twelfth Series, **3** : 1–64.

LYNES, H. 1925. On the Birds of North and Central Darfur, with notes on the West-central Kordofan and North Nuba provinces of British Sudan. *Ibis* : Twelfth Series, **1** : 541–590.

MACKWORTH-PRAED, C. W. & GRANT, C. H. B. 1957. *African Handbook of Birds*, Series 1, vol. 1.

SMITH, K. D. 1957. An annotated check list of the birds of Eritrea. *Ibis* **99** : 307–337.

WHITE-WINGED COLLARED DOVE　　　　　*Streptopelia reichenowi*

Turtur reichenowi Erlanger, Orn. Monatsb., 9, 1901, p. 182.

 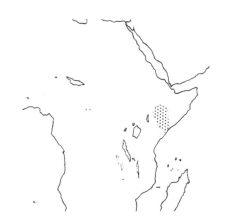

DESCRIPTION : Slightly smaller than a Barbary Dove and similar in proportions. Head dark bluish grey, some of the feathers tipped brownish, shading to paler bluish grey on face, breast, and flanks and creamy white on throat, belly and under tail coverts. Upperparts dull earth brown, a broad black half-collar dividing the grey head from the brown mantle. Outer wing coverts pale blue grey with broad whitish outer edges to most feathers forming a conspicuous white band across the open wing. Primaries and primary coverts blackish. Central tail feathers earth brown, others brown edged grey and tipped white. Underside of tail greyish white, basal third blackish. Irides silvery orange or yellowish. Bill blackish. Feet and legs pink.

The female has the grey areas more suffused with brown. The juvenile is paler and browner with buff or tawny fringes to most feathers.

DISTRIBUTION AND HABITAT : Occurs in southern Abyssinia, the Juba River Valley in Somaliland, and near the Daua River in Kenya. Found among Borassus palms near water.

FEEDING AND GENERAL HABITS : Little recorded. Evidently feeds on the ground and largely on seeds like most other turtle doves.

NESTING : Recorded nesting in Borassus Palms. Nest presumably as in other turtle doves.

VOICE : Has been described (advertising coo ?) as a 'harsh coo'.

DISPLAY : No information.

OTHER NAMES : Reichenow's Dove ; White-winged Ringdove.

REFERENCE

MACKWORTH-PRAED, C. W. & GRANT, C. H. B. 1957. *African Handbook of Birds.* Series 1, vol. 1. London.

MOURNING COLLARED DOVE   *Streptopelia decipiens*

Turtur decipiens Hartlaub and Finsch in Finsch and Hartlaub, Vög. Ostafr., 1870, p. 544.

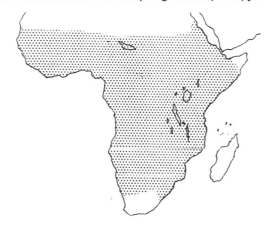

This large ring-necked turtle dove is very like the Red-eyed Dove in general appearance, differing only in minor details of colour and marking. Its voice is, however, quite distinct.

DESCRIPTION: Much as the Red-eyed Dove (q.v.) but looking in life rather more heavily built and with slightly larger head in proportion. Mauve-pink of breast usually lighter and shading into grey or white on the belly. Grey of forehead and crown usually extended to sides of face. Tail pattern somewhat different (see sketches) and with light parts of tail white or greyish white. Under tail coverts greyish-white or grey with white tips. Upperparts usually lighter sometimes a light sandy brown. Irides light yellow to light orange-yellow, sometimes with dark outer ring; orbital skin reddish.

The above is a composite description of the many recognised races of this species which differ slightly in size and/or depth of colour.

DISTRIBUTION AND HABITAT: Africa, from Senegal and the Sudan south to the Limpopo and Zambesi valleys, Eastern Transvaal, northern Bechuanaland, Kaokoveld and Angola. Frequents dry sandy areas where there are trees (typically thorn scrub) and where surface water can be obtained.

FEEDING AND GENERAL HABITS: Feeds chiefly, perhaps entirely, on the ground. Recorded foods are seeds of various weeds and cultivated grain. Often feeds in cultivated land and about cattle kraals and human dwellings.

NESTING: Usual pigeon nest in tree or shrub. Two white eggs (sometimes only one *fide* Mackworth-Praed & Grant). Incubation period, in England, 13 to 14 days (Newman, 1909). Recorded breeding February to April and June to October in the Sudan; June, July in southern Africa.

VOICE: The advertising coo is a loud, pleasant 'Cŏŏ, cōo-ōo' with the accent on the middle syllable. It is usually repeated several times. The same version is used when nest-calling. The display coo is muffled and deep in tone and appears to be variable. I noted the display coos of four different captive males as follows 'Cōo-ōo-cŏŏ-cŏŏ', 'Crōo-ōo-ŏŏ', 'Cŏŏ-ŏŏ-cŏ-cŏ' and 'Cōo, cru-cru-cru-cru-cru'.

The excitement cry is a sharp, growling purr which can be well imitated by forcibly blowing air sharply between the closed and pursed lips.

DISPLAY: The bowing display is almost identical with that of the Barbary Dove but the bows are, perhaps, a very little quicker in tempo.

OTHER NAMES: Deceptive Turtle dove; Angola Dove; Mourning Dove; Dongola Dove.

REFERENCES

CHAPIN, J. P. 1939. The birds of the Belgian Congo. *Bull. Amer. Mus. Nat. Hist.* **75**: 157–159.
MACKWORTH-PRAED, C. W. & GRANT, C. H. B. 1957. *The African Handbook of Birds.* Series 1, vol. 1. London.
McLACHLAN, G. R. & LIVERSIDGE, R. 1957. *Roberts Birds of South Africa*, revised edition. Cape Town.
NEWMAN, T. H. 1909. The Deceptive Turtle-dove. *Avicult. Mag.*, Third Sereis, **1**: 120–126.

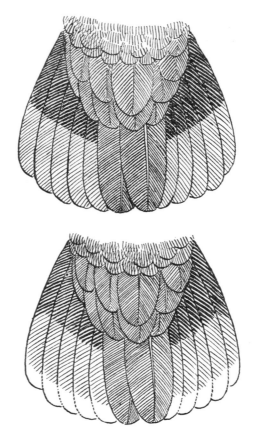

FIG. 41:   Tails of Red-eyed Dove (top) and Mourning Collared Dove (bottom),
to show difference in colour pattern.

RED-EYED DOVE   *Streptopelia semitorquata*

Columba semitorquata Ruppell, Neue Wirbelth., Vög., 1837, p. 66, pl. 23, f. 2.

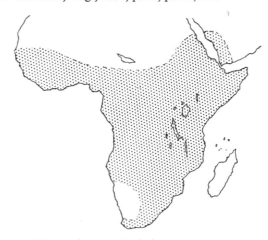

The largest and darkest of the African ring-necked doves.

DESCRIPTION: Somewhat larger than a Barbary Dove, indeed often nearly as large as a small Feral
Pigeon.   Upperparts dark greyish-brown, primaries near blackish.   Outer wing coverts (wing edge)

dark slaty blue, underwing coverts, flanks and sides of rump bluish grey. Basal half of tail feathers blackish, terminal half light brownish grey (light silver-grey on undersides). Black half-collar on neck edged silver-grey frontally. Forehead pale bluish-grey or silvery shading to bluish-grey on crown. Neck, breast and underparts dark mauve-pink to wine red. Bill blackish. Feet and orbital skin purplish red. Irides usually deep golden or orange, sometimes yellowish, red or orange-brown.

Juvenile duller and browner with reddish-brown or reddish-buff edges and ill-defined dark subterminal bars on most of the feathers. Indication of (future) collar at sides of neck only. Feet, orbital skin and irides dull.

FIELD CHARACTERS: Advertising coo (q.v.) diagnostic. Distinctive light and dark patterned tail *without any white* and darker general coloration than other related species. Easily confused with *S. decipiens* if tail not clearly seen.

DISTRIBUTION AND HABITAT: Africa, south of the Sahara and south-western Arabia. Found in well wooded and well-watered areas, including lowland forest which other ring-necked doves tend to avoid. In forest areas it is, however, found near open areas such as river-beds or clearings. Sometimes in more open country with scattered trees or in or near reedbeds.

FEEDING AND GENERAL HABITS: Feeds chiefly on the ground but also takes some berries from trees. Often feeds on cultivated ground and around cattle kraals and farmsteads. Takes seeds of many kinds including cultivated grains and peanuts when available. Also small red peppers, small tubers and termites; probably other invertebrates also at times. Usually in pairs, singly or in small parties but large numbers may aggregate at good feeding grounds.

NESTING: Usual pigeon nest in tree or shrub; at varying heights. Two eggs; one egg clutches recorded, perhaps due to predation or bird having been forced to lay one elsewhere. Incubation, in England, 12 to 13 days. First egg laid in evening, second on morning of next day but one (Newman, 1907). Breeding season prolonged, probably breeds whenever food supplies plentiful.

VOICE: The advertising coo is a loud cheerful-sounding 'cōō-cōō, cŏŏ-cŏŏ-cŏŏ, cŏŏ-cōō', or 'cōō-cōō, cŏŏ-cŏŏ, cŏŏ-cŏŏ, cōō-cōō', usually repeated twice or more. The same form is used when nest-calling but is then often repeated more times without pause. The display-coo suggests a muffled and much speeded-up version of the advertising coo. The excitement cry is a sharp, rather high-pitched note that could almost be described as a short scream. To me it suggests the defensive 'spitting' of a domestic cat in its suddeness and emphasis. My captive specimens often gave the excitment cry when handled, particularly if they were struggling to escape. Here it seemed to express extreme fear but I was not able to detect any difference in the excitement cry given by a frightened bird in the hand and that given when angry or after copulation. The usual distress call is similar to that of the Barbary Dove and other pigeons.

DISPLAYS: In the bowing display, as compared with that of the Barbary Dove, the bows are quicker and more shallow and, at the culmination of each, the head is held at a different angle, so that (frontally) the pale forehead is fully exhibited but the median part of the black collar is not visible. It is no coincidence, perhaps, that in this species the median part of the collar is often less well developed or even obsolescent.

The display flight, like that of other turtle doves, consists of towering upwards, checking, and then gliding with wings and tail outspread.

Nodding, although less emphatic than in the *Columba* species, is more so than in the Barbary Dove. The nods of this species being always easily distinguishable from the 'aiming' flight-intention movements.

The pre-copulatory displacement-preening is not confined to the usual 'behind the wing' movement. The Red-eyed Dove also lowers its head and makes a preening movement among the feathers of its underparts. At high intensity this may culminate in an odd waggling movement of the head suggestive of (and probably homologous with) that used when retrieving eggs or adjusting their position.

OTHER NAMES: Half-collared Dove; Black Dove; Black Pigeon. These latter rather misleading names are given, in parts of Africa, to this species in distinction from other paler-coloured doves.

REFERENCES

GOODWIN, D. 1956. Observations on the voice and displays of certain pigeons. *Avicult. Mag.* **62**: 17–33 and 62–70.
MACKWORTH-PRAED, C. W. & GRANT, C. H. B. 1957. *African Handbook of Birds*. Series 1, vol. 1. London.
NEWMAN, T. H. 1907. The Half-collared Turtle Dove. *Avicult. Mag.*, new series **5**: 318–324.

RING-NECKED DOVE   *Streptopelia capicola*

Columbam vinaceam var. capicolam (Accusative case) Sundevall, Kongl, Sv. Vet-Akad. Handl. (N.S.) 2, No. 1, 1857, Art 3, p. 54.

DESCRIPTION: Very similar to the Vinaceous Dove with which it may be conspecific but slightly larger and with the brown and pink parts more suffused with grey. The nominate form *S. c. capicola* from Transvaal and Zululand to Cape Province is slightly smaller than a Barbary Dove. Throat whitish, forehead and face light bluish grey; crown darker bluish grey with a narrow black stripe from bill to eye. Nape, sides and front of neck mauvish pink, more or less suffused with grey, the grey suffusion being more pronounced on breast and underparts. Ventral area and under tail coverts white. Black half-collar on hind neck. Mantle, scapulars and inner wing coverts dark drab brown shading to dark bluish grey on outer wing coverts, rump and upper tail coverts. Primary coverts, primaries and outer secondaries dull black with pale fringes to outer webs of primaries. Underwing dark bluish grey. Irides dark brown, orbital skin yellowish. Bill black or purplish black. Legs and feet reddish purple, dark purple or greyish purple. The female usually has the grey parts suffused with, and on the rump largely replaced by drab brown. The juvenile has rusty fawn or buffish fringes to most feathers and has the black collar indicated by a patch on each side of the neck.

The above description is of the nominate form; *S. c. damarensis* from most of the dryer parts of South Africa is paler and greyer, the male typically being pale bluish grey on head and outer wing coverts, light drab grey on the mantle and pale greyish mauve on the breast, the female is slightly browner. *S. c. ongouati* from Ongouati and surrounding areas in the Kaokoveld of South West Africa is slightly paler and greyer than *damarensis*. *S. c. tropica* from most of tropical eastern Africa is a little paler than the nominate form, much more strongly tinged with mauve-pink on neck and breast, with little or no grey suffusion on the face and the grey of the crown suffused with pink.   *S. c. hilgerti* from northern Somaliland is like *tropica* but paler and with a grey face and crown that usually contrasts with the pinkish of the hind neck dividing the grey crown from the black half-collar.   Other races have been described but, except for *S. c. dryas* which is said to be intermediate between *S. c. tropica* and *S. vinacea* they all closely resemble one of those described above.

DISTRIBUTION and HABITAT: Africa from the southern Sudan and Abyssinia to South Africa.   Also found throughout the Comoro Islands, possibly through introduction by man (Benson pers. comm.).   Inhabits most types of fairly dry and open country with trees or bushes, including cultivated areas and arid regions.   Avoids dense forest.

FEEDING AND GENERAL HABITS: Feeds chiefly on the ground.   Food mainly seeds, including cultivated grains but will eat winged termites (Curry-Lindahl, 1960) and probably takes other invertebrates also. Commonly in pairs, small parties or (when mate sitting) singly but often in large flocks.   Sometimes and perhaps usually, such flocks consist of aggregations of individuals or small groups at feeding or watering places.

NESTING: Usual pigeon nest in tree or shrub, occasionally on a ledge of a building.   Two white eggs. Incubation period 12 days, young fledge at 16 to 17 days (McLachlan & Liversidge, 1957).   Breeding season prolonged, nests with eggs have been found at all times of year (Vincent, 1946).   Distraction display in which bird flies from nest, then alights and violently beats its wings has been recorded by Vincent.

VOICE: The advertising coo is harsh and trisyllabic with the accent usually on the second syllable, has been transcribed 'Kookōro', 'How's fāther?', 'Coo-cōō-coo', 'Cascāra'. etc.   It is usually repeated many times.   The display coo is a short 'Cŏŏk' or 'Cuk' uttered with each bow.   The excitement cry is a harsh, snarling 'Kōorrr' or 'Kēērrr' difficult to transcribe adequately, sometimes sounding di-syllabic 'Keerrick' and (at low intensities?) softer and shorter 'Chirr'.

DISPLAY: In the bowing display the bows are made quickly (Vincent, 1946).   The display flight involves flying upwards with slow flapping wings and then gliding around or downwards with wings and tail outspread (Vincent, 1934).

OTHER NAMES: Cape Turtle Dove; Turtle Dove (in South Africa); Cape Ringdove; Damara Dove; Dark-eyed Ringdove.

REFERENCES

CURRY-LINDAHL, K. 1960. *Ecological Studies on the Mammals, Birds, Reptiles and Amphibians in the Eastern Belgian Congo.* Pt. 2 (Report No. 1 of the Swedish Congo Expeditions, 1951–2 and 1958–9), p. 103.
MCLACHLAN, G. R. & LIVERSIDGE, R. 1957. *Roberts birds of South Africa* (revised edition), pp. 168–169. Cape Town.
VINCENT, A. W. 1946. On the breeding habits of some African Birds. *Ibis* **88**: 48–67.
VINCENT, J. 1934. The Birds of Northern Portuguese East Africa. *Ibis* **4**: Thirteenth Series, 305–340.

VINACEOUS DOVE   *Streptopelia vinacea*

Columba vinacea Gmelin, Syst. Nat., 1, p. 2, 1789, p. 782.

DESCRIPTION: Appreciably smaller than a Barbary Dove (although very much larger than a Diamond Dove) and with rather more sloping forehead.   Head, neck, breast and underparts a soft vinous pink or fawnish pink, sometimes with a slight tinge of grey on crown and nape, shading to creamy white on the ventral area and white on the under tail coverts.   A narrow black stripe from bill to eye.   Broad black half-collar on hind neck.   Upper parts light drab brown shading to pale bluish grey on outermost wing coverts.   Outer secondaries black, washed with silver grey.   Primaries and primary coverts black, or brownish black with narrow whitish fringes to outer webs.   Central tail feathers greyish brown, outer ones black at base with end half greyish white.   Underside of tail, basal half black, end half white.   Underwing bluish grey.   Irides dark brown.   Bill black, usually purplish at gape.   Legs and feet purplish red or purple.

Sexes alike but female tends to have the pinkish areas less vinous and more brownish but this is only an average tendency not a definite difference.   Juvenile duller, with pale buffish or pale rufous fringes to most feathers and collar indicated only by a blackish patch at each side of neck.

DISTRIBUTION AND HABITAT: Africa from Senegal and Liberia to Uganda and Eritrea. Inhabits dry savanna and thorn scrub country. Often common in or near cultivation but also typically the commonest dove of uninhabited dry open thorny savanna (Bates, 1930). Locally migratory (Chapin, 1939).

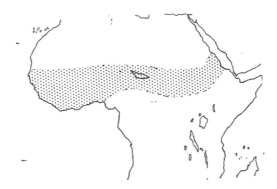

FEEDING AND GENERAL HABITS: Feeds chiefly, probably entirely, on the ground. Known to take seeds, including cultivated grains when available. Probably takes termites and other invertebrates also. Usually in pairs, small parties or singly but sometimes in flocks and large numbers may aggregate at good feeding places. Locally migratory.

NESTING: Usual pigeon nest in tree or shrub. Often low down and among thorns. Two white eggs. Breeding season prolonged but usually in the dry season. Recorded breeding in Nigeria from November to March, and also in June and September, in the Congo (Uelle District) October to December, in southern Sudan January to April (Mackworth-Praed & Grant, 1957; Serle, 1939).

VOICE: What is evidently the advertising coo is usually described as being rather harsh, hurried in tempo and of four syllables, e.g. 'Coo-coo-coo-coo' (Harwin, 1963), 'Coo-cu-cu-coo' (Welman in Bannerman, 1931) but Chapin (1939) describes it as sometimes trisylabic. What is probably the excitement cry is described by Chapin as 'a protracted vibrant "K-k-k-k-koo"'.

DISPLAY: I can find nothing recorded, probably identical with the Ring-necked Dove (q.v.).

OTHER NAMES: Vinaceous Turtle Dove; Vinaceous Ring Dove.

REFERENCES

BANNERMAN, D. A. 1931. *The Birds of Tropical West Africa*: 343–348.
BATES, G. L. 1930. *Handbook of the Birds of West Africa*: 14–15.
CHAPIN, G. P. 1939. The Birds of the Belgian Congo. *Bull. Amer. Mus. Nat. Hist.* LXXV: 161–162.
HARWIN, R. M. 1963. Thoughts on a five weeks stay in Northern Nigeria. *Bokmakierie* 15: 2: 10–12.
MACKWORTH-PRAED, C. W. & GRANT, C. H. B. 1957. *African Handbook of Birds*. Series 1, 1: 475–476.
SERLE, W. 1939. Field observations on some Northern Nigerian Birds. *Ibis* 3: Fourteenth Series, 654–699 (683).

RED COLLARED DOVE   *Streptopelia tranquebarica*

Columba tranquebarica Hermann, Obs. Zool., 1804, p. 200.

DESCRIPTION: About a quarter smaller than a Barbary Dove and slightly more compact in form (see sketch) with proportionately longer and more pointed wings and shorter tail. Throat whitish. Head bluish grey shading to whitish grey immediately above the bill and just in front of the black half-collar on the hind neck. Mantle, upper back, wing coverts, scapulars and inner secondaries deep mauvish pink, inclining to brick red in worn plumage. Neck, breast and belly a slightly paler and more greyish pink shading to pinkish grey and then to white on the under tail coverts.   Lower back, rump, upper tail coverts dark bluish grey.   Central tail feathers drab grey, outer ones with basal half dark grey, rest greyish white, outermost pair have the outer webs entirely white.   Underwing whitish grey or pale bluish grey.   A small amount of bluish grey on outer wing coverts at edge of folded wing.   Primaries blackish.   Underside of tail boldly patterned with black basal half and rest white.   Irides brown, dark brown or brownish black.   Orbital skin greyish.   Bill black or greyish black.   Legs and feet dark purplish red or purplish black.

The female differs strikingly from the male being a dull drab brown where he is vinous pink, and brownish grey where he is bluish grey, except under the wing where she is the same colour as the male.   The juvenile female resembles the adult in ground colour but is paler and has conspicuous buffish edges to most feathers. The juvenile male is similar but with a more reddish tinge.

The above description applies to the nominate form, *S. t. tranquebarica*, from most of India.   The form found from north-eastern India (where many birds are intermediate) eastwards, *S. tranquebarica humilis*, is darker in all its colours being in the male predominantly dull purplish red and dark bluish grey and, in the female, dark drab brown.

FIELD CHARACTERS: Combination of small size, white-tipped outer tail feathers, shortish tail and dark pink or dark drab general colour distinguish it from all sympatric species.

DISTRIBUTION AND HABITAT: Eastern and south-eastern Asia from north-western India, east to north-eastern Tibet and northern China, south to southern India, Burma, Siam, Indo-China, the northern Philippine Islands, and the Andaman Islands.   Normally only a vagrant in Ceylon.   A summer resident only in the more northern parts of its range.

Inhabits open country with some trees, open cultivated country, scrub jungle and dry woodland.

FEEDING AND GENERAL HABITS: Feeds chiefly, perhaps entirely on the ground.   Known to take seeds, including grass-seeds and cultivated grains, buds and young leaves.   Large numbers frequently gather on suitable feeding grounds and sometimes, unlike most turtle doves, such flocks move about as cohesive units even when away from the feeding area.   Usually more afraid of man than most small doves; probably this shyness is due to persecution by sportsmen and shown most in areas where the latter are common. Flight very swift and straight.   When alarmed usually flies some distance before re-alighting.

NESTING: Usual pigeon's nest in tree or shrub but seldom very low down and often quite high up in large trees.   Two white or creamy white eggs.   In the warmer parts of its range may breed at any time when food is available, further north it is, naturally, a summer breeder.

VOICE: The advertising coo is a series of short, rather guttural but vibrant and not unpleasant notes 'Crōō, crŏŏ-crŏŏ-crŏŏ', or 'Crŏr, crŏ-crŏ-crŏ-crŏ', repeated several times.   The first note is longer and more accented than the others (but not so long as most dove notes), the next three are shorter and run together but with the last of the three a little bit more accented than the other two. The phrase '*Now! How-are-you?*' gives some idea of the tempo and emphasis. The nest call is the same.

The display coo is a hurried 'crŏŏ(wa) crŏŏ(wa) crŏŏ(wa) the (wa) being an inspiration (?) only audible at fairly close quarters, the whole series of notes very hurried and very similar to the display coos of *S. turtur* and *S. chinensis*.

DISPLAY: In the bowing display the male bobs his head rapidly in much the same manner as the Spotted Dove, *S. chinensis*, but the head is not bowed so deeply as in that species or *risoria*.

OTHER NAMES: Red Ringdove; Red Turtle Dove.

REFERENCES

BAKER, E. C. S. 1913. *Indian Pigeons and Doves.* London.
RIPLEY, S. D. 1961. *A synopsis of the birds of India and Pakistan.* Madras.
SMYTHIES, B. E. 1953. *The Birds of Burma.* London.

MADAGASCAR TURTLE DOVE — *Streptopelia picturata*

Columba picturata Temminck, Pig. et Gall., 1, 1813, p. 315, 480.

DESCRIPTION: Between Barbary Dove and Feral Pigeon in size. More heavily built and longer-legged than other *Streptopelia* species. Head bluish grey. Display plumage on sides and, to some extent, back of neck consists of more or less bifurcated feathers with blackish bases and slightly iridescent mauve pink or greenish mauve tips. Rest of neck and breast dark pinkish purple shading to a darker reddish purple on mantle and inner wing coverts and greyish to buffish white ventral regions. Greater wing coverts, dark dull brown, tinged purplish red. Secondaries and primaries dark dull brown with narrow reddish buff fringes. Rump and upper tail coverts dark bluish grey, sometimes intermixed with dark brown. Under tail coverts white. Central tail feathers dark greyish brown, outer ones greyish black with broad greyish white terminal band. Iris brown, shading to red at outer edge (perhaps sometimes paler as in other races, q.v.). Orbital skin purplish red. Bill bright bluish grey at tip, purplish at base. Legs and feet reddish or reddish mauve. Newman (1908) noticed that the iris is nearly round in a dull light but contracts to a very narrow oval in bright sunlight, a condition he had not observed in any other species. Female duller, with less extensive purplish red on wings and darker (grey) terminal band to tail. Juvenile a general dull greyish brown with most feathers on the breast and upperparts edged with chestnut or rufous-buff.

The above description applies to the nominate race from Madagascar. *S. p. comorensis* from the Comoro Islands is a little browner in general tone and has the head brownish purple, not bluish grey. The population on Grand Comoro has pale red or reddish brown eyes; those on the other islands have irides with a yellow inner ring and purplish red outer ring (Benson, 1960). *S. p. rostrata* from the Seychelles is very similar to *comorensis* but darker and greyer. *S. p. aldabrana* from the Aldabra Islands is like *comorensis* but paler with less extensive reddish purple on the wing coverts and greyish under tail coverts.

DISTRIBUTION AND HABITAT: Madagascar, the Comoro, Seychelles, Amirante and Aldabra Islands. Introduced to Mauritius and Diego Garcia; the Madagascar form has also been introduced to the Seychelles and interbred with the local race there. Inhabits evergreen forest, secondary growth, thickets and patches of scrub in various types of country. Sometimes feeds in plantations and open areas but usually near to cover.

FEEDING AND GENERAL HABITS: Feeds on the ground; largely on seeds but also takes insects and other invertebrates. From the rather conflicting evidence it would appear to keep usually in pairs or singly with quite large numbers sometimes aggregating at good feeding places.

NESTING: Usual pigeon nest in tree or shrub. Two white eggs, rather larger for size of bird than is usual with pigeons (Newman, 1904). Nesting recorded in July, September and October in Madagascar (Rand, 1936) and October and November in Comoros. Distraction display regularly seen from a captive female when put off the nest (Newman, 1908).

VOICE: The advertising coo and the display coo would appear to be similar. Described by Newman as 'cŏŏ-cŏ-ō-ō-ō', the last part very much drawn out, this note is low and of considerable sweetness, and by Benson as 'a series of five quite melodious "Coo-oo's"' the first being slightly lower pitched than the remainder. Benson and Penny found the advertising coo of the Aldabran form differed from that of Comoro birds, it being a not very loud 'Coo-c-r-r-r-r', or 'Coo, coo-r-r-r-r' repeated three or four times. Excitement cry, of nominate form, a hoarse, nasal 'hē-hē-hē' (Newman).

DISPLAY: In the bowing display the male draws himself up stiffly and then makes a very low bow (Newman, 1908). Distraction display given by captive female when forced off nest with small young.

OTHER NAMES: Painted Dove; Red Turtle Dove.

REFERENCES

BENSON, C. W. 1960. The birds of the Comoro Islands. *Ibis* **103B**: 5–106.
BENSON, C. W. & PENNY, M. J. The land birds of Aldabra. (In Press).
NEWMAN, T. H. 1908. The Madagascar Turtle-dove. *Avicult. Mag.*, New Series. **6**: 79–84.
RAND, A. L. 1936. The Distributions and Habits of Madagascar Birds. *Bull. Amer. Mus. Nat. Hist.* **72**: Art. 5, 143–499.

SPOTTED DOVE   *Streptopelia chinensis*

Columba chinensis Scopoli, Del. Flor. et Faun. Insubr., fasc. 2, 1786, p. 94.

DESCRIPTION: About the size of a Barbary Dove but with proportionately shorter wings and longer tail. Forehead, crown and face bluish grey more or less tinged with pink. Chin whitish. Nape, sides of upper neck, throat and breast deep wine pink shading to buffish and grey on the lower belly. A narrow black line from mouth to eye.   Large patch of display plumage on back and sides of neck, the individual feathers comprising which are bifurcated, black at the base and with white tips.   Those on the hinder area of the display patch have pinkish buff tips.   Back, most of wings, rump, upper tail coverts and central tail feathers dull drab brown or sepia with paler and (when new) somewhat rufescent edges to most feathers. Line along wing edge, formed by outermost coverts, and underwing coverts slate blue.   Outer tail feathers greyish black, broadly tipped white.   Sexes alike.   Irides yellow, orange or pinkish, orbital skin mauve or purplish red.   Legs and feet red, pink or purplish.   Bill dark brown or blackish.   Juvenile generally pale drab with paler reddish buff fringes to most feathers.

The above description applies to the populations of China and Formosa, *S. c. chinensis* and *S. c. szetzeri*.   These differ considerably from the Indian and Ceylonese populations, *S. c. suratensis* and *S. ceylonensis* whose description follows: appreciably smaller than a Barbary Dove (or a Chinese Spotted Dove) and differing in colour from the Chinese form as follows.   Head only slightly suffused with grey. Head and breast a paler and more mauvish pink shading to creamy white on the lower belly.   Under tail coverts white, usually with small blackish tips.   The dull brown feathers on back and wing coverts have blackish wedge-shaped marks at the end flanked on each side by a pale mauve-pink (fading to buff) spot. Blue grey area on wing 'edge' paler and more extensive.   The general effect is of a rather pastel-hued spotted bird whereas the Chinese form appears a rather dark bird with only a patch of spotted feathers on the neck.

The form found in Burma and the Malayan regions, *S. c. tigrina*, is somewhat intermediate in appearance although on the whole closer to the Indian than to the Chinese form.   Intermediates between *chinensis* and *tigrina* have been taken in western Yunnan.   See also discussion on p. 119.

FIELD CHARACTERS: A dark, or pale and spotted, rather long-tailed and short-winged turtle dove. The spotted wing coverts of the Indian form distinguish it from the related Laughing Dove and throughout its range the black, white-spotted neck patch is diagnostic.

DISTRIBUTION AND HABITAT: India, Ceylon, Indo-Malayan region, southern China.   Introduced and established in parts of Australia, California and Hawaii.   Frequents woodlands, forest edge, agricultural country with trees and gardens.   Not usually in arid or treeless areas or in heavy forest.   In most parts of its range found in or near cultivated regions.

FEEDING AND GENERAL HABITS: Feeds chiefly on seeds picked up on the ground.   Usually seen in pairs or small parties.   Walks and runs nimbly on ground.   When disturbed rises almost vertically with a noisy clatter of wings, but seldom flies far.   Where not persecuted has little fear of man.   Often feeds on roads and paths in towns and villages.   Suffers heavy casualties when motor cars become common in towns where they have previously been rare or non-existent.

NESTING: Usual pigeon nest in tree, bush or in or on a building.   Usually at no great height, often in quite exposed situations.   Two white eggs.   Breeding season prolonged.   Nests throughout the year in Burma (Smythies, 1953).   Distraction display frequent (Thompson, in Baker, 1913).   Both male and female of a captive pair, of the Ceylon form, spent the night together on the nest, and were often on it together by day, when they had hatching eggs or newly hatched young.

VOICE: Advertising coo an emphatic 'cŏŏ, crōo-ōo, crōo-ōo', or 'cŏŏcŏŏ, crōor-crōor' subject to much minor variation.   It has a rising cadence and an excited 'cheering' tone unlike that of any other dove whose voice is known to me.   The female utters quieter and less distinct versions of this rather more freely than most female turtle doves do.   The nest-call does not differ from the advertising coo.

The display coo is a simplified form of the above 'cŏŏ, crōor' or 'cŏŏ, crōo-ōor' given while bowing and repeated with each bow.

The distress call is loud for so small a dove and perhaps rather longer-drawn than in other turtle doves. There appears to be no excitement cry.

The above description is of the voice of Spotted Doves of the Ceylonese and Indian forms which I have kept and observed in captivity.   The calls of introduced birds in Australia, phenotypically *S. c. chinenis* and *S. c. tigrina* were similar but deeper in tone and their advertising coos variable and often ending rather abruptly: 'Cŏŏcŏŏ, crōō-ōō, kŏŏk' and variants; sometimes 'Cŏŏ, crōō-ōō, kŏŏk' very like Collared Dove's in rhythym.

DISPLAY: In the bowing display the head is held with the bill at an angle of about 80 to 90 degrees from the substrate at the culmination of each bow. Thus the erected display plumage on sides and back of neck is fully exhibited, forming a broad collar framing the lowered head. The bows are not quite so (relatively) slow and deliberate as those of the Barbary and Collared Doves but slower than the quick bobbing bows of the Turtle Dove. Display flight similar to that of other turtle doves, flies steeply upwards, clapping wings loudly, and then glides down with outspread wings and tail.

Distraction display apparently similar to that of Turtle Dove (q.v.) has been recorded from birds flushed from (? hatching) eggs.

OTHER NAMES: Necklace Dove; Pearl-necked Dove; Indian Turtle Dove; Chinese Turtle Dove.

REFERENCES

BAKER, E. C. S. 1913. *Indian Pigeons and Doves.* London.
SCHÄFER, E. 1938. Ornithologische Ergebnisse zweier Forschungsreisen nach Tibet. *Journ. f. Orn.* **86**: Sonderheft.
SMYTHIES, B. E. 1953. *The birds of Burma.* London.

LAUGHING DOVE   *Streptopelia senegalensis*

Columba senegalensis Linnaeus, Syst., Nat., Ed. 12, 1, 1766, p. 283.

DESCRIPTION: About one quarter smaller than a Barbary Dove and with proportionately shorter wings and longer tail. Head, neck and breast a rather dark mauve-pink shading to creamy white on the lower belly and white on the under tail coverts. A broad band of display plumage on sides and front of neck of which the individual feathers are bifurcated and have black bases and glossy golden-copper tips. Mantle, scapulars and inner wing-coverts bright reddish brown. Outer wing coverts slate blue. Secondaries a darker greyer slate colour. Primaries dark brownish grey with narrow dull white outer edge. Lower back and rump slate blue more or less intermixed with brown. Upper tail coverts dark greyish brown with paler and redder tips. Central tail feathers greyish brown, outer ones patterned in dark grey and white. There is a good deal of minor individual and local variation, some birds being, even when in fresh plumage, rather paler than the above description and with whitish chins. Female paler and not such a reddish brown on the upper parts. Irides brown or dark brown. Feet and legs purplish red or dull purplish pink. Bill blackish. The juvenile is pale dullish brown where adults are red-brown and dull tawny grey where they are pink, with pale fringes to most feathers (See pl. ?)

The above description applies to the birds found in most of Africa and western Arabia. The Laughing Doves from the Nile Valley and the Nile Delta, *S. senegalensis aegyptiaca*, are a little larger and usually rather darker and redder in colour. The populations from the oases of north-western Africa, *S. senegalensis phoenicoptera*, show much local variation but tend to be rather larger in size and duller in colour as do specimens from Turkey. Those from the island of Sokotra, *S. senegalensis sokotrae*, are very small, those from São Thomé, *S. s. thomé*, are small and with brighter pink heads. The only really well-differentiated form is, however, that found in India and eastern Arabia, *S. senegalensis cambayensis*, which is smaller and much duller, the upper parts being a light drab brown with no trace of the rusty orange hue of the African form and with very little blue grey on the rump.

FIELD CHARACTERS: Smallish, reddish brown dove with longish white-edged tail and much slate blue on wings.

DISTRIBUTION AND HABITAT: Africa, Arabia, India, Afghanistan and Turkestan. Also locally in Palestine, Syria, the Lebanon, Turkey and Malta, in all these places probably as a result of human introduction as in parts of western Australia where it is now well established.

Appears to be naturally a bird of arid scrub or thorn bush country in the vicinity of permanent water. Over most of its range it has, however, become adapted to a man-altered environment and is pre-eminently a bird of cultivated oases, gardens, villages and towns.

FEEDING AND GENERAL HABITS: Feeds on the ground, principally on seeds. Much of the natural food consists of very small seeds of various wild plants, but it will swallow such large cultivated grains as maize besides millet, wheat and dari. Flight usually (for a turtle dove) rather slow, but faster in colder weather, and can put on a surprising turn of speed when chased by a hawk.

Where not (or not much) molested has very little fear of man. Wild-caught adults will commence nesting in captivity within a few hours of being trapped and caged.

NESTING: Usual pigeon nest in a tree or bush, at base of a palm frond or on some sheltered ledge, beam, or nook in or on a building. Two white eggs. Incubation period 12½–14 days.

VOICE: The advertising coo is a soft, rather musical phrase of four, five or six notes Cŏŏ-cŏŏ, cŏŏ-ōō', 'Cŏŏrŏŏcŏŏ-cŏŏ-cŏŏcōō', or 'ŏŏ-gŏŏrŏŏtōō. It has a somewhat bubbling quality and, although difficult to describe, is quite unlike that of any other *Streptopelia* species and easily recognised. The nest call is similar. Display coo a hurried-sounding Cōō-ōō-ŏŏ-cŏŏ-cŏŏ.

DISPLAY: In its bowing display the Laughing Dove bows rather rapidly and at the lowest point of the bow the bill is held little if any below the horizontal. Thus the display plumage on front and side of neck is fully visible to the bird displayed to.

In display flight towers up with clapping wings and then glides down, often in a circle or half-circle, with wings and tail widely spread.

Copulation preceded by displacement preening behind wing by one or both birds, and billing in which female inserts her bill into male's and they make a slight head movement. Probably no actual feeding of female. Immediately after copulation male stands with head well up and neck feathers puffed out, much as male Turtle Dove but body posture less erect, and female 'parades' with feathers of rump and neck erected.

OTHER NAMES: Senegal Dove; Palm Dove; Egyptian Turtle Dove; Little Brown Dove; Town Dove; Village Dove; Garden Dove.

THE GENUS *APLOPELIA*

The lemon doves of the genus *Aplopelia* are found only in Africa where they inhabit forest, spreading much of their time on the ground in or near dense undergrowth. They show a considerable resemblance to the American doves of the genus *Leptotila* not only in general coloration but also in their posture, gait and flight intention movements. They have usually been considered most closely related to *Leptotila* and such other largely ground-living forms as the New World and Old World quail doves, *Geotrygon* and *Gallicolumba*, but I think this is, probably, an incorrect assessment.

In spite of the strong general resemblance between them *Aplopelia* differs from *Leptotila* in having a broad instead of a sharply attenuated outer primary; in lacking any bright chestnut colour on the underside of the wing and in the quite different colour pattern of its outer tail feathers. If their resemblance was due to a close phylogenetic relationship it would be difficult to think of any reason why *Aplopelia* should lack these three characters of *Leptotila* or *vice versa*. I think that their resemblance in general coloration, form and some behaviour patterns is due to convergence. The same probably holds good for the lesser degree of similarity of colouring between *Aplopelia* and the Blue-headed Dove, *Turtur brehmeri*. Here again details differ, particularly the colour pattern of the outer tail feathers, a character that is remarkably homogeneous in *Turtur* and its near allies. *Aplopelia* shows some general similarity of colouring to two forest species of *Columba*, *C. iriditorques* and *C. delegorguei*, with which it is sympatric. Here again details of colour pattern differ (besides differences of proportions) but one African *Columba* species, *C. albinucha*, has a tail pattern somewhat like that of *Aplopelia*. I think, however, that *Aplopelia* is probably most closely related to *Streptopelia*.

It is found on the continent where the greatest number of forms of *Streptopelia* occur. The colour pattern of its tail feathers is almost identical with that found in *Streptopelia semitorquata* but it lacks the contrasting neck markings found in the *Streptopelia* species. It also differs in having iridescence on its neck. In these characters, however, it is approached by *Streptopelia picturata*, from Madagascar and the islands of the Indian Ocean, which is intermediate between *Aplopelia* and the other species of *Streptopelia*. *S. picturata* has relatively inconspicuous neck markings and a slight but quite visible iridescence on the neck. It is also darker and more uniformly coloured, more heavily built, has longer legs and is more terrestial in habits than other species of *Streptopelia*. Moreover *picturata* frequents dense woodland as does *Aplopelia* on the African mainland. Although *picturata* is rightly included in *Streptopelia*, it shows how an *Aplopelia*-like form might arise from *Streptopelia* stock. The evidence thus suggests that *Aplopelia* originated in Africa, either from *Streptopelia*, from some form ancestral to present day *Streptopelia* species or, possibly, from some form ancestral to both *Streptopelia* and *Columba*.

The lemon doves were formerly regarded as two species, the Lemon Dove or Cinnamon Dove *A. larvata* of south and eastern Africa and the Western Lemon Dove *A. simplex* of parts of west and west-central Africa. As, however, there are no known differences of voice or behaviour, the two forms are allopatric and their major plumage differences are largely bridged by the races *jacksoni* and *samiliyae*, they are all treated here as forms of a single polytypic species *Aplopelia larvata*.

Lemon Dove   *Aplopelia larvata*

Columba larvata Temminck, in Knip, Les Pigeons, 1810, Les Colombes, p. 71, pl. 31.

DESCRIPTION: Rather larger than a Barbary Dove, with longer legs, proportionately shorter tail and wings and rather large head with steeply sloping forehead and large eyes. Forehead, face and throat white to greyish white shading to rich pinkish rufous on neck and breast. Nape, hind neck, upper mantle and, to a lesser extent, sides of neck and breast with rich iridescence, that appears mauve pink, bronzy pink or bronze green according to incidence of light. Rest of underparts rufous shading to darker brown on flanks and underwing and deep chestnut on under tail coverts. Upperparts, including central tail feathers dark olive brown, tinged rufous. Outer tail feathers blackish with very broad pale grey terminal band. Irides crimson, dark brownish red, brown or pinkish, sometimes (? female only) with silver-white inner ring, eye rims dark red or purplish red; orbital skin dark red or greyish with dark red carunculations. Bill blackish. Feet and legs dark red or purplish red.

Female tends to be a little duller but sexual differences slight as compared with those of western forms of the species. Juvenile has most of the cover feathers either barred rust brown and blackish or with a blackish subterminal bar and broad rufous tip giving it a generally barred and rusty appearance.

The above description is of the nominate form *A. l. larvata* which is found from Cape Province north through eastern Africa to extreme south-east Sudan. *A. l. bronzina* from the highlands of Ethiopia is similar but a little smaller. *A. l. jacksoni* from the eastern Congo to Uganda and western Tanganyika is slightly larger, the female is very similar to *larvata* but is pale greyish on forehead and face and paler and less reddish on belly and under tail coverts. The male has the upper parts a darker and colder olive brown and the breast grey or brownish grey shading to pale grey on ventral regions and under tail coverts. Irides are often or usually mauve or purplish grey; orbital skin sometimes, perhaps usually, grey without any red. *A. l. plumbescens* of southern Cameroon is similar to *jacksoni* but the male is blackish grey on back, wings, rump and central tail feathers, a purer grey below nearly white on the under tail coverts. Irides grey, the female is a little paler below and has whitish under tail coverts. *A. l. inornata* of Cameroon Mountain and the Cameroon-Nigerian highlands is similar to *jacksoni* but a little darker. *A. l. simplex* of São Thomé Island and Rollas Islet is like *plumbescens* but the male is not quite so dark and both sexes, but especially the female, tend to have very pronounced bronze green iridescence on hind crown and mantle. *A. l. poensis* from Fernando Po Island and *A. l. hypoleuca* from Annobon are very like *simplex*. *A. l. principalis* from Principe (Princes Island) is very like nominate *larvata* but duller, with greyish forehead, paler underparts and white under tail coverts. It shows less sexual dichromatism than other western races differing only in the male being more tinged with purplish pink on breast and belly. *A. l. samiliyae* from north-western Rhodesia (Mwinilunga) is intermediate between *larvata* and *jacksoni* in most of its colouring but is darker on the upperparts than either, the male being purplish black and the female very dark brown, tinged with purple.

DISTRIBUTION AND HABITAT: Africa from Ethiopia and interior of Kenya south through Natal to Cape Province, Cameroons, Congo, Angola and Northern Rhodesia. Recently found in Liberia (near Mount Nimba), from which country there was only one previous record (Chapin 1939, Forbes-Watson). Inhabits forests, in eastern Africa especially mountain forests; also cocoa plantations, planted forests of exotic trees and tree-grown gardens or cultivated areas.

FEEDING AND GENERAL HABITS: Feeds on the ground, usually in shade of trees. Takes seeds, fallen berries, insects and molluscs; locally in South Africa has learned to eat bread and scavenges for crumbs at picnic sites. Keeps much to cover, in or near dense undergrowth. When flushed rises with a clatter and either flies a short distance and alights on the ground again or perches in a tree. Usually in pairs or singly. Difficult to see in cover but not usually very shy of man and once seen often quite easy to watch.

The flight intention movement is very like that of *Leptotila*. The head is pulled back rather slowly and then jerks quickly forward to, approximately, the normal resting position.

NESTING: Nest in tree or shrub, often low down and commonly more substantial than pigeons' nests usually are. Two creamy-white, cream or very pale buff eggs. Young fledge in 20 to 21 days (Van Someren, 1956).

VOICE: The advertising coo of a captive bird was a soft but very deep $\overline{oo}$-$\overline{oo}$. Allowing for slight differences of transliteration this appears to be the call that various observers have most often heard from wild individuals but 'a deep hoarse R-r-r-roo' and 'a deep dull Oomp' (Mackworth-Praed & Grant, 1957) may refer to other calls.

DISPLAY: No information.

OTHER NAMES: Cinnamon Dove (the races *larvata* and *bronzina*); Forest Dove.

REFERENCES

BATES, G. L. 1930. *Handbook of the birds of West Africa.* London.
CHAPIN, J. P. 1939. *The Birds of the Belgian Congo, Pt. 2:* 164–166.
FORBES-WATSON, A. D. (In press and pers. comm.).
MACKWORTH-PRAED, C. W. & GRANT, C. H. B. 1957. *African handbook of birds.* Series, vol. 1. London
McLACHLAN, G. R. & LIVERSIDGE, R. 1957. *Roberts Birds of South Africa*, revised edition. Cape Town.
VAN SOMEREN, V. G. L. 1956. Days with birds. *Fieldiana: Zoology*, vol. 38.

CUCKOO DOVES AND LONG-TAILED PIGEONS

The cuckoo doves or brown pigeons are found in the Oriental and Australasian regions. They are characterised by their more or less barred brown plumage and strongly graduated tails with very long and broad central tail feathers.

The cuckoo doves are birds of jungle and forest where they feed both in trees and shrubs and on the ground. Their barred plumage and long tails are responsible for the usual name of cuckoo dove, their long tails and iridescence for the alternative pheasant dove or pheasant pigeon, a name better applied to the more truly pheasant-like *Otidiphaps*. Their relationships are obscure but it seems most probable that they represent a rather early offshoot from the same ancestral stock as produced the emerald doves and their allies (q.v.). This is suggested particularly by the similarity in colour-patterns of the outer tail feathers and, although less convincingly, by their geographical distribution and the resemblances of their juvenile plumages. The brown, usually barred adult plumage of the cuckoo doves has much in common with the juvenile plumages of other groups and like them is almost certainly of protective character. It is significant that the related but much larger long-tailed pigeons do not show this type of over-all coloration although they agree with the cuckoo doves in some details of colour pattern.

The cuckoo doves fall into two main groups which differ in size. The group of larger forms consists of the Bar-tailed Cuckoo Dove *Macropygia unchall*, the Pink-breasted Cuckoo Dove *M. amboinensis*, the Large Brown Cuckoo Dove *M. phasianella*, the Large Cuckoo Dove *M. magna*, and the Andamans Cuckoo Dove *M. rufipennis*. Most of these are allopatric and all are unquestionably very closely related but the Bar-tailed and Large Brown Cuckoo Doves now overlap in Sumatra and Java and the Pink-breasted and the Large Cuckoo Dove may overlap in the extreme southern tip of Celebes. Thus they cannot all be treated as members of a superspecies or even races of a single species, nor, on present evidence, would the affinities of some forms be at all certain even if the group were divided into two superspecies.

The Bar-tailed Cuckoo Dove has barred central tail feathers and bluish grey on the outer tail feathers, characters which, *in combination*, distinguish it from all other species. It should, however, be noted that some females of the race *tusalia* show only very obscure barring on their central tail feathers and a reduced amount of blue grey on the outer ones; also that in other cuckoo doves there is often (as with many other birds) a suggestion of barring, in 'water mark' on the tail feathers. The Pink-breasted Cuckoo Dove differs from *unchall* in lacking the blackish bars on the central and the blue grey on the outer tail feathers. It is generally smaller than *phasianella*, *magna* and *rufipennis*. Its pale forehead, darker underwing, pink tinge on the breast and the fine type of barring on its breast all distinguish most individuals of most races of *amboinensis* from the above three forms but I can find no single character to distinguish all forms of the Pink-breasted Cuckoo Dove from all forms of the Large Brown Cuckoo Dove.   In appearance the Pink-breasted Cuckoo Dove is largely intermediate between *unchall* and *phasianella*.   The available descriptions of its voice suggest a possibly greater affinity with the former with which it also agrees in some points of behaviour (Gifford, 1941) but no comparative descriptions are available for *phasianella*.   To put the Pink-breasted Cuckoo Dove in a superspecies together with either the Bar-tailed or the Large Brown Cuckoo Dove would I feel be misleading as it would wrongly suggest that there was good evidence for considering it more closely related to one than the other.

The Large Cuckoo Dove is very similar to the Large Brown Cuckoo Dove although its male is much more strongly barred.   The two can certainly be considered as members of the same superspecies and may prove conspecific.   The Andaman Cuckoo Dove is very close to both the above forms and indeed on visual characters it might well be placed as a race of either.   However, its distribution suggests that it is at least as likely to be an offshoot of *unchall* stock.   The differences of colour pattern between it and the Bar-tailed Cuckoo Dove being typical of those between mainland and island forms.   For this reason alone I think it better not to prejudice future studies by linking *rufipennis* definitely to any other form.   Detailed observations on behaviour, voice and display of all the larger cuckoo doves are urgently needed.   I suspect, however, that signficant differences might only exist in areas of overlap where they had evolved as isolating mechanisms.

Of the three smaller species the Lesser Bar-tailed Cuckoo Dove *M. nigrirostris* can be distinguished by its central tail feathers which are barred rufous and black in all plumages.   Its bill is rather short and thicker in proportion than in other species.   It has bifurcated breast feathers as in the other small species. The Little Cuckoo Dove *M. ruficeps* and Mackinlay's Cuckoo Dove *M. mackinlayi* are very similar morphologically although geographically separated.   The following characters taken together serve to distinguish them.   In *ruficeps* the top of the head is reddish brown or golden brown contrasting with a greyish, iridescent or barred hind neck.   In *mackinlayi* the crown colour does not contrast sharply with that of the hind neck.   The upper parts of *ruficeps* are more or less barred on mantle and wing coverts, even, to some extent, in adult males.   In *mackinlayi* the upper parts are almost uniformly reddish or grey with fine darker speckling or 'peppering' on some feathers.   In *ruficeps* only some of the breast feathers show traces of bifurcation.   In *mackinlayi* strongly bifurcated breast feathers are usually present in numbers.   It is doubtful if the above characters are of specific significance but in view of the geographical position of the more strongly differentiated *nigrirostris* it seems preferable to consider them members of a superspecies rather than races.   As there is no evidence of an actual overlap in the New Guinea area between *nigrirostris*, which inhabits the mainland and larger islands, and *mackinlayi* which is confined to small islands (Mayr, 1941) it seems best to treat all three small Cuckoo Doves as members of a superspecies.

The long-tailed pigeons of the genus *Reinwardtoena* differ from the cuckoo doves in being larger, having proportionately thicker bills and more conspicuously patterned and (when adult) unbarred plumage. They resemble them, however, in shape and in the colour pattern of their outer tail feathers which, together with their distribution, suggests that they and the cuckoo doves are closely allied.   They are confined to the Moluccan and New Guinea regions and are largely arboreal although at least one of them may nest in caves.

Reinwardt's Long-tailed Pigeon *R. reinwardtsi* and Brown's Long-tailed Pigeon *R. browni* replace one another geographically and have similar plumage patterns although the colour of most of the upperparts differs and *browni* has a thicker bill.   The Crested Long-tailed Pigeon *R. crassirostris* is the Solomon Islands representative of the same stock but is more strongly differentiated having an even thicker and more strongly curved bill than *browni* and a long crest.   I agree with those who think that these differences do not justify retention of the monotypic genus *Coryphoenas*.

The two predominately slaty-black pigeons of the genus *Turacoena*, the White-faced Pigeon *T. manadensis* and the Timor Black Pigeon *T. modesta* much resemble the cuckoo doves in shape but have less strongly graduated, more rounded tails and very different coloration. They are usually considered to be most closely related to the cuckoo doves.

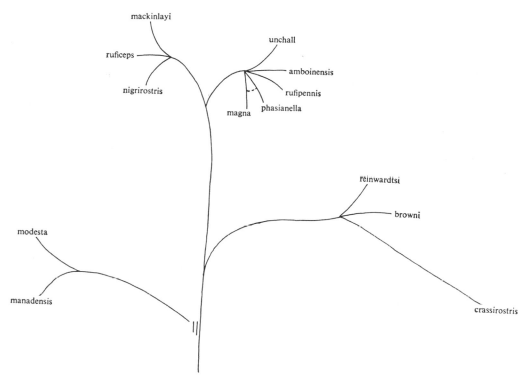

FIG. D.4: Presumed relationships of species in the genera *Macropygia, Reinwardtoena* and *Turacoena*.

This view is also favoured by one of the calls of *T. manadensis* being very similar to that of *Macropygia* species (Stresemann, 1941). On the other hand the coloration of the *Turacoena* species is very like that of *Columba vitiensis* and its allies and it is possible that *Turacoena* might be an offshoot of *Columba*. The genus *Turacoena* is here maintained not as elsewhere (Stresemann, 1941) 'out of convention' but because I am not entirely convinced that its component species are most closely related to *Macropygia*.

REFERENCES

GIFFORD, E. W. 1941. Taxonomy and habits of pigeons. *Auk* **58**: 239–245.
MAYR, E. 1941. *List of New Guinea Birds.* Published by the American Museum of Nat. Hist., N.Y.
STRESEMANN, E. 1941. Die Vögel von Celebes, pt. 3. *Journ. f. Orn.* **89**: 1–102.

BAR-TAILED CUCKOO DOVE   *Macropygia unchall*

Columba Unchall Wagler, Syst. Av., 1827, Columba sp. 38.

DESCRIPTION: Somewhat larger than a Barbary Dove in bulk but typical cuckoo dove shape. Forehead and throat buff shading into greyish pink on crown, ear coverts and nape. Hind neck iridescent green and/or purplish pink (predominantly green in most lights). Sides of neck and breast mauve pink with black subterminal bands on feathers giving a lightly barred effect; most of the feathers of these regions show some green iridescence in certain lights. Rest of underparts greyish pink shading to buff on belly and under tail coverts and dusky on flanks. Back, wings and central tail feathers closely barred black and dark chestnut.　Outer tail feathers blue grey (nearly white on basal half of outer webs of outermost pair) with broad black subterminal band.　Irides usually with a yellow or whitish inner ring, then a pink or reddish ring and, often, a grey or brownish outermost ring.　Eyelids purplish; orbital skin bluish grey.　Bill black.　Feet and legs purplish.

The female differs from the male in having the head and breast bright reddish brown shading into buff on the face and belly and everywhere closely barred with black.　Some green iridescence on the tips of the feathers of the hind neck.　Basal part of inner webs of outer tail feathers chestnut.

Juvenile like female but the young male slightly darker and redder in tone.

The above description is of the nominate form, *M. u. unchall*, from the Malay Peninsula, Sumatra, Java and Lombok.　The form found in the Himalayas east to Assam and south to Burma, *M. u. tusalia*, is slightly larger and darker with a richer pink tinge on head and breast.　The form from Southern China, Laos, Annam, and Hainan, *M. u. minor*, is very similar to it.

DISTRIBUTION AND HABITAT:　Himalayas from Kashmir and Garhwal east to Assam, Southern China, Laos, Annam, northern Siam, Hainan, Burma, Malay Peninsula, Sumatra, Java and Lombok.　Throughout its range a bird of mountain forest.　In some places, however, as in northern India, occurring in the foothills and sometimes even in the adjacent plains in winter.　Found in both primeval and secondary forest, often in open glades and clearings.

FEEDING AND GENERAL HABITS:　Feeds both in trees and on the ground.　Recorded taking berries, small fruits, seeds, grain, acorns, buds and young shoots.　When on ground usually carries the tail slightly raised.　Often tame and unsuspicious of man.　When flushed from ground or low cover rises vertically for six to ten feet then levels out and sails away.

NESTING:　Usual pigeon nest in tree or shrub.　Commonly from five to twenty feet high.　Clutch usually consists of one pale buff or cream coloured egg.　Rarely (or locally?) egg may be white and, in any case, collected eggs often fade to near-white.　Two egg clutches have been recorded but this occurrence needs confirming.　In northern India recorded breeding April to September, in the high mountains of Selangor from December to March.

VOICE:　The advertising coo has been described as a booming 'croo-oom', very deep and vibrating. What may be the same call has been rendered also as a very deep 'coo' ending in 'a curious gurgle'.

DISPLAY:　The bowing display has been described by Gifford, who kept the species in captivity.　The displaying male expands his neck so that crop region touches the ground, bows slightly, slowly raising and lowering the front of the body.　His tail is kept horizontally and slightly spread.　In the display flight the bird flies up with clapping wings for about fifty feet, then glides back to its perch in a spiral with wings held straight and body feathers, especially those on the rump, erected.　The display flight normally starts from a high perch at the top of a tree.

OTHER NAMES: Larger Indian Cuckoo Dove; Larger Malay Cuckoo Dove.

REFERENCES

BAKER, E. C. S. 1913. *Indian Pigeons and Doves*. London.
GIFFORD, E. W. 1941. Taxonomy and habits of pigeons. *Auk* **58**: 239–245.
ROBINSON, H. C. & CHASEN, F. N. 1928. *The Birds of the Malay Peninsula*. Vol. 2. London.

PINK-BREASTED CUCKOO DOVE   *Macropygia amboinensis*

Columba amboinensis Linnaeus, Syst. Nat., ed. 12, 1, 1766, p. 286.

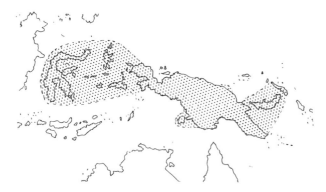

DESCRIPTION: Somewhat larger than a Barbary Dove, slimmer and longer bodied with long broad tail. General colour of upperparts reddish brown, darkest on the wing coverts, where the feathers are largely blackish but with more or less extensive reddish tips. Primaries and secondaries brownish black with narrow rusty or tawny edges to outer webs. Forehead and face deep orange brown shading to deep red-brown on crown. Feathers of mantle (and to a lesser extent those elsewhere) rust brown with fine 'peppering' of blackish giving a general dark red-brown effect. Feathers of sides and back of neck similar but with broad iridescent silvery green and/or silvery pink fringes. Throat pale yellow brown. Breast feathers golden brown, more or less suffused with pink and narrowly barred with blackish, the brownish pink tips of these feathers fade to a creamy straw colour. Owing to this and the slow rate of body feather moult in pigeons, most individuals have a greater or lesser amount of pale mottling on the breast. Belly and under tail coverts more or less uniform chestnut. Long central tail feathers dark red brown, short outer tail feathers chestnut with broad black subterminal bands. Irides; inner ring grey or blue, outer ring of red, orange, or yellow. Bill black or brown. Feet brownish purple to bright red.

Female lacks the iridescence on neck feathers and generally appears redder and more barred above than male. The forehead and crown are usually a nearly uniform red brown, often with black bases showing, giving a speckled effect. Wing coverts with dark blackish bases and broad rust red, or red brown fringes to feathers. Hind neck and upper mantle red brown or tawny with fine dark 'peppering' and vermiculations to feathers. Distinct pale streak under eye which is lacking in male.

Juvenile like female but feathers of mantle with black subterminal bars and tawny or rusty fringes. Underparts redder and less closely barred than in adult.

The above description is of the nominate form, *M. a. amboinensis*. Throughout its range this species shows much variation and consequently several local races have been differentiated and named. The forms found in New Guinea tend to be less strongly barred with, in males, a stronger pink tinge on the breast, paler face and forehead and, especially in the race *M. a. kerstingi* from Central New Guinea, a strong blue-grey tinge on crown and nape. The birds from the Bismarck Archipelago, *M. a. carteretia*, are similar to New Guinea forms but paler, the male having a buff forehead and face, light pink breast and light tawny underparts, and the female pale whitish buff or whitish grey centres to the throat and breast feathers which gives the breast a scaled or spotted appearance. In the form from Numfor Island the male has the crown and nape slate grey, and the gloss on the hind neck is mainly green; the female is intermediate in appearance between the female of *carteretia* and the nominate form.

   In the form from South Celebes, *M. a. albicapilla*, the male has rich dark chestnut upperparts, a cream-coloured forehead, grey tinted crown, and strongly barred breast with very pale tips to the barred feathers and no pink tinge; the female is similar to the nominate form but redder. The remaining races all closely resemble one or other of those described above.

DISTRIBUTION AND HABITAT: Sangir and Talaut Islands, Celebes, Peling, Banggai, Kalidupa, Buton, Sula Islands. The Moluccas, Kei Islands, New Guinea and nearby islands and archipelagoes.
   Inhabits both forest and also small clumps of trees and narrow strips of woodland fringing streams in open grassland.

FEEDING AND GENERAL HABITS: Little recorded. Known to feed on berries and seeds, which are often taken from the ground. Commonly found in pairs.

NESTING: Nest sometimes, perhaps usually, rather large and bulky for a pigeon. Placed in a tree or shrub, frequently on the large leaf of a Pandanus, or on the frond of a large fern. One egg is the normal clutch.

VOICE: What is presumably the advertising coo is described as 'koo, koo' or 'Hoopoo', the second note less loud than the first. Heinrich (in Stresemann, 1941) describes a growling note when the male is bowing to the female.

DISPLAY: Heinrich appears to have seen a bowing display but does not describe it.

OTHER NAMES: Amboina Cuckoo Dove.

REFERENCES

GILLIARD, E. T. & LEROY, M. 1961. *Bull. Amer. Mus. Nat. Hist.* **123**: art. 1.
OGILVIE-GRANT, W. R. 1915. *Ibis* Jubilee Supplement No. 2.
RAND, A. L. 1942. *Bull. Amer. Mus. Nat. Hist.* **79**: art. 4.
STRESEMANN, E. 1941. Die Vögel von Celebes. *Journ. f. Orn.* **89**: 11–101.

LARGE BROWN CUCKOO DOVE   *Macropygia phasianella*

Columba phasianella Temminck, Trans. Linn. Soc. London, 13, pt. 1, 1821, p. 129.

DESCRIPTION: About the size of a smallish Feral Pigeon but typical cuckoo-dove shape. Back, wing coverts, rump and central tail feathers dark reddish brown, the feathers of the wing coverts with redder, brighter, more rusty-red fringes. Outer primaries and secondaries brownish black with rufous fringes. Head, neck and breast warm reddish brown tinged pink on the upper breast and shading to golden brown on lower breast, throat and underparts. Feathers on breast, neck and underparts sometimes faintly barred, vermiculated or 'peppered' with blackish grey. Nape and hind neck glossed with light mauve-pink and bronzy green. Under tail coverts light chestnut. Underwing dark chestnut. Outer tail feathers chestnut with broad black subterminal bands. Irides white or bluish, often with orange or red outer ring. Bill black or dark brown. Legs and feet red. Female has a rich rufous crown. Lacks the pink iridescence on the neck and the pink tinge on the breast. Greyish vermiculations and speckling on feathers of neck and underparts much more prominent than in most males. Juvenile much as female but still more noticeably barred.

The above description is of the Australian form of the species, *M. p. phasianella*, from eastern Australia. The many other races that have been recognised throughout the species' range are mostly of a richer red-brown colour and with more or less conspicuous black and rufous, or black and tawny, barring on the neck and underparts of the female.

DISTRIBUTION AND HABITAT: Eastern Australia, Kangean Island, Java, Sumatra, Lombok, Klagger Island, Sumbawa, Flores, Engaro, the Mentawi Islands, Nias Island, Simalur Island, the Batan Islands, Botel Tobago, Calayan Island, Northern Borneo and the Philippines.

Inhabits forest. In eastern Australia it is one of the commonest pigeons in many of the remaining patches of rain forest. Frequents especially glades and small openings within forest.

FEEDING AND GENERAL HABITS: Feeds largely on fruits and berries taken both from trees and shrubs and from the ground. When feeding in trees or shrubs the spread tail is often used as a support (Austin, 1950). The Australian form is said to appear clumsy when flying among trees. This is probably a false impression as the long tail – which is often said to look as if it impedes the bird – must certainly be an adaption to flying and balancing among the branches. Flies swiftly when travelling over open country.

NESTING: Usual pigeon nest in a tree or shrub. Usually low down, but nests up to thirty feet high recorded. One creamy white egg. Two egg clutches have been recorded but their validity seems questionable. In Australia nests have been found in November, December and January.

VOICE: A loud tri-syllabic coo, variously written 'whoop-a-whoop', 'did-you-walk', etc., is probably the advertising coo. I can find no account of any other calls, although it probably has others.

DISPLAY: The bowing display is said by Gifford (1941) to be the same as in the Bar-tailed Cuckoo Dove *M. unchall* (q.v.).

OTHER NAMES: Brown Pigeon; Slender-billed Cuckoo-Dove; Dark Cuckoo-Dove.

REFERENCES

AUSTIN, C. 1950. Further notes on the birds of Dunk Island, Queensland. *Emu* **49**: 225–231.
COOPER, R. P. 1962. A Revision of the Distribution of the Brown Pigeon. *Emu* **61**: 253–269.
GIFFORD, E. W. 1941. Taxonomy and habits of pigeons. *Auk* **58**: 242–245.

LARGE CUCKOO DOVE   *Macropygia magna*

Macropygia magna Wallace, Proc. Zool. Soc. London, 1863 (1864), p. 497.

DESCRIPTION: About the size of a small Feral Pigeon but usual cuckoo dove shape. Head golden brown to chestnut red, inconspicuously barred with blackish. Throat pale straw colour. Neck, upper mantle, breast and underparts light golden brown to buff, barred with blackish. Back and rump rather darker with obscure barring. Wing coverts barred blackish and rufous freckled with dark grey, general effect being of a dark red brown colour. Primaries and outer secondaries blackish with narrow tawny fringes. Underwing chestnut. Under tail coverts light chestnut. Tail feathers dull reddish brown, the outermost pair with obscure blackish subterminal bands.   Irides blue grey with pink, red or orange outer ring.   Orbital skin ? ? ?.   Bill brown or blackish with pale tip to lower mandible.   Feet purplish red or brownish red.

Female much as male but breast appears predominantly reddish brown with only faint barring and pale spots.   The individual feathers of this area have pale greyish centres, a narrow blackish subterminal band and broad rufous tips.   Juvenile very like female.

The above description is of nominate form, *M. m. magna*, from Timor, Alor Wetar, Roma, Kisar, Letti, and Moa.   The form found on south Celebes and the Island of Salayer, *M. m. macassariensis*, and that from Djampea and Kalao tua islands, *M. m. longa*, are very different in appearance.   They bear about the same relation to the nominate form as does the grey phase of *M. mackinlayi* to the rufous phase of that species.   In these two races of *magna* (which differ only very slightly in size) the head and upperparts are greyish brown, the feathers on the nape and back and sides of the neck being finely freckled with greyish and cream or buff, giving a 'pepper and salt' effect.   The throat is pale buff and the breast and underparts pale buff to creamy white barred with drab grey.   There is only a small area of pale chestnut under the wing.

The female is slightly browner above and more warmly buff below than the male.   The young are much browner than the adults, deeper buff and more strongly barred below, their heads barred rufous and black, and black subterminal bands and reddish tawny or chestnut fringes to most of the wing coverts.

The form of the species found in the Tenimber Islands, *M. m. timorlaoensis*, is like the nominate form in pattern and markings but much less red in colour being, in the latter respect, intermediate between it and the greyish forms *M. m. longea* and *M. m. macassariensis*.

DISTRIBUTION AND HABIT: Southern Celebes, Islands of Salayer, Djampea, Kalao tua, Timor, Alor, Wetar, Roma, Kisar, Letti, Moa, and the Tenimber Islands.

FEEDING AND GENERAL HABITS: No information.

NESTING: No information.

VOICE: No information.

DISPLAY: No information.

ANDAMANS CUCKOO DOVE   *Macropygia rufipennis*

Macropygia rufipennis Blyth, Journ. As. Soc. Bengal, 15, 1846, p. 371.

DESCRIPTION: Very similar to the Large Brown Cuckoo Dove.   About size of a smallish Feral Pigeon.   Head and nape pinkish rufous to chestnut, lighter on cheeks and shading to pale rufous on throat. Hind neck reddish brown to pale yellow brown, barred and speckled with blackish. Sides of neck and breast reddish brown to light chestnut barred with black shading to a yellow brown with dusky bars and speckling on belly. Under tail coverts chestnut. Mantle, back and wings dark brown, most cover feathers with blackish subterminal bars and rusty fringes. Underwing mainly chestnut. Rump,

upper tail coverts and central tail feathers dull reddish brown. Outer tail feathers lighter with ill defined blackish basal area and subterminal bands. Irides with inner ring pale bright blue, outer ring purplish red. Orbital skin greyish blue. Bill dull pinkish or pinkish purple, slightly brighter at base. Legs and feet dull pinkish red or horny pink.

Female has crown more rusty and with black bases and edges to feathers giving speckled effect. Sides of neck, breast and underparts rusty chestnut with little or no dark barring or speckling. Broad rusty chestnut tip to wing coverts and primaries and secondaries predominantly rusty chestnut although tipped and speckled blackish brown. General appearance much redder than male. Juvenile very like female but hind neck and mantle more clearly barred and general tone of plumage often less reddish.

DISTRIBUTION AND HABITAT: The Andaman and Nicobar Islands. Inhabits secondary growth, gardens and clearings as well as forest.

FEEDING AND GENERAL HABITS: The only first-hand observations I can find are those of Davison (in Hume, 1874). He found this species to feed, in his experience, exclusively on the small Nepal or Birds-eye chillies which grow, or at any rate then grew abundantly all over both islands.

NESTING: A nest and eggs found by Davison that may have been of this species was similar to those of the Emerald Dove.

VOICE: No information.

DISPLAY: No information.

OTHER NAMES: Nicobar Cuckoo Dove.

REFERENCE

HUME, A. O. 1874. The Islands of the Bay of Bengal. *Stray Feathers* **1**: 266–269.

LESSER BAR-TAILED CUCKOO DOVE *Macropygia nigrirostris*

Macropygia nigrirostris Salvadori, Ann. Mus. Civ. Genova, 7, 1875, p. 972.

DESCRIPTION: Somewhat smaller than a Barbary Dove, usual Cuckoo Dove shape. General appearance (of male) rich chestnut red, darker on the wings and somewhat paler below. Outer primaries and secondaries brownish-black with narrow rufous edgings. Indistinct blackish barring on upper tail coverts. Central tail feathers rich chestnut barred with black. Outermost tail feathers pale chestnut with broad black subterminal bands. Breast feathers bifurcated. Iris with a red, orange or yellow outer ring, and then a brown or black median ring and a pale grey or white inner ring.   Sometimes, apparently, entirely red, orange, pink or yellow.   Orbital skin plum red (from a few records only).   Feet red, reddish brown, or chocolate.   Bill black, brownish black, or brown.

Female a lighter chestnut, often golden-buff on face and underparts with all feathers marked with black so that she appears barred and spotted all over.   Tail, as male's, but more clearly barred.   Juvenile like female, but details of pattern, especially on tail feathers, somewhat different.

DISTRIBUTION AND HABITAT: New Guinea, Jobi; larger islands of the Bismarck Archipelago, Lihir Islands and D'Entrecasteaux Archipelago.   Presumably inhabits woodland like other cuckoo doves, but little recorded of its habits.

NESTING: No information.

VOICE: No information.

DISPLAY: No information.

OTHER NAMES: Black-billed Cuckoo Dove.

MACKINLAY'S CUCKOO DOVE   *Macropygia mackinlayi*

Macropygia mackinlayi Ramsay, Proc. Linn. Soc. New South Wales, 2, 1878, p. 286.

DESCRIPTION: In its New Hebridean populations this species shows marked dimorphism or, to be more precise, dichromatism; some individuals being rufous in colour, others grey.   This situation is found in many species of owls and some nightjars but is unique among pigeons.

About the size of a Barbary Dove but with the usual cuckoo dove shape.   The rufous phase of this species is a deep reddish brown colour, darkest on the upperparts and somewhat lighter on the head, neck, and underparts which may show a tawny tinge.   Outer primaries and secondaries brownish black with narrow rufous fringes.   Central tail feathers dark red brown, outer ones paler with greyish rufous tips and broad blackish subterminal bands.   Breast feathers bifurcated with blackish bases and red brown tips.   Irides orange, yellow, red-brown or red.   Bill black.   Feet and legs red.

The female is duller and greyer on the head and of a general yellow brown suffused with grey on neck and breast.   This effect being due to the individual feathers being finely vermiculated or 'peppered' with dull greyish on a tawny ground.

Juvenile much as female but redder and of a general barred appearance.   Most of the feathers of the upperparts have blackish subterminals and conspicuous rufous tips.   Feathers of breast barred red brown and blackish, those of belly reddish tawny and grey.

Grey Phase: Upperparts dark grey with broad pale grey fringes to most feathers. Head and underparts pale grey, the forehead, throat and breast being sometimes a very pale tawny silver colour. The individual feathers of most parts are very finely speckled with minute spots and freckles of darker grey on the pale silver, or buffish grey, ground giving a 'pepper and salt' effect.

Female as male, but with more pronounced black bases to the bifurcated breast feathers and more pronounced buffish tinge on underparts. Juvenile: Feathers of crown and breast blackish with conspicuous pale buffy grey tips. Otherwise mainly dark grey above and pale grey below with blackish subterminal bars and pale greyish buff tips to most feathers.

Some specimens (mostly females) occur that are intermediate, to varying degrees, in colour between the rufous and grey phases. These are of a predominantly greyish-tawny hue.

The above description is of the nominate form of the species, *Macropygia m. mackinlayi*, from the New Hebrides, Santa Cruz Islands and Banks Islands. The other races of the species are not dimorphic, or are only exceptionally so, and resemble the rufous phase of the nominate form – most of them being, however, rather richer in colour. This is particularly so with the Solomon Islands form, *M. m. arossi*, in which the male is a beautiful rich chestnut red with a purple tinge on the upperparts. Its female is equally handsome being only a slightly paler and more golden-rufous on face and breast with the black bases to the bifurcated breast feathers very prominent giving a fine spotted effect.

DISTRIBUTION AND HABITAT: Santa Cruz Islands, Banks Islands, New Hebrides, Solomon Islands, Dampier Island, St. Matthias, Squally, Uaton and Witu Islands, Talasea district of New Britain.

Inhabits woodland; in the Solomons is found in and about clearings, gardens, second growth and broken areas in forest at all elevations from coast to mist forest.

FEEDING AND GENERAL HABITS: Feeds both in trees and on ground. Very agile when feeding in trees and shrubs, often hanging upside down; long tail (as in other cuckoo doves) used for balancing. Feeds on berries and small fruit; no doubt other foods also.

NESTING: Apparently usual pigeon nest 'not too high' in trees or palms. One white egg. (Meyer, 1933.)

VOICE: What is probably the advertising coo has been described as a loud 'moo-kau' sounding at a distance like the call of the European Cuckoo.

DISPLAY: No information.

OTHER NAMES: Rufous-brown Cuckoo Dove; Rufous Cuckoo Dove; Rufous Pheasant Pigeon.

REFERENCES

CAIN, A. J. & GALBRAITH, I. C. J. 1956. Field notes on birds of the eastern Solomon Islands. *Ibis* **98**: 100–134.
MEYER, P. O. 1933. Vogeleier und Nester aus Neubrittanien, Sudsee. *Beitr. zur Fortplanzungsbiologie der Vögel* **9**: 122–135.

LITTLE CUCKOO DOVE   *Macropygia ruficeps*

Columba ruficeps Temminck, Pl. col. livr., 95, 1834.

DESCRIPTION :   The Little Cuckoo Dove shows considerable geographical variation in size and colour so that a single description cannot serve for all forms of the species.   The race found in Pantar, Flores, Sumbawa, and Lombok, *M. ruficeps orientalis*, is about the size of a Barbary Dove but with the typical slender outline, small bill and long broad tail of a cuckoo dove.   General appearance reddish brown, darkest above and palest on head and belly.   Mantle, back and wing coverts a dull reddish brown, the fringes of the feathers somewhat redder and lighter.   Head and face light rufous or golden brown, paler on the throat and somewhat darker and more reddish on neck and breast.   Some of the feathers on the breast with pale creamy tips.   Feathers on back and sides of neck 'peppered' with blackish and with light bronzy green and/or wine-pink iridescence.   Primaries and outer secondaries dull brownish black. Central tail feathers dark red brown, outer ones chestnut with black subterminal band.   Underwing coverts and basal parts of underside of wing quills chestnut.   Irides pale blue to white.   Orbital skin dark grey.   Bill brown.   Legs and feet red or purplish red.

Female slightly duller and paler than male but often with broader and more closely defined rust red edges to mantle and wing covert feathers.   Little or no iridescence on neck.   Breast feathers have their sides except at tip, blackish so that upper breast may appear spotted.

Juvenile similar to female but redder and more barred and mottled in appearance, the majority of feathers having pronounced rufous or rust edges set off by a blackish subterminal area.

The form found in Java and Bali, *M. r. ruficeps*, is very similar to that described above, but somewhat smaller and a brighter reddish brown in general.   That from Burma and Tenasserim is like the Javanese form but is slightly lighter in colour with the pale fringes to the male's breast feathers and the 'spots' on the female's more pronounced.

The form found in Borneo, *M. ruficeps nana*, is appreciably smaller than a Barbary Dove in body size. In colour the general impression given is that of a more richly coloured bird than the form previously described ; redder above, paler on the underparts and with a conspicuously spotted or mottled breast. This appearance is due to the upperparts being of a redder tone with broad, but ill-defined, rusty chestnut fringes to the wing and mantle feathers, a richer and chiefly wine-red iridescence on the hind neck, broad blackish areas on the sides (except at extreme tip) of most of the breast feathers, and lighter golden brown lower breast and belly.

The female differs from the male in being duller below, having more pronounced dark mottling on the breast ; hind neck and upper mantle feathers barred blackish or iridescent green and rusty fawn and more contrasting chestnut edges, and blackish bases to the wing coverts.   The forms from Malaya and Sumatra are extremely similar.

DISTRIBUTION AND HABITAT :   Burma, Northern Siam, Indo-China, Laos, Malay States, Borneo, Sumatra, Java, Bali, Simalur, Sumbawa, Flores, Pantar and Timor.   Found in forest, usually, but not always, at rather high elevations.   Often frequents clearings and cultivated plots.

FEEDING AND GENERAL HABITS: Feeds both on ground and in trees. Known to take berries, seeds, rice and chillies. Usually in pairs or small parties.

NESTING: Usual pigeon nest in tree or shrub. Sometimes, however, the nest consists chiefly or entirely of a pad of moss. It seems likely in such cases that the pad of moss got in place by some other agency and the doves merely found and exploited it as a nest site. One buff, cream or white egg. Two egg clutches have been recorded, probably in error.

VOICE: What is probably the advertising coo has been described as a rapidly repeated 'croo-wuck, croo-wuck, croo-wuck', the 'croo' so soft that it can only be hears at close quarters, but the 'wuck' audible some distance. What may be the same call has been described also as a quickly repeated 'oo-who-who-oo'. In Malaya a 'very peculiar and monotonous coo' has been heard from parties feeding on the ground. Possibly this is the display coo.

DISPLAY: No information.

OTHER NAMES: Lesser Red Cuckoo Dove; Red-headed Cuckoo Dove; Red-faced Cuckoo Dove.

REFERENCES

BAKER, E. C. S. 1913. *Indian Pigeons and Doves*. London.
ROBINSON, H. C. & CHASEN, F. N. 1928. *The Birds of the Malay Peninsula*. Vol. 2. London.
SMYTHIES, B. E. 1960. *The Birds of Borneo*. London.

REINWARDT'S LONG-TAILED PIGEON

Reinwardtoena reinwardtsi

Columba reinwardtsi Temminck, Pl. col. livr. 42, 1824, pl. 248.

DESCRIPTION: About the size of a largish Feral Pigeon but with a very long and strongly graduated tail (see sketch) and rather stout bill with strongly arched culmen. Throat, white. Head, neck, breast and underparts pale bluish grey shading to somewhat darker bluish grey on flanks and under tail coverts. Breast often tinged with vinous pink and with pale pinkish, creamy, or white fringes to many feathers. Mantle, back, rump, upper tail coverts and the visible parts of the long, broad central tail feathers dark rich chestnut. Wing coverts and scapulars dark chestnut, the outermost ones shading into blackish. Primaries, primary coverts and secondaries black. Outermost pair of tail feathers have outer webs greyish white with black subterminal band, inner webs broadly banded black, grey, black, with grey tips. The next pair are blackish at base with a central band of grey and subterminal band of black intermixed with chestnut. The next pair have broad chestnut ends. Subsequent feathers show progressively more chestnut and the central ones have only a little concealed grey and black basally. Underwing grey and black. Irides white, yellowish white or yellow with pink or red outer ring. Orbital skin purplish pink to wine red. Bill brown, base of bill and cere dull purplish pink. Legs and feet red, pink, or purplish red.

Sexes alike in plumage, but female's eye is more often yellowish, male's more often white on inner ring. Orbital skin of female sometimes duller and more brownish red than male's. Juvenile sooty brown, darkest on wings and palest on throat where near dirty white. Rump and upper tail coverts reddish brown with darker fringes. Central tail feathers sooty brown tinged with chestnut. Some feathers of mantle and wing coverts with faint rufous fringes. See Pl. 1.

The above description is of the form *R. r. griseotincta* which inhabits New Guinea and adjacent islands where the species has been most often collected and observed. The nominate form, *R. r. reinwardtsi*, from the Moluccas, and *R. r. brevis*, from Biak Island are rather smaller and paler especially on the breast which is almost white.

In life this species is easily picked out by its long broad tail, relatively short rounded wings, and the pale head and breast contrasting with the dark wings.

DISTRIBUTION AND HABITAT : The Moluccas and New Guinea, and adjacent and intervening islands. Inhabits mountain forest. In New Guinea found up to the limit of the tree line at 11,100 feet (Mayr and Gilliard, 1954). Perhaps dependant on suitable rock formations for nesting sites.

FEEDING AND GENERAL HABITS : Known to feed on fruit taken from trees. On Ceram (and doubtless elsewhere) often in flocks feeding on fruiting trees. Has a very agile, silent, twisting flight.

NESTING : In New Guinea the natives told Gilliard that Reinwardt's Pigeon nests on ledges in caves and river gorges. Gilliard himself saw an adult fly up in tight spirals out of a deep pothole hundreds of feet deep. Shaw-Mayer found a nest of usual pigeon type in a bush four feet above ground. It had one egg which was white with a faint olive-buff tinge (Harrison and Frith). Juveniles have been taken in July, October and November (in New Guinea) suggesting a prolonged breeding season.

VOICE : A 'soft cooing note' has been recorded by Ripley (1964).

DISPLAY : Has a display flight in which it flies up in slanting flight from a high perch, makes a wide circle and glides back to the same tree or one near it.

OTHER NAMES : Chestnut and Grey Pigeon ; Maroon and Grey Pigeon.

REFERENCES

GILLIARD, E. T. & LECROY, M. 1961. *Bull. Amer. Mus. Nat. Hist.* **123** : art. 1, p. 37.
HARRISON, C. J. O. & FRITH C. B. Nests and eggs of some New Guinea birds. *(in press).*
MAYR, E. & GILLIARD, E. T. 1954. *Bull. Amer. Mus. Nat. Hist.* **103** : art, 4, p. 338.
STRESEMANN, E. 1914. Die Vögel von Seran (Ceram). *Novit. Zool.* **21** : 25–135 (51).
TUBB, J. A. 1945. Field Notes on some New Guinea birds. *Emu* **44** : 249–273.

BROWN'S LONG-TAILED PIGEON   *Reinwardtoena browni*

Macropygia browni Sclater, Proc. Zool. Soc. London, 1877, p. 110.

DESCRIPTION: Similar in size and shape to the previous species and very similar in colour pattern except for a lack of any chestnut in the plumage. Forehead, crown and hind neck silvery grey shading to white or nearly white on face and breast and to dark bluish grey on the flanks and under tail coverts. Mantle, back, rump, upper tail coverts, central tail feathers and wings black. The outer tail feathers are patterned with grey. Irides red. Legs and feet dull red. Bill dark grey. These soft part colours are from the data on only two specimens and may not be very exact. The species has extensive orbital skin whose colour was not recorded by the above collector.

I have only seen one young bird of this species which had nearly completed its first moult. The juvenile feathers remaining suggest that the juvenile plumage is predominantly sooty grey, very similar to that of *R. reinwardtsi*.

DISTRIBUTION AND HABITAT: New Britain and Duke of York Island. Presumably in forest.

FEEDING AND GENERAL HABITS: Known to eat berries.

NESTING: No information.

VOICE: No information.

DISPLAY: No information.

OTHER NAMES: Black and White Long-tailed Pigeon: Black and Grey Long-tailed Pigeon.

CRESTED LONG-TAILED PIGEON   *Reinwardtoena crassirostris*

Turacoena crassisrostris Gould, Proc. Zool. Soc. London, 1836, p. 136.

DESCRIPTION: Similar in size and shape to the previous species but with long crest formed by elongated and rather hairy-textured feathers of crown and nape. In Museum specimens the crest appears loose and straggly but in life is said (Ramsay, 1883) to look very similar to that of the Crested Pigeon *Ocyphaps lophotes*. Bill slightly stouter and upper mandible strongly hooked. Head and crest pale purplish grey. Throat whitish. Breast and sides of neck clear silvery bluish grey darkening to a darker bluish grey on rest of underparts and hind neck. Some individuals have the breast and underparts suffused with yellowish fawn or with yellowish fawn fringes to the feathers. Upperparts black with a bluish-silver bloom, especially on the wings. Central tail feathers black. Outermost pair have outer web greyish white at base shading to grey, then a black sub-terminal bar and grey tips; inner web black with broad oblique grey central band and narrow grey tip. Rest black with grey central band. Irides yellow with red outer ring, yellow or orange. Orbital skin purplish red or carmine red. Bill yellow or orange at tip, red or purplish red at base. Legs and feet red, dull red or purplish red.

Sexes often alike but very few females have clear grey breasts, most showing yellowish fawn fringes to the feathers. These pale fringes seem, however, to be largely due to wear and the pronounced yellow hue shown by some specimens to be due to staining. The juvenile has the black on the wing coverts duller and each feather with a rusty edging. Its head feathers are dusky with blackish subterminal bars and rusty tips. Those on the crown are slightly elongated but not long and hairy like the adults. Its underparts are dull brownish grey with faint rusty fringes to most feathers.

DISTRIBUTION AND HABITAT: The Solomon Islands. Apparently inhabits hill forest.

FEEDING AND GENERAL HABITS: I can find little information. Galbraith (1956) saw only a solitary individual and noted that in flight the crest was not noticeable. Morton (in Ramsay, 1883) recorded that it was 'strictly a ground pigeon', frequented dense scrub and when flushed flew to the lower boughs of the nearest tree. Since he also says that it has similar habits to the cuckoo doves, it is possible that it is largely a ground feeder but hardly likely that it is, in fact, 'strictly a ground pigeon'.

NESTING: Said by French (1953) to lay one egg. He gives no other details.

VOICE: No information.

DISPLAY: No information.

OTHER NAMES: Crested Pigeon.

REFERENCES

CAIN, A. J. & GALBRAITH, I. C. J. 1956. Field notes on birds of the Eastern Solomon Islands. *Ibis* **98**: 100–134.
FRENCH, W. 1957. Birds of the Solomon Islands. *Ibis* **99**: 126–127.
GALBRAITH, I. C. J. & E. H. 1962. Land birds of Guadalcanal and the San Cristoval Group, Eastern Solomon Islands. *Bull. Brit. Mus. (Nat. Hist.) Zoology*, Vol. 9, No. 1.
RAMSAY, E. P. 1883. Notes on the Zoology of the Solomon Islands, Pt. 4. *Proc. Linn., Soc. New South Wales* **7**: 16–43.

WHITE-FACED PIGEON   *Turacoena manadensis*

Columba manadensis Quoy and Gaimard, Voy. 'Astrolabe', Zool. 1, 1830, p. 248.

DESCRIPTION: Rather smaller than the average Feral Pigeon with a longer tail which is graduated but not to the same degree as in the cuckoo-doves (*Macropygia*). Forehead, face and throat white. Rest of plumage slaty black with intense green or purple (according to angle of light) iridescence on the neck and slight iridescence elsewhere on the cover feathers. Irides light red or purplish red; orbital skin purplish red. Legs and feet blackish. Sexes alike. The juvenile, or at least the single specimen I have been able to examine, is like the adult but duller and with the face suffused with grey.

DISTRIBUTION AND HABITAT: Celebes, Buton Island and adjacent islands, Peling Island and the Sula Islands. In Celebes (and no doubt elsewhere also) inhabits lowland areas, particularly small patches of dense woodland in otherwise open country and in wooded gorges.

FEEDING AND GENERAL HABITS: Little recorded. Heinrich (in Stresemann, 1941) found that it kept much to cover, not perching on exposed treetops as imperial pigeons do. Probably feeds much on berries. Said to eat the flesh of Papayas in native gardens. Also takes fruits of *Lantana camara*. Drinks in the evening. On Muna Island Bemmell (1951) found it in company with the Pink-breasted Cuckoo Dove.

NESTING: No information.

VOICE: Heinrich (in Stresemann, 1941) records a two-syllabled deep 'kookook' suggestive of the call of some cuckoos and, except in modulation, rather like that of the various *Macropygia* species.

DISPLAY: No information.

OTHER NAMES: White-faced Black Pigeon; White-faced Cuckoo Dove; White-headed Pigeon; White-faced Black Cuckoo Dove.

REFERENCES

BEMMELL, A. C. V. VAN. 1951. On the birds of the islands of Muna and Buton, South Celebes. *Treubia* 21, 1: 94–95.
STRESEMANN, E. 1941. Die Vögel von Celebes. Pt. 3. *Journ. f. Orn* 89: 1–102.

TIMOR BLACK PIGEON *Turacoena modesta*

Columba modesta Temminck, Pl. col. liver., 93, 1835, pl. 552.

DESCRIPTION: Size and shape as in the last species (q.v.). Colour entirely dark bluish slate shading to nearly black on tail and wings, and rather paler on head and underparts. Fringes of feathers on crown, nape, neck, breast and upper mantle with light green and/or amethyst iridescence. Irides brownish red or with yellow inner ring and red outer ring. Orbital skin yellow. Feet and legs bluish black. Sexes alike. Juvenile brownish slate with narrow blackish subterminal bands and pale fawny-white fringes to most feathers.

DISTRIBUTION AND HABITAT: Timor. Presumably in woodland.
FEEDING AND GENERAL HABITS: No information.
NESTING: No information.
VOICE: No information.
DISPLAY: No information.
OTHER NAMES: Black Cuckoo Dove; Slate-coloured Cuckoo Dove.

AFRICAN SPOT-WING DOVES

This group of pigeons is composed of the five species of wood doves of the genus *Turtur* and the Masked Dove or Namaqua Dove, *Oena capensis*. The wood doves are plump, compact little pigeons, the largest of them, the Blue-headed Dove or Maiden Dove, *Turtur brehmeri*, being about as large as a domestic Barbary Dove but plumper in shape and with a larger head. The four others are considerably smaller.

All these have chestnut colouring on the inner webbing of the primaries, iridescent areas on the scapulars and greater wing coverts that form two dark shining spots on the closed wing; blue-grey outer tail feathers with a blackish subterminal band, and a pale band bordered with two darker ones across the lower back. This last feature is less pronounced in the dark-coloured Tambourine Dove, *Turtur tympanistria*, than in the Green-spotted, Blue-spotted and Black-billed Wood Doves, *Turtur chalcospilos*, *T. afer* and *T. abyssinicus*, and is obsolescent in some individuals of the Blue-headed Dove. The *Turtur* species are forest or scrub-haunting birds which feed on the ground but nest on bushes or trees, usually at no great height. The Masked Dove differs markedly from the wood doves in appearance, due to its very long tail, small size, and the striking black face and breast of the male. Its colour pattern and its geographical distribution clearly indicate, however, that it and the wood doves are closely related.

The Green-spotted, Blue-spotted and Black-billed Wood Doves are extremely alike in appearance; and no marked differences in their voices have been recorded. *T. afer* overlaps widely with *T. chalcospilos* and *T. abyssinicus*. The only colour difference which seems likely to serve as a species-specific recognition mark is its predominantly red bill, the bills of the other two being blackish. It is very unlikely that the slightly darker general tone of *afer* or its slightly smaller wing spots could function as isolating mechanisms. *T. afer* shows different habitat preferences, but it and either *chalcospilos* or *abyssinicus* are often found in fairly close proximity.

T. chalcospilos and *T. abyssinicus* appear to be even more closely related to one another than either is to *T. afer*. The only constant differences in colour are the paler pinkish breast of *abyssinicus* and its slightly smaller iridescent wing markings that do not extend so far towards the end of the feathers as do those of *chalcospilos*. Other differences such as the generally paler coloration of *abyssinicus*, the colour of the iridescent wing spots (usually purple-black to greenish blue in *abyssinicus* and golden-green to bluish green in *chalcospilos*) and the colour of the stripe from gape to eye (always black in *abyssinicus*, usually grey, of a tone darker than rest of face, in *chalcospilos*) are valid only for a majority of individuals of each form.

I have seen no individuals that appear to be undoubted intergrades or hybrids between the two but in view of the very slight differences it is questionable whether such would be recognisable. It may be significant that a specimen of *T. chalcospilos* from the Didinga Mountains in the southern Sudan has a black facial stripe and wing spots that in colour nearly match those of some specimens of *abyssinicus* (B.M. Nos. 1915.12.24.279, 1922.12.28.109 and 1900.1.3.388) from Darfur, Roseires and Beni Schongul. There are, however, some similar specimens of *chalcospilos* from further south.

The distributions given in some regional works (e.g. Mackworth-Praed and Grant, 1957) suggest that *abyssinicus* and *chalcospilos* are sympatric in Eritrea and Ethiopia. I have been unable to find evidence of both forms occurring at the same place. The nearest among the many British Museum specimens of both from East Africa are a *chalcospilos* from Eros in the Didinga Mountains of southern Sudan and an *abyssinicus* from Gondoroko on the White Nile, southern Sudan. Moltoni (1944) who gives a list of localities from which both have been obtained in the former Italian colonies does not record both from the same place. There thus seems no evidence that the two forms actually occur, much less breed, in the same locality.

Whether *chalcospilos* and *abyssinicus* should be considered as races of the same species or as members of a superspecies must, on present evidence, be an open question. The latter course has been adopted here because the example of *T. afer* shows that in this group specific level may be accompanied by only a very slight amount of morphological difference.

The Tambourine Dove differs strikingly from the above species in coloration and in its sharply attenuated first primary.   These are undoubtedly adaptations to living in denser and generally more shady cover. The colour pattern of the head and breast shows a remarkable but not surprising convergence towards that of some *Gallicolumba* species that also frequent dense vegetation.   In all essentials, however, the plumage pattern of *tympanistria* is identifiable with that of the other *Turtur* species.   The Blue-headed Wood Dove has diverged further in size and coloration but its affinities are obvious when skins or even more when living specimens are compared and it is rightly included in this genus.

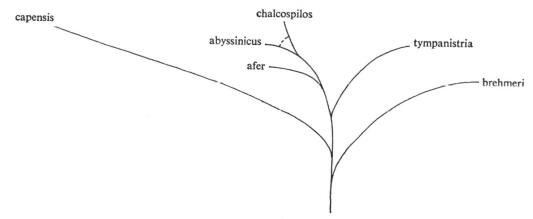

Fig. D.5:   Presumed relationships of species in the genera *Turtur* and *Oena*.

The female Masked Dove is very similar in colour pattern to the three scrub-haunting *Turtur* species. She differs chiefly in lacking any pink on the breast and in having a dark stripe along the lower inner edge of the folded wing formed by blackish edges to the inner webs of the inner secondaries.   The juvenile plumage is also similar to that of the three light coloured *Turtur* species but the male differs strikingly from any *Turtur* in his black face and breast and both sexes in their long graduated tails and more pointed wings.   These can, I think, be considered as adaptations to a rather different ecology which (often at any rate) appears to involve exploiting temporary supplies of food and water in arid country and then flying considerable distances to find suitable conditions elsewhere.   This greater mobility has, in all probability, been the factor enabling *Oena capensis* to extend its range to Arabia and Madagascar. Although its relationship to *Turtur* is unquestioned the sum total of its morphological and behavioural differences seem just sufficient to justify retention of the monotypic genus *Oena*.

The nearest relatives of the African spot-wing doves appear to be the emerald doves *Chalcophaps*, the Australian bronzewings, and, probably rather more distantly, the American ground doves and their allies.

REFERENCES

MACKWORTH-PRAED, C. W. & GRANT, C. H. B. (1957).   *African Handbook of Birds*.   Series 1.   Volume 1.   London.
MOLTONI, E.   1944.   *Gli Uccelli Dell' Africa Orientale Italiana*.   Part 2.   Milan.

GREEN-SPOTTED WOOD DOVE   *Turtur chalcospilos*

Columba Chalcospilos Wagler, Syst. Av., 1827, Columba, sp. 28.

DESCRIPTION: About two-thirds the size of a Barbary Dove or rather less.   Plump and compact in shape.   Top of head bluish grey shading to white or pale grey on forehead.   Narrow black line from gape to eye.   Sides of neck and underparts light mauve-pink shading to whitish on chin and centre of belly.   Upperparts light brown to pale greyish fawn.   Iridescent areas on some of the inner secondaries and greater coverts form two large brilliant patches on the closed wing.   These are usually shining emerald green or golden green, less often bluish-green.   The lower back is crossed by two blackish bands which enclose a whitish fawn band between them.   Blackish tips to the upper tail coverts form two (sometimes three) dark bands across the base of the tail. Central tail feathers dull greyish brown with broad ill-defined black tips. Other tail feathers bright bluish grey with broad black tips, the outermost on each side with basal half of outer web white. Tips and outer webs of primaries and outer secondaries blackish, rest bright chestnut, as is the underside of the wing. Underside of tail and the longest under tail coverts mainly black. Irides brown or dark brown. Legs and feet purple or dull purplish red. Bill black or near black, usually tipped with reddish purple at the base. Sexes alike. The juvenile has most of the feathers more or less barred with buff or rufous on a dusky ground with dark subterminal bars and conspicuous pale buff tips. Wing patches smaller and less lustrous.

DISTRIBUTION AND HABITAT: Africa from Ethiopia and northern Somaliland in the east and Katanga and Angola in the west south to the Cape. Inhabits dry veldt, thornscrub and dry woodland with little or no undergrowth. Said (Benson and White, 1957) to occur away from water but other observers have recorded it as always found within easy reach of surface water.

FEEDING AND GENERAL HABITS: Feeds largely on seeds, including seeds of grasses, picked up from the ground. Also takes termites, small molluscs and some other invertebrates as well. Commonly feeds in clearings, on roads, paths and similar places. Flight rapid, often in zig-zag course, and commonly flies only short distances. Raises tail once or twice on alighting.

NESTING: Usual pigeon nest in bush, shrub, or tree, usually not above eight feet high. Two cream-coloured eggs. Has been recorded breeding at various times of year in different areas, e.g. April to June in Ethiopia and Somaliland, irregularly at most seasons further south in eastern Africa; August and September, and February and March, in South Africa.

VOICE: What is evidently the advertising coo has been described by Vincent as 'a series of soft coos, in double utterances at the commencement, very softly and slowly delivered, becoming louder and more run together, ending with a long series of quickly uttered and more evenly space coos and finally dying away'. The description of other observers agree essentially with the above. Softer versions are sometimes uttered but if the display coo and the nest coo differ essentially from the advertising coo they would appear not to have been recorded.

DISPLAY: No information.

OTHER NAMES: Emerald-spotted Dove; Emerald-spotted Wood Dove.

REFERENCES

BENSON, C. W. & WHITE, C. M. N. 1957. *Check-list of Birds of Northern Rhodesia*, 1957. Lusaka.
MACKWORTH-PRAED, C. W. & GRANT, C. H. B. 1957. *African Handbook of Birds*. Series 1, Volume 1. London.
MCLACHLAN, G. R. & LIVERSIDGE, R. 1957. *Roberts Birds of South Africa*, revised edition. Cape Town.
VAN SOMEREN, V. G. L. 1956. Days with birds. *Fieldiana : Zoology* **38**; July 20th, 148–151.
VINCENT, A. W. 1946. On the breeding habits of some African birds. *Ibis* **88**; 48–67.

BLACK-BILLED WOOD DOVE   *Turtur abyssinicus*

Chalcopelia abyssinicus Sharpe, Bull. Brit. Orn. Cl., 12, 1902, p. 83.

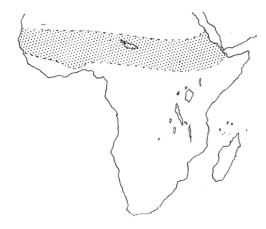

DESCRIPTION : Like the Green-spotted Wood Dove (q.v.) but very slightly paler and greyer in colour. The chief plumage difference is that in the present species the iridescent wing patches are smaller and either entirely dark blue and/or purple or with a hint of green, but predominantly purple or blue.

DISTRIBUTION AND HABITAT : The drier parts of tropical Africa, north of the range of *T. chalcospilos*, from Senegal to Eritrea and northern Ethiopia. Would appear to frequent dry scrub and woodland similar to that favoured by the Green-spotted Wood Dove further south.

FEEDING AND GENERAL HABITS : Feeds largely on seeds picked up from the ground.

NESTING : Usual pigeon nest in tree or shrub. Two dark cream-coloured eggs.

VOICE : From descriptions apparently very similar to that of the Green-spotted Wood Dove.

DISPLAY : No information.

OTHER NAMES : Abyssinian Wood Dove; Black-billed Blue-spotted Wood Dove.

REFERENCES

BANNERMAN, D. A. 1951. *The Birds of Tropical West Africa*, Volume 8. London.
HOLMAN, F. C. 1947. Birds of the Gold Coast. *Ibis* **89**; 623–650.
MACKWORTH-PRAED, C. W. & GRANT, C. H. B. 1957. *The African Handbook of Birds*. Series 1, Volume 1. London.

BLUE-SPOTTED WOOD DOVE   *Turtur afer*

Columba afra Linnaeus, Syst. Nat., ed. 12, 1, 1766, p. 284.

DESCRIPTION : Like the Green-spotted Wood Dove (q.v.) but with the brown parts of a darker and less greyish shade. Pink on breast darker and less mauvish, belly mostly buffish. Iridescent wing-spots much smaller and purple, and/or dark blue with little or no green. The most obvious colour distinction is that of the bill which in this species is red, usually pale and yellowish at the tip and often purplish at the base.   The legs and feet tend to be redder and less purplish than those of the other two closely-related species.

DISTRIBUTION AND HABITAT :   Africa south of the Sahara, east to Ethiopia and south to Angola, Southern Rhodesia and the Transvaal.   Inhabits wooded country, especially wood or scrub near streams and rivers, also about native cultivation and clearings in evergreen forest.   Replaced by the Green-spotted and Black-billed Wood Doves in drier areas and by the Tambourine Dove in denser forest.

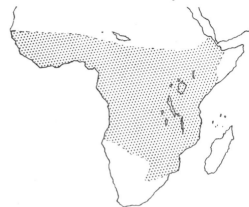

FEEDING AND GENERAL HABITS :   Apparently as Green-spotted Wood Dove, except for the differences in habitat.

NESTING :   Usual pigeon nest in a bush or tree.   Two cream-coloured or buff eggs.

VOICE :   The (presumed) advertising coo is described as being very similar to that of the Green-spotted Wood Dove 'but more muffled, the call slower and cut off in the middle of the final descending run'.

DISPLAY :   No information.

OTHER NAMES :   Sapphire-spotted Dove; Red-billed Wood Dove; Red-billed Blue-spotted Wood Dove.

REFERENCES

MACKWORTH-PRAED, C. W. & GRANT, C. H. B.   1957.   *African Handbook of Birds*.   Series 1, Volume 1.   London.
McLACHLAN, G. R. & LIVERSIDGE, R.   1957.   *Roberts Birds of South Africa*, revised edition.   Cape Town.

TAMBOURINE DOVE   *Turtur tympanistria*

Columba Tympanistria Temminck, in Knip, Les Pigeons, 1810, les colombes, p. 80, pl. 36.

DESCRIPTION: Size and general appearance and colour pattern very like the Green-spotted Wood Dove (q.v.) though coloration different and with attenuated first primary. Forehead, area around and behind eye, throat, breast and underparts white. Black band from gape to eye. Upperparts dark brown with a slight olivaceous tinge and a strong grey suffusion on head and neck. Lower back crossed by two obscure blackish bands with a light band between them. Iridescent wing spots less lustrous than in the other wood doves, of a blackish purple or dark bluish green, looking black except in a good light. Most of inner webs of primaries and underwing chestnut. Central tail feathers dark purplish brown, outer ones blue grey with broad bluish subterminal bands and grey tips. Under surface of tail dark with ill-defined markings. Under tail coverts dark brown. Irides brown or dark brown. Bill reddish purple tipped blackish or dark brown. Legs and feet purplish red. The female has the white parts suffused with grey, usually her neck and breast are predominantly grey. The juvenile has most feathers barred with rufous buff and blackish.

DISTRIBUTION and HABITAT: Africa from Sierra Leone and southern Ethiopia southwards and the Comoro Islands (Benson pers comm.). Inhabits forest, riparian woods and dense rich scrub.

FEEDING AND GENERAL HABITS: Feeds chiefly or entirely on the ground. Takes seeds, especially the seeds of the castor oil plant, and berries. Also termites and probably other small invertebrates, as in captivity it readily takes mealworms and other insects. Can fly swiftly through thick cover, dodging expertly round trunks and branches in its way.

NESTING: Usual pigeon nest in tree or shrub. Two creamy white to dark cream-coloured eggs. Both sexes incubate and brood. One male recorded as feeding the brooding female at the nest (Van Someren, 1956). Breeding recorded October to February in southern parts of Africa, March to November further north.

VOICE: The advertising coo is very like that of the Green-spotted Wood Dove but deeper and more muffled in tone. Van Someren records that the 'two long first notes' given repeatedly in a very low and tender tone was given by both sexes just before feeding young.

DISPLAY: No information.

OTHER NAMES: White-breasted Wood Dove; Forest Dove; White-breasted Pigeon.

REFERENCES

MACKWORTH-PRAED, C. W. & GRANT, C. H. B. 1957. *African Handbook of Birds*. Series 1, Volume 1. London.
MCLACHLAN, G. R. & LIVERSIDGE, R. 1957. *Roberts Birds of South Africa*, revised edition. Cape Town.
VAN SOMEREN, V. G. L. 1956. Days with Birds. *Fieldiana: Zoology* 38; 148-151.

BLUE-HEADED WOOD DOVE   *Turtur brehmeri*

Chalcopelia Brehmeri Hartlaub, Journ. F. Orn., 13, Mar. 1865, p. 97; Ibis Apr. 1865, p. 236.

This beautifully and unusually coloured pigeon was at one time placed in the monotypic genus *Calopelia*. It is, however, in my opinion preferable to include it in the genus *Turtur* since its affinities with the other wood doves is obvious in spite of its larger size and longer tail.

DESCRIPTION: Rather smaller than a Barbary Dove, very slightly smaller than a Mourning Dove but plumper and proportionately larger headed. General plumage dark chestnut brown strongly tinged with reddish purple on the mantle, neck and wing coverts, less so on the rump and tail and with little or no purple tinge on underparts. Iridescent areas on scapulars and inner greater coverts form two shining golden-bronze or golden-copper spots on the inner side of the folded wing. Primaries dusky. Outer tail feathers blue-grey with black subterminal and chestnut terminal band. Lighter chestnut band

across lower back with bluish brown borders.　　Head bright greyish blue, palest on the forehead and fore-crown and darkest on the hind crown and nape.　　Dark purple stripe from gape to eye.　　Underwing chestnut, primaries tinged blackish.　　Irides very dark brown.　　Feet purplish red.　　Bill dark purplish at base, distal half dull greenish.

The juvenile has a barred chestnut-brown and blackish plumage.

The above description applies to the nominate race *T. b. brehmeri*.　　The populations from the coastal forest regions of Sierra Leone and the Gold Coast to the Cameroon Mountains, *T. b. infelix*, have the wing spots shining green and the banding on the lower back more often obscure or obsolescent.　　The two races intergrade.

DISTRIBUTION AND HABITAT:　　West African forest regions from the coastal forest of Sierra Leone through the Cameroons, Rio Benito, French Congo and northern Belgian Congo.　　Inhabits forest; said not to come into clearings and only rarely found in secondary growth.

FEEDING AND GENERAL HABITS:　　Probably largely or entirely a ground feeder.　　Seeds of different kinds, and slugs have been found in shot birds.

NESTING:　　The usual pigeon type.　　The few that have been found have been in trees at no great height.

VOICE:　　The advertising coo of three captive birds in a zoo (probably all males) was a series of deep, rather musical coos.　　The first few louder and widely spaced, the succeeding ones progressively less loud and run together till the final notes suggest distant, rapid drum beats.　　Could perhaps be written ‘Ōō-Ōō-Ōō, o͞o-o͞o, o͞o-o͞o-o͞o, ŏŏ-ŏŏ, ŏŏ, ŏŏ, ŏ, ŏ, ŏ, ŏ!

The nest-call, like that of the Wood Pigeon, appears to be just the first notes of the advertising coo in slightly altered form, ‘C͞oo, C͞oo-o͞oo’, varying to ‘C͞oo, cŏŏ, co͞oo’, or ‘C͞oo, cŏŏ, cooo-co͞oo’. Descriptions of the cooing of wild birds suggest that the above are the normal versions of the calls.

DISPLAY:　　When nest calling the bird gives pronounced upward flicks of the closed wings and there is a slight upward movement of the tail also.　　I have no doubt that this movement of the wings serves to exhibit (or ‘flash’) the iridescent wing spots to the approaching or watching mate.

A captive male courting an indifferent female Common Bronzewing strode after her with head held high and feathers of forehead and crown sleeked down and bill at an angle of about 45 degrees.　　When it reached the other it stood still and bowed its head deeply once or (more often) twice without calling or inflating its neck.   Then it stood still and gave the advertising coo.   While it did this the Bronzewing each time wandered away over the aviary floor and the Blue-headed Dove strode after it and repeated the performance.   Presumably this performance is the equivalent of the bowing display of other pigeons, but further observations are required.   The nodding of a nest-calling bird was like that of *Columba* species.

OTHER NAMES :   Maiden Dove; Blue-headed Dove.

REFERENCE

HOLMAN, F. C. 1947.   Birds of Gold Coast. *Ibis* **89**; 623–650.

MASKED DOVE   *Oena capensis*

Columba capensis Linnaeus, Syst. Nat., ed. 12, 1, 1766, p. 286.

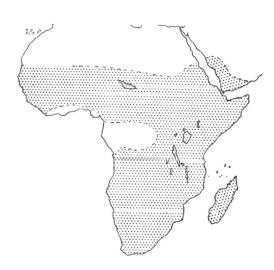

DESCRIPTION :   A small dove, only a little larger than a Diamond Dove, with very long, graduated tail.   Forehead, face, throat and frontal area of breast black, narrowly bordered with greyish white. Rest of head, sides of neck, sides of breast and most wing coverts light bluish grey.   Hind neck, mantle, inner wing coverts, scapulars and inner secondaries light fawnish drab to dull earth brown.   Two iridescent purplish black to dark bluish green patches on wing formed by markings on some of the inner greater coverts and inner secondaries.   Primaries chestnut with brownish black tips and outer webs edged brownish black.   The dull drab back and rump are crossed by a whitish band, bordered by two blackish bands, on the lower back.   Upper tail coverts grey to brownish grey with black tips that form a bar across base of tail.   Underwing black and chestnut.   Central tail feathers dull silver grey at base shading to black at tip, much individual variation as to amount of black.   Outer tail feathers blue grey with broad black subterminal bars, the outermost pair with white on the outer webs as far as the black band.   Underside of tail black except for white outer webs of outermost pair of feathers and grey tips to some others.   Irides dark brown; orbital skin purplish grey to grey.   Bill purplish red to (less often) orange-red at base, orange to yellow-orange at tip.   Legs and feet purplish red.   (See pl. 2).

The female lacks the black mask and has a whitish grey face with black line from gape to eye and greyish drab head, neck and breast.   Her outer wing coverts are a less pure prey than the male's and her bill is purplish black.   The juvenile has a speckled appearance due to most of its cover feathers having blackish subterminal bars and yellowish fawn or whitish tips.   Its primaries are tipped with chestnut. Some (but not most) juvenile males have the breast feathers dull blackish with pale fawn tips.   The young male moults directly from juvenile to adult dress.

The above description is of the nominate form *O. c. capensis* which inhabits most of the species' range. The form from Madagascar *O. capensis aliena* is slightly darker and greyer.

DISTRIBUTION AND HABITAT: Africa from Senegal, the southern Sahara and Red Sea coast south to Cape Province, Socotra Island western and south-western Arabia and Madagascar. Inhabits dry open country with some scrub; less often open dry wooded areas. Often in gardens, cultivated areas, villages and towns.

FEEDING AND GENERAL HABITS: Known to feed largely on small seeds. Usually feeds where the ground is bare in open spaces among thorn scrub, roadsides, paths, old gardens and similar places. Walks and runs about quickly when feeding. Flight very swift. Raises tail and then lowers it more slowly after alighting. Like its ecological counterpart in Australia, the Diamond Dove, it appears to be a sun lover. Usually comes to drink during the middle hours of the day not in early morning and evening as most other African doves usually do. Perches on bushes, fences, stones and other low elevations seldom, if ever, high in trees. Seen singly and in pairs also in small and large parties, the latter perhaps usually aggregates at good feeding grounds.

NESTING: Usual pigeon nest, proportionately small and often rather firmly constructed, in a bush, shrub, dead branch, grass tuft or other support. Never high up, usually within a few feet of the ground and sometimes on it. Two cream-coloured eggs, white eggs occasionally recorded. Fledging period 16 days (*fide* McLachland and Liversidge). When flushed from the nest either parent will often fly to a nearby perch and flutter its wings (Vincent, 1946). More intense forms of distraction display appear not to have been recorded.

VOICE: What is, probably, the advertising coo is a rather deep, low-pitched coo, usually double but sometimes single (? perhaps different calls); some have described the first coo of the double call as 'explosive'. When nest calling a captive male uttered a single deep gruff note (Harrison, pers. comm.).

DISPLAY: In the bowing display (Gifford, 1941) the male lowers his head, raises his tail without spreading and 'moves both wings slightly and rhythmically at the rate of about one hundred times per minute'. Gifford also describes as part of the courtship behaviour a 'hovering, descending flight with tail spread' performed in front of the female. When nest calling Harrison's bird made upward movements of its wings and tail.

OTHER NAMES: Namaqua Dove; Cape Dove; Long-tailed Dove.

REFERENCES

ARCHER, G. & GODMAN, E. M. 1937. *The Birds of British Somaliland and The Gulf of Aden.* Vol. 2. London.
GIFFORD, E. W. 1941. Taxonomy and Habits of Pigeons. *Auk* **58**; 239–245.
HOESCH, W. & NIETHAMMER, G. 1940. Die Vogelwelt Deutsch-Sudwestafrikas. *Journ. f. Orn.* **88**; Sonderheft.
MACKWORTH-PRAED, C. W. & GRANT, C. H. B. 1957. *African Handbook of Birds.* Series 1, Volume 1. London.
McLACHLAN, G. R. & LIVERSIDGE, R. 1957. *Roberts Birds of South Africa*, revised edition. Cape Town.
VINCENT, A. W. 1946. On the Breeding Habits of some African Birds. *Ibis* **88**; 48–67.

EMERALD DOVES AND BRONZEWINGS

The emerald doves or green-winged doves are plump, compact, rather long-legged pigeons that take their names from their iridescent green wing coverts. They are woodland dwellers that feed and spend much time on the ground although usually nesting and roosting in trees or bushes. They are swift fliers and at least one of the two species appears to perform considerable migrations or nomadic wanderings. They probably feed much on invertebrate animals as well as on seeds and other vegetable foods.

The emerald doves appear to link the African spot-winged doves and the Australian bronze-wings. They resemble the former in their rump markings and some of both groups in the pattern of their outer tail feathers, their chestnut-marked primaries and the iridescence on their wings although in them this is more extensive. They are probably also fairly closely allied to the Old World quail doves and the cuckoo doves. They consist of two closely related species which are allopatric throughout most of their ranges but which overlap in south-eastern New Guinea and the Celebes.

The Emerald Dove *Chalcophaps indica* is a widespread, abundant and thriving species. Several races have been described but the main distinction is between the forms in which the male has a whitish forehead and blue-grey crown (*C. i. indica*, *C. i. robinsoni*, *C. i. maxima*, *C. i. natalis*, *C. i. sanghirensis* and *C. i. minima*) and those in which the head of the male is brownish purple (*C. i. chrysochlora*, *C. i. longirostris*, *C. i. timorensis* and *C. i. sandwichensis*). The latter form usually has a larger white shoulder patch and more extensive chestnut on the wing. It is not known to overlap with the Oriental form (although both occur relatively near one another in the Lesser Sunda Islands), and they seem, on present evidence, best treated as conspecific. The possibility that the Oriental and Australasian forms of *indica* may have reached specific level and be mutually exclusive through competition where they meet cannot be excluded.

The Brown-backed Emerald Dove *C. stephani* probably originated, or rather became differentiated from the parent stock of both itself and *indica*, in the New Guinea region. It overlaps with the Oriental form of *indica* in Celebes and with the Australasian in south-eastern New Guinea. In Celebes there appears to be some ecological separation between the two, *stephani* being found inside the humid tropical forest and *indica* at the forest edge and in thickets in more open or deforested areas (Stresemann, 1941) but in New Guinea no habitat differences appear to be known (Mayr, 1941). It is likely that such exist, however, and that *indica* and *stephani* can only inhabit the same area when this is sufficiently extensive and diverse to permit ecological separation between such closely related and very similar forms. Both are said to occur on the Kei Islands but I have been able to find no record of both species being taken on the same island. With the above possible exception only one of the two occurs on each of the smaller islands or archipelagoes and it seems likely that this is due to competition between them. Their present distribution suggests strongly that *stephani* may once have inhabited the Moluccas, all of the Western Papuan Islands and the Louisade Archipelago but has been eliminated from those islands where *indica* managed to establish itself.

The Black Bronzewing *Henicophaps albifrons* and the New Britain Bronzewing *H. foersteri* form a superspecies. Although much larger and with a uniquely large and strong bill *Henicophaps* is, I think, a close relative of *Chalcophaps*. The plumage pattern of *H. albifrons* is very similar to that of *Chalcophaps* although the general coloration is much darker and the iridescence on the wings more restricted. Some specimens of *Henicophaps* show an ill-defined paler band across the rump that appears to be a homologue of the rump markings of *Chalcophaps*. In body size *Henicophaps* is similar to the larger Australian Bronzewings, such as *Phaps chalcoptera*. It may possibly represent an early offshoot from Australian stock and be more closely related to *Phaps* than to *Chalcophaps*. I think, however, that the reverse is the case and that the great differences in size and type of bill between *Henicophaps* and *Chalcophaps* is indicative only of adaptations to different ecological niches by two closely related and long sympatric forms.

The Australian Bronzewings well illustrate the principle of adaptive radiation. Within this group whose colour-patterns, behaviour and geographical distribution all indicate their phylogenetic affinity we find several genera that are morphologically distinct. These differences are due to adaptation to differing habitats, for among the bronzewings are both woodland and open country forms, far, strong fliers and partridge-like terrestial species.

The bronzewings take their name from the iridescent markings on their wings. These are most brilliant and extensive in the Common Bronzewing and almost obsolete in the (Australian) rock pigeons. They also show a characteristic light and dark facial pattern. This is most strikingly developed in the Harlequin

Bronzewing or Flock Pigeon and the partridge bronzewings, but has been completely lost in the Crested Pigeon.

They are all either predominantly or entirely ground feeders that feed principally on seeds. Some of them take grubs or larvae freely in captivity and doubtless do so in the wild also. In all species whose behaviour is known the bowing display involves a frontal presentation of the partly spread wings and the spreading and erecting of the tail. A comparison of all the bronzewings, particularly the fact that many have iridescent areas *concealed* by overlapping feathers, suggest that their evolution has involved reduction of iridescent areas. It seems reasonable to postulate that the 'ancestral bronzewing' was a form with the wing coverts and scapulars wholly or largely iridescent as in the emerald doves. Apart from the Wonga Pigeon and the geopelias which are, I believe, related to them, the bronzewings appear to be most nearly related to the emerald doves, and, more distantly, to the American ground doves and the African spot-winged doves.

Six genera of bronzewings are usually recognised. I here recognise three: *Phaps, Petrophassa* and *Ocyphaps*, treat *Histriophaps* as a synonym of *Phaps* and *Lophophaps* and *Geophaps* as synonyms of *Petrophassa*. The Flock Pigeon, although a very distinctive species is not sufficiently so, in my opinion, to justify its retention in a monotypic genus. Its wing and tail proportions do not differ much more from those of *Phaps chalcoptera* than do those of the latter form *Phaps elegans*. In colour pattern it shows considerable resemblance to *elegans*, especially when females are compared. It flies with continuous wing beats like *chalcoptera* and *elegans* although usually flying higher. *Lophophaps* differs from *Geophaps* in its smaller size and possession of a long crest. In other respects they are much alike and indeed in some aspects of its colour pattern and in its robust bill *Geophaps smithii* seems a connecting link between *Lophophaps* and *G. scripta*. Both *Petrophassa* and *Geophaps* have (Austin, pers. comm.) a partridge-like flight similar to that of *Lophophaps*. It seems best to recognise the close relationship of all these forms by including them in the single genus *Petrophassa*.

The Common Bronzewing *Phaps chalcoptera* and the Brush Bronzewing *P. elegans* overlap geographically in parts of southern Australia and Tasmania. They would appear to differ somewhat in ecology. It seems likely that *chalcoptera* evolved in the interior, probably during a very arid period. Its drinking habits (q.v.) suggest that at some period it suffered intense predation from diurnal birds-of-prey when at the water, presumably as a result of having a very restricted choice of available drinking places.

The Flock Pigeon *Phaps histrionica* is to some extent the Australian counterpart of the open-country dwelling, ground feeding *Columba* species of Eurasia and Africa. It has, however, become highly nomadic in adaptation to the variable rainfall (or lack of it) and consequent fluctuating food supplies of its range and, like many other Australian pigeons, it nests on the ground.

The Crested Pigeon *Ocyphaps lophotes* is a very distinct species but in life shows more resemblance to '*Lophophaps*' than would be deducible from examination of museum specimens. It also agrees closely with '*Lophophaps*' in the pattern of its wing coverts and scapulars. That this long-tailed and relatively long-winged form should have the same partridge-like flight as *Petrophassa* suggests that both derived from a common ancestor that had already become terrestrial. Subsequently the ancestral *Ocyphaps* took again to trees for roosting and nesting.

This re-acquisition of partly arboreal habits was, probably, a factor that enabled it successfully to populate more diverse habitats and a much wider geographical area than any one of its terrestial allies. I think it probable that *lophotes* may be phylogenetically as close to *plumifera* and *ferruginea* as are the other species included with them in *Petrophassa* but its greater divergence seems best indicated by retention of the genus *Ocyphaps*.

The Red Plumed Pigeon *Petrophassa ferruginea* and the White-bellied Plumed Pigeon *P. plumifera* are allopatric in their known ranges and Mayr, 1951, is in favour of treating them as races of a single species. As, however, they are not known to intergrade, are said to differ in voice (Whitlock, 1923) and have hitherto been regarded as separate species they are here treated as members of a superspecies. This, has, however, been done largely for reasons of convenience. Mayr separated the West Kimberleys form of *plumifera* on the ground of its being redder in colour than *G. p. plumifera* of northern Australia or *G. p. leucogaster* of central Australia. I have examined the series of *proxima*, including the type, in the American Museum of Natural History and they do not seem to differ in colour from *leucogaster* when specimens of the same sex and in the same state of plumage are compared. Specimens of *plumifera* are a little duller and more yellowish hue than either *leucogaster* or *proxima* but not at all noticeably so. Wear and bleaching is evidently both extensive and rapid. On the same specimen old feathers will be pale sandy yellow where new ones are a dark reddish brown. Plumed pigeons that have moulted in captivity often show increased melanin and have the entire crown and the long crest feathers bluish grey instead of this colour being restricted to the forehead and forecrown as in wild specimens.

The Partridge Bronzewing *Petrophassa scripta* and the Bare-eyed Partridge Bronzewing *P. smithi* appear to be geographical representatives which have diverged considerably in bill size and colour pattern.

The White-quilled and Red-quilled Rock Pigeons *Petrophassa albipennis* and *P. rufipennis* form a super-species and are allopatric. They are probably most closely related to 'Geophaps'.

REFERENCE

MAYR, E. 1951. Notes on some Pigeons and Parrots from Western Australia. *Emu* **51**: 137-145.

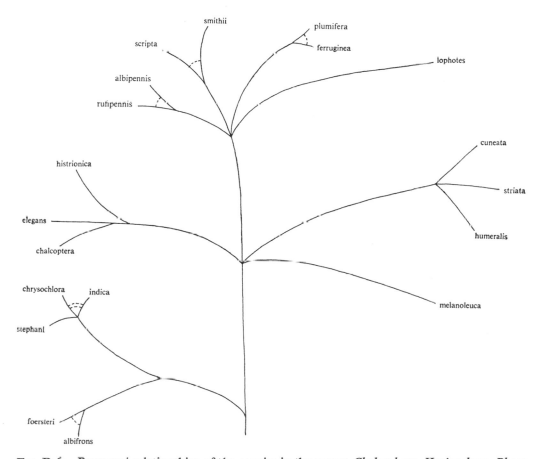

FIG. D.6: Presumed relationships of the species in the genera *Chalcophaps, Henicophaps, Phaps, Petrophassa, Ocyphaps, Leucosarcia* and *Geopelia*. In this and subsequent dendrograms two dotted lines connect very distinct and geographically separated races of the same species.

EMERALD DOVE   *Chalcophaps indica*

Columba indica Linnaeus, Syst. Nat. Ed. 10, 1, 758, p. 164.

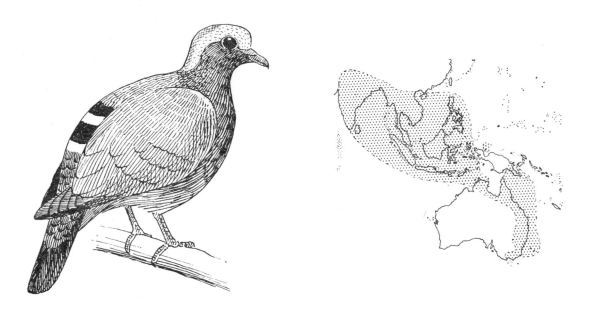

Many slightly differing races of this widely distributed species have been recognised. The only marked racial differences, however, are those between the Oriental form which, in its various very slightly differentiated races, is found over most of the species, range, and the Australasian form which is found in Australia, south-eastern New Guinea, New Caledonia, the New Hebrides and the Lesser Sunda Islands west to Wetar and Timor.

DESCRIPTION : About the size of a Barbary Dove but plumper and more heavily built with shorter tail. Forehead and stripe over and extending behind eye white. Crown and nape bluish-grey. Neck and breast dark brownish purple more or less tinged with blue-grey along the median line of the hind neck and shading to vinous grey on belly and flanks. A small ill-defined white patch (formed by white-tipped feathers) on shoulder. Mantle, scapulars, wing coverts and inner secondaries iridescent emerald green or bronze green ; some individuals show much coppery red hue, in others the green is a pure shining emerald green with no coppery tint. Most are intermediate between the above extremes. Primaries and outer secondaries slaty black with some chestnut on inner webs. Underwing chestnut. Lower back blackish, slightly glossed with copper red or, less often, green and crossed by two pale grey bands. Rump and upper-tail coverts dark grey, the feathers tipped black, in some individuals so broadly that these areas look quite black. Central tail feathers greyish black, outer ones blue grey with broad black or purplish subterminal bands and pale grey tips. Irides dark brown with purplish or flesh-coloured orbital skin. Bill orange-red or red, with purplish base. Legs and feet red or pinkish.

The female is rufous or chestnut brown where the male is purple. She lacks the white on the shoulder and has the grey and white of the head restricted to the front of the forehead and a stripe over the eye. This feature is rather variable and almost lacking in some individuals. Females in which the brown areas are predominantly dull drab rather than chestnut are common in the Moluccas and occur in a minority elsewhere.

The juvenile has predominantly red-brown plumage with blackish bars and a much smaller area of iridescence on mantle and wings. It soon, however, starts to moult into adult dress. (See pl. 3).

The Australasian form differs in that the male has no white or grey on the head or neck ; the white wing patch is larger and more clearly defined and there is a greater area of chestnut on the wing quills.

The female usually has grey only on the two outermost tail feathers the grey being replaced by chestnut on the others. She has the male's white wing patch indicated by a small grey mark.

DISTRIBUTION AND HABITAT: Oriental and Australasian regions from northern India, Assam and Hainan southwards and eastwards to the Philippines, New Guinea and eastern Australia. Inhabits wooded country both in flat and hilly districts.

FEEDING AND GENERAL HABITS: Feeds on the ground chiefly, perhaps entirely. Known to eat various seeds, including seeds of castor-oil plant and candle nut tree; rice and wheat, fruits and termites, and to visit 'salt-licks'. Comes freely to feed in clearings, paths, camp-sites and about human dwellings in forest areas. Usually seen singly (? when one of the pair is on nest) or in pairs. Sometimes in small parties. Walks and runs nimbly on ground. Flies low and swiftly, dodging neatly around trees and shrubs. Apparently often mistakes white-washed walls for openings in the cover and fails to see wire fences and, as a result, injures or kills itself by flying at full speed into them. Little is known about its movements or migrations but it has often been taken at sea on ships and at lighthouses.

NESTING: Nests in trees or shrubs. Nest is usually rather more substantial than that of most pigeons. Two creamy or buffish eggs,, laid on alternate days (Sprankling, 1921). Incubation period (in England) 14 days. Young fledge at 12 to 13 days. In north-eastern Australia nests with eggs found in January, February, August and December (Lavery *et al.*).

VOICE: Several authors describe a soft, deep coo, variously rendered as 'hoo', 'tnk-hoo', 'hoo-hoo', 'hoon, with a nasal ending' etc. Hyem (1936) records 'a loud bellowing note' for the Australian form.

DISPLAY: Thomasset (1901) described what is evidently the bowing display of the male in which 'he depressed the head and breast, raising the closed wings over his back, thus presenting the whole of his glittering green plumage'. I have seen a captive male approach the female and face her in an upright posture with head 'pulled in' on breast and wings slightly raised but not opened.

OTHER NAMES: Green-winged Dove; Little Green Pigeon; Green-backed Dove.

It is much to be regretted that the name 'Bronzewing Pigeon' previously applied only to *Phaps chalcoptera*, has been used for this species in recent books on regional avifaunas.

REFERENCES

ALI, S. 1949. *Indian Hill Birds*. pp. 171–172. Oxford.
AUSTIN, C. 1950. Further notes on the Birds of Dunk Island, Queensland. *Emu* **49**: 225–231.
BAKER, E. C. S. 1913. *Indian Pigeons and Doves*. pp. 121–125. London.
FRITH, H. J. 1952. Notes on the Pigeons of Richmond River, N.S.W. *Emu* **52**: 89–99.
HYEM, E. L. 1936. Notes on the Birds of Mernot, N.S.W. *Emu* **36**: 109–127.
LAVERY, H. J. *et al.* Breeding seasons of birds in north-eastern Australia (in press).
SPRANKLING, E. 1921. Indian Green-wing Doves. *Bird Notes*. Series 3, **4**: 87–91.
THOMASSET, B. C. 1901. Nesting of Green-winged Doves. *Avicult. Mag.* **7**: 159–160.

BROWN-BACKED EMERALD DOVE *Chalcophaps stephani*

Chalcophaps stephani Pucheran. Voy. Pole Sud., Zool., 3, 1853, p. 119; Atlas, pl. 28, F. 2.

DESCRIPTION: Very similar to the Emerald Dove but slightly smaller and with slightly more rounded tail. General colour chestnut brown, darkest on the scapulars and central tail feathers, palest on the underparts. Strongly tinged with bluish purple on the crown and nape. and with reddish purple on the back and sides of neck. Forehead pure white, sharply demarcated from the purplish chestnut crown. Most wing coverts and part of inner secondaries iridescent emerald green or bronze-green, rarely with a coppery-red tint. Outermost tail feathers grey, or chestnut on inner web and grey on outer web with broad blackish subterminal bar and chestnut tip. Other outer tail feathers chestnut with more or less defined black subterminal areas.   Lower back blackish brown crossed and bordered with two buffish bars. Underwing chestnut.   Irides dark brown.   Bill red or orange, darker red at base.   Legs and feet dull purplish red.   The female has a grey forehead and shows less purple on her head and neck.   The juvenile resembles that of *indica*.

DISTRIBUTION AND HABITAT: Celebes, New Guinea and adjacent islands and archipelagoes and the Solomon Islands.   Inhabits lowland forest in New Guinea.   Schodde & Hitchcock (1969) found it at forest margins and in secondary growth.   In Celebes found within the humid evergreen forest (Stresemann, 1941).

FEEDING AND GENERAL HABITS: Little recorded.   Apparently similar to previous species but perhaps keeps more to dense cover.   Sometimes feeds under colonies of *Aplonis metallica* on the undigested berry seeds disgorged by these starlings, flies fast and direct through trees (Schodde & Hitchcock).

NESTING: Meyer (1930, 1933) says that the nest is never high and is not hidden and that two nonglossy yellowish eggs laid but gives no further details.

VOICE: No information.

DISPLAY: No information.

OTHER NAME: Brown-backed Green-winged Dove.

REFERENCES

MEYER, P. O.   1930.   Uebersicht uber die Brutzeiten der Vögel auf der Insel Vuatom.   *Journ. f. Orn.* **78** : 19–138.
—— 1933.   Vogeleier und Nester aus Neubritannien, Sudsee.   *Beitr. z. Fortpflanz.   der Vogel* **9** : 122–135.
SCHODDE, R. & HITCHCOCK, W. B. 1968. Contrib. Pap. Orn., Div. Wildlife Res. paper no. 13. Pub. by CSIRO, Australia.

BLACK BRONZEWING   *Henicophaps albifrons*

Henicophaps albifrons G. R. Gray, Proc. Zool. Soc. London, 1861 (1862).   p. 432, pl. 44.

DESCRIPTION: About the size of an average Feral Pigeon.   Medium length tail and wings.   Remarkable for its very large, heavy and long bill with only a suggestion of the soft cere usual in pigeons.   Forehead and crown white or buffish-white.   Nape, hind neck, and upperpart of mantle very dark, dull purple which shades to somewhat lighter on sides of neck, breast and flanks through to light purplish grey on belly and throat. Lesser wing coverts (where not iridescent) dark reddish purple. Large iridescent areas on many of the lesser, median and greater wing coverts and the inner secondaries form large shining coppery red and bronze green patches on the folded wing. The amount of iridescence and its exact shade vary individually. That on the secondaries is always predominantly green but on the coverts some birds are bronze green or golden green, others coppery red. Rest of upperparts including wings and tail slaty black. Under tail coverts dark chestnut. Irides dark brown or brown. Bill dull slate or blackish, usually with lower mandible paler and sometimes pinkish at base. Legs and feet red, salmon or pink. Female slightly duller with pale grey forehead and buffish crown. Juvenile like adult but not quite so dark, the purple areas more reddish and with very little iridescence on the wings.

DISTRIBUTION AND HABITAT: New Guinea and adjacent islands. Inhabits wooded country both in lowlands and in hills up to about 1,400 metres (Mayr, 1941).

FEEDING AND GENERAL BEHAVIOUR: To judge from very few observations of wild birds and behaviour of captives, feeds and spends much time on the ground. It digs for food with its powerful bill and probably, like *Lophophaps* but unlike most pigeons, uses it as a pickaxe to break up food too large to swallow.

NESTING: No information.

VOICE: A 'series of low coos' was heard from one of two birds seen flying from branch to branch in the forest (Rand, 1942).

DISPLAY: Grant (in Grant, W.R.O., 1915) records birds 'showing off after the manner of a Wood Pigeon'. This probably is a general description for a bowing display like that of, for example, *Phaps chalcoptera* (which see).

OTHER NAMES: White-capped Bronzewing; New Guinea Bronzewing; White-capped Ground Pigeon; Long-billed Bronzewing.

REFERENCES

GRANT, W. R. O. 1915. Report on the birds collected by the British Ornithologists' Union Expedition and the Wollaston Expedition in Dutch New Guinea. *Ibis*, Jubilee Suppl. No. 2: 311–312.
RAND, A. L. 1942. *Bull. Amer. Mus. Nat. Hist.* **79**: 306.

New Britain Bronzewing   *Henicophaps foersteri*

Henicophaps foersteri Rothschild and Hartert, Bull. Brit. orn. Cl. 91, 1906, p. 28.

DESCRIPTION: Similar to the Black Bronzewing but with buffish forehead and underparts, whitish face and chestnut crown, nape and hind neck. Irides dark brown, bill blackish brown, feet red.

DISTRIBUTION: New Britain.

FEEDING AND GENERAL HABITS: No information.

NESTING: No information.

VOICE: No information.

DISPLAY: No information.

Common Bronzewing   *Phaps chalcoptera*

Columba chalcoptera Latham, Ind. Orn. 2, 1790, p. 604.

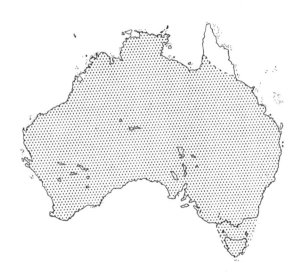

Description: About size of a Feral Pigeon but with proportionately broader and more rounded body and smaller head. Forehead creamy buff to rufous buff bordered posteriorly by a purplish band across crown which continues along side of head behind eye. Dark stripe from bill to eye with a white or cream stripe under it which continues below and beyond eye. Throat whitish. Sides of neck bluish grey. Breast deep mauve-pink to salmon pink shading to brownish grey on ventral regions and under tail coverts. Upper parts drab brown with pale rufous to pale buff fringes to most feathers giving a cryptic laced or mottled effect. Outer wing coverts partly bluish grey and with large iridescent spots or patchet that give a brilliant effect, and form a predominantly barred pattern in the living bird. These iridescens areas are bronze-red to emerald green in colour but a similar iridescent patch on the secondaries is purplish-red to blue-green. Underwing light chestnut. Primaries and central tail feathers dark drab brown with paler fringes. Outer tail feathers bluish grey with broad blackish brown subterminal band. Irides dark brown or reddish brown. Orbital skin narrow and fleshy grey. Bill purplish black. Legs and feet pinkish red or purplish pink.

The female has a dull greyish forehead, except for a narrow white line extending from base of bill to above the eye, the purplish head markings of the male are replaced by less well defined rusty brown ones and the breast buffish drab only slightly, if at all, tinged with pink. Some females have the iridescent wing markings of a green hue that looks purple in some lights but never bronze or red, although others have these wing markings as in the male. Juvenile a dull drab brown with rusty fawn fringes to most feathers and lacking the iridescent wing markings. Young males have a buffish forehead and can be sexed by this feature even before they leave the nest.

The above description fits the species generally. On the whole the populations of south-eastern Australia are largest and darkest, those from central, south and south-west Australia are slightly redder in colour and those of northern and north-western Australia are palest and smallest.

FIELD CHARACTERS: When seen in flight from above looks a dark, brownish pigeon with no light areas visible unless the sun catches the iridescent wing spots, which is relatively seldom the case. If seen at eye level or from below the light chestnut underwing is conspicuous. When on ground or perched the whitish facial streak and pale forehead are noticeable but the plumage is highly cryptic and non-moving birds are often very hard to pick out.

DISTRIBUTION AND HABITAT: Australia and Tasmania. Inhabits various types of woodland, usually more or less dry and open in character; dry scrubland, open country with some shrubs and trees and partly cultivated areas.

FEEDING AND GENERAL HABITS: Feeds on the ground, taking seeds of various plants and cultivated grains, especially wheat, when available. In many places the seeds of mulga trees, *Acacia sp.*, are an important food. Its bones and entrails, but not its flesh, become poisonous when it has been feeding on the seeds of the box-poison tree *Gastrolobium bilobum*. Has also been recorded taking berries. In captivity it readily eats earthworms and other invertebrates and probably does so at times in the wild also.

Usually drinks in the twilight after sunset, many individuals not doing so until it is almost dark. When coming in to water some few individuals fly straight to the waters' edge but the majority alight at some distance, usually not less than about 100 yards, from the water, where they wait about for some time and then walk to the waters' edge. Sometimes the birds may first alight at a considerable distance and then make a second and shorter flight on their way to the water. Also drinks in the early morning just before dawn but is uncertain whether the same individuals drink twice in the 24 hours. On two occasions when I watched at drinking places both in the evening and the following morning only about one third the number of birds came before dawn. A few individuals may drink while it is still quite light in the evening and often they begin to arrive then and to gather on the ground under cover nearby. I once came on a bird bathing in a trough (to which many hundreds came nightly to drink) in bright sunlight at 10 a.m.

The habit of drinking after dusk or before dawn is shared by Bourke's Parakeet *Neophema bourkii* but not by other sympatric species of pigeons and parrots. It is almost certainly an anti-predator device in reference to diurnal birds-of-prey but the gathering in the vicinity of the water probably also has a social function. It probably facilitates the meeting of mateless individuals and subsequent pair formation.

When, apparently, ill at ease but reluctant to fly, it slightly lowers one wing and then flicks it back into position, sometimes moving both wings alternately, in the same way as does the Crested Pigeon (q.v.).

Usually, by day, in pairs or singly, less often small parties of two or more pairs. Spends much time on the ground, usually in shade or semi-shade under trees or shrubs. Flight swift and strong with regular wing beats like that of *Columba* species. Flies low through the trees or shrubs seldom, if ever, above the tree tops. When flying only a short distance and not alarmed may fly quite slowly. Rises with a clattering of wings like a *Columba* not such a whirring sound as *Lophophaps*.

NESTING: Usual pigeon nest in a tree or shrub, sometimes in a hollow of a tree, occasionally on a ledge or in a hollow of a rock or on the ground. Two white eggs. May nest at any time of year (Serventy and Whittell, 1948) but apparently, most often between August and December.

VOICE: The advertising coo is a deep, low-pitched repeated 'ōōm, ōōm', suggestive in its tone of the lowing of cattle. A slight bow of the head is given as it is uttered. Also I often heard a softer, more rapidly repeated 'ŏŏm, ŏŏm', from unseen birds gathered near water. According to Whitman (1919) the nest call is similar to the advertising coo but usually less loud and the display coo is a short, rather soft 'coo, coo-coo' the second and third notes shorter and closer together. Whitman also records clucking sounds being uttered when driving the female and during the copulation ceremony. The distress call is the usual panting grunt but intensifies to a growl when the bird is defending its nest against an intruding hand. The begging call of the young is a whistling squeak as in other pigeons but it also utters (fide Whitman) a soft, mellow whistling twitter, apparently as a contact call.

DISPLAY: In the bowing display the bird makes a quick down stroke of head and bill, the wings are half spread and tilted forward to show the iridescent markings and the tail is raised. No noticeable inflation of neck but on the few occasions I have seen this display the bird did not utter the display coo. Male also erects feathers of rump, slightly droops the folded wings so that the iridescent area appears to be increased in size and hops towards the female. When nest calling the wing movements consist of a slow up and down movement of the wings which are held folded but raised from the sides (to a varying degree) so that the iridescent markings are emphasised. These slow wing movements are in the same tempo as the wing movements of the begging young.

In the copulation ceremony the male bows and then may offer his open bill. Female may respond by bowing and/or inserting her bill into male's. Male then reaches his neck over back of female's neck and presses her down. She may respond by crouching or by reaching her neck over male's in turn. When male mounts the female he utters 'clucking' notes. He may then droop his wings, then leap off the female's back, clapping his wings loudly over his back and uttering a loud explosive clucking cry as he does so. On alighting he lowers and slightly lifts his wings so that their tips and his spread tail press the ground, arches his neck and, with open bill, rushes up to or around the female. He then mounts again and, if coition now takes place it is followed by the male recovering his position on the female's shoulders, lowering his head, uttering a series of (usually) seven clucking notes which increase in loudness and rapidity and finally leaping off with a loud wing clap and explosive cry as above described. The female often mounts the male but Whitman did not, apparently, record any reversed coition in which the female showed all the male's copulating behaviour sequence although he may have seen it as he wrote 'Her behaviour is that of the male, it is merely less energetic'.

OTHER NAMES: Bronzewing Pigeon; Forest Bronzewing.

REFERENCES
CAYLEY, N. W. 1931. *What bird is that?* Sydney.
MATHEWS, G. M. 1910–11. *The birds of Australia.* Vol. 1. London.
NEWMAN, T. H. 1929. The Bronze-winged Pigeon. *Avicult. Mag.* Fourth Series 7: 1–3.
SERVENTY, D. L. & WHITTELL, H. M. 1948. *Birds of Western Australia.* Perth.
WHITMAN, C. O. 1919. *The behaviour of Pigeons.* Posthumous works of C. O. Whitman. Vol. 3. Carnegie Inst. Washington.

BRUSH BRONZEWING   *Phaps elegans*

Columba elegans Temminck, in Knip, Les Pigeons, 1810, les colombes, p. 56, pl. 22.

DESCRIPTION: Rather smaller than a Feral Pigeon. Plump, rounded and small-headed in shape with proportionately shorter tail and wings than the Common Bronzewing. Forehead reddish buff to deep golden brown, sometimes grey only slightly tinged with buff. Crown and nape dark bluish grey. Cheeks bluish grey, usually tinged with buff. A dark blackish chestnut line from gape to eye and a broader dark chestnut band continuing from behind eye and enclosing the grey nape. A narrow whitish line below the dark line on face and adjacent to it. Throat patch dark chestnut. Hind neck, sides of upper part of neck dark chestnut. Upperparts warm olive brown, more or less (in different individuals) tinged with chestnut and shading to predominantly pinkish chestnut on outer wing coverts. Two shining bands on wings formed by iridescent, grey-edged markings on the median and greater coverts. These iridescent areas are coppery red through bronze to golden green except on inner greater coverts where they are predominantly purple or blue. Primaries dull brown with basal and median parts of outer webs edged chestnut and inner webs chestnut except at tip so wings show chestnut patch in flight. Underwing chestnut. Outer tail feathers bluish grey with blackish brown subterminal band. Breast, sides of neck and underparts medium to light bluish grey. Irides dark brown. Bill purplish grey to black. Legs and feet purplish pink or pink.

The female is duller, with the chestnut markings only slightly indicated and the grey of the underparts tinged with brown. Juvenile paler and browner than adult with buff or rufous fringes to most feathers and the iridescent wing markings indicated only by obscure dark patches.

DISTRIBUTION AND HABITAT: South-west and south-east Australia and Tasmania. Inhabits scrub and 'heathland', that is places with abundant cover of bushy growth or stunted trees. Most often in coastal districts. Has decreased in many areas, possibly owing to predation by introduced mammals such as cats and foxes.

FEEDING AND GENERAL HABITS: Feeds chiefly or entirely on the ground. Known to take seeds, berries and some invertebrates. Usually seen in pairs or singly (when mate on nest?). When flushed usually flies a short distance and then alights on the ground, not in a tree. Flight direct and straight with continuous wing beats like that of Common Bronzewing (Austin).

NESTING: Usual pigeon nest, usually placed low down in a shrub or fallen tree or on the ground. Two white eggs. Known to breed from October to January (Cayley, 1931). A pair breeding in captivity in England laid eggs (three clutches in all) on alternate days. Incubation period 16 days. Young left nest and could fly well at 22 days (Seth-Smith, 1904).

VOICE: The advertising coo is a rather mournful-sounding $\overline{coo}$, $\overline{coo}$, $\overline{coo}$, or $\overline{hoop}$, $\overline{hoop}$, $\overline{hoop}$. The display coo is a softer, more grunting coo (Seth-Smith, 1904). It probably has other notes but they do not appear to have been recorded.

DISPLAY: Bowing display as in other bronzewings with lifted, frontally presented wings and tail raised and spread. Nodding and wing movements accompany nest-calling.

REFERENCES

Austin, C. N. (pers. comm.).

Cayley, N. W. 1931. *What bird is that?* Sydney.

Mathews, G. M. 1910–1911. *The birds of Australia.* Vol. 1. London.

Serventy, D. L. & Whittell, H. M. 1948. *Birds of Western Australia.* Perth.

Seth-Smith, D. 1904. Notes on the habits in captivity of the Brush Bronzewing Pigeon *Phaps elegans.* Avicult. Mag. New Series **2**: 211–214 and 263–266.

FLOCK PIGEON   *Phaps histrionica*

Peristera histrionica Gould, Bds. Austr. pt. 2. Mar. 1841, pl. (13) = 5, pl. 66 of Bound Volume.

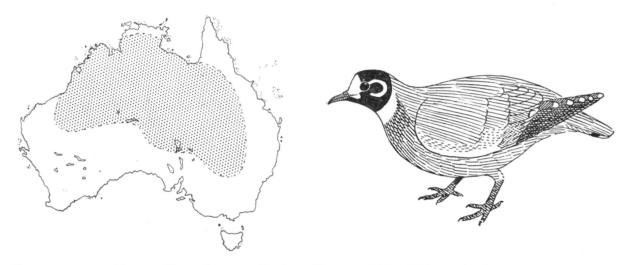

DESCRIPTION: About midway between Barbary Dove and Feral Pigeon in size; plump and compact in shape with short tail and longish wings. Head strikingly patterned in black and white (see sketch). Underparts, below the broad white band in front of neck, bluish grey shading to rusty buff with greyish centres on the under tail coverts. Hind neck, mantle, back, inner wing coverts, scapulars and inner-most secondaries, rump, upper tail coverts and central tail feathers are almost uniform bright reddish brown which fades to light sandy brown when worn and bleached. Outer tail feathers blue grey with black subterminal bands and broad white tips. Outer wing coverts bluish grey, those of the alula and primary coverts tipped white and those on the carpal area white, or partly white, forming a white line along the upper edge of the folded wing. Some of the inner secondaries with iridescent areas forming a glossy purple and green patch on folded wing. The two innermost of the group of 'inner central' secondaries that are thus ornamented have blue grey ends with a conspicuous large white spot. Pri-maries grey with rufous edgings to outer webs and concealed rufous patch on inner web, and white tips. Irides dark brown or blackish. Bill black or dark brown. Feet and legs purplish or dark grey.

The female lacks the white forehead and black crown of the male, and has the rest of the facial pattern only obscurely indicated in greyish black and buffy white. Her upper breast and flanks are light tawny brown, which colour often more or less suffuses the grey of her lower breast and belly. The brown of her upperparts is slightly less bright and reddish than the male's, and she shows the wing markings in much reduced form. The juvenile female is duller than the adult and has pale fawn fringes to most feathers. The brown feathers show some trace of a 'peppered' or speckled pattern such as is found more clearly in the young of *Geophaps* (q.v.). I have not seen a male juvenile.

FIELD CHARACTERS: Large-winged, very short-tailed pigeon with strong flapping flight with continuous wing beats. When settled bright sandy-brown upperparts and crestless black and white head (grey and buffish in female) equally diagnostic.

DISTRIBUTION AND HABITAT: The interior of Australia; from Northern Australia south to the Minilya River in West Australia, north-eastern South Australia and north-western New South Wales. Vagrant in coastal districts. Inhabits open country and plains, both grassland and semi-desert, not avoiding areas with scattered trees.

FEEDING AND GENERAL HABITS: Feeds on the ground. Known to eat seeds of grasses and other plants and small young leaves. Flight strong, with regular wing beats, usually fairly high. Nomadic, commonly or usually in large dense flocks. When coming to water such large flocks often indulge in much circling, twisting and hesitation before swooping down to the water from which they rise again in apparent fright before all have had time to drink from the edge. Fletcher (in Campbell, 1901) suggests that this behaviour may be due to the Aborigines who regularly preyed on Flock Pigeons coming to drink. His description of the Aboriginals' hunting technique is of great interest. It depended, apparently, on temporarily disorganising the descending birds by fixing artificial 'bushes' near the water's edge which caused the 'front ranks' to check and, at the precise moment of the resulting confusion, the Aborigines hiding near would jump up and hurl boomerangs into the milling and confused flock. The white man with his guns has, however, long taken over from the Aborigine in the matter of Flock Pigeon destruction and often for less justifiable motives.

Sometimes alights on the surface to drink.

NESTING: A slight scrape or depression, usually with little or no nesting material, on the ground in the shelter of a clump of grass, or low bush. Two creamy white eggs. Apparently breeds at any time when food is plentiful, chiefly near the end of a rainy period or soon after when the grass is long and green.

VOICE: Fletcher records a 'delicate soft coo-coo' heard only when the birds are breeding.

DISPLAY: No information.

REFERENCES
CAMPBELL, A. J. 1901. *Nests and Eggs of Australian Birds*. Pt. 2. Sheffield.
MacGILLIVRAY, W. D. K. 1932. The Flock Pigeon. *Emu* **31**: 169–174.

CRESTED PIGEON   *Ocyphaps lophotes*

Columba lophotes Temminck, pl. Col. Live; 24, 1882, pl. 142.

DESCRIPTION: Rather larger than a Barbary Dove with, for a pigeon, a rather slim build, with longish, slightly graduated tail, medium-short wings, a small bill and a jaunty Lapwing-like crest. Head medium grey, throat, breast and underparts pale grey. Crest blackish. Sides of lower neck and breast salmon pink. Upperparts drab brown, more or less glossed with bronze green, except on hind neck and upper tail coverts. Most wing coverts strikingly barred, each feather being light purplish brown with a black subterminal bar and a wide light fawn tip. Those parts of the greater coverts and inner secondaries visible when the wing is folded are iridescent green and iridescent purple respectively, in each case the glossy parts of each feather being bordered with white. Primaries dark greyish, the third from outermost primary is very short and narrow. Two central tail feathers dark drab, somewhat glossed with green and with narrow white tips. Outer tail feathers darker with bluish, purplish and/or greenish iridescence and broad white tips. Irides orange, yellow or orange-red. Orbital skin purplish-pink or pinkish red. Feet pinkish red. Bill black or greenish black, greyish at base.

The juvenile is duller with only a slight suggestion of iridescence on the wings and tail.

FIELD CHARACTERS: At a little distance appears an almost uniform light grey and this general colour combined with its distinctive flight (q.v.) and/or its long, dark crest and longish tail at once identify it.

DISTRIBUTION AND HABITAT: Most of Australia except the heavy rainfall regions and east of the great dividing range in eastern Australia. Inhabits various types of arid and (at least by European standards) more or less open woodland, open arid country with some shrubs or trees and cultivated areas provided some tree or scrub cover is available. Normally always within easy flying distance of surface water. Habitually uses such artificial water sources as dams and cattle troughs. Often common around farms and homesteads.

FEEDING AND GENERAL HABITS: Feeds on the ground, chiefly on seeds. Known to take the seeds of several herbaceous plants, of *Acacia* trees, young green vegetation and small bulbs.

Usually in pairs or small flocks of from four to thirty individuals but much larger flocks, up to a thousand or more, may aggregate in good feeding areas or near water during dry periods. At Innamincka, in northern South Australia, where large numbers of this species were present in April 1965, I found them roosting in pairs in small densely foliaged trees. These trees were in ratio of about 1 to 40 of other, less dense species, so clearly this represented choice not chance.

Flight usually swift and consisting of several rapid wing beats alternating with gliding during which the wings are held still and more or less horizontal. When flying more slowly only one wing beat may intersperse the glides. When flying upwards, as when rising from water in a deep gully or steep-banked river, the wings are, naturally, beaten continuously.

Usually comes to water about half to one hour after sunrise, before feeding, and fills its crop with water. Many (but probably not the same individuals), however, come to drink in the early evening. The Crested Pigeons that I watched in the wild usually showed signs of fear when coming to drink and hence although often arriving in pairs or small parties, tended to sit about on trees near the water, giving distress calls, until a bold individual flew down and began to drink when its example was at once followed. When first putting their bills to the water many slightly tilted and spread their tails, a flight-intention movement. When drinking from natural waters many individuals wade in and drink with the breast and belly in contact with the water but I never saw one bathe.

When nervous at the proximity of a human being frequently and repeatedly makes a quick 'hitching up' movement of one wing. This appears to involve a slight opening and lowering of the wing which is then quickly flicked back to its normal resting position. This is seen in some other species as an apparent comfort movement but in *Ocyphaps* and *Phaps chalcoptera* it appears to be compulsive in certain situations where there is apparent conflict between fear and whatever impulse prompts the bird not to fly away.

In what is, probably, an innate escaping behaviour pattern normally having reference to birds of prey, the bird flies at great speed to a thick-foliaged tree or bush, plunges into it and then crouches motionless. This may, rather rarely, be shown when the bird is frightened by a human being, especially just before dusk. Often Crested Pigeons disturbed by man will fly down to and perch on a bush or shrub, and then make repeated movements in which the head is lowered and the bird 'peers into' the bush. These appear to be intention-movements of entering and hiding although, if more closely approached the bird flies away. Walks and runs swiftly on the ground.

NESTING: Usual pigeon nest placed in a tree or bush. Two white eggs. Breeding has been recorded at almost all seasons but chiefly in the Spring and Summer.

VOICE: The advertising coo is a soft, plaintive but rather musical 'Co͞o-ŏŏ' or 'ŏŏ-rŏŏ' subject to some variation but the first note always a little longer and more emphatic than the second. It sounds, especially at a little distance, very like the advertising coo of the Stock Dove *Columba oenas* but less loud and, I think, higher pitched. The display coo is short and grunting with an audible inspiration after each coo – could perhaps be written 'ŏŏ (wa)' but at a distance sounds monosyllabic 'ŏŏ'. It is repeated rapidly in time with the bows. The nest call is a soft, rapidly repeated 'O͞oro͞o'. The distress call is a short, panting 'coo' more musical and less grunting in character than the homologous calls of most pigeons.

DISPLAY: In the bowing display there is little or no inflation of the neck, the wings are partly opened and tilted frontally and the tail raised and spread so that the iridescent areas on wings and tail flash fully into view. The bows are rather rapid in tempo. The bowing display is given by fighting males 'between rounds' as well as when courting a female. The display flight consists of flying up at a steep angle, loudly clapping the wings and then gliding steeply down, often in a part circle. A male at liberty in England was observed (Alston, 1903) to give a very intense and spectacular form of this display flight. I have also seen both sexes approach and parade around each other with head lowered and pointed forward, wings slightly spread to emphasise the display plumage and crest lowered flat against neck and back. This occurred after male had given bowing display and was followed by allo-preening.

When nest-calling the Crested Pigeon's wing-twitching consists of a series of quick movements rapidly repeated, then a pause of longer duration, then another series of rapid movements. A clear example of how in this and many other species the wing movements used when nest-calling are given in the same rhythm as the usual wing movements when flying.

In flight a distinctive whistling rattle is produced during the wing beats. It is said to be produced by the modified primary but very similar sounds are made in flight by Bourke's Parakeet *Neophema bourkii*. This sound may function as a contact call but when a large flock of Crested Pigeons are in flight there appears to be no attempt to synchronise the wing movements.

OTHER NAMES: Crested Bronzewing; Crested Dove; Topknot Pigeon; Toppy; Whistle-winged Pigeon.

REFERENCE

ALSTON, G. 1903. Peculiarities in the Flight of Birds. *Avicult. Mag.* New Series 1: 150–151.

WHITE-BELLIED PLUMED PIGEON   *Petrophassa plumifera*

Geophaps plumifera Gould, Bds. Austr., pt. 7, 1842, p. (6) = 5, pl. 69 of bound volume.

DESCRIPTION: A plump compact quail-like little dove, a shade smaller than a Barbary. General colour bright yellowish-brown with an orange or rusty tinge, barred with black and grey on the upperparts. The individual feathers of the back and wing coverts are bluish-grey with black subterminal bands and sandy brown tips. An iridescent green and purple patch on the wing, largely obscured when the wing is fully folded, is formed from iridescent areas on some of the inner secondaries. Primaries light chestnut with blackish tips. Central tail feathers dull sandy-brown, outer ones black. Head, except for the sandy-brown crown and long pointed crest, strikingly patterned in black and white with blue-grey forehead and area of bare red skin extending from gape to and behind eye. The sandy-brown of the underparts broken by a white band across the lower breast, bordered below with a narrow band of grey and black and a large white patch on the belly. Irides golden yellow. Extensive bare facial skin bright brick red in front of eye and orange or orange-red behind eye, sometimes entirely red.   Legs purplish black.   Bill, including cere, black.   Sexes alike; juvenile duller.   (See pl. 1).

The above description is of the Central Australian form *L. plumifera leucogaster* which is the only one I have seen alive.   Nominate *L. p. plumifera* from further north is slightly smaller and is said to be duller but this may be due to comparing specimens in different degrees of plumage wear.

FIELD CHARACTERS: General bright sandy-brown colour, short tail, buffish (not black) crest and black and white markings at once distinguish it from Crested Pigeon, the only species with which it could be confused.

DISTRIBUTION AND HABITAT: Central Australia and the interior of northern tropical Australia. Inhabits dry areas where there are rocky hills or outcrops, surface water (often only small rock holes in gullies) and spinifex.   It seems unlikely that the spinifex is a major factor in determining its distribution in spite of its alternative name.

FEEDING AND GENERAL HABITS: Feeds on the ground.   Known to eat seeds, including those of Mulga trees *Acacia* sp.   Has been recorded (Ellis, 1957) visiting fowl yards when the fowls were fed, presumably to eat grain.   I have seen captive individuals break up whole (shelled) peanuts by hammering them with the point of the closed bill.   The strong, stout, hard bill is doubtless used in this manner on some natural foods also.

On the ground walks and runs actively and jumps up onto rocks or stones in a manner remarkably similar to that of partridges of the genera *Alectoris* and *Ammoperdix*.   Freely visits and feeds in the beds of (dry) creeks and gullies, among and under bushes and shrubs but appears usually to roost and nest in more open, rocky ground on the slopes and plateaux.   Usually in pairs or small parties, often larger aggregations at feeding or resting places.   Tame and easily approached from below or on a level but flees much sooner if the approaching human is above it, e.g. walking downhill towards it. When flushed rises with a rapid whirring clatter of wings then glides on stiffly held, horizontal wings.   Just before alighting, a few rather slow wing flaps are given.　When flying longer distances (which it often does in spite of statements to the contrary) the flight is just like that of the Crested Pigeon (q.v.) except that it does not throw up its tail after alighting.

Roosting sites that I found near the Pass of the Abencerrages in Western Australia were on gentle slopes on or near the hill tops; all on the lee side of some small (and usually very flat) shrub, large stone or (less often) clump of spinifex.　The birds appeared in each case to have roosted in some slight depression on bare sand, soil or small stones, not perched on a large stone.　No bird had roosted *inside* a shrub, under overhanging twigs or foliage or right against a large rock or spinifex clump, presumably because such a position might make instant flight from some nocturnal predator difficult.

Seen to come to drink, at rock holes in gullies, about mid-day but may also, perhaps more usually, drink at other times of day.　Appears not to 'flick up' one wing as do *Ocyphaps* and *Phaps chalcoptera* when nervous but a possibly homologous flight-intention (?) movement consists of very quickly partly opening both wings and snapping them shut again.

NESTING:　The nest is a slight scrape in the ground, often with little or no nesting material.　Often placed beside a clump of spinifex or a stone or among low vegetation.　Two white eggs.　Recorded breeding in August and September (Whitlock, 1924).

VOICE:　The display coo is a rather musical 'ŏŏ, cōōrh(wa)-cōōrh(wa)' or cŏŏ, ōōr(ŏŏ)-ōōr(ŏŏ).　The distress call is a low 'cōō-ŏŏ' which although of a 'cooing' quality is uttered without any visible inflation of the neck.　It is more plaintive and less emphatic in sound than the display coo but not so 'panting' in tone as the distress call of most pigeons.　A short growling 'grrŏŏr' was uttered, apparently in threat, by a captive bird.　Whitlock (1924) describes the 'call note' as sounding like 'Nturuta', this probably refers to the display coo.

DISPLAY:　In the bowing display the bird bows deeply with bill at about right angles to the substrate at lowest point of bow, raising and somewhat spreading its folded wings and erecting and spreading its tail.　Seen from above the wing movements look slight.　I have, however, often had a captive male display at me 'head on' a few inches from my face.　Then one sees the display as another dove would and it is most striking.　The shining patches on the secondaries flash into view at the same moment as the black outer tail feathers, and the pupils contract so that the golden eyes seem about to burst from their red setting in the piebald face.　This display is not always directed at the mate or another pigeon.　Often the male, standing on top of a large stone or some other small eminence, will give apparently undirected bows as he coos.　At such times the bows often appear less deep and probably this is a generalised self-assertive display equivalent to the turning round and cooing of the Rock Pigeon (q.v.).　It is significant that both species are sociable and the displaying individual often has others (apart from its own mate) around and in sight of it.　May try to bow and coo when running after another bird but is then, like other species, unable to perform the full display.

Has a threatening posture in which the bird faces its opponent with head more or less in line with the (horizontal) back and crest depressed and lying flat.　Has a display, probably the homologue of nodding, in which it adopts a horizontal posture with head lowered and crest depressed (but not lying quite flat) then thrusts forward and shakes the bill and head.　It appears to give a lateral shake while moving the head forward and down through a small arc.　The shaking, which could well be an emphasised form of the 'twig-fixing' movement such as is shown when nodding by the *Geopelia* species, serves to emphasise the crest which moves from side to side very noticeably.　This display appears to be shown both as a greeting between members of a pair and in threat or defiance towards outsiders.　The male drives his mate away from other males if she approaches close to them.

OTHER NAMES:　Plumed Ground Dove; Spinifex Pigeon; Plumed Rock Pigeon; Crested Ground Dove.

REFERENCES

ELLIS, R.　1957.　A note on the Plumed Pigeon.　*Emu* **57**: 5: 340.
WHITLOCK, F. L.　1924.　Journey to Central Australia in search of the Night Parrot.　*Emu* **23**: 4: 254–5.

RED PLUMED PIGEON　　　　　　　　　　　　　　　　　*Petrophassa ferruginea*

Lophophaps ferruginea Gould, Handb. Bds. Austr. 2, 1865. p. 137.

DESCRIPTION:　As the last form but rather smaller with no white on the breast and belly.

DISTRIBUTION AND HABITAT:　Northern and western Australia, in the same type of country as *L. plumifera*.

FEEDING AND GENERAL HABITS:　As *L. plumifera*.

NESTING:　As *L. plumifera*.　P. Colston found a nest among scattered herbage in flat open country over a mile from the nearest rocky area.　It contained two eggs.　One parent was incubating and the other close by (Colston, pers comm.).

VOICE:　Said to differ (? how) from that of the white-bellied form, but different calls might have been compared.

DISPLAY:　As *L. plumifera*.

OTHER NAMES:　Red Plumed Ground Dove; Red Crested Quail Dove.

PARTRIDGE BRONZEWING　　　　　　　　　　　　　　　　*Petrophassa scripta*

Columba scripta Temminck, Trans. Linn. Soc. London, 13, 1821, p. 127.

DESCRIPTION: Somewhat smaller in body than the average Feral Pigeon. Compact and partridge-like in shape, with short wings and tail. General plumage drab brown with pale, buffish tips to the wing coverts and scapulars and faint pale fringes elsewhere. Face and throat strikingly patterned in black and white. Lower breast and belly bluish grey with large white area at sides. Ventral regions buffish. Inner greater coverts with an iridescent green and purple area on their outer webs, forming a small glossy patch on the closed wing. Two central tail feathers drab brown, rest black with drab bases. Irides dark brown. Orbital skin bluish white, greyish blue or creamy white with an area of pink, yellow and pink or purplish red both in front of and behind the eye, towards 'corners' of bare space. Legs and feet dull purple. Bill black.

Juvenile plumage similar to adult but with the pale feather edges more clearly defined, the drab areas somewhat vermiculated with buffish and the grey and iridescent areas only slightly indicated. Young captive-bred birds were in adult plumage at about two months old.

DISTRIBUTION AND HABITAT: Inland districts of north-eastern and eastern Australia. Inhabits open country, usually near water or within easy distance of it. Has decreased greatly owing to persecution by man and, probably, owing to the effects of introduced sheep and cattle on its habitat. Probably has also suffered from the introduction of the fox and other exotic predators.

FEEDING AND GENERAL HABITS: Known to feed on seeds of grasses and knot-grass (*Polygonum*). Probably also takes other foods. Almost entirely terrestrial in habits but when flushed will often fly into a tree. When alarmed (but not sufficiently to induce it to take wing) it 'freezes', crouching low on the ground or lengthwise along the branch of a tree. It has the game-bird-like habit of frequently standing up on tip-toe and flapping its wings. In a wild state often found in flocks and Newman (1908), who kept and bred it in captivity, found that the parents, unlike most species of pigeons, showed no hostility towards the young of their first brood when the second brood hatched. His captive birds roosted near each other on the ground, facing outwards. This partridge-like habit having no doubt evolved, in both groups of birds, as a protection against mammal predators. This formation evidently giving the best chance of one or other individual hearing or seeing an approaching enemy and allowing all to take wing in an emergency without striking into one another. Flight like that of the Plumed Pigeon (q.v.), but the initial impetus may enable the bird to rise in height while gliding (Austin).

NESTING: The nest is a slight scrape in the ground, usually lined with a few stems, grasses or leaves. Two cream-coloured eggs are laid. The newly hatched young have dark fawn down, which is *not* more abundant than that of most nestling pigeons, and a well developed egg-tooth on both mandibles but that on the lower mandible flattened and semicircular instead of triangular (Newman, 1908). Appears to nest according to local conditions, usually from September to January.

Newman's birds gave distraction display when driven from the nest.

VOICE: Paired birds call frequently to one another with low crooning notes appearing to 'keep up a running conversation'. The nest-call (? and advertising coo) is a 'low soft note', the display coo a 'thrice-repeated hurried coo'. This information is all taken from Newman's observations on his captive birds.

DISPLAY: Bowing display with somewhat opened, frontally presented wings and raised and spread tail as in other bronzewings. Newman's captive male often nodded its head and raised the feathers of head and back on meeting the female.

ALTERNATIVE AND LOCAL NAMES: Squatter Pigeon; Blue-eyed Partridge Bronzewing.

REFERENCES

AUSTIN C. N. (pers. comm.).
CAYLEY, N. W. 1931. *What Bird is that?* pp. 88–89.
MATHEWS, G. M. 1910–11. *The birds of Australia.* Vol. 1. London.
NEWMAN, T. H. 1908. Nesting of the Partridge Bronzewing Pigeon. *Avicult. Mag.* New Series **6**: 337–343.

BARE-EYED PARTRIDGE BRONZEWING   *Petrophassa smithii*

Columba Smithii Jardine and Selby, Illustr. Orn., 2, 1830, pl. 104.

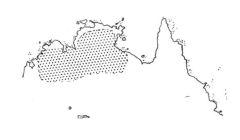

DESCRIPTION: Size and shape as last species. General colour drab brown. Face and throat boldly patterned with white (see sketch), the white areas narrowly edged with blackish. A small patch of pale blue-grey feathers with narrow black subterminal bands on centre of breast. Below this patch the brown of the underparts is strongly tinged with vinous pink. White patch on flanks and under wing. Ventral area buffish. Under tail coverts drab with broad buff edges to each feather. Iridescent blue, or green and blue areas on some of the inner greater coverts, and iridescent green, or green and purple, on the inner secondaries form two shining patches which are largely concealed when the wing is fully closed. Irides white freckled with brown or grey, whitish, or grey. Orbital skin red or yellow. Feet and legs purplish or red. Sexes alike.

Juvenile a general warm brown, paler and pinker where adult is pinkish or grey but differs strikingly in that the feathers are speckled or 'peppered' with brownish black. They also mostly have ill-defined blackish subterminal bars and fawn or pale rufous tips.

The population from around Napier Broom Bay is said to differ in having buffish-yellow orbital skin but it does not seem certain on present evidence whether this character is geographical or due to condition of the individual or its food. The former seems probable as many birds all with ochre yellow orbital skin were seen at Kalamburu (Mees 1968).

FIELD CHARACTERS: Conspicuous red or yellowish facial skin and white head markings on *crestless* head. In life shows white crescent-shaped mark just in front of folded wing when not alarmed (Frith & Freeman pers comm.).

DISTRIBUTION AND HABITAT: The Kimberley Division and Northern Territory of Australia. Inhabits grassland with some trees.

FEEDING AND GENERAL HABITS: Feeds on the ground. The only foods definitely recorded appear to be seeds of Acacia trees and of grasses. Often seen in small parties of five to twenty individuals. Terrestial, but frequently flies into trees and perches on large branches. Flight as in previous species.

NESTING: The nest is a shallow scrape or depression in the ground or in a grass clump, lined with a few or many grass stems or blades. Two cream-coloured eggs. Hill (1911), to whom is owed most of the relevant observations of this species in the wild, found it breeding in the region east of Napier Broome Bay from March until late June.

VOICE: The then Marquis of Tavistock (1914) recorded that some he kept at liberty in England uttered a purring 'corrw-coo' at frequent intervals when moving about on the ground feeding, and a loud purring 'corrw' in the bowing display.

DISPLAY: Bowing display with partly open wings, and raised, spread tail as in related species.

OTHER NAMES: Red-eyed Partridge Bronzewing; Naked-eyed Partridge Bronzewing; Squatter Pigeon.

REFERENCES

FREEMAN, D. & FRITH, C. B. (pers. comm.).
HILL, G. F. 1911. Field Notes on the birds of Kimberley, N. W. Australia. *Emu* **10**: 258–290.
MEES, G. F. 1968. Colour of orbital ring in Partridge-Pigeon. Emu 67: 294.
TAVISTOCK, MARQUIS OF. 1914. Foreign doves at liberty. *Avicult. Mag.* Third Series **5**: 123–132.

CHESTNUT-QUILLED ROCK PIGEON *Petrophassa rufipennis*

Petrophassa rufipennis. Collett, Proc. Zool. Soc. London, 1898. p. 354, pl. 28.

DESCRIPTION: About mid-way in size between a Barbary Dove and a smallish Feral Pigeon, but with the plump broad shape usual in the Australian bronzewings. General coloration a dark sepia brown but the feathers on head, neck, mantle and breast have opalescent grey centres, then a broad border of dark sepia and then a narrow lighter brown fringe giving a pale-spotted appearance. Throat and a narrow stripe above and below eye white. Primaries and primary coverts bright chestnut with tips of both webs and basal half (approximately) of outer webs dark sepia. Small concealed iridescent greenish or purplish spots on one or more inner secondaries and on one, two, or more of the inner greater coverts appear to be all that this species retains of the display plumage common to the group. Sometimes these vestigial spots are absent. Irides brown. Legs black or dark brown. The orbital skin and bill would appear, so far as one can tell from skins, to be grey or blackish in life.

FIELD IDENTIFICATION: Chestnut of wings conspicuous in flight.

DISTRIBUTION AND HABITAT: The region of the South and East Alligator rivers in the Northern Territory of Australia. Found in and about rocky gullies, ravines and cliffs. The country where it is found is extremely rugged but many kinds of native figs and other trees grow among the huge tumbled rocks.

FEEDING AND GENERAL HABITS: Little has been recorded about this species but Mr. Claude Austin who has observed it in its native haunts has very kindly supplied the following information.

The Chestnut-quilled Rock Pigeon lives on and under the rocks. Mr. Austen has never seen one perched in a tree. It flies with a very noisy clattering even for a pigeon. Flight fast with alternate beating and gliding. Shows little fear of man. Feeds on the ground, presumably mostly on seeds. When nervous, slightly lowers wings, slightly raises tail (which is usually held low) and gives a quick vertical bobbing of the head, probably a flight-intention movement (Frith, pers. comm.).

NESTING: Presumably nests on the ground or on a rock surface and lays cream-coloured eggs like its congenor the White-quilled Rock Pigeon. Mr. Austin thinks that it may, at any rate in some instances, nest in shelter under the rocks. Frith (pers. comm.) found an old nest (bird nearby) in a longitudinal sheltered crevice in a vertical rock face.

VOICE: No information.

DISPLAY: No information.

OTHER NAMES: Red-winged Rock Pigeon; Rufous-quilled Rock Pigeon.

REFERENCES

AUSTIN, C. N. (pers. comm.).
FRITH, C. B. (pers. comm.).

WHITE-QUILLED ROCK PIGEON   *Petrophassa albipennis*

Petrophassa albipennis Gould, Proc. Zool. Soc. London 1840 (1841) p. 173.

DESCRIPTION: In general appearance very like the Chestnut-quilled Rock Pigeon from which it chiefly differs in having the light parts of the wings white instead of chestnut. It is often reddish brown rather than greyish sepia in general colour. Reddish individuals of both sexes occur. All of the few sexed greyish specimens I have seen were females. A male in the American Museum of Natural History collected at Forest River is redder in colour than any other specimen but a female from the same locality is the greyest of all and forms the greatest contrast to the male. A feather from the neck of this 'red' male had its central (visible) area a brown-tinged opalescent grey, then a broad dark reddish brown border, then a rusty fawn fringe, the corresponding areas on a feather from the 'grey' female were clear opalescent grey, dark blackish brown and pale fawn with no rusty tinge. In life the iridescent wing spots are usually, perhaps always, concealed when bird is at rest (Frith, pers. comm.). The form from Victoria river, *P.a. boothi*, has little or no white on the wings (Goodwin 1969).

FIELD CHARACTERS: In flight the largely white primaries at once identify the nominate form.

DISTRIBUTION AND HABITAT: Kimberly Division of Western Australia and adjacent areas of the Northern Territory. Found in areas where there are sandstone cliffs and scattered rocks within easy reach of some source of water.

FEEDING AND GENERAL HABITS   Hill (1911) found that in the Kimberly District this species fed chiefly on the fallen seeds of Acacia. It has also been seen, near Wyndham, feeding on the roadside in company with Common Bronzewings. Spends much time by day in shallow caves or under shelter of boulders or rock overhangs. Seen to come to water at different times. Flight alternate loud flapping and gliding on stiff horizontal wings; when flying upwards only very short pauses punctuate the flapping. On alighting wings are at once snapped shut. Has a low crouching stance and walks in same posture so that legs are seldom visible (Frith pers. comm.).

NESTING: Nests found by Hill (1911) and by Freeman (pers. comm.) were on exposed surfaces of rocks and composed of only a few twigs. Kilgour (1904) found a nest on the ground, a slight hollow in the sand lined with grass stems. Two cream coloured eggs are laid.

VOICE: No information.

DISPLAY: No information.

OTHER NAMES: White-winged Rock Pigeon; White-winged Bronzewing.

REFERENCES

FREEMAN, D. J. (pers. comm.) ⎫ Observations made when with the Harold Hall Australian Expedition.
FRITH, C. B. (pers. comm.)   ⎭
GOODWIN, D. (1969). A new sub-species of white-quilled Rock Pigeon. Bull B.O.C. **89**: 131–132.
HILL, G. F. 1911. Field Notes on the birds of Kimberley, N.W. Australia, *Emu* **10**: 258–290.
KILGOUR, J. F. 1904. A trip to the Ord River. *Emu* **4**: 37–43.

THE WONGA PIGEON AND THE GEOPELIAS

The affinities of the large and striking Wonga Pigeon *Leucosarcia melanoleuca* are questionable. In my opinion it is most likely to be an offshoot of the Australian bronzewings (q.v.). It has often been considered close to the bleeding-hearts and their allies in the genus *Gallicolumba* and to the large Grey Ground Pigeon *Trugon terrestris* of New Guinea. The latter is also predominantly grey in colour but does not otherwise much resemble *Leucosarcia*. The Wonga Pigeon has a rather similar dark and white underwing pattern to some of the *Gallicolumba* species but does not otherwise resemble them in colour pattern. I think its resemblances to *Gallicolumba* are due to convergence (in a group derived originally from stock related to *Gallicolumba*) rather than to its being an Australian representative of *Gallicolumba*.

When we compare the Wonga Pigeon with the bronzewings, however, we find that it much resembles *plumifera* and *scripta* in plumage pattern though not in size. The head markings of the Wonga Pigeon could well be a simplified version of those found in *scripta* and most other bronzewings. Unlike the bronzewings *Leucosarcia* has no iridescent markings on its wings. However, comparison of the different species of Australian bronzewings suggests that they probably evolved from an ancestral form with more extensive iridescent areas and that in the course of their adaptive radiation and evolution the tendency has been towards reduction of the iridescent areas. In some species, such as *Phaps chalcoptera*, some of the iridescent markings are confined to concealed parts of the feathers. In *Petrophassa rufipennis* this reduction of the iridescent areas has progressed so far that only obsolescent iridescent spots on concealed parts of some of the feathers are present.

In its bowing display *Leucosarcia* erects and spreads its tail, as do the various bronzewings. A piece of negative evidence in favour of bronzewing origin is that unless the Wonga Pigeon is a representative of this group then the otherwise versatile bronzewings failed to evolve a rain forest form. The Emerald Dove, although a relative, does not seem to fill the bill as its relatively slight degree of differentiation suggests that it reached Australia much later than the ancestral bronzewings.

The three doves that comprise the genus *Geopelia* bear considerable superficial resemblance to turtle doves. This is especially so in the case of the largest of them the Bar-shouldered Dove, *Geopelia humeralis*. They are, however, most probably an offshoot of the Australian bronzewings with which they agree in many aspects of their behaviour, in their tendency to loquacity and their geographical distribution. They have the outermost primary attenuated, unlike either turtle doves or (other) bronzewings. The *geopelias* also lack the contrasting head pattern found in most bronzewings but so does the Crested Pigeon *Ocyphaps lophotes*, an unquestionable member of the bronzewing group. In colours and colour pattern also the Crested Pigeon much resembles the Bar-shouldered Dove, particularly when the juvenile plumages are compared. The rock pigeons *Petrophassa albipennis* and *P. rufipennis* are in some respects intermediate in colour pattern between the Bar-shouldered Dove and the Crested Pigeon although the barring on their dark, cryptic plumage is less prominent than in either. The white dark-edged wing spots of the Diamond Dove *Geopelia cuneata* appear, from their position, to be homologous with the iridescent wing spots of the common Bronzewing *Phaps chalcoptera*.

Like the bronzewings the *Geopelias* erect and spread their tails in the bowing display, whereas the *Streptopelia* species do not although they spread and exhibit their similarly patterned tails in the display flight. The mating ceremonies of the *Geopelias* are very similar to those of such bronzewings whose behaviour is known and relatively unlike that of *Streptopelia*. Their resemblance to turtledoves is, I think, superficial and due to convergence.

DIAMOND DOVE   *Geopelia cuneata*

Columba cuneata Latham, Index Orn., Suppl. 1801. p. LXI.

This delicate-looking little dove is now domesticated, like the Budgerigar, it is kept and bred in aviaries throughout the world.

DESCRIPTION: About the size of a Skylark or House Sparrow but with a longer tail and rather plumper body. Head, neck, breast and wing coverts soft slate grey, sometimes tinged with brown. Back and scapulars soft dark brown. The wing coverts and scapulars are ornamented with small white spots, each with a narrow blackish edging.   The four long central tail feathers are brownish grey, the next pair have white tips and the remaining feathers have rather more than the apical half white.   The undersides of the primaries, except for the tips, and those parts of their uppersides that are hidden when the wings are closed, are chestnut.   Irides bright red or orange-red, sometimes with a narrow silver inner ring.   Orbital skin bright orange-red.   Feet and legs flesh pink.   Bill dull brownish or blackish.   The female usually has her grey parts more suffused with brown and the orange-red orbital skin paler than the male's.   Pale grey ('silver'), fawn, and white varieties have been bred in domestication.

The juvenile has all the grey and brown areas duller and browner with a blackish sub-terminal and buffish terminal band on each feather and a black outer edging to some of the scapulars.   Eyes and orbital skin and feet dull greyish.

FIELD CHARACTERS: Small darkish grey dove with long, white-edged tail.   Contrasting white belly and (in flight) chestnut primaries distinguish it from (Australian form of) Zebra Dove.

DISTRIBUTION AND HABITAT: Northern and inland Australia; occasionally 'erupting' into coastal areas of southern Australia.   Inhabits various types of more or less open woodland, mulga scrub, gum creeks and open country with some shrubs and trees within reach of water.

FEEDING AND GENERAL HABITS: Roosts, nests and often perches in trees and bushes, but feeds and spends much of its time on the ground. a great sun lover often resting in the full glare of the sun at times when other birds have sought the shade.   Has a quick, toddling run often used when seeking food on ground, also walks more slowly.   Feeds on seeds, many of them very small, of various herbaceous plants and of some grasses.   Also sometimes takes the larger seeds of *Acacia* sp.   Probably also takes young leaves and shoots since domestic birds readily peck pieces from growing chickweed, young grass, etc.

Usually seen in couples, not always of opposite sexes, or small parties, sometimes in flocks of twenty or more.   Single birds sometimes seen but even incubating or brooding birds tend to feed and rest in company during their 'off duty' periods.

Flight parakeet-like, usually very fast, a series of rapid wing beats followed by a closure of the wings causing a downward dip or swoop similar to but usually less pronounced than that in the flight of many passerines.   Particularly when flying some distance the wing closures may only be momentary and the consequent 'dips' in flight only very slight.   May fly well above tree top height, unlike most other dry-country Australian pigeons.

NESTING: Usual pigeon's nest, but proportionately small, in a tree, bush, tangle of débris in a dry river-bed, etc. Usually low down. Two white eggs which, at least in captive birds, are laid at 24 hour intervals and in the morning. Incubation takes about 12 to 13 days and young can fly at 11 to 12 days old.

VOICE: Very loquacious and 'talkative' like most of its relatives. It has two quite distinct advertising coos. One is a pleasant 'cōo-cōo, cōo, cōo-cōo' or cōo-ŏŏ, cōo-cōo with a sad – or at any rate mournfully 'resigned' tone. The other is a two-note phrase consisting of a harsh, nasal-sounding coo (very suggestive of a human snore) followed by a 'normal' coo. One could, perhaps write it as 'cor-cōo' or 'coorh-cōo'.

At full intensity the advertising coos are quite loud and all the notes, except for the snoring 'cor' are very clear and pure in tone. At lower intensities they are less loud and clear and sometimes broken or varying in pitch. When studying captive birds I could find no difference in the function or causation of the two forms of advertising coo, and my male birds would habitually vary their songs, uttering one or two 'cor-cōos' followed by one or more 'cōo-cōo, cōo, cōo-cōo' and so on.

The cor-cōo is also used as a nest-call. It is then usually less clear and more drawn out with the nasal tone of the 'cor' often permeating the final 'coo'. The female's notes are much less loud than the male's but a female calling at high intensity may sound very like a low intensity variant of the same call from a male.

Paired birds frequently utter rather soft calls with the same nasal snoring or growling quality as the 'cor' note. These are given when the male and female are together on the nest site; when one alights near the other and as contact notes. These low calls intergrade completely into the full versions of the advertising coo and might be considered low intensity varients of it, but they do not appear to be uttered by solitary birds which, naturally, give the advertising-coos loud and often. They do not appear to be used in aggressive contexts and are thus not equivalent to the excitement-cries of the turtle doves although they are used in some situations where a *Streptopelia* would give its excitement-cry.

The display coo is an emphatic 'oh (wa)' or 'coorh (wa)', the (wa) being, apparently, an inspiration following the cooing note. The distress call is, like that of other doves, a panting gasp but has a more whistling, less grunting, tone than in larger species. Usually a whole series of these gasping distress notes are given run together before pausing.

When the male strikes at the female prior to copulation (q.v.) he gives a loud explosive-sounding cry, suggestive of the defensive 'spitting' of a domestic cat.

DISPLAY: In the bowing display the bird bows rather rapidly up and down, the tail being erected and fully spread at the culmination of each bow. Commonly the bow is frontal but if the hen is to one side of the displaying male he tilts himself somewhat towards her. The bowing display seems only to be used in sexual contexts.

Wing-lifting display in which the male holds his folded wings horizontally as does the Rock Pigeon, but head is bent downwards sometimes given in a horizontal posture as a response to another flying above, sometimes an upright posture if female is behind and on a level with or lower than the male.

Copulation commonly initiated by male displaying to female then flying a little way from her and going into an upright wing-lifting display on alighting, and usually preceded by billing. The male then mounts the female, gives a single coo, dismounts, at once utters a loud cry and strikes at the hen with his wing. She crouches, however, and his wing appears to go *just* over her head and not actually to hit her. Immediately after this they (usually) bill again for a second or so, then male remounts and repeats the process, but this time jumping down to the other side of his mate and striking with the other wing. He then mounts a third time, gives a double coo and copulates. Immediately afterwards the male makes as if to attack the female but does not (as a rule) actually touch her, she flies only a foot or so and they are friendly again in a few moments.

Head-shaking and nodding occur in the same situations as in other pigeons. The Diamond Dove usually makes a quivering 'twig-fixing' movement at the culmination of each nod, but this is less pronounced than in its relative the Bar-shouldered Dove.

OTHER NAMES: Little Dove; Little Turtledove.

REFERENCE

GOODWIN, D. 1960. Some observations on the Diamond Dove. *Avicult. Mag.* **66**: 97–105.

ZEBRA DOVE   *Geopelia striata*

Columba striata Linnaeus, Syst. Nat., ed. 12, 1, 1766, p. 282.

DESCRIPTION: About half the size of a Barbary Dove. Tail long, the central tail feathers of equal length but the three outer pairs progressively shortened so that the tail is graduated when spread. First primary attenuated, forehead, face and throat light bluish grey; top of head a pale drab brown. Hind neck finely barred whitish drab and blackish. Sides of neck, breast and flanks barred black and white. Centre of breast mauve-pink to salmon pink shading to white on belly and under tail coverts. Upperparts light earth brown shading to grey on wing coverts, with black fringes to feathers giving a barred effect. Secondaries and primaries dark greyish drab with some chestnut on basal parts of the inner webs forming an obscure patch on underside of wing. Underwing coverts pale rufous barred blackish. Central tail feathers drab, the four outermost on either side blackish broadly tipped white. Irides white, blue or grey or some intermediate hue. Orbital skin blue, greenish blue or greyish blue. Bill grey or greyish brown at tip shading through bluish grey to gre-blue or blue at base. Feet and legs dull pink or (especially in Australian forms) mottled dark purple and flesh-pink or whitish.

Juvenile paler and browner, barred as much as the adult but the barred feathers on back and wing coverts with buff fringes.

The above plumage descriptions apply to the nominate race, *G. s. striata*, which is found widely in the Indo-Malayan regions and has been introduced elsewhere. The Australian forms *G. s. placida*, *G. s. tranquilla* and *G. s. clelandi* are paler with the barring extending right across the front as well as sides of breast. They have no chestnut on the inner webs of the wing quills but their underwing coverts are a barless dark chestnut. The form found in the eastern Lesser Sunda Islands, *G. s. maugeus*, is darker with the entire breast strongly barred, pure white belly and extensive chestnut areas on the wing quills, and chestnut underwing coverts.

FIELD CHARACTERS: The Australian form (the only one I have seen wild) looks a small, grey long-tailed dove. Paler general colour, less contrasting pale belly, drab primaries and, at close quarters, blue orbital skin distinguish it from Diamond Dove with which it is easily confused at a distance.

DISTRIBUTION AND HABITAT: Indo-Malayan and Australasian regions from southern Tenasserim south and east to Luzon in the Philippines, the Lesser Sunda Islands, Tenimber and Kei Islands, southern New Guinea and Australia.   Has been successfully introduced into Madagascar, St. Helena, the Hawaiian Islands and elsewhere.

Inhabits open country with some trees and bushy growth.   Also, at least in Australia, wooded creek-beds intersecting more open arid scrubland.   Seldom or never in primeval jungle or forest other than at the edges or in clearings.   Over much of its range a characteristic bird of cleared areas, gardens and agricultural land.

FEEDING AND GENERAL HABITS: Feeds and spends much of its time on the ground.   Food chiefly small seeds of grasses and herbaceous plants but some insects and other small invertebrates also eaten. Although chiefly a feeder on small seeds it will, at least in some areas, readily learn to take cultivated grains and even artificial foods such as bread and biscuit crumbs.

Commonly in pairs or family parties but large numbers of pairs or individuals may gather at good feeding grounds.   Similar but smaller gatherings may occur, at anyrate with non-breeding birds, at favourite sun-bathing or resting places.   Flight like that of Diamond Dove (q.v.) but typically with the wing closure and consequent dipping flight path more pronounced.

NESTING: Usual pigeon nest in tree or bush from a few inches to a dozen feet from the ground.   Two white eggs.   Probably breeds whenever conditions suitable.   In Victoria, Australia, from November to February.   In the Malay Peninsula in 'early months of the year'.   In North Australia, Immelmann (1960) found it breeding during the rains in spite of appearing physically distressed by them.

VOICE: Little seems to have been recorded of the calls of the nominate form.   Most writers familar with it in life describe it as 'koo-kurr-kurr', or something similar.   The nest call of a male of this form that I observed in captivity was a soft, 'liquid-sounding' note between a coo and a soft scream, followed by a series of soft clucking sounds.   I wrote it down as 'cröōō, clk-clk-clk-clk'.   His advertising coo was rather similar but louder, the notes longer-drawn and more mellow.   'Crōōōdle, Clu-clu-clu-clu' the first note (crōōōdle) being a most peculiar sound difficult to describe other than as 'between a coo, a whistle and a scream'.   The calls I heard in northern South Australia were a much softer 'cōō-cōō,cŏŏ' or 'oo-oo, cŏŏk' and a 'co-co, co-co, co-co' both with a very 'morse code-like' tone.

Lowe (1956) in his excellent study on a population in southern Australia described the following calls. A double 'coo-luc, coo-luc' and a triple 'coo-a-luc, cōō-a-luc', both apparently used as an advertising coo. A bubbling croon 'heard during love-making and nest-building'.   A 'long drawn-out croo-ool', also apparently used as an advertising coo; a peculiar hoarse cry which is uttered during copulation (Lowe thinks by the female), and a series of urgent sounding coos like 'oow-oow-oow', used when giving the bowing display.   Also a mewing distress call and bill-clicking when giving defensive-threat display.

DISPLAY: Bowing display with raised and fanned tail as in other *geopelias*.   Display flight in which bird rises with clapping wings and then glides down to perch or ground (Lowe, in litt.).   Copulation ceremonial (of introduced population of nominate form on Seychelles) very like that of *G. cuneata*.   After billing male mounts female for a few seconds, then 'dismounts, holding its head high and uttering a single "cro-o-o-o" sound'.   The process is repeated a second time.   At the third mounting the male gives three consecutive 'cro-o-o-o cro-o-o-o' notes and then copulates (Loustau-Lalanne 1962).   Nodding as in *Geopelia humeralis* (q.v.).

OTHER NAMES: Peaceful Dove (Australia); Barred Ground Dove; Barred Dove.

REFERENCES

IMMELMANN, K.   1960.   Im Unbekannten Australien.   Pfungstadt/Darmstadt, Germany.
LOUSTAU-LALANNE, P.   1962.   Land birds of the granitic islands of the Seychelles.   *Seychelles Soc. Occ. Publ.* **1**: 18–19.
LOWE, U. T.   1956.   The Way of a Dove.   *Emu* **56**: 167–182.
ROBINSON, H. C.   1927.   The Birds of the Malay Peninsula, Vol. 1.   London.
SCHWARTZ, C. W. & E. R.   1951.   Food Habits of the Barred Dove in Hawaii.   *Wilson Bull.* **63**: 149–156.
TUBB, J. A.   1945.   Field Notes on some New Guinea Birds.   *Emu* **44**: 249–273.

BAR-SHOULDERED DOVE   *Geopelia humeralis*
Columba humeralis Temminck, Trans. Linn. Soc. London, 13, pt. 1, 1821, p. 128.

DESCRIPTION: About the size of a Barbary Dove but with proportionately longer tail and shorter wings. Upperparts light greyish drab, paler and tinged with pink on the wing-coverts.   Hind neck and upper part of mantle light coppery buff.   Forehead pale bluish grey; rest of head, sides of neck and breast bluish grey.   Underparts buffy-white with a strong salmon pink tinge on the lower breast and sides. All the cover feathers of the upperparts, except on the forehead, have narrow blackish terminal bands giving a scaled effect.   Primaries with blackish outerwebs and tips, otherwise chestnut.   Underwing chestnut.   Four central tail feathers greyish drab, rest dull chestnut with broad white tips.   Irides yellow or greenish.   Orbital skin and bill bluish grey.   Feet dull red.

The juvenile is duller with ill-defined dark subterminal bars, buff edgings to most feathers and barred buff and brown feathers on the parts that are grey in the adult.   There is a certain amount of geographical variation, birds from New Guinea tend to be a little darker; those from Western Australia more strongly tinged with salmon pink.   Mayr (1951) has discussed this geographical variation in detail.

DISTRIBUTION AND HABITAT: Northern and eastern Australia and the lowlands of southern New Guinea.   Inhabits wooded areas near water.   Chiefly in or near the gallery forest along water courses. Also sometimes common in dry scrub, as near Townsville, Queensland and also, in small numbers, in rain forest and open forest (H. Lavery, pers. comm.).

FEEDING AND GENERAL HABITS: Largely a ground feeder, possibly entirely so, but its habitat suggests the probability that it may also feed in trees or shrubs.   Known to take seeds.

NESTING: Usual pigeon nest in a tree or shrub at no great height.   Two white eggs.   In north-eastern Australia found breeding in all months except April, May and June (Lavery, *et. al.*).

VOICE: Advertising-coo a loud, cheerful-sounding 'kŏŏ, kōō-ŏŏ' repeated several times, the first two notes sounding much like the call of a male Cuckoo (*Cuculus canorus*), but the final 'ŏŏ' shorter than even the first note.   This may be used as a nest-call also.   Various low intensity forms are used that vary somewhat from the above and can intergrade with an odd growling chatter which is often used when 'nodding' and also in apparent greeting between paired birds.   The display-coo is less loud and long than the advertising coo.   It could be written 'cŏŏ-ōōh' but is sometimes monosyllabic.

DISPLAY: Bowing display with raised and fanned tail.   Like that of the Diamond Dove but with the head held nearly horizontal at the culmination of the bow.   Frontally the coppery neck feathers show conspicuously on either side of the head during the bowing.   From Whitman's (1919) description the copulation ceremonial would appear to be very similar to that of the Diamond Dove (which see).   Immelmann (1960) recorded, from wild individuals, a display flight in which it flies up with clapping wings, then glides down with wings and tail outspread.   Nodding occurs in both hostile and sexual situations and each nod terminates in the shuddering 'twig-fixing' movement that is part of the nest-building repertoire.

OTHER NAMES: Bronze-necked Dove; Copper-necked Dove.

REFERENCES

LAVERY, H. *et al.* Breeding Seasons of birds in north-eastern Australia. (in press).
IMMELMANN, K. 1960. Im Unbekannten Australien. Pfungstadt, / Damstadt, Germany.
WHITMAN, C. O. 1919. *The Behaviour of Pigeons.* Vol. 3 of the posthumous works of C. O. Whitman. Carnegie Inst., Washington.

WONGA PIGEON   *Leucosarcia melanoleuca*

Columba melanoleuca Latham, Ind. Suppl., 1801, p. LIX.

DESCRIPTION: About the size of a Wood Pigeon but plumper in build and with proportionately smaller head and shorter wings and tail. Tail rounded. Wings rounded with stiff and rather narrow and decurved primaries. Blackish band from gape to eye. Forehead and throat white shading to greyish white on crown and face. Breast and upperparts slate grey, banded with white at sides of breast. Primaries and secondaries a more brownish slate, narrowly fringed whitish on outer webs. Outer tail feathers tipped white. Underparts white with black centres to feathers forming a boldly spotted pattern on flanks. Under tail coverts whitish buff, spotted with dark grey. Underwing coverts spotted black and white. Irides very dark brown, orbital skin pink or pinkish red, blue grey at outer edge. Legs and feet purplish, purplish pink or pinkish red. Bill purplish pink or purplish red at base, dark purplish or purplish black at tip. Sexes alike, females perhaps averaging a little smaller and very slightly less bluish in tone. Juvenile duller and browner, especially on wing coverts.

DISTRIBUTION AND HABITAT: Eastern Australia. Inhabits rain forest.

FEEDING AND GENERAL HABITS: Feeds on the ground, largely on seeds. Usually feeds in the early morning and late afternoon. Unless alarmed usually walks, even over distances of up to half a mile. When flushed rises with a loud wing flap and flies only a short distance before alighting on a branch or the ground where it stays quite still and is hard to pick out. Apparently territorial, pairs usually being found regularly in the same area. May aggregate in numbers at good feeding places. Most of the above information is taken from Frith's (1952) observations.

NESTING: Usual pigeon nest in tree or shrub. Apparently usually rather high up, from 10 to 40 feet above ground. Two white eggs. Nesting recorded from October to January and also in July (Campbell, 1901).

VOICE: The advertising coo is a repeated loud and high pitched series of fluting coos. 'Coo-coo-coo-coo-coo . . .'. Each 'coo' is exactly the same in pitch and tempo as all the others, which gives a curious but not unmusical effect. Both sexes give the advertising coo in very similar if not identical form. The nest call I have only heard on a few occasions from captive birds (a male and two females) it did not differ, to my ears, from the advertising coo. The display coo is a soft throaty 'croor' quite unlike the advertising coo; probably this is subject to variation. I have only heard it from two captive individuals and Frith (1952) described that of a wild male as 'clucking'.

DISPLAY: In the bowing display lowers head and raises and spreads tail. May give this display while walking around or after female (Frith, 1952) and then, apparently, with little or no elevation of the tail. Copulation seen once by Frith: the hen crouched in solicitation immediately after bowing display of male and without any preliminary billing. When nest-calling the wing movements are slower and more 'flappy' than in *Columba* species and the wing (or wings) are slightly spread. Very similar to the homologous wing movements of the Common Bronzewing.

REFERENCES

CAMPBELL, A. J. 1901. *Nests and eggs of Australian Birds.* Part 2, 696–697.
FRITH, H. J. 1952. Notes on the Pigeons of the Richmond River, N.S.W. *Emu* **52**: 89–99.

THE MOURNING DOVE GROUP

In this assemblage I include the Mourning Dove, *Zenaida macroura*, the Eared Dove, *Z. auriculata* and the Zenaida Dove, *Z. aurita*, the White-winged Dove, *Z. asiatica*, the Galapagos Dove, *Z. galapagoensis* and the extinct Passenger Pigeon, *Ectopistes migratorius*.

The species in *Zenaida* are mostly rather smaller than a Barbary Dove although one is a little larger. They are quietly clad in soft greys, browns and pinks usually enlivened with iridescence on the neck and black and white markings on wings and tail. All have a blackish stripe across the lower part of the face and an iridescent patch on the neck immediately behind it. Most have black spots on the wing-coverts and white on the outer tail feathers. Their tails vary in size and shape from wedge-shaped in the Mourning Dove to only slightly rounded in the larger White-winged Dove. They perch and usually nest in trees and shrubs but feed and spend much time on the ground. One species, the Galapagos Dove, is very largely terrrestial. All lay two eggs.

Zenaida macroura and *Z. auriculata* are allopatric and agree very closely in morphology and behaviour. They seem best considered as members of a superspecies. *Z. aurita* differs from them in having 12 instead of 14 tail feathers and proportionately larger feet and legs. In these characters, as in its colour pattern and more terrestial habits it forms a connecting link between *auriculata* and the Galapagos Dove *Z. galapagoensis*. This latter has a still shorter tail, larger bill with more decurved culmen and is highly terrestial. Whitman (1919) suggested that *galapagoensis* represents a form ancestral to both *aurita* and *asiatica*. I think it is more likely that *aurita* and *galapagoensis* are geographical representatives. *Z. asiatica* stands well apart from the others and shows, expecially in its large South American race *melpoda*, considerable resemblance to some American species of *Columba*.

Although the above species show a considerable amount of differentiation *inter se* their relationship is obvious when they are compared and they are, in my opinion, all best included in *Zenaida*.

The Passenger Pigeon *Ectopistes migratorius* shows obvious affinities to the Mourning Dove *Z. macroura* and they may be, phylogenetically, more closely related to one another than *macroura* is to *asiatica*. The Passenger Pigeon differs, or did differ, from *Zenaida* species in its larger size, in lacking the characteristic facial stripe, in its pronounced sexual dichromatism, in laying only one egg to a clutch, in its remarkably distinct voice and behaviour and in its ecology. Taken together these differences seem just sufficient to justify the retention of *Ectopistes* as a monotypic genus.

The nearest relatives of the mourning dove group are almost certainly not the Old World turtle doves, to which some of them bear some superficial and convergent resemblance, but the American ground doves, and the American quail doves.

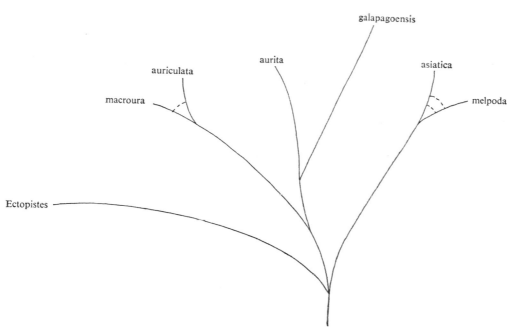

FIG. D.7: Presumed relationships of species in the genera *Zenaida* and *Ectopistes*.

PASSENGER PIGEON   *Ectopistes migratorius*

Columba migratoria Linnaeus, Syst. Nat., ed. 12, 1, 1766, p. 285.

The Passenger Pigeon shares with the Dodo the doubtful fame of being one of the two best known species that have been exterminated by man.

DESCRIPTION: Rather smaller than a Feral Pigeon and slimmer in build with a long pointed tail. Head and upperparts bluish grey with black streaks on scapulars and black spots on wing coverts (see sketch).   Secondaries and primaries greyish black, the latter edged whitish on inner webs.   Lower throat and breast a rich pinkish rufous shading to a paler orange pink on lower breast and flanks, and white on ventral regions and under tail coverts.   Patch of shining pink or purple-pink iridescence at side of neck which spreads to some extent over hind neck.   Central tail feathers dark grey, outer ones greyish white with black patch near base of inner web and base of inner web chestnut.   Irides bright red.   Orbital skin purplish flesh.   Bill black.   Legs and feet red.

Female much duller than the male.   Browner grey above, light greyish drab on the breast, a smaller iridescent pink patch on neck, more profuse black spots on the wing coverts, orange irides and greyish orbital skin.   Juvenile similar to female but browner above and on breast, with whitish edgings to most feathers giving it a pronounced scaly effect and light chestnut edges to the primaries.

DISTRIBUTION AND HABITAT: The eastern half of North America from central and southern Canada to Louisiana and Florida, wintering south of the breeding range.   Inhabited forest and, to a limited extent for feeding purposes, cultivated areas in or adjacent to forest.   Now extinct.

FEEDING AND GENERAL HABITS: Fed both on the ground and in trees and shrubs taking beech nuts, seeds of many kinds including cultivated grains, berries, earthworms and other invertebrates.   Had a special behaviour pattern of catching earthworms by stalking and suddenly seizing them by the head (Whitman, 1919).   Intensely gregarious; normally migrating, nesting and feeding in enormous flocks although even when it was still abundant nesting in scattered pairs also occurred.   The species' way of life was, however, adapted to living and breeding colonially.   It evidently relied for nesting success on breeding in such large numbers in one area that the local predators could not normally take sufficient toll to prevent successful reproduction.   Once civilised man with his resources became a predator on the species it was doomed.   A very large amount of literature on it exists.   This has been collected together and the relevant information extracted by Schorger (1955) whose book on the Passenger Pigeon should be read by all who wish for fuller details on its history and life-history than can be given here.

NESTING: Usual pigeon nest in a tree, usually in dense colonies with many nests in each tree.   One white egg.   The siting of nesting colonies was often, and perhaps usually, dependent upon there having been a good crop of beech mast the previous autumn, the beech nuts still on the ground providing a major food for the nesting birds in Spring.   Incubation period thirteen days; young fledge at fourteen days; probably usually only one brood (of one young) reared per year in the wild.   There is good evidence (see Schorger, 1955) that the males roosted away from the nesting colonies when the females were incubating.

Schorger (p. 119) states that (unlike all other pigeons whose behaviour is known) the young Passenger Pigeon was abandoned by its parents while still in the nest; that it remained in the nest for a day or so, then fluttered to the ground, after which it was another three or four days before it could fly properly. I find it difficult to believe that this was normal behaviour and think that such accounts are due to observations on young whose parents had been killed and/or on instances where persistent harrying by man or other abnormal circumstances had, perhaps, caused most of the adults to desert.   It may well be that towards the end of the nesting cycle attachment to the young was less intense and that the constant human interference and persecution commonly caused the adults to desert *en masse*.   If so, this side-effect of human predation may well have been a major factor in exterminating the species.

VOICE: The most complete and authentic account of the calls and displays of the Passenger Pigeon is given by Craig (1911) from whose work the information under this and the following headings are compiled.   Most of its calls were harsh, loud clucking or chattering notes.

The excitement cry, or its apparent equivalent, was a loud harsh and rather high-pitched 'keck!' generally given singly but sometimes twice or thrice in succession, but with a short pause between each.   It was apparently used in threat and also, probably, in sexual excitement.   'Scolding, chattering and clucking' were used by Craig 'to represent the wide variations of this most characteristic and frequent utterance'. This call would appear also to have fulfilled some of the functions of the excitement cry but also to have functioned as a contact call or advertising coo.   It was, apparently, given in all kinds of social contexts and subject to much modulation in pitch, loudness and speed of delivery.   In many situations it appears to have been functionally equivalent to the self-assertive version of the display coo of *Columba livia*.

The vestigial coo, or 'keeho', was a soft disyllabic note which was often uttered after the 'keck' cry or the chattering call.   The nesting call a moderately loud half-musical call, 'a great mixture of high and low notes' each series always ending in a 'keeho'. Only low clucking and croaking calls and a feeble counterpart of the male's 'keeho' were heard from females.

DISPLAY: When uttering the 'keck' cry or the chattering call the male would often give a single flap of his wings. Craig also thought that a continuous wing-flapping given while perched may have been a display although his description sounds very like the wing flapping 'exercise' commonly indulged in by young pigeons of most species shortly prior to fledging and by closely confined captive adults.

Nodding consisted of a 'movement of the head in a circle, back, up, forward and down, as if the bird were trying to hook his head over something . . . body and tail remained all the while stationary'. This form of nodding may well have correlated with the movement of putting the neck over the female's and pressing on her. The pre-copulatory behaviour consisted of the male, or the female if she was more eager, pressing up against its mate putting its neck over the mate's and 'hugging' or pressing downwards. This followed a brief billing in which the bills were momentarily shaken together. The copulation which followed involved much trampling and fluttering by the male before the female would crouch. These copulations were, perhaps, not typical. After copulation both sexes uttered soft clucking, the female might strike at the male or allo-preening might take place. Allo-preening in this species was always rough and perfunctory.

OTHER NAMES: Wild Pigeon; Migratory Pigeon.

REFERENCES

CRAIG, W. 1911. The Expression of Emotion in the Pigeons. 3. The Passenger Pigeon (*Ectopistes migratorius* Linn.). *Auk* **28**: 408–437.
SCHORGER, A. W. 1955. *The Passenger Pigeon*. Madison, U.S.A.
WHITMAN, C. O. 1919. *The Behaviour of Pigeons*. Posthumous works of C. O. Whitman. Vol. 3. Carnegie Inst., Washington.

MOURNING DOVE   *Zenaida macroura*

Columba macroura Linnaeus, Syst. Nat., Ed. 10, 1, 1758. p. 164.

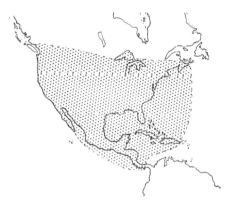

DESCRIPTION: A little smaller than a Barbary Dove and slighter in build with very thin, delicate-looking bill, neat head and rather long graduated tail. Upperparts a light greyish drab with a slight buffy tinge, shading to bluish grey on centre of crown and nape and outer part of wing. Black markings on wing coverts and scapulars as in *auriculata* (q.v.). Primaries blackish drab with narrow pale edgings to outer web. Upper part of throat whitish. Rest of head, except for grey area on crown reddish buff with short black facial streaks behind and below eye. Buff of face shades into deep vinous pink on breast and then into buff on lower breast and belly and under tail coverts. Flanks and underwing blue grey. Central tail feathers drab; outer ones grey at base with black central band and extensive greyish white (near centre) or white tips. The outermost pair entirely white on outer web. Patch of pink, purplish pink and/or bronze iridescence on sides of neck.   Irides dark brown.   Orbital skin narrow and greenish blue or light blue.   Bill blackish, red at gape edge.   Legs and feet dull red or purplish red.

The female is rather paler and duller with less grey on the head, less iridescence on side of neck and little or none of the rich buff and pink hues on head and breast.   Her tail is slightly shorter than the male's. The juvenile is like the female in ground colour but has conspicuous pale buffish fringes to most feathers and blackish or dusky marks on sides of some feathers on head and breast.   This gives it a spotted, scaly appearance unlike the adults'.

The above description is of the race *Z. macroura carolinensis* from eastern North America.   *Z. m. marginella* from western North America tends to be slightly paler in colour.   Nominate *Z. m. macroura* from Cuba, the Isle of Pines and Hispaniola is a little smaller and darker in colour.   *Z.m. tresmariae* from the Tres Marias Islands off western Mexico is similar to *Z. m. carolinensis* but has darker buff on the head. *Z. m. clarionensis* from Clarion Island off western Mexico is larger and darker, with a larger bill.   The form from Socorro Island, *Z. m. graysoni*, has diverged still further so that it is considered by some to merit specific rank.   It is appreciably larger (being larger than a Barbary Dove) and darker in colour with earth brown upperparts and forehead, face, breast and underparts deep buffish rufous.   Its calls do not differ (Gifford, 1927).

DISTRIBUTION AND HABITAT: North and Central America; breeding from British Columbia, Manitoba, southern Ontario and Nova Scotia south to Florida, Mexico, the Bahamas, Cuba, the Isle of Pines and Hispaniola.   A summer resident in the more northern parts of its range.   Inhabits open woodland, cultivated country with some trees or bushes, arid areas, semi desert and desert areas within reach of water. Unless very intensely persecuted it generally increases in range and numbers where man destroys the original vegetation and replaces it with cultivation and secondary growth and pasture.

FEEDING AND GENERAL HABITS: Feeds on the ground, chiefly on seeds of various annual weeds but also takes cultivated grains, especially wheat.   The grain taken is, however, usually only that which has been spilled in harvesting and is going to waste.   Also takes small snails and, probably, other small invertebrates.   Has been recorded picking seeds from pine cones still in the trees.

Normally in pairs, small loose-knit parties and single birds (whose mates are incubating or brooding). Often large numbers gather at good feeding grounds and at communal roosts.   Flight swift and darting, the wings making a characteristic whistling sound.   Throws up tail just after alighting and as a flight-intention movement.

NESTING: Usual pigeon nest in tree or shrub.   Very often on the old nest of some other species, sometimes on the ground or on the ledge of a building.   Two white eggs; the first is laid in the evening and the second in the early morning of the next day but one after.   Incubation period 14 to $15\frac{1}{2}$ days.   Young fledge at 13 to 15 days.   Distraction display frequent; in the most intense form the bird drops or flutters to the ground near the nest and flutters wildly about.   More often less intense forms are shown in which the bird flies from the nest, then flutters a little on the ground, stops and waves its wings, then walks further away, waving or flapping its wings and sometimes making little jumps into the air.

VOICE: The advertising coo consists of a very faint di-syllabic coo followed by two or three much louder coos 'cŏo-ŏo ŌŌ, ŌŌŌ' or 'cŏo-ōō, ŌŌ, ŌŌ, ŌŌ'.   Craig (1911) gives the musical notation for this call and points out that a fourth 'coo' is sometimes included though more often not.   The advertising coo has a very clear, melodious and somewhat sad tone and I agree with Craig that 'for romantic sweetness there is no pigeon song . . . which can approach that of . . . (the) Mourning Dove'.   The display coo does not differ from the advertising coo except, possibly, by being given with slightly greater intensity.   The nest call that I heard from a captive male was a fairly loud Cōo-ōō of the same quality as the louder notes of the advertising coo.   Craig (1911) states, however, that the nest call is usually much less loud and although very variable, 'its typical form is of three notes, a low, a high and a low'.   The advertising coo is also given by the female but in 'thin weak voice and staccato tones' (Craig).   The excitement cry is a faint growling note which according to Craig (1919) is given only immediately after copulation.   Whitman (1919), however, also records it given by the male when approaching his mate.   The distress call is a short, grunting note like that of other pigeons.

DISPLAY: In the homologue of the bowing display the male walks or runs towards or after the female, often leaping towards her in the self-assertive posture with head held low and body raised on the tips of the toes. He then stops, just behind her, with lifted head and thickened neck, stands quite still and coos. The neck is inflated and the iridescent areas thus emphasised but there is no bowing movement. When nest calling the tail is spread just enough to show the white tips of the outer feathers at the first note, as soon as this first note is passed the tail closes again (Craig, 1911), wing-twitching rather rapid and 'shuddering'. When 'parading' the self assertive posture is similar to that of many other species, with 'arched' back and lowered head. The nodding described by Craig would appear to be the flight-intention movement as he describes the upward, backward and then a downward (or forward) movement of the head as being correlated with an upward and downward movement of the tail. In *Z. m. graysoni*, and presumably in other races, copulation is preceded by billing and displacement preening and followed by both birds standing erect, the male with spread tail and swollen neck (Gifford, 1927).

The display flight consists of towering upwards, often with noisy wing beats, and then gliding downwards or in sweeping curves on wide-spread wings. Displacement preens behind wing as in other pigeons. Copulation preceded by billing, in which food is not always, perhaps not usually, passed, and followed by both sexes uttering the excitement cry.

OTHER NAMES: Carolina Dove; Soccoro Dove; Grayson's Dove.

REFERENCES

BENT, A. C. 1932. Life histories of North American Gallinaceous birds. *U.S. Nat. Mus. Bull.* 162:

CRAIG, W. 1911. *The Expression of Emotion in the Pigeons.* 2. *The Mourning Dove (Zenaidoura macroura* Linn.).

GIFFORD, E. W. 1927. Grayson's Pigeon in Captivity. *Auk* XLIV: 513–519.

NICE, M. M. 1922 & 1923. A study of the nesting of Mourning Doves. *Auk* **39**: 4. 437–474. **40**: 1. 37–58.

WHITMAN, C. O. 1919. *The Behaviour of Pigeons.* Posthumous works of C. O. Whitman. Carnegie Inst., Washington, publ. 257, Vol. 3.

EARED DOVE   *Zenaida auriculata*

Peristera auriculata Des Murs, in Gay's Hist. Fis. Pol. Chile, Zool., 1, 1847. p. 381; Atlas, 2, Orn. P . (7).

DESCRIPTION: This widespread polymorphic species is very similar in general appearance to the Mourning Dove, *Z. macroura*, with which it forms a superspecies. General appearance, including colour pattern and coloration, very like Mourning Dove except for the shorter and much less strongly graduated tail and, proportionately, rather less slender and delicate bill.

Size a little smaller than a Barbary Dove. Crown and nape bluish grey or tinged with this colour. Rest of head, neck and breast pale dull buffish pink to deep purplish pink, shading to reddish buff or pale cream (or any intermediate shade) on belly, ventral regions and under tail coverts. Upperparts warm olive brown to light greyish drab with black markings on wings (see sketch).   Primaries and outer secondaries dark brownish grey to greyish black with slightly paler tips and narrow whitish edges to outer webs.   Underwing grey.   Facial markings as in Mourning Dove but the lower one more pronounced and dark iridescent blue instead of dull black.   Iridescent bronze and/or pink and amethyst patch on side of neck.   Central tail feathers dull olive brown or drab, sometimes with an ill-defined blackish central bar.   Next pair grey with black central bar.   Rest with grey base, black central bar and pale grey to greyish white ends, outermost pair with outer webs and ends white.   Irides brown, dark brown, reddish brown or dark red.   Orbital skin bluish, greenish blue or grey.   Bill dark grey or blackish.   Legs and feet red, dark red or purplish red.

The female is usually duller with less intense pink on the breast but there is much individual variation. The juvenile is browner and lacks the pink and grey tints.   It has pale fringes to most feathers and a triangular whitish terminal spot in the centre of each feather on breast and sides of neck, the same markings are present on the wing coverts to a lesser degree.   Thus the juvenile appears conspicuously freckled or spotted, unlike the adult.

The above is a composite description covering the three very similar and intergrading races. *Z. a. auriculata*, *Z. a. chrysauchenia* and *Z. a. hypoleuca* that are found from Argentina and Chile north and northwest to southern Brazil, Ecuador and Peru.   *Z. a. stenura* from the southern Lesser Antilles, Tobago and Trinidad, Venezuela, British Guiana and parts of Northern Brazil and Eastern Columbia is slightly smaller and darker in colour.   The whole of its underparts, including the under tail coverts, are a deep vinous pink.   The tail feathers are light pinkish chestnut where those of the previous described forms are white.   The female is duller on the breast and head but otherwise similar.   *Z. a. penthera*, from the temperate zone of the eastern Andes of Columbia and the Sierra of Mérida in western Ecuador is like *Z. a. stenura* but rather larger and even darker and redder in colour with the face and underparts a deep rufous pink and the ends of the outer tail feathers rich chestnut.   Many other races of this dove have been named but all are similar to or intermediate between one or more of those described here.

DISTRIBUTION AND HABITAT: South America, Trinidad, Tobago and other islands in the southern Caribbean Sea and the southern Lesser Antilles in the West Indies.   Inhabits arid or semi-arid open country usually with some trees, bushes, or patches of woodland and cultivated areas.

FEEDING AND GENERAL HABITS: Very much as the Mourning Dove (q.v.).   Feeds principally on seeds picked up off the ground.   In the more southern parts of its range (and probably elsewhere) partly nomadic.   Usually in pairs or small groups, although large numbers may gather at a good feeding ground. Sometimes flies in large flocks.   Often roosts communally.

NESTING: Usual pigeon nest in a tree or shrub or on the ground; when on the ground often very little nesting material used.   In the West Indies ground nests are relatively rare (Bond, 1960) but in southwestern Ecuador eight of fourteen nests found (Marchant, 1960) were on the ground.   Usually nests singly, although often many pairs within a relatively small area as with most other pigeons, but in parts of northeastern Brazil it breeds in enormous colonies (Ihering, 1935).   These nesting colonies are in woods in semi-arid regions.   Most of the nests are on the ground, the numbers of nesting pairs present are suggestive of the former flocks of Passenger Pigeon and, like them, suffer intense human persecution.   Two white eggs.   Incubation period about 14 days.

VOICE: The advertising coo can be written 'O$\overline{oo}$, cr$\overline{oo}$-cr$\overline{oo}$, cr$\overline{oo}$-cr$\overline{oo}$', or (another version) 'O$\overline{oo}$! cr$\overline{oo}$, cr$\overline{oo}$-cr$\overline{oo}$', the first note loud and 'pure' with no 'R' sound, the second hoarse and with a strong 'R' sound, the succeeding two or three less loud and with a faint 'R' sound.   The display call (heard only a few times) is a deep short 'Cr$\breve{o}\breve{o}$-$\breve{o}\breve{o}$', the two syllables slurred together.   The above description is of captive specimens of the British Guiana form *Z. a. stenura*.   At least the advertising coo of other forms is probably very similar; Wetmore (1926) describes that of nominate *Z. a. auriculata* as 'a low sad-toned whoo, whoo, whoo, whoo-oo in a guttural tone'.   The nest call as described by Whitman (1919) is 'a low, single, abrupt hoarse muffled note . . . cut short and barely audible'.

DISPLAY: The bowing display, or rather its homologue, consists merely of standing still and cooing with inflated neck, exactly as in the Mourning Dove. In display flight (Wetmore, 1926) glides with set wings in short circles with throat inflated. Wing and tail movements when nest calling as in Mourning Dove (q.v.).

OTHER NAMES: Violet-eared Dove; Torpedo Dove; Blue-eared Dove; Bronze-necked Dove; Gold-necked Dove.

REFERENCES

IHERING, R. VON. 1935. La Paloma *Zenaida auriculata*, en el Noreste del Brazil. *Hornero* **6**: 37–47.
MARCHANT, S. 1960. The breeding of some S.W. Ecuadorian Birds. *Ibis* **102**: 349–382.
WETMORE, A. 1926. Observations on the birds of Argentine, Paraguay, Uruguay and Chile. *U.S. Nat. Mus. Bull.* **133**: 180–182.
WHITMAN, C. O. 1919. *The Behaviour of Pigeons.* Posthumous works of C. O. Whitman. Carnegie Inst., Washington, publ. 257, No. 3.

ZENAIDA DOVE
Zenaida aurita

Columba aurita Temminck, in Knip, Les Pigeons, 1810, les colombes, p. 60. pl. 25.

DESCRIPTION: A little larger than a Barbary Dove but plumper and more compact in shape with proportionately longer legs and shorter tail. Throat whitish. Head and upper part of neck rufous, tinged with mauve on crown. Two dark iridescent streaks on face, behind and below eye (see sketch). Upper sides of neck iridescent pinkish purple, purple or amethyst. Breast mauve pink, usually with more or less silvery wash, shading to paler mauve pink on flanks and white on belly and under tail coverts. Upperparts warm reddish brown with black and black, white-edged spots on wings. Outer secondaries black with broad white tips that show as a conspicuous white mark on wing. Underwing bluish grey. Primaries brownish black narrowly edged dull white. Central tail feathers reddish brown with obscure blackish central band. Outer ones grey, more or less tinged rufous on outer web, with black central bar and pale grey or greyish white terminal band. Outermost pair with outer webs nearly all white. Irides dark brown, reddish brown or brownish black. Bill dark horn or blackish, red at edge of gape. Feet and legs reddish flesh, purplish red or dull red.

The female is paler and has the brown of the upperparts of a less reddish tint. Juvenile very like female but no iridescence on neck and rufous buff fringes to feathers of back and wings.

The above description is of nominate *Z. a. aurita* from the Lesser Antilles. In the northern Lesser Antilles this form intergrades with *Z. a. zenaida* from the Greater Antilles, Cuba, Jamaica and the Bahamas. This form is darker and less reddish brown above and darker below with the belly and under tail coverts a dark mauve pink intermixed with bluish grey. The terminal band on its outer tail feathers and the outer web of the outermost pair are bluish grey, not whitish.

The form from the Yucatan Peninsular and adjacent Islands, *Z. a. salvadorii*, has the upperparts a pale greyish or olive brown only slightly tinged (in the male only) with reddish. There is a strong greyish mauve tinge on forehead and crown. Face and upper neck sandy fawn; breast and underparts, including belly and under tail coverts, mauve pink. Tips of outer tail feathers greyish white.

DISTRIBUTION AND HABITAT: The West Indian Islands, including Cuba, the Bahamas, Isle of Pines, Jamaica, the Cayman Islands, Hispaniolu, Mona, Puerto Rico, Virgin Islands, Sombrero, Anguilla, St. Martin, St. Bartholomew, Barbuda, St. Eustatius, St. Kitts, Nevis, Antigua, Monserrat, Guadeloupe, Dominica, Martinique, Santa Lucia, St. Vincent, Barbados, Grenada and the Grenadines, Yucatan coast and adjacent islands. Formerly also the Florida Keys. Inhabits open woodlands, mangroves, bushy and scrubby areas, marshes, old fields and cultivated regions. Avoids dense forest and profits by man's use of the land which results in forest being replaced by second growth, scrub or cultivation. Usually in lowland areas.

FEEDING AND GENERAL HABITS: Feeds chiefly on seeds picked up on the ground, including those of wild legumes, mallows, knotweed and pigweed, also waste grain in cultivated regions. Also takes some small fruits and berries (Wetmore, 1927). Comes to water frequently. Flight strong and direct with land wing clapping when flushed. Now a common bird at the built-up areas in Bridgetown, Barbados (Haverschmidt, in press).

NESTING: Usual pigeon nest in tree or shrub, on the ground in cover of plants or bushes or in a hole or niche among rocks. Two white eggs.

VOICE: The advertising coo is very similar to that of the Mourning Dove but often deeper in tone (Pough, 1951) and (Bond, 1960) rather more curtailed. Bond also records 'a short OOA-OO' like that of the Eared Dove but more resonant.

DISPLAY: In display flight the male sails in circles with wings held stiffly (Wetmore, 1927).

OTHER NAMES: Wood Dove; Seaside Dove; Pea Dove.

REFERENCES

BOND, J. 1960. *Birds of the West Indies.* pp. 104–105. *Ibis* **111**: 613.
HAVERSCHMIDT, F. The Zenaida Dove on Barbados.
POUGH, R. H. 1951. *Audubon Water Bird Guide.* pp. 308. New York.
WETMORE, A. 1927. *The Birds of Porto Rico and the Virgin Islands. Scientific Survey of Porto Rico and the Virgin Islands.* Vol. 9. Pt. 3. pp. 394–398.

GALAPAGOS DOVE   *Zenaida galapagoensis*

Zenaida Galapagoensis Gould, in Darwin's Zool. Voy. 'Beagle' Birds, Pt. 9, 1839. p. 115; Pt. 15, 1841, pl. 46.

DESCRIPTION: About the size of a Barbary Dove but thicker set with longer legs and short tail. Very similar to the Zenaida Dove but more partridge-like in shape and with a slightly stronger and more decurved

bill. Head, neck and breast dull wine red to purplish pink shading to buffish on the belly and pale grey on the under tail coverts. Narrow black border round orbital skin. Two black facial stripes below and behind eye, enclosing a white or cream stripe. Iridescent pink and bronze patch at side of neck. Upper parts dull reddish brown or earthy brown, most of the wing coverts and scapulars with black and white or black markings, giving a spotted and streaked effect. Primaries black, most with dull brown tips and narrow white fringe to outer webs. Underwing dark bluish grey. Central tail feathers dull brown with narrow black subterminal bar; outer ones brown and dark grey or dark grey with broad black subterminal bar and slightly narrower bluish grey terminal bar. Irides brown. Orbital skin light blue or greenish blue. Legs and feet purplish red or purplish pink. The female tends to be slightly paler and duller in colour with the mauve pink of the breast usually more or less washed with dull brown and this colour predominating on the head. The juvenile is paler and duller with rusty fringes to many of the cover feathers. The above description is of the nominate form *Z. g. galapagoensis*. The form found on Wenman and Culpeper Islands, *Z. g. exul* is slightly larger and is said to have darker blue orbital skin.

DISTRIBUTION AND HABITAT: The Galapagos Islands. Inhabits the dry rocky low country, usually where there are some trees, bushes or tree cacti (*Opuntia*).

FEEDING AND GENERAL HABITS: Feeds on the ground. Known to take seeds, and also recorded eating green grass and cactus pulp. Digs for food by flicking the soil towards itself like a gamebird as well as using the sideways flicking movement which other ground feeding pigeons use. It also uses this movement when sunning itself after a bath and Nicolai (1962) who has kept and bred this species, thinks it may be in process of developing dust bathing. Walks and runs with great agility, has been compared to Mourning Dove in this respect but captive birds I have seen struck me as rather more highly developed pedestrians than Mourning Doves. Flight less swift and graceful than other *Zenaida* species.

When the Galapagos Islands were first visited this species showed no fear of man. It is still remarkably tame in spite of intense human predation. Wild caught birds breed freely in captivity as, apparently, do their descendants for a few generations but, so far, no continuously reproducing captive stock has been established. There seems therefore little chance of its avoiding extinction when the human populations on, or visitors to the Galapagos Islands increase in numbers.

NESTING: Usual pigeon nest, often very little material, in hollows and crevices in the rocks or on the ground, usually in a depression and sheltered by overhanging rock ledges or vegetation. Two white eggs. Incubation period 13 days. Young fledge at 17 days and can then fly but, at least in captivity, spend much time on the ground and return to the nest to roost for a few more nights (Nicolai, in Prestwich, 1959). Distraction display recorded by several observers. Breeding recorded from March to September (Gifford, 1913) but said to be normally from March to June with a peak in March and April (Lack, 1950).

VOICE: Proebsting (1959) describes voice of male 'including display call' as a soft deep 'bob-bob-bob-rururur-bububurr'; also a deep, rolling 'bororororororrr' used to attract female to food or a roosting site. Voice of female 'burrr'. Apparently not loud – Gifford (1931) refers to a 'scarcely audible coo' given by the male when displaying.

DISPLAY: In the bowing display or its equivalent the male stands with head down and slightly spreads his tail (Gifford, 1931). Proebsting describes homologue of bowing display in which male calls with lowered head, neck inflated, wings drooped and twitching, body jerking and tail erected and partly spread. The same posture and movements are used when nest-calling. Pair also run around each other on ground during courtship. Copulation ceremony in which male feeds female then flies up and circles briefly above her before mounting.

REFERENCES

GIFFORD, E. W. 1913. The Birds of the Galapagos Islands. *Proc. Calif. Acad. Sci* (4) **2**: 6–11.
—— 1931. The Galapagos Dove. *Avicult.* (2) **3**: 17–19.
LACK, D. 1950. Breeding seasons in the Galapagos. *Ibis* **92**: 268–278.
NICOLAI, J. 1959. See under Prestwich.
—— 1962. Über Regen –, Sonnen-und Staubbaden bei Tauben (Columbidae). *J. Orn.* **103**: 125–139.
PRESTWICH, A. A. 1959. The Galapagos Dove in Freedom and Captivity. *Avicult. Mag.* **65**: 66–76.
PROEBSTING, F. 1959. Galapagostauben. *Gefied. Welt.* **83**: 155–156.

WHITE-WINGED DOVE   *Zenaida asiatica*

Columba asiatica Linnaeus, Syst. Nat. Ed. 10, 1, 1958, p. 163.

DESCRIPTION : About the size of a Barbary Dove or slightly larger and of similar general shape except, proportionately, slightly larger wings and bill. Forehead, face, neck and breast warm buff shading to greyish around base of bill and whitish at top of throat. Sides of lower neck and breast more or less tinged with vinous pink. Crown, nape and hind neck deep mauve-pink. A conspicuous black mark on side of head below and behind eye and immediately behind it a pale bronzy iridescent patch. Mantle, inner wing coverts, scapulars and central tail feathers light slightly reddish drab. Broad white ends to most of the outer wing coverts form a broad, conspicuous white band along the wing when folded and across it when opened. Outer secondaries and primaries brownish black and former tipped white, forming a second and much smaller white mark on the folded wing. Underparts below breast pale bluish grey. Lower back and rump bluish grey, slightly intermixed with drab brown. Outer tail feathers bluish grey with narrow ill-defined black subterminal bar and broad white or greyish white terminal band. Underside of tail black with broad white terminal band. Irides orange or red. Orbital skin blue or greyish blue. Bill black, legs and feet red.

The female is slightly duller with less intense mauve-pink suffusion on head and neck and usually none on the breast. Juvenile like female but duller and paler. The above description is of the nominate form *Z. a. asiatica* from the West Indies, the lower Rio Grande Valley of Texas, eastern Mexico and central America. The form from Arizona, Western Mexico and California *Z. a. mearnsi* is slightly larger and slightly paler and duller in colour. The South American form *Z. a. meloda* is more strongly differentiated. It is paler and greyer in general coloration with little or no pink tinge on crown and nape, face and neck pale grey rather than buff and greyish pink breast. The terminal band on its outer tail feathers is pale grey not white. Its irides are greyish brown and its orbital skin bright blue or purplish blue.

DISTRIBUTION AND HABITAT : Southern U.S.A. in New Mexico, southern Arizona, south-eastern California, southern Lower California and the lower Rio Grande Valley, Texas ; Mexico through central America to pacific coast region of Costa Rica ; Bahiá Parita on the coast of Herrera and Cocti, in Panama ; southern Bahamas on Great Inagua Island ; Old Providence Island, Jamaica, Cuba and Hispaniola. In South America in the arid tropical zone of south-western Ecuador in Santa Elena and on Puna Island and Pacific coastal region of Peru to northern Chile in the provinces of Taina and Tarapacá. Inhabits chiefly arid regions with scrubby thickets but also wooded and cultivated areas and, in Panama, mangrove swamps.

FEEDING AND GENERAL HABITS : Feeds on seeds picked up on the ground, including cultivated grains, especially wheat, when available. Also takes berries and fruits from the branches, and perches on ears of sorghum to eat the grains.   Wetmore (1920), from whose account of the species' habits much of the information here is derived, recorded the purple drupes of the shrub *Condalia spathulata* and the fruits of the giant cactus as favourite foods.   Often roosts and nests colonially.   Flies singly, in pairs or small parties, large numbers aggregating at good feeding grounds.   When nervous jerks up, spreads and then closes tail in a similar manner to when displaying.   Flight swift and direct.   Tends to alight among foliage rather than on a bare or exposed branch.

NESTING: Usual pigeon nest in tree or shrub.   In the arid parts of the southern U.S.A. often nests in large colonies in mesquite thickets.   In such situations there are, however, not more than two or three nests in each tree, often only one and pairs apparently maintain a territory around their nest.   Nesting of single pairs or a few pairs together also occurs.   In Ecuador Marchant (1960) found the southern form only in scattered pairs.   Two buff, cream or white eggs, the more richly coloured eggs usually fading during incubation or (more especially) after being blown.   Breeding recorded in June in Arizona, in March and April (the dry season) in Costa Rica, January and June in the West Indies and March in Ecuador.   Distraction display in which the incubating bird drops from the nest and flutters over the ground is common (Wetmore, 1920).

VOICE: Like the Diamond Dove this species has two different forms of advertising coo.   Wetmore (1920) describes these as, firstly 'who hoo who hoo-oo', the first three notes gruff and abrupt, the last are strongly accented and somewhat prolonged.   The other he describes as 'who hoo, whoo hoo, hoo-áh, hoo-hoo-áh, who-oo', the first section short and low, the second louder and almost merged with the third; the third and fourth more musical and strongly accented and the last part lower and more slurred.   The nest call is, apparently, similar to the first described form of advertising coo, possibly identical with it. Whitman (1919) describes it as being of five syllables, three in the first half and two in the second half, a single growling note (first syllable) followed by two barking notes (second and third syllables) connected together and with rising emphasis in the second bark, then two barking notes together with a falling inflection and the last one somewhat prolonged.   What is probably the excitement cry is a low, querulous-sounding muttered or snarling note which is given in various agonistic or sexual situations.

DISPLAY: In the bowing display the tail is lifted high, spread and then closed with a quick flash of the black and white markings.   When nest calling within sight of the female momentarily and slightly spreads his wings and at the same time spreads his tail (Whitman, 1919).   In display flight the male flies out and up with quick, emphatic wing strokes and then glides in circles with the tips of the outspread wings decurved. The above descriptions are based mainly on Wetmore's (1920) observations.

OTHER NAMES: Singing Dove; Mesquite Dove; Whitewing.

REFERENCES

COTTAM, C., TREFETHEN, J. B. *et al.* 1968. Whitewings. D. Van Nostrand Co. Inc., Princetown.
MARCHANT, S.   1960.   The breeding of some S.W. Ecuadorian birds. *Ibis* **102**: 349–382.
SKUTCH, A. F.   1964.   Life histories of Central American Pigeons. *Wilson Bull*. **76**: 211–247.
WETMORE, A.   1920.   Observations on the habits of the White-winged Dove. *Condor* **22**: 140–146.
WHITMAN, C. O.   1919.   The behaviour of Pigeons. Postworks of C. O. Whitman, Vol. 3 Carnegie Inst. Wash.

THE AMERICAN GROUND DOVES

This group of pigeons is not too happily named as although they are all ground feeders and many of them spend much time on the ground; they are not so terrestrial as, for example, the quail doves or some of the bronzewings.   They vary in size from the tiny and beautifully coloured Mauve-spotted Dove, which is no larger than a Diamond Dove, to the Black-winged Dove which is only slightly smaller than a Barbary Dove.   Typically they are compact, plump little pigeons with rather short tails, but they include some long-tailed forms. Most of them are quietly clad in soft browns, greys and pinks with black or iridescent bands and spots on their wings. They inhabit South and Central America and the Southern U.S.A. They have produced forms adapted to high elevations, rain forest and bleak mountain plateaux as well as lowland forms.

When all the species in this group are compared their affinities are obvious. In spite of the amount of adaptive radiation and consequent morphological differentiation among them there can be little, if any, doubt that they are all more closely related *inter se* than any of them is to any pigeon of another group. Owing to the amount of difference shown between species and the existence of forms intermediate between groups of species there has been much disagreement as to how many genera should be recognised. I formerly recognised the five genera *Columbina, Scardafella, Claravis, Metriopelia* and *Uropelia* (Goodwin, 1959). I still think this is the best arrangement. The only reasonable alternative would be to include all the species here discussed in a single genus. The difficulty of defining such a morphologically hetero-geneous group would seem to outweigh the advantages gained by thus more sharply emphasising the close phylogenetic relationship of all these forms. I think that it is probable that the species within each genus recognised are most nearly related to others in the same genus but discussion of specific affinities is particularly necessary for this group.

The Scaly-breasted Ground Dove *Columbina passerina* and the Plain-breasted Ground Dove *C. minuta* are sibling species. They now show a wide overlap in range but their close relationship is obvious. It seems possible that *passerina* is at present the more successful species and is in process of replacing *minuta* in some or all of the areas that both now occupy. Buckley's Ground Dove *C. buckleyi* is similar to *minuta* in general coloration but in plumage pattern of both sexes, and coloration of the female is almost identical with the Ruddy Ground Dove *C. talpacoti*. I fully agree with Hellmayr & Conover (1942) in considering *buckleyi* 'more nearly related' to *talpacoti*. These two are allopatric and I consider them as forming a superspecies.

The Picui Dove *C. picui* and the Gold-billed Ground Dove *C. cruziana* are allopatric and show many close similarities of colour and plumage pattern although differing in proportions. In spite of their present differences they are, I think, geographical representatives. The Blue-eyed Dove *Columbina cyanopis* stands a little apart. It has an attenuated first primary like *Claravis* and appears to form a connecting link between that genus and *Columbina* but on the whole seems best included in the latter. The Mauve-spotted Ground Dove *Uropelia campestris* much resembles two of the *Claravis* species in its wing markings although otherwise nearer in appearance to some *Columbina* species. Until more is known about it I think it is preferable to recognise the genus *Uropelia*.

The blue ground doves are very closely related to the *Columbina* species. They differ in their larger size, greater sexual dimorphism and attenuated first primary. None of those differences are very funda-mental but taken together they seem to me just sufficient to justify retention of the genus *Claravis*. Of the three species the Blue Ground Dove *C. pretiosa* overlaps the geographical ranges of both the Purple-barred Ground Dove *C. godefrida* and the Purple-breasted Ground Dove *C. mondetoura* although they frequent different habitats and are ecologically separated. *C. godefrida* and *C. mondetoura* are allopatric and are considered here as members of a superspecies. The *Claravis* species show a more or less notch-like emargination on the central part inner webs of eighth or, in *mondetoura*, sixth, seventh and eighth primaries. I do not agree with Johnston (1961) in thinking that this has no significance in relation to the similar emarginations on the seventh or sixth and seventh primaries of *Columbina* species but rather that it is one more indication of their close relationship.

The genus *Metriopelia* represents an offshoot from *Columbina* stock that has become adapted to life at high altitudes. The Bare-faced Ground Dove *Metriopelia ceciliae* and Morenoi's Ground Dove *M. morenoi* are allopatric and are almost certainly geographical representatives although in plumage colour *morenoi* is closer to *melanoptera*. The Black-winged Ground Dove *M. melanoptera* and the Bronze-winged Ground Dove *M. aymara* differ in size but are remarkably alike in colour. They also agree in having proportionately larger wings than any other American ground doves and with the 'cut away' indentations on the inner webs of ninth and tenth primaries more developed than in *morenoi* or *ceciliae* (in which latter species it is almost or quite missing on the ninth). *M. aymara* is the only *Melanoptera* species which retains iridescent wing markings similar to and homologous with those of *Columbina* species. *M. melanoptera* appears, however, to be in process of developing a white shoulder patch. Except for *aymara*, all the *Metriopelia* species have an extensive area of bright yellow or orange orbital skin which contrasts with the iris colour and probably 'compensates' for lack of display plumage in intraspecific encounters. *M. aymara* and *M. melanoptera* are sympatric but they are, I think, more closely related to each other than to *ceciliae* or *morenoi* whose ranges they also overlap.

The genus *Scardafella* consists of two allopatric forms, the Inca Dove *Scardafella inca* and the Scaly Dove *S. squammata*. These seem best treated as members of a superspecies rather than as races of a single species as apart from differences of size and coloration their calls also differ. Johnston (1961) is in favour of including these species in *Columbina*, partly on the grounds of similarities in the emargination of the primaries, the extension of the barbs on the inner web of the first primary to form a faint fringe on the trailing edge (a feature also found in other genera). Although these, and some of their other characters certainly indicate relationship with *Columbina* they differ in their longer tails, in lacking iridescent signal markings on the wings and, to some extent, in their colour pattern. *C. picui* has a tail nearly as long as that of *Scardafella* but differently marked and it (*picui*) also has the characteristic wing markings. The colour pattern of *Scardafella's* tail is very like that of *Metriopelia ceciliae* and it may well be as closely related to *Metriopelia* as to *Columbina*. Johnston may be right in thinking the distinctive bowing display of *Scardafella* species a specific character of no phylogenetic significance although too few displays of the American ground doves have as yet been recorded in enough detail to be sure. In some other groups, such as the Old World *Columba* species and the turtle doves, there is a decided correlation between the form of the bowing display and the degree of phylogenetic affinity; the most closely related species have the most similar display movements although the display plumage exhibited thereby usually differs.

Scardafella shows a remarkable general resemblance to the Australian genus *Geopelia* in appearance, shape and even the form of the bowing display. Both of these genera differ from most of their nearest relatives in possessing long tails boldly patterned in black and white, a similar and homologous 'scaly'

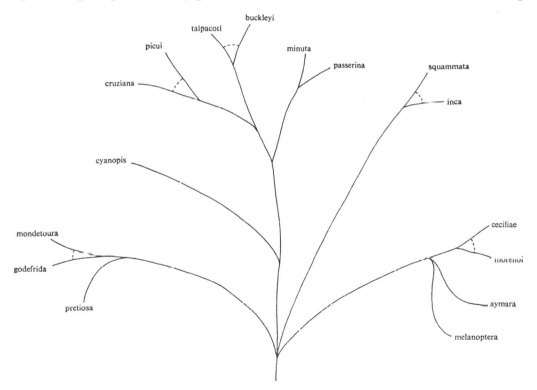

Fig. D.8: Presumed relationships of species in the genera *Columbina*, *Claravis*, *Metriopelia* and *Scardafella*.

plumage pattern and in lacking iridescent signal markings on the wings.   There is no reason to suppose any direct connection between *Scardafella* and *Geopelia*, I think their similarities are not due entirely to convergence but that, as Harrison (1960) has suggested, the groups to which they belong are related and the ancestral stocks of both had, probably, rather similar genetic potentialities.

The American ground doves appear to be most closely related to the mourning dove group, which many of them much resemble in wing markings and general coloration, and, therefore, to other American groups related to *Zenaida*.   Their nearest affinities outside America are probably, as has been suggested, the bronzewings and geopelias.

REFERENCES

GOODWIN, D. 1959. Taxonomic notes on the American ground dove. *Auk* **76**: 510–516.
HARRISON, C. J. O. 1960. Signal plumage and phylogenetic relationship in some Doves. *Bull. B.O.C.* **80**: 134–140.
HELLMAYR, C. E. & CONOVER, B. 1942. Catalogue of birds of the Americas. *Field Mus. Nat. Hist., Zool. Ser.* **13**: Pt. 1, No. 1: 1–636.
JOHNSTON, R. F. 1961. The genera of American ground doves. *Auk* **78**: 372–378.

SCALY-BREASTED GROUND DOVE   *Columbina passerina*

Columba passerina Linnaeus, Syst. Nat. Ed. 10, 1, 1758, p. 165.

DESCRIPTION: Slightly larger than a House Sparrow or Diamond Dove, but plump and compact in shape with shortish tail.   Forehead, face, sides of neck, breast and underparts dull rose pink, mauve pink, pinkish grey or silvery pink.   Crown, nape and hind neck blue grey, silver grey or greyish pink. The feathers of the above areas mostly have darker margins except those of the breast and sides of neck which have dark centres.   This gives the bird's foreparts a scaly and spotted appearance when seen at close quarters.   Upper parts greyish-brown, drab brown, greyish fawn or pale dull grey except for the wing coverts and outer secondaries which are mainly pinkish and pale grey with iridescent purplish black or dark blue markings (see sketch).   Primaries chestnut with drab or blackish tips and outer webs. Underwing and axillaries chestnut.   Central tail feathers dull brown or grey.   Outer ones black with more or less grey at base.   Outermost ones with small white tips, chiefly on outer web.   Undertail coverts greyish brown with pale tips to white with faint darker centres.   Irides dark red, brownish red, orange or pinkish.   Bill red, orange, yellow or flesh coloured at base, dusky or blackish at tip – sometimes all blackish.   Feet flesh coloured, light pinkish or dull pink.

The female is much duller than the male being pale drab to brownish white where the male is pink and only slightly tinged with grey on the head.   Her iridescent wing markings are purplish brown or dull chestnut with a purple tinge.   The juveniles are much like the female but have pale buff fringes to the feathers of the upperparts and wings, and the young males have a faint tinge of pink about the neck.

Throughout its wide range this species varies somewhat in shade of colour and many different races have been described. The above is a composite description which will fit the species wherever found.

FIELD IDENTIFICATION: Very small size combined with short tail and scaly neck pattern.

DISTRIBUTION AND HABITAT: Southern North America, from South Carolina and south-eastern Texas, south through Mexico, Central America and the West Indian Islands to northern South America south to central Ecuador and northern Brazil (Bahia).

Inhabits open country with trees and bushes, sandy reefs, open sandy areas in forest and savannah, but over much of its range now primarily a bird of cultivated land, villages and towns.

FEEDING AND GENERAL HABITS: Feeds on the ground, largely on small seeds. Locally will freely take crumbs of bread and other scraps of human food. Spends much of its time on or very near the ground. Usually in pairs, sometimes in small parties. Not often persecuted and consequently usually unafraid of people.

NESTING: Usual pigeon nest, allowing for small size of bird and consequently of nesting material, in a tree or shrub or on the ground. Ground nests, which are usual in some parts of its range, are usually in the shelter of a plant or tuft of grass. Two white eggs. Incubation period 13 to 14 days.

Young can fly at 11 days. Nesting season varies in different parts of its range, usually prolonged. Like most pigeons it appears to nest whenever food supplies are plentiful.

VOICE: A soft low coo (? advertising coo) variously described as 'woot', 'coowa', etc. Display coo described as 'low short wout or wout-wout-wout'. Sharp 'wut-wut' when threatening. An 'angry, nasal, rasping note' when in defensive threat display on nest.

DISPLAY: Evidently has a bowing display or at least lowers its head when cooing at female. Chases female with lowered head and flicks wings. Raises wings in threat when about to attack as well as in defensive contexts.

OTHER NAMES: Passerine Dove; Rosy Ground Dove; Sparrow Dove; Scaled Ground Dove; Tobacco Dove; Common Ground Dove; Speckled Ground Dove.

REFERENCES

BENT, A. C. 1932. Life Histories of North American Gallinaceous Birds. *U.S. Nat. Mus. Bull.*, 162.
NICHOLSON, D. J. 1937. Notes on the Breeding of the Florida Ground Dove. *Wilson Bull.* 49: 101–114.
YOUNG, C. G. 1928. Ornithology of the Coastland of British Guiana. *Ibis* 4: Twelfth Series, 748–781.

PLAIN-BREASTED GROUND DOVE *Columbina minuta*

Columba minuta Linnaeus, Syst. Nat. Ed. 12, 1, 1766, p. 285.

DESCRIPTION: About the same size as the Scaly-breasted Ground Dove or a little smaller. Its colours and markings are very similar, the chief points of difference being that the present species, as its name denotes, lacks the dark edgings and centres of neck and breast feathers that give *passerina* its scaly appearance.   Forehead, crown and nape bluish grey.   Face and throat pale pinkish shading to deeper mauve-pink on breast and underparts.   Under tail coverts dull white with dark greyish central areas. Rest of plumage and sexual dimorphism as in the Scaly-breasted Ground Dove (q.v.).   Irides yellow, yellow-brown or dull orange.   Bill greyish or brown.   Legs and feet pink or pinkish red.

FIELD IDENTIFICATION: Lack of spotty or scaly appearance on neck and breast and redder feet distinguish it from *passerina*, smaller size from *buckleyi*.

DISTRIBUTION AND HABITAT: Although its range is geographically wide this species tends to be locally and patchily distributed.   Found in south-eastern Mexico, Guatemala, El Salvador, British Honduras, tripical zone of south-western Costa Rica, south along the Pacific slope of Panama to northern Colombia, Island of Trinidad, Venezuela and the Guianas, Brazil, Paraguay and the Pacific coastal region.

Inhabits savannah country, open wastelands, savannah, second-growth woodland and cultivated areas.

FEEDING AND GENERAL HABITS: As recorded, does not differ in feeding and general behaviour from the Scaly-breasted Ground Dove although it seems highly likely that, at least when the two occur together, ecological differences between them do in fact exist.

NESTING: Most observers describe the usual type of pigeon nest, but Belcher & Smooker (1936) state that (in Trinidad) nests of this species always contain 'a definite pad of feathers'.   The nest is placed in a bush, shrub or tree from two to three feet above the ground, sometimes on the ground.   Two white eggs, incubation period (in Europe) 14 days (Nicolai, 1965).   Distraction display recorded.

VOICE: Astley (1900) heard from a captive male 'a tiny coo' of three short, somewhat whistling notes 'wuh wuh wuh' but did not say in what situation it was uttered.   Wetmore (Ms.) describes one call as like 'co way, co way', uttered rapidly and repeatedly and another as 'a low woo-ah woo-ah woo-ah'.

DISPLAY: No information.

OTHER NAMES: Grey Ground Dove; Little Ground Dove; Pygmy Dove.

REFERENCES

ASTLEY, H. D.   1900.   Pygmy Doves.   *Avicult. Mag.* **7**: 85–86.
BELCHER, C. & SMOOKER, G. D.   1936.   Birds of the Colony of Trinidad and Tobago.   Pt. 3.   *Ibis* **6**: Thirteenth Series, 1–35.
NICOLAI, J.   1965.   *Vogelhaltung-Vogelpflege.*   p. 48.   Kosmos, Stuttgart.
YOUNG, C. G.   1928.   Ornithology of the Coastland of British Guiana.   *Ibis* **4**: Twelfth Series, 748–781.
WETMORE, A.   1964.   Manuscript for a book on Birds of Panama.

BUCKLEY'S GROUND DOVE   *Columbina buckleyi*

Chamaepelia buckleyi Sclater and Salvin, Proc. Zool. Soc. London, 1887, p. 21.

DESCRIPTION: Very similar in colour to the Plain-breasted Ground Dove but larger, about as big as the Ruddy Ground Dove (q.v.).   Of similar proportions to the latter bird and probably at least as closely related to it as to *minuta*.   Forehead and face pale greyish pink shading to slightly deeper mauve-pink, suffused with grey, on breast and underparts.   Crown and nape bluish grey.   Upperparts pale brownish grey, wing coverts pinkish grey spotted and barred with black (see sketch).   Primaries and outer secondaries mainly black.   Central tail feathers greyish, rest black with some grey at base, outermost ones tipped white.   Axillaries and under wing coverts black.

Female rather browner and less pinkish, especially on breast.   Juvenile brown with pale or rusty edges and/or centres of feathers in areas where adults are pinkish or greyish.

DISTRIBUTION AND HABITAT: North-western Ecuador south to north-western Peru. Confined to the arid tropical zone.

FEEDING AND GENERAL HABITS: No information.

NESTING: No information.

VOICE: No information.

DISPLAY: No information.

RUDDY GROUND DOVE   *Columbina talpacoti*

Columba talpacoti Temminck, in Knip, Les Pigeons, 1811, Les Columbigallines, p. 22, pl. 12.

DESCRIPTION: About mid-way between Diamond Dove and Barbary Dove in size. Plump and compact in form with shortish tail. Forehead, crown and nape bluish grey. Face and throat pale dull pinkish. Rest of plumage dark purplish pink or pinkish chestnut (according to degree of wear) with black markings on wings forming a spotted and streaked pattern (see sketch). Primaries brownish black, sometimes tinged rufous on inner webs. Under wing coverts black. Central tail feathers as back; outer ones black, narrowly tipped pinkish chestnut. Irides dark reddish brown, red or orange; whitish once recorded (? sick bird), bill brown, blackish brown, greyish or horn coloured usually darker at tip. Legs and feet flesh pink or pale purplish.

Female much duller. Generally dull earth brown above and paler, greyish brown below, tinged with rufous on rump, upper and under tail coverts and central tail feathers and with grey on the crown. Her irides are usually paler than the male's, often buff or yellowish. The juvenile female resembles the adult but is paler, has less intense wing markings and buff fringes to most of the cover feathers. The juvenile male is similar but a more reddish brown and with rusty buff feather edges.

The above description is of the nominate form *C. t. talpacoti* from South America. The form from Central America and north-eastern South America *C. talpacoti rufipennis* differs in having the primaries chestnut with dark drab tips. The secondaries are also largely chestnut and the general colour averages a little paler than in the nominate form. This tendency to paleness is more pronounced in the populations from western Mexico which are, as a result, sometimes separated subspecifically as *C. t. eluta*.

DISTRIBUTION AND HABITAT: Central and South America from Mexico (Sinaloa in west, southern Vera Cruz in east) south to Rio Grande do Sul, Paraguay and northern Argentina. Not west of the Andes in South America.

Inhabits sandy savannas, open sandy area on reefs and ridges in swampy country, cultivated land, plantations, gardens, second growth forest with open areas and waste lands near human settlements. Usually in low-lying country.

FEEDING AND GENERAL HABITS: Feeds on the ground. Known to take seeds of various kinds. In some areas has learnt to eat spilled grain and crumbs of bread and other human food. Perches, roosts and nests above ground. Usually seen in pairs or singly but numbers may aggregate at a good feeding place.

NESTING: Nest commonly rather more compact and deep than those of pigeons usually are. In tree or shrub, sometimes on old nest of some other bird. Usually low down but sometimes very high up. Two white eggs normal clutch but there are records of apparent one-egg clutches. The evidence as to times of laying seems to me insufficient to be certain whether the eggs are laid on alternate days since, owing to the female sitting on the nest for some time before laying, it is unclear whether the first egg is laid in the late evening or early morning. Incubation period 11 to 13 days (Haverschmidt & Skutch), 13 or 14 days (Snow), 14 days in captivity in Europe (Nicolai). Young fledge at 10 to 14 days, usually at 11 to 13 days (Snow).

Voice: The advertising coo is a soft ŏŏ'ōo, ŏŏ'ōo repeated several times and at a little distance sounding more like 'kitty-woo, kitty-woo' as Skutch (1956) paraphrases. The nest call appears to be very similar, perhaps identical but I have heard it only from a few captive specimens. Neither Skutch (1956) nor Haverschmidt (1953) specifically mention a nest call which seems to confirm my records that it is the same as the advertising coo.

DISPLAY: Wing twitching is pronounced and used in most (probably all) situations involving sexual or aggressive excitement. Displacement preening behind wing and pre-copulatory billing also recorded. In display flight the male flies upwards, claps his wings loudly and then glides downwards on outspread wings.

OTHER NAMES: Stone Dove; Blue-headed Ground Dove; Cinnamon Dove; Talpacoti Dove.

REFERENCES

HAVERSCHMIDT, F. 1953. Notes on the Life History of *Columbigallina talpacoti* in Surinam. *Condor* **55**: 21-25.
NICOLAI, J. 1965. *Vogelhaltung-Vogelpflege*, p. 48. Kosmos, Stuttgart.
SKUTCH, A. F. 1956. Life History of the Ruddy Ground Dove. *Condor* **58**: 188-205.
SNOW, D. W. 1969. *In litt.*

PICUI DOVE   *Columbina picui*

Columba Picui Temminck, Pig. et Gall., 1, 1813, p. 435, 498.

DESCRIPTION: Much smaller than a Barbary Dove but appreciably larger than a Diamond Dove, with shortish wings and medium-long rounded tail. Forehead and throat whitish with narrow black stripe from mouth to eye.   Crown and nape light ash grey shading to brownish grey on mantle, back, rump, innermost wing coverts and secondaries, upper tail coverts and central tail feathers.   Central wing coverts pale pinkish fawn with iridescent blackish blue stripe across lesser coverts.   Broad white fringes to outer wing coverts and outer secondaries form a broad white stripe along the wing when closed or across it when opened.   Primaries and primary ~ ~ ~ ~ ~ ~ A dull black edge to the inner secondaries forms a black stripe at ~~~ ~ ~~~~ east pale greyish pink shading to near white on belly and ~~~ ~~~~~most tail feathers white.   Underwing coverts and axillari~ ~~~~~~~ ~~~~ ~~~sh at base of lower mandible.   Legs and feet purplish.

The female is a little duller than the male with the grey and pinkish tones less clear and more suffused with brown.   The juvenile is duller and browner with pale fringes to most feathers and reddish buff or buff central areas to most of the wing coverts and breast feathers.

DISTRIBUTION AND HABITAT: South America, from north-eastern Brazil, south to Argentina (Mendoze and Buenos Aires provinces), Uruguay and central Chile.   Inhabits forest edge, savanna country, open grassland with some trees and cover, cultivated areas and gardens in towns and cities.

FEEDING AND GENERAL HABITS: Feeds on the ground, largely on seeds, including cultivated grains. Has been recorded gathering in hundreds to fields of hemp that had been allowed to go to seed.   Usually in small parties or flocks; said to be very social but some of the evidence given merely suggests numbers of birds aggregating at a good food supply.   Flight described as swift and darting.

NESTING: Usual pigeon nest in shrub or tree.   Two white eggs.   Recorded breeding in January, February and March in Mendoza, northern Argentina.

VOICE: No information.

DISPLAY: No information.

OTHER NAMES: White-winged Ground Dove; Steel-barred Dove; Long-tailed Ground Dove.

REFERENCE

WETMORE, A.   1926.   Observations on the Birds of Argentina, Paraguay, Uruguay and Chile.   *U.S. Nat. Mus. Bull* **133**: 178 180.

GOLD-BILLED GROUND DOVE   *Columbina cruziana*

Columba Cruziana 'D'Orbigny' Prevost, in Knip, Les Pigeons, ed. 2, 2, 1838–1843, p. 89, pl. 48.

DESCRIPTION: A small, plump, shortish-tailed Dove about half as large again as a Diamond Dove or House Sparrow, with a proportionately larger bill than most small doves. Head bluish grey, nearly white on the chin, shading into soft brownish grey on the upperparts, and a darker brownish grey on the central tail feathers. Wing coverts a paler pinkish grey, the inner wing coverts and scapulars have dark purple or blue-black spots and blotches (see sketch) that form a regular pattern on the closed wing. Some of the inner wing coverts have reddish purple tips forming a short bar across the upperpart of the wing. Most of the secondary coverts have a whitish subterminal area which, together with the whitish edge of the longest inner secondary, form a contrast with the black tip of the secondary coverts and the blackish outer secondaries and primaries. Underwing greyish with a pale pinkish central area and jet black underwing coverts and axillaries. Breast and underparts mauve-pink. Outer tail feathers black with very narrow whitish tips. Iris reddish-brown or red with cream or white inner ring; sometimes succeeding narrow rings of red-brown, black or blue and yellow or cream can be distinguished. Orbital skin yellow. Bill black, contrasting with its basal portion which is vivid yellow, golden yellow or orange. Feet pink.

The female lacks the blue-grey and pink hues of the male, being a light drab brown above and a pale creamy brown or light greyish brown below. Her wing markings and soft parts are as in the male but usually less intense. The juvenile much resembles the female but has rather ill-defined buffish tips to many of the feathers.

DISTRIBUTION AND HABITAT: The arid and semi-arid regions of the Pacific coast of South America in Ecuador, Peru and northern Chile.

FEEDING AND GENERAL HABITS: Little recorded. Known to eat seeds and to feed chiefly, perhaps entirely, on the ground.

NESTING: Usual pigeon nest in bushes or trees, also on ledges of buildings, low cliffs or banks, and in open-fronted nest boxes. Sometimes on the ground. Two white eggs, but Marchant, to whose observations in Ecuador most of what is known of its breeding habits, is due, also found clutches of one and three eggs and thought these were not due to loss or two hens laying in one nest. The incubation period is about fourteen days and the young leave the nest when ten or eleven days old, often earlier if frightened. In south-western Ecuador, nests were started in all months except August, September and October but away from human habitation the breeding season appears less prolonged and the majority of pairs only start to breed about four to six weeks after the first good rainfall (Marchant, 1959).

VOICE: No information.

DISPLAY: No information.

OTHER NAMES: Peruvian Ground Dove; Gold-ringed Ground Dove.

REFERENCES

MARCHANT, S. 1957. The Birds of the Santa Elena Peninsula S.W. Ecuador. *Ibis* **100**: 349–387.
—— 1959. The Breeding Season in S.W. Ecuador. *Ibis* **101**: 137–152.

BLUE-EYED GROUND DOVE *Columbina cyanopis*

Peristera cyanopis 'Natterer' Pelzeln, Orn. Bras., Abth. 3, 1870. p. 277. 336. (orig. descr.).

DESCRIPTION: Slightly larger in body than a Diamond Dove with a medium long graduated tail. Outer primary attenuated. General colour reddish brown above dullest on mantle, back and scapulars and deepening to a rich purplish rufous on head, neck, wing coverts and upper tail coverts. Dark iridescent blue spots and markings on wings forming a pattern similar to that on the Ruddy Ground Dove *C. talpacoti*. Throat whitish. Breast purplish rufous shading paler and duller on lower breast, abdomen and flanks. Under tail coverts white. Outer primaries dusky brown with some chestnut on inner webs, the inner ones chestnut with dusky tips. Underwing rufous. Central tail feathers rufous. Outermost two or three pairs black tipped white, rest blackish tipped rufous. Irides blue, orbital skin greyish. Bill blackish. Legs and feet flesh pink. Female slightly duller and paler, especially on the underparts. I have only seen one specimen partly in juvenile plumage. From this the juvenile appears to be paler and duller with rufous fringes to many feathers and obscure wing markings.

DISTRIBUTION AND HABITAT: Interior of Brazil from Cuyabá, Matto Grosso to Itapura near the confluence of the Teeté and Paranà rivers in northern São Paulo.

FEEDING AND GENERAL HABITS: I can find nothing recorded of the habits of this dove which, so far as one can judge from the numbers of specimens in museums and lack of field observations, is extremely rare. Almost certainly a ground feeder. Probably feeds largely on small seeds.

NESTING: No information.

VOICE: No information.

DISPLAY: No information.

REFERENCES

HELLMAYR, C. E. & CONOVER, B. 1942. Catalogue of Birds of the Americas. Pt. 1, No. 1. *Zool. Ser. Field Mus. Nat. Hist.* Vol. 13.
PINTO, O. 1949. Esboço Monográphico dos Columbidae Brasilieros. *Arquivos de Zoologia do Estado de São Paulo* **7**: Art. 3. 241–324.

BLUE GROUND DOVE   *Claravis pretiosa*

Peristera pretiosa Ferrari-Perez, Proc. U.S. Nat. Mus., 9, 1886, p. 175.

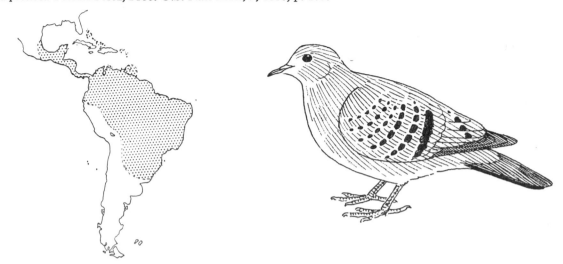

DESCRIPTION: Rather more than half the size of a Barbary Dove. Compact in shape but less so than the Ruddy and Little Ground Doves. First primary attenuated. General colour a clear bluish-grey, paler on the underparts and shading to nearly white on the forehead and throat. Black markings, edged with silver-grey, on the wing coverts and secondaries form a barred and spotted pattern on the folded wing. Primaries blackish grey. Two central tail feathers dark bluish grey, outer tail feathers black. Irides red, pink or yellowish. Bill greenish or greenish brown. Legs and feet pink or reddish. The female is a warm dark brown, paler beneath and inclining to greyish on the belly and flanks. Her tail coverts and central tail feathers are a warm reddish brown, the dark markings on her wings are dull purplish red and the black of her outer tail feathers more or less intermixed with chestnut.

The juvenile female resembles the adult but is paler and has buffish or pale rufous fringes and ill-defined dusky subterminal areas on most of the cover feathers. Its wing spots are duller and ill-defined and its tail coverts and tail a paler and brighter rufous. The juvenile male resembles the juvenile female but is darker and has dull purplish black wing spots. The first primary of the juvenile is much less markedly attenuated than that of the adult.

DISTRIBUTION AND HABITAT: Central and South America from south-eastern Mexico to Peru, Bolivia, northern Argentina and southern Brazil. Found in woodland but tends to inhabit areas free from under-growth and with clearings, secondary growth and other relatively open areas rather than the heavy rain forest which is the natural climax vegetation in most parts of its range.

FEEDING AND GENERAL HABITS: Feeds largely, perhaps entirely, on the ground. Eats seeds and, probably, other foods as well, but little has been recorded of its diet. 'When alighting the head is darted forward, then quickly pulled back to its normal position' (Gifford, 1941). Commonly in pairs.

NESTING: Nests in trees or shrubs. Skutch, who has studied this and other doves in Costa Rica, found that the Blue Ground Dove's nest was 'rather consistently' slighter and frailer than that of any other species. Two eggs. Incubation period fourteen days. The second egg is laid in the morning between 7 and 10 a.m. In one case (possibly all) the first egg had been laid about 24 hours previously.

VOICE: What is, presumably, the advertising coo is described by Dickey and Van Rossem (1938) as a repeated single, hooting note with a characteristic explosive quality, Skutch records only a 'low, soft monosyllable "coo" or perhaps better "coot".'

DISPLAY: Wetmore (MS) describes bowing display in which the male spreads and raises its tail, droops its wings and bows. Gifford (1941) says that 'in cooing to the hen the cock lifts his feet very high and then puts them down slowly' but does not otherwise describe the bowing display.   Billing in which female appeared to be fed by male recorded by Skutch.

OTHER NAMES: Ashy Dove; Blue Dove; Cinereous Dove.

REFERENCES

DICKEY, D. R. & VAN ROSSEM, A. J.   1938.   The Birds of El Salvador.   *Zool. Ser. Field Mus. Nat. Hist* **23**: 194–195.
GIFFORD, E. W.   1941.   Taxonomy and Habits of Pigeons.   *Auk* **58**: 242–245.
NICOLAI, J.   1965.   *Vogelhaltung-Vogelpflege*, p. 48.   Kosmos, Stuttgart.
SKUTCH, A. F.   1959.   Life History of the Blue Ground Dove.   *Condor* **61**: 65–74.
WETMORE, A.   1964.   Manuscript for a book on the Birds of Panama.

PURPLE-BARRED GROUND DOVE   *Claravis godefrida*

Columba godefrida Temminck, in Temminck and Knip, Les Pigeons, 1, colombes, p. 125, 1811.

DESCRIPTION: Similar in size, shape and type of sexual dimorphism to the Blue Ground Dove.   Male darkish blue-grey, paler below.   The folded wing shows two broad bands of deep purple (fading to chestnut sometimes when worn) narrowly edged with blackish and pale grey and a smaller but otherwise similar band of dark bluish-purple on the lesser coverts.   Central tail feathers grey.   Four outermost ones white, others mainly greyish-white with grey bases.   Female brown with the wing bands slightly paler than male's and edged black and pale buff.   Central tail feathers brown, outer ones with black bases and broad pale buff tips.   Juveniles bear same relation to adults as in the Blue Ground Dove.

DISTRIBUTION AND HABITAT: South-eastern Brazil and adjacent parts of Paraguay.   Possibly elsewhere in South America.   Inhabits wooded country.

FEEDING AND GENERAL HABITS: No information.

NESTING: No information.

VOICE: No information.

DISPLAY: No information.

OTHER NAMES: Geoffroy's Dove.

PURPLE-BREASTED GROUND DOVE   *Claravis mondetoura*

Priestera mondetoura Bonaparte, Compt. Rend. Acad. Sci. Paris, 42, p. 765, 1856.

DESCRIPTION: Very similar to the Purple-barred Ground Dove with which it may be conspecific.   The male differs from that of *C. godefrida* in being slightly darker and in having a greyish white forehead, face and chin and a dark reddish-purple breast.   Irides light orange brown; orbital skin yellow.   Bill black. Legs and feet dull red.   (These soft part colours are from one specimen only.)   The female is slightly darker than the female of *godefrida* with a sandy rufous forehead and face and only narrow light tips to her outer tail feathers.   (See pl. 2).

DISTRIBUTION AND HABITAT: Central and south America from Mexico to Peru.   Inhabits forested sub-tropical mountain zones where it apparently replaces *C. pretiosa* which is the lowland species.

FEEDING AND GENERAL HABITS: Little recorded.   Wetmore (MS) found it in small numbers on the ground in forest with heavy undergrowth.

NESTING: No information.

VOICE: Wetmore (MS) records a 'coo-ah, coo-ah' very like the cooing of the Blue Ground Dove but with a rising inflection.

DISPLAY: No information.

OTHER NAMES: Maroon-chested Ground Dove; Mondetour's Dove.

REFERENCE

WETMORE, A.   1964.   Manuscript for a book on the Birds of Panama.

BARE-FACED GROUND DOVE   *Metriopelia ceciliae*

Columba (Chamoepelia) Ceciliae Lesson, Echo du Monde savant, 12th 1er semestre, 1845, col. 8.

DESCRIPTION: About half-way in size between Diamond Dove and Barbary Dove, plump and compact in form.   General coloration drab brown or greyish brown with paler tips to most feathers.   On the wing coverts and secondaries the whitish or buff feather tips are larger, giving a spotted effect.   Neck and breast grey, more or less tinged with vinous pink.   Belly and under tail coverts buffish.   Primary coverts, primaries, outer secondaries and under wing coverts blackish.   Area on inner webs and under sides of primaries rufous.   Central tail feathers drab, outer ones black with white tips.   Irides blue or bluish white.   Orbital skin extensive and bright yellow, golden, or orange; narrowly bordered with black (feathering).   Feet and legs flesh, pale pink or dull pink.   Sexes alike but male usually with more pronounced pink tinge on breast.   Juvenile like adult except for looser texture of plumage and duller soft parts.

The above description applies to the nominate form, *M. c. ceciliae*, from most of the Peruvian range of the species (q.v.).   The form from the Upper Marañon Valley and its tributaries in northern Peru, *M. c. obsoleta*, is slightly paler and greyer.   That from extreme southern Peru, Chile and Bolivia, *M. c. gymnops*, is a warmer brown above, a more definite pink tinge on the breast and warmer buff on the belly and (? sometimes) yellowish irides.

DISTRIBUTION AND HABITAT: Peru, Bolivia and Northern Chile. Inhabits the arid temperate and Puña zones but in some areas at least (Dorst, 1957) absent from the actual Puya stands where *M. melanoptera* occurs. Locally at lower elevations in towns and villages (F. Vuillieumier, *pers. comm.*).

FEEDING AND GENERAL HABITS: Feeds on the ground, largely on seeds. Runs rapidly like a small game-bird. The only pigeon known to dustbathe (Nicolai, 1962). Has been recorded roosting in holes in buildings (Dorst, 1957) and probably roosts in holes and sheltered rock ledges where buildings not available. Abundant in many villages and towns, including Lima.

NESTING: Little recorded. Almost certainly nests in holes and crevices of rocks and buildings. In captivity chooses enclosed nest-boxes in preference to more open sites.

VOICE: No information.

DISPLAY: Gifford (1941) recorded that when cooing and sexually excited it slightly raises and lowers the tail without spreading it, but did not give fuller details.

OTHER NAMES: Bare-eyed Ground Dove; Yellow-eyed Dove; Spectacled Dove; Cecilia's Dove.

REFERENCES

DORST, J. 1957. The Puya Stands of the Peruvian High Plateaux as a Bird Habitat. *Ibis* **99**: 594–599.
GIFFORD, E. W. 1941. Taxonomy and Habits of Pigeons. *Auk* **58**: 239–245.
NICOLAI, J. 1962. Über Regen, Sonnen und Staubbaden bei Tauben (*Columbidae*). *Journ. f. Orn.* **103**: 125–139.

MORENO'S BARE-FACED GROUND DOVE   *Metriopelia morenoi*

Gymnopelia morenoi Sharpe, Bull. Brit. Orn. Cl. 12, 1902, p. 54.

DESCRIPTION: Similar in size to the previous species, *M. ceciliae,* but with proportionately longer tail and shorter upper tail coverts. Outer webs of second to fifth primaries strongly emarginated. Upperparts dull brown tinged with grey on head and mantle and with rufous on the upper tail coverts. Throat whitish grey. Rest of underparts pale brownish grey shading to buffish on ventral area and dull reddish brown on under tail coverts. A narrow black line bordering the orbital skin. Primaries, outer secondaries, and underwing black. Outer tail feathers black, tipped white. Irides brown, one specimen recorded as white. Orbital skin extensive and bright orange. Legs and feet pink or pinkish flesh. Sexes alike, probably in life orbital skin of female less brilliant. Juvenile like adult but with rufous fringes to feathers of crown and upperparts and rufous tinge on inner webs of primaries. The above description is based on only four specimens. Further records, especially as to coloration of soft parts, are needed.

DISTRIBUTION AND HABITAT: The temperate and Puña zones of north-western Argentina, in the provinces of Jujuy, Salta, Tucumán, Catamarca and La Rioja. Inhabits hilly and mountainous country, usually at fairly high elevations. In Tucumán at a height of 2,000 metres upwards (Dinelli, 1929).

FEEDING AND GENERAL HABITS: Little apparently recorded. Almost certainly a ground feeder. Found in flocks (Dinelli, 1929).

NESTING: Said to nest in clay walls so presumably nests in holes and crevices like its relative *M. ceciliae*.

VOICE: No information.

DISPLAY: No information.

REFERENCE

DINELLI, L. 1929. Notas Biologicas Sobre Aves del Nordeste Argentino. *El Hornero* 4: 273–277.

BLACK-WINGED GROUND DOVE   *Metriopelia melanoptera*

Columba Melanoptera Molina, Sagg. Stor. Nat. Chili, 1782, p. 236, 345.

DESCRIPTION: About a quarter smaller than a Barbary Dove and with proportionately shorter tail. Outermost primary 'scooped' on inner web, next two deeply emarginated on outer web. Upperparts light greyish brown or earth brown, faintly tinged with pink, paler and more greyish on outer wing coverts. A white patch on shoulder and along edge of underwing. Primaries, primary coverts and outer secondaries and most of underwing black.   Central tail feathers dark greyish brown, outer ones black.   Throat whitish, rest of underparts fawnish pink, palest on the belly and shading to greyish on the flanks.   Under tail coverts and underside of tail black.   Irides bright green, blue, or violet, sometimes (? or always) with narrow reddish outer ring.   Orbital skin bright yellow, orange or salmon pink.   Legs and feet dark brown or blackish.   Bill blackish.   The irides fade to pale blue or whitish after death.

Female less pinkish on underparts.   Juvenile without pink tinge and with narrow pale buff edgings to most cover feathers.

The above description applies to the nominate form which is found in the southern parts of the species' range.   The form found in Ecuador and southern Colombia *Metriopelia melanoptera saturatior* is slightly darker in colour above and less pinkish below.

DISTRIBUTION AND HABITAT: Temperate and Puña Zones of Peru, Bolivia, Chile, from Taina south to Colchagua, western Argentina south to the western Rio Negro, and the Paramo Zone of Ecuador, and extreme south of Colombia.

Found in high valleys and wooded hillsides, arid country with scrub and cactus and in the Puya stands of the high Andes.   Local migration to lower levels, in some places even to coastal areas, for the winter. Sometimes common about houses and farms where not persecuted.

FEEDING AND GENERAL HABITS: Little recorded, feeds largely, perhaps entirely, on the ground. When feeding associates in parties and small flocks.   In the Puya zone of Peru Dorst (1957) found that it habitually roosted in the shelter of a Puya, perched on a leaf and close to the centre of the plant as possible.   Many individuals were killed, however, by becoming entangled in the hooked spines of the Puya leaves and unable to escape.   When flushed from the ground rises a few feet with a loud rattling sound, made by the wings, and then darts swiftly away (Wetmore, 1926).

NESTING: Usual pigeon nest, in the Puya zone among the Puya leaves, probably in shrubs and trees elsewhere.   Presumably lays two eggs like its relatives.

VOICE: No information.

DISPLAY: In display flight flies upwards and then glides down.   In the downward glide may approach another individual to whom the white shoulder patches of the displaying bird would then almost certainly be very visible (F. Vuilleumier, *pers. comm.*).

REFERENCES

DORST, J.   1957.   The Puya Stands of the Peruvian High Plateaux as a Bird Habitat.   *Ibis* **99**: 594–599
WETMORE, A.   1926.   Observations on the Birds of Argentina, Paraguay, Uruguay and Chile.   *U.S. Nat.. Mus, Bull.* **133**: 177–178.

BRONZE-WINGED GROUND DOVE

Metriopelia aymara

Columba Aymara 'D'Orb' Prevost, in Knip, Les Pigeons Ed. 2, 2, 1838–1843, p. 62, pl. 32.

DESCRIPTION: About half the size of a Barbary Dove. Plump and compact with shortish tail and long pointed wings, small short bill and dense soft plumage. The two outermost primaries with deep indentations on the inner web and the next two after the outermost with deeply emarginated outer web (see page 10). General coloration pale fawnish brown above strongly tinged with vinous pink except when feathers well worn. Underparts vinous pink shading to white on the throat and buff on the belly. Central tail feathers greyish brown tipped black (the long fawn upper tail coverts reach nearly to the end of closed tail), outer ones purplish black. The longer under tail coverts are blackish as are the primaries, except for a chestnut area at their bases which form a chestnut patch on underside of wing, and primary coverts. Iridescent golden bronze spots on the lesser coverts form a bar near shoulder of closed wing. Two partially concealed purplish black patches on scapulars and innermost secondaries. Irides brown. Bill black. Feet and legs pink or flesh colour. Sexes alike. Juvenile like adult but paler, with pale fringes to feathers of wing coverts, little or no pink tinge and lacking the golden bronze wing bar.

DISTRIBUTION AND HABITAT: Southern Peru, Bolivia, Chile (south to Atacama) and the Argentine (south to Mendoza), Inhabits the Puña zone.

FEEDING AND GENERAL HABITS: No information.

FIELD CHARACTERS: Chestnut on primaries and underside of wing usually conspicuous in flight and, with the short tail, distinguish from other doves in same regions (F. Vuilleumier, *pers. comm.*).

NESTING: No information.

VOICE: No information.

DISPLAY: No information.

INCA DOVE   *Scardafella inca*

Chamaepelia inca Lesson, Descr. Mamm. Et. Ois. Recémm. Decouv. 1847, p. 211.

DESCRIPTION: Between Diamond Dove and Barbary Dove in size, nearer to the former and rather similarly shaped. The tail, although long, is not, however, proportionately as long as a Diamond Dove's. Throat whitish. Forehead pale pinkish grey shading to pale brownish pink on crown, face and neck. Upperparts pale greyish brown shading to whitish grey on outer median and greater wing coverts. Breast pale dull pink shading to buffish white on belly and white on under tail coverts. All these cover feathers are narrowly edged with dusky grey giving a scaly effect except on the breast and forehead where the dark feather fringes are usually absent or obsolescent. Outer secondaries dark drab grey and primaries chestnut with tips, and most of outer webs of outermost four pairs, blackish drab; underwing chestnut with black patch. Central tail feathers greyish brown; next two pairs black and drab with trace of white at tips, outer ones black with white ends, the white area increasing to the outermost pair which are black only at base of outer web and about half length of inner web. Irides orange, red-orange or red. Bill black. Legs and feet flesh pink to purplish pink.

Sexes nearly alike but female tends to have less intense pale pink on breast and dusky feather fringes on breast and forehead less reduced than in male. Juvenile like female but with ill-defined but conspicuous buff subterminal bars on feathers of back and wings.

DISTRIBUTION AND HABITAT: Southern North America and Central America from Arizona, southern New Mexico and central Texas south to Nicaragua and north-western Costa Rica. Inhabits open country with some scrub or tree cover. Common in parks and gardens in or near towns, cultivated areas and about farmsteads.

FEEDING AND GENERAL HABITS: Feeds on small seeds picked up from the ground. Will take wheat dari and other cultivated grains of similar size when available although most of the wild seeds it eats are much smaller than these. Flight strong with rapid wing beats but often jerky and slow when flying short distances. Makes a characteristic buzzing noise in flight, believed to be produced (Johnston, 1960) by the emarginated outer webs of the eighth and ninth primaries. About one second after alighting the tail is abruptly raised two or three inches. Usually shows little fear of man. Adults usually in pairs (when one not on nest) but numbers may aggregate at good feeding areas. Non-breeding adults and immatures form loose flocks, usually small except around very good feeding grounds. Much time spent sunning. Roost in evergreens, usually communally. Two or more individuals roost side by side in physical contact. Roosting actually on the backs of other members of the flock has been recorded on several occasions (Bent, 1932; Johnston, 1960).

NESTING: Usual pigeon nest in tree or bush, often on old nests of other birds. Two white eggs. Young fledge at 14–16 days. Breeding season prolonged. Records of nests in New Mexico from March to August. In Mexico City from October to July and in Salvador throughout the year (Bent, 1932; Heilfurth, 1934; Johnston, 1960).

VOICE: The advertising coo is on disyllabic or trisyllabic cooing variously described as 'a slowly uttered Coe-coo or Co-o-oh coo-oo, the first slightly shorter, high pitched, coarser and with 'o' as in 'go', the second lower, with a typical 'oo' sound as in 'room' (Simmins in Bent, 1932); a 'sleepy Voo-hooor or Voo-hoo-hoop' (Heilfurth, 1934, transcription of call anglicised by present writer) and coo-coo (Johnston, 1960). The display coo is described by Johnston as a soft throaty 'cut-cut-ca, doah'; audible only for a short distance. An apparent derivative from or intensification of the display coo is used in threat between males. This Johnston has named the aggression call and transcribed as 'cut-cut-cut-ca-doah'; 'of a throaty quality, with the last three syllables accented . . . The alarm call a soft 'cut' difficult to 'pinpoint'.

DISPLAY: Bowing display involves assumption of a horizontal posture but, apparently, little or no head movement. The tail is raised nearly vertical and fanned out to exhibit the black and white markings. A bobbing movement of the head in which head is raised high, followed by an abrupt downward movement of head and neck with bill kept more or less horizontal is probably homologous with nodding of *Columba* species and used in comparable situations. Allo-preening between members of a pair and even between individuals who may not subsequently pair is common. The aggressive call is accompanied by raising the tail, but not so high as in the bowing display, and slightly spreading it. In threat or aggressive chasing a horizontal posture is adopted. One wing is frequently raised in agonistic situations sometimes, apparently, in aggressive rather than defensive threat. Early in the breeding season males often mount females and sometimes other males but are usually soon dislodged. Johnston interprets this behaviour as attempts at copulation rather than aggression. This section is compiled from Johnston's work on the species which is the most detailed I have read.

REFERENCES

BENT, A. C. 1932. Life Histories of North American Gallinaceous Birds. *U.S. Nat. Mus. Bull.* **162**.
HEILFURTH, F. 1934. Zu den Lebensgewohnheiten von *Scardafella inca* in Mexico. *Orn. Monatsb XLII*, **4**: 103–110.
JOHNSTON, R. F. 1960. Behaviour of the Inca Dove. *Condor* **62**: 7–24.

SCALY DOVE   *Scardafella squammata*

Columba squammata 'Temm', Lesson. Traite D'Orn., Livr. 6, 1831, p. 474.

DESCRIPTION: Size and general appearance very similar to the Inca Dove with which it forms a superspecies. Upper parts greyish brown tinged with vinous on hind neck and upper mantle. Those parts of the outer wing coverts visible when wing closed predominantly white, forming a conspicuous white band along lower part of wing. Forehead, face and breast very pale greyish pink shading to white on throat, belly and under tail covert. Blackish borders to all these cover feathers give a conspicuous scaly effect. These dark feather edgings are least pronounced on breast and forehead and absent or obsolescent on throat and under tail coverts. Primaries blackish on tips and outer webs, otherwise chestnut. Underwing black and chestnut. Central tail feathers brownish grey; outer ones patterned black and white. Irides dark reddish brown or dark red. Bill blackish or dusky, sometimes paler at base. Feet flesh pink.

Sexes alike. Juveniles differs from adult in same ways as that of the previous species, *Scardafella inca*. The above description is of the nominate form *S. s. squammata* from Brazil and Paraguay. *S. squammata ridgwayi*, from northern South America, has the dark edges to the feathers, especially on the back and wing coverts, broader and more intensely black.

DISTRIBUTION AND HABITAT: The arid tropical zone of north-eastern South America from the Santa Marta region of Colombia to the Orinoco-Coura Basin in Venezuela, Margarita Island and Trinidad. Also the Brazilian table-land from Maranhão, Piahuy and Ceará south to western Minas Geraes, São Paulo, Paranã and Matto Grosso, and Paraguay. Inhabits arid regions with open ground and some tree or scrub cover. Commonly in cultivated areas, gardens and about human habitations.

FEEDING AND GENERAL HABITS: Probably very similar to, if not identical with, those of the Inca Dove.

VOICE: The only detailed records of voice that I can find are those made by Harrison (1961) on males and a female specimen of the nominate form and my own on these same individuals and on two males of the northern form in the New York Zoo. The differences noted most probably reflect a difference in voice between the northern (*ridgwayi*) and southern (*squammata*) populations. For convenience of phrasing this will be assumed in the following descriptions but the possibility that the differences are individual rather than geographical cannot be entirely ruled out until more individuals of each form have been observed.

The advertising coo of *squammata* is a trisyllabic call whose clear, incisive and monotonous character is reminiscent of the well-known call of the Common Quail *Coturnix coturnix*. Harrison describes it as 'Quor-cu-cor, the first note very emphatic, the second short and subdued and the third emphasized, but not as much as the first'. The advertising coo of *ridgwayi* is less explosive and incisive and has a definite 'R' sound in the first note. I paraphrased it as 'Croo! co-co'.

The display coo of *squammata* is described by Harrison as 'an abrupt, relatively high-pitched, loud Corrok' the 'Corrok' notes being often interspersed with and sometimes, in low intensity display, replaced by a 'less intense, subdued cut note'. I have not seen the full bowing display of *ridgwayi*. When threatening or defying each other the two males I watched uttered a soft 'Crōo-ōo, crr-crōo - ōo' apparently the equivalent of the 'Aggression Call' of the Inca Dove.

The nest call of *squammata* is identical with that of *ridgwayi* and similar to their display coos described above. In *ridgwayi* I paraphrased it as 'Crroo' or 'Croo(a)'.

The alarm call at low intensity is a 'soft suddened cut'. In greater fear *squammata* utters 'an abrupt, loud Quok, rather high-pitched . . . with pitch and volume similar to the advertisement call'. In intermediate states of alarm Harrison records 'a lower pitched, rolling Crorr'.

DISPLAY: The bowing display, with raising and fanning of the tail and the threatening and attacking postures are the same as in the Inca Dove (q.v.). Nest calling is accompanied by raising and slightly opening the tail which is not, however, raised so high or opened so fully as in the bowing display. Wing twitching is represented by a violent shuddering movement of the folded wings. I saw this movement given by males of *ridgwayi* when defying or threatening one another. Head bobbing as described by Harrison, differs from that of the Inca Dove (q.v.) in that the bill points slightly upwards at the initial throw back of the head which then describes a forward and downward arc, so that the bill points downwards at the culmination of the movement.

OTHER NAMES: Mottled Dove; South American Zebra Dove.

REFERENCES

HARRISON, C. J. O. 1961. Notes on the Behaviour of the Scaly Dove. *Condor* **63**: 450–455.

MAUVE-SPOTTED GROUND DOVE *Uropelia campestris*

Columbina campestris Spix, Av. Bras., 2, 1825, p. 57, pl. 75, F. 2.

DESCRIPTION: About the size of a Diamond Dove and rather similar in shape, with short rounded wings and long, graduated tail. Forehead and forecrown bluish grey. Upperparts light drab brown, tinged pinkish on hind neck. Two iridescent purple and black, white-bordered bands on wing formed by markings on the median and greater coverts. Row of large black or purple and black spots on outer webs of inner secondaries. Underwing black and white. Throat, sides of neck and breast pale mauve-pink shading to white on belly and under tail coverts. Central tail feathers drab brown; outer ones black broadly tipped white. Sexes alike, in life female probably paler round eye. Irides bluish grey or light blue. Orbital skin, feet and legs yellow, orange-yellow or orange. Bill dusky. Juvenile has buff fringes to many cover feathers and is chestnut and buff where the adult is iridescent purple and white on its wings. (See pl. 1).

DISTRIBUTION AND HABITAT: The Campos of Brazil, from the island of Marajo, Maranhão, Piahuy and Ceará south to western Minas Geraes, Goyaz and Matto Grosso and adjacent parts of eastern Bolivia in the department of Santa Cruz. Apparently inhabits grasslands, usually in vicinity of water.

FEEDING AND GENERAL HABITS: Little apparently recorded. Probably feeds mainly on seeds picked up on the ground. Reiser (1924) observed it lifting its tail as it ran about in the sand by a small lake, and that it was fearless of man.

NESTING: No information.

VOICE: No information.

DISPLAY: No information.

REFERENCES

REISER, O. 1924. Ergebnisse der Zoolog. Expedition der Akad. der Wissenschaften nach Nordostbrasilien im Jahre 1903 Vögel. *Denkschr. Akad. Wien* 76: 107–252.
PINTO, O. 1949. Esboço Monográphico dos Columbidae Brasilieros. *Arquivos de Zoologia do Estado de São Paulo* 7: Art. 3, 241–324.

THE DOVES OF THE GENUS *LEPTOTILA*

These are between Feral Pigeon and Barbary Dove size with rather long legs with bare ankle ('knee') and tarsus and medium to short-medium tails of 12 feathers. They have the end of the outermost primary abruptly and sharply attenuated. They have rich rufous or light chestnut red on the axillaries and under side of the wing and white-tipped tails but otherwise lack distinctive markings. In their shape, gait and general coloration they show a considerable resemblance to the African genus *Aplopelia*. This resemblance is almost certainly due to convergence in two different groups that have independently become adapted to a very similar way of life. The *Leptotila* doves spend much time on the ground in forest or scrub, walking about swiftly and nimbly and keeping either under cover or within a short distance of it. They perch freely in trees and shrubs, sometimes at a considerable height. In habits and build they suggest a link between the mourning doves and ground doves and the American quail doves and it is to these other American pigeons that I think they are most closely related.

The *Leptotila* species are all very similar in external characters and were they all allopatric would be considered all forms of one or at most two species. The forms *verreauxi, megalura, jamaicensis, wellsi, rufaxilla, plumbeiceps, pallida, cassini, ochraceiventris* and *conoveri* are usually treated as species. I have followed this course here because it seems less likely to lead to confusion in our present state of knowledge. Further information on the precise breeding distribution of the continental forms, their ecology, calls and behaviour will be necessary to elucidate their exact relationship. On present evidence their relationships appear to me to be as follows.

L. verreauxi is a widespread polytypic species. *L. megalura* appears to be closely related to it and they would certainly be treated here as conspecific but for the fact that they are said to overlap widely in north-western Argentina (Hellmayr & Conover, 1942). *L. rufaxilla* and *L. plumbeiceps* replace one another geographically and although here provisionally treated as members of a superspecies will probably prove to be conspecific. *L. pallida* also clearly belongs to this group. It is said to occur in the same faunal region as *L. plumbeiceps* (Hellmayr & Conover, 1942) but there seems no evidence that it has occurred in exactly the same areas (H. & C. de Schauensee, 1948–49), and it therefore seems justifiable to regard it as a representative of this group. *L. wellsi* is, as Bond (1963) has pointed out, another member of this group. All these can be considered as members of a superspecies, to which *L. jamaicensis* probably also belongs as it seems to resemble this group more closely than it does *L. verreauxi*. Also *jamaicensis* and *verreauxi* may overlap in Yucatan although they are probably ecologically separated.

L. battyi of Coiba Island is considered here as a race of *L. plumbeiceps*. It is certainly a geographical representative of *plumbeiceps* rather than *cassini* but it is, for a *Leptotila*, rather distinctively coloured and Dr. Wetmore has informed me (*pers. comm.*) that its most usually uttered coo differs in sound from that of *plumbeiceps*. The possibility of *battyi* having reached specific level cannot be excluded. Further information on the allegedly intermediate form *L. p. malae* is needed in this connection.

L. cassini overlaps both *plumbeiceps* and *verreauxi*. It seems likely that the rather differently coloured *L. ochraceiventris* of western Ecuador is its geographical representative. *L. conoveri* in spite of its different head colour appears to be closest to *ochraceiventris*. *L. conoveri*, *L. ochraceiventris* and *L. conoveri* are probably best considered as representatives of the same superspecies.

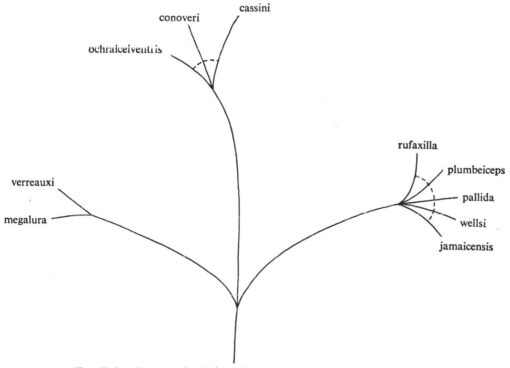

FIG. D.9: Presumed relationships of species in the genus *Leptotila*.

WHITE-FRONTED DOVE   *Leptotila verreauxi*

Leptotila verreauxi Bonaparte, Compt. Rend. Acad. Sci. Paris, 40, 1855, p. 99.

DESCRIPTION: About mid-way between Barbary Dove and Feral Pigeon in size. Typical *Leptotila* shape. Forehead pinkish white to pale pink or greyish pink shading to a slightly iridescent purplish

16—P & D

brown or purplish grey on crown and light pinkish brown or pinkish grey, shot with iridescent light red-purple and bronze green on nape and hind neck.   Upperparts light greyish olive brown with narrow pale tawny fringes to outer webs of outer secondaries.   Central tail feathers greyish brown, outer ones blackish, broadly tipped white.   Throat white.   Face, breast and sides of neck pale greyish pink shading to white on belly and under tail coverts.   Underwing chestnut.   Irides golden, golden brown, yellow or orange.   Orbital skin light blue, greenish blue or greyish blue.   Bill blackish or very dark horn colour. Legs and feet dark red or purplish red.

The female is usually a little duller, having the pink areas of the head and breast less clear and, usually, suffused with greyish brown.   The juvenile has reddish buff fringes to most of the cover feathers and reddish buff or rufous shaft streaks to those of head and neck.

The above description is of the nominate form *L. v. verreauxi* of southern Central America, northern and eastern Colombia, northern Venezuela and adjacent islands.   *L. v. brasiliensis* from the Guianas southward to the Amazon Valley and west to the Rio Solimoes is a shade darker above, more reddish on the head with a richer iridescence on hind neck and a slighly darker, more buffy pink on the breast.   *L. v. approximans* from most of north-eastern Brazil is like *brasiliensis* but more tinged with grey on head and back.   *L. v. decolor* of western Columbia, western and central Ecuador and nothern Peru is rather larger, paler in colour and with the neck iridescence usually showing more green.   *L. v. chlorauchenia* is very similar to *decolor* but not quite so pale in colour.   *L. v. fulviventris* of south-eastern Mexico, Yucatan, British Honduras and north-eastern Guatemala is similar to *brasiliensis* but slightly larger and paler and with the belly, flanks and under tail coverts predominantly buff.   *L. v. angelica* from Texas and most of Mexico is slightly larger than *fulviventris* and duller in colour.   It is predominantly white on the belly and under tail coverts and a rather cold olive brown above and dull greyish pink on the breast.   It much resembles the race *chlorauchenia* from southern South America in general appearance but has richer red iridescence. Many other races have been recognised but they all very closely resemble one or other of those described above.

A specimen from Uruguay (race *chlorauchenia*) and others from Salvador (race *bangsi*) have been recorded with a dull red spot in the loral region and one in the apical corner of the otherwise blue or grey orbital skin.   On present evidence it seems uncertain to what extent this is a geographical or an individual character.

DISTRIBUTION AND HABITAT: Southern North America, Central America and South America; from the Lower Rio Grande Valley, Texas south to southern Brazil, Uruguay and eastern Argentina.   Inhabits bushy country, forest edge, open woodlands and groves or thickets in cultivated areas in both temperate and tropical zones. Typically in semi-arid or arid districts and replaced by allied species in humid forest areas.

FEEDING AND GENERAL HABITS: Feeds chiefly, perhaps entirely, on the ground. Known to take various seeds and berries. Keeps much in cover of trees or shrubs but readily comes out into open spaces, glades or trails when seeking food. Usually in pairs or singly but often very many individuals in a comparatively small area. Commonly flies up and perches in trees when flushed from the ground. Some rather quiescent individuals that I watched at the Bronx Zoo frequently jerked their tails down and then upwards. This was almost certainly, as in *Leptotila jamaicensis* (q.v.), a low intensity flight intention movement.

NESTING: Nest in tree or shrub, often more substantial than most pigeons' nests. Two white, cream or pale buff eggs. Incubation period 14 days (Skutch). Breeding season apparently prolonged, at any rate in Central America, but not during May or June in Costa Rica (Skutch, 1964). In Trinidad breeds most of the year (Snow).

VOICE: Sennet (in Bent, 1932) describes what is evidently the advertising coo of the northern race, *angelica*, as somewhat prolonged, ending with a falling inflection and very low in pitch. Wetmore (1926) describes one call, probably the advertising coo, of the South American forms *ochroptera* and *chlorauchenia* as 'a low, resonant whoo-whoo-oo, a sound similar to that produced by blowing across the top of a wide-mouthed bottle', and another as 'a low "coo-coo" barely audible at a distance of 10 metres'. Skutch describes a deep, long-drawn moaning 'coo-ooo' and a higher pitched 'coo woo' from Costa Rican birds.

DISPLAY: Wetmore (1926) records that 'occasionally one bowed low with elevated tail' but does not give details of the circumstances. Possibly this was the fear response of crouching with somewhat raised tail that is common to many species.

OTHER NAMES: White-tipped Dove; Solitary Pigeon; Wood Pigeon; Pale-fronted Dove.

REFERENCES

BENT, A. C. 1932. Life Histories of North American Gallinaceous Birds. *U.S. Nat. Mus. Bull.* 162.
DICKEY, D. R. & VAN ROSSEM, A. J. 1938. The Birds of El Salvador. *Zool. Ser. Field Mus. Nat. Hist.* 23: 197–199.
REISER, O. 1923. Ergebnisse der Zoology. Exped. der Akad der Wissenschaften nach Nordostbrasilien im Jahre 1903. Vögel. *Denkschr. Akad. Wien* 76: 107–252.
SKUTCH, A. F. 1964. Life Histories of Central American Pigeons. *Wilson Bull.* 76: 211–247.
SNOW, D. W. (*Pers. Comm.*).
VOOUS, K. H. 1957. Studies on the Fauna of Curaçao and other Caribbean Islands. 27: 29. The Birds of Aruba, Ciuraçao and Bonaire.
WETMORE, A. 1926. Observations on the Birds of Argentina, Paraguay, Uruguay and Chile. *U.S. Nat. Mus. Bull.* 133: 174–177.

WHITE-FACED DOVE   *Leptotila megalura*

Leptolia megalura Sclater and Salvin, Proc. Zool. Soc. London, 1879. p. 640.

DESCRIPTION: Very similar to White-fronted Dove. Slightly larger than the race of *verreauxi* with which it overlaps and differs in having the white at the throat more extensive, the feathers around the eye and sometimes those of most of the face, also white, the underparts slightly darker and the upperparts strongly tinged with reddish purple. On mantle, back, rump and wing coverts new feathers are reddish olive brown fringed with dull reddish purple but with wear they fade and lose the purple colour. Moulting individuals thus present, at close view, a slightly mottled appearance. Irides yellow. I have not seen a juvenile of this species but it is almost certainly similar to that of *verreauxi*.

DISTRIBUTION AND HABITAT: The subtropical zone of Bolivia, Argentina in provinces of Jujuy, Salta and Tacuman.

FEEDING AND GENERAL HABITS : I can find nothing recorded.
NESTING : No information.
VOICE : No information.
DISPLAY : No information.
DISPLAY : No information.
OTHER NAMES : Long-tailed Dove.

GREY-FRONTED DOVE   *Leptotila rufaxilla*

Columba rufaxilla Richard and Bernard, Actes. Soc. Hist. Paris. 1, 1792, p. 118.

DESCRIPTION : Between Barbary Dove and Feral Pigeon in size, nearer to the former, typical *Leptotila* shape. Forehead greyish white or very pale bluish grey shading to medium bluish grey on crown and greyish purple with slight iridescence on nape and hind neck. Throat and narrow line of feathers bordering orbital skin in front of, above and below eye pinkish white or white. Rest of face pinkish buff or rusty buff. Breast and sides of neck greyish pink shading to white on belly and under tail coverts, the latter marked brown on outer web. Upper parts olive brown with suggestion of bronze-green lustre and purplish tinge on upper mantle and inner wing coverts. Primaries slightly darker and less olivaceous with narrow buff fringes to outer webs. Under wing coverts and central area of underside of primaries chestnut. Central tail feathers olive brown, outer ones blackish, conspicuously tipped white. Irides yellow or brown or, and probably usually, with a dark brown inner ring and a yellow, greenish yellow, whitish or light brown outer ring.   Orbital and loral skin dull red or red.   Bill black.   Legs and feet pinkish red or red.

The female has more brown or olivaceous suffusion on flanks and a certain amount sullying the pink of neck and breast.   Her upperparts usually show a more pronounced green tinge and lack all trace of the purple tinge shown by males.   Juvenile similar to female but with many cover feathers edged rusty and breast barred rusty buff and drab.

The above description is of the nominate form *L. v. rufaxilla* from South America in the Guianas and northern Brazil.   *L. rufaxilla bahiae* from Brazil (Bahia to southern Matto Grosso) is a little larger and more reddish in colour, the mantle and wing coverts being strongly tinged with reddish purple in the male and slightly in the female and the breast a rich buffy pink or salmon pink with only a faint vinous tinge.   *L. rufaxilla reichenbachi* is very similar to *bahiae* but less reddish above and usually a darker pink on neck and breast, the female is strongly green tinged above.   *L. rufaxilla pallidipectus* is paler and greyer with a pale buffish mauve breast and paler olive brown upper parts with little or no reddish tinge.   Several other races have been recognised but they are all either very similar to one of those here described or intermediate between two of them.

This species may be conspecific with the Grey-headed Dove *L. plumbeiceps*.

DISTRIBUTION AND HABITAT: South America from the tropical zone of eastern Colombia at the eastern base of the eastern Andes east to the Guianas and north-eastern Brazil and south to south-eastern Brazil, Rio Grande do Sul, Paraguay and Misiones.   Inhabits humid forest.

FEEDING AND GENERAL HABITS: Feeds largely on ground but also above it; seen to take fruits of *Costus* from the fruiting heads (Snow).

NESTING: Usual pigeon nest in tree or shrub.   In Trinidad Belcher & Smooker (1936) recorded nests usually from 10 to 20 feet above ground.   Two cream coloured eggs.   In Trinidad nests breeds in all months with possible exception of August, September and October (Snow).

VOICE: Presumed advertising coo 'crrr crrr cooooooooo'; the first two notes much softer, purring and not audible at a distance; the coo rising in loudness and intensity with a slight dying away effect at the end (Snow).

DISPLAY: No information.

REFERENCES

BELCHER, C. & SMOOKER, G. D.   1936.   Birds of the Colony of Trinidad and Tobago, Pt. 3.   *Ibis* **6**:   Thirteenth Series 1–35.
SNOW, D. W. (*Pers Comm.*).

GREY-HEADED DOVE   *Leptotila plumbeiceps*

Leptotila plumbeiceps Sclater & Salvin, Proc. Zool. Soc. London, 1868, p. 59.

DESCRIPTION: Between Barbary Dove and Feral Pigeon in size, but nearer to the former.   Typical *Leptotila* proportions.   Forehead very pale bluish grey shading to medium bluish grey on crown, nape, upper mantle and sides of neck, in these latter areas the grey is tinged with mauve. Face and ear coverts pinkish buff shading to a more definite soft pale pink on breast. Throat, belly and under tail coverts white. Upper parts dark olive brown with a slight rufous tinge. Under wing chestnut. Central tail feathers dark olive brown, outer ones blackish, tipped white. Bill black. Legs and feet flesh pink. The soft part colours here given are based on only one collector's data. Female has the breast more or less suffused with greyish fawn. Juvenile generally more olivaceous above, with dark subterminal bars and rusty red or rusty fawn tips to many of the cover feathers. Feathers of breast mostly drab brown with tawny shafts and tawny tips, giving a barred appearance.

The above description is of the typical form which inhabits most of the species range. *L. p. battyi* from Coiba Island, off the Pacific Coast of Panama, differs in having the nape and hind neck as well as the crown bluish grey and the upper parts a rich reddish brown or chestnut. Irides dull yellow. Orbital skin grey but skin of loral area, between gape and eye, which joins it, dull red. Legs and feet dull red. *L. p. malae* from the Cape Mala Peninsula, Veraguas, western Panama is intermediate between the above-described forms.

DISTRIBUTION AND HABITAT: Tropical zone of south-eastern Mexico in States of Tamaulipas, Vera Cruz, Mexico, Oaxaca and Tabasco south through eastern Guatamala, British Honduras, Nicaragua, western Costa Rica and Panama to western Columbia. Also the Cape Mala Peninsular of western Panama and Coiba Island. In Mexico inhabits chiefly humid lowland forest (Blake, 1953); on Coiba Island, Wetmore (1957) found it common both in swampy woods near the river mouths and in the forests of the interior.

FEEDING AND GENERAL HABITS: Feeds and spends much time on the ground. Keeps much in cover but comes out onto trails and open areas, especially in the early morning. When mildly alarmed (by man) flies up onto a low branch or log; when badly frightened flies swiftly away to more distant cover. The above information is based chiefly on Wetmore's (1957) observation of the species on Coiba Island.

NESTING: Presumably much as other *Leptotila* species but I can find nothing recorded.

VOICE: What is probably the advertising coo of the form *battyi* is described by Wetmore as 'a single hooting note . . . highly ventriloquial'; and a call of the form *notius* from western Panama as a 'curious low "Cwuh-h-á" '.

DISPLAY: No information.

REFERENCES
BLAKE, E. R. 1953. *Birds of Mexico.* University of Chicago Press.
WETMORE, A. 1957. The Birds of Isla Coiba Panama. *Smithsonian Miscellaneous Collections* **134**: No. 9, 36–37.
—— 1964. Manuscript for a book on Birds of Panama.

PALLID DOVE — *Leptotila pallida*

Leptotila pallida Berlepsch and Taczanowski, Proc. Zool. Soc. London, 1883 (1884), p. 575.

DESCRIPTION: Between Barbary Dove and Feral Pigeon in size; typical *Leptotila* proportions. Forehead, face and throat white shading through pale grey on crown to pinkish grey on nape and hind neck and pale greyish pink on sides of neck and breast. Belly and under tail coverts white. Upper parts rich chestnut brown inclining to chestnut red on outer wing coverts, upper tail coverts and central tail feathers and with a purplish tinge in very new feathers. Slight purplish iridescence on hind neck and upper mantle. Primaries dark greyish brown (where visible when wing folded) with rusty fringes. Underwing chestnut. Outer tail feathers dark chestnut with ill-defined blackish subterminal band and conspicuous white tip. Irides yellow. Legs and feet pinkish red or brownish red. Bill blackish. These soft part colours are based on two specimens only.

Female a slightly less reddish brown above and with the pink and grey areas less clear and bright. I have not seen a juvenile; it probably bears the same relation to the adults as in other *Leptotila* species.

DISTRIBUTION AND HABITAT: The tropical zone of the Pacific coast region of western Columbia and western Ecuador, from the Rio San Juan to province of Loja.

FEEDING AND GENERAL HABITS: I can find nothing recorded. Presumably much as other *Leptotila* species.

NESTING: No information.

VOICE: No information.

DISPLAY: No information.

GRENADA DOVE   *Leptotila wellsi*

Engyptila wellsi Lawrence, Auk, New Ser., 1, p. 180. 1884.

DESCRIPTION: Throat white; face and forehead pale pinkish shading through greyish to dull brown on crown and nape. Neck and upper breast pinkish buff shading to pure white on lower breast, belly and under tail coverts. Flanks light brownish. Upper parts bronzy olive brown, fading to greyish drab on old feathers. Underwing chestnut. Irides buff, orbital skin blue. Bill black. Legs and feet bright carmine red. The above description is based on only a few specimens. I have not seen a juvenile.

DISTRIBUTION AND HABITAT: The Island of Grenada, West Indies. On Grenada inhabits the lower parts (Bond, 1960).

FEEDING AND GENERAL HABITS: I can find nothing recorded. Presumably similar to *Leptotila rufaxilla* with which it may prove conspecific.

NESTING: Unrecorded in the wild. Bond says that it has nested in captivity, laying two eggs per clutch.

VOICE: Bond (1960) thinks that a 'single booming note' very like that of *L. verreauxi*, heard near Grand Anse, was probably uttered by this species.

DISPLAY: No information.

OTHER NAME: Well's Dove.

REFERENCE

BOND, J. 1960. *Birds of the West Indies*. London.

WHITE-BELLIED DOVE   *Leptotila jamaicensis*

Columba jamaicensis Linnaeus. Syst. Nat. Ed. 12, 1, 1766, p. 283.

DESCRIPTION: Between Barbary Dove and Feral Pigeon in size and typical *Leptotila* proportions with rather plump, compact shape, high steeply sloping forehead and longish legs. Forehead face and throat white shading through pale grey on hind crown to iridescent amethyst or purple on nape. Back and sides of neck richly iridescent; this iridescence being, in most lights, primarily green and/or purple on hind neck and golden bronze, more or less shot with purple, at sides of neck. Breast pale greyish pink with a creamy tinge; in life a small white band shows at side of breast just in front of the folded wing. Belly and under tail coverts white. Upperparts olive brown with faint bronzy tinge. Narrow whitish edges to outer webs of primaries. Underwing chestnut. Central tail feathers greyish brown; outer ones greyish black with conspicuous white tips. Irides silvery white or with a whitish inner ring and reddish outer ring. Orbitall skin dull purple. Bill greyish black, powdery grey at base. Legs and feet red. Female usually has the neck iridescence slightly less brilliant. The juvenile is duller with sandy rufous fringes to most cover feathers and the areas of neck and breast that are bronze or pinkish in the adult are barred with dull brown and sandy rufous.

The above description is of nominate *L. j. jamaicensis* from Jamaica. *L. j. gaumeri* from Northern Yucatan and Cozumel, Mugeres and Holbox Islands is slightly smaller, more olivaceous above and with less vivid iridescence on the neck and slightly darker pink on the breast. *L. j. neoxena* from the Island of St. Andrews is intermediate between the two forms described. *L. j. collaris* from Grand Cayman is like the nominate Jamaican form but averages slightly smaller.

DISTRIBUTION AND HABITAT: Jamaica, Grand Cayman Island, St. Andrews Island, Northern Yucatan and Cozumel, Mugeres and Holbox Islands. Inhabits areas with shrub or tree cover, usually at low level. Commonest in semi-arid districts.

FEEDING AND GENERAL HABITS: Feeds largely on seeds picked up on the ground. Keeps much under cover of bushes or shrubs and walks about rapidly when seeking food (Field, 1894). The flight intention movement consists of jerking the head back a little and then throwing it strongly forward; at the culmination of the movement the head is about in line with the back and bill pointing downwards at an angle of about 30 degrees. As the head is jerked back the tail is somewhat lowered and then jerks strongly upwards to slightly above its normal position as the head is thrown forward. A slight upward flick of the tail, given by an otherwise quiescent bird, appears to be a very low intensity form of flight intention movement.

NESTING: Usual pigeon in tree or shrub, seldom very high up. Sometimes nests on the ground. Two white eggs.

VOICE: The advertising coo would appear to be a four syllabled cooing phrase with the last note drawn out and more strongly accented. The nest call, as heard from a captive bird, was 'C$\overline{oo}$-c$\overline{oo}$-c$\overline{ooo}$ (o͞o)', very pure and musical in tone. It is transcribed as 'Cu-cu-cuoo' by Bond (1960) and 'Hoo, hoo, hoo, hoo, by Alderson (1903). The display coo, which I have heard several times from the males of two pairs in the London Zoo, is best written 'Crr$\overline{oo}$; $\overline{oo}$, c$\overline{oo}$-c$\overline{oo}$-c$\overline{ooo}$ (oo)' the first note low and purring, the next 'oo' very faint, the last phrase loud and musical, suggestive in both tone and tempo of the advertising coo of the Picazuro Pigeon.

DISPLAY: In the bowing display the male lowers his head and adopts a rather hunched posture with neck inflated and/or neck feathers partly erected so that the head is framed in the purple and bronze areas of the back and sides of neck. In this posture he runs towards the female, then stops still and utters the display coo. There is no appreciable movement of the tail or head during either the initial approach or in the final phase. In this respect the bowing display is very like those of the Mourning and Eared Doves. Alderson (1903), however, writes of the male 'bowing very low' which suggests that this species may, at times, make the initial approach to the female in a more upright posture. Her description otherwise fits the displays I saw given by the London Zoo birds.

In aggressive (? and sexual) excitement bird may take long hops when on the ground. Nodding occurs in hostile and sexual contests and is very similar in form to that of the Rock Pigeon although the nods are, perhaps, not usually so deep. Wing twitching consists of a rapid, shuddering movement of the folded wing as in the Mourning and Inca Doves. It appears to be used both in defensive and sexual situations but I have only seen it on a few occasions.

OTHER NAMES: Jamaican Dove; White-fronted Dove; Violet Dove; Ground Dove.

REFERENCES

ALDERSON, R. 1903. Nesting of the White-fronted or Violet Dove *Leptotila jamaicensis*. *Avicult. Mag.* New Series, **1**: 393–397.
BOND, J. 1960. *Birds of the West Indies*. London.
FIELD, G. W. 1894. Notes on the Birds of Port Henderson, Jamaica, West Indies. *Auk* **11**: 117–127.

CASSIN'S DOVE   *Leptotila cassin*

Leptotila cassini Lawrence. Proc. Acad. Nat. Sci. Philad., 1867, p. 94.

DESCRIPTION: Rather larger than a Barbary Dove; usual *Leptotila* shape but perhaps rather plumper and shorter tailed than average for the genus. Forehead dull pinkish grey. Crown and nape dark dull reddish brown. Throat white. Neck, face and breast a slightly purplish grey shading to a slightly iridescent greyish purple on hind neck and through greyish pink on lower breast to buffish white on belly. Flanks dull brown. Under tail coverts white, marked with dull brown. Upperparts dark olive brown with a subdued bronze-green lustre and slight purplish tinge on mantle and inner wing coverts. Primaries and tail feathers slightly darker and less olivaceous than rest of upperparts. Only two outermost pairs of tail feathers tipped white, sometimes only a trace of white on second from outermost pair. Under wing coverts chestnut and some chestnut on underside of primaries but less than in most *Leptotila* species. Irides greyish yellow, yellow or greenish yellow. Orbital skin grey except at posterior angle and in loral area where it is dull red. Legs and feet red or purplish red.

The female is duller and darker than the male, less olivaceous on the upperparts and with the grey and pinkish areas of the underparts suffused, with dull brown.   The juvenile has most of its cover feathers more or less barred with dark brown and rusty fawn.

The above description is of the nominate form *L. c. cassini* from Northern Colombia and much of Panama.   *L. cassini rufinucha* from south-western Costa Rica and western Panama is lighter in colour has the neck and breast more strongly tinged with purplish pink and has the crown and nape a rusty buff or light chestnut colour forming a conspicuous contrast to the pale forehead and purplish hind neck.   Its orbital skin has been described as red but is probably red and grey as in the nominate form.   The difference between the sexes is less marked, though similar in kind, to that shown in the nominate form.   *L. cassini cerviniventris* from further north is similar to *rufinucha* but has only an ill-defined and much less bright reddish brown area on crown and nape, the purplish pink tinge on the breast is more pronounced and the lower breast, at least of the male, is predominantly a dark vinous pink or salmon pink.

DISTRIBUTION AND HABITAT: The tropical zone of the Caribbean Lowlands of extreme south-eastern Mexico through central America to western Colombia.   Inhabits humid lowland forest, groves, thickets and locally shady pastures and gardens, up to 3,000 feet in Costa Rica (Skutch, 1964).

FEEDING AND GENERAL HABITS: Little recorded.   Known to take seeds, including maize when available, and fallen berries.   Feeds chiefly, probably entirely, on the ground.   Keeps much to cover.

NESTING: Usual pigeon nest in trees, shrub; Skutch found nests at heights from three to fifteen feet. They were always situated in thickets or at woodland edge never deep in the rain forest.   Two white or creamy eggs.   Skutch saw distraction display, which took the form of a slow, deliberate and conspicuous beating of the wings, from *rufinucha* but never from the nominate form.   An incubating male of the latter race bent his head and slightly spread his wings, thus concealing his pale forehead and underparts, when toucans were in the tree tops above him.   Nests have been found in February, March, April, July, August and September in Costa Rica and February to December in Panama.

VOICE: What is probably the advertising coo has been described by Skutch as 'a repeated, long-drawn, rather mournful 'cooo'; that of the form *rufinucha* as a long-drawn "cooo-oo"' like that of *verreauxi* but less resonant.

DISPLAY: No information.

OTHER NAMES: Grey-chested Dove; Grey-breasted Dove.

REFERENCES

HALLINAN, T., 1924.   Notes on Some Panama Canal Zone Birds with special reference to their food.   *Auk* **41**: 304–326.
SKUTCH, A. F.   1949.   Life History of the Ruddy Quail-Dove.   *Condor* **51**: 3–19.
—— 1954.   The Parental Strategems of Birds.   *Ibis* **96**: 544–564.
—— 1964.   Life Histories of Central American Pigeons.   *Wilson Bull.* **76**: 211–247.

BUFF-BELLIED DOVE

Leptotila ochraceiventris

Leptotila ochraceiventris Chapman. Bull. Amer. Mus. Nat. Hist., 33, 1914, p. 317.

DESCRIPTION: Rather larger than a Barbary Dove, typical *Leptotila* shape. Forehead whitish pink, shading through rusty purple on the crown to a slightly iridescent violet-purple on hind neck and upper mantle. Rest of upper parts dark olive brown with a very subdued bronze-green lustre and tinge of purple on mantle and wing coverts. Throat white. Front of neck warm buff. Breast mauve-pink. Lower breast, flanks and belly warm buff. Under tail coverts white tinged buff. Underwing chestnut. Central tail feathers dark brown; outer ones blackish, tipped white. Irides of one male were yellow.

DISTRIBUTION AND HABITAT: The tropical and sub-tropical zones of south-western Ecuador.

FEEDING AND GENERAL HABITS: No information.

VOICE: No information.

DISPLAY: No information.

OTHER NAMES: Ochraceous-bellied Dove.

CONOVER'S DOVE

Leptotila conoveri

Leptotila conoveri. Bard and de Schaunsee, Not. Naturae, No. 122, p. 1, May 1943.

DESCRIPTION: I have not seen this species. It is described as having the crown dark grey, throat white; hindneck vinaceous brown glossed with violet. Upper mantle vinaceous grey, glossed with shining violet: rest of upperparts dark grey with a purple sheen. Breast vinaceous pink sharply demarcated from the buff lower breast and belly. Under tail coverts white. Under wing chestnut. Tail slaty, the outer feathers tipped white.

DISTRIBUTION AND HABITAT: Colombia in the sub-tropical zone of the east slope of the Central Andes from Tolima south to Huila.

FEEDING AND GENERAL HABITS: No information.

NESTING: No information.

VOICE: No information.

DISPLAY: No information.

OTHER NAMES: Tolima Dove.

REFERENCE

DE SCHAUNSEE, R. M. 1964. *The Birds of Colombia.* Pennsylvania.

THE AMERICAN QUAIL DOVES

These superficially partridge-like, long-legged and largely terrestrial pigeons are very like the Old World quail doves in general appearance and, to some extent, in overall colouration. They do not, however, show resemblance to them in details of colour pattern except, in some cases, in the pattern of black and white on the underwing coverts and I think that the resemblances between the New and Old World quail doves are more likely due to convergence than to very close relationship. Most of the New World quail doves show distinctive facial markings which, although more elaborate, are similar to and probably homologous with those found in the American doves of the genus *Zenaida*. I think it probable that this resemblance indicates phylogenetic affinity and that the quail doves and *Zenaida* have diverged from a common stock subsequent to the latter's establishment in America.

Except for their characteristic facial markings the American quail doves largely lack striking or contrasting plumage patterns. Most of them are predominantly brown or purplish in hue and appear rather sombre when seen in a poor light or at a distance. At close quarters however, their deep lustrous greens and purples or rich browns and chestnuts make them decidedly handsome. They are largely terrestrial but usually nest and roost above ground, keep in or near cover and lay buff or cream-tinted eggs.

The Costa Rican Quail Dove *G. costaricensis* and Lawrence's Quail Dove *G. lawrencii* are obviously closely allied and might be treated as conspecific if their distribution did not overlap on the Caribbean coast of Costa Rica (Hellmayr and Conover, 1942). It is, however, not certain whether the breeding ranges overlap. If not these could certainly be considered members of a superspecies, together with Goldman's Quail Dove *G. goldmani*. The Purple Quail Dove, *G. saphirina* appears to be a geographical representative of the above group. It has sometimes been placed in a separate genus, *Osculatia*, on account of its attenuated outer primary; the other alleged plumage characters on which this genus was recognised, the short tail and rather narrow and pointed primaries, are not peculiar to it (Goodwin, 1958). This group appears to be represented on Cuba and Hispaniola by the Grey-headed Quail Dove *G. caniceps* and on Jamaica by the Crested Quail Dove *G. versicolor*. These island forms have, however, diverged more widely so that their affinities, within *Geotrygon*, are necessarily hypothetical. In most plumage characters they show considerable resemblance to *G. costaricensis* and its relatives but unlike them they have a largely chestnut underwing. In this feature they resemble the Veragua Quail Dove *G. veraguensis*, a species that now overlaps widely with the *costaricensis* group but is clearly very closely related to them.

The White-faced Quail Dove *G. linearis* and the Pink-faced Quail Dove *G. frenata* are both polytypic species that are almost entirely allopatric. I should consider them conspecific but both are said to occur together in western Colombia (Hellmayr & Conover). It is not, apparently, known whether the breeding ranges of the two overlap but, in view of the possibility, it is more convenient to treat them separately here.

The Key West Quail Dove *G. chrysia* and the Bridled Quail Dove, *G. mystacea* are here treated as members of a superspecies. The Violaceous Quail Dove, *G. violacea*, a very widespread mainland form may be related to the Key West and Bridled Quail Doves, the former of which it much resembles in coloration. It differs, however, in only possessing the faintest traces of the typical facial pattern. Indeed with its almost unmarked but pale fronted head its appearance suggests a link between the quail doves and the *Leptotila* species. It does not, however, show any trace of the few characteristic *Leptotila* features.

The Ruddy Quail Dove, *G. montana*, appears to be the most successful as it is certainly the most widely distributed species. In its size and shape, its strong sexual dimorphism, its enormous range and apparent tendency to migration or nomadism it remarkably parallels the equally successful Old World Emerald Dove, *Chalcophaps indica*.

The Blue-headed Quail Dove, *Starnoenas cyanocephala* is at once the most aberrant and the most beautiful of the New World quail doves. The main elements of its distinctive head pattern are, basically, the typical *Geotrygon* facial markings but it possesses a unique feature in the black, white-bordered breast bib. This, the hexagonal scales on the front of its legs and its laying white eggs, seems, perhaps, sufficient to justify retaining it in a monotypic genus. Its morphological characters do not suggest that the Blue-headed Quail Dove is more closely related to one particular existing *Geotrygon* species than to any other.

It probably represents a very early invasion of Cuba by some form ancestral both to it and to the present *Geotrygon* species or else a form whose mainland representative has since become extinct. The striking colour pattern of its head and breast doubtless functions as an isolating mechanism in reference to the other Cuban quail doves, *G. caniceps*, *G. chrysia* and *G. montana* and may have evolved, or become intensified for this purpose in reference to them or to some previously existing form(s).

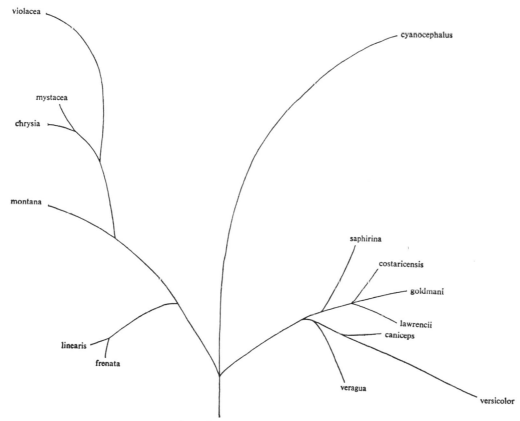

FIG. D.10: Presumed relationships of species in the genera *Geotrygon* and *Starnoenas*.

REFERENCES

GOODWIN, D. 1958. Remarks on the Taxonomy of some American Doves. *Auk* **75**: 330–334.
HELLMAYR, C. E. & CONOVER, B. 1942. Catalogue of Birds of the Americas. *Field Mus. Nat. Hist., Zool. Ser.*, 13, Pt. 1, 610 and 619.

LAWRENCE'S QUAIL DOVE   *Geotrygon lawrencii*

Geotrygon lawrencii Salvin, Ibis (3), 4: 329.

DESCRIPTION: Rather larger than a Barbary Dove and usual quail dove shape, plump and compact with short tail (see sketch of *G. saphirina*). Forehead greyish white shading through bluish grey to dull greyish green on crown, nape, hind neck and upper edge of mantle. Rest of mantle and innermost lesser wing coverts dull purple. Rest of upperparts dark olive brown, tinged reddish on outer wing coverts and secondaries. Primaries dark brownish grey, the next three after the outermost strongly emarginated and edged with pale buff on the outer web. Central tail feathers dull purplish brown, outer ones blackish with dull grey tips. Face and throat white with two conspicuous black lines, one from bill to eye and the other below the eye.   Neck and breast grey tinged greenish at sides.   Centre of belly and under tail coverts pale creamy buff.   Flanks umber brown.   Irides red or brownish orange; orbital skin grey with red spot in front of eye and red eye rims.   Bill reddish at base, black at tip with pale patch on underside of lower mandible.   Feet and legs reddish.   The sexes are alike.

The juvenile lacks the grey areas and has the green and purple of the mantle and the conspicuous face pattern less strongly developed.   Most of its cover feathers have narrow blackish sub-terminal bars and rusty-buff fringes.

The above description is of the nominate form, *G. l. lawrencii* from Panama and Costa Rica.   The form found in Mexico, *G. l. carrikeri*, is somewhat paler and brighter in colour.

DISTRIBUTION AND HABITAT: Caribbean slopes of western Panama and Costa Rica and in Mexico, in south-eastern Vera Cruz.   Also recorded from Tenerio on the Pacific side of Costa Rica, but may not be regular there.   Inhabits humid mountain forest.

FEEDING AND GENERAL HABITS: Large seeds, seeds of sedge (*Scleria* sp.) and cockroach egg-capsules found in crop of a shot male (Olson, *et al.* 1968).   On the Cerro de Tuxtla, in Vera Cruz, found on the ground in deep shade.   When flushed it usually flew a little distance and alighted again on the ground, but sometimes perched in trees (Wetmore, 1943).

NESTING: Usual pigeon nest in bush or shrub.   One buff or pinkish egg.

VOICE: A "soft, low-pitched 'who whō-oo' the first part of the second note more emphatic" has been described by Andrle (1967), and a 'loud coo-ah' repeated at short intervals and with a nasal, rather frog-like tone by Wetmore.

DISPLAY: No information.

OTHER NAMES: Purplish-backed Quail Dove.

REFERENCES
WETMORE, A.   1943.   The Birds of Southern Vera Cruz.   *Proc. U.S. Nat. Mus.* **93**: 215–340.
ANDRLE, R. F.   1967.   Birds of the Sierra de Tuxtla in Veracruz, Mexico.   *Wilson Bull.* **79**: 163–187.
OLSON, S. L. *et al.*   1968.   *Condor* **70**: 179.

COSTA RICAN QUAIL DOVE   *Geotrygon costaricensis*

Geotrygon costaricensis Lawrence, Ann. Lyc. Nat. Hist. N.Y., 9, p. 136, 1868.

DESCRIPTION: Similar in size and markings to the previous species (*G. lawrencii*), with which it may prove to be conspecific.   Differs in colour in having the upperparts reddish purple and reddish brown suffused with purple instead of dull purple and olive brown; the forehead buff instead of greyish white and in lacking the buff fringes to the primaries.   Bill dusky, reddish at base.   Irides brown.   Orbital skin dull red.   Legs and feet dull red.   I have not seen a juvenile but from descriptions it appears, as would be expected, to bear the same relation to the adult as does the juvenile of Lawrence's Quail Dove (q.v.).

DISTRIBUTION AND HABITAT: Sub-tropical rain forest zone of Costa Rica and western Panama. Inhabits dense forest at from 3,000 feet to 10,000 feet (Skutch, 1964).

FEEDING AND GENERAL HABITS: Little is recorded. Feeds on the ground and has been said to 'scratch like chickens' when seeking food. This seems most unlikely and it probably uses only the bill when food seeking like other doves.

NESTING: A single nest found by Skutch (1964) was 10 feet high on the horizontal branch of a shrub growing among bamboo undergrowth in heavy oak forest. The nest was partly made of green mosses and liverworts that were common in the forest nearby and contained one young one that was later taken by some predator.

VOICE: No information.

DISPLAY: No information.

OTHER NAMES: Red-backed Quail Dove; Purple-backed Quail Dove.

REFERENCE

SKUTCH, A. F. 1964. Life Histories of Central American Pigeons. *Wilson Bull.* **76**: 211–247.

GOLDMAN'S QUAIL DOVE *Geotrygon goldman*

Geotrygon goldmani Nelson, Smiths, Misc. Coll., 60, No. 3, p. 2, 1912.

DESCRIPTION: Very similar to Lawrence's Quail Dove (q.v.) but differs as follows. Top of head bright rufous, face warm buff above the black facial stripe. Only a very faint greenish tinge on a small area of the otherwise purple mantle. Wings and upperparts a deep reddish brown, tinged with purple. Grey of breast less sharply demarcated from the dull brown flanks and whitish grey belly. Iris orange; orbital skin dull grey with red spot in front of eye and red eye rims and gape. Bill black. Feet and legs dull red. These soft part colours from one male specimen (Wetmore MS). Female has grey of breast more tinged with brown and the brown of the wings and back a little less reddish. I have not seen a juvenile of this species. It is described (Wetmore MS) as being dull cinnamon brown above and dusky brown edged with reddish buff below. The above description is of the nominate form; *G. goldmani oreas* from the isolated Cerro Chucanti, near the eastern end of the Province of Panama is darker.

DISTRIBUTION: The sub-tropical zone of eastern Darien, Panama.

FEEDING AND GENERAL HABITS: Little recorded; known to eat seeds. Has usually been encountered on the ground in forest undergrowth but once perched high in a tree (Wetmore MS).

NESTING: Nothing recorded.

VOICE: One call is a 'hollow cooing sound like that made by blowing in a bottle', very different from the (known) call of *Geotrygon lawrencii* (Wetmore MS).

DISPLAY: No information.

OTHER NAMES: Mount Pirri Quail Dove.

REFERENCE

WETMORE, A. 1964. A Manuscript for a book on the Birds of Panama.

PURPLE QUAIL DOVE   *Geotrygon saphirina*

Geotrygon saphirina Bonaparte, Compt. Rend. Acad. Sci. Paris, 40, No. 3, p. 101, Jan. 15, 1855.

DESCRIPTION: About size of a Barbary Dove but shape very different being even plumper and more compact than that of other quail doves. First primary attenuated, tail very short. Forehead, throat and face below eye white, a blackish purple stripe from the base of the lower mandible extends below and beyond the ear forming a striking facial pattern (see sketch). Top of head bluish grey glossed with bronze green on nape. Hind neck bronzy brown with green, golden and purplish pink iridescence. Mantle, back and inner wing coverts deep, slightly iridescent reddish purple (purple or reddish brown in some lights) shading to dark purplish brown on outer wing coverts and secondaries and blackish brown on primaries and inner secondaries one of which latter has a small conspicuous white spot. Rump and upper tail coverts iridescent bluish purple or greenish blue. Central tail feathers blackish, outer ones blackish with blue-grey tips. Breast pale grey shading into white on the belly and warm buff on the flanks and under tail coverts. The sexes are alike, but female tends to be less brilliant. The juvenile is a general dark reddish brown above with darker subterminal bands and rusty fringes to feathers. White areas duller; sides of breast barred dusky pale and pale rufous. Face markings as adult but less intense. I have been unable to find any authentic description of eye, foot or bill colour. (See pl. 1).

The above description is of the nominate form, *G. s. saphirina*, from eastern Ecuador. The form found in south-eastern Peru, *G. s. rothschildi*, is very similar. The form found in western Ecuador and western Colombia, *G. s. purpurata*, differs more. It is darker and has the crown and nape deep blackish purple contrasting very sharply with the white forehead and it lacks the white spot on the wing. It has light red irides, grey and black bill, and reddish feet and legs.

DISTRIBUTION AND HABITAT: Colombia west of the western Andes, western Ecuador, eastern Ecuador, and the Marcapata Valley in south-eastern Peru. In all the above countries it occurs only in the tropical zone. Presumably inhabits wooded country but little recorded.

FEEDING AND GENERAL HABITS: No information.

NESTING: No information.

VOICE: No information.

DISPLAY: No information.

OTHER NAMES: Sapphire Quail Dove.

GREY-FACED QUAIL DOVE   *Geotrygon caniceps*

Columba caniceps Gundlach, Journ. Boston Soc. Nat. Hist., 6, 1852, p. 315.

DESCRIPTION: Slightly larger than a Barbary Dove but typical quail dove shape with plump compact body, longish legs and short wings and tail. Forehead greyish-white, crown, face and throat medium grey with slight iridescence on back of head. Underparts dull grey shading to near cream on centre of belly and tawny rufous on tibial and ventral regions and under tail coverts. Underwing, the basal

17—P & D

parts of the inner webs and a narrow edging on outer webs of primaries chestnut. Mantle and sides of breast deep glossy purple shading to bluish-purple on lower back, rump and upper tail coverts. Wings and tail dark grey. The female is slightly duller than the male. I have not been able to examine a juvenile but Ezra (1925), who bred this species in captivity, describes the juvenile as dark brown above, the feathers edged with reddish buff and chestnut brown on the underparts with brownish grey forehead and pale grey throat.

The above description is of the Cuban form, *G. c. caniceps.* The Dominican race, *G. caniceps leucometopsis* is darker with a richer iridescence, especially on the hind crown, and a purer white forehead.

DISTRIBUTION AND HABITAT: The tropical lowland forests of Cuba (where it is now very rare and perhaps verging on extinction) and the mountain rain forests of Dominica.

FEEDING AND GENERAL HABITS: Little or nothing recorded of its feeding habits in the wild. In captivity will eat mealworms and other insect foods – as will other ground-living pigeons.

NESTING: Nests in low undergrowth (Bond, 1960). A captive pair (Ezra, 1925) always laid one deep buff egg to a clutch but Bond states that in the wild both one and two-egg clutches occur.

VOICE: What is probably the advertising coo is described by Wetmore and Swales (1931) as 'a low hoot hoot hoot repeated with great rapidity and audible for only a few yards' which changes suddenly to 'a hollow, resonant coo' uttered in 'slow, throbbing beats often for the space of a minute, a sound that carried for a long distance . . .'.

DISPLAY: I am indebted to Dr. Nicolai for the following information on his two captive male specimens. When nest-calling the male erects his tail, twitches his wings, and then suddenly spreads them fully on either side. This is always done facing a prospective mate or rival. When displacement-preening behind the wing as an invitation to billing, the male stands in an upright posture with his back to the other bird, depresses and spreads his tail and 'preens' first to one side then the other.

An amazing convergence in behaviour towards game-birds is that the male offers food to prospective mate (or actual mate?) by picking up the morsel and letting it drop several times, whilst twitching his wings and spreading his tail. He does not utter any call as he does so but the behaviour attracts the other bird to come and eat the titbit.

OTHER NAMES: Hispaniolan Quail Dove; Grey-headed Ground Pigeon.

REFERENCES

BOND, J. 1960. *Birds of the West Indies.* p. 108.
EZRA, A. 1925. The Grey-headed Ground Pigeon (*Geotrygon caniceps*). *Avicult. Mag.* **3**: Fourth Series, 198–299.
WETMORE, A. & SWALES, B. H. 1931. The Birds of Haiti and the Dominican Republic. *U.S. Nat. Mus. Bull.* **155**: 207–209.

CRESTED QUAIL DOVE   *Geotrygon versicolor*

Columbi-Gallina versicolor Lafresnaye, Rev. Zool. 1846, p. 321.

DESCRIPTION: Rather larger than a Barbary Dove, plump and compact in build with rather larger head, in proportion, than most quail doves. Head and nape feathers form a short cap-like crest (see sketch). Forehead blackish grey shading to blue grey on crown and buffish grey on nape. Broad reddish buff malar stripe extends across face below eye, median line of throat also reddish buff. Rest of face, neck and underparts grey with intense bronzy gold, bronzy green and pink iridescence on nape and hind neck, and less iridescence on sides of neck and breast. Mantle and lesser wing coverts iridescent reddish purple shading to deep bluish purple on scapulars, lower mantle and innermost secondaries.

Primaries bright chestnut with some blackish grey on inner webs. Rest of upperparts, including tail, greenish black with slight purple iridescence. Belly and flanks purplish chestnut. Irides red. Eye-rim scarlet. Orbital skin greyish. Legs and feet pinkish. Bill black. Female usually pale and browner than male on neck and belly. Juvenile duller and with rusty edges to most feathers.

DISTRIBUTION AND HABITAT: The island of Jamaica. Inhabits forest.

FEEDING AND GENERAL HABITS: Little first hand information. Feeds and probably spends most of its time on the ground. Gosse (1847) records various seeds including castor oil nuts, and a small snail as having been eaten by specimens he dissected.

NESTING: Usual pigeon nest placed in low trees or shrubs, sometimes on ground. Two buff eggs.

VOICE: A very sad, haunting coo was given, I think as an advertising coo, by a rather sickly captive formerly in the London Zoo. So far as I can remember this was monosyllabic but I have lost my notes on it and may be wrongly remembering or the bird may only have cooed at low intensity. Bond (1960) describes the voice (advertising coo) as 'A doleful cooo-cu, the second note softer and lower in pitch'. Gosse (1847) as 'two loud notes, the first short and sharp, the second protracted and descending with a mournful cadence. At a distance the first note is inaudible and the second reiterated at measured intervals, sounds like the groans of a dying man'.

DISPLAY: No information.

OTHER NAMES: Mountain Witch; Jamaican Quail Dove.

REFERENCES

BOND, J. 1960. *Birds of the West Indies*. p. 107. London.
GOSSE, P. H. 1847. *The Birds of Jamaica*. pp. 316–320. London.

VERAGUA QUAIL DOVE   *Geotrygon veraguensis*

Geotrygon veraguensis Lawrence, Ann. Lyc. Nat. Hist. N.Y., 8, p. 349, 1867.

DESCRIPTION: About size of Barbary Dove but typical quail dove shape. Forehead greyish white, buffish white, or reddish buff shading through a narrow band of grey on the crown to dark purple or reddish purple on hind crown, nape and neck. Throat and facial stripe (see sketch) white or whitish buff, sometimes reddish buff. Centre of belly white or pale buff, flanks and under tail coverts dark reddish buff. Underwing chestnut. Rest of plumage dark olive brown, in some individuals more purplish brown. Subdued purple and greenish iridescence on neck, breast and upperparts. Irides yellow, straw-yellow or greyish white. Orbital skin purplish red. Bill black. Legs and feet reddish. Sexes alike, but females more often with buff foreheads and little or no grey on crown. The juvenile is similar to the adults but less iridescent and has rusty fringes to most feathers.

DISTRIBUTION AND HABITAT: Caribbean Costa Rica south through Panama to western Colombia and north-western Ecuador. Inhabits humid tropical forest.

FEEDING AND GENERAL HABITS: Little recorded. Wetmore (MS) notes that when disturbed they usually rise with a slight rattle of wings and fly further into the undergrowth but may merely walk aside. Remains of seeds, a berry and a beetle were found in the stomach of a shot specimen.

NESTING: No information.

VOICE: No information.

DISPLAY: No information.

REFERENCE

WETMORE, A. 1964. Manuscript for a book on the Birds of Panama.

WHITE-FACED QUAIL DOVE   *Geotrygon linearis*

Columbi-Gallina linearis Prevost, in Knip, Les Pigeons, Ed. 2, 2, 1838–43, p. 104, pl. 55.

DESCRIPTION: Rather smaller than the average Feral Pigeon and typical quail-dove shape. Forehead pinkish-buff to rufous shading to deep purplish brown on crown. A broad pale grey or bluish grey band from behind the eye passes across the nape; it is emphasised at the sides by a whitish border. Face below eye buffish white to very pale brown with the usual quail-dove pattern of a dark streak from bill to and beyond the eye and another below it from malar region to below and beyond ear coverts. Upperparts generally dark reddish brown except the mantle which is predominantly reddish purple and the dark brownish sepia primaries, the outermost of which have narrow buffish fringes. Feathers of hind neck with iridescent purple and/or bronze-green tips. Breast pale grey or brownish grey shading to purplish at sides and deep buffy fawn on belly, flanks and under tail coverts. Bill black. Irides orange, orange-red, brownish orange or yellow. Eye-ring and post-ocular area of orbital skin red, rest of orbital skin blue grey. Legs and feet red. Female similar to male but grey of breast more suffused with brown. Juvenile redder in appearance and most of its plumage barred reddish brown and blackish, but with the black facial stripes as in the adult.

The above description is of the nominate form, *G. l. linearis* of eastern Colombia. The form from Costa Rica and western Panama, *G. linearis chiriquensis*, is much redder in general colour, has the breast warm reddish buff tinged with pink, and forehead and crown bluish grey. The form from Mexico, *G. linearis albifacies*, has a whitish forehead, the facial markings absent or obsolescent, but a conspicuous neck pattern formed by the feathers at side of neck being reduced in size and having pale shiny brown, buff or pinkish tips and dark bases, giving a similar appearance to the neck feathers of the Laughing Dove, *Streptopelia senegalensis*. Several other races of this dove have been named, but they all closely resemble one or other of the forms described above.

DISTRIBUTION AND HABITAT: Southern Mexico through Central America to northern South America in northern and eastern Colombia, Venezuela, Trinidad and Tobago. Inhabits humid mountain forest.

FEEDING AND GENERAL HABITS: Little recorded. Know to feed chiefly, and probably entirely, on the ground. Dr. D. W. Snow informs me (in litt.) that in Trinidad he found it regularly visited the courts of male manakins in order to eat the berry seeds disgorged undigested by these fruit-eating birds. Usually encountered singly but this might perhaps be due to collectors having come across breeding birds whose mates were incubating or brooding.

NESTING: Dickey and van Rossem (1938) found a nest in a tangle of vines, about 20 feet high. Probably often nests lower down. Eggs creamy buff.

VOICE: Said to utter 'deep and very loud notes'.

DISPLAY: A captive bird (in London Zoo), of the race *albifacies*, when sexually excited, walked round another individual with head low, back arched, and wings folded but slightly raised. It made quick deep nods with a scooping movement of its bill, and jerked its tail up to an angle of about 85 degrees as it did so but without spreading it. During this the display feathers on the neck were very prominent with a pattern of dark creases between them.

OTHER NAMES: Brown Quail Dove; Chiriqui Quail Dove; Lined Quail Dove.

REFERENCE

DICKEY, D. R. & VAN ROSSEM, A. J. 1938. The Birds of El Salvador. *Publ. Field Mus. Nat. Hist., Zool. Ser.* **23**: 199–200.

PINK-FACED QUAIL DOVE   *Geotrygon frenata*

Columba frenata Tschudi, Arch. Nature., 9 (1), p. 386, 1843.

DESCRIPTION: Very similar to *G. linearis* with which it may be conspecific. Differs chiefly in having the forehead and face below eye and above malar stripe mauvish pink. Also slightly darker in colour, especially noticeable in the deep purple of the mantle. Three forms have been described but they differ only very slightly; chiefly in colour of crown and nape which (between them) varies from bluish grey through pinkish grey to purplish brown. In all females show less grey than males.

Some females of the Ecuadorian form, *G. frenata bourcieri*, are more dark and reddish in colour than most and were formerly considered a separate species Salvadori's Quail Dove, *Geotrygon erythropareia*.

DISTRIBUTION AND HABITAT: The subtropical zones of northern Bolivia, Peru, Ecuador and central and western Colombia. Inhabits forest.

FEEDING AND GENERAL HABITS: No information.

NESTING: No information.

VOICE: No information.

DISPLAY: No information.

OTHER NAMES: Bourcier's Quail Dove; Alamor Quail Dove; Peruvian Quail Dove.

KEY WEST QUAIL DOVE   *Geotrygon chrysia*

Geotrygon chrysia Bonaparte, Compt. Rend. Acad. Sci. Paris, 40, 1855, p. 100.

DESCRIPTION: About the size of a Barbary Dove but plumper and of the usual quail dove shape. Upperparts chestnut brown with a rich iridescence which, in most lights, is predominantly bronze green and amethyst on crown, nape and hind neck and purple, or purplish red, on mantle, back, rump and inner wing coverts. The inner secondaries and tips of the primaries are suffused with dusky olive brown.

Throat and a broad conspicuous stripe passing from the lower mandible under and beyond the eye (see sketch) white.   A deep brown area separates the lower edge of the white facial stripe from the white throat.   Sides of neck and breast mauvish pink or pinkish grey shading to near white on the belly and dusky brown on the flanks.   Under tail coverts greyish buff with white tips.   Bill brownish at tip, dull red at base.   Irides yellow, orange or red.   Orbital skin dull red.   Legs and feet pinkish or red.

The female is slightly duller than the male, her wing coverts and scapulars are predominantly olive brown. The juvenile has little or no iridescence and broad rusty fringes to most of its feathers.

DISTRIBUTION AND HABITAT: The Bahama Islands, Cuba, Isle of Pines and Hispaniola.   Has occurred on Key West, in Florida, U.S.A., hence its name.   Inhabits lowland forest and scrub usually in semi-arid country but sometimes in moist areas.   Now rare in most parts of its range.

FEEDING AND GENERAL HABITS: Feeds on the ground, usually beneath the cover of trees or shrubs but where the forest floor is itself relatively clear or in small lanes or clearings.   Takes seeds, fallen berries, insects and other invertebrates.

NESTING: Usual pigeon nest in tree or shrub, usually low down.   Sometimes nests on the ground. Two buff eggs; one egg clutches have been recorded from a captive bird although two is the usual number laid in captivity.

VOICE: The advertising coo has been described (by several authors) as a loud, resonant and protracted booming call.   The nest call is similar or identical.   Distress call a short whirring note.

DISPLAY: No information.

REFERENCES

BOND, J. W.   1960.   *Birds of the West Indies*.   London.
NAETHER, C.   1963.   Successful Nesting of the Key West Quail Dove.   *Game Bird Breeders, Pheasant Fanciers' and Aviculturists' Gazette* **12**: 6: 12–13.

BRIDLED QUAIL DOVE   *Geotrygon mystacea*

Columba mystacea Temminck, in Temminck & Knip, Les Pigeons, 1, les colombes, p. 124, pl. 56, 1811.

DESCRIPTION: Very similar to the last species (q.v.) to which it is very closely related.   Differs in being duller and darker in colour.   The upperparts are dark olive brown with chestnut on the primaries and outer tail feathers and green and purple iridescence on nape, hind neck and the upperpart of the mantle only.

DISTRIBUTION AND HABITAT: West Indies: Virgin Islands (except for Anegada and most of the smaller cays) and the Lesser Antilles from Saba and Barbuda south to St. Lucia.   Inhabits forest and woodland, usually in dry localities.

FEEDING AND GENERAL HABITS: Feeds on the ground. Known to take seeds and snails. Usually found in dark undergrowth in dense forests and woody ravines. Flight agile, zig-zagging through trees, seldom noisy in flight (Voous, 1955).

NESTING: Usual pigeon nest, usually low down in undergrowth. Clutch size said to vary, sometimes one and sometimes two buff eggs (Bond, 1960).

VOICE: Said to be like that of the Key West Quail Dove (q.v.)

DISPLAY: No information.

REFERENCES

BOND, J. 1960. *Birds of the West Indies.* London.
VOOUS, K. H. 1955. *De Vogels van de Nederlandse Antillen..* Utrecht.

VIOLACEOUS QUAIL DOVE   *Geotrygon violacea*

Columba violacea Temminck, in Knip, Les Pigeons, 1810, les colombes, p. 67, pl. 29.

DESCRIPTION: A little smaller than a Barbary Dove. Plump and compact but less so perhaps than most quail doves and with a proportionately smaller head. Forehead greyish white shading through greyish mauve on the crown to rich iridescent amethyst or reddish purple on hind neck and mantle. Rest of upperparts rich chestnut brown, more or less overlaid with amethystine, purple red or reddish violet iridescence except on the primaries, outer secondaries and outer wing coverts. Throat white. Face pale mauvish grey with only a faint suggestion of the pale stripe from the malar region running below the eye which is such a feature of most other quail doves. Breast and sides of neck pale pinkish mauve. Belly and under tail coverts white. Flanks buff. Underwing mottled white, blackish and chestnut. Irides orange brown or buff. Bill, legs and feet crimson red; these soft part colourings are based on records for only two individuals, both males.

Female duller and browner than male with much less iridescence and head and neck brownish rather than mauve or grey. Wing coverts duller, more olivaceous brown but tail coverts and tail as in male. Juvenile much as female but with dark subterminal bars and rufous fringes to most feathers.

The above description is of the nominate form *G. v. violacea* from South America. The Central American form, *G. violacea albiventer*, is slightly smaller and darker in colour, the male having the head darker and more purplish and a richer, usually more bluish purple, iridescence on the mantle. In appearance this species forms a link between the quail doves and the doves of the genus *Leptoptila* although too little is known of the behaviour of either to say whether behavioural evidence indicates this also.

DISTRIBUTION AND HABITAT: South America, in eastern Brazil and adjacent parts of Argentina, Bolivia, Paraguay, Dutch Guiana and northern Venezuela and southern Central America from Nicaragua to northern Colombia. Inhabits thick woods.

FEEDING AND GENERAL HABITS: Presumably much as other quail doves but little recorded. Said to inhabit wooded country (Pinto, 1949).

NESTING: No information.

VOICE: No information.

DISPLAY: No information.

OTHER NAMES: White-bellied Quail Dove; Violet Quail Dove.

REFERENCE

PINTO, O. 1949. Esboço monográphico dos Columbidae Brasilieros. *Arquivos Zoologia do Estado de São Paulo* **3**: Art. 3, 241–324.

RUDDY QUAIL DOVE
Geotrygon montana

Columba montana Linnaeus, Syst. Nat. 10th Ed., 1, p. 163, 1758.

DESCRIPTION: About the size of a Barbary Dove but typical quail dove shape, plump, long-legged and short-tailed. Upperparts, including wings, rich chestnut with purple-red iridescence on nape, back and sides of neck, mantle, inner wing coverts and rump. Face (below eye) pale fawn or pinkish white with two purplish chestnut stripes, one from gape below eye and one from malar region to ear coverts. Breast deep purplish pink or pinkish brown shading to warm buff on belly, flanks and under tail coverts. Small patch of pale buff feathers at side of breast adjacent to front edge of folded wings. Bill purplish red at base, dark brownish at tip. Axilliaries and under wing coverts patterned in blackish and pale chestnut. Irides yellow, buff, orange, yellowish brown or orange brown. Orbital skin, legs and feet purplish red.

There is marked sexual dimorphism. The female is olive brown with a slight greenish gloss where the male is chestnut or purplish, and bronzy buff, more or less suffused with dusky olive, where he is pink. Her feet and orbital skin are paler red than the male's.

The juveniles (which are also sexually dimorphic) are duller in ground colour than adults of same sex and have broad pale chestnut or reddish buff tips to many of the cover feathers, especially the outer wing coverts.

The above description is of the nominate form, *G. m. montana*, which is found over most of the species' wide range. The form, *G. montana martinica*, from the Lesser Antillean islands of Guadeloupe, Dominica, Martinique and St. Lucia, is somewhat larger and darker in colour. The population from St. Vincent and Grenada appear to be intermediate.

DISTRIBUTION AND HABITAT: Most of tropical America from Mexico through central America and the West Indies, Cuba, Jamaica and Trinidad, south to Peru, Bolivia and northern Paraguay. Inhabits forest, usually humid forest at low elevations, but in places up to 3,000 or 4,000 feet. Also locally in coffee and cacao plantations.

FEEDING AND GENERAL HABITS: Feeds on seeds, fallen fruits, small slugs and other invertebrates. In captivity very eager for live food, taking gentles, mealworms, small pale-coloured slugs, small snails, and earthworms readily. Usually keeps in cover of trees or undergrowth but will come out on to open paths and small open spaces. In Trinidad (and doubtless elsewhere also) regularly visits the display courts of manakins to feed on disgorged fruit seeds. Possibly also takes invetebrates attracted by the pellets or droppings of the mannakins. Perches freely but usually low down.

NESTING: Nests in tree or shrub, most often low down in undergrowth, sometimes on the ground. Usual pigeon nest but lined (? always) with leaves which are fresh or at least not completely dried when brought to nest. Two buff or buffish brown eggs. Skutch (1949), who appears to be the only person to have made a study of this species in the wild, found that unlike most other pigeons the parents left the first egg uncovered in the nest until the second was laid. This particular observation seems to have been made only for one nesting of a single pair but may represent normal behaviour. When its mate came to relieve it the incubating bird would fly off the nest when it saw its mate approaching over the ground, not waiting till it arrived at the nest as other pigeons (at least those whose behaviour is known) usually do.

The parents, again unlike the majority of pigeons whose nesting habits are known, keep the nest clean by eating the droppings of the young. They also eat the hatched eggshells instead of carrying them away. The incubation period is from ten to twelve days. Distraction display in which the bird flies from nest to ground and then 'walked . . . with wings spread and flapping loosely' (Skutch, 1949), or 'fluttering and tumbling across the floor' (Jones, 1948) has been observed in both wild and captive individuals. The young can fly at ten days old.

Nests found by Skutch, in Costa Rica, from March till August, including the months of May and June when some sympatric doves appear not to breed (Skutch, 1964).

VOICE: The scanty observations by other authors (that I have been able to find) do not in any way conflict with Jones' (1948) descriptions of the voice and display of his captive pairs. I am, therefore, quoting the latter extensively in this and the following section.

Advertising coo; 'a fairly high-pitched sad coo repeated at about ten second intervals'. Skutch, however, describes this coo, perhaps a more intense version, as a 'soft deep coo'. and Bond (1960) as 'a prolonged booming note reminiscent of the doleful sound of a fog-buoy'. When nest calling (see also under 'Display') a 'short throaty coo' precedes the wing movements and a single coo, identical with the advertising coo, follows them. The display coo is a 'single rather low coo'. The distress call is a 'series of short sharp cu-cu-cus'.

DISPLAY: In the bowing display the male flies down 'using exaggerated clapping wing beats . . . on landing with a bump a little in front of the hen, he bows to her once, beak to the ground and tail fanned out' (and erected). . . . 'This action is rather similar to the display of the Wood Pigeon, except that the bow is made only once'. This display is also given immediately after copulation.

A special display movement accompanies nest calling in both sexes. 'This begins with a short throaty coo, the wings are then raised fully stretched above the back, the bird then giving the normal sad coo. This coo-flap-coo is repeated at about twenty second intervals.'

The distraction display is described in the section on Nesting.

OTHER NAMES: Partridge Dove; Red Mountain Dove; Rufous Quail Dove.

REFERENCES

BOND, J. 1960. *Birds of the West Indies*. London.
JONES, T. 1948. The Red Mountain Dove. *Avicult. Mag.* **54**: 48–50.
SKUTCH, A. F. 1949. Life History of the Ruddy Quail Dove. *Condor* **51**: 3–19.
—— 1964. Life Histories of Central American Pigeons. *Wilson Bull.* **76**: 211–247.

BLUE-HEADED QUAIL DOVE *Starnoenas cyanocephala*

Columba cyanocephala Linnaeus, Syst. Nat., 10th Ed. 1, p. 163, 1758.–Based on 'The Turtle Dove from Jamaica' Albin, Nat. Hist. Bds, 2, p. 45, pl. 49.

DESCRIPTION: Slightly smaller than a Feral Pigeon, typical quail dove shape but with proportionately smaller head and flatter forehead than most other quail doves. Tail shortish medium length and rounded. Entire top of head a bright greyish blue or deep powder blue bordered by a black line that runs from the mouth, to and behind eye, meeting at the nape. This black stripe is set off by a white stripe that runs from below the upper mandible to the sides of the nape. Throat and lower part of face black, most feathers except those on centre of throat tipped blue. Black of throat expands into a velvety black breast bib, narrowly bordered with white. Breast immediately around and below the bib delicate pinkish purple shading to olive brown tinged with purple on sides and back of neck and mantle and buffy brown on belly. Rest of plumage dark buffish brown with an olive tinge, primaries somewhat darker. Outer tail feathers slaty grey with a slight silvery sheen. Irides dark brown. Bill greyish, dark red at base. Legs and feet purplish pink or light purplish red. Sexes apparently alike but I have seen only half a dozen specimens, most of them unsexed, and two live birds whose sex was uncertain. The juvenile is said to be like the adult but duller and with narrow rufous edgings to the feathers of the back and wing coverts.

DISTRIBUTION AND HABITAT: Cuba, has been recorded in the Isle of Pines and the Florida Keys but records doubtful. Formerly in Jamaica, presumably introduced, but now extinct there. Inhabits chiefly lowland forest and shrubbery but locally in highland forest. Appears to need areas with fairly thick overhead cover but where the forest floor is open enough for it to walk about freely. Now much rarer and less widespread than formerly owing to human persecution and destruction of its habitat by man.

FEEDING AND GENERAL HABITS: Little recorded. Feeds chiefly, probably entirely, on the ground. Said to take seeds, fallen berries and snails (Gundlach, in Bent, 1932).

NESTING: Usual pigeon nest, in tree or shrub, at low height or on the ground. Two white eggs. Sometimes only one egg per clutch (*fide* Bond, 1960).

VOICE: One call has been described as 'two hollow-sounding notes, Hu-up, the first syllable long drawn out, the second short and uttered very quickly' (Bendire, in Bent, 1932), another as a 'rapid Hup-up, rather deep, like a small fog-horn' (Bond, 1960). I noted down the display coo of a captive bird in the London Zoo as 'a low pitched, single coo'. Bendire (in Bent, 1932) also recorded a 'low muttering'.

DISPLAY: The bowing display of a captive bird (presumed male) was a fairly deep bow, given frontally and fully exhibiting the head colours. At culmination of the bow the wings jerk open a little with the primaries partly spread.

OTHER NAMES: Blue-headed Ground Pigeon; Black-bearded Dove.

REFERENCES

BENT, A. C. 1932. *Life Histories of North American Gallinaceous Birds.* *U.S. Nat. Mus. Bull.* No. 162, pp. 456–458.
BOND, J. 1960. *Birds of the West Indies.* pp. 110. London.

THE NICOBAR PIGEON

Few groups of pigeons are more distinct from all others than is this species whose relationships are quite uncertain. I think it probable that it is most closely related to *Gallicolumba* and derived from some stock ancestral both to it and to modern *Gallicolumba* species. Its alimentary tract is adapted to a diet that includes large hard seeds. It digests the stones of some fruits which are swallowed by both it and *Ducula* species, the latter digest only the pulp and void the seeds whole. It has a threat display reminiscent of those of some green pigeons. This is possibly convergence. A detailed study of the display behaviour patterns of the Nicobar Pigeon in comparison with those of *Ducula*, *Treron*, *Columba*, *Gallicolumba*, *Chalcophaps* and *Didunculus* is much to be desired.

NICOBAR PIGEON   *Caloenas nicobarica*

Caloenas nicobarica Linnaeus, Syst. Nat., Ed. 10, 1, 1758, p. 164.

DESCRIPTION: About same size as a Wood Pigeon but very differently shaped with long legs and wings, short tail and close hard plumage except on the neck. Heavy bill and rather vulture-like stance and carriage. Feathers on head very short, those on front of neck and upperpart of hind neck somewhat elongated and hairy in texture. Feathers elsewhere on hind neck elongated to form long shining hackles which hang over the mantle and shoulders when neck is retracted.

Head and the hairy upper neck feathers dark blackish grey with a silvery purple bloom like that on a ripe plum. Primaries and secondaries dark blue, glossed more or less with green and purple, inner webs blackish. Tail white. Upperparts shining dark green or dark green shot with coppery red. Underparts dark, iridescent green or green and blue as are the longest upper and under tail coverts. Irides brown, sometimes whitish. Bill and cere blackish or dark grey. Feet purplish or dark purplish red with yellow or pale brown claws. Female slightly smaller than male with less protuberant cere, hackles less exuberant, usually more coppery red gloss on mantle.

Juvenile like female but duller, neck feathers not hackled. Tail entirely blackish green. Feet blackish.

The above description is of the widely distributed nominate race, *C. n. nicobarica*. The form from the Pelew Islands, *C. n. pelewensis*, is a little smaller and somewhat more bluish in colour. Its neck hackles are shorter and some of them are bifurcated at the tip.

FIELD CHARACTERS: Short white tail and otherwise dark plumage diagnostic.

DISTRIBUTION AND HABITAT: Most of the Indo-Australasian region from the Nicobars and Mergui Archipelago eastwards to the Philippines, New Guinea and the Solomon Islands. Found throughout its range only on small wooded islands and the islets off the larger land masses. Migrates or wanders between various groups of islands.

FEEDING AND GENERAL HABITS: Feeds on seeds and fruits, probably also takes some invertebrates. So far as is known a ground feeder, but in spite of its wide range and abundance has been little studied. Flight swift and strong. In captivity it usually spends the day resting on some perch and only becomes active at dusk (Nicolai, pers. comm.). In the wild state, however, it certainly feeds by day at times, although perhaps usually in semi-gloom on the forest floor. The large eye and white tail appear to be adaptions to such activity in semi-darkness. Observations as to its times of activity in the wild are needed.

NESTING: Nests in colonies, sometimes very large, on islands. Usual pigeon nest in tree or bush. On Batty Malve, where Davison found it breeding in thousands, the nests were from ten to thirty feet above ground in thick bushy trees. Often several nests in one tree. One white egg. Nestling said to be 'devoid even of down like a newly hatched Domestic Pigeon'; an ambiguous statement.

VOICE: Whitman (1919) records a pig-like grunting given when threatening others. Heinroth (1902) a short, deep but soft cooing.

DISPLAY: Two observers have described a bowing display with most of the plumage erected, but the descriptions were not detailed. Whitman describes a threat display in which the bird erects its neck and back feathers and throws its head forward opening its bill widely and grunting as it does so. A male at a zoo, that is reacting socially to humans, usually reacts to my speaking to it by parading up and down close to my face (wire between) with slightly lowered head. The folded wings are partly spread, and lowered; the neck hackles hang straight down on either side. Sometimes it utters soft grunts. It also has a display, perhaps its equivalent of nodding, in which it bows its head quickly so that only top of head is visible at climax of movement. It looks as if bill must be upside-down and near horizontal but the hanging neck plumage make it impossible to see from side. This display is usually frontal. I can often elicit it by nodding my own head deeply.

OTHER NAMES: Hackled Pigeon; White-tailed Pigeon; Vulturine Pigeon.

REFERENCES

BAKER, E. C. S. 1913. *Indian Pigeons and Doves*. London.
HEINROTH, O. 1902. Ornithologische Ergebnisse der '1 Deutschen Sudsee Exped. von Br. Mencke'. *Journ. f. Orn.* **4**: 390–457.
NICOLAI, J. 1962. Über Regen, Sonnen- und Staubbaden bie Tauben. *Journ. f. Orn.* **103**: 125–139.
WHITMAN, C. O. 1919. *The Behaviour of Pigeons*. Posthumous works of C. O. Whitman. Vol. 3. Carnegie Inst. Washington.

THE OLD WORLD QUAIL DOVES OR GROUND DOVES

These are long-legged pigeons with plump, compact bodies and short to medium length wings and tails. They show a superficial resemblance to partridges in shape and gait. They range in size from as large as a Feral Pigeon to about a third smaller than a Barbary Dove. They tend to have pale but often strikingly patterned faces and breasts and dark, richly iridescent upperparts. Some show strong sexual dichromatism. All have the tarsus and ankle ('knee') bare. They usually have 14 tail feathers but some species have only 12 and many individuals that are otherwise 'normal' have 16 tail feathers. They are forest or cover haunting species which spend most of their time on or near the ground. They feed on seeds, berries, young shoots and invertebrate animals. Judging from their behaviour and dietary needs in captivity it is probable that they take more animal food than do most other pigeons.

They fall into two main groups. The first consists of the bleeding-hearts of the Philippines, characterised by having a patch of red or orange highly modified feathers on the breast, the smaller and less ornamented Golden-heart *Gallicolumba rufigula* of New Guinea, and the Celebes Quail Dove *G. tristigmata*. All these are geographical representatives of the same stock; the bleeding-hearts can certainly be considered members of a superspecies, the Golden-heart is very closely related to them. The Celebes Quail Dove is a very distinctive species. If its unique specific features are discounted, its colour pattern is, however, closest to that of the Bleeding-hearts to which it is evidently most closely allied.

The second main group comprises those forms that were put in a separate genus, *Terricolumba*, by Hachisuka. They show rich purplish iridescence at least on the carpal area of the wing and usually more extensively on wings and mantle and have the throat and breast pale in colour and sharply demarcated from the rest of the plumage; this demarcated 'breast shield' being, however, reddish brown and less sharply demarcated in the females of the sexually dichromatic species. They are also said to differ from the bleeding-heart group in never crouching with lowered head and raised tail when alarmed (Gifford, 1941) as the other Old World quail doves and many other pigons do.

The White-breasted Ground Dove *Gallicolumba jobiensis*, The Truk Island Ground Dove *G. kubaryi*, the Society Islands Ground Dove *G. erythroptera* and the White-throated Ground Dove *G. xanthonura* all agree closely in plumage characters, except in so far as some show sexual dichromatism. The Friendly Ground Dove *G. stairi* and the Santa Cruz Ground Dove *G. sanctaecrucis* should I think be included in the same superspecies with them. These last two appear, from their plumage characters, to stand a little further apart from *jobiensis* than the others. This suggests that *erythroptera* probably represents a separate invasion from the New Guinea area rather than colonisation of the Society Islands via Tonga or Samoa. The extinct *Gallicolumba* (?) *norfolciensis* appears to have been a member of this group.

The very distinct Marquesas Ground Dove, *G. rubescens*, is intermediate in size and coloration (if its specific white markings are discounted) between the *jobiensis* superspecies and the Grey-breasted Ground Dove *G. beccarii*. I do not, however, agree with Hachisuka (1931) when he implies that it is most closely related to *beccarii*. I think that it probably results from an early colonisation of the Marquesas by some form ancestral to both *jobiensis* and *beccarii*. Such an ancestral quail dove may also have populated the other groups of islands but become extinct there as a result of competition with the later invaders of *jobiensis* stock. In this connection it is noteworthy that most islands or archipelagoes support only one species of *Gallicolumba*; only New Guinea and some adjacent archipelagoes supporting more than one species. The Grey-breasted Ground Dove is closely related to the Palau Ground Dove *G. canifrons* which is clearly its geographical representative. The Thick-billed Ground Dove *G. salamonis* is known only from two specimens (Mayr, 1945) of unknown sex. It is possibly the geographical representative of *jobiensis* stock and, if so, most closely related to *sanctaecrucis* and *stairi*. The Wetar Ground Dove *G. hoedtii* differs from the others in its strongly attenuated first primary. Its grey head is reminiscent of *canifrons* but on the whole its characters suggest to me that it probably is an early derivative of *jobiensis* stock. Although at first glance it looks very different from typical *jobiensis* yet *stairi* is intermediate between them in the degree to which it has developed chestnut on the wing quills and become more restricted in its purple iridescence.

It seems probable that this group of pigeons represent an early offshoot from the same stock as produced the emerald doves (q.v.) and their relatives. Their geographical distribution, colour patterns, and some aspects of their behaviour point, though admittedly far from conclusively, to such an affinity. Whether they are directly related to the American quail doves, which they closely resemble in form and in some aspects of behaviour, is uncertain. I think it more likely, however, in view of differences in colour pattern, that the New World and Old World quail doves have evolved independently (although from related stocks) and that where they resemble each other closely this is due to convergent adaption to a similar way of life.

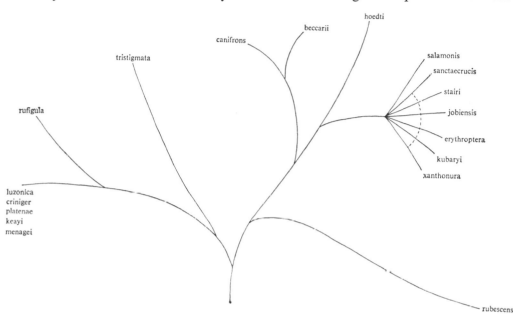

FIG. D.11: Presumed relationships of species in the genus *Gallicolumba*. The bleeding-hearts, superspecies *luzonica*, are listed together to indicate their extremely close relationship with each other.

REFERENCES

GIFFORD, E. W. 1941. Taxonomy and Habits of Pigeons. *Auk* **58**: 239–245.
HACHISUKA, HON. M. 1931. Notes sur les oiseaux des Philippines. *L'Oiseau Nouv. Ser.* **1**: 23–29.
MAYR, E. 1945. *Birds of the southwest Pacific*. New York.

LUZON BLEEDING-HEART   *Gallicolumba luzonica*

Columba luzonica Scopoli, Del. Flor. et Faun. Insubr., fasc. 2, 1786, p. 94.

DESCRIPTION: This is the most striking of all the bleeding-hearts since its breast markings appear just like a deep still-bleeding wound. Indeed, many people unfamiliar with the species think – when they first see a live specimen – that it has just been deeply gashed in the breast.

About the size of a small Feral Pigeon but typical quail dove shape and stance (see sketch). Forehead and wing coverts light blue-grey, the latter with dark red-brown markings that form three bars across the closed wing. Crown, nape, sides of breast, mantle, back and rump dark greyish but with broad iridescent fringes to the feathers so that all the upperparts usually appear a beautiful amethystine purple or, in some lights, bronzy-green. Primaries, secondaries and central tail feathers dark dull brown. Underwing largely chestnut. Outer tail feathers blue-grey with blackish subterminal bands. Throat, breast and underparts white tinged with pale pink below the breast patch and more deeply pinkish-red immediately adjacent to it. Longitudinal patch of blood-red feathers of hairy texture in centre of breast. In life the feathers of this red patch usually form a groove or indentation between the surrounding 'blood-stained' white plumage, thus enhancing the wound-like appearance. Sexes alike.

Irides greyish violet. Orbital skin grey. Bill blackish, grey at base. Legs and feet red. I have not seen a juvenile of this species but it would almost certainly be very similar to the juvenile of *G. criniger* (q.v.).

DISTRIBUTION AND HABITAT: The Philippine Islands of Luzon and Polillo. Inhabits forests.

FEEDING AND GENERAL HABITS: Feeds and spends much of its time on the ground. Feeds on seeds, fallen berries and probably a good many insects or other invertebrates since it cannot thrive without such fare (or its equivalent) in captivity. Roosts in shrubs and trees. When flushed usually flies only a short distance then alights and runs farther away.

NESTING: Probably nests in bushes, vines or trees at no great height as some of its relatives are known to do. Said to lay two eggs to a clutch, unlike the closely related *G. criniger* (Delacour, 1964).

VOICE: The advertising coo is a low-pitched but clear and very mournful-sounding 'cōooō or cōo' ōo', varying somewhat in loudness and intensity. The display coo is quite different, a hurried almost gruff 'crōo-cŏŏ-cŏŏ-cŏŏ-cŏŏ'. The above is based, however, on observations extending over many years, of a single captive male at the London Zoo.

DISPLAY: In the equivalent of the bowing display the male runs rapidly after the bird to be displayed at then suddenly stops, depresses his tail and throws his breast upwards so that the vivid 'blood mark' is fully presented frontally. Then he bows his head forward to its usual position, or a little below, uttering the display coo as he does so. When nest-calling rapidly shivers one or both wings (according to position of bird eliciting nest-calling) and raises them, still folded to horizontal plane thus exhibiting the barred pattern. These wing movements also used by both sexes in other situations.

OTHER NAMES: Luzon Punalada; Luzon Blood-breasted Pigeon.

REFERENCES

DELACOUR, J. 1964. Bartlett's Bleeding-heart Pigeon. *Letter in Avicult. Mag.* 70: 118.
MCGREGOR, R. C. 1909. *A Manual of Philippine Birds.* Pt. 1. Manila.

BARTLETT'S BLEEDING-HEART   *Gallicolumba criniger*

Pampusanna criniger Pucheran, Voy. Pole Sud. Zool., 3, 1853, Mamm. et Ois, p. 118.

DESCRIPTION: General colour pattern similar to that of the Luzon Bleeding-heart but differing as follows: Forehead darker grey. Iridescence on head, neck and mantle predominantly bronze-green in most lights. Back, inner wing coverts, secondaries and central tail feathers chestnut. Breast patch larger and composed of very harsh 'hairy' feathers of deep blood red.   Lower breast (below the red patch) deep reddish buff shading to creamy-buff on belly.   Irides brown.   Bill blackish.   Feet red.

Juvenile predominantly reddish brown with no blue grey at all in plumage.   Wing coverts barred buff and dark brown instead of blue grey and chestnut.

DISTRIBUTION AND HABITAT: The Philippine Islands of Mindanao, Leyte, Samar and Basilan.   Inhabits forest.

FEEDING AND GENERAL HABITS: Very little recorded of wild birds.   Apparently not known to differ from *luzonica* (q.v.).

NESTING: Presumably as *luzonica*.   Newman, who bred this species in captivity, found that his pair laid one cream coloured egg to a clutch.

VOICE: The display coo was described as a 'rumbling coo' by Newman (1909).   The display coo of the female was like that of the male but less loud.

DISPLAY: Newman describes a display in which the cock turns in the direction of the hen, stands quite still and at regular intervals of a few seconds, slowly raises his wings to their fullest extent.   This display might be continued for a considerable time and was only done when the hen was in sight.

The equivalent of the bowing-display, as described by Newman, appears identical with that of *luzonica*. It was usually preceded by the male 'lowering his head and arching his wings so . . . the bars became very conspicuous'.   Pursuit of the female and the 'bowing display' commonly followed this wing arching posture.   Newman saw less intense versions of this display, without any preliminary wing arching, from a female.

OTHER NAMES: Bartlett's Blood-breasted Pigeon; Bartlett's Punalada; Hair-breasted Pigeon; Hair-breasted Bleeding-heart.

REFERENCES

NEWMAN, T. H.   1909.   Bartlett's Bleeding-heart Pigeon.   *Avicult Mag.*, new series, 7: 225–234.

MINDORO BLEEDING-HEART   *Gallicolumba platenae*

Phlegoenas platenae Salvadori, Cat. Birds Brit. Mus., 21, 1893 (in Key), 588

DESCRIPTION: General colour-pattern much like that of the Luzon Bleeding-heart but differs as follows: Forehead dark grey.   Upperparts a rich dark chestnut, vividly glossed with reddish purple (bronze-green in some lights) on mantle and back.   Area of pale grey, dark-spotted feathers near bend of wing and triangular pale grey marks at tips of some median wing coverts.   Breast patch much smaller and orange in colour.   White of underparts tinged cream on breast and greyish on flanks.   No blood-stained appearance.   Upper tail coverts and tail a bluer grey, contrasting with the chestnut rump.

I have not seen a juvenile of this species.   It probably bears the same relation in colour to the adult as the juvenile of *criniger* (q.v.).

DISTRIBUTION AND HABITAT: Philippine Island of Mindoro. Inhabits forest.

FEEDING AND GENERAL HABITS: Little recorded. As *luzonica* so far as known.

NESTING: Usual pigeon nest in tree or shrub from three to six feet above ground. Two pale cream coloured eggs.

VOICE: No information.

DISPLAY: Distraction display has been seen in a female flushed from a nest where she was brooding two young (Bourns & Worcester, in McGregor, 1909).

OTHER NAME: Mindoro Punalada.

REFERENCES

HACHISUKA, HON. M. 1932. *The Birds of the Philippine Islands*. Vol. 1. London.
McGREGOR, R. C. 1909. *A Manual of Philippine Birds*, Pt. 1. Manila.

NEGROS BLEEDING-HEART   *Gallicolumba keayi*

Phlogoenas keayi Eagle Clarke, Ibis, 1900, p. 359, pl. 8.

DESCRIPTION: Very similar to the Mindoro Bleeding-heart in general colour pattern, differing from it as follows: Crown, nape, upper part of mantle, sides of neck and innermost lesser wing coverts iridescent green. Grey colour on wing even paler and forming a single greyish-white band across the folded wing. Upper tail coverts and central tail feathers chestnut like the back. Breast patch larger (but smaller than that of *luzonica*) and blood red.

DISTRIBUTION AND HABITAT: The Philippine Island of Negros. Inhabits forests and woodland. Said to have been common in the last century but believed rare now.

FEEDING AND GENERAL HABITS: No information.

NESTING: No information.

VOICE: No information.

DISPLAY: No information.

OTHER NAMES: Keay's Bleeding-heart; Negros Blood-breasted Pigeon; Negros Punalada.

TAWI-TAWI BLEEDING-HEART   *Gallicolumba menagei*

Phlogoenas menagei Bourns and Worcs. Occ. Papers Minnesota Acad. Nat. Sci., 1, No. 1, 1894, p. 10.

DESCRIPTION: I have not seen a specimen of this rare and beautiful species.   From descriptions it appears rather similarly marked to *criniger* but with the iridescent green of the neck spreading almost completely across the breast and enclosing a bright orange breast patch below which the underparts are greyish white.   Irides silver grey,   Bill black at base, dark grey at tip.

DISTRIBUTION AND HABITAT: The Philippine Island of Tawi-Tawi.

FEEDING AND GENERAL HABITS: No information.

NESTING: No information.

VOICE: No information.

DISPLAY: No information.

OTHER NAME: Tawi-Tawi Punalada.

GOLDEN-HEART   *Gallicolumba rufigula*

Peristera rufigula Pucheran, Voy. Pôle Sud. Zool., 3, 1853, Mamm et Ois., p. 118.

DESCRIPTION: Slightly larger than a Barbary Dove but typical quail dove shape.   Forehead bright rusty-buff or light rufous.   Band above and behind eye bluish grey.   Face pinkish fawn.   Upperparts and sides of breast rich reddish brown or chestnut, strongly washed with purplish pink on neck, sides of breast and upper mantle. Wing coverts broadly tipped with pale mauvish grey so that closed wings show a barred grey and chestnut pattern. Primaries dusky drab, outer webs dull rufous. Axilliaries and underwing coverts boldly patterned black and white (broad white tips to black feathers). Throat and underparts white, central area of breast light pinkish gold, golden yellow or creamy gold and feathers of this part hairier in texture. This creamy gold colour also tinges the lower breast and belly to a greater or lesser extent and fades greatly in old skins. Flanks and under tail coverts reddish buff. Central tail feathers purplish chestnut, outer ones grey with broad chestnut and black central band.

Irides purplish or purplish red with pale purplish inner ring, dark reddish brown or red. Orbital skin dark purplish or red. Bill dark purplish, purplish grey or reddish brown with lighter tip. Legs and feet dark purplish red, dark red or (one only) bright red. Sexes alike but female averages a little paler on breast and forehead. Juvenile with rusty fawn tips to most cover feathers, especially noticeable on wing coverts and underparts. Central region of breast reddish brown.

The above description is of the nominate form *G. r. rufigula* from western New Guinea and the western Papuan Islands. *G. r. alaris* from southern New Guinea lacks the grey markings on the head, the corresponding areas being pinkish brown. *G. r. helviventris* from the Aru Islands is like *alaris* but has the grey bands on the wings suffused with purplish and so less conspicuous. Other races have been described all of which closely resemble one or other of those described above.

DISTRIBUTION AND HABITAT: New Guinea, the western Papuan Islands of Misol, Salawati and Waigeu and the Aru Islands. Inhabits lowland and hill forest up to 1,600 metres.

FEEDING AND GENERAL HABITS: Little recorded. Feeds and spends much time on ground.

NESTING: Three nests found (Rand, 1942) were from three to seven feet above ground in dark shady forest. One on a 'shelf-like platform provided by a "birds nest" fern', one on a flat palm frond and one on several crossed pandanus leaves. Two of the nests were of flat dead leaves, one also had some twigs. One creamy white egg.

VOICE: No information.

DISPLAY: Gifford (1941) says that 'part of the courtship' consists of raising both wings high above the back but gives no further details. He implies that the bowing display is the same as in the bleeding-hearts.

OTHER NAMES: Chestnut Quail Dove; Rufous Quail Dove; Rufous Ground Dove; Yellow and Brown Quail Dove.

REFERENCES

GIFFORD, E. W. 1941. Taxonomy and habits of Pigeons. *Auk* **58**: 239–245.
RAND, A. L. 1942. Results of the Archbold Exped. No. 42. *Bull. Amer. Mus. Novit.* **79**: 289–366 (306).

CELEBES QUAIL DOVE — *Gallicolumba tristigmata*

Columba tristigmata Bonaparte, Compt. Rend. Acad. Sci. Paris, 40, 1855, p. 207.

DESCRIPTION: About the size of a Feral Pigeon but typical quail dove shape (see sketch). Forehead bright golden, crown of head grey, feathers tipped with bronze green. Broad deep purple half-collar on back of neck. Face pale grey shading to whitish grey on throat, and slightly darker grey suffused with greenish gold on breast and sides of neck. Lower breast pale creamy golden shading to near white on belly and under tail coverts. Flanks and sides of body buffish drab. Hind neck, mantle and upper back olive brown with a strong reddish-mauve or, in some lights, pinkish-green or bronze-green iridescence. Rest of upperparts warm olive brown shading to a reddish brown on wing coverts and outer secondaries. Primaries darker brown. Underwing coverts patched white and brown. Irides brown or dark brown. Feet purplish red or red. Bill dark purplish grey.

Female slightly less bright than male.   The juvenile is mainly brownish with rusty edges to feathers, rusty cream where adult is whitish or golden.   Neck band dull purplish brown.

The above description is of the nominate race, *Gallicolumba t. tristigmata*, from northern Celebes. The forms found in central and southern Celebes, *G. t. auripectus* and *G. t. bimaculata*, differ in being whiter on throat, having a paler gold forehead and brighter golden on the breast, and in having a purple patch on either side of the neck instead of a continuous band across the back of the neck.

DISTRIBUTION AND HABITAT: Celebes.   Inhabits primeval forest from sea-levels to high elevations but nowhere numerous.

FEEDING AND GENERAL HABITS: Little known, most of the information available being owed to Heinrich (in Stresemann, 1941).   He found it 'a true ground bird'.   When flushed by a human being flies only a short distance then alights and runs further.   Feeds on seeds of trees picked up on the ground. Presumably also on other foods.

NESTING: No information.

VOICE: Heinrich records a repeated 'oocoocoocoocoocoo' like the call of a Hoopoe, but deeper and less loud.

DISPLAY: No information.

REFERENCE

STRESEMANN, E. 1941. Die Vögel von Celebes. *Journ. f. Orn.* **89**: 1–102.

WHITE-BREASTED GROUND PIGEON   *Gallicolumba jobiensis*

Phlogoenas jobiensis A. B. Meyer, Mitt. Zool. Mus. Dresden Heft 1, 1875, p. 10.

DESCRIPTION: Somewhat smaller than a Barbary Dove and of typical quail dove shape with plump compact body, short tail and long legs with bare ankle ('knee').   Head and face greyish black with a broad conspicuous white stripe extending from base of upper mandible over and behind eye.   Throat and breast white, sometimes showing a faint creamy tinge in fresh plumage.   Hind neck, sides of neck and area bordering sides of white 'breast shield', mantle, scapulars and wing coverts – except the outermost greater coverts, predominantly a vivid dark purple.   Rest of upperparts and basal parts of the purple feathers slaty black with a faint greenish gloss on back, rump and inner secondaries.   Tail feathers slaty black the outer ones with grey tips.   Underparts below breast shield very dark slate grey.   Irides dark brown.   Bill black.   Feet and legs dark purplish red.

Female differs from the male in having the white breast suffused with pinkish grey or buffish pink.   The purple tips to the feathers of back and wing coverts tend to be less extensive than in the male so that the purple areas may appear more or less mottled with greenish black.   Her underparts, except for the dark area bordering the breast shield, are of a paler slate grey.   I have seen a few specimens said to be females that were of typical male colour but I suspect these may have been wrongly sexed by the collector.

Juvenile dark brownish grey with rufous fringes to most feathers, these often being wide enough to give the bird a predominantly rufous appearance.   In its first moult the juvenile usually grows whitish grey (male), or dull grey (female) feathers on the throat and breast.   These would appear to be retained for only a short time as most juveniles that have nearly completed their first moult already have some fully adult (white or cream) feathers on the lower breast.   In some juveniles the majority of breast feathers first grown are white.   Probably the difference is due to the age at which moulting begins, but observations on live birds are needed to discover the facts.

The above description applies to the nominate form, *G. j. jobiensis*, from New Guinea, Bismarck Archipelago and adjacent islands.   The form found in the Solomon Islands, *G. j. chalconota* differs in having a slightly heavier bill and the purple on the upperparts confined to a band across the upper parts of the mantle and the lesser wing coverts.

DISTRIBUTION AND HABITAT: New Guinea, the Bismark Archipelago, Jobi, Dampier, Vulcan and Goodenough Islands and the Solomon Islands of Vella Lavella and Guadalcanal.   Inhabits forest.

FEEDING AND GENERAL HABITS: Little recorded.   A captive pair which bred in an aviary were said by their owner to spend much time perched and little on the ground.   However, a single captive bird I watched on many occasions in the London Zoo spent much time walking about the floor of its enclosure.

NESTING: In captivity builds the usual pigeon nest above ground and lays two eggs.

VOICE: A grunting call has been recorded from captive birds (Bright, 1922) and also a call sounding 'like a small claxon horn' (Stokes, 1924).

DISPLAY: No information.

OTHER NAMES: Jobi Island Dove; White-breasted Ground Dove; Purple Ground Dove.

REFERENCES

BRIGHT, H. 1922. Notes on Breeding the White-breasted Ground Pigeon. *Avicult. Mag.* Third Series, **13**: 168–170.
STOKES, H. S. 1924. Some Winter Notes. *Avicult. Mag.* Fourth Series, **2**: 159–163.

TRUK ISLAND GROUND DOVE   *Gallicolumba kubaryi*

Phlogoenas Kubaryi Finsch, Journ. F. Orn. 28, 1880, p. 292.

DESCRIPTION: Very similar to the male of the last species (*Gallicolumba jobiensis*), but slightly larger and with appreciably longer legs and bill. Chiefly differs from *jobiensis* in colour by having the forehead white, the purple on the upperparts and wing coverts of a redder and less vivid hue, the underparts below the white breast shield dark grey, nearly black and dark grey bases to the outer tail feathers. The sexes are practically alike, but the female is a little paler (due to tawny feather tips) on the underparts. Juvenile like that of *jobiensis* but with wider and brighter golden rufous fringes and lighter more olivaceous bases to the feathers.

DISTRIBUTION AND HABITAT: Eastern Caroline Islands, in the Ruk and Ponapé Island groups. Inhabits wooded areas. Has been recorded (by different observers) both in forest and in fairly open country (Baker, 1951).

FEEDING AND GENERAL HABITS: Little recorded. At least on Ponapé a ground feeder. Known to take small snails, seeds and worms (Baker, 1951).

NESTING: Little information. Has been said to nest on top of tree ferns and lay one egg.

VOICE: Said to have a deep moaning coo also a whistling call.

DISPLAY: No information.

OTHER NAMES: White-breasted Ground Dove; White-fronted Ground Dove; Purple Ground Dove; Ponapé Ground Dove; Caroline Islands Ground Dove.

REFERENCE

BAKER, R. H. 1951. The Avifauna of Micronesia, its evolution and distribution. Univ. Kansas Publ. Mus. Nat. Hist.
    3: 1–359.
MAYR, E. 1945. *Birds of the southwest Pacific.* New York.

SOCIETY ISLANDS GROUND DOVE   *Gallicolumba erythroptera*

Columba erythroptera Gmelin, Syst. Nat., 1, Pt. 2, 1789, p. 775.

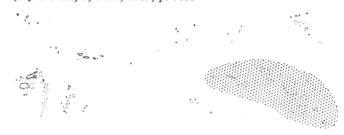

DESCRIPTION: The male is very similar indeed to the male of the preceding species, differing in colour only in having the grey of the head and underparts not so dark and blackish in tone, the central area of the mantle dark olive grey with slight purple and green iridescence, the grey of the outer tail coverts lighter, and the purple on the hind neck and wing coverts more apt to fade or bleach to a dull chestnut red. The female differs greatly in colour being of a general bright reddish brown strongly tinged with reddish purple on crown, neck and wing coverts, and more or less dark olive on mantle, back, rump and innermost wing-coverts. Her wing quills are blackish olive edged tawny, and the grey areas of her tail strongly tinged with rufous. The breast shield – although not very clearly demarcated – is usually of a paler reddish brown than the rest of the underparts. The head markings of the male are also slightly indicated in the female. Her plumage is very apt to fade and bleach with wear, the brown parts becoming (in extreme cases) pale fawn, and the olive areas pale dust grey. In such worn specimens the breast shield and head markings are more clearly demarcated. Worn birds in moult have a spotted or mottled appearance. On Hiti Island some (perhaps all) males have all-white heads.

Juvenile much like that of the preceding species.

DISTRIBUTION AND HABITAT: The Society and Taumotu Islands. Inhabits forest.

FEEDING AND GENERAL HABITS: No information.

NESTING: No information.

VOICE: No information.

DISPLAY: No information.

OTHER NAMES: Taumotu Islands Ground Dove; White-breasted Ground Dove.

WHITE-THROATED DOVE   *Gallicolumba xanthonura*

Columba xanthonura 'Cuv', Temminck, Pl. Col. Livr., 32, 1823, Pl. 190.

DESCRIPTION: Slightly larger than a Barbary Dove and of plumper and more compact shape with shorter tail and longer legs. Crown of head, nape, hind neck, and a small adjacent area just below and behind eye pale pinkish rufous. Rest of head, neck and breast shield white with a strong salmon-pink suffusion except along extreme border of breast shield. In worn, bleached plumage the entire head and breast may be almost pure white. In some males, which judging from moulting juveniles (q.v.) are those in their first year, the pale pinkish rufous areas are replaced by dark grey, more or less intermixed with rufous, and the forehead and throat and upper breast are pinkish buff rather than off white. A band of rich purple runs from the sides of the breast in front of the wings across the upper part of the mantle dividing the pale hind neck from the dark bronzy olive or bronzy purple-brown of the upperparts. Lesser wing coverts predominantly rich purple and the median wing coverts broadly tipped with the same colour. The purple may fade to light tawny red in very bleached plumage. Wing quills and underwing blackish. Underparts below breast shield greyish black, feathers mostly fringed dull rufous. Central tail feathers very dark brownish grey with ill-defined broad black tips, outer ones dark grey with broad black subterminal bands. Irides brown. Orbital skin yellowish white. Bill black or dark brownish. Legs and feet purplish red.

Female predominantly tawny brown below and olivaceous above. Forehead and crown golden brown to dark rufous. Neck and underparts tawny brown, the feathers having greyish bases and rufous or tawny tips, the depth of the two shades varying individually so that some (but not most) females appear more grey-brown than tawny. Mantle, back, rump and wing coverts bronzy olive green with tawny-rufous fringes to the feathers. Central tail feathers dull reddish brown suffused with olive and with an ill-defined dark subterminal band. Outer tail feathers rufous with black subterminal bands. Irides grey or brown. Orbital skin grey. Legs purplish red. Male-plumaged females occur, but, apparently, rarely. The only such specimen I have seen, No. 332263, in the collection of the American Museum of Natural History, had well developed eggs in its ovary when it was killed so there is no doubt of its sex. In colour it resembles the darker headed type of male (see above), but is a little more suffused with rufous on the breast shield and not quite so dark on the underparts. Juvenile female like female (brown and green type) but with much broader and more conspicuous tawny rufous feather fringes. Juvenile male with darker bases to feathers and with even broader and richer rufous tips to feathers than in the young female. Young of both sexes, but especially the juvenile male, appear predominantly bright rufous in colour. The young male in his first moult begins to grow dark grey feathers on forehead and crown and greyish feathers on throat and breast. These appear to be shed very soon and replaced with full adult plumage. Specimens still partly in the rufous juvenile plumage have, for example, a mixture of juvenile, grey and new growing pinkish-white feathers on the breast shield.

DISTRIBUTION AND HABITAT: Marianas Islands and Yap Island. Inhabits forest but often seen in flight high over valleys and ridges.

FEEDING AND GENERAL HABITS: Unlike most *Gallicolumba*, Marshall (1949) found this species strictly arboreal. Feeds in trees on fruits, berries and seeds. Often perches on ferns in freshwater marshes to sun itself but does not feed there. Usually in pairs, females keep more to cover than do males which perch conspicuously and often fly long distances in the open. Flight very slow and laboured in appearance with vigorous deep wing strokes and body inclined upwards as if fighting a strong headwind.

NESTING: Recorded nesting in high trees, in January, February, March and May (Baker, 1951).

VOICE: The advertising coo is a low, deep moaning 'Ooo' uttered at intervals of ten to twelve seconds. What is probably the excitement cry or its equivalent is a long snarling call.

DISPLAY: No information.

OTHER NAMES: White-throated Ground Dove; White-throated Quail Dove; Marianas Quail Dove; Yap Quail Dove, White-breasted Quail Dove.

REFERENCES

BAKER, R. H. 1951. The Avifauna of Micronesia, its origin, evolution and distribution. *Univ. Kansas Publ. Mus. Nat. Hist.* 3: 1–359 (206).
MARSHALL, J. T. JNR. 1949. The Endemic Avifauna of Saipan, Tinian, Guam and Palau. *Condor* 51: 200–221.

NORFOLK ISLAND DOVE   *Gallicolumba (?) norfolciensis*

Columba norfolciensis Latham, Index Orn., Suppl., 1801, p. 60.

There seems abundant evidence (Hindwood, 1965) that a dove formerly existed on Norfolk Island. From the description of its coloration (q.v.) I think it was, in all probability, a *Gallicolumba*, very similar in appearance to *G. xanthonura* and showing similar sexual dimorphism.   It is, however, possible that the bird described as the female was, in fact, an Emerald Dove *Chalcophaps indica*, even though no mention is made of the rump markings which are a conspicuous feature of *Chalcophaps*.

DESCRIPTION: Length 14 inches.   Head, neck and breast white.   Underparts below the breast black. Back and wings dusky purple with a few darker markings.   Tail dull purple with inner webs of the feathers dusky.   Bill black; legs red.   Female dusky purple with green back and reddish brown head, neck and breast.   The above description is taken from Latham.   There is, however, a picture by John Hunter of the 'Dove of Norfolk Island' which (*fide* Hindwood, 1965) has the head, neck and breast white, the rest of the plumage a deep warm brown with a purple patch on the shoulder of the wing.   Whether this represents the same species and the discrepancy is due to different plumage phases or individual variation or whether it represents another species, closer in coloration to *G. stairi*, is uncertain.

DISTRIBUTION: Norfolk Island; now extinct.

REFERENCES

HINDWOOD, K. A.   1965.   John Hunter: A Naturalist and Artist of the First Fleet.   *Emu* 65: 83–95.
LATHAM, J.   1801.   *Supplementum Indicis Ornithologici*: 60.
——— 1801a.   *General Synopsis of Birds, Supplement*. 2: 374.

FRIENDLY QUAIL DOVE   *Gallicolumba stairi*

Caloenas (Phlegoenas) Stairi, G. R. Gray, Proc. Zool. Soc. London, 1856, p. 7, pl. 115.

DESCRIPTION: About the size of a Barbary Dove or a little larger, but typical quail dove shape.   Forehead, face, sides of neck and upper breast deep mauvish grey, vinous pink or pinkish rufous shading through cream to near white along the borders of the breast shield.   The feathers just behind the white border are tipped with purple thus forming a dark iridescent border to the white one.   Crown and nape grey, more or less overlaid with bronze-green iridescence, shading into brownish green on hind neck. Upperparts dark slightly reddish brown with a purple or bronze-green lustre.   Inner and median wing coverts broadly tipped with rich purple or reddish purple.   Primaries dark olive brown narrowly edged with yellowish brown.   Underwing mainly chestnut.   Central tail feathers dark brown, outer ones dull

grey edged brown on outer webs and with broad blackish subterminal bars and brownish tips.   Underparts below breast shield dark olive brown.   Irides brown.   Bill black.   Legs and feet red.

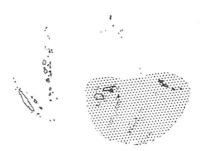

Females, at least in the Fiji Islands where the species has been most collected, are dimorphic. Some
resemble males except for having little or no grey on the outer tail feathers.   The other colour phase
of female has a reddish brown head, light reddish brown or tawny neck and breast and mantle, back
and wings olive brown with a subdued but beautiful bronzy-green lustre.   The juveniles of males
and male-like females are a general reddish brown above, most of the feathers having ill-defined blackish
brown bases and broad rufous edges.   Breast shield dull pinkish-rufous shading to dingy cream near its
lower border.   Rest of underparts rusty brown.   The juvenile of the brown phase female has the breast
shield only slightly paler and redder than the rest of the underparts.

DISTRIBUTION AND HABITAT: Fiji, Tonga and Samoan Islands.

FEEDING AND GENERAL HABITS: No information.

NESTING: A clutch of two white eggs was laid by a captive pair kept by the Rev. S. J. Whitmee
(1875).

VOICE: No information.

DISPLAY: No information.

OTHER NAMES: Friendly Ground Dove; Purple-shouldered Quail Dove; Samoan Quail Dove;
Tongan Quail Dove; Fiji Quail Dove.

REFERENCES

WHITMEE, S. J.   1875.   List of Samoan Birds, with Notes on their Habits.   *Ibis*, Third Series, **5**: 436–447.

SANTA CRUZ GROUND DOVE   *Gallicolumba sanctaecrucis*

Gallicolumba sanctaecrucis Mayr, Am. Mus. Novit., No. 820, 1935, p. 1.

DESCRIPTION: Smaller than the last species (*G. stairi*) to which it is very closely allied, being smaller
than a Barbary Dove though of the more plump and compact quail dove outline.   Face, sides of neck
and forehead pale grey shading into dull brown on the crown and nape and pinkish cream on the breast;

posterior border of breast shield white.   Upperparts dark olive brown, most feathers broadly tipped with slightly iridescent reddish purple.   Feathers at sides of neck bordering breast shield and lesser wing coverts predominantly bright pure purple.   Tail feathers purplish brown with greyer basal areas, dark subterminal band and lighter tips only very faintly indicated on the outer tail feathers.   Underparts below breast shield and underwing blackish brown.   Irides brown.   Bill black.   Feet and legs purplish red or red.

Female has the head and neck deep rufous shading to a paler and brighter hue on the breast.   Underparts below breast shield light drab brown.   Mantle, back, rump, wing coverts and central tail feathers dark olive with a bronze-green gloss.   Outer tail feathers dull rufous with ill-defined blackish subterminal bars.   I have not seen a juvenile of this species.   It is probably very similar to that of *G. stairi* (q.v.).

DISTRIBUTION AND HABITAT: The islands of Tinakula and Utupua in the Santa Cruz Archipelago and Espiritu Santo in the New Hebrides.

FEEDING AND GENERAL HABITS: No information.

NESTING: No information.

VOICE: No information.

DISPLAY: No information.

OTHER NAMES: Santa Cruz Ground Pigeon; Santa Cruz Quail Dove.

REFERENCE

MAYR, E.   1945.   *Birds of the southwest Pacific.*   New York.

TANNA GROUND DOVE   *Gallicolumba ferruginea*

Columba ferruginea Wagler (nec. Forster), Isis, 1829, p. 738.

DESCRIPTION: Very similar to the two previous species and sometimes considered to be referable to *stairi*, a mistake having been made as to the place of origin of the described specimens (see Peters, 1937). It seems more likely, however (Stresemann, 1950), that a species of *Gallicolumba* did formerly inhabit Tanna Island.

DISTRIBUTION AND HABITAT: Tanna Island, now extinct.

FEEDING AND GENERAL HABITS: No information.

NESTING: No information.

VOICE: No information.

DISPLAY: No infromation.

REFERENCES

LYSAGHT, A. 1959. *Some Eighteenth-century Bird Paintings in the Library of Sir Joseph Banks* (1743–1820).
PETERS, J. L. 1937. *Checklist of Birds of the World*, **3**: 136.
SALVADORI, T. 1893. *Catalogue of the Columbae or Pigeons in the Collection of the British Museum*: 605.
STRESEMANN, E. 1950. Birds collected during Capt. James Cook's last expedition. (1776–1780). *Auk* **67**: 66–88.

THICK-BILLED GROUND DOVE
Gallicolumba salamonis

Phlogoenas salamonis Ramsay, Proc. Linn. Soc. New South Wales, 7, p. 299 (1882).

DESCRIPTION: Apparently very similar to *G. stairi* but has thicker bill with more deeply curved culmen. General colour above, dark reddish brown with purple iridescence, especially on the mantle and wing coverts. Head chocolate, paler on face. Breast 'shield' light reddish brown, small purple patch at each side of breast, rest of underparts dark reddish brown. I have not seen this rare dove which is known only from two specimens of unknown sex.

DISTRIBUTION AND HABITAT: The Solomon Islands of Ramos and San Cristobal. Presumably in woodland.

FEEDING AND GENERAL HABITS: No information.

NESTING: No information.

VOICE: No information.

DISPLAY: No information.

MARQUESAS GROUND DOVE
Gallicolumba rubescens

Columba rubescens Vieillot, Nouv. Dict. Hist. Nat., 26, 1818, p. 346.

DESCRIPTION :   About a quarter smaller than a Barbary Dove.   Plump and compact but tends to hold itself in a hunched posture with wings somewhat drooped.   Head, neck, throat and breast light to medium ash grey, rarely pale whitish grey.   In the lighter examples a trace of the head markings of related species is shown by the areas of the head and face that are dark in them being of a distinctly darker grey.   Back and sides of hind neck, lesser wing coverts, and parts of the median wing coverts, rich purple, fading to dull reddish chestnut when worn.   Rest of plumage greenish black above and dull black below.   Basal half (rather more in specimens with pale grey breasts) of primaries and tail feathers white so that when spread the wings and tail show large white areas.   Irides brown.   Bill black.   Legs and feet purplish black or reddish black.

Female like male but grey of head and breast usually darker and suffused with brown.   Very pale females are, however, paler than most males.

Juvenile duller and browner with rust-brown fringes to most feathers.   The back, wings and head have such broad rufous fringes that they appear predominantly reddish brown.   Very little white in wings and none on tail feathers (as a rule) which are grey at the base.

DISTRIBUTION AND HABITAT :   The Marquesas Islands of Fatuhuku and Hatutu.   Presumably frequents forest or brush, but little seems to have been recorded about it in the wild although large numbers of specimens have been collected.

FEEDING AND GENERAL HABITS :   The only observations on its habits that I have been able to find were made by E. W. Gifford (1925) who kept and successfully bred this species in captivity in California.   He found them to be ground feeders, readily taking and thriving on a diet of seeds and mealworms.   They were very like rails or game-birds in their general deportment, and much more constantly active than captive doves usually are.   They were constantly digging in the soil and turning over dead leaves and other débris, using the bill only, of course.   The wings were often carried in a somewhat drooped posture, if the birds were at ease and not alarmed.   They would jump for a seeding grass head, seize and pull it down with the bill, then hold it under one foot while plucking the seeds from the ear.   If one got any thread or fibre entangled around its foot it did not just struggle along as best it could (as other doves do) but would pause quietly, inspect its toes and, if possible, pull off the fibre with its bill.   It would be most interesting to know if any (or all) of the other Old World quail doves share the above habits.   They were fond of sun bathing and bathing in rain or the fine spray from a hose, but never bathed in a pool or dish of water.

NESTING :   In captivity the usual type of pigeon nest is made in the usual way.   Two white eggs per clutch.   Incubation thirteen to fifteen days.

VOICE :   Gifford records the only call he (apparently) heard from his birds was an 'undove-like rasping snarling sound . . . given very infrequently, and then either in paying addresses to the female or another male' . . . Females coo, but apparently rarely.   The young squeak when begging for food, like other pigeons.

DISPLAY: When about to fight (? in conflict between aggression and fear) the bird pecks at the ground or at food.   Usual defensive threat posture with far wing raised and near one used to strike the opponent Adults do not press home attacks on juveniles but caress them, usually roughly, instead.

Gifford's statement that 'there is no spreading of the wing or tail for display as in the bronzewing doves, but the plumage of the neck is somewhat distended', suggests that the species has a bowing display, although he does not describe it.

Copulation preceded by caressing, displacement preening and billing.   Billing may be interspersed several times by both male and female 'parading back and forth'.

OTHER NAMES: Grey-hooded Quail Dove, Grey-hooded Ground Dove; Marquesan Quail Dove.

REFERENCES

GIFFORD, E. W.   1925.   The Gray-hooded Quail Dove (*Gallicolumba rubescens*) of the Marquesas Islands, in captivity. *Auk* **XLII**: 388–396.

GREY-BREASTED QUAIL DOVE   *Gallicolumba beccarii*

Chalcophaps beccarii Salvadori, Ann. Mus. Civ. Genova, 7, 1875 (1876), p. 974.

DESCRIPTION: About half the size of a Barbary Dove, with the typical plump compact quail dove shape (see sketch).   Forehead and area above and behind eyes darkish blue-grey shading into dark iridescent greenish on crown and nape and pale grey on breast, lower breast and posterior edge of breast shield greyish white.   Feathers bordering breast shield tipped purple at sides and blackish purple on lower breast.   Rest of underparts blackish grey to dark drab.   Hind neck, upperparts, median and greater wing coverts and inner secondaries dark olive green with a bronze-green gloss.   Lesser wing coverts dark purple.   Primaries and outer secondaries black.   Central tail feathers as back, outer ones dark grey with ill-defined black subterminal bands and brownish tips.   Underwing blackish grey with slight suffusion of chestnut.   Irides brown, orbital skin grey.   Bill black.   Feet and legs purplish red. The female lacks the purple on wings and sides of breast.   The grey of her head and neck is suffused with brown, the white and grey breast shield of the male is represented by a light yellowish rufous area, the rest of the underparts are pale drab.   Juvenile like the female but duller and browner and with rufous fringes to feathers on wings and breast and, to a slight extent, elsewhere.

The above description is of the nominate form, *G. b. beccarii*, from New Guinea.   *G. b. johannae* from Dampier Island in the Bismark Archipelago is slightly larger, its brown parts are a little lighter and more reddish and the upperparts of the male are glossed with bronzy purple or red-purple as well as – or instead of – bronzy green.   *G. b. admiralitatis*, of the Admiralty Islands is like *G. b. johannae*, but has head entirely blue-grey and the blue-grey of breast shield shades into white only at median part of border, its female has a fairly clearly demarcated dark grey breast shield.   The populations from Nissan Island have been considered referable to this form but the males are paler and the females have very clearly defined breast shields.   A few other races have been described which all very closely resemble one or other of those described above.

DISTRIBUTION AND HABITAT :   Mountains of New Guinea, Admiralty Islands, Dampier Island, Solomon Islands and Rennell Island.   Inhabits mountain forest in New Guinea and doubtless elsewhere as well.

FEEDING AND GENERAL HABITS :   Little recorded.   Keeps to dense cover on or near ground.   When flushed rises quickly, flies a short distance and then dives to the ground again.

NESTING :   Usual pigeon nest.   Said always to nest low down.   The only definite description I have found is of a nest found in New Britain by Eichhorn on 7th March 1925.   This was built on a rotten log and contained one egg only.

VOICE :   No information.

DISPLAY :   No information.

OTHER NAMES :   Grey-throated Ground Dove ; Quail Dove.

REFERENCES
EICHHORN. 1925. Data on a slip referring to an egg collected ; in British Museum (Natural History), London.
MEYER, P. O. 1933. Vogeleier und Nester aus Neubritannien, Sudsee. *Beiträge zur Fortpflanzungsbiologie der Vögel* 9 : 122–135.

PELEW GROUND DOVE   *Gallicolumba canifrons*

Phlegoenas canifrons Hartlaub and Finsch, Proc. Zool. Soc. London, 1872, p. 101.

DESCRIPTION :   About a third smaller than a Barbary Dove, typical quail dove shape.   Throat whitish. Forehead, face and sides of neck pale bluish grey shading to dark bluish grey on the crown and whitish grey tinged with pink on centre of upper breast, the pink tinge increasing on lower breast but becoming white at posterior edge of the 'breast shield'. Rest of underparts dark greyish brown tinged with rufous, blackish brown immediately adjacent to 'breast shield'. Nape (slightly crested), hind neck and sides of lower neck chestnut. Lesser wing coverts and small adjacent patch at side of breast rich purple. Primaries chestnut but dusky brown at tip and on outer webs where visible when wing is folded. Central tail feathers purplish brown, outer ones with blackish purple central areas and rufous tips. Rest of upperparts bronzy olive with narrow rufous fringes to most feathers. Irides dark brown; orbital skin bright pink or pinkish red. Bill black. Legs and feet bright pink or pinkish red.

Sexes apparently alike. I have, however, only seen one male and one (presumed) female specimen of which the latter was more rufous on the underparts and less pink on the breast. I have not seen a juvenile or a description of one.

DISTRIBUTION AND HABITAT: The Pelew (Palau) Islands. Marshall (1949) found that it inhabits only woodland growing on rocky ridges.

FEEDING AND GENERAL HABITS: Known to take berry seeds. Feeds on the ground particularly on accumulations of soil and leaf mould on flat rocks, bottoms of ravines and similar places. Walks swiftly and gracefully. When flushed leaps from the ground with a loud wing clap, flies very swiftly for a short distance then alights and hides behind a tree trunk for a few minutes. The advertising coo is given from a fixed song perch about ten feet above ground and screened by vines. Each male can be found daily at its song post (Marshall, 1949).

NESTING: No information.

VOICE: The advertising coo is 'a series of seven or eight gentle coo's each with an upward "questioning" inflection, and very soft' (Marshall, 1949).

DISPLAY: No information.

OTHER NAMES: Palau Ground Dove; Grey-fronted Ground Dove.

REFERENCE

MARSHALL, J. T. JNR. 1949. The Endemic Avifauna of Saipan, Tinian, Guam and Palau. *Condor* **51**: 200–221.

WETAR ISLAND GROUND DOVE *Gallicolumba hoedtii*

Leptotila Hoedtii Schlegal, Nederl. Tijdschr. Dierk., 4, 1871, p. 30.

DESCRIPTION: A little smaller than a Feral Pigeon, similar proportions to other quail doves. Outer primary strongly attenuated, next four emarginated on outer web. Head light bluish grey shading to greyish white on throat. Hind neck reddish brown shading through pale rufous on sides of neck to cream or reddish cream on breast. A band of shining purple or bluish purple borders the breast on either side and there is a patch of same colour on the 'shoulder' of the wing. Underparts below the breast shield dark brownish grey to dull black.   Upperparts chestnut except for the purple patch on the wing and the tip and parts of outer webs of primaries which are blackish drab.   Central tail feathers dark reddish brown; outer ones brownish grey with ill-defined dark subterminal bar.   Underwing chestnut.   Underside of the tail blackish.   Irides blackish brown.   Bill black.   Legs and feet reddish purple.

Female has head, neck and breast a light rusty chestnut.   Upperparts and belly a rather reddish-tinged olive brown.   Tail feathers chestnut with only trace of a subterminal bar on inner webs.   I have not seen a juvenile specimen.   The above descriptions are based on only a very few specimens so that confirmation, especially of the soft part colours, is desirable.

DISTRIBUTION AND HABITAT :   Wetar Island, north of Timor.

FEEDING AND GENERAL HABITS :   No information.

NESTING :   No information.

VOICE :   No information.

DISPLAY :   No information.

THE THICK-BILLED GROUND PIGEON

This large ground-living pigeon is very distinct.   Its shape, colour-pattern and distribution all suggest that it may form a connecting link between the Old World quail doves *Gallicolumba* and the Solomon Island Crowned Pigeon *Microgoura*.   That this form, in some respects intermediate between *Gallicolumba* and *Microgoura*, exists, heightens the likelihood of such more aberrant forms as *Didunculus*, *Goura* and *Otidiphaps* being, as I think they are, offshoots of this group.

In its colour pattern *Trugon* shows most resemblance to *Microgoura* although the black and white underwing pattern closely resembles that of some *Gallicolumba* species.   To a less extent some parts of the colour pattern are suggestive of those of the Wonga Pigeon but this seems likely to be due to convergence rather than to any very close affinity.

THICK-BILLED GROUND PIGEON   *Trugon terrestris*

Trugon terrestris G. R. Gray, 1849, Genera Birds, 3, appr., p. 24.

DESCRIPTION :   About size of Feral Pigeon but gamebird-like in general shape with rather short, rounded wings with stiff, arched and rather narrow primaries, a wedge-shaped tail of 12 (sometimes 14) feathers which in life is carried in 'roofed' or arched shape like a fowl's, and long, bare legs.   Forehead dull pinkish white shading to dark bluish grey on crown and nape.   Throat and ear coverts buffish white, divided by a broad pale bluish grey malar stripe.   A band of short, unusually small, blackish feathers extend from below the cheeks around the back of the neck, no doubt making the longer nape feathers appear as a peak or crest when neck is at all stretched.   Rest of neck, breast and mantle dark bluish grey.   Innermost lesser wing coverts dull purplish chestnut, rest of wing dull grey with some chestnut tinge on coverts and pale chestnut edges to outer webs of primaries and outer secondaries.   Rest of upperparts, including tail, dull dark grey, slightly bluish but much less so than breast and mantle.   Underwing coverts and axilliaries mottled black and buffish white.   Belly creamy white in centre shading through warm reddish buff to pale chestnut on flanks and outer webs of under tail coverts.   Irides orange or red; orbital skin dark grey.   Bill flesh-coloured to pinkish white at tip, dark grey at base.   Legs and feet flesh pink. Sexes alike.   I have not seen a juvenile.

The above description is of the most widespread race *Trugon terrestris leucopareia* from southern and south-eastern New Guinea. *T. terrestris mayri* from northern New Guinea has the pale parts of the face grey rather than whitish, paler belly and flanks and only a slight tinge of chestnut on the wing coverts. Nominate *T. t. terrestris* from north-western New Guinea is like *T. t. leucopareia* but has the wing coverts entirely grey.

DISTRIBUTION AND HABITAT: New Guinea and the adjacent island of Salawati. Inhabits lowland forest.

FEEDING AND GENERAL HABITS: Presumably feeds on ground but I can find nothing recorded of its feeding habits. Always found on the ground. Rand (1938) noted that it would flush within a few yards and fly for some distance with a 'whirring, grouse-like flight' before alighting again on the ground. Grant (1915) also recorded that it was never seen in trees.

NESTING: Three nests described by Rand (1938) were all on the ground against a buttressed tree in the angle between two buttresses. Each consisted of a substantial platform of twigs, on top of and at the back of which was the nest proper which was flat, consisted of rootlets with a few bits of moss and leaves. One white egg. These nests were found in June, July and October.

VOICE: Apparently unrecorded.

DISPLAY: No information.

OTHER NAMES: Slaty Ground Pigeon; Grey Ground Pigeon.

REFERENCES

GRANT, W. R. O. 1915. Report on the Birds collected by the British Ornithologists' Union Expedition and the Wollaston Expedition in Dutch New Guinea. *Ibis*, Jubilee suppl. No. 2. p. 315.
MAYR, E. 1941. List of New Guinea Birds. *Amer. Mus. Nat. Hist.*
RAND, A. L. 1938. Results of the Archbold Expedition, No. 19. *Amer. Mus. Novit.* No. 990.

SOLOMON ISLAND CROWNED PIGEON   *Microgoura meeki*

Microgoura meeki Rothschild, Bull, Brit. Orn. Cl., 14, 1904, 77.

This is one of the most distinct of pigeons, and appears to be a connecting link between larger crowned pigeons of the genus *Goura* and *Trugon*.

DESCRIPTION: About the size of a Wood Pigeon but with longer legs and shorter wings and tail.

Forehead and face black; skin of face behind the black area reddish and very sparsely feathered. Top of head, including the hairy-looking crest, neck, breast and mantle dark bluish grey, shading to brown on the lower back. Wings and rump olive brown. Tail very dark brown glossed with purple. Underparts buffish chestnut. Bill with black upper mandible and red lower mandible. Gallinule-like frontal shield pale whitish blue. Irides brown. Legs purplish red. Sexual differences (if any) and juvenile plumage not known.

DISTRIBUTION AND HABITAT: Choiseul, Solomon Islands. Not found since 1904.

FEEDING AND GENERAL HABITS: No information.

NESTING: Said to lay one cream-coloured egg on the ground with no nest material (Meek, 1913).

VOICE: No information.

DISPLAY: No information.

REFERENCE

MEEK, A. S. 1913. *A Naturalist in Cannibal Land.* London.
PARKER, S. A. 1957. Bull, B.O.C. (*in press*).

PHEASANT PIGEONS

The pheasant pigeons form a very distinct group of forms which are probably best considered as races of a single polytypic species. They have several anatomical peculiarities (Glenny and Amadon 1955) including a greatly reduced furcula, relatively small and very rounded wings and large fowl-like tail of 20 or 22 feathers.

They are highly adapted to a terrestrial or nearly terrestrial life and in appearance and movements appear at first sight to be some extremely elegant fowl or pheasant until we get a good view of the dainty and very typically pigeon-like head.

Their relationships are quite obscure. Whether they have any very close affinities with *Goura* and *Microgoura* is an open question. In life they look very different from the heavy, clumsy looking *Goura* except in so far as both suggest some sort (but a very different sort) of galliform bird. In their colour pattern they are slightly suggestive of some species of *Gallicolumba* and still more like the equally aberrant Tooth-billed Pigeon *Didunculus* but the resemblances, even in the latter case, are certainly not sufficient to rule out the possibilities of convergence. It is, however, probable that both they and *Didunculus* are very divergent offshoots of *Gallicolumba* or 'Protogallicolumba' stock.

The breeding behaviour, as recorded from captive individuals, appears to be unusual in that the cock feeds the brooding hen during the first week of the nestling's life.   It seems unlikely that this can be an incorrect or imaginative observation as the other details of breeding biology recorded (Black, 1930) are such as are normal or frequent in many other species.   Further observations on behaviour are, however, highly desirable.

PHEASANT PIGEON   *Otidiphaps nobilis*

Otidiphaps nobilis Gould, 1870, Ann. Mag. Nat. Hist. (4) 5, p. 62.

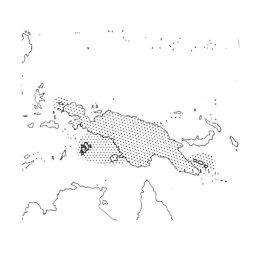

DESCRIPTION: About a third larger than a Wood Pigeon, in fact nearly as large as a smallish domestic fowl.   Very suggestive of a fowl or pheasant in general appearance except for its typical pigeon head. Body plump and compact, wings short and rounded, the large tail is, in life, laterally compressed like that of a fowl (*Gallus*) or kaleege pheasant (*Lophura, Gennaeus*).   Long, slender legs, slender neck and small head give it a most elegant appearance.   Head with short nuchal crest black, glossed green and blue.   Breast and underparts blackish richly glossed purple or purple and blue except on belly where gloss tends to be less intense and more greenish.   Nape and upper part of hind neck iridescent green or (in some lights) amethyst.   Immediately behind this is a patch of deep golden bronze, more or less shot with pink and purple.   Mantle and back iridescent reddish purple shading to chestnut on outer wing coverts and secondaries.   Underwing dull black.   Lower back dark purple shading to dark purplish blue on the upper tail coverts.   Tail black with slight greenish gloss.   Irides orange or orange-red; orbital skin red.   Bill bright red, sometimes orange at tip.   Legs and feet red or purple at tarsal joint and down side of leg, frontal plates of leg yellow or salmon coloured.   Feet black or red suffused with black.

Sexes alike.   Juvenile with extremely woolly-textured plumage, greyish black where adult is purplish black and dark rufous on mantle and wings, and with the hairy, black pale tipped down feathers being retained for a long time on ends of the juvenile feathers.   The above description is of the nominate form *O. n. nobilis* (Bronze-naped or Green-naped Pheasant Pigeon) from western New Guinea.   The form from the Aru Islands, *O. nobilis aruensis* (White-naped Pheasant Pigeon), has little or no nuchal crest, the iridescence on the breast often more greenish and the nape and hind neck silvery white in striking contrast to the black head and purplish red mantle.   (See pl. 1).   *O. nobilis cervicalis* (Grey-naped Pheasant Pigeon) from south-eastern New Guinea resembles *O. n. aruensis* but has the neck patch pale grey and a bronze area immediately behind it, and its lower back and rump are, in most lights, dark green or bluish green rather than purple or blue.   The form from Fergusson Island, *O. nobilis insularis*, has the mantle and wings chestnut without any purple gloss and its greenish lower back contrasts somewhat with its dark purple rump and upper tail coverts.   The nuchal crest is absent or at least barely noticeable in the white-naped form *aruensis* and, so far as can be judged from two skins, in the other island form, *insularis* also.

DISTRIBUTION AND HABITAT :   New Guinea, Batanta and Waigeu Islands, the Aru Islands and Fergusson Island.   Inhabits hill and mountain forest.

FEEDING AND GENERAL HABITS :   Little recorded in a wild state.   Evidently feeds and lives on the forest floor, rising with a loud clatter of wings when flushed (Mayr and Rand, 1937).   I noticed that a captive of the white-naped form, in the London Zoo, jerked its tail up and down in the same way as does a Golden Pheasant *Chrysolophus pictus*.   As with the pheasant this appeared to be a flight-intention movement and was done most intensly when the bird appeared somewhat alarmed.

NESTING :   I can find no account of this species' nesting habits in the wild.   The following information is taken from an article written by an aviculturist in California who was, apparently, very successful in breeding the nominate form in captivity (Black, 1930).   A low nest site was chosen.   Usual pigeon nest. One bright cream-coloured egg.   Incubation period normally 23 to 26 days.   (It is claimed that female squabs take 26 days, males only 23 days!) but up to 29 days in adverse weather.   Incubation by both sexes for usual periods but female taking over from male for about half an hour at mid-day also.   When the egg is hatching both sexes sit on the nest together with bills together and heads lowered close to the nest.   For the first week after hatching the male feeds the female on the nest and she feeds the squab. After this period the two parents brood in turn (as during incubation) both, presumably, feeding the young.

VOICE :   What is probably the advertising coo has been described (Grant in Ogilvie-Grant, 1915) as 'a sort of moaning coo' that 'can be heard at a great distance'.

DISPLAY :   No information.

OTHER NAMES :   Green-naped Pheasant Pigeon ; Bronze-naped Pheasant Pigeon ; Green-collared Pigeon ; Bronze-collared Pigeon (*O. n. nobilis*) ; Grey-naped Pheasant Pigeon ; Grey-collared Pigeon (*O. n. cervicalis*) ; White-naped Pheasant Pigeon (*O. n. aruensis*).

REFERENCES

BLACK, A. R. 1930. Breeding the Green-naped Pheasant Pigeon in California. *Avicult. Mag.* 8. Fourth Series **6** : 158–160.
GLENNY, F. H. & AMADON, D. 1955. Remarks on the Pigeon *Otidiphaps nobilis* Gould. *Auk* **72** : 199–203.
    GRANT, C. H. B. in OGILVIE-GRANT, W. R. 1915. *Ibis*, Jubillee Supplement, No. 2, p. 316.
MAYR, E. & RAND, A. L. 1937. Results Archbold Expeditions 14. Birds 1933–34 Papuan Expedition. *Bull. Amer. Mus. Nat. Hist.* **73** : 43.

THE CROWNED PIGEONS

The crowned pigeons or gouras form a very distinct group with several anatomical peculiarities besides their great size and generally fowl-like appearance.   They have no oil gland or gall bladder, reticulated scaling on their strong thick legs and 16 tail feathers.   Their most visually striking features are their large erect laterally compressed fan-shaped crests.   The crest feathers have long and separated barbs (except near the feather tips in one species) which give them an attractive lace-like appearance.

In their behaviour they do not differ significantly from other forest dwelling and largely ground living pigeons.   Like the green pigeons of the genus *Treron* they show an up and down movement of the tail, instead of the more usual wing twitching, in agonistic and sexual situations. Their coloration is predominantly blue and purplish red with a contrasting patch of white or pale grey on the wing. There is some inverse correlation between development of crest and wing patch, the species with the most highly ornamental crest, *G. victoria*, being the one with the least strongly contrasting wing patch.

The three forms of crowned pigeon all inhabit New Guinea. They are very closely related and although their distribution is mainly allopatric two of them, *G. victoria* and *G. cristata*, meet and hybridise in the Siriwo River region of north-western New Guinea. On present evidence it must be largely a matter of opinion whether they should be treated as members of a superspecies or as very well marked races of one species. The former course has been taken in most recent systematic lists and is certainly the more convenient so I shall follow it here.

The Solomon Island Crowned Pigeon *Microgoura meeki* may form a link between the genera *Goura* and *Trugon*. It is, however, a very distinct form with no very close relatives.

Blue Crowned Pigeon   *Goura cristata*

Goura cristata Pallas, 1764, in Vroeg's Cat., Adumbr., p. 2.

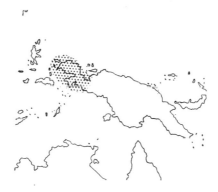

DESCRIPTION: About size of a large Domestic Fowl (Chicken) or small hen Turkey, heavily built with rather long and stout legs and large laterally-compressed crest of lacy feathers. Broad, rounded wings and medium-length round-ended tail. General coloration a medium to dark greyish blue. Crest a paler blue-grey with a silvery or creamy tinge. Wings and tail a rather darker and more slaty tint then elsewhere, the tail with a paler greyish blue teminal bar. Upper part of mantle and most wing coverts dark purplish red or dark wine red. White patch on wing formed by white, purple-tipped outer greater coverts. Area around base of bill, lores and a broad stripe extending around and behind eye black. This species is much subject to partial melanism, and individuals with varying and often extensive areas of black, especially on the head, upper tail coverts and ventral regions, are common.

Irides red, bill black, legs and feet dark red. Sexes alike. Juvenile like adult but white wing patch suffused cream and grey and wine-red of wings replaced by chestnut. The above description is of the nominate form. *G. cristata minor*, from the Western Papuan Islands, shows no noticeable difference but seems even more prone to melanism than the nominate form.

DISTRIBUTION AND HABITAT: North-western New Guinea eastward to the Etna Bay in the south and to the Siriwo River in the north. Also the Western Papuan Islands of Misol, Salawati, Batanta and Waigeu. Inhabits lowland forest including marshy and partly flooded areas.

FEEDING AND GENERAL HABITS: Spends most of its active time on the ground but perches on large branches of trees and flies up into trees when alarmed. Known to feed on fallen fruits; probably takes other food such as seeds and molluscs.

NESTING: Nests above ground in sites comparable, when allowance is made for bird's size and weight, with those chosen by other tree-nesting pigeons. Nest tends to be proportionately larger and more compact than most pigeon's nests. One white egg. Incubation period (in captivity in Europe) 28 to 29 days and young leaves nest at 30 to 36 days but is fed by its father for some time after, until 56 days old in one instance (Johst, 1961). Both sexes incubate in the same way as with other pigeons.

VOICE: The display coo is a deep booming Ŏŏhmp-ŏŏhmp. It is loud but has a very deep and muffled tone, suggestive, to my ears at least, of a ship's foghorn, or the 'drumming' of an Emu. When I first heard this call, from a captive bird only a yard from me in a Zoo, I thought it must have come from some much larger animal at a distance away. Johst, however, describes the display coo of a captive male as 'a long drawn buuuuuuh' which, from his account (Johst, 1961) was also used in aggressive contests and as the advertising coo. It is uncertain how much this difference is due to differences of individuality or intensity in the calling birds or in our interpretations of them. Heinroth (1903) describes a deep grumbling conversational note and 'a very loud call like that made by the Papuans on their drums'.

DISPLAY: I saw the bowing display of this species many times but only from one captive bird, presumably a male. In it the bird spread and erected its tail, partly opened its wings and bowed its head quickly forward into an inverted position. The spread tail was slightly twisted to one side towards the bird displayed at and the inverted head also, at least sometimes, slightly tilted so as to show it to full advantage. After displaying, without response from its companion, it usually displacement-preened behind one wing in the typical pigeon manner. In the pre-copulatory display of a captive pair (Johst, 1961) the male combined the bowing display with 'dancing' on the ground with upstretched wings. The female responded by also lifting high her spread wings and running around the male or running beside him with slightly bent legs, holding her bill close to his and uttering short, harsh, hissing calls. This usually continued for some time then the female solicited in a somewhat crouched posture, the male ran once or twice round her and then mounted and copulated.

In aggressive as well as defensive threat display, one or both wings are raised and the tail jerked up and down. This movement appears to be the equivalent of the similar and probably homologous tail movements of the green pigeons *Treron* and the wing-twitching of other pigeons.

OTHER NAMES: Common Crowned Pigeon; Grey Crowned Pigeon; Blue Goura; Grey Goura.

REFERENCES

HEINROTH, O. 1903. Ornithologische Ergebnisse der '1. Deutschen Sudsee Exped. von Br. Mencke'. *Journ. f. Orn* **4**: 65–125.

JOHST, G. & E. 1961. Über Verhalten und Brutpflege Gekäfigter Krontauben (*Goura cristata*). *Journ. f. Orn.* **102**: 88–195.

SETH-SMITH, D. 1931. The Breeding of the Crowned Pigeon. *Avicult. Mag.* **9**: Fourth Series, 20–21.

MAROON-BREASTED CROWNED PIGEON   *Goura scheepmakeri*

Goura scheepmakeri Finsch, 1876, (1 Apr.) Proc. Zool. Soc. London (1875), p. 631, pl. 68.

DESCRIPTION: Like the previous species, *Goura cristata*, but crest feathers even longer and more lacy. The nominate form *G. s. scheepmakeri*, from south-eastern New Guinea from Hall Sound to Orangerie Bay, differs in colour from the Blue Crowned Pigeon (q.v.) in having the breast (below the neck) and belly dark purplish red, the mantle and lesser wing coverts dark greyish blue like the rest of the upperparts and the wing patch very pale whitish grey. The form found in southern New Guinea from the Mimika River to the Fly River has a white wing patch, purplish red lesser and median wing coverts and the purplish of the breast shading into grey blue on the lower breast and belly. Irides deep red. Bill dark bluish grey.

Legs and feet purplish red. Sexes alike. The juvenile differs from the adult in the same way as in the previous species. Also prone to partial melanism.

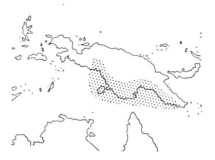

DISTRIBUTION AND HABITAT: Southern and south-eastern New Guinea. Inhabits both dry and flooded forests.

FEEDING AND GENERAL HABITS: Known to eat small crabs (Grant, 1915) as well as berries and fruits. Habits, at least such as so far recorded, as previous species. Flight strong, straight and heavy when crossing rivers.

NESTING: Five nests found by Rand (1942) were in typical situations, allowing for size of bird, in trees at heights varying from 12 to 50 feet. The nests were (for pigeons) solid and compact but small, made of sticks, stems, palm leaves and tendrils. One white egg.

VOICE: Unrecorded?

DISPLAY: Probably similar to or identical with that of previous species. I once saw, from a distance, two captive birds dashing around the floor of their enclosure frequently lifting both wings high over the back and holding them so while running about. When I got near their excitement had subsided but both birds were jerking their tails up and down a little. This tail movement was intensified, in both birds, whenever one approached the other. It appeared homologous with the tail movements of *Treron*.

OTHER NAMES: Scheepmaker's Crowned Pigeon; Sclater's Crowned Pigeon.

REFERENCES

GRANT, C. H. B. in OGILVIE-GRANT, W. R. 1915. Report on the Birds collected by the British Ornithologists' Union Expedition and the Woollaston Expedition in Dutch New Guinea. *Ibis*, Jubilee Supplement No. 2, pp. 316–318.
RAND, A. L. 1942. Results of the Archbold Expedition No 42. *Bull. Amer. Mus. Nat. Hist.* LXXIX, Art. IV, pp. 289–366 (307).

VICTORIA CROWNED PIGEON   *Goura victoria*

Lophyrus victoria Fraser, 1844, Proc. Zool. Soc. London, p. 136.

DESCRIPTION: Very similar to the other crowned pigeons but the crest feathers have the barbs at their ends only slightly separated. These normal areas on the otherwise loose and lacy feathers are dark blue tipped broadly with white and make this species' crest even more striking and beautiful than those of its congenors. General coloration dark greyish blue. Breast dark purplish red. Wing patch pale greyish blue, edged dark purple. Irides red or purplish red. Bill dark grey. Legs and feet purplish red. Sexes alike. Juvenile duller, purple parts more brownish and feathers of pale wing patch with dull grey, not purple tips. Prone to melanism.

The above description is of the form *G. victoria beccarii* from northern New Guinea. *G. v. victoria* from Japan (Jobi) Island is slightly smaller and slightly darker in colour.

DISTRIBUTION AND HABITAT: Northern New Guinea from the Siriwo River to Astrolabe Bay; Collingwood Bay between Holnicote Bay and Mount Maneao. Also Japen (Jobi) Island and Biak Island where it may have been introduced. Inhabits forest.

FEEDING AND GENERAL HABITS: Little recorded of the species in a wild state; presumably much as other crowned pigeons. In captivity will eat sliced fruit, grapes, lettuce, maize, carrots, peanuts and is especially fond of the fruits of the wild fig *Ficus macrophylla* (Fleay, 1961).

NESTING: Probably as other *Goura* species in the wild. In captivity (Fleay, 1931) lays one white egg. Incubation period, for one egg in Queensland, Australia, 30 days. Young fledged at four weeks old when it could fly well although only about a quarter the bulk of the adult. It was fed by the parents until 13 weeks old.

VOICE: What appears to be the advertising coo is described by Fleay (op. cit.) as 'prolonged, lugubrious "moos" like someone blowing strongly over the top of an empty milk bottle'. The display coo he describes as a 'booming "Boom-Pa! Boom-Pa! Boom-Pa!" ' He also describes a 'rumbling' threat call and a 'soft but penetrating' alarm call.

DISPLAY: From Fleay's description the bowing display appears to be identical to that which I saw from the Blue Crowned Pigeon (q.v.). The up and down tail movement would appear also to be used by the begging juvenile and, perhaps, by adults as a flight-intention movement even in non-agonistic situations. Fleay records the female as sometimes 'working her beak' when the male approached her to take over on the nest. He considered this an indication that feeding of the female by the male occurs but it seems to me more likely that this bill movement is shown, like the similar bill movement of *Ducula* and *Treron*, in agonistic situations equivalent to those in which 'nodding' is shown by such pigeons as the *Columba* species.

OTHER NAMES: White-tipped Crowned Pigeon; Victoria Goura; White-tipped Goura.

REFERENCE

FLEAY, D. 1961. Gouras of New Guinea. *Animal Kingdom LXIV*: 4: 106–110. New York.

THE TOOTH-BILLED PIGEON

The Tooth-billed Pigeon takes its generic name *Dididuncucus* indicates, from its unique and some-what dodo-like bill. Its affinities are obscure but it seems most likely to be a relative of *Gallicolumba* and the various aberrant forms, such as *Trugon* and *Otidiphaps* that are, probably, also related to *Gallicolumba*. Its colour pattern is too simplified to be of much help but certainly suggests possible relationships with *Otidiphaps*. The unique form of the bill may have evolved relatively rapidly in response to specialised feeding habits and may not be indicative of any great phylogenetic gap between it and more 'normal-billed' forms.

TOOTH-BILLED PIGEON   *Didunculus strigirostris*

Gnathodon strigirostris Jardine, Ann. and Mag. Nat. Hist., 16, 1845, p. 175, p. 9.

This aberrant species seems most likely to be an early offshoot from the same stock as produced the Old World quail doves. Its unique bill bears some resemblance to that of the Dodo but at least as much to some *Treron* species. Its method of eating seeds would appear to be different from that of all other pigeons but at least one quail dove, *Gallicolumba rubescens*, shares its habit of using the feet when feeding.

DESCRIPTION: About size of average Feral Pigeon but thicker set with tight plumage, short tail and unique stout curved bill with two notches and three projections on each side of the lower mandible from which the bird gets its name. Head, neck, breast and mantle blackish green with a silvery blue lustre on the hind neck and, to a lesser extent on sides of neck. Underparts below the breast duller and with the feather fringes grey rather than bluish silver or greenish. Back, rump, tail, under tail coverts, wing coverts and inner secondaries dark chestnut. Primaries, primary coverts, outer secondaries and underwing greyish black. Irides brown. Bill yellow, red at base. Orbital skin red. Legs and feet red. Female has a little less silvery sheen on neck than male. The juvenile has a barred plumage, chestnut and black on the underparts (except for the blackish areas on the wings) and head. Blackish and tawny brown on the breast and underparts, and greenish with small terminal spots or bars, on the hind neck and upper mantle. The juvenile tail feathers show traces of black barring giving a freckled effect.

DISTRIBUTION AND HABITAT: Samoa: Upolu Island and Savaii Island. Said to inhabit wooded mountain sides.

FEEDING AND GENERAL HABITS: Williams (in Ramsay, 1864) described it as being 'strictly a ground pigeon' that fed on berries, fruit and the mountain plantain. Bennet (1864) who closely observed two captive individuals said that when eating they nibbled into minute bits the seeds of loquats, almonds and hemp seed 'with the same action as observed in the parrot tribe'. Boiled potatoes they tore up and swallowed in large pieces. They used their feet to hold down stale bread while tearing it with the bill.

When still fairly plentiful, was usually found in flocks of ten to twenty (Williams). Jardine (in Armstrong, 1932) said that when flushed it flies off with loudly beating wings for about thirty yards, then glides for about fifty yards and settles in a tree. Flies below the height of the branches of the larger trees. Mayr (1945) says that it flies with agility through undergrowth, perches in low trees but is said to roost in high ones. Jardine (op. cit.) says that the adult has a waddling walk but that a young bird he watched walked in a rail-like manner without waddling. Probably this difference has reference to different types of gait that are used in different circumstances rather than being characteristic of adults or juvenile birds. A young bird frightened when walking crouched flat with head tucked down in front. Adults always flew when alarmed, even at a hundred yards distance, by man and did not run or crouch.

NESTING: It is often stated that this species formerly nested on the ground but, since the havoc brought by pigs, it now nests in trees. I have not been able to find any definite information of its nesting habits.

VOICE: A plaintive, repeated coo was given in apparent alarm by a captive bird (Bennett, 1864). The same individual, when watched, would go to a perch and utter 'deep guttural growls, followed by a vibration of the whole body, uttering at the same time its plaintive notes of "Goo, goo, goo", repeated in quick succession'.

DISPLAY: No information.

REFERENCES

ARMSTRONG, J. S. 1932. *A Hand-list to the Birds of Samoa.* London.
BENNETT, G. 1864. Notes on the *Didunculus strigirostris* or Tooth-billed Pigeon. *Proc. Zool. Soc. London* 1864: 139–143.
MAYR, E. 1945. *Birds of the South-west Pacific.* New York.
RAMSAY, E. P. 1864. On the *Didunculus strigirostris* or Tooth-billed Pigeon from Upolo. *Ibis* 6: 98–100.

THE BROWN FRUIT DOVES

The brown fruit doves form a distinct group of fruit pigeons, consisting of only two species. Both are confined to the Philippine Islands. The populations of both species have diverged on different islands but the differences between these races are relatively slight. Their affinities are obscure. The colour pattern of their plumage does not suggest very close relationship with other fruit pigeons. The alimentary tract of the only specimen of brown fruit dove I have dissected was similar to those of seed-eating pigeons and the green pigeons (*Treron*) and unlike those of most fruit pigeons.

The two species *P. leucotis* and *P. amethystina* are closely related and probably evolved relatively recently from a common stock. They are now, however, widely sympatric and although much alike in colour differ in size and relative bill size. Presumably the differences in bill size are correlated with different foods but very little appears to be known about their ecology.

LESSER BROWN FRUIT DOVE   *Phapitreron leucotis*

Columba leucotis Temminck, Pl. col. livr. 32, 1823, pl. 189

DESCRIPTION: Rather smaller than a Barbary Dove, compact in shape with shortish tail. Forehead pale to medium grey shading to vinous brown on crown and nape. Rest of plumage a dark warm brown, paler on the underparts and more rufescent on the throat. Nape, hind neck and mantle strongly glossed with bronze-green and purple. Most other feathers of upper parts also show (in some lights) a purple or bronzy-olive lustre. Central tail feathers dark purple brown with dull grey tips. Outer tail feathers with broad dark purplish subterminal band and broad pale grey tips. Under tail coverts pale grey. A conspicuous black stripe with a still more conspicuous white one below it runs across the face from the bill under and past the eye. Irides brown, purplish, grey, or pinkish (varying racially) often (? or normally) with a narrow outer ring of pale blue or white. Eyelids purplish; orbital skin yellowish green to bluish green. Feet and legs pink or red. Bill black. Several races, differing only slightly.

The juvenile is paler and redder in colour. The wing coverts, secondaries and primaries have broad and rusty fawn fringes, the outermost primaries are, however, very similar to those of the adult. Little or no iridescence on neck. Facial markings indicated but not so clear as in adult. Plumage of the underparts of a very 'woolly' texture, even for a juvenile pigeon.

DISTRIBUTION AND HABITAT: The Philippine Islands. Inhabits woodland, including open woodland and borders of cultivated areas.

FEEDING AND GENERAL HABITS: Known to eat fruits taken from trees.

NESTING: Nest of usual pigeon type, often built of tendrils in a small tree.

VOICE: Advertising coo a clear musical 'Wōok, wōok, wōok, wōok, wōok, wōok' increasing in loudness and tempo. I also heard a captive (possibly the same individual) utter a soft, rapidly repeated series of short coos that I wrote as 'Cŏŏ-cŏŏ-cŏŏ-cŏŏ-cŏŏ-cŏŏ'.

DISPLAY: No information.

OTHER NAMES: Pigeon; Brown Fruit Pigeon; White-eared Fruit Pigeon.

REFERENCE

HACHISUKA, M. 1932. *The Birds of the Philippine Islands*. Vol. 1, pt. 2. London.

GREATER BROWN FRUIT DOVE *Phapitreron amethystina*

Phapitreron amethystina Bonaparte, Consp. Av., 2, 1855, p. 28.

DESCRIPTION: A little larger than the previous species but more heavily built and with a proportionately, as well as actually, much larger bill. Coloration and markings similar but of a generally darker and colder brown with much more intense iridescence on hind neck and mantle. This iridescence is predominantly violet blue and purple not green and reddish purple. Under tail coverts reddish buff. Irides yellowish, golden-brown or reddish. Orbital skin pinkish or dull red, sometimes inclining to bluish. Feet red. Bill black.

Juvenile has markedly 'woolly' plumage and is paler than adult with only a trace of gloss on the hind neck, reddish fawn edges to wing coverts and secondaries and obscure facial markings.

The above description is of the nominate form *P. a. amethystina*, which is found on the islands of Luzon, Polillo, Samar, Leyte, Panaon, Dinagat, Bohol and Mindanao. Of the other races found elsewhere in the Philippines the most distinct is *P. a. maculipectus*, which occurs on Negros. The male of this form has the breast light grey shading to dusky on the flanks and pale greyish tawny on the belly. The female is similar but has the breast suffused with tawny brown with a faint pink tinge. In both sexes, but more so in the female, the breast has a slightly spotted or scaled appearance due to the bases and fringes of the feathers being slightly darker than the central area.

DISTRIBUTION AND HABITAT: The Philippine Islands. Found in deep forest.

FEEDING AND GENERAL HABITS: No information.

NESTING: No information.

VOICE: What is probably the advertising coo has been described as 'a . . . loud honking call . . . like the honk-honk-honk of an old car horn'.

DISPLAY: No information.

OTHER NAMES: Amethyst Fruit Dove; Amethystine Brown Pigeon; Greater White-eared Fruit Pigeon.

REFERENCES

HACHISUKA, M. 1932. *The Birds of the Philippine Islands*. Vol. 1, pt. 2. London.
RIPLEY, S. D. & RABOR, D. S. 1956. Birds from the Canlaon Volcano in the highlands of Negros Island in the Philippines. *Condor* **58**: 283–291.

THE GREEN PIGEONS

The members of this group differ from other fruit pigeons, at least from those in which the point has been investigated, in having a long narrow gut and grinding gizzard similar to what is found in typical seed-eating pigeons. They feed largely on wild figs, the seeds of which are not voided intact but ground up and digested (Cowles & Goodwin). They are found in the Ethiopian and Oriental regions, a few of them just reaching the Palaearctic region in eastern Asia.

As their name suggests they are predominantly green in colour, not the glittering iridescent green or rich grass-green found in some other fruit pigeons, but a soft green with usually a yellowish or olive tinge. Most of them have black and yellow markings on the wings and many are beautifully marked with mauve, purplish-chestnut, orange or yellow. The majority have a scalloped or 'scooped out' indentation on the inner web of the third from outermost primary which varies in degree both between and within species.

They are rather thickset birds, mostly with shortish tails, although a few have long rounded or pointed tails. They vary in size, from smaller than a Barbary Dove to as large as a Wood Pigeon. They are highly arboreal, even preferring to drink by sidling down a branch that hangs into or projects from the water. Most are swift flyers, probably all of them when they have need to be. They have odd whistling or fluting cries but most appear to lack any cooing notes. However, so far as I know, a detailed account of the full range of voice of any green pigeon as compared with any 'ordinary' pigeon has yet to be made.

Except in regards to their alimentary system the green pigeons appear to have diverged further from 'ordinary' members of their family than have the other fruit pigeons. This may, however, be a faulty impression. The green and yellow coloration depends on yellow carotenoid pigments in the plumage. If for any reason, such as unsuitable feeding in captivity, a green pigeon lacks or fails to develop these pigments the result is a grey and purplish, white-marked bird whose coloration is like that of many typical pigeons. It is possible that some of their other differences may also depend on only one or two factors.

The reasons for considering all the green pigeons best included within the single genus *Treron* have been discussed in detail by Husain (1958). This treatment is preferable, in my opinion, to splitting the green pigeons up into several genera. They fall into the following groups, not all of which are equally well differentiated. The African Green Pigeon *Treron calva* and its island relatives, the Yellow-bellied Green Pigeon *T. waalia* and the Yellow-legged Green Pigeon *T. phoenicoptera* were placed together in the subgenus *Vinago* by Husain. They form a valid species group but I doubt if they merit even subgeneric rank. The pin-tailed green pigeons *T. apicauda*, *T. seimundi* and *T. oxyura* form a morphologically discrete group but in colour pattern are remarkably similar to the first group and where they differ serve, in this respect, to link them with other Asiatic forms. The Wedge-tailed Green Pigeon, *T. sphenura*, the Formosan Green Pigeon *T. formosae* and Siebold's Green Pigeon *T. sieboldii* form another closely related group that, like the pin-tailed forms, mainly inhabit mountain regions. I do not concur with Husain in thinking the Thick-billed Green Pigeon, *T. curvirostra*, and its allies more closely related to this group than they are to the Pink-necked and Orange-breasted Green Pigeon *T. vernans* and *T. bicincta*, but rather that the remaining Asiatic Green Pigeons including the aberrantly large-sized *T. cappellei*, are, probably, all more closely related to one another than any of them are to Wedge-tailed, Siebolds and Formosan Green Pigeons.

It is necessary to discuss the affinities of some closely related forms and the reasons for the nomenclatorial status which they will be given here. Most recent authors have treated all the mainland African Green Pigeons, with the exception of the Yellow-bellied *T. waalia* of the northern savannas, as conspecific with the green pigeons of Madagascar. Two exceptions were Peters (1937) and Chapin (1939). Chapin, who had wide experience of African birds in the field, was convinced that the two were specifically distinct although he did not detail reasons for this opinion. The African and Madagascar forms appear to have been first united by Grote (1931) who says that his studies led him to the certain conviction (Sicheres Ueberzeugung) that they were conspecific but does not give further details. Husain treated the African and Madagascar green pigeons as conspecific yet gave the São Thomé Green Pigeon *T. s. thomae* and the Pemba Island Green Pigeon *T. pembae* specific rank.

The green pigeons of Madagascar and the nearby Comoro Islands all have a rather small bill with a small greyish cere. In this they differ strikingly from all the African mainland forms in which the cere is red, orange or pink and more extensive than in Madagascar birds. Amadon (1953) wrote that ' . . . *australis* is more like the race *calva* of West Africa than are some races of eastern and southern Africa' but this is true only of the shade of green of the plumage. The head of *calva* with its very extensive red or orange cere differs greatly in appearance from that of *australis*. In the matter of plumage colour, there is a range of intermediate forms between the West African *calva* and the other mainland races that least resemble the West African forest form in this respect, the Madagascar Green Pigeon is less close in plumage colour to those mainland forms to which it is nearest geographically. I think, like Chapin, that the mainland and Madagascar forms are best treated as species within the same superspecies. In view of the difference in cere colour, which greatly alters the appearance of the living birds, it is likely that if *australis* and *calva* ever came into contact they would not interbreed. Indeed it seems highly probable that the difference in cere colour between the two species *T. calva* and *T. waalia* has functioned as an isolating mechanism between them.

I concur with Husain (1958) in giving specific rank, within the same superspecies, to *s. thomae* and *pembae* as these two island forms have also differentiated sufficiently to suggest long isolation and the probability that they would not now interbreed with mainland forms were they to meet. These two forms, geographically so far apart but both confined to small islands, show remarkable convergence in coloration both being much duller and greyer than mainland forms. Apart from the coloration of its underparts and small size *pembae* is quite close to the mainland form *delalandii*. The São Thomé form differs markedly from the mainland forms, and from the forms on Fernando Po and Principé not only in its greyer colour but even more in its very small cere and stout bill with strongly arched culmen.

There appears to be intergradation between virtually all of the mainland forms. That from the southern and south-eastern lowlands, *delalandii*, with its grey head and underparts and brilliant yellow-green upperparts is the most distinct. However, it evidently interbreeds with *salvadorii* in southern Rhodesia where intermediates have been obtained. Also the voices and habits of the two are said not to differ (Benson, 1956; Vincent, 1934).

The Pompadour Green Pigeon, *Treron pompadora*, the Thick-billed Green Pigeon *Treron curvirostra* and their island derivatives would be regarded as members of a superspecies and/or races of a polytypic species but for the fact that they overlap widely. The last detailed revision of these pigeons was by Mayr (1944) who listed all the conspicuous characters and recognised seven species – *curvirostra*, *pompadora*, *griseicauda*, *chloroptera*, *floris*, *teysmanni* and *psittacea*. The recognition of the last four species, which are island forms of limited distribution being largely because of the difficulty of assigning them correctly to one rather than another of the three wider-ranging forms which are given specific rank. Husain (1958) followed Mayr's nomenclature but placed *chloroptera*, *griseicauda*, *floris*, *teysmanni* and *psittacea* in the same superspecies as *pompadora*. He admitted however, that this was done as a provisional measure of convenience and did not given any specific reasons for considering all or any of these species closer to *pompadora* than to *curvirostra*.

If we take this group as a whole we find the variation in the main shows the common tendency towards increase of size and loss of sexual dichromatism in forms that inhabit small islands. The tendency towards duller colouring in island forms is shown to a limited extent in *teysmanni*, *floris*, and *psittacea* but not in *aromatica* and *chloroptera* where an apparent reduction of melanin results in extensive bright yellow and bright yellowish green areas. Where *curvirostra* and *pompadora* overlap they show constant and clearly visible differences. On the Asiatic mainland areas of overlap the male Thick-billed Green Pigeon (race *nipalensis*) has the base of bill, at sides, a brilliant red, extensive expanse of green orbital skin, throat and breast green with *faint* golden or buffish yellow wash, under tail coverts pale rufous buff, the shorter ones green tipped with white. The Pompadour Green Pigeon (race *phayrei*) has no red on bill, bright yellow-green face and throat, pronounced orange-buff patch on breast, under tail coverts entirely rich chestnut. The females of both lack those differences involving chestnut or orange colours.

In the Philippines the two forms overlap in Mindoro (Mayr, 1944). Here both *curvirostra* (race *erimacra*) and *pompadora* (race *axillaris*) have red on the base of the bill. They differ strikingly however, in the colour of the iris, which is predominantly red in *curvirostra* and bluish in *pompadora* and the under tail coverts which are chestnut in *curvirostra* and white in *pompadora*. The ventral area and tibial feathers of *curvirostra* are marked dark green and yellow, those of *pompadora* dark green and yellowish white. A further difference in this area is that *pompadora* has greyish green feet whereas the feet of *curvirostra* are red, as are those of *pompadora* elsewhere in its range.

T. griseicauda is intermediate in the amount of feathering on the cere between *curvirostra* and *pompadora*. In its other characters it seems to me to be nearest to *curvirostra*. This is particularly the case if it is compared with the geographically nearest forms of *pompadora* and *curvirostra*. It agrees with the latter in having chestnut under tail coverts and red feet and legs as well as being closer to it in the relative size of bill and curvature of culmen, wide expanse of orbital skin and distribution of grey on the head. I would consider *griseicauda* conspecific with *curvirostra* but for the fact that it may possibly overlap with the latter in the islands of the Sundra Strait (Stresemann, 1934; Mayr, 1944). Provisionally, therefore I treat it as a species but still consider it best treated as a member of the same superspecies as *curvirostra*.

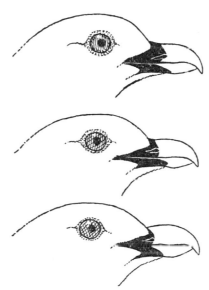

FIG. 110: Heads of *Treron psittacea* (top), *T. floris* (middle) and *T. teysmanni* (bottom) to show differing amounts of bare skin (cere) at base of bills.

The small island forms can now be considered. I concur with Mayr (1944) in thinking that *aromatica* from Buru is best considered a race of *pompadora*. Although a well-marked form it differs less from the Philippine races of *pompadora* (*axillaris* and *everetti*) than these do from the mainland forms. The Nicobars-Andamans form *chloroptera* appears clearly referable to *pompadora* rather than *curvirostra*. It differs from the former only in its rather large size and heavy bill and in the reduction of the purplish-chestnut area on the male which is confined to the lower mantle and scapulars, the shoulders being green as in the female. The differences do not seem to me greater than those between other forms treated as races of *pompadora* and I think it best to treat *chloroptera* as a race of *pompadora*.

Mayr (1944) comments on the striking differences between *teysmanni*, from Sumba Island, with its feathered cere and purplish chestnut back (in the male) and *psittacea*, from Timor and Samau, with its green back and naked cere. However, the two are, so far as these characters are concerned, linked by *floris* from the Lesser Sunda Islands, Lombok to Alor, in which the amount of feathering on the cere is intermediate and in which the male, although at first glance green like the female, shows a mauvy-bronze wash on the mantle. It is interesting that these three island forms could, if judged by the amount of feathering on their bills, be assigned respectively to *curvirostra*, *griseicauda* and *pompadora*. This would clearly be wrong in view of their distribution and obvious affinities. It is far more likely that they all are representatives of *curvirostra* or *griseicauda* stock that have diverged slightly in isolation, *psittacea* having developed a bare cere like that of *pompadora*, than that *psittacea* represents a separate invasion of Timor by *pompadora*.

In his taxonomic and zoogeographic study of the genus Husain (1958) pointed out that the Wedge-tailed Green Pigeon *Treron sphenura*, Siebold's Green Pigeon *Treron sieboldii* and the Formosan Green Pigeon *Treron formosae* would be considered members of a superspecies or even as conspecific if they did not overlap in distribution. He also said the same for the Pin-tailed Green Pigeon *Treron apicauda*, the White-bellied Pin-tailed Green Pigeon *Treron seimundi* and the Yellow-bellied Pin-tailed Green Pigeon *Treron oxyura*. He did not, however, discuss the characters of the species in reference to their status in the areas of sympatry. His table of taxonomic characters is taken from each species as a whole and thus tends to conceal some possibly significant geographical variation.

Treron sphenura, T. sieboldii and *T. formosae* are extremely alike in colour, colour pattern and morphology. All are birds of mountains or hilly regions and no differences in habitat preference or ecology between any two of them appear to be known. I know of no comparative description of their voices. That of nominate *sphenura* (Dodsworth, 1912) would appear to be unlike the few described calls of *sieboldii* (Yamashina, 1961) or the call recorded for *formosae* (Swinhoe, 1866). It is therefore possible, but by no means certain, that there may be significant vocal differences between them, at any rate between any two of them that occur in the same area.

T. sphenura delacouri overlaps *T. sieboldii murielae* in Annam. There are specimens of both forms taken from Hué in the British Museum collection. Nominate *sieboldii* overlaps *formosae* in Formosa according to the ranges given by Husain (1958) and Peters (1937). Where *sphenura* and *sieboldii* overlap the latter has a strong golden wash on crown and breast and *sphenura* has not although elsewhere *sphenura* shows a pronounced golden tinge on crown and breast. Similarly nominate *sieboldii* has only a very faint golden tinge (if any) on the crown whereas *formosae*, with which it overlaps, has a rich golden-bronze crown and no yellow on the breast. The two Formosan forms clearly represent a double invasion of the same stock. Except for its rich golden-bronze crown nominate *f. formosae* shows differences from *sieboldii* such as are characteristic of island forms in its darker and generally duller plumage. Such differences have advanced still further in the form from the Riu-Kiu islands, *T. formosae permagna* which is predominantly dark green with no bronze or yellow about its head or breast.

Treron apicauda lowei and *T. seimundi modestus* overlap in central Annam. There are specimens of both from Hué in the British Museum collection. Where they overlap *apicauda* has the loral region feathered whereas it is bare, like that of *seimundi*, in other forms of *apicauda*. This difference involves only the interposition of a narrow 'bridge' of feathers between bill and eye, but would considerably alter the appearance of the living bird's head. Although nominate *apicauda* shows (in the male) a pronounced golden tinge on the breast this is absent in both forms in the area of overlap with *seimundi*.

Thus in both the wedge-tailed and pin-tailed green pigeons there are some morphological differences and evidence of character displacement between overlapping forms where they are sympatric. The visual differences involved affect chiefly those parts of the body (head, breast and under tail coverts) which are used by some species of *Treron*, and almost certainly by these also, in sexual and agonistic displays. It is, therefore, likely that these differences function as isolating mechanisms and may have evolved or become emphasised subsequent to the forms in question coming into contact. The rather slight degree of difference so far achieved may be due to other isolating mechanisms, such as voice, being more important. I think, however, it is more probable that in each case the secondary invasion of the area has been relatively recent and we are, probably, witnessing a comparatively early stage in the evolution of colour differences as isolating mechanisms.

More information is needed, particularly in regard to voice, behaviour and ecology in the areas of overlap and to what extent the apparently sympatric forms are truly sympatric when breeding. It is surprising that there seems to be little evidence of any difference in colour of irides or orbital skin between overlapping forms. In the very similarly-coloured ring-necked African doves of the genus *Streptopelia* there are specific differences of iris colour as well as of voice. As some ornithologists have suggested that the presence or absence of a golden wash on the breast in these and some other *Treron* species is a matter of age only it seems as well to discuss this point briefly here. Although in forms in which it is normally present the gold on the breast may be absent or nearly absent in some few individual males I know of no instance where this has been proved to be due to immaturity. A juvenile male specimen of the Pin-tailed Green Pigeon in the British Museum collection, no. 1889.2.2.1435, which is in its first moult, already has some pink and golden feathers growing on its breast.

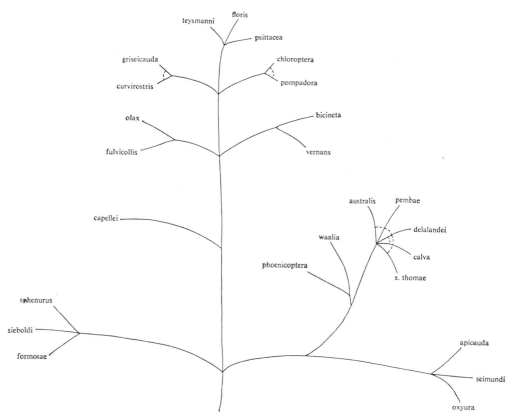

FIG. D.12: Presumed relationships of species in the genus *Treron*.

REFERENCES

AMADON, D. 1953. *Avian systematics and evolution in the Gulf of Guinea.*
BENSON, C. W. 1956. *Occ. Papers Nat. Mus. S. Rhodesia.* Vol. 3, No. 2b.
—— 1960. The Birds of the Comoro Islands. *Ibis* **103b**: 50–51.
CHAPIN, J. 1939. The Birds of the Belgian Congo. Pt. 2, p. 175. *Bull. Amer. Mus. Nat. Hist.,* Vol. LXXV.
COWLES, G. S. & GOODWIN, D. 1959. Seed digestion by the fruit-eating pigeons *Treron. Ibis* **101**: 253–254.
DODSWORTH, P. T. L. 1912. Notes on some habits of the Kokla or Wedge-tailed Green Pigeon in confinement. *Avicult. Mag.* Third Series, Vol. 3, No. 5. pp. 129–135 and 163–169.
GOODWIN, D. 1959. Taxonomy of the genus *Columba. Bull. Brit. Mus. (Nat. Hist.) Zool.* Vol. 6, No. 1.
—— 1960. Taxonomy of the genus *Ducula. Ibis* **102**: 526–535.
GROTE, H. 1931. Die Gliederung des Formenkreises *Treron australis. Anzeiger Ornith. Gesellschaft Bayern,* **2**: 140–141.
HUSAIN, K. Z. 1958. Subdivisions and Zoogeography of the genus *Treron* (Green Fruit-pigeons). *Ibis* **100**: 334–348.
MAYR, E. L. 1944. The Birds of Timor and Sumba. *Bull. Amer. Mus. Nat. Hist.* **83**: Art. 2, pp. 130–194.
PETERS, J. L. 1937. *Check-list of Birds of the World.* Vol. 3.
SWINHOE, R. 1866. Ornithological Notes from Formosa. *Ibis* **2**: New Series, 392–406.
VINCENT, J. 1934. The Birds of Northern Portuguse East Africa. *Ibis* **4**: Thirteenth Series, 495–527.
YAMASHINA, Y. 1958. *Birds in Japan,* p. 167. Tokyo.

CINNAMON-HEADED GREEN PIGEON

Treron fulvicollis

Columba fulvicollis Wagler, Syst. Av., 1827, Columba, sp. 8.

DESCRIPTION: About the size of Barbary Dove but plumper in shape with short tail. Head and neck rusty purplish chestnut shading to dark greenish gold on the breast and dark reddish purple on the mantle and lesser wing coverts. Belly dull yellowish green shading to greenish grey on the flanks. Tibial feathers spotted pale yellow and dark green (dark tips to each feather). Under tail coverts light chestnut. Outer wing coverts, secondaries and primaries black with usual bright yellow edgings as in most *Treron* species. Underwing dark grey. Inner secondaries, rump and central tail feathers olive green. Outer tail feathers greenish grey with black subterminal and pale grey terminal bar. Irides buffy pink or with blue inner and pink outer ring. Orbital skin greyish green or bluish green. Bill white tinged with bluish green, base bright dark red. Feet purplish pink, claws white.

The female differs strikingly from the male. She completely lacks the chestnut colour which is replaced by dark olive green above and yellowish green on the breast. Her forehead and crown are grey, her under tail coverts white or yellowish white marked with green. The juvenile is much like the female.

The above description is of the nominate form, *T. f. fulvicollis* from most of the species range. *T. f. oberholseri* from the Natuna Islands of Sirhassen and Bunguran, and *T. f. melopogenys* from Nias Island are very similar. *T. f. baramensis* from North Borneo, northern Sarawak and the North Bornean Islands differs in the male having the breast purplish chestnut like the head and the belly grey, only slightly tinged with green.

DISTRIBUTION AND HABITAT: Tenasserim south through Malaya and the Malay Archipelago, Sumatra, Rhio Archipelago, Borneo, islands of Billiton and Banka, North Bornean Islands, Natura Islands and Nias Island. One record from Cochin China. Most often in mangroves or other woodlands not far from the coast. Apparently uncommon and migratory or nomadic throughout its range.

FEEDING AND GENERAL HABITS: Little recorded. Known to take fruit from the branches like other green pigeons.

NESTING: Usual pigeon nest in tree or shrub. Two white eggs. Only a few nests appear to have been found (Baker, 1913).

VOICE: No information.

DISPLAY: No information.

OTHER NAME: Chestnut-headed Green Pigeon.

REFERENCES

BAKER, E. C. S. 1913. *Indian Pigeons and Doves*. London.
ROBINSON, H. C. & CHASEN, F. N. 1936. *The Birds of the Malay Peninsula*. Vol. 3. London.

LITTLE GREEN PIGEON   *Treron olax*

Columba olax Temminck, Pl. col., liver. 41, 1823, p. 241.

DESCRIPTION: A little smaller than a Barbary Dove; plump, compact and short-tailed. Head, upper half of neck and hind neck darkish blue grey shading to pale blue grey on forehead and chin. Breast dark orange-gold shading to yellow-green on lower breast and belly. Flanks grey. Tibial feathers chestnut and grey. Long under tail coverts dark chestnut. Mantle and inner wing-coverts dark reddish purple. Rest of wing black with narrow pale yellow edges to outer greater coverts and secondaries. Underwing, rump and upper tail coverts dark grey. Tail feathers greyish black with narrow pale grey terminal band (obsolescent on central pair). Irides inner ring white or cream, outer ring orange, brick red, buff or cream. Edge of eyelids yellow. Orbital skin light blue or greenish blue. Bill whitish, pale green or greenish yellow with light blue or greenish blue base and cere. Feet red or purplish red.

The female has no purple, orange or chestnut and is a general dark olive green above and yellowish green below, with grey forehead and crown, buff and dark green ventral region and buff under tail coverts. The juvenile much resembles the female but the young male has chestnut fringes to the inner wing coverts and scapulars.

DISTRIBUTION AND HABITAT: The Malay Peninsula, Sumatra, Rhio Archipelago, Java, Borneo and Bunguran Island. Inhabits forest and wooded areas, locally in parks and large gardens. Usually in foothills or lowlands, rarely at high elevations.

FEEDING AND GENERAL HABITS: Little recorded. Known to feed on wild figs (*Ficus*) taken from the branches. Usually flies in small parties of up to eight individuals (Robinson & Chasen, 1936).

NESTING: No information.

VOICE: Robinson & Chasen (loc. cit.) record a 'soft whistling coo'.

DISPLAY: No information.

REFERENCE

ROBINSON, H. C. & CHASEN, F. N. 1936. *The Birds of the Malay Peninsula*. Vol. 3. London.

PINK-NECKED GREEN PIGEON *Treron vernans*

Columba vernans Linnaeus, Mantissa, 1771, p. 526.

DESCRIPTION: About the size of a Barbary Dove but plumper and more compact with, proportionately, shorter tail and longer wings. Head and median area of hind neck and mantle light bluish grey more or less suffused with pale green on cheeks and throat and with vinous pink on the hind neck. Sides of neck and breast and a band across the upper breast delicate mauve-pink. Lower breast (except at

sides) bright tawny-orange. Underparts yellowish green shading to yellow on ventral regions and grey green, with some feathers edged yellow, on the flanks. Back and wing coverts bright olive green with the yellow edges to some feathers forming the usual yellow wing markings. Wing quills (and some outer coverts) black. Central tail feathers mainly blue-grey, others blue-grey with broad black subterminal bands and narrow grey tips. Upper tail coverts with loose tawny fringes. The long under tail coverts are chestnut. Irides with a pink or red outer ring and a blue inner one. Bill white, grey or pale greenish blue with a darker yellowish or greenish base. Legs and feet pink, purple or reddish. Female predominantly darkish olive green above and yellowish green below, lacking the pink, orange and grey of the male. Her under tail coverts are paler, the feathers usually broadly edged with pale yellowish and their chestnut areas paler and suffused with green. Juvenile similar to female but a greyer green above and with buff and/or yellow fringes to many feathers. (See pl. 1).

DISTRIBUTION AND HABITAT : South-east Asia from southern Tenasserim through Indo-China, Sumatra and Java to the Philippines and Celebes. Found in forested country but, in some areas, more in open country with trees and at forest edge than in dense forest. In the Malayan regions at any rate, usually in coastal districts. Ward (1968) found it on dry beach ridges with sparse vegetation, in mangroves and in gardens but not in true jungle or hill country.

FEEDING AND GENERAL HABITS : Recorded feeding on fruits, particularly those of *Melastoma* and wild figs. Often in pairs or small parties but large numbers congregate at good feeding places and at communal roosts. The latter are often in mangroves, particularly on mangrove-covered islands.

NESTING : Usual pigeon nest in tree or shrub, often quite low down. Two white eggs.

VOICE : Described (Davison, in Baker, 1913) as 'a soft low whistle ending in a sort of coo' and 'a double, whistling coo, the second note much prolonged (Robinson & Chasen, 1936). I have found no detailed desription ; the London Zoo birds never called while I was watching them.

DISPLAY : I have seen from captive birds an apparent threat with widely open mouth which made the dark mouth cavity strikingly visible. As with other green pigeons an up and down wagging of the tail seems to be used as an equivalent of the wing-twitching (q.v.) of more typical pigeons. When this movement is performed on the nest-site it reminds one at once of the similar movements of the male Lapwing and in both cases the chestnut under tail coverts are prominently displayed.

REFERENCES

BAKER, E. C. S. 1913. *Indian Pigeons and Doves*. London.
ROBINSON, H. C. & CHASEN, F. N. 1936. *The Birds of the Malay Peninsula*. Vol. 3. London.
WARD, P. 1968. Origin of the avifauna of urban and suburban Singapore. *Ibis* **110**: 241–255.

ORANGE-BREASTED GREEN PIGEON   *Treron bicincta*

Vinago bicincta Jerdon, Madras Journ. Lit. Sci., 12, 1840, p. 13.

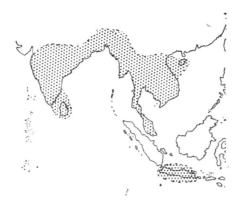

DESCRIPTION: Very similar to the Pink-necked Green Pigeon (q.v.) from which it principally differs in having the forehead, face and throat yellowish green, a more restricted mauve-pink area on the upper breast, and a different tail pattern, the outer tail feathers being blackish with a broad pale grey terminal band.   The female differs from the female of *vernans* in having a grey nape and hind neck and different tail pattern.   It is also, on the whole, a slightly larger and heavier-billed bird.

DISTRIBUTION AND HABITAT: India, Indo-Malayan region, Hainan, Java and Ceylon.   Chiefly in well-wooded country but also at any rate temporarily, in orchards and in clumps of fruit-bearing trees in open country.

FEEDING AND GENERAL HABITS: As described does not appear to differ from other small green pigeons such as the last species.   Has been recorded feeding on many kinds of fruits including wild figs, wild dates, lantana berries, cinnamon berries and guavas.

NESTING: The nest, like that of other green pigeons, is of usual type but generally very small and frail-looking.   Situated in a tree or shrub, often one that stands beside a path or opening or in a clearing.   Two white eggs.   Incubation by both parents recorded (Henry, 1955).

VOICE: A beautifully modulated mellow whistle and, when threatening, a harsh repeated croaking note and a chuckling-call have been variously, but similarly, described by several authors.

DISPLAY: Has the vertical tail-wagging movement as in (all ?) other green pigeons as Henry says it 'waves its tail up and down'.

REFERENCES

BAKER, E. C. S.   1913.   *Indian Pigeons and Doves*.   London.
HENRY, G. M.   1955.   *A Guide ot the Birds of Ceylon*.   Oxford.

POMPADOUR GREEN PIGEON   *Treron pompadora*

Columba pompadora Gmelin, Syst. Nat., 1, pt. 2, 1789, p. 775.

DESCRIPTION: A polytypic species whose affinities are discussed in the introduction to this group. Nominate *T. p. pompadora* from Ceylon is between Feral Pigeon and Barbary Dove in size but plumper and shorter-tailed.   Forehead, face and throat bright yellow-green shading to pale soft green on breast and belly and greyish green on hind neck.   Crown of head bluish grey.   Mantle, scapulars and lesser wing coverts dark purplish chestnut. Rest of wing black with bright yellow edges to the outer median and greater coverts and outer secondaries. Rump and central tail feathers yellowish olive green. Outer tail feathers dark grey washed with olive at base, blackish central band and broad pale grey terminal band. Under tail coverts whitish marked with greyish green. Underwing dark grey. Irides with blue inner ring and red or pink outer ring. Eye-rims green. Bill bluish grey or pale grey, green at base. Legs and feet red or purplish red.

The female is olive green where the male is purplish chestnut. The first (nestling) plumage is in general light olive with yellow fringes to most feathers. As in other *Treron* species this is very soon partly or completely replaced by an immature plumage very similar to that of the adult female.

T. pompadora affinis, from western India, has forehead and nape, as well as crown, light bluish grey. The green parts of its plumage are paler and brighter. The ventral areas and tibial feathers marked dark green and bright yellow. The longer under tail coverts of the male are chestnut. *T. pompadora phayrei*, from Bengal east and south to Laos, Siam, Cochin China and Tenasserim is much like *affinis*, but the male has a pinkish gold or ochraceous gold breast and the purplish chestnut of his mantle is a little lighter. *T. pompadora axillaris*, from the Philippines is slightly larger and thicker-billed. The under tail coverts of the male (and female) are whitish. The yellow markings on the wings are broader and brighter. The base of the bill is red. The iris usually appears predominantly blue or green. *T. p. everetti*, from the Sulu Archipelago is similar but has the green parts slightly brighter and yellower. *T. p. aromatica*, from Buru is very like *everetti* but a little smaller. It has no red on the bill, its shoulder and most of the lesser wing coverts are dark grey. Its green parts are brighter and yellower, and the yellow wing markings even brighter and more extensive. *T. p. chloroptera* of the Andaman and Nicobar Islands resembles *aromatica* but is larger, has the green parts of the neck and underparts duller, but the rump a very bright yellow-green. The shoulders and lesser wing coverts are olive green in both sexes, the male having the purplish chestnut confined to the mantle and scapulars.

DISTRIBUTION AND HABITAT: Ceylon, Western India from Bombay to southern Travancore, north-eastern India through south-east Asia to Tenasserim, continental Siam and Cochin China, the Philippine Islands, the Sulu Archipelago, Buru and the Andaman and Nicobar Islands. Inhabits forest and woodland. Readily comes into fruiting trees in cultivated areas. Found in both hilly and lowland country but seldom at any great elevation.

NESTING: Usual pigeon nest in tree or shrub, generally within ten feet of the ground. Two white eggs. A pair watched by Baker (1913) behaved in typical pigeon manner, the male bringing the twigs and the female building the nest. Breeds at different times in different parts of its range (e.g. April to August in Bengal and Assam; December to June and sometimes August to September in Ceylon; January to April in western India). Probably whenever food supplies are plentiful.

FEEDING AND GENERAL HABITS: Feeds largely on fruits and berries taken from the branches. Wild figs are favourite foods, as with other green pigeons. It has been recorded (Baker, 1913) coming to the ground to feed on strawberries and termites and also eating buds. Flight swift and direct; when frightened performs snipe-like turns and changes of direction.

VOICE: Most people who know this bird in life note that it utters a beautifully modulated whistling call Baker (1913) also heard a deep soft crooning 'coo, coo' uttered by a male when near his nest.

DISPLAY: No information.

OTHER NAMES: Grey-fronted Green Pigeon; Ashy-headed Green Pigeon; Andaman Green Pigeon.

REFERENCES

BAKER, E. C. S. 1913. *Indian Pigeons and Doves*, pp. 27–45.
HENRY, G. M. 1955. *A Guide to the Birds of Ceylon*, pp. 243–244.
MAYR, E. 1944. The Birds of Timor and Sumba. *Bull. Amer. Mus. Nat. Hist.* **83**: Art. 2.

THICK-BILLED GREEN PIGEON   *Treron curvirostra*

Columba curvirostra Gmelin, Syst. Nat. 1, pt. 2, 1789, p. 777.

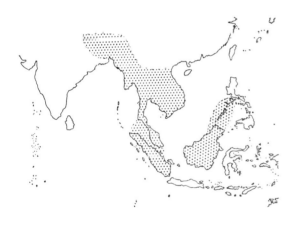

DESCRIPTION: From somewhat smaller to somewhat larger than a Barbary Dove but typical thick-set green pigeon shape and with a rather thick bill. Forehead and crown bluish grey. Face, throat, neck, underparts, rump and central tail feathers light green tinged with gold or yellow on rump, central tail feathers and breast and with grey on hind neck and belly. Flanks, tibial feathers and the shorter under tail coverts dark green broadly tipped with white giving a spotted effect. Long under tail coverts pale chestnut. Mantle and inner wing coverts dark purplish maroon. Rest of wings dark green or black with broad yellow edges to most feathers, forming conspicuous yellow stripes on the closed wing. Underwing slate grey. Outer tail feathers dark grey at base, pale grey at tips with a black central band. Irides with dark blue or dark brown inner ring and yellow, gold, orange or red outer ring. Orbital skin bright green or bluish green. Bill pale yellowish, pale green, or whitish, with red patch at base on either side. Feet and legs coral red.

The female has all the under tail coverts green and white and is dark green or olive green on the back where the male is purplish maroon. Juvenile like female, but duller and greyer with yellowish or, in one specimen, fawn fringes to many of the covert feathers. There are relatively very few specimens even partly in juvenile plumage in collections.   Their appearance suggests that the first plumage may be very quickly changed for a female-like subadult dress, but more young specimens or, better, observations on live individuals from hatching to the acquisition of adult dress, will be needed to prove or disprove this idea.   Many races of this species have been described.   Most of them differ only in size or very minor details of coloration.   The above is a composite description.

DISTRIBUTION AND HABITAT: Nepal, Bengal, Assam, Burma, continental Siam, Tonkin, Annam, Hainan, Cambodia, Cochin China, Malay Peninsula, Sumatra, Borneo and intervening islands, Bunguran Islands, Simalur, Nias and adjacent islands, the Philippine islands of Balabac, Mindoro and Palawan and Borneo.

Found in or near forest in both hills and level country.   In the Malay Archipelago especially in moist lowland forest.   Sometimes in open country with groups of trees, but less often than many other green pigeons.

FEEDING AND GENERAL HABITS: Takes fruits and berries.   In Borneo said to feed more on hard fruits than on wild figs, but elsewhere has been recorded flocking to fruiting fig trees.   Has been recorded feeding on wild strawberries on the ground and on cultivated rice and millet.

Usually in small parties, sometimes in large flocks.   Flight described as swift and strong by some observers but others note it as flying less high and fast than *Treron vernans*.

NESTING: Usual pigeon nest in tree or shrub, often in horizontally growing bamboo.   Two white eggs.   In north-eastern India (Cachar and Khasia Hills) nesting has been noted from late March to August inclusive.

VOICE: Utters harsh half-hissing and half-guttural notes when feeding, probably in threat.   Softer low pitched versions of the same throaty notes and whistled phrases similar to those of other green pigeons. I have, however, found no detailed published description of the voice of this or any other green pigeon.

DISPLAY: Has been recorded bowing and bobbing and calling with widely-open mouth when threatening.   A pair which I watched fighting over food in a Zoo sprang at one another in silence and lowered their heads immediately on landing after such an attack.   Before and after making actual aggressive movements they wagged their tails up and down in the usual *Treron* manner.

REFERENCES
BAKER, E. C. S.   1913.   *Indian Pigeons and Doves.*   London.
SMYTHIES, B. E.   1960.   *The Birds of Borneo.*   London.

GREY-FACED THICK-BILLED GREEN PIGEON   *Treron griseicauda*

Treron Griseicauda Bonaparte, 1854 (nec of Gray 1856), Consp. Gen. Av., 2: 10.

DESCRIPTION: Very similar to the last species, *Treron curvirostra*, with which it forms a superspecies. Similar to *curvirostra* except as follows: Male has a pinkish gold patch (often obscure) on side of lower neck, central area of breast always green. Both sexes have the grey of the crown extending on to the face and upper parts of the throat. Cere green or blackish, sometimes with a yellowish or buff patch on top. The feathering on the cere, and consequent profile intermediate between *curvirostra* and *popmadora*. Orbital skin green and extensive as in *curvirostra*.

DISTRIBUTION AND HABITAT: Southern Sumatra, Java, Bali, Kangean Islands, Celebes, Peling, Banggai, Djampea, Kalao, Madu, Kalao Tua, Tukang Besi Islands and Sanghir Islands. In the Celebes recorded (Heinrich, in Stresemann, 1941) as inhabiting cultivated regions and fairly open country with patches of woodland or groups of trees.

FEEDING AND GENERAL HABITS: Little apparently recorded. Often in large flocks in the Celebes (Stresemann, 1941). Presumably similar in essentials to *curvirostra*.

NESTING: No information.

VOICE: No information.

DISPLAY: No information.

REFERENCE

STRESEMANN, E. 1941. Die Vögel von Celebes. *Journ. f. Orn.* **89**: 1–102.

SUMBA ISLAND GREEN PIGEON   *Treron teysmanni*

Treron Teysmanni Schlegel, Notes Leyden Mus., 1, 1899, p. 103.

DESCRIPTION: About the size of a small Feral Pigeon but plumper in shape. Cere feathered. General coloration a soft greyish green shading to bright yellow-green on forehead, lores, throat, rump and upper tail coverts. Lower part of mantle, scapulars and some inner wing coverts purplish chestnut. Outer median and greater coverts and secondaries black edged bright yellow. Primaries greyish black with narrow whitish edges. Underwing grey. Ventral area, tibial feathers and under tail coverts marked green and yellowish white. Central tail feathers yellow-green, outer ones dark grey at base with ill-defined darker central bar and apical half greyish white. I can find no record of the soft part colours of this species. Judged from the appearance of museum skins the bill and feet are, probably, similar to those of *psittacea* (q.v.). The female lacks the purplish chestnut on the upperparts and has the wing markings yellowish white, not bright yellow. A juvenile female was very like the adult except, of course, in texture of plumage. I have not seen a juvenile male.

DISTRIBUTION AND HABITAT: Sumba Island.

FEEDING AND GENERAL HABITS: No information.

NESTING :   No information.

VOICE :   No information.

DISPLAY :   No information.

REFERENCE

MAYR, E.   1944.   The Birds of Timor & Sumba.   *Bull. Amer. Mus. Nat. Hist.* **83**: Art. 2: 127–194.

FLORES GREEN PIGEON   *Treron floris*

Treron floris Wallace, Proc. Zool. Soc. London 1863 (1864), p. 496.

DESCRIPTION : About the size of a small Feral Pigeon but plumper and more compact in shape.   Cere partly feathered.   General coloration soft green with a slight yellow tinge on underparts and breast. Forehead, face and crown pale grey.   Male with a faint purplish bronze wash on mantle.   Colour pattern otherwise as next species, *Treron psittacea* (q.v.) but yellow on wings pale in both sexes.   Irides light brown.   Bill greenish grey with yellowish or whitish green tips.   Feet red.   These soft part colours are from only two specimens.   I have not seen a juvenile of this form.

DISTRIBUTION AND HABITAT :   The Lesser Sunda Islands : Lombok, Sumbawa, Flores, Solor, Lomblen, Pantar and Alor.

FEEDING AND GENERAL HABITS :   No information.

NESTING :   No information.

VOICE :   No information.

DISPLAY :   No information.

TIMOR GREEN PIGEON   *Treron psittacea*

Columba Psittacea Temminck, in Knip, Les Pigeons, 1808, les columbars, p. 28, pl. 4.

DESCRIPTION :   About the size of a small Feral Pigeon or a little smaller but plump and compact.   Tail nearly square-ended.   General coloration soft, slightly greyish green shading to brighter yellow-green on throat, rump and upper tail coverts.   Carpal edge and innermost secondaries dark grey.   Outer median coverts, greater coverts and outer secondaries greyish black, broadly edged bright yellow.   Primaries grey-black. Underwing grey. Tibial feathers white. Ventral region and under tail coverts white marked with green. Central tail feathers yellowish green, outer ones pale grey at base, dark grey central band, apical half greyish-white. Irides inner ring olive yellow, outer ring orange. Orbital skin pale bluish green. Bill horn white, basal half dull bluish. Feet dark, dull purplish red.

The female is slightly duller green than the male and has the wing markings yellowish white not bright yellow as in the male. I have not seen a juvenile of this species.

DISTRIBUTION AND HABITAT : The islands of Timor and Samau.

FEEDING AND GENERAL HABITS : No information.

NESTING : No information.

VOICE : No information.

DISPLAY : No information.

REFERENCES

HARTERT, E. 1898. List of Birds collected in Timor by Mr. Alfred Everett. *Nov. Zool.* **5**: 111–124.
MAYR, E. 1944. The Birds of Timor and Sumba. *Bull. Amer. Mus. Nat. Hist.* **83**: Art. 2: 127–194.

LARGE GREEN PIGEON   *Treron capellei*

Columba capellei Temminck, Pl. col., liver. 24, 1823, pl. 143.

DESCRIPTION : Rather larger than a Feral Pigeon and much more heavily built with close, rather harsh (for a pigeon) feathering; large head and heavy bill (see sketch). General coloration light greyish olive-green, palest on underparts and darkest on mantle and wing coverts. Outer wing coverts and secondaries dark grey, primaries blackish grey. Bright yellow edges to outer webs of outer greater and median coverts and central secondaries forming bright yellow stripes on closed wing. Breast dark golden or dull orange-yellow. Underwing slate grey. Outer tail feathers dark grey with pale grey terminal band, central ones olive green. Flank feathers tipped buff. Long under tail coverts dark chestnut. Irides dark reddish brown or dark brown, sometimes (sick or aberrant birds?) white, pale yellowish or greyish. Orbital skin pale yellow to golden yellow. Bill greenish white to pale green at tip, base and cere darker green. Feet and bare part of legs yellow.

The female has the breast greenish yellow and the under tail coverts buff and greenish grey. Juvenile like female but the young male has a yellower breast than the adult female and pale chestnut under tail coverts.

DISTRIBUTION AND HABITAT : Malay Peninsula, Sumatra, Java and Borneo. Inhabits forest, in the Malay Peninsula usually in old and fairly open jungle.

FEEDINGS AND GENERAL HABITS: Little detail recorded. Presumably feeds on fruits taken from the branches, probably taking larger species than its relatives. In the Malay Peninsula Robinson & Chasen (1936) found it gregarious, flying in large flocks. In Borneo Banks (in Smythies, 1960) found it flying in ones and twos, never in flocks, although large numbers might gather to feed on fruiting trees.

NESTING: No information.

VOICE: Robinson & Chasen (loc. cit.) record a 'deep booming coo' more like that of *Ducula* than that of other green pigeons. Banks (loc. cit.) a 'gurgling note when feeding'. The descriptions presumably refer to different calls.

DISPLAY: No information.

OTHER NAMES: Large Thick-billed Green Pigeon; Great Green Pigeon.

REFERENCES

BANKS, E. (In B. E. Smythies' *Birds of Borneo*, p. 227, 1960, London.)
ROBINSON, H. C. & CHASEN, F. N. 1936. *The Birds of the Malay Peninsula*. Vol. 3, pp. 39–40. London.

YELLOW-LEGGED GREEN PIGEON   *Treron phoenicoptera*

Columba phaenicoptera Latham, Ind. Orn. 2, 1790, p. 597.

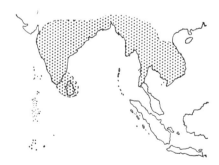

DESCRIPTION: About the size of an average Feral Pigeon but rather more heavily built. Three outermost primaries very narrow at tip and pointed, succeeding one less so; 'scooped' inner margin to third primary. Top of head, nape and cheeks bluish grey, more or less washed with yellowish green on forehead. Throat yellowish green shading into bright mustard yellow on neck and breast and a rather darker mustard yellow on hind neck. Pale grey band across mantle, dividing the dark yellow of hind neck from the yellowish green upperparts. Pale mauve patch on shoulder of wing. Primaries and secondaries blackish, edged light yellow. Broader yellow edges to the greyish green greater wing converts. Basal half of tail feathers washed with yellowish green, rest slate grey. Underparts below breast pale bluish grey washed with yellowish green, and feathers on flanks edged whitish or yellow. Feathers on tibia and upper part of tarsus bright yellow. Under tail coverts purplish chestnut with broad buffish tips. Underside of tail blackish basal half, rest silver grey. Underwing bluish grey. Irides with a blue inner ring and the outer ring purple, red, pink or orange. Orbital skin pale greenish or pale grey. Bill greyish white, pale grey, or pale greenish, rather darker at base. Legs (where not feathered) and feet bright yellow or yellowish orange.

Female similar to male but averaging a little less bright and with smaller mauve patch on shoulder. Juvenile duller and paler with little or no mauve on shoulder.

The above description applies to the nominate form of the species, *T. p. phoenicoptera*, from northern India. Those from central and southern India, *T. p. chlorigaster*, differ in having most of the underparts greenish yellow instead of pale grey and little or no trace of greenish yellow on the forehead or tail feathers. The Ceylon form *T. p. phillipsi*, resembles the south Indian bird but is smaller and duller with the green of the upperparts strongly tinged with grey. The form from Burma and north western Siam, *T. p. viridifrons*, resembles that from northern India but has a bright greenish yellow forehead, little or no yellowish green suffusion on the grey underparts and is slightly smaller. The form from eastern Siam, Laos, Annam and Cochin China, *T. p. annamensis*, is like *viridifrons* but duller, especially in the green and yellow parts of its plumage which are of dull olive green and mustardy-olive hues. All these forms, with the exception of the geographically isolated Ceylonese one, intergrade and birds intermediate between any two of the above-described forms occur.

DISTRIBUTION AND HABITAT: India and Ceylon east through Assam, Burma and northern Tenasserim to Siam, Laos, southern Annam and Cochin China. Inhabits forest and scrubland; also visiting fruiting trees in open country and built-up areas for feeding purposes. Locally in trees in parks and gardens. Found both in hilly and level country but not in high mountain ranges.

FEEDING AND GENERAL HABITS: Feeds on fruits and berries, especially wild figs. Also recorded taking buds, young shoots and cultivated grains, especially maize, while still in the unripe 'milky' stage. Normally arboreal when feeding but will come to the ground to eat earth at salt-licks and to obtain grit. Like other fruit pigeons usually drinks by sidling down a branch hanging into or projecting above the water's surface.

Commonly in small parties of up to ten individuals, sometimes in larger flocks and very large numbers may congregate to feed in the same fruiting tree or group of trees. Clambers, clings and, if necessary, hangs upside down when feeding. Feeds in the early morning and again in the late afternoon, the morning flight being usually very straight and following a traditional line. This habit, shared by other green pigeons, makes them highly vulnerable to sportsmen. Flight swift and strong.

NESTING: Usual pigeon nest in a tree or shrub. Two white eggs. Often two or more pairs nest near each other, sometimes even in the same tree. Eggs said to take fourteen days to hatch. Recorded breeding from March to June in northern and central India.

VOICE: Various observers mention a melodious whistling call or series of calls, but give no detailed information.

DISPLAY: Stuart Baker describes a display in which 'The male . . . puffs out his throat and breast, lowers his wings, ruffles out his feathers, then prances solemnly up and down a branch, continually bowing his head and whistling softly as he makes his way backwards and forwards to and from the female . . . ' The female will, he says, sometimes respond with a low intensity version of the same display.

OTHER NAMES: Common Green Pigeon; Yellow-footed Green Pigeon; Bengal Green Pigeon;

Southern Green Pigeon; Ceylon Green Pigeon; Burmese Green Pigeon.　All except the first two are of course applied only to a particular race or population of the species.

REFERENCES

BAKER, E. C. S.　1913.　*Indian Pigeons and Doves.*　London.
ALI, S.　1941.　*The Book of Indian Birds.*　Bombay.

YELLOW-BELLIED GREEN PIGEON　　　　　　　　　　　　　　*Treron waalia*

Columba waalia F. A. A. Meyer, Syst.-Sum. Uebers. Zool. Entdeck., 1793, p. 128.

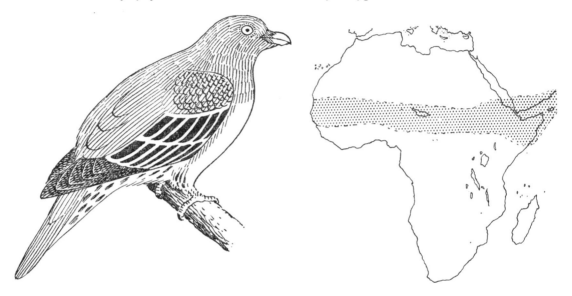

DESCRIPTION:　About the size of a smallish Feral Pigeon but rather plumper and more compact in shape.　Head, neck and breast light greenish grey or greyish green.　Mantle, back, rump, scapulars, much of wing coverts and innermost secondaries light yellowish olive-green.　Central part of lower breast and belly bright yellow bordered at sides by greyish green.　Flanks and tibial feathers dark green with whitish borders.　The long under tail coverts chestnut or mixed olive and chestnut with broad creamy tips.　Lesser wing coverts mostly light purple forming large patch on 'shoulder' of wing.　Primaries, outer secondaries and outermost greater wing coverts blackish, the former fringed narrowly and the latter broadly with yellow, forming conspicuous yellow marks on closed wing.　Tail feathers dark grey, usually washed with green, with broad light grey tips, the two central ones almost uniform grey or greenish grey.　Underside of tail feathers blackish, conspicuously and broadly tipped pale grey.　Underwing slate grey washed greenish.　Irides bright blue or purple usually with a red, yellowish, or cream-coloured outer ring.　Bill bluish white or pale bluish grey with dark purple, lilac or dull purplish red base.　Legs and feet yellow or orange with pale greenish grey or whitish claws.　Sexes alike but female averaging a little smaller and less bright.　Juvenile at first greyer and duller with very 'woolly' plumage and only trace of purple on bend of wing.

DISTRIBUTION AND HABITAT:　Dry savannah and thorn scrub regions of northern Africa from Senegal east to Eritrea, south to northern Ghana and the drier northern parts of Uganda, Kenya, Abyssinia and southern Somaliland, Socotra Island and south-west Arabia.　Frequents thickly foliaged trees near water, densely wooded valleys and parklike open country, less often in open thorn-scrub or juniper forest.

FEEDING AND GENERAL HABITS: Known to feed largely on wild figs of various species. Usually seen in pairs or small parties, but large numbers may flock at fruiting fig trees. Conflicting statements exist as to whether it drinks regularly or at all. Possibly this depends on the water content of its food at any particular time. Much persecuted by man and usually shy and timid as a result.

NESTING: Usual pigeon nest in tree or shrub. Often in peripheral twigs of some thick tree at from eight to fifteen feet above ground. Two white eggs, sometimes only one (? incomplete clutch). Recorded breeding January to May.

VOICE: Has at least two calls, variously described as a 'quarrelsome chatter' and a 'crooning whistle' a 'long soft call followed by two shorter ones', and a 'sort of clucking, whistling yap.'

DISPLAY: No information.

OTHER NAMES: Bruce's Green Pigeon.

REFERENCES

BANNERMAN, D. A. 1931. *The Birds of Tropical West Africa*. Vol. 2. London.
BATES, G. L. 1930. *Handbook of the Birds of West Africa*. London.
CHAPIN, J. P. 1939. The Birds of the Belgian Congo. *Bull. Amer. Mus. Nat. Hist.* **75** : 173–174.
MACKWORTH-PRAED, C. W. & GRANT, C. H. B. 1957. *The African Handbook of Birds*. Series 1, Vol. 1. London.

MADAGASCAR GREEN PIGEON *Treron australis*

Columba australis Linnaeus, Mantissa, 1771, p. 526.

DESCRIPTION: About the size of a smallish Feral Pigeon but plumper in shape though less so than many *Treron* species. Head, neck and breast bright yellow-green with an olive tinge, shading to greyish green on flanks. Ventral regions and tibial feathers mottled dark green and yellow. Upperparts greyish green. Shoulder of wing light mauve. Primaries and secondaries black. Pale yellow edges to outer median and greater coverts and secondaries forming yellow stripes on wing. Central tail feathers bluish grey; outer ones with ill-defined blackish central bar and broad pale grey terminal band. Underwing grey. Under tail coverts chestnut tipped buffish white. Irides inner ring blue, outer ring purple or reddish. Bill pale grey, darker grey at base. Feet and legs yellow or orange-yellow.

Sexes nearly alike but female usually with less mauve on the lesser wing coverts. I have not seen a juvenile but it almost certainly bears the same relation to the adult as does the juvenile of the African Green Pigeon, *Treron calva*.

The above description is of the nominate form from Madagascar, east of the High Plateau. The form from the central parts of western Madagascar, *T. australis xenia*, is slightly paler and more tinged with grey, with little or no green on the bright yellow tibial feathers. *T. australis griveaudi* from Moheli in the Comoro Islands is much greyer on head and upperparts but a deep yellow green on breast, belly and upper tail coverts. Its long under tail coverts are chestnut without any white tips and its legs and feet are reddish purple not yellow.

DISTRIBUTION AND HABITAT: Madagascar and Moheli Island in the Comoros. In Madagascar

Rand (1936) found it in relatively open woodland near the coast, in the denser parts of the savannah, gallery forests in the savannah, forest edges, areas of secondary growth and plantation. The Moheli form has been recorded (Benson, 1960) only in evergreen forest in the upper parts of Moheli.

FEEDING AND GENERAL HABITS: Usually in twos and threes. Sometimes large numbers gather in a fruiting tree. Feeds on fruits taken from the branches; will feed in low bushes as well as trees. Flight very rapid according to Rand from whose field-notes the above is largely compiled. Newton (1863) thought the flight of those he saw was 'slow and heavy for pigeons'. Probably this reflects different types of flight within the species' repertoire.

NESTING: No information.

VOICE: Rand (1936) records 'a loud rich call of several notes'. Griveaud (in Benson, 1960) describes 'a long drawn-out whistling trill followed by three higher pitched shorter whistles, these three notes sometimes (given) . . . on their own'.

DISPLAY: No information.

OTHER NAMES: Moheli Green Pigeon (*T. a. griveaudi*).

REFERENCES

BENSON, C. W. 1960. The Birds of the Comoro Islands: Results of the British Ornithologists' Union Centenary Expedition 1958. *Ibis*, **103B**: 1: 1–106 (50–51).
NEWTON, E. 1863. Notes of a second visit to Madagascar. *Ibis*, **5**, First Series; 452–461.
RAND, A. L. 1936. The Distribution & Habits of Madagascar Birds. *Bull. Amer. Mus. Nat. Hist.* **72**: Art. **5**: pp. 143–499.

AFRICAN GREEN PIGEON   *Treron calva*

Columba calva Temminck, in Knip, Les Pigeons, 1808, Les Columbars, p. 35, pl. 7.

DESCRIPTION: This species varies considerably throughout its range and many races have been named and described. Most of them intergrade and only the more divergent will be described here. The general trend is from yellow-footed, large-cered, grey-tailed forms in the west to red or orange-footed small-cered forms with green or green-tinged tails in the east and south-east. Forms from humid tropical areas tend to be a darker and duller green, those from dryer areas a paler and more yellowish green.

The nominate form, *T. c. calva*, from Lower Guinea, northern Angola and the western Congo is rather smaller than a Feral Pigeon but plumper and heavier in build with a large cere extending far back beyond the nostrils. General plumage dark olive green slightly tinged with yellow on head and underparts. An ill-defined grey patch on hind neck and upper mantle. Dark mauve patch on shoulder of wing. Outer secondaries and primaries black, the former with pronounced and the latter with faint pale yellow edges to outer webs. Broader pale yellow edges to greater coverts forming, as with most other green pigeons, a prominent yellow stripe on the folded wing. Flanks mottled dark green and yellow. Tibial feathers yellow. Shorter under tail coverts dark green tipped white, longer under tail coverts chestnut with pale buff tips. Central tail feathers bluish grey, sometimes with faint green wash. Outer ones dark grey, sometimes faintly washed green, with broad grey terminal band. Underside of tail blackish at base, pale grey at end. Irides inner ring blue or purplish blue, outer ring blue grey and brown, brown, cream-coloured, red or purple. Bill grey or bluish grey with paler tip, base of bill and cere red or deep pink. Legs and feet yellow, dark yellow or orange yellow. Sexes almost alike but cere of female usually smaller and less bright and her plumage slightly duller. Juvenile much like adult in colour but yellower on belly and body plumage much softer and more mossy looking with ill-defined yellow-green fringe to most feathers of upperparts which are otherwise greyer than the adults. No mauve on wing. Irides reddish brown, feet and cere dull purplish. Much (but not all) of this first plumage is quickly replaced by plumage intermediate between it and the adult's and before the bird is full grown it is moulting into adult dress. *T. c. poensis* from Fernando Po Island is rather larger and more yellowish green below. *T. c. virescens* from Principé is like *calva* but a slightly duller green. *T. c. nudirostris* from Senegal, Gambia and Portuguese Guinea has a slightly smaller cere and is much paler and brighter in colour than *calva* being a beautiful bright light yellow-green on head, neck and breast and a pale greyish green above. *T. c. brevicera* from eastern Kenya and north-eastern Tanganyika is much like *nudirostris* in colour but not quite so pale and bright, and has a well-defined clear blue-grey patch on the hind neck and upper mantle. Its flanks are mottled dark green and whitish but the tibial feathers bright yellow as in western forms. It has a much smaller cere than the west African forms. The cere is often orange or yellow, the feet are red or orange. The most strikingly differentiated form is *T. c. delalandii* from the lowland regions of eastern Africa from Mombasa south to Natal and the eastern half of Cape Province. It has a greenish grey head, neck, breast and underparts and the green of its upperparts is a very bright yellowish green, the tail feathers predominantly dark yellow-green with a broad whitish green terminal band. The forms not mentioned here are either very similar to one of the forms described above discussed or intermediate between two or more of them. See introduction to this group for reasons for treating *delalandii* as a race of *calva*.

DISTRIBUTION AND HABITAT: Africa from Senegal and Gambia east to south-west Ethiopia southward to southern Africa, the islands of Principé and Fernando Po in the Gulf of Guinea. Inhabits both forest and savannah; frequenting especially areas of secondary growth and clumps of trees and strips of riverside woods in fairly open country.

FEEDING AND GENERAL HABITS: Feeds chiefly on fruits and berries taken from the branches. Wild figs and the fruits of the parasol tree *Musanga* are major foods when available. Also takes buds of mangroves (probably also of many other trees) and, locally, cultivated millet when the grains are in the 'milky' stage. Recorded coming to the ground apparently to eat earth at bare patches in the forest (Chapin, 1939). Climbs, clings and hangs upside down when feeding. Usually in small parties but large flocks may gather at good feeding trees. Flight very swift. When in a tree it 'freezes' when alarmed (but not sufficiently so to fly away) and is then most difficult to see among the foliage. In some areas sedentary but over most of its range indulges in local migration or nomadism, probably in reference in food supplies.

NESTING: Usual pigeon nest, often very small and frail, in a tree. Usually fairly high up and among thick foliage. One or two white eggs. This is one of the few species of pigeon whose clutch size is known to differ in different parts of its range. In east and south Africa the clutch is usually two eggs but sometimes only one. In west Africa and the Congo clutch size is usually, perhaps always, one only. It seems probable that this difference is correlated with a difference in the quality or quantity (or both) of food available in the different areas. It may have significance in this connection that the breeding season would appear to be prolonged in the west African tropical regions (Bates, 1930; Chapin, 1939), but restricted to a fairly short period in southern Africa (Benson, 1953; McLachlan & Liversidge, 1957).

VOICE: The descriptions of most observers all appear, most probably, to refer to versions of the same call. All describe (in slightly different terminology) a high-pitched whistling or whinneying of several musical notes followed by three or four harsher notes, these latter with a disgusted or contemptuous intonation. Some record a similar call but ending in a purr or throaty coo, or clicking popping sounds. Mrs. Snow (in litt.) frequently heard a loud 'kick-a-week, kick-a-week' which was made by a bird when chasing another and is probably a cry of aggression or general excitement. I know of no comprehensive or comparative account of the voice of this species. A captive pair I often watched in the London Zoo were always silent.

DISPLAY: These notes are based mostly on observations of a captive pair of one of the West African races (either *T. c. calva* or *T. c. sharpei*) at the London Zoo. The equivalent of nodding, seen in both friendly context between the pair and in a hostile context towards other green pigeons in the same aviary, is a quick shuddering to-and-fro movement of the head. The head is held more or less horizontally and at the same time the mandibles open and close rapidly.

The equivalent of the wing twitching of typical pigeons is an up and down movement of the tail whilst the wings are held closed and perfectly still. It is used both when threatening enemies and towards the approaching mate when on the nest site, just as is the wing twitching of other species. In Kenya Mrs. Snow saw a display performed by two of three birds together in a tree in which they turned away from one another, when about a yard apart, and erected their tails, thus presenting the brightly marked under tail coverts.

OTHER NAMES: Green Fruit Pigeon; African Fruit Pigeon.

REFERENCES

BATES, G. L. 1930. *Handbook of the Birds of West Africa*. London.
BENSON, C. W. 1953. *Check List of Nyasaland Birds*. Blantyre & Lusaka.
CHAPIN, J. P. 1939. The Birds of the Belgian Congo, Pt. 2. *Bull. Amer. Mus. Nat. Hist.* Vol. LXXV.
MACKWORTH-PRAED, C. W. & GRANT, C. H. B. 1957. *The African Handbook of Birds*. Series 1, Vol. 1 (2nd ed.). London.
McLACHLAN, G. R. & LIVERSIDGE, R. 1957. *Roberts' Birds of South Africa*. Revised ed. Cape Town.

PEMBA ISLAND GREEN PIGEON   *Treron pembaensis*

Treron pembaensis Pakenham, Bull. B.O.C. 60, 1940, p. 94.

DESCRIPTION: Between Barbary Dove and Feral Pigeon in size; very similar to the African Green Pigeon, with which it may be conspecific, but smaller and darker. Head, neck, breast and underparts slate grey tinged with green. Dark mauve patch on shoulder of wing. Upperparts greyish olive green, brighter on rump and upper tail coverts, otherwise as *Treron calva* (q.v.). Irides inner ring blue, outer ring purple. Bill greyish white at tip, base and cere dull red. Legs and feet yellow or orange.

DISTRIBUTION AND HABITAT: Pemba Island, off the East African coast. Frequents forest and well-wooded areas, including gardens and the neighbourhood of houses.

FEEDING AND GENERAL HABITS: Pakenham (1940 & 1943) to whom we owe what is known about this species in life, recorded that it feeds much on the young fruits of the betel palm *Areca catechu*. When breeding in trees around houses he found it showed little alarm at the presence of people.

NESTING: Usual pigeon nest in tree. Two white eggs. Breeds from December to February, probably also at other times.

VOICE: Pakenham describes a soft 'kiu-tiu-kiutiu, kiwrikek-wrikek' followed by a still soft purring 'krrr, rrr, rrr'.

DISPLAY: No information.

REFERENCES

PAKENHAM, R. H. W. 1940. A new Green Pigeon from Pemba Island. *Bull. B.O.C.* **60**: 94–95.
——1943. Field Notes on the Birds of Zanzibar and Pemba. *Ibis*, **85**: 165–189.

SÃO THOMÉ GREEN PIGEON   *Treron s. thomae*

Columba S. Thomae Gmelin, Syst. Nat. 1, Pt. 2, 1789, p. 778.

DESCRIPTION: Very similar to the duller West African races of *Treron calva* from which it differs most noticeably in its heavy, strongly arched bill and small cere. About the size of a Feral Pigeon but more heavily built. Head, neck and most of underparts dark greenish grey. Ventral region and tibial feathers patched bright yellow and dark green. Mantle, back, rump and wing coverts dark olive green. Dark mauve patch on shoulder. Primaries and secondaries blackish. Pale yellow edges to greater coverts and very narrow pale yellow edges to secondaries. Underwing blue grey. Tail grey washed olive with ill-defined blackish central band. Under tail coverts chestnut with creamy tips. Irides blue (one record, probably really blue with purple or red outer ring as in related species). Bill and foot colour not recorded but from the appearance of museum specimens it seems likely that the cere is dark in life, not bright red or orange as in the African Green Pigeon. Sexes alike. I have not seen a juvenile.

DISTRIBUTION AND HABITAT: São Thomé Island and Rollas Islet in the Gulf of Guinea. Boyd Alexander (in Bannerman, 1915) found it in tall forest.

FEEDING AND GENERAL HABITS: Little recorded. Presumably much as other green pigeons but the rather aberrant bill may have reference to some difference in feeding habits or foods taken.

NESTING: The only record I can find (Amadon, 1953) is of a nest, usual pigeon type, eight feet high in a cocoa tree. It contained one fresh egg. The clutch size is therefore uncertain.

VOICE: A bi-syllabic 'crooning rattle' recorded by Alexander (in Bannerman, 1915).

DISPLAY: No information.

REFERENCES

AMADON, D. 1953. Avian Systematics and Evolution in the Gulf of Guinea. *Bull. Amer. Mus. Nat. Hist.* **100**: Art. 3: 394–451.

BANNERMAN, D. A. 1915. Report on the Birds collected by the late Mr. Boyd-Alexander during his last expedition to Africa, Pt. 2, The Birds of St. Thomas' Island. *Ibis*, **3**: Tenth Series: 89–121.

PIN-TAILED GREEN PIGEON   *Treron apicauda*

Treron apicauda 'Hodgson' Blyth, Journ. As. Soc. Bengal, 14, Pt. 2.

DESCRIPTION: Rather smaller than a Feral Pigeon and less heavily built than most green pigeons with rather broad wings and long pointed tail (see sketch). General coloration bright yellowish green, palest on the underparts and darkest on the wing coverts and scapulars. Breast more or less golden, yellow-gold or pinkish gold (the feathers of this area are pink with gold or yellowish tips). An ill-defined greyish band across the mantle. Outer secondaries and primaries black. Yellow edges to median and greater coverts and (less pronounced) secondaries form yellow stripes on the closed wing as in other green pigeons. The two long pointed central tail feathers are bluish grey, washed with green at their tips. The remaining feathers in the otherwise wedge-shaped tail are bluish grey with black bases. Flanks green, feathers tipped whitish. Under tail coverts chestnut, tipped buffish. Underwing slate grey. Irides bright blue with outer ring of pink, red, orange, or reddish brown. Orbital skin blue. Bill pale greenish or whitish blue at tip, bright blue at base. Legs and feet red or purplish red.

Female duller than the male with, at most, only a trace of gold on the breast and grey on the mantle. Her long central tail feathers are much shorter than the male's and her under tail coverts are dull yellow-brown and whitish with grey-green central streaks. I have seen no very young birds. Immature males much resemble the female.

The above description applies to the nominate form, *T. a. apicauda*, of the Himalayan foothills from western India to Assam and south to Tenasserim. The form found in central Annam, *T. a. lowei*, is a little duller and less yellowish green generally but has very bright greenish yellow rump and upper tail coverts.   The form from northern Annam, Laos and Tonkin, *T. a. laotinus*, is similar but duller, lacking the very bright upper tail coverts.

DISTRIBUTION AND HABITAT: Himalayan foothills up to 6,000 feet from western India (Kumaon) to eastern Assam and south to Tenasserim.   The mountains of Laos, Tonkin and northern Annam and the mountains of central Annam and adjacent areas of Laos.   Inhabits woodland, particularly evergreen hill forest.   Locally in forest or wooded country in the plains, usually only when not breeding.   In Annam descends into the plains of Annam for the dry season, May to September, when many trees bear fruit.

FEEDING AND GENERAL HABITS: Recorded feeding on fruit and berries, particularly wild figs.   When feeding climbs about the branches with lowered head and tail close to the branch in a very parakeet-like manner and will hang head downwards when necessary.   Tail often thrown up vertically as the bird reaches forward.   Flight less swift and more direct than that of most green pigeons.   Usually in pairs or small parties but may congregate in larger numbers at food sources.   In early morning often suns itself on top branches of some dead tree.

NESTING: Usual pigeon nest in tree or bush, commonly about five to twenty feet high.   Two white eggs.   Apparently breeds at most times of the year, presumably whenever local conditions are suitable.

VOICE: Apparently has very musical whistling call, very like those of other green pigeons; guttural notes that are used in apparent threat and a subdued chattering.   I can find no detailed information as to the significance of its calls.

DISPLAY: No information.

OTHER NAMES: Long-tailed Green Pigeon.

REFERENCES

ALI, S.   1962.   *The Birds of Sikkim.*   Oxford.
BAKER, E. C. S.   1913.   *Indian Pigeons and Doves.*   London.

YELLOW-BELLIED PIN-TAILED GREEN PIGEON   *Treron oxyura*

Columba oxyura 'Reinw' Temminck, pl. col., livr. 41, 1823, pl. 240.

DESCRIPTION: Similar to the previous species, *Treron apicauda*, except as follows: Tail shorter and less strongly pointed.   General colour a darker and duller green; extensive bright yellow area on belly and ventral regions, but no yellow on the wings.   Irides with blue inner ring and mauve, pink or orange outer ring.   Orbital skin light green or bluish green.

DISTRIBUTION AND HABITAT: Sumatra and western Java. Inhabits mountainous country.

FEEDING AND GENERAL HABITS: Little recorded. Probably similar to *T. apicauda*.

NESTING: No information.

VOICE: No information.

DISPLAY: No information.

WHITE-BELLIED PIN-TAILED GREEN PIGEON   *Treron seimundi*

Sphenocercus seimundi Robinson, Bull. B.O.C. 25, 1910, p. 98.

DESCRIPTION: Very similar to the Pin-tailed Green Pigeon but darker in general colour with a conspicuous large white belly patch and less strongly pointed tail. Between Feral Pigeon and Barbary Dove in size. General colour a rather dark, olivaceous green tinged with coppery gold on the forehead and crown and lighter on the breast, rump, and upper tail coverts. Pinkish orange patch on sides of neck, varying amount of grey on hind neck and mantle. Small reddish purple patch on lesser coverts on the carpal area of the wing. Outermost greater wing coverts and secondaries black broadly edged with bright yellow on outer webs. Underwing grey. Belly snow white. Under tail coverts bright lemon yellow. Central tail feathers dark bluish grey. Outer ones greyish black with pale grey terminal band. Irides with outer ring pink, red, orange or yellow and inner ring blue or mauve. Orbital skin blue or purplish blue. Bill greyish or greenish grey at tip, base and cere blue or purplish blue. Feet red or purplish red. The female lacks the purple on wings and the orange-pink flush at side of neck. I have not seen a juvenile of this species.

The above description is of the nominate race, *T. s. seimundi* from the Malay Peninsula and Siam. In the form *T. seimundi modestus* from Annam the male lacks the pinkish orange patches on the sides of the neck and the golden tinge on the crown.

DISTRIBUTION AND HABITAT: Main mountain range of the Malay Peninsula, Annam, also recorded from south-western coast of Malay Peninsula and Siam (Bangkok). Inhabits mountain ranges and foothills. In Annam said to descend to the plains and nest there in winter.

FEEDING AND GENERAL HABITS: Apparently little known. Robinson (1928) recorded it as found feeding in high trees and flying at great height across a valley from one hill to the other.

NESTING: No information.

VOICE: No information.

DISPLAY: No information.

OTHER NAMES: Seimund's Green Pigeon.

REFERENCES

DELACOUR, J. & JABOUILLE, P. 1931. *Les Oiseaux de l'Indochine Française*. Vol. 2. Paris.
ROBINSON, H. C. 1928. *The Birds of the Malay Peninsula*. Vol. 2. London.

WEDGE-TAILED GREEN PIGEON   *Treron sphenura*

Vinago sphenura Vigors, Proc. Comm. Zool. Soc. London, 1831 (1832), p. 173.

DESCRIPTION: A little smaller than a Feral Pigeon. Less heavily built than most green pigeons. Central tail feathers longer, outer ones progressively shorter so that tail is a rather blunt wedge-shape when spread or partly spread. Head, neck and underparts bright yellowish-green, shading into coppery gold on the crown and breast. The golden breast feathers are salmon-pink except at the tips. Flanks and ventral regions streaked pale yellowish and dark green. The long under tail coverts pale yellowish chestnut. Hind neck bright green shading into vinous grey on upper part of mantle. Inner wing coverts and a varying extent of the mantle dark purplish chestnut. Rest of upperparts dark green or greyish green. Outer secondaries and primaries blackish. Narrow yellow edgings to greater coverts, secondaries and primaries. Central tail feathers as back, outer ones grey with blackish subterminal band. Underwing slate grey. Underside of tail light grey. Irides with pink, red, or pinkish-buff outer ring and blue inner ring; a minority of specimens in museum collections are stated to have had the inner ring of the eye red and the outer blue; it is uncertain whether this reversal of the usual condition does occur or whether errors have been made by the collectors. Orbital skin light blue. Bill light blue at base, whitish blue or greyish at tip. Feet bright red or deep pink.

Female lacks the maroon and golden colours of the male, her head and breast being entirely pale yellowish green and her upperparts dark green. Her under tail coverts are pale yellow with dark green centre stripes. The juvenile is much like the female but duller. Young males start to acquire adult plumage early, usually having some maroon feathers before they are fully grown.

The above description is of the nominate form which occurs from Kashmir to Burma, the form from Yunnan and northern Tonkin has been separated as *T. s. yunnanensis*, but differs only in the female being a slightly darker green. *T. s. robinsoni* from Malay Peninsula and *T. s. annamensis* from Annam are slightly smaller and darker, and the males usually show little or no golden colour on head and breast. *T. s. korthalsi* from Sumatra, Java, and Lombok has (in the male) darker golden on the breast and darker chestnut on the under tail coverts. The form from Hainan, *T. s. oblitus*, is said to be small and a very bright green but it was described from a single female.

DISTRIBUTION AND HABITAT: Mountains and hill country of northern India from Kashmir to Assam, east and south to Burma, Yunnan, Annam, Tonkin, the island of Hainan, the main mountain range of the Malay Peninsula and the mountains of Sumatra, Java, and Lombok. Inhabits various types of forest and wooded areas of mountains between 2,000 and 8,000 feet. Locally migratory, at any rate in northern India where the higher and more northerly parts of its breeding range are deserted in winter. In spite of its feeding habits it may occur in conifer as well as in evergreen or deciduous forests.

FEEDING AND GENERAL HABITS: Feeds on fruits and berries taken from the branches. Probably other food also taken at times. Dodsworth, who studied this species in northern India and to whom we owe most of the detailed information on it, found the berries of *Myrica sapuida* to be an important food in the wild. When feeding shows the usual fruit pigeon agility at clambering, clinging and hanging among the branches. Feeds most intensely in morning and evening.

Usually seen singly (in breeding season when mate is on nest?), in pairs or small parties, rarely in large flocks. Flight said by some observers to be direct and not (as pigeons go) very swift, by others to be direct *and* swift. Smythies, however, writing of the species in Burma, describes the flight as deeply undulating like a woodpecker's. This latter suggests a display flight rather than the normal flight especially in view of the statements of others.

NESTING: Usual pigeon nest in a tree, but tends to nest higher than tree-nesting pigeons commonly do, up to fifty feet and usually over twenty feet, although sometimes much lower. Nest more often than not on a large bough. Two white eggs; incubation period, in captivity in England, 14 days or less; young fledged at 12 days (Baily, 1917). The Wedge-tailed Green Pigeon is one of the many species that often nests near to the occupied nest of a pair of drongos (*Dicrurus* sp.) presumably this has survival value owing to the drongos' ferocity and success in attacking avian nest predators such as crows and some hawks. In northern India breeds from April to August.

VOICE: What is, probably, the advertising coo is a very rich and musical series of whistling or fluting notes which have been variously transliterated but have impressed all hearers with their richness and beauty. Dodsworth considered Blyth's description of it the best and quotes him as follows: 'The notes bear some resemblance to the human voice in singing and are highly musical in tone, being considerably prolonged and modulated, but always terminating abruptly, and every time the stave is repeated exactly as before, so that it soon becomes wearisome to a European ear!' Dodsworth also records a 'low coo' when displaying (q.v.) and a low 'coo-coo' when nest calling. His most detailed observations were, however, based only on one pair of birds of which one (the female) died when less than a year old.

DISPLAY: Dodsworth's captive male, when sexually excited, would hop from perch to perch with bowed head, puffed out throat and wings and tail spread. This was done as a preliminary to nest-calling in a corner of the cage. When the female joined the nest-calling male both would 'pretend to pick up something from the ground'. This last probably refers to incipient or abortive nest building movements. Further detailed observations on this and other green pigeons are much to be desired.

OTHER NAMES: Kokla; Singing Green Pigeon.

REFERENCES

ALI, S. 1962. *The Birds of Sikkim.* Oxford.

BAKER, E. C. S. 1913. *Indian Pigeons and Doves.* London.

BAILEY W. S. 1917. The Breeding of the Green Fruit Pigeon. *Bird Notes*, New Series, **8**: 158–159.

DODSWORTH, P. T. L. 1912. Notes on some habits of the Kokla or Wedge-tailed Green Pigeon *Sphenocercus sphenurus* (Vigors) in confinement. *Avicult. Magazine*, Third Series, **3**: 129–135 and 165–169.

SMYTHIES, B. E. 1953. *The Birds of Burma.* London.

WHITE-BELLIED WEDGE-TAILED GREEN PIGEON   *Treron sieboldii*

Columba sieboldii Temminck, pl. col., liver. 93, 1835, pl. 549.

DESCRIPTION: Very similar to the previous species (*Treron sphenura*) to which it is closely related. Differs in having less pronounced golden tinge on breast and very little on crown and forehead, paler (nearly white) belly and under tail coverts blotched or streaked with grey green on a whitish yellow ground. Irides with blue inner ring and purple, pink or red outer ring. Bill cobalt blue or greyish blue at base, greyer at tip. Feet red or purplish red. Female lacks the purple on wing coverts and has breast and forehead yellowish green.

The above description is of the nominate form which occurs in Japan. The Formosan form *T. sieboldii sororius* shows no appreciable difference. In the form from Tonkin and Annam, *T. s. murielae*, the male has a rich golden tinge on forehead, crown and breast.

DISTRIBUTION AND HABITAT : Japan, Formosa, Tonkin and extreme southern China south to central Annam. In the northern parts of Japan a summer resident only. Inhabits woods and forests. In Japan both deciduous and mixed woodlands but with a strong preference for the remaining areas of primeval forest. Most often in wooded hills or wooded mountain slopes.

FEEDING AND GENERAL HABITS : Feeds largely on fruits. Wild cherries and acorns of *Pasanai cuspidata* and *Quercus glauca* definitely recorded. Most food taken from branches but also (*fide* Yamashina,1961) sometimes feeds on the ground. Usually in pairs or small parties of up to ten individuals. Flight swift and straight with jerky wing-beats often, however, making rapid turns or changes of direction in flight. The above is compiled chiefly from the observations of Yamashina (1961) and Jahn (1942) on the species in Japan.

NESTING : Usual pigeon nest in tree or shrub. Two white eggs (Yamashina, 1961).

VOICE : What is probably the advertising coo has been described by Yamashina as a 'very mournful . . . extended oaooh, oaooh', by Jahn as 'a high and a deep (note) something like o-vuuo-vuuo-vuuo-vououo-oo', uttered together and suggestive of a crying child. Has a short alarm note rendered as 'pyu' by Yamashina.

DISPLAY : No information.

OTHER NAMES : Siebold's Green Pigeon ; Japanese Green Pigeon.

REFERENCES

JAHN, H. 1942. Zur Oekologie und Biologie der Vögel Japans. *Journ. f. Orn.* **90**: 7–301 (267–269).
YAMASHINA, H. 1961. Birds in Japan. Tokyo.

FORMOSAN GREEN PIGEON   *Treron formosae*

Treron formosae Swinhoe, Ibis, 1863, p. 396.

DESCRIPTION : Very similar to the two previous species, *Treron sphenura* and *T. sieboldii*, to which it is very closely allied. It differs as follows : Tail less wedge-shaped ; the general plumage a darker green, the breast a deep and only slightly yellowish green. Belly and ventral regions pale yellow marked with green. Crown of head deep golden bronze. Irides (from one specimen only) with purple and black inner rings and blood-red outer ring. The female lacks the dull purple patch on the shoulder and the golden bronze on the head.

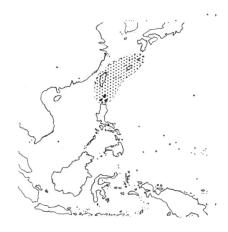

The above description is of the nominate race from Formosa. The form from the Philippine Islands, *T. f. australis* is similar but its irides have blue inner ring and pink outer ring, (McGregor, 1909). I have not seen a specimen. The forms from the Riu Kiu (Loo Choo) islands, *T. f. permagna* and *T. f. medioximus*, are larger and darker and lack the golden bronze on the crown.

DISTRIBUTION AND HABITAT: The mountains of Formosa. The Riu Kiu (Loo Choo) islands and the Philippine islands of Batan, Calayan and Camiguin.

FEEDING AND HABITS: Presumably much as the other wedge-tailed green pigeons but I can find nothing recorded.

NESTING: No information.

VOICE: Swinhoe (1866) described one call of this species as 'like a man with a bad ear and a bad voice trying to coo like a dove'. The voice of the Philippine form, as described by McGregor (1909) ounds very like that of *Treron seeboldii* (q.v.).

DISPLAY: No information.

REFERENCES

McGREGOR, R. C. 1909. *A Manual of Philippine Birds*, Pt. 1, p. 26. Manila.
SWINHOE, R. 1866. Ornithological Notes from Formosa. *Ibis*, 1866, **2**, New Series: 392–406.

THE FRUIT DOVES

The fruit doves or smaller-sized fruit pigeons are currently placed in the genus *Ptilinopus*. They are very closely related to the imperial pigeons of the genus *Ducula*. Indeed such species as *Ducula poliocephala* and its near allies form a link between the two genera which have a similar geographical distribution.

In general, however, the fruit doves are smaller than the imperial pigeons, they comprise a greater number of species and, as would therefore be expected, show a greater variety of colour-patterns. Some of them are among the most richly and beautifully coloured of any birds. Most of them are predominantly green in colour, usually with bands and patches of bright or contrasting colours on the underparts and with pink or purple caps. Some species, however, such as the vivid Orange Dove, diverge considerably from this general pattern.

They vary in size from the Dwarf Fruit Dove, which is about as large as a House Sparrow, to the Australian form of the Magnificent Fruit Dove which is as large as a Wood Pigeon. Most of them, however, are about the size of a Barbary Dove, but heavier in build and shorter-tailed.

They nest above ground in trees or shrubs and lay one egg, or at least those species whose clutch-size is known do so. All of them feed on berries and fruits. Probably they also feed on buds and young foliage and some forms of invertebrate life.

The amount of speciation that has taken place, particularly in New Guinea, the number of sympatric species and consequent variety of species-specific markings make it difficult to assess relationship within the genus *Ptilinopus*. There is a lack of any detailed information on display or other points of behaviour that might help. Some species show characters intermediate between or common to both of almost any two definable groups. Cain (1954) subdivided the genus and discussed its taxonomic characters, and the affinities of the component species. The species are discussed here in reference to Cain's work.

Cain placed in the subgenus *Leucotreron*, the Pink-necked Fruit Dove, *P. porphyrea*, The Black-backed Fruit Dove, *P. cincta*, The Banded Pigeon, *P. alligator* and the Red-naped Fruit Dove, *P. dohertyi*.

These all agree largely in plumage pattern (see species descriptions) having a concolorous or simply patterned head, neck and breast divided from the rest of the plumage by a narrow whitish line and, on the breast, by a dark bar immediately behind it, unmarked wings with attenuated first primary and rather large size (for fruit doves). Cain treats *alligator* as a race of *cincta* but in view of the rather considerable colour differences I prefer to treat them as members of a superspecies, together with *dohertyi*. The Pink-necked Fruit Dove overlaps the Black-backed Fruit Dove only on Bali and is otherwise its geographical representative but it differs considerably in colour, in having bifurcated breast feathers and in lacking, or almost lacking indented ends to its inner primaries.

Marche's Fruit Dove, *P. marchei*, Merrill's Fruit Dove, *P. merrilli*, Fischer's Fruit Dove, *P. fischeri*, the Black-chinned Fruit Dove *P. leclancheri* and the Dark-chinned Fruit Dove *P. subgularis* are placed together by Cain in the subgenus *Rhamphiculus* which he defines as 'Medium-sized to large *Ptilinopids* (wing length 150 to 170 mm) with the most deeply coloured patches of head ornamentation (excepting the chin stripe) lateral, sometimes meeting on the hind neck to form a ring, (A red cap occurs in *Pt. merrilli faustinoi.*). No tendency to ornamentation of the wings, nor to a pale line bounding the whole of the anterior parts as in *Leucotreron*. First primary emarginate, usually very obviously. Philippines and Celebes'.

This definition is not entirely accurate as *P. marchei* and *P. merrilli* have very striking ornamentation on the wings produced by highly modified areas on the outer webs of many of their secondaries and *P. fischeri* certainly shows 'a tendency to ornamentation' in the bright yellow edges to the outer webs of its secondaries. Cain places *marchei* and *merrilli* in the one subgroup and *occipitalis* and *fischeri* in another. I agree with *occipitalis* and *fischeri* being treated as members of a superspecies but *occipitalis* seems to give every indication of being at least as closely related to *marchei* as *merrilli* is. It has a very similar plumage pattern on head and breast to that of *marchei* whereas *merrilli* which has similarly modified secondaries to *marchei* otherwise differs considerably from it. In particular it has chestnut axilliaries and under wing coverts, the only fruit dove with this feature except *P. formosus* which shows it to a lesser degree. The close relationship of these four species is beyond doubt. The differences between *fischeri*, *merrilli* and *marchei* which probably developed or intensified as species-specific characters in reference to each other after they became sympatric and the immediately apparent resemblances between the allopatric *marchei* and *occipitalis* need not therefore imply that they are the most nearly related among the four species. They do, however, in my opinion, make it inadvisable to link *marchei* more closely with *merrilli* than with *occipitalis*.

P. leclancheri and *P. subgularis* are, as Cain points out, closely related and best treated as members of a superspecies. They seem to me to stand in an intermediate position between the four species discussed above and others not included by Cain in his subgenus *Rhamphiculus*. *P. subgularis* is closely related to the Scarlet-breasted Fruit Dove *P. formosus*, one of the two species formerly placed in the genus *Megaloprepia* and not included in Cain's paper. It agrees with *formosus* in shape and proportions, in its chestnut under tail coverts and in general details of plumage pattern. It differs in its dark throat patch and in having an attenuated first primary. The colour pattern of the two has more in common than at first appears. Where *subgularis* is grey on head and breast, *formosus* is grey washed with yellowish green (head) or slightly greyish green; where *subgularis* is chestnut on the flanks and ventral area *formosus* has a more extensive area of feathers that are chestnut at the base but greenish gold on the exposed tips; *subgularis* has a buff patch on the lower breast instead of a scarlet one. Thus most of the more obvious colour differences between the two could probably have been brought about simply by loss of some carotenoid pigments by one or their acquisition by the other. The two are allopatric and are I think, closely allied to the Magnificent Fruit Pigeon, *P. magnificus* of New Guinea. Except for its yellow wing spots and much more extensive purple (instead of scarlet) colour on the underparts *magnificus* is very close to *formosus* in colour pattern while in many individuals the purple of the breast is continued up the median line of the throat (becoming duller and less dark) until it nearly reaches the base on the lower mandible where it is suggestive of the throat stripe of *subgularis*. These three species have diverged rather too far from each other to be treated here as members of a superspecies (besides the colour differences *subgularis* has a strongly attenuated first primary and *magnificus* indented ends to some of the inner primaries) but they are certainly geographical representatives.

The Jambu Fruit Dove, *P. jambu* is a very distinct species. Its characters suggest to me that it is most closely allied to species placed by Cain in the subgenera *Leucotreron* and *Rhamphiculus* and I do not concur with Cain's opinion that it might on the other hand be more closely related to *P. melanospila*. It resembles *P. leclancheri* in having a similar dark throat patch, chestnut under tail coverts, similarly patterned tail and a similar general size and coloration of the upperparts. The distinctive red, pinks and creamy white on the male's head and breast are very similar in tone and texture to those of *P. dohertyi* although their distribution is somewhat different. As Cain points out the patterns on the head and breast are rather like those seen in *P. marchei*, a species which, incidently, possesses a brown throat patch which although larger and paler is probably the homologue of those of *subgularis*, *leclancheri* and *jambu*. In distribution *jambu* is allopatric to *marchei*, *dohertyi*, *subgularis* and *leclancheri* and I think, as did Salvadori (1893), that its affinities are with these forms.

The remaining species, together with *P. jambu*, are all placed by Cain in his subgenus *Ptilinopus* which he defines as containing 'Small to medium-sized Ptilinopids (wing length 90 to 160 mm only in *Pt. huttoni* 170 mm), with strong tendencies to ornamentation of the wing coverts and scapulars and of the underparts, either a pectoral or abdominal patch or both being almost always present. The most deeply coloured patches on the head (excepting the chin stripe) are dorsal and median, forming a cap. First primary often clearly emarginate, sometimes obscurely so or merely tapering to the tip'.

The Ornate Fruit Dove, *P. ornatus*, the Pink-spotted Fruit Dove, *P. perlatus*, the Orange-fronted Fruit Dove, *P. aurantiifrons*, Wallace's Fruit Dove *P. wallacii* and the New Hebrides Fruit Dove, *P. tannensis* are placed together by Cain in a species group. *P. ornatus* and *P. perlatus* which are placed by Cain in a subgroup are obviously closely allied and present the unusual case of two closely related sympatric species of similar size having a virtually identical colour pattern of head (including bill and eye colour) and breast. Presumably the differently coloured wing spots, pink in *perlatus*, grey in *ornatus*, and the purple shoulder bar of the latter serve as recognition marks together, perhaps, with vocal differences. The above statements apply to the form of *ornatus* found in south-eastern New Guinea. This form with its greenish gold head overlaps, in part of its range, with the carmine-capped *P. wallacii*. Possibly selection for isolating mechanisms in reference to *wallacii* are, at least partly, the reason for its failure to develop different head colouring from *perlatus*, as the northern form of *ornatus*, which does not overlap with *wallacii*, has a reddish purple head.

P. aurantiifrons and *P. wallacii* have features in common with *ornatus* and *perlatus* and are probably most closely related to them although I hesitate to follow Cain in bracketing them together in a subgroup of which they are the only members.

They resemble each other in having a similar patterning of silver grey spotting on mantle and wing coverts and to a lesser extent, in the distribution of grey (silver grey in *wallacii*, deep bluish grey in *aurantiifrons*) but in other points of colour pattern seem to link the *ornatus* subgroup with other species. If *wallacii* is compared with the superb Fruit Dove, *P. superbus*, it will be seen that their plumage patterns are remarkably alike although the colours differ, *wallacii* having no purple and rust red on breast and hind neck, a white instead of a blackish blue pectoral band, silver grey instead of blackish blue wing spots and an orange belly patch.   The last feature is one common to species, as *P. richardsii* and *P. regina*, whose colour patterns indicate relationship to *superbus*.   Silver grey, white or pink spots or bars although giving a very different appearance, and hence of use for species-specific recognition, need not imply any lack of fairly close affinity with forms with similarly placed dark markings.   The difference is visually very similar to that shown by barred or chequered Domestic Pigeons *C. livia* that carry the 'stencil' factor and 'normal' barred or spotted birds and a similar relatively 'simple' genetic factor might be involved in the pale rather than dark spotting of these wild species.

P. tannensis would, as Cain suggested, appear to be an offshoot of *ornatus* stock.   It lacks bright markings on head and breast but although otherwise showing the relative dullness common in island forms it has not only developed bright silver spotting on its shoulders but also yellow wing spots comparable in appearance to those of *magnificus*.

The many apparently closely related fruit doves with (usually) bright-coloured caps and spotted wings were included by Cain (1954) in his *purparatus* group which he defined as 'Small to medium species (wing length 95 to 145, 170 mm in *Pt. huttoni*) with a bright red, purple or blue cap bordered behind with yellow (or with vestiges of such a cap), and with clearly or obscurely bifid breast feathers.   Scapular and wing covert spots present, dark blue, pink, pale purple, or emerald green, often not clearly marked.   Abdomen ornamented with a large patch and a darker transverse bar or spot, reduced or absent in a few forms.   Under tail coverts plain red, orange or yellow (spotted only in *Pt. superbus*).   First primary emarginate, almost always very clearly'.   The Blue-capped Fruit Dove, *P. monacha*, Grey-green Fruit Dove, *P. purparatus*, the Purple-capped Fruit Dove, *P. porphyraceus*, the Rarotonga Fruit Dove, *P. rarotongensis*, the Henderson Island Fruit Dove, *P. insularis*, the Marianas Fruit Dove, *P. roseicapilla*, the Pink-capped Fruit Dove, *P. regina*, the Silver-capped Fruit Dove, *P. richardsii*, Grey's Fruit Dove, *P. greyii*, the Rapa Island Fruit Dove, *P. huttoni*, together with the two pairs of overlapping species, the Lilac-capped Fruit Dove, *P. coronulatus*, and the Crimson-capped Fruit Dove, *P. pulchellus* of New Guinea and the White-capped Fruit Dove, *P. dupetithouarsii*, and the Red-moustached Fruit Dove, *P. mercierii*, are all considered by Cain to represent 'one superspecies with two doublets'.   Although this treatment results in a superspecies, plus doublets, with some rather strongly divergent members I am in favour of it except as regards *P. monacha*.   This very distinct species is a geographical representative of the *purpuratus* group but in view of its degree of differentiation I prefer not to include it in the same superspecies.   The sympatric forms of the *purpuratus* superspecies are in both instances very similarly sized and with basically very similar plumage patterns but with striking differences in appearance due to different coloration of the head and underparts.   This is especially noticeable in *dupetithouarsii* and *mercierii* which have an indentical plumage pattern but the former has a white cap and malar patches and orange belly patch and the latter a purplish crimson cap and malar patches and an entirely yellow belly.   In this connection it is likely that the differences between *P. richardsii* and *P. greyii* (purple cap and belly patch, poorly developed pinkish grey markings on scapulars and inner secondaries in *greyii*, silver-grey cap, orange belly patch and well developed bright pink wing markings in *richardsii*) may have developed in reference to each other.   They are not known to occur together but in view of their respective ranges may well have done so in the recent past.

The Rapa Island Fruit Dove *P. huttoni* shows considerable divergence in its much larger size, proportionately longer bill and loose 'hairy' plumage.   These differences suggest that it may have been longer isolated than any other form.   *P. purpuratus* has evidently progressed further than *huttoni* towards the loss of species-specific markings but in size and plumage texture is nearer the average for the group.   The Pelew Island Fruit Dove, *P. pelewensis* seems better given specific rank than considered as a race of *P. porphyraceus*.

Cain puts the Many-coloured Fruit Dove *P. perousii* and the Superb Fruit Dove *P. superbus* together as the only two members of a separate subgroup which he defines as having 'lower neck and upper back with a more or less extensive bright brownish red or dark red band.   Wide transverse abdominal band present'.   Elsewhere (Cain, 1954a) he gives as reasons for linking *perousii* with *superbus* rather than with the *purpuratus* species group as Ripley and Birckhead (1942) had done, its red mantle bar, the very pale abdomen of the male and its sexual dimorphism. I think Ripley and Birckhead were right and that *perousii* is more closely related to the *purpuratus* superspecies than to *superbus*. The purplish crimson band extending from the innermost wing coverts across the mantle of *perousii* seems to be analogous to not homologous with the rusty orange band extending from the sides of the neck across the hind neck of *superbus; perousii* has no equivalent of the purple-blue carpal patches of *superbus*. The pale belly of the male *perousii* is part of its general pallor and does not necessarily indicate relationship to *superbus* where the similarly coloured belly is marked with two conspicuous green lateral patches of which *perousii* shows no trace. *P. superbus* and *P. perousii* have very different types of sexual dimorphism. The female *superbus* has a rather juvenile-like green plumage with a distinctive blue-black patch on the nape. In *perousii* both sexes have a similar purplish red cap and similar display plumage on the breast. The sexual dimorphism seems to have involved only the male becoming paler, apparently through partial loss of melanim pigments and on tail and wings of carotenoid pigments also and his acquisition of the purplish red band on the mantle. The cap of *perousii* is identical with that of most members of the *purpuratus* superspecies and differs from that of *superbus* in being divided from the eye (or rather the orbital skin) by a pale area (see sketch) and in not extending onto the nape.

Both sexes of *perousii* have bright purplish pink under tail coverts. This character is shared, to the same or a lesser degree, by five members of the *purpuratus* superspecies (*greyii, richardsii, porphyraceus, pelewensis* and *huttoni*) but not by *superbus* in which both sexes have the under tail coverts white blotched with green like those of *P. wallacii*. The display plumage on the breast of both sexes of *perousii* is certainly very like that of the male *superbus* but it is equally like that of *pelewensis*, a member of the *purpuratus* superspecies. I think that *perousii's* closest affinities are with Cain's *purpuratus* subgroup. It and *P. porphyraceus* with which it overlaps with, however (*fide* Ripley and Birckhead), some ecological separation represent another 'doublet' similar to those discussed above.

Some of the resemblances of plumage pattern between *P. suberbus* and *P. wallacii* have already been pointed out when discussing the latter's affinities. In addition they have similar green markings on the flanks and under tail coverts, the shape and extent of the cap of *wallacii* is the same as that of the male *superbus*, and *wallacii* has a dark orange shoulder patch where *superbus* has a dark bluish one. I think that *superbus* is a connecting link between the *purpuratus* group and *wallacii* and is probably more closely related to the latter than to the former.

The next group separated by Cain is his *viridis* species group which he defines as 'Forms medium-sized for this genus (wing length 115 to 135 mm). Pectoral patch large, sharply defined and coloured white, yellow or deep red. Abdominal patch reduced and dark purple or absent. Wing covert spots present, dark blue or grey. First primary not or only slightly emarginate". In this are included two subgroups, one containing the White-bibbed Fruit Dove, *P. rivoli*, and the Yellow-bibbed Fruit Dove, *P. solomonensis*, and the other the Red-bibbed Fruit Dove, *P. viridis*. I am not convinced that these two subgroups are necessarily more closely related to each other than to other fruit doves. Their colour patterns are not particularly close, neither the wing spots nor the coloured 'bib' occupying the same position. *P. rivoli* and *P. solomonensis* seem to have as many features in common with such forms as *purpuratus* and *wallacii* as they have with *viridis*.

I follow Cain in treating *ocularis* as a race of *solomonensis* as, in spite of the difference in colour pattern of the head, intermediate forms occur. I also agree with Cain's arguments for considering *pectoralis* a race of *viridis*. I think, however, that the White-headed Fruit Dove, *P. eugeniae*, is best considered as a species, forming a superspecies, with *viridis*, not as a race of the latter. Not only would the great difference in the coloration of the head and orbital skin between *eugeniae* and the geographically nearest forms of *viridis* probably act as an isolating mechanism were they to come together but the fact that there is no evidence of introgression suggests that it may already have functioned to prevent either form from interbreeding with stragglers of the other.

The Orange-bellied Fruit Dove, *P, iozonus*, the Knob-billed Fruit Dove, *P. insolitus*, the Grey-headed Fruit Dove, *P. hyogastra*, the Carunculated Fruit Dove, *P. granulifrons*, the Black-naped Fruit Dove, *P. melanospila* and the Dwarf Fruit Dove, *P. naina* are placed by Cain in the *hyogastra* species group which he defines as 'medium-sized to small for this subgenus (wing length 90 to 130 mm). Breast, neck and back plain green, unornamented. Abdomen with an orange or violet patch (absent in *Pt. melanospila*). Head plain green or grey unornamented or with a chin stripe and nuchal spot. First primary indistinctly emarginated or merely tapering'. Within it he puts together *P. iozonus* and *P. insolitus* in one subgroup and the remaining species together in another.

I fully concur with Cain in thinking *iozonus* and *insolitus* best considered members of a superspecies; they are allopatric and alike in colour pattern but differ in the enormously developed cere of *insolitus*. I consider, however, that *hyogastra* and *granulifrons* which differ from each other in a similar way (the former having an enlarged cere which is, however, carunculated not smooth as in *insolitus*) are closely related to *insolitus* and *iozonus* and best placed in the same superspecies. All four are allopatric in distribution, not known to differ in habits, of similar size and their colour patterns are almost identical except that *granulifrons* and *hyogastra* have grey heads and a purple instead of orange belly patch.

P. melanospila is a very distinct species but I agree that its affinities are most probably with the *hyogastra* species group to the other members of which it is allopatric. I do not think it advisable to ally *P. naina* with this, or any other group within *Ptilinopus* on present knowledge. Its small size, in which it is approached most nearly by *P. monacha* and the apparently vestigial grey patches at the side of the breast suggest a possible affinity with the *purpuratus* group. Its bright yellow wing markings obviously derive from a retention and intensification of the juvenile pattern. The lack of any conspicuous head or breast markings (and their probable loss in the course of evolution) have no doubt been due to greater predation pressure as a result of its small size and the fact that its diminutive size alone probably functions as a species-isolating mechanism in reference to the other and much larger species with which it is sympatric.

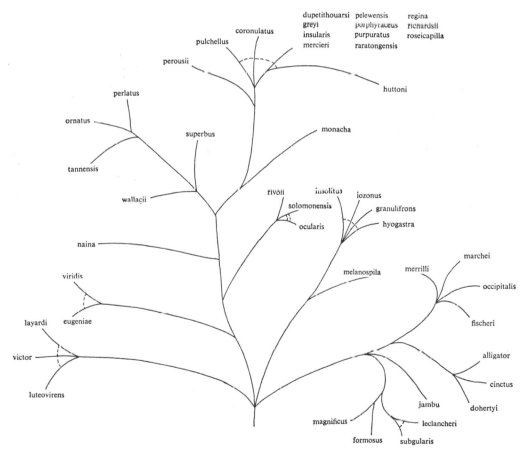

FIG. D.13: Presumed relationships of species in the genus *Ptilinopus*.

The very distinctive Orange Dove, *P. victor*, Golden Dove, *P. luteovirens* and Yellow-headed Dove *P. layardi* form a superspecies and, as Amadon (1943) has pointed out, represent a very early colonisation of Fiji by *Ptilinopus* stock.

In view of the species that appear to occupy an intermediate position I think it better not to recognise subgenera with *Ptilinopus*.

The Cloven-feathered Dove, *Drepanoptila holosericea*, is clearly an offshoot of *Ptilinopus* stock and has a colour pattern very similar to some *Ptilinopus* species. In view of the great amount of difference in structure of the primaries and shape of wing, besides other lesser differences it is, however, justifiable to maintain it in a monotypic genus.

REFERENCES

AMADON, D. 1943. Birds collected during the Whitney South Sea expedition. 52 Notes on some non-passerine genera, 3. *Amer. Mus. Novit.* No. 1237.

CAIN, A. J. 1954. Subdivisions of the genus *Ptilinopus*. *Bull. Brit. Mus.* (*Nat. Hist.*) *Zool.* 2: 8.

——1954a. Affinities of the fruit pigeon *Ptilinopus perousii* Peale. *Ibis*, 96: 104–110.

RIPLEY, S. D. & BIRCKHEAD, H. 1942. Birds collected during the Whitney South Sea expedition, 51. On the fruit pigeons of the *Ptilinopus purpuratus* group. *Amer. Mus. Novit.*, No. 1192.

BLACK-BACKED FRUIT DOVE   *Ptilinopus cincta*

Columba cincta Temminck, in Knip, Les Pigeons, 1810, Les Colombes, p. 58, pl. 23.

DESCRIPTION: Between Barbary Dove and Feral Pigeon in size. Head, neck and breast pale yellow or yellowish white, pure white on forehead and at border between the pale and dark areas on lower breast and mantle. Mantle and wings black, shading to dark olive green on lower back and rump. Upper tail-coverts dark grey. Tail feathers greyish black with grey or greyish white terminal band. A broad black band across lower breast. Belly and flanks yellowish olive or mustard yellow. Under tail coverts greenish grey, tipped yellow. Tibial feathers greenish grey. Bill yellow, greenish yellow or orange. Irides orange, orange-brown or red. Feet purple or pinkish purple. Female often with faint fine grey speckling on head and neck.

Juvenile with feathers of yellowish white areas vermiculated with pale greenish grey. Feathers of areas that are black in adult dark bronzy green with yellow fringes.

The above description is of nominate *P. c. cincta* from Timor, Wetar and Roma. *P. c. lettiensis* from Letti, Moa, Luang, Sermatta and Teun has a wider and greyish white terminal tail bar. *P. c. ottonis* from Damar and Babar is similar but has the tail bar merging into the dark colour of the rest of the tail and an olive green rump. *P. c. everetti* of Pantar and Alor has the neck and upper breast finely speckled with pale grey but with a white line dividing the greyish areas from the black of mantle and breast band. *P. c. albocinctus* of Lombok, Sumbawa, Flores and Bali has a greyish white head and pale blue-grey neck and breast bordered by a white band narrow above and broad on the breast.

DISTRIBUTION AND HABITAT: The Indonesian Islands of Timor, Wetar, Roma, Lombok, Sumbawa, Flores, Pantar, Alor, Letti, Moa, Luang, Sermatta, Teun, Damar and Babar. Inhabits forest and wooded areas.

FEEDING AND GENERAL HABITS: Little apparently recorded. Known to feed on fruits and berries taken from the branches.

NESTING: No information.

VOICE: No information.

DISPLAY: No information.

OTHER NAMES: Banded Fruit Dove; White-headed Fruit Dove; White-headed Pigeon.

BLACK-BANDED PIGEON   *Ptilinopus alligator*

Ptilinopus (Leucotreron) alligator Collett, Proc. Zool. Soc. London, 1898, p. 354, pl. 29.

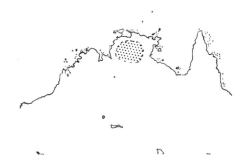

DESCRIPTION: About size of a smallish Feral Pigeon with a rather longish tail for a fruit dove. Very similar to the previous species with which it may be conspecific. Head white, tinged with yellow shading to yellowish cream on hind neck and breast bordered posteriorly with a narrow white band. Broad black band across lower breast; belly and flanks light bluish grey shading to very pale grey on the under tail coverts. Mantle adjacent to whitish areas black. Rest of mantle, back and wing coverts mixed grey and black with a somewhat laced or spangled appearance, the individual feathers being a darkish silver grey with black edges and black shaft streaks. Lower part of rump and upper tail coverts almost clear silver grey. Tail black with very broad silver grey terminal band. Primaries and outer secondaries black with slight greenish gloss. Underwing slate grey. Iris red or yellowish. Bill orange. Feet red. I have not seen a juvenile. The above description was taken from the type, a female, and two other specimens, a male and a female of which the former had the yellow parts of the neck very faintly speckled with pale grey.

FIELD CHARACTERS: Whitish head, neck and breast separated from pale grey underparts by black band. In flight dark wings and centre of tail probably contrast conspicuously from pale tail coverts and end of tail.

DISTRIBUTION AND HABITAT: The Northern Territory of Australia. Known from the region about the headwaters of the South Alligator River. Inhabits high rocky ridges and gullies in sandstone country where trees grow where they can find roothold among the tumbled boulders. Has not been found in true forest or along river banks. This and all other information here on ecology and behaviour is derived from the observations of Austin *et al.* (1963 and pers. comm.) who rediscovered this species.

FEEDING AND GENERAL HABITS: Known to feed on fruits of wild figs and probably takes other fruits and berries also. Makes a noisy whistling sound with its wings when flying. Has been observed both singly and in small groups.

NESTING: No information.

VOICE: The only call that has been recorded is a deep booming similar to that of the Common Bronzewing *Phaps chalcoptera* but slower and continuing for up to a minute. (Austin *et al.* 1963).

DISPLAY: No information.

REFERENCE

AUSTIN, C. N., BROWN, A. G., OFFICER, H. R. & WETTENHALL, H. N. B. 1963. Notes on the Black-banded Pigeon. *Emu*, **62**: 238–240.

RED-NAPED FRUIT DOVE   *Ptilinopus dohertyi*

Ptilopus dohertyi Rothschild, Bull. Brit. Orn. Club 5, 1896, p. 46.

DESCRIPTION: Between Feral Pigeon and Barbary Dove in size but nearer to the former. First primary acuminated, inner primaries square-ended and notched on tip of inner web. Head and upper part of neck yellowish white or cream-coloured. Lower part of neck and breast a beautiful pale, but bright, shell pink bordered narrowly yellowish white. Upper parts dark iridescent blue or purplish blue, most of the feathers edged with very dark bronzy green, this latter colour predominating on mantle and inner wing coverts. Broad dark purple band across underparts immediately below the whitish breast border. Belly and flanks dull greyish green. Under tail coverts streaked green and yellow. Central tail feathers and outer webs of outer ones dark lustrous purple. A large patch of crimson, hairy and somewhat elongated feathers on nape and hind neck. Underwing and underside of tail greyish black. Bill grey or greyish blue with yellow tip. Irides greyish or greyish brown. Orbital skin greenish white. Feet purplish grey. Sexes alike, but only three males and five females examined.

I have only seen one juvenile specimen.   This, a female, had the areas that are pink and white in the adult with greenish white feathers, faintly barred with pale olivaceous.   Its upperparts, and the underparts where purple in adult, were dark bronzy green, the feathers narrowly fringed with yellow.   Its underparts, where green in adult, were similar but paler.

DISTRIBUTION AND HABITAT: Sumba Island in Indonesia.   Probably in forest but I can find nothing recorded about it.

FEEDING AND GENERAL HABITS: No information.

NESTING: No information.

VOICE: No information.

DISPLAY: No information.

OTHER NAMES: Doherty's Fruit Dove; Purple-tailed Fruit Dove.

PINK-NECKED FRUIT DOVE   *Ptilinopus porphyrea*

Columba porphyrea 'Reinw.' Temminck, pl. col., liver. 18, 1823, pl. 106.

DESCRIPTION: A little larger than a Barbary Dove.   Head, neck and upper breast bright purplish pink deepening to foxglove red on the middle breast which is bordered by a band of white, then one of greenish black, from the grey belly.   Rest of plumage mainly rich green tinged with gold and mixed with yellow on the ventral regions.   Primaries and outer secondaries blackish tinged with green.   Central tail feathers bronzy olive-green, outer ones greenish black with grey terminal bands.   Irides red or orange.   Bill greenish or yellow olive, darker at base.   Feet pink or red.   The female is a little smaller with less clearly defined breast bands, and the pink of the breast and neck more or less obscured by greenish yellow edges to the feathers.   Juvenile predominantly green with yellow fringes to most feathers and with first primary not so sharply attenuated as the adult's.

DISTRIBUTION AND HABITAT: Sumatra, Java and Bali.   Found in forested areas.

FEEDING AND GENERAL HABITS: No information.

NESTING: No information.

VOICE: No information.

DISPLAY: No information.

MARCHE'S FRUIT DOVE   *Ptilinopus marchei*

Ptilopus (Rhamphiculus) Marchei Oustalet, Le Naturaliste, 1, 1880, p. 325.

DESCRIPTION: About the size of a smallish Feral Pigeon but plumper and with shorter wings. Outermost primary moderately attenuated, wings rather short. Throat orange-brown. Area above, behind, and in front of eye rusty orange, freckled blackish. Ear coverts black forming a large black patch on side of head. Forehead, crown, nape and malar region rusty carmine. Sides of neck and breast pale grey, this colour extending in a narrow band over the hind neck and in a narrow projection between the brown throat and carmine malar stripe. Front of breast bright reddish orange shading posteriorly into a broad crimson border. This is followed by a broad, ill-defined band of whitish yellow intermixed with grey. Rest of underparts light grey with yellowish fringes to some feathers. Under tail coverts with greenish grey inner and buffish outer webs, giving a spotted effect. Mantle, back and inner wing coverts black shading to dark bronzy green on outer wing coverts. A crimson patch on each wing formed by decomposed hair-like fringes on parts of the outer webs of the inner secondaries. Owing to the texture of the plumage forming them these crimson patches are not remarkably brilliant when viewed from the side or above, as then the dark underlying feathers show through. If, however, the bird is held in the hand and looked at from in front, with the wings very slightly held out from the body, they appear as two solid patches of a most brilliant and vivid red. (See pl. 1).

I have no doubt the species has some display in which they are thus exhibited. Tail dark greyish green with pale greenish grey terminal band. Irides, inner ring yellow, outer ring red. Bill dull red, tipped yellow. Feet dark red.

Female like male but with more pronounced green on rump, tail, wings and tail coverts. The juvenile is a generally dark bronzy green and paler greenish or grey tipped with green where adult is grey. It has a brown throat like the adult but lacks the red coloration although the forehead and crown feathers are tipped with rusty orange.

DISTRIBUTION AND HABITAT: The Philippine Islands of Luzon and Polilio. It is rare and is found among stunted trees near the tops of mountains.

FEEDING AND GENERAL HABITS: Presumably much as other fruit pigeons, but I can find no details recorded. Macgregor (1909) notes that the native Igorots say that at certain times these pigeons become so fat that they catch them alive, simply by chasing them till they are exhausted.

NESTING: No information.

VOICE: No information.

DISPLAY: No information.

OTHER NAMES: Marche's Fruit Pigeon; Black-eared Fruit Pigeon.

REFERENCE

McGREGOR, R. C. 1909. *A Manual of Philippine Birds*. Manila.

MERRILL'S FRUIT DOVE   *Ptilinopus merrilli*

Leucotreron merrilli McGregor, Phil. Journ. Sci., 11, sect. D, 1916, p. 269, f. 1.

DESCRIPTION: About midway between Barbary Dove and Feral Pigeon in size, but plumper and more compact. General colour a rich deep, but not very bright, green, shading to pale grey, more or less tinged with green on head, neck, and breast. Throat whitish. A narrow band of dark green divides the grey of the breast from the yellowish buff or cream colour of the lower breast and belly. Flanks dark green. Feathers on legs and under tail coverts greenish with creamy buff tips. Outer secondaries dark green with pale yellow edges to outer webs. Primaries greenish black. Some of the central secondaries have a dark blue stripe stripe on their outer edges the blue area being fringed with decomposed hair-like crimson barbs. The resultant patch is similar in character to that of Marche's Fruit Pigeon (q.v.). It appears purplish when viewed from the side but bright crimson (a little darker than the vivid red of *marchei*) when viewed frontally. Tail dark green with obscure pale terminal band on outer feathers. Underside of tail pale grey. Underwing chestnut. Irides red, orbital skin dark red. Bill dark red at base, dull yellow at tip. Feet dark red. Sexes alike. I have not seen a juvenile specimen.

The above description is of the nominate form *P. m. merrilli* from eastern and southern Luzon and Polillo. *P. m. faustinoi* from Mt. Tabuan, Cagayan Province, Northern Luzon, has a brownish red patch on the crown.

DISTRIBUTION AND HABITAT: The Philippine Islands of Luzon and Polillo. Inhabits mountain forest; rare.

FEEDING AND GENERAL HABITS: Recorded feeding on fruits of the small tree *Symplocos ahernii*.

NESTING: No information.

VOICE: No information.

DISPLAY: No information.

REFERENCES

DELACOUR, J. & MAYR, E. 1946. *Birds of the Philippines*. New York.
McGREGOR. 1916. *Phil. Journ. Sci.*, 11, sect. D, p. 269.

YELLOW-BREASTED FRUIT DOVE   *Ptilinopus occipitalis*

Ptilinopus occipitalis G. G. Gray, Gen. Bds., 2, 1844, p. (467), col. pl. (118).

DESCRIPTION: Between Barbary Dove and Feral Pigeon in size.   Plump and heavily built with short legs and small bill.   Outermost primary attenuated.   Throat whitish yellow or pale yellow.   Front of face, forehead, crown and sides of breast light bluish grey sometimes tinged with yellow or green.   Cheeks, hind crown and nape dark reddish purple.   Central part of breast dark golden yellow with a greenish tinge, sometimes slightly intermixed with red.   A broad band of reddish purple across lower breast or upper belly immediately posterior to the yellow area.   Lower belly greyish.   Flanks and ventral areas and under tail coverts green and yellowish white.   Upper parts rich darkish green.   Primaries greenish black.   Narrow pale yellow edges to outer webs of outer secondaries and primaries.   Outer tail feathers with pale greenish grey terminal bands.   Underside of wings and tail grey.   Irides yellowish brown, yellowish olive, or greenish gold.   Eyelids grey.   Bill bright red with yellow or greenish yellow tip.   Feet bright red.

The sexes are alike.   The juvenile lacks the red and yellow markings and is green and greenish grey with yellowish fringes to the feathers of the underparts.

DISTRIBUTION AND HABITAT: Philippine Islands, except those north of Luzon.   Inhabits primeval forest at low altitudes and up to 3,000 feet.

FEEDING AND GENERAL HABITS: No information.

NESTING: No information.

VOICE: No information.

DISPLAY: No information.

OTHER NAMES: Sulphur-breasted Fruit Dove; Yellow-breasted Fruit Pigeon.

REFERENCE

DELACOUR, J. & MAYR, E. 1946.   *Birds of the Philippines.*   New York.

FISCHER'S FRUIT DOVE   *Ptilinopus fischeri*

Ptilinopus Fischeri Bruggemann, Abh. Naturwiss. Ver. Bremen, 5, 1876, p. 82, pl. 4.

DESCRIPTION: About size of a smallish Feral Pigeon but shorter winged and plumper.   Outermost primary strongly attenuated.   Head pale whitish grey.   Dark crimson patch on each side of head connected across nape by a black band. Breast and sides of neck pale grey shading to dark grey on hind neck and upper parts of mantle. Lower breast and belly pale dull gold, or greenish gold, often intermixed with grey as the gold is only on the tips of most feathers. Ventral areas, leg feathers and under tail coverts mottled and blotched greenish grey and cream. Upper parts dark green, brightest on

the wings. Outer secondaries with yellow fringes on outer webs. Primaries greenish black. Underwing dark grey. Central tail feathers dark green. Outer ones black and green with broad light grey terminal bands. Underside of tail blackish with broad pale grey terminal band. Irides brown. Bill green-Feet purplish.

The juvenile is like the adult but has the grey areas duller and tinged with green, lacks the black nucha band and has the red face patch much duller and less well defined.

The above description is of the nominate form, *P. f. fischeri* from Northern Celebes. *P. f. centralis* from central and south-eastern Celebes has the back and mantle dark grey. *L. f. meridionalis* from the mountains of the southern peninsula of Celebes is strikingly different in appearance. It is green only on the lower part of the rump, upper tail coverts and tail. Its mantle, back, and wings are greyish black with narrow yellow edges to outer secondaries. Its breast and belly are pale grey with only a faint tinge of yellow or cream colour on the tips of the belly feathers. Its irides are orange. I have not seen a juvenile of this form.

DISTRIBUTION AND HABITAT: Celebes. Inhabits mountain forest according to Heinrich (see Stresemann, 1941) usually about the 2,000 metre zone, upwards to 3,000, but hardly ever below 1,000 metres.

FEEDING AND GENERAL HABITS: No information.

NESTING: Heinrich found a nest with one egg under the root of an old tree on a mountainside.

VOICE: Heinrich records a 'one-syllabled huh . . . huh repeated with small pauses between each note.'

DISPLAY: No information.

REFERENCE

STRESEMANN, E. 1941. Die Vögel von Celebes, pt. 3. *Journ. f. Orn.* **89** : 1–102.

JAMBU FRUIT DOVE   *Ptilinopus jambu*

Columba Jambu Gmelin, Syst. Nat., 1, pt. 2, 1789, p. 784.

DESCRIPTION: About the size of a Barbary Dove but heavier and plumper in build. Outermost primary strongly attenuated. Median line of throat blackish brown. Face, forehead and forecrown bright pinkish crimson, usually slightly paler on top of head than elsewhere. A large patch of bright but pale and delicate pink on the breast. Underparts yellowish white or cream-coloured, the yellow tinge being slight or lacking on front and sides of neck. Under tail coverts dark chestnut. Upperparts rich darkish green. Primaries blackish green. Outer secondaries and inner primaries with narrow yellow fringes. Underwing dark grey. Outer tail feathers dark green at base with paler terminal band which is light greenish on outer webs and pale grey on inner webs. Underside of tail dark grey with pale grey terminal band. Irides brown or reddish. Orbital skin whitish. Bill yellow or orange.

The female is much duller than the male. She is predominately darkish green in colour with chestnut throat, dull purplish pink head (sometimes only a tinge of this colour), whitish belly and pale fawnish chestnut under tail coverts. The juvenile is very like the female but young males soon moult into full adult plumage.

DISTRIBUTION AND HABITAT: Malay Peninsula, Rhio Archipelago, Sumatra, Banka, Billiton and Borneo. Inhabits forests and wooded areas, including mangrove swamps and small islets. At least partly migratory. In September and October of 1965 large numbers were discovered crossing the main mountain range of the Malay Peninsula from east to west. It is thought that these migrating birds are on passage to Sumatra (K. W. Scriven, in litt.).

FEEDING AND GENERAL HABITS: Has been recorded (Smythies, 1960) feeding on the ground on fruits knocked down by hornbills and monkeys. Probably more often takes berries and fruits from the branches. Little recorded of its habits. Indulges in migration or nomadism and when thus engaged often comes to grief by alighting at lighthouses, on ships, or in cities.

NESTING: Usual pigeon nest in tree or shrub. One white egg.

VOICE: A 'soft coo' is the only note I can find recorded.

DISPLAY: No information.

OTHER NAMES: Jambu Fruit Pigeon; Pink-headed Fruit Dove; Crimson-headed Fruit Dove.

REFERENCES

ROBINSON, H. C. & CHASEN, F. N. 1939. *Birds of the Malay Peninsula*, **4**: 329–330. London.
SMYTHIES, B. E. 1960. *The Birds of Borneo*. London.

DARK-CHINNED FRUIT DOVE   *Ptilinopus subgularis*

Ptilopus subgularis A. B. Meyer & Wiglesworth, Abh. Berlin Mus., Dresden, 1896/7, No. 2, pp. 4, 6, 19.

DESCRIPTION: About midway between Barbary Dove and Feral Pigeon in size with rather longer and more rounded tail than most fruit doves. Outermost primary strongly attenuated. Small patch on upper throat very dark chestnut. Head, neck and most of underparts pale silvery grey tinged with green on hind neck and flanks and with buffish yellow on breast. A large buff patch on lower breast. Under tail coverts and ventral area dark chestnut. Tibial feathers chestnut and greyish green. Upperparts rich green, darker and bluer on (visible parts of) primaries. Tail with ill-defined, narrow pale terminal bar. Underside of tail grey with paler tip. Irides orange red or brownish orange. Orbital skin blue (*fide* Wallace, 1865). Bill yellow. Feet red or purplish red. Sexes nearly alike but females have the neck more strongly and extensively tinged with green. I have not seen a juvenile.

The above description is of *P. subgularis epia* which is found in Celebes. The nominate race *P. s. subgularis* from Peling and Banggai Islands has darker chestnut under tail coverts and the buff breast patch only faintly indicated. The form from the island of Sula Mangoli, *L. s. mangoliensis* has the neck and under parts predominantly greenish yellow, all the feathers of these areas having broad greenish yellow tips.

DISTRIBUTION AND HABITAT: Celebes and the nearby islands of Peling, Banggai and Sula Mangoli. On Celebes, and doubtless elsewhere as well, inhabits dense primeval forest at low elevations (Heinrich, in Stresemann, 1941).

FEEDING AND GENERAL HABITS: I can find little recorded. Known to take fruits from the branches.

NESTING: No information.

DISPLAY: No information.

REFERENCE

STRESEMANN, E. 1941. Die Vögel von Celebes. *Journ. f. Orn.* **89**: 1–102.

BLACK-CHINNED FRUIT DOVE   *Ptilinopus leclancheri*

Trerolaema leclancheri Bonaparte, Compt. Rend. Acad. Sci. Paris, 41, 1855, p. 247.

DESCRIPTION: Very similar to the previous species, *P. subgularis*, but slightly smaller and with proportionately shorter tail. 'Chin' black. Head, neck and breast silver grey, tinged with green on nape and hind neck. A broad blackish chestnut band across the lower breast dividing the grey breast from the dull green belly. Ventral areas pale buffish. Under tail coverts light chestnut. Upperparts rich green with narrow yellow fringes to outer webs of outer secondaries. Primaries blackish green with conspicuous yellow edges to outer webs. Irides bright red. Bill yellow, base of lower mandible purplish red or dark red. Feet dark red or purplish red.

Female has head, neck and breast green, more or less suffused with grey, forehead often clear grey. Her throat mark is usually tinged with brown and her dark pectoral band much smaller than the male's.

Juveniles, at least those I have seen or read descriptions of, are like the female but lack the pectoral band and have only a faint dark smudge on the throat. None of the juvenile specimens I have seen were, however, recently fledged and the plumage described here may, therefore, be an intermediate one.

DISTRIBUTION AND HABITAT: The Philippine Islands. Inhabits forest.

FEEDING AND GENERAL HABITS: Known to feed on fruits taken from the branches. Little recorded of its habits.

NESTING: Usual pigeon nest in tree or shrub. One white egg.

VOICE: No information.

DISPLAY: No information.

OTHER NAMES: Black-throated Fruit Dove; Leclancher's Pigeon.

REFERENCE

McGREGOR, R. C. 1909. *A Manual of Philippine Birds*, Pt. 1. Manila.

SCARLET-BREASTED FRUIT DOVE   *Ptilinopus formosus*

Carpophaga (Megaloprepia) formosa G. R. Gray, Proc. Zool. Soc. London, 1860 (1861), p. 360.

DESCRIPTION: A shade smaller than a Barbary Dove but with a longer and much broader tail. General plumage rich deep green shading to a paler duller green on neck and breast. Head pale yellowish grey shading into the green of the neck. A patch of bright scarlet red in the middle of the green lower breast. Belly deep buffish gold shading into golden yellow on the under wing coverts. Under tail coverts chestnut

Inner webs of primaries and undersides of wing and tail quills dark greyish. The female has a pale greyish green head and lacks the scarlet breast patch.

DISTRIBUTION AND HABITAT: Northern Moluccas, Ternate, Batjan, Obi. Inhabits dense bamboo growth from feet of mountains to the highest peaks (Heinrich).

FEEDING AND GENERAL HABITS: I can find nothing recorded. Probably similar to that of the last species.

NESTING: Usual pigeon nest. One white egg. Two of three nests found by Heinrich were on fern leaves, quite low down, one in a small tree. Two nests with, respectively, a well-incubated and a fresh egg, were found in July; one with a young nestling in late April.

VOICE: Heinrich describes a deep but not very loud oohoo and an odd-sounding growling call.

REFERENCE
HEINRICH, G. 1956. Biologische Autzeichnungen über Vögel von Halmahera und Batjan. *Journ. f. Orn* 97: 31–40.

MAGNIFICENT FRUIT DOVE   *Ptilinopus magnificus*
Columba magnifica Temminck, Trans. Linn, Soc. London, 13, Pt. 1, 1821, p. 125.

DESCRIPTION: About the size of a Wood Pigeon but with longer, rounded tail and shorter wings. General colour green, more or less suffused with golden yellow. Secondaries and greater coverts a more brilliant and less yellowish green, outer primaries blackish green. Yellow patches on (some) wing coverts form an ill-defined band across the folded wing. Head and neck pale greenish grey. Median part of front of neck and upper breast, lower breast, and belly dark purple. Ventral area and underwing coverts deep yellow. Undersides of wing quills dull greyish and chestnut. Under tail coverts dull yellowish. Irides orange or red. Orbital skin green, greyish green or bluish green. Legs and feet green, yellowish green, or greenish orange. Bill yellow or greenish yellow, red at base.

The above description is of the nominate Australian form of the species which occurs in southern Queensland, New South Wales and Victoria. The forms from further north within the species' range become progressively smaller. Few birds, and no other species of pigeon, show such great size differences between geographical races.

The form from north-western New Guinea, *P. m. puella*, which is one of the smallest, is hardly larger than a Barbary Dove. The spots on its wing coverts are smaller and paler, it has little or no yellow suffusion in the green part of its plumage, the purple on its underparts is of a brighter and redder tone, and the red of its bill restricted to a small patch behind the nostril. The populations from northern Australia and southern New Guinea are more or less intermediate in size and appearance between the extremes here described. The sexes are alike in this species except that females tend to be very slightly paler on the purple areas.

I have not seen a juvenile of this species. Ripley (1964) describes one that appears to have been in partly juvenile plumage as having the breast 'patched with blackish brown'.

DISTRIBUTION AND HABITAT: New Guinea and adjacent islands and eastern Australia. Inhabits both lowland and hill forest.

FEEDING AND GENERAL HABITS: Feeds on fruits and berries. In Australia favourite foods are the fruits of white cedar *Melia azederach*, white fig *Ficus infectoria* and small-leaved fig *Ficus eugenniodes* (Frith, 1952). Feeds largely in the branches but has also been seen feeding on the ground.

NESTING: Usual pigeon nest in tree or shrub. One white egg. Nests found by Rand (1942) in New Guinea were from twelve to twenty feet high and made largely of woody tendrils of creepers.

VOICE: What is probably the advertising coo or its equivalent of the Australian form has been variously described 'a deep bubbling Wollack a Woo', 'a loud monotonous note', 'the almost shouted Bah-rook, Bah-roo', etc. Frith also records 'a conversational low pitched 'Pack-pack-pack' uttered only when the birds are feeding and 'a guttural deliberate Bah-roo'. S. Parker (pers comm.) heard a deep guttural '(g)'whompoo, (g)'whompoo'; the '(g)' sound only audible at close quarters. Grant (in Ogilvie-Grant, 1915) described the usual call of the Northern New Guinea form as 'Coo-uk-coo . . . the middle syllable rendering it easily recognisable . . . .'

DISPLAY: No information.

OTHER NAMES: Wompoo Pigeon; Purple-breasted Fruit Dove; Purple-bellied Pigeon.

REFERENCES

FRITH, H. J. 1952. Notes on the Pigeons of the Richmond River, N.S.W. *Emu* **52**: 89–99.
OGILVIE-GRANT, W. R. 1915. Report on the birds collected by the British Ornithologists' Union Expedition and the Wollaston Expedition in Dutch New Guinea. *Ibis*, Jubilee Suppl. No. 2, pp. 300–301.
RAND, A. L. 1942. Results of the Archbold Expedition No. 42. *Bull. Amer. Mus. Nat. Hist.* LXXIX, Art. 4, pp. 289–366.

PINK-SPOTTED FRUIT DOVE   *Ptilinopus perlatus*

Columba perlata Temminck, 1835, pl. col., Livr. 94, 1835, pl. 559.

DESCRIPTION: A little smaller than a Feral Pigeon but plump and thick-set in shape, with shortish tail. Head greenish yellow with an olive tinge, very narrowly bordered at nape with bronzy gold and separated from the green upperparts by a pale bluish grey collar which is continuous with the whitish grey of the throat and malar region. Extreme upper breast and narrow margin to the grey collar golden bronze, rest of breast brownish bronze. Lower breast and belly dark yellowish green. Upperparts rich, more or less bronze-tinged, green. Bright pink central areas to many lesser wing coverts and scapulars form extensive pink spotting on inner part of closed wing. Secondaries and greater coverts darker, more bluish green with narrow yellow edges to outer webs. Primaries dark green, inner webs blackish. Underwing slate grey. Tail with pale greenish silver terminal band. Under tail coverts whitish yellow, marked sparsely with light greyish green.

Irides with yellow or greenish yellow inner ring and orange-yellow, orange or light-red outer ring; orbital skin greenish yellow. Bill yellow or pale yellow at tip, greenish orange, dark greenish yellow or yellowish olive at base. Feet purplish red or dark red. Sexes alike. I have not seen a juvenile of this species.

The above description is of the form *P. perlatus zonurus* from the Aru Islands, south New Guinea from Kapare River to Milne Bay and D'Entrecasteaux Archipelago. Nominate *P. p. perlatus* from north-western New Guinea and adjacent islands has the tail bar absent or nearly so (on the upper side of the tail) the silvery areas being reduced to spots on the inner webs. *P. perlatus plumbeicollis* from north-eastern New Guinea from Astrolabe Bay to Huon Gulf has the head tinged with grey and a broader grey collar.

DISTRIBUTION AND HABITAT: New Guinea, the Western Papuan Islands of Waigeu and Salawati, Japen Island, the Aru Islands and D'Entrecasteaux Archipelago (Fergusson, Goodenough and Normanby Islands). Inhabits forest and forest edge, riverside woodland, parks and cultivated areas with trees from sea level to about 4,000 feet (Watson *et al.* 1962).

FEEDING AND GENERAL HABITS: Has been seen eating wild figs from the branches; the same observers (Watson *et al.*, 1962) noted it as being active early in the morning but usually more quiescent later in the day.

NESTING: No information.

VOICE: Said to resemble that of *P. regina* (Watson, *et al.*, 1962).

DISPLAY: No information.

OTHER NAMES: Pink-spotted Fruit Pigeon.

REFERENCES

MAYR, E. 1941. List of New Guinea Birds. *Amer. Mus. Nat. Hist.*
OGILVIE-GRANT, W. R. 1915. *Ibis*, Jubilee Suppl. No. **2**: 294–295.
WATSON, J. D., WHEELER, W. R. & WHITBOURN, E. 1962. With the R.A.O.U. in Papua, New Guinea. *Emu* **62**: 31–50.

ORNATE FRUIT DOVE   *Ptilinopus ornatus*

Ptilinopus ornatus 'von Rosenberg' Schlegel, Nederl. Tijdschr. Dierk., 4, 1871, p. 52.

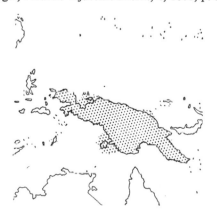

DESCRIPTION: Colour pattern and coloration as in the previous species, *P. perlatus*, except as follows – pale grey of throat and collar less extensive and golden of upper breast correspondingly more so. Bronze brown of breast and green of underparts darker, upper part of mantle more or less strongly tinged with golden bronze or bronzy brown, no pink spots on wings but a dark purple patch on 'shoulder', a less well defined silver grey patch below, scapulars golden green with pale grey centres giving a pale, spotted effect. Terminal tail bar tinged strongly with yellow. Irides inner ring orange, outer orange-red.

The above description is of *P. ornatus gestroi* which is found throughout most of the species' range. The form from Vogelkop, north-western New Guinea *P. o. ornatus*, is slightly smaller and darker and has the upperparts of the head dark purple instead of mustard yellow.

DISTRIBUTION AND HABITAT: New Guinea. Inhabits lowland forest and hill forest up to about 4,500 feet.

FEEDING AND GENERAL HABITS: Known to take fruit from the branches. Large numbers may gather at a fruiting tree. Flight swift and straight (Grant, in Ogilvie-Grant, 1915).

NESTING: No information.

VOICE: Grant (in Ogilvie-Grant, 1915) describes a call which consists of 'five or six quickly repeated "coos" '.

OTHER NAME: Gestroi's Fruit Dove.

REFERENCES

MAYR, E. 1941. List of New Guinea Birds. *Amer. Mus. Nat. Hist.*
OGILVIE-GRANT, W. R. 1915. *Ibis*, Jubilee Suppl. No. 2.

SILVER-SHOULDERED FRUIT DOVE   *Ptilinopus tannensis*

Columba tannensis Latham, Ind. Orn., 2, 1790, p. 600.

DESCRIPTION: Between Barbary Dove and Feral Pigeon in size but of usual plump and compact fruit dove shape. Forehead, crown and face dark greenish yellow shading into the rather dark green of the rest of the plumage (except as noted). Tips and outer webs of primaries dark bluish green, inner webs blackish. Yellow tips or fringes to outer webs of most greater coverts and secondaries form two yellow patches on wing. Innermost lesser wing coverts silvery white edged green, forming a patch of silver spots on shoulder of wing. Underwing slate grey. Central tail feathers green with ill-defined silvery green subterminal band; outer ones dark bright green with clearer silvery subterminal bands. Broad yellow tips to feathers of ventral regions and under tail coverts. Irides greyish or yellowish. Bill bluish grey or dark bluish. Feet and legs purplish or purplish red.

Female lacks the silver spots on the wing. Juvenile green with yellow edges to all feathers giving it a laced or scaled effect.

DISTRIBUTION AND HABITAT: New Hebrides and Banks Island.

FEEDING AND GENERAL HABITS: Recorded flocking to fruiting Banyan Trees.

NESTING: No information.

VOICE: No information.

DISPLAY: No information.

OTHER NAMES: Yellow-headed Fruit Dove; Tanna Island Fruit Dove; New Hebrides Fruit Dove.

ORANGE-FRONTED FRUIT DOVE   *Ptilinopus aurantiifrons*

Ptilinopus aurantiifrons G. R. Gray, Proc. Zool. Soc. London, 1858, p. 185, p. 137.

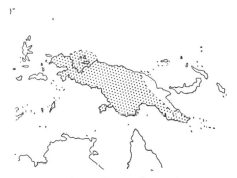

DESCRIPTION: Slightly larger than a Barbary Dove but plumper and more heavily built with short tail. Forehead bright orange or yellow-orange. Throat and lower part of face white. Crown, nape and upper part of face green with a bronze or golden tinge. Broad band of bluish grey includes most of neck and upper breast. Ventral regions pale greenish grey. Under tail coverts yellowish white and dull green. Rest of plumage green with a bronze or golden tinge except on primaries and outer secondaries which are dark green with blackish inner webs. Bluish grey bases to the feathers form spots on the wing coverts and upper mantle. Outer tail feathers tipped grey and white on inner webs. Irides red, orange or yellow, often or usually with bluish or whitish inner ring. Orbital skin greenish yellow. Bill red at base, greenish yellow at tip. Feet bright purple or purplish-red. The sexes are alike but the female tends to have the orange and blue grey areas slightly less bright. I have not seen a juvenile of this species: it probably bears the same relationship to the adult in appearance as in the closely related *P. wallacii* (q.v.).

DISTRIBUTION AND HABITAT: The western Papuan islands of Misol, Batanta and Salawati, Japen and Aru Islands, the D'Entrecasteaux Archipelago and New Guinea except for the north-east coast between Sepik River and Collingwood Bay. Inhabits lowlands up to 300 metres, in wooded savannah, coastal woods, riparian forest and mangrove swamps.

FEEDING AND GENERAL HABITS: Little recorded. Known to eat fruits and berries taken from branches. Flight swift and dashing. Often in pairs or groups of three.

NESTING: Usual pigeon nest (often more substantial than most *Ptilinopus* nests) in tree or shrub. One white egg.

Four nests found by Rand (1942) were between 8 and 12 feet above ground. The parents, whether incubating eggs or brooding young, left the nest when Rand was about 50 yards away and usually flew some distance before alighting.

23—P & D

VOICE: One call has been described as a 'low soft "coo" '.

DISPLAY: No information.

OTHER NAMES: Golden-fronted Fruit Dove; Yellow-fronted Fruit Pigeon.

REFERENCES

OGILVIE-GRANT, W. R. 1915. Report on the Birds collected by the British Ornithologists Union Expedition and the Wollaston Expedition in Dutch New Guinea. *Ibis*, Jubilee Suppl. No. **2**: 295.

RAND, A. L. 1942. Results of the Archbold Expeditions No. 42. *Bull. Amer. Mus. Nat. Hist.*, Vol. LXXIX, Art. 4: 289–366.

WALLACE'S FRUIT DOVE   *Ptilinopus wallacii*

Ptilonopus wallacii G. R. Gray, Proc. Zool. Soc. London, 1858, p. 185, pl. 137.

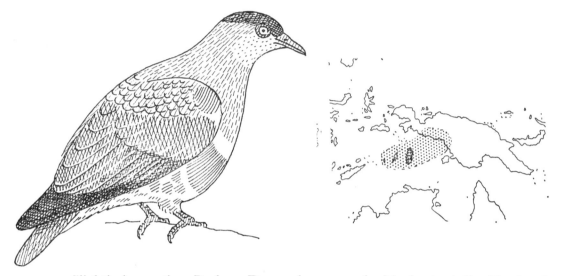

DESCRIPTION: Slightly larger than Barbary Dove, plumper and with shorter tail. Forehead and top of head dull crimson or carmine. Throat and lower part of face white. Rest of head, neck, breast and upper mantle pale bluish grey. A white band divides the grey of the breast from the large orange belly patch which becomes yellow posteriorly. Flanks, ventral regions and under tail coverts pale yellow and greenish. Patch of golden bronze on carpal region of wing. Mantle and inner wing coverts bluish grey, each feather edged with yellowish green or golden-bronze giving a scaled effect. Primaries and secondaries dark glossy green, black on areas not visible when wing is folded. Narrow yellow edges to secondaries and greater coverts. Back, rump, and upper tail coverts yellowish green. Central tail feathers green with pale terminal band; outer ones darker and with terminal band, except on edge of outer webs, greyish white. Irides golden or yellow with red or orange outer ring. Orbital skin bluish. Bill yellow or greenish yellow with paler tip. Feet purple or pinkish. Female like male but with grey parts tinged with green (faint green bar on many feathers) and orange belly patch less brilliant. Juvenile with red cap edged and somewhat intermixed with dark green, feathers of mantle and wing coverts glossy green with yellow tips; grey of breast and orange of belly more or less suffused with green.

DISTRIBUTION AND HABITAT: Babar Island, Banda, Timor Laut, South-east Islands (Kur and Tayandu), Kei, Aru Islands and south New Guinea (Mimika and Noord Rivers). Inhabits lowland forest.

FEEDING AND GENERAL HABITS: No information.

VOICE: Advertising coo (?) of a captive male 'o̅o̅o̅o̅! o̅o̅o̅, o̅o̅o̅, o̅o̅o̅, o̅o̅o̅'; sad, musical and quite loud, each note spaced out but with a longer pause after the first. Excitement cry a gruff 'wŏŏ', uttered with mouth widely open. When cooing bird bows head low on breast and appears 'hump-backed'.

DISPLAY: No information.

OTHER NAMES: Golden-shouldered Fruit Dove; Crimson-capped Fruit Dove; Wallace's Fruit Pigeon.

SUPERB FRUIT DOVE   *Ptilinopus superbus*

Columba Superba Temminck, in Knip, Les Pigeons, 1810, Les Colombes, p. 75, pl. 33.

DESCRIPTION: Nearly the size of a Barbary Dove but more compact in shape and with proportionately shorter tail. Most of upperparts, including areas of head behind the eye bordering the cap, a beautiful rich golden green with a coppery tinge. Median and greater coverts narrowly edged yellow. Blue-black patch on carpal joint, and blue-black spots on inner wing coverts, secondaries and scapulars. Cap vivid reddish purple. Hind neck and upper part of mantle rusty orange. Tail, except for the two greenish central feathers, greenish black with greyish-white terminal band. Throat silver grey. Feathers of breast bifurcated, grey and purple with pale grey tips. Lower breast grey, divided by a broad blue-black band from the belly and flanks which are white patched with dark green at the sides. Under tail coverts white blotched with green. Primaries and outer secondaries black with narrow yellow margins. Irides yellow or (some females) greenish. Legs and feet red. Bill greyish-green, greenish, or slate.

Female predominantly a dark rich green with a bluish tinge. Wing spots obscure and bluer (less dark) than those of male. A blue-black patch on the nape. Throat greyish. Tips of the bifurcated breast feathers tinged with silver grey. Feathers on lower breast green with narrow yellow edges. White on flanks and belly tinged with yellow.

Juvenile similar to female but a more yellowish green and broad yellow edges to wing coverts, and no nape patch. Bill, eyes and feet at first dull but soon changing.

The above description is of nominate *P.s. superbus.* In *P.s. temminckii,* from Celebes and the Sulu Archipelago, the female has a dull purple cap and the male has the lower breast above the blackish band, pinkish purple.

FIELD IDENTIFICATION: The dark green and white flank markings serve to identify it when perched high up or at a distance (Rand, 1942).

DISTRIBUTION AND HABITAT: Celebes and the Sulu Archipelago, east through the Moluccas, western Papuan islands, New Guinea and nearby islands and archipelagos to north-eastern and eastern Australia. Inhabits both lowland and hill forest, also in secondary growth at previously cleared places, forest edge and river banks and in open agricultural country with some trees.

FEEDING AND GENERAL HABITS: Known to take berries and small fruits from the branches. **Has a** whirring flight, commonly singly or in pairs, but large numbers may aggregate at feeding places.

NESTING: Nest of usual pigeon type, generally very small and slight. In tree or shrub, usually (? or those most usually found) low down, not more than ten feet above ground. One white or creamy white egg. Two egg clutches have been recorded (see Mathews, 1910) but probably in error.

VOICE: One call has been described (to give two divergent renderings) as 'a loud "Mwoot" repeated several times', and 'a gruff succession of "ooms" repeated slowly'. What is probably, a different call as a 'rather quickly repeated "Boobooboobooboo"'.

DISPLAY: Cain and Galbraith (1956) saw a display flight in which the male, who had been perched at the female's side, glided away from her with wings and tail fully spread 'looking like an inverted saucer'.

OTHER NAMES: Purple-capped Fruit Dove; Purple-crowned Fruit Dove; Purple-crowned Pigeon.

REFERENCES

CAIN, A. J. & GALBRAITH, I. C. J. 1956. Field notes on birds of the eastern Solomon Islands. *Ibis* **98**: 100–134.
CAYLEY, N. W. 1931. *What Bird is that?* p. 16. Sydney.
MATHEWS, G. M. 1910. *The birds of Australia*, **1**: Pt. 2: 109–111.
MAYR, E. & GILLIARD, E. T. 1954. Birds of central New Guinea. *Bull. Amer. Mus. Nat. Hist.* **103**: Art. 4: 315–374.
RAND, A. L. 1942. Results of the Archbold Expeditions No. 42. *Bull. Amer. Mus. Nat. Hist.* Vol. LXXIX: Art. 4: 289–366.
STRESEMANN, E. 1941. Die Vögel von Celebes. *Journ. f. Orn.* **89**: 1–102.

MANY-COLOURED FRUIT DOVE   *Ptilinopus perousii*

Ptilinopus perousii Peale, U.S. Expl. Exped., 8, 1848, p. 195.

DESCRIPTION: Rather smaller than a Barbary Dove and more compact in shape. Outermost primary sharply attenuated. Forehead, crown and a broad band from inner wing coverts across mantle, purplish crimson. Rest of head, including stripe above eye, and neck yellowish white or pale primrose yellow (individual feathers have primrose yellow edges and/or subterminal bars, the former soon fading) shading to deeper yellow faintly barred with purplish pink just before the mantle bar. Breast with bifurcated feathers which have bright purple-pink subterminal bands and white tips giving a spotted white and pink effect. Below this an obscure reddish orange band (pink, orange-tipped feathers), belly and flanks yellowish white. Under tail coverts bright purplish-pink. Wings silver grey, feathers edged greenish yellow; outer secondaries bronze green, primaries blackish green. Back and rump greenish yellow.

Tail silver grey with faint yellowish edges to feathers. Irides yellowish buff, orange yellow or reddish orange. Bill dark greyish green or green with horn-coloured tip. Legs and feet greyish green or dark green. (See pl. 1).

Female has upperparts a slightly bronzy green. Back of head and neck light greyish green; pink on breast darker and more restricted; lower breast and belly dull greenish yellow or pale greyish green (grey-green feathers with pale or yellowish tips). Central tail feathers bronze green; outer ones with inner webs dark greyish with an ill-defined greyish white subterminal bar. Cap and under tail coverts as in male. Juvenile generally green with yellow fringes to most cover feathers and yellowish belly, juvenile female a more bronzy, less pure green above than male. Some juvenile plumage replaced, on upperparts, by self-coloured green feathers but at about same time adult feathers are also growing and usually no complete intermediate plumage is worn although males in first adult plumage may show stronger green tinge on back and rump and green markings on scapulars and greater coverts.

The above description is of the nominate *P. p. perousii* from Samoa. In *P. perousii mariae* from Fiji and Tonga the pale parts of the male tend to be whiter and the female has pale yellow or yellow and pink under tail coverts.

DISTRIBUTION AND HABITAT: The Samoan, Fijian and Tongan Islands of Savaii, Upolu, Tutuila, Ofu, Tau, Viti Levu, Ovalau, Wakaia, Ngau, Mango, Niue (Savage Island) and Tongatabu. Inhabits forest, including small patches of 'bush' in grassland. Locally in parks and gardens.

FEEDING AND GENERAL HABITS: Feeds on fruits and berries taken from the branches. The fruits of the banyan *Ficus prolixa* appear to be an important food (Whitmee, 1875) but also takes other fruits including those of the introduced African Tulip Tree. Keeps much to top of trees but will come low down into trees or shrubs to feed. Said by Mayr (1945) to live in flocks. Porter (1935) found it associated in flocks but with the pair as the basic social unit. Very active when feeding, flight said (Porter, 1935) to be 'exceedingly swift and totally unlike that of any other pigeon'.

NESTING: No information.

VOICE: What is probably the advertising coo has been described as a 'distinctive Coo-coo-coo coocoocoo diminuendo' (Morris, 1964), 'a quickly-repeated Hoo-hoo-hoo-hoo' (Mayr, 1945) and as '. . . Dove-like, beginning in a high crescendo . . . ends in a series of gasps' (Bahr, 1912).

DISPLAY: No information.

OTHER NAMES: Nutmeg Dove; Rainbow Dove; Painted Dove.

REFERENCES
ARMSTRONG, J. S. 1932. *Hand-list to the Birds of Samoa*. London.
BAHR, P. H. 1912. Notes on the Avifauna of the Fiji Islands. *Ibis* 6: Ninth Series: 282–314.
MAYR, E. 1945. *Birds of the south-west Pacific*, p. 113. New York.
MORRIS, R. O. 1964. Unpublished MSS on Birds observed in Fiji, and pers. comm.
PORTER, S. 1935. *Notes on Birds of Fiji*. *Avicult. Mag.* 8: Fourth Series: 164–171.
WHITMEE, S. J. 1875. List of Samoan Birds with notes on their Habits. *Ibis* 5: Third Series: 436–447.

PURPLE-CAPPED FRUIT DOVE   *Ptilinopus porphyraceus*

Columba porphyracea Temminck, Trans. Linn. Soc. London, 13, 1821, p. 130.

DESCRIPTION: Slightly smaller than a Barbary Dove but plumper and more compact in shape. Forehead and crown bright purple obscurely bordered with greenish yellow. Throat yellowish white. Face, nape, neck and breast a pale silvery green, feathers on centre of breast bifurcated. Obscure dark green and purplish belly patch. Ventral region and under tail coverts yellow, the latter tinged pink or orange. Mantle, back, rump and wing coverts bluish green to bronze green, scapulars and inner secondaries with iridescent blue-green central areas forming spots. Tail dark green (grey on inner webs of outer tail feathers) with silver-grey terminal bar on outer tail feathers and suggestion of same on two central feathers. Flanks and tibial feathers green. Sexes nearly alike but belly patch of female less distinct. Irides yellowish buff or yellow. Bill greyish green, green or, in one specimen, dark brown. Feet purple or purplish red. Juvenile generally bright moss green with yellow fringes to most feathers giving a barred and freckled effect.

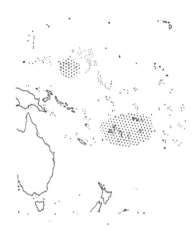

The above description is of nominate *P. p. porphyraceus* from the Fijian and Tongan Islands. *P. porphyraceus fasciatus* from the Samoan Islands has pinkish grey iridescent spots on the scapulars and inner secondaries, the purple belly patch is brighter and bordered posteriorly with a dark rusty orange patch and the tail bar more defined and yellow or white and yellow in colour. *P. porphyraceus ponapensis* from the Caroline Islands is like the nominate form but has the neck and breast tinged with yellow and a broad yellow terminal bar on its tail, whitish to pale brown irides and a lead grey bill.

DISTRIBUTION AND HABITAT: The Fijian, Tongan, Samoan and Caroline Islands of Taviuni, Wakaia, Ovalau, Mango, Kambara, Vavau, Niüe, Nomuka, Tongatabu, Eva, Savaii, Upolu, Tutuila, Ofu, Olosenga, Tau, Uala (Moen), Ponapé, Kusaie and Ebon. Inhabits forest and wooded areas. In the Caroline Islands Brandt (1962) found it only in heavy forest on volcanic peaks. In Samoa Yaldwin (1952) found it 'very common all over the Samoan Islands' in 1950–51.

FEEDING AND GENERAL HABITS: Known to feed on fruits and berries, especially wild figs, taken from the branches. Usually in pairs or singly. Whitmee (1875) states that it is not gregarious but Mayr (1945) that it sometimes lives in small flocks. Possibly some 'flocks' recorded are mere aggregations at sources of food.

NESTING: Usual pigeon nest in tree or shrub, sometimes high up (over 30 feet) in large trees (Brandt, 1962). One white egg. In the Truk Islands (Caroline Islands) nests were found in February, June, July, August, November and December.

VOICE: What is probably the advertising coo has been described as $\overline{\text{Coo}}$-$\overline{\text{coo}}$-cŏŏcŏŏrŏŏ (Mayr, 1945) and 'a loud call' (Brandt, 1962).

DISPLAY: No information.

OTHER NAMES: Crimson-crowned Fruit Dove, Ponapé Dove.

REFERENCES

BRANDT, J. H. 1962. Nests and eggs of birds of the Truk Islands. *Condor* 64: 416–437.
MAYR, E. 1945. *Birds of the south-west Pacific*. New York.
WHITMEE, S. J. 1875. List of Samoan Birds with notes on their Habits. *Ibis* 5: Third Series: 436–437.
YALDWIN, J. C. 1952. Notes on the present status of Samoan Birds. *Notornis* 5: 28–30.

PELEW FRUIT DOVE   *Ptilinopus pelewensis*

Ptilinopus pelewensis Hartlaub & Finsch, Proc. Zool. Soc. London, 1868, p. 7.

DESCRIPTION: Very similar to the Purple-capped Fruit Dove (q.v.) but differs in being slightly smaller, having the central breast feathers with purple subterminal bars, a large orange belly patch and pinkish purple, orange-tipped under tail coverts. Bill dark grey with greenish white tip. Feet dark blood red.

DISTRIBUTION AND HABITAT: The Pelew (Palau) Islands of Babeltop (Babelthuap), Koror, Garakayo, Peleliu, Ngabad and Anguar. Inhabits woods and thickets.

FEEDING AND GENERAL HABITS: Feeds on berries and fruits, mostly from large trees but some taken from shrubs and ground plants. Usually found singly, sometimes in pairs (Baker, 1951).

NESTING: Usual pigeon nest in tree or shrub. One white egg. Baker found two nests in September.

VOICE: Advertising coo a series of coos with a downward inflection each distinct and separate and with pauses (denoted by asterisks) in first part of call: 'Coo, coo, * coo-cu, *, coo, coo-cu *, coo, cu, cu, cu, cu'. Habitually calls at night; initially one bird calls in response to the similarly-sounding call of the Pelew Owl, others answer it (Marshall 1949).

DISPLAY: No information.

REFERENCES

BAKER, R. H. 1951. The Auifauna of Micronesia, its origin, evolution and distribution. *Univ. Kansas Publ. Mus. Nat. Hist.* 3, 1951: 185–187.
MARSHALL, J. T. 1949. The endemic avifauna of Saipan, Tiniam, Guam and Palau. *Condor* 51: 200–221.

RAROTONGAN FRUIT DOVE   *Ptilinopus rarotongensis*

Ptilinopus rarotongensis Hartlub & Finsch, Proc. Zool. Soc. London, 1871, p. 30.

DESCRIPTION: Very similar to the Purple-capped Fruit Dove with which it may be conspecific. Differs in having neck and breast paler and greyer with only obscure dull yellow-green subterminal bars on the feathers. Belly patch olive-yellow with pinkish purple central area shading to creamy yellow on ventral areas and under tail coverts. Tail with broad yellowish silver terminal bar.

DISTRIBUTION AND HABITAT: Raratonga Island in the Hervey Group.   Presumably in woodland.

FEEDING AND GENERAL HABITS: No information.

NESTING: No information.

VOICE: No information.

DISPLAY: No information.

MARIANAS FRUIT DOVE   *Ptilinopus roseicapilla*

Columba roseicapilla Lesson, Traite D'Orn, Liur. 6, 1861, p. 472.

DESCRIPTION: About size of Barbary Dove but more compact and with shorter tail.   Forehead and crown and malar patch deep purplish pink, the 'cap' bordered with greenish yellow.   Throat pale yellowish. Rich green or golden-green except where otherwise stated.   Breast feathers bifurcated, with silvery tips. A small purple patch on lower breast running into a larger orange patch and shading to yellow on ventral regions and pinkish or yellowish orange on under tail coverts.   Scapulars and inner secondaries with rich dark blue centres and yellowish green fringes giving a brightly spotted effect.   Outer part of wing iridescent green with yellow fringes to most feathers.   Tail with broad greyish white, green-tipped terminal bar. Irides yellow.   Bill dark green.   Feet and legs dark red.

Sexes nearly alike but some (perhaps all ?) females a little less bright than males.   Juvenile, so far as can be judged from a few specimens that have begun the post-juvenile moult, green with yellow feather edges as in most other fruit doves.

DISTRIBUTION AND HABITAT: The Marianas (Marianne) Islands of Saipan, Tinian, Rota and Guam. Inhabits woodland.   Believed to be decreasing on Guam (Baker, 1947).

FEEDING AND GENERAL HABITS: Feeds on fruits, berries and flowers taken from the branches.   Usually feeds in the upper parts of the trees walking along horizontal twigs and reaching up or to either side to pluck food.   On alighting usually either 'freezes' motionless for about 15 minutes or does so after first walking further into the foliage.   Not shy of man when once it begins to feed in company.   Flight very swift and straight, at tree-top level.   Does not usually, if ever, form cohesive flocks but large numbers gather in the same fruiting tree to feed.   When feeding tends to work from inside the tree, not from the periphery as does *Ducula oceanica*.   These and other data on behaviour are derived from Marshall's (1949) observations.

NESTING: No information.

VOICE: What is probably the advertising coo is described by Marshall as a 'sequence of mellow "coo's", all beginning on the same pitch (starting) with two or three long notes definitely separated from each other, each inflected upwards in the middle'. This inflection imparts to the opening notes a particularly 'demanding' or 'insistent' character. They are followed by a rolling series of notes becoming faster, then slower towards the end, followed by three or four longer notes with a rising inflection. This ... can be represented (commas indicate pauses): 'cooo,cooo,cooo,cu-cucucucu-cu-cu coo coo coo.'

DISPLAY: No information.

OTHER NAME: Rose-capped Fruit Dove.

REFERENCES

BAKER, R. H. 1947. Size of Bird Populations at Guam, Mariana Islands. *Condor* **49**: 124–125.
MARSHALL, J. T., Jnr. 1949. The endemic avifauna of Saipan, Tinian, Guam and Palau. *Condor* **51**: 200–221.

PINK-CAPPED FRUIT DOVE *Ptilinopus regina*

Ptilinopus purpuratus var. *Regina* Swainson, Zool. Journ. 1, 1825, p. 474.

DESCRIPTION: About a fifth smaller than a Barbary Dove with proportionately shorter tail. Upper parts mainly rich green, often with a golden-bronze tinge. Greater wing coverts and secondaries edged yellow. Dark iridescent bluish centres of feathers form bright spots on scapulars and inner secondaries and suggestion of same on coverts. Hind neck more or less tinged with grey, sides of neck and tips of the green-based bifurcated breast feathers silver grey. Cap light mauve-red narrowly bordered with yellow. Chin yellowish. Bright mauve-pink patch on lower breast. Rest of lower breast orange. Belly and ventral areas yellow, the under tail coverts broadly tipped with tawny orange. Tail green above, grey below, with broad yellow tips on all but the two central feathers. Irides yellow, orange, orange-brown or reddish; orbital skin olive green, tinged yellow. Bill olive green, green or greyish green. Legs and feet bluish grey tinged with olive, greenish grey, greenish brown or green. Female like male but slightly less brilliant with the silver-grey on neck and breast less pronounced. Juvenile mainly green with yellow edges to most feathers.

The above description is of the nominate race *P. r. regina* of eastern Australia. In the northern territory of Australia and on Melville Island lives a paler race, *P. regina ewingi*, with a pink cap and breast spot. *P. r. flavicollis* from the islands of Flores, Savu, Samoa and Timor is very similar but paler and with a strong yellow-green suffusion on neck and breast. *P. regina xanthogaster* found in the Banda and Kei Islands and the islands of Damar, Sermattu, Babar, Teun, Nila and Timorlaut, has the cap and breast spot a pale silvery grey. *P. regina roseipileum* from the Wetar, Roma, Kisar, Moa, and Letti islands is even paler with cap and breast spot a very pale pinkish silver, often quite white on the forehead.

DISTRIBUTION AND HABITAT: Banda and Kei Isles, eastern Lesser Sunda Isles, northern and eastern Australia. Found in wooded areas; in Australia in coastal or riverine forests ('brushes') not in the drier woodlands of the interior.

FEEDING AND GENERAL HABITS: Known to feed on berries and small fruits taken from the branches. When feeding 'crawls about the trees with a parrot-like appearance'. Often feeds and nests in low trees or undergrowth. When frightened darts away through the trees, does not rise above the canopy. Will visit very small patches of forest in otherwise fairly open country. Nomadic or migratory, at least in eastern Australia (Frith, 1952).

NESTING: Usual pigeon nest; one white egg. Breeding season in Richmond River area of New South Wales mid October to March.

VOICE: What is, probably, the advertising coo is described by Frith as a very loud series of 'boo' notes at different tones, commencing slowly and deliberately and increasing rapidly in speed. Has a melancholy tone. Display coo a single 'Whoo' (Wheeler, 1939).

DISPLAY: Wheeler records a bowing display which involved 'blowing out the sides of the breast; stretching the head up and then with arched neck, bowing to touch the branch with its beak. . . .'

OTHER NAMES: Blue-spotted Fruit Dove; Grey-capped Fruit Dove; Red-crowned Pigeon; Pink-crowned Pigeon; Rose-crowned Fruit Dove.

REFERENCES

FRITH, H. J. 1952. Notes on the Pigeons of the Richmond River, N.S.W. *Emu* **52**: 89–99.
WHEELER, R. 1959. The R.A.O.U. Camp-out at Noosa Heads, Queensland, 1958. *Emu* **59**: 230–249.

SILVER-CAPPED FRUIT DOVE   *Ptilinopus richardsii*

Ptilinopus richardsii Ramsay, Nature, 25, 19th Jan., 1882, p. 282.

DESCRIPTION: About size of Barbary Dove but plumper in shape with shortish tail. Forehead, crown and malar patch silver grey to pale bluish grey. Inconspicuous yellow-green line runs over the eye and borders the 'cap'. Throat pale yellow and rest of head, neck, breast and upper part of mantle pale yellowish green more or less tinged with silver grey. The feathers of the central area of breast are bifurcated, with pale shining silvery green tips and yellow-green bases. Large belly patch bright orange. Flanks yellowish green. Tibial and ventral feathers yellowish green tipped with orange. Under tail coverts bright orange, often tinged or intermixed with pink. Back, rump, upper tail coverts and inner wing coverts rich moss green. Outer part of wing shining bluish green with bronze green fringes to the coverts and narrow yellow fringes to the secondaries. Bright pale pink areas on scapulars and innermost secondaries form bright spots and streaks on inner edge of wing. Tail dark green with pale greenish yellow terminal bar. Irides orange, buffish orange or orange-red with pale yellow, greenish or golden inner wing. Bill dull dark green at base, pale yellowish green at tip; cere dull purple. Legs and feet bluish purple to purplish red.

Sexes alike. Juvenile mainly green with grey tinge on forehead, yellow belly patch and under tail coverts and yellow fringes to feathers except on head and neck. The above description is of nominate *P. r. richardsii* from Ugi and Santa Anna. *P. richardsii cyanopterus* from Rennell Island is said to have bluer wings and a smaller bill but the four specimens that I have seen do not show any marked difference from a series of the nominate form, although they are rather more pink on the under tail coverts and the orange belly patch has a pinkish tinge.

DISTRIBUTION AND HABITAT: The eastern Solomon Islands of Ugi and Santa Anna and Rennell Island. On Ugi inhabits both lowland and hill forest and is abundant (Cain & Galbraith, 1956).

FEEDING AND GENERAL HABITS: Feeds on berries and small fruits taken from the branches. Large numbers gather in fruiting trees. Flight rapid and direct with head held low.

NESTING: Usual pigeon nest in tree or shrub. One white egg.

VOICE: What is, probably, the advertising coo has been described as 'Whooh-ghoo-ghoo-ghoo' repeated up to nine times with continuously falling pitch and decreasing strength (Bradley & Wolff, 1956). A 'soft high-pitch trilling "wrrrroo" is also thought to be a call of this species' (Cain & Galbraith, 1956).

DISPLAY: No information.

OTHER NAMES: Richard's Fruit Dove; Pink-spotted Fruit Dove.

REFERENCES

BRADLEY, D. & WOLFF, T. 1956. The birds of Rennell Island. *The Natural History of Rennel Island, British Solomon Islands* 1 : 97.
CAIN, A. J. & GALBRAITH, I. C. J. 1956. Field notes on birds of the eastern Solomon Islands. *Ibis* 98 : 100–134.

GREY-GREEN FRUIT DOVE   *Ptilinopus purpuratus*

Columba purpurata Gmelin, Syst. Nat., 1, pt. 2, 1789, p. 784.

DESCRIPTION: Slightly smaller than a Barbary Dove, plumper and more compact in shape though less so than many fruit doves. Outermost primary only slightly attenuated. Forehead and forecrown pale mauve with an ill-defined greenish yellow border posteriorly. Throat yellowish white. Rest of head, neck, breast, and underparts light greenish grey palest and most silvery on neck and breast and dullest on belly and flanks. Breast feathers bifurcated with silvery grey tips and obscure yellow-green sub-basal bars. Ventral areas and the rather short under tail coverts pale yellow. Upperparts predominantly bronzy green inclining to bluish green on scapulars and tail. Primaries dark green where visible when wing is folded, otherwise blackish slate. Narrow pale yellow fringes to outer webs of secondaries. Pale silvery grey bands on inner webs and part of outer webs of tail feathers form an interrupted pale and rather narrow subterminal bar when tail is spread. Underwing slate grey. Irides yellow or orange. Eye-rim yellowish. Bill greenish yellow or yellow with orange or reddish cere. Feet and unfeathered part of legs purplish. Sexes alike, but female tends to have the grey of neck and breast more suffused with yellowish green. Juvenile duller than adult with yellow fringes to feathers of underparts and wings and without the mauve cap. The above description is of the nominate form, *P. p. purpuratus*, from Tahiti. *P. p. frater*, from Moorea, is very similar but, perhaps, a little brighter and with the outermost primary more attenuated. *P. p. chrysogaster*, from the western islands in the Society Group, has a paler, more silvery neck and breast, yellow throat, clearly marked greenish yellow posterior edge to the pale mauve cap, greenish yellow lower breast and belly, brighter yellow ventral regions and under tail coverts, and the pale markings on the tail more extensive so they form a broad terminal band. *P. purpuratus chalcurus*, from Mahatea in the Tuamotu Archipelago, is intermediate in general plumage colour between *purpuratus* and *chrysogaster*, but differs from both in having a deep reddish purple cap. *P. purpuratus coralensis*, from most of the islands in the Tuamotu Group, is very like *chrysogaster* but has the cap light reddish purple and more restricted in area as immediately above the bill its forehead is grey. Both it and *coralensis* are said to have red feet and irides. All these latter forms have a more strongly attenuated outer primary than nominate *purpuratus*.

DISTRIBUTION AND HABITAT: The Society Islands and the Tuamotu (Puamotu) or Lau Archipelago. Arboreal but little recorded of its habits or habitat preferences. In 1907 Wilson recorded that it was still common on Tahiti and 'does much damage to the vanilla'.

FEEDING AND GENERAL HABITS: Has been recorded taking wild figs, fruits of the Chili pepper and Vanilla flowers.

NESTING: No information.

VOICE: No information.

DISPLAY: No information.

OTHER NAMES: Tahitian Fruit Dove; Tuamotu Fruit Dove; Purple-capped Fruit Dove.

REFERENCE

WILSON, S. B. 1907. Notes on Birds of Tahiti and the Society Group. *Ibis* **1**: Ninth Series: 373–379.

GREY'S FRUIT DOVE   *Ptilinopus greyii*

Ptilinopus greyii Bonaparte, Iconogr. Pigeons, 1857, pl. 20.

DESCRIPTION: Rather smaller than a Barbary Dove and plumper and more compact in shape. Outermost primary strongly attenuated. Forehead and crown pinkish purple to purplish red bordered by a narrow yellow stripe running from in front of and over the eye. Throat pale yellow. Rest of head, neck, breast and underparts pale greyish green, the breast feathers bifurcated, with silvery green tips and darker yellowish green bases. Pinkish purple belly patch, more or less intermixed with yellow ventrally. Under tail coverts pale pinkish purple. Upper parts green, more or less tinged with bronze. Narrow yellow fringes to secondaries and greater coverts. Pale greyish mauve central areas on scapulars and some inner secondaries form partly concealed spots at inner edge of wing. Primaries dark green, slaty-black where not visible when wing is folded. Pale greenish grey terminal band on tail. Underwing grey. Irides brownish yellow or orange sometimes (or usually ?) with one golden and one brown ring. Bill light green. Feet and unfeathered part of legs dark pink, red, or purplish red.

Sexes alike. Juvenile paler and duller with yellow fringes to most body feathers, creamy fringes and tips to primaries, no pinkish purple on the head and only a little on underparts. From this the young bird appears to moult soon into a plumage like that of the adult, but more strongly suffused with yellow, the parts that are greyish in the adult being predominantly yellow-green and with the purple belly patch and under tail coverts strongly suffused and intermixed with yellow or orange.

DISTRIBUTION AND HABITAT: Gower Island, southward through the Santa Cruz Islands, Banks Group, New Hebrides, Loyalty Islands, New Caledonia and Isle of Pines. Inhabits wooded areas. Layard (1878) in the New Hebrides, found it 'generally scattered thro' the bush'.

FEEDING AND GENERAL HABITS: Little recorded. Was, apparently intensely hunted for sport and food as early as the latter part of the last century.

NESTING: Little recorded. Layard (1880) found them breeding abundantly on Lifu in August but beyond saying that the eggs are pure white gives no further details.

VOICE: No information.

DISPLAY: No information.

REFERENCES

LAYARD, E. I. & E. L. C. 1878. Birds collected or observed in the New Hebrides. *Ibis* 2: Fourth Series: 267–280.
——— 1880. Notes on the Avifauna of the Loyalty Islands. *Ibis* 4: Fourth Series: 220–234.

RAPA ISLAND FRUIT DOVE   *Ptilinopus huttoni*

Ptilonopus huttoni Finsch, Proc. Zool. Soc. London, 1874, p. 92.

DESCRIPTION: Rather larger than a Barbary Dove and with proportionately longer tail than most fruit doves. In coloration very much a large, dull version of *Ptilinopus greyii*. Forehead, crown, a small malar patch, upper part of throat, belly patch and under tail coverts pinkish purple, this colour being palest on throat and under tail coverts and darkest on the belly patch. Ventral area whitish yellow. Neck and breast silvery grey tinged with green, breast feathers bifurcated. Rest of plumage dull green shading to blue-green on wings. Ill-defined dark bluish spots formed by central areas of inner secondaries which are also very narrowly fringed with pink and yellow or yellow. Primaries dark green and blackish. Tail dark shining green with blackish inner webs to all but the central feathers, and narrow yellowish white fringes. Irides yellow. Bill yellow, pink at base. Feet red. Sexes alike. Juvenile duller and bronzier with yellow fringes to feathers of wings and underparts.

DISTRIBUTION AND HABITAT: Found only in Rapa Island in the Austral Group.

FEEDING AND GENERAL HABITS: No information.

NESTING: No information.

VOICE: No information.

DISPLAY: No information.

OTHER NAMES: Hutton's Fruit Dove; Long-billed Fruit Dove.

WHITE-CAPPED FRUIT DOVE   *Ptilinopus dupetithouarsii*

Columba Du Petithouarsii Neboux, Rev. Zool., 1840, p. 289.

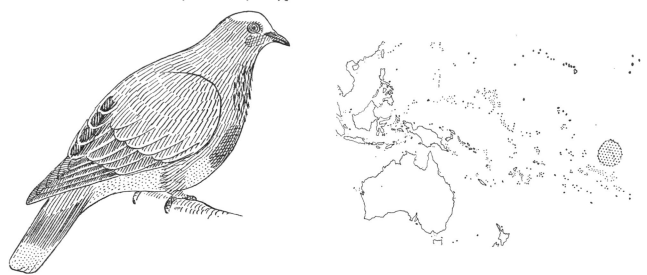

DESCRIPTION: Rather smaller than a Barbary Dove. Plumper and more compact in shape than this species but less so than many fruit doves. Wings rather long and pointed with outer primary strongly attenuated. Breast feathers of adult bifurcated. General plumage has a slightly hairy texture. Forehead and crown white. A small greyish-white malar patch. A narrow but conspicuous orange and yellow line encircles and borders the cap, terminating in front of the eye where the cap joins the malar patch. Throat pale yellow. Nape and neck silvery grey tinged green. The tips of the bifurcated breast feathers are silver, the visible parts of their bases yellowish green. Large orange belly patch, usually with some bright mauve-pink in its frontal area. Flanks greenish and yellow. Ventral regions and under tail coverts bright yellow. Mantle, back, rump, upper tail coverts and wing coverts bright yellowish olive-green. Scapulars, some greater coverts and inner secondaries have dark bright blue or green and blue central areas and yellow-green or yellow fringes, forming bright contrasting spots and patches on the folded wing. Primaries dark green with narrow yellow fringes except on the outermost ones. Parts of primaries not visible when wing is folded are blackish. Underwing light and dark grey. Tail dark green with broad yellowish-white terminal band. Irides grey, brown or yellowish. Bill greenish or apple green with paler tip, cere purple. Feet red, pinkish red or purplish pink. Female very like male but has the bifurcated breast feathers less developed, the grey parts of neck and breast more tinged with green, and the belly patch usually less brilliant. Juvenile duller and greener in colour with an obscure greenish grey, green-edged cap; yellow fringes to most of the cover feathers; and dark terminal markings to the tail giving a spotted white and dark tail band.

The above description is of the nominate form, *P. d. dupetithouarsi*, from the southern islands in the Marquesas Group. The form from the northern islands of Nukuhiva, Huapu and Huahuna, *P. d. viridior*, has the green parts more strongly tinged with yellow, its grey areas are strongly suffused with greenish yellow and its cap cream-coloured rather than white or yellowish white.

DISTRIBUTION AND HABITAT: The Marquesas Islands: Nukuhiva, Huapu, Huahuna, Hivaoa, Tahuata, Motane and Fatuhiva. Presumably in woodland but I can find nothing recorded as to its habits or habitat.

FEEDING AND GENERAL HABITS: Known, from stomach contents of collected specimens, to take buds and flowers as well as fruit.

NESTING: No information.

VOICE: No information.

DISPLAY: No information.

OTHER NAME: Marquesan Fruit Dove.

RED-MOUSTACHED FRUIT DOVE   *Ptilinopus mercierii*

Kurukuru mercierii Des Murs & Prevost, Voy. 'Venus', Zool., 1849, p. 266.

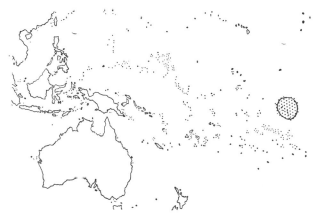

DESCRIPTION: About a fifth smaller than a Barbary Dove. Plump and compact in shape. First primary sharply attenuated. Texture of body plumage slightly hairy. Breast feathers of adult bifurcated. Forehead, crown and malar patch bright purplish crimson. A bright yellow band from in front of the eye passes over the eye and encircles the red cap. Throat yellowish. Nape, neck and breast silver-grey tinged with green. Lower breast, belly and under tail coverts bright golden yellow. Ventral regions bright yellow. Feathers on legs (tibia and upper part of tarsus) grey. Mantle, back, rump and wing coverts rich green with a golden tinge. Scapulars and inner secondaries with blue or greenish-blue centres and yellow-green edges forming bright spots on folded wing. Parts of primaries and outer secondaries visible when wing is closed shining green or bluish green. Tail dark green with broad whitish terminal band. Irides dull yellow, light olive or greenish brown. Orbital skin drab (based on one specimen only). Bill dull olive green. Feet greyish purple. Sexes nearly alike but female has grey parts more strongly tinged green and bifurcation of breast feathers less developed. I have not seen a juvenile but it probably bears the same relationship to the adult as does that of the closely related White-capped Fruit Dove (q.v.).

The above description is of the form, *P. mercieri tristrami* from Hivaoa. The nominate form, *P. m. mercieri*, from Nukuhiva differs in having a more extensive red cap with no golden border and being more generally tinged with greenish yellow. I have not, however, been able to examine specimens of this form.

DISTRIBUTION AND HABITAT: Marquesas Islands of Nukuhiva and Hivaoa.

FEEDING AND GENERAL HABITS: No information.

NESTING: No information.

VOICE: No information.

DISPLAY: No information.

OTHER NAMES: Yellow-bellied Fruit Dove; Red-capped Marquesas Fruit Dove.

HENDERSON ISLAND FRUIT DOVE   *Ptilinopus insularis*

Ptilinopus insularis North, Rec. Austral. Mus., 7, 1908, p. 30.

DESCRIPTION: As large as a Barbary Dove this species is very similar in general appearance to the related Red-moustached Fruit Dove but is larger and proportionately longer-tailed than the latter. Feathers of breast bifurcated, but this rather obscured by the somewhat hairy texture of the body plumage. Forehead and crown bright purplish crimson narrowly bordered with greenish yellow. Throat white. Nape, sides of head, neck and breast silvery grey tinged with green. Belly patch yellowish green. Ventral regions yellowish white. Feathering on legs greenish grey. Under tail coverts pale yellow. Upper parts green with same pattern and markings as in the previous species, *P. mercieri*, but the greens and blue-greens darker, the yellow edges less golden in tinge and the pale terminal band on the tail narrower, greyish instead of white and absent from the central feathers. Irides dark yellow, yellowish, orange or reddish orange. Bill yellowish green, bright green or dark yellowish. Feet red or pinkish red. Sexes nearly alike but female more strongly tinged with green on the grey areas. I have not seen a juvenile specimen.

DISTRIBUTION AND HABITAT: Henderson Island, in the Pitcairn group. Arboreal, but I can find nothing recorded of its ecology and habitat preferences. Williams (1960) recorded that it was still common and tame on Henderson Island and implied that it was killed by the Pitcairners when they visit the island. He did not, however, give further details about it.

FEEDING AND GENERAL HABITS: No information.

NESTING: No information.

Voice: No information.

Display: No information.

Other names: Wood Pigeon (Pitcairn Islanders' name for it); Henderson Island Fruit Pigeon.

REFERENCE

Williams, G. R. 1960. The birds of the Pitcairn Islands. *Ibis* **102**: 58–70.

LILAC-CAPPED FRUIT DOVE   *Ptilinopus coronulatus*

Ptilinopus coronulatus G. R. Gray, Proc. Zool. Soc. London, 1858, p. 185, pl. 38.

Description: Rather smaller than a Barbary Dove but plump and compact in shape, with short tail. First primary attenuated; feathers on upper breast bifurcated. Forehead and crown bright pinkish mauve or lilac, narrowly edged posteriorly with dark reddish purple and then bordered with a narrow rich yellow band. Nape and hind neck deep green or bluish green often shading into grey green on cheeks. Throat yellowish. A bright mauve patch on lower breast. Belly and under tail coverts bright yellow. Rest of plumage rich green slightly tinged with golden bronze on the upper parts and strongly tinged with golden yellow on breast and flanks. The central areas of the outer wing coverts, scapulars, secondaries and outer tail feathers are a more bluish green. The scapulars and inner secondaries are narrowly fringed with bright yellow. Underside of wing and tail slate grey. Irides, inner ring yellow, outer ring orange. Orbital skin light green or yellowish green. Bill light green. Feet red or purplish red.

Sexes alike, but female often paler on yellow areas. To judge from one half-moulted specimen the juvenile is similar to, but duller than the adult and lacks the lilac crown. However, Captain H. S. Stokes (1923) who successfully bred this species in captivity, noted that the juveniles at fourteen days old showed lilac patches on head and belly but later these seemed to disappear and at a month old could not be seen. Presumably this was due to abrasion or shedding of the lilac feather tips.

The above description is of the nominate form, *P. c. coronulatus*, from the south coast of New Guinea from the Mimika River to Milne Bay and the Aru Islands. *P. c. huonensis* from the northern coast of south-eastern New Guinea from Huon Gulf to Goodenough Bay is slightly smaller and richer in colour. *P. c. quadrigeminus* from Manam Island and northern New Guinea between Humboldt Bay and Astrolabe Bay is paler lilac on the head and has the lilac belly patch more or less surrounded by rusty orange. *P. c. geminus* from northern New Guinea from Takar west to Manokwari and the Japen and Kurudu islands has the crown very pale lilac, almost silver grey, and the belly patch largely rusty orange. *P. c. trigeminus* from Salawati and the western part of the Vogelkop is very similar to *P. c. geminus*.

Distribution and Habitat: New Guinea and adjacent islands. Inhabits lowland forest and wooded savanna up to about 1000 metres.   Appears to favour forest edge, areas of secondary growth and savanna areas immediately adjacent to forest.

FEEDING AND GENERAL HABITS :   Know to feed on berries and small fruits taken from the branches. Breeding captive birds took large amounts of sponge cake soaked in milk even though fruit was available (Stokes).   Often, perhaps usually, feeds low down in shrubs and secondary growth rather than in high trees.   Rand (1942), found that when he disturbed a number feeding some would usually fly off at once but others 'froze' and remained motionless for some time.

NESTING :   Usual pigeon nest in tree or shrub.   Most nests recorded by Rand were very frail and supported on palm fronds or accumulation of dead leaves.   In one case a green leaf supported the nest and may have been placed in position by the bird.   One white egg.   Incubation period in captivity eighteen days (Stokes) and a young captive-bred bird left the nest and flew strongly when twelve days old.

VOICE :   No information.

DISPLAY :   No information.

OTHER NAMES :   Lilac-crowned Fruit Dove ; Lilac-crowned Fruit Pigeon.

REFERENCES

MAYR, E.   1941.   List of New Guinea Birds.   *Amer. Mus. Nat. Hist.*
RAND, A. L.   1942.   Results of the Archbold Expeditions No. 42.   *Bull. Amer. Mus. Nat. Hist.* **79** : Art. 4 : 289–366.
STOKES, H. S.   1923.   Breeding of the Lilac-crowned Fruit Pigeon.   *Avicult Mag.* **1** : Fourth Series : 119–200.
TUBB, J. A.   1945.   Field notes on some New Guinea Birds.   *Emu* **44** : 249–273.

CRIMSON-CAPPED FRUIT DOVE   *Ptilinopus pulchellus*

Columba pulchella Temminck, pl. col. Livr. 95, 1835, pl. 564.

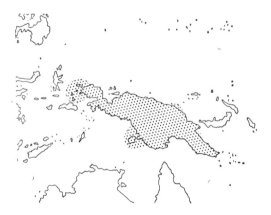

DESCRIPTION :   About a third smaller than a Barbary Dove.   Plump and compact in shape.   First primary sharply attenuated.   Often with some breast feathers more or less bifurcated.   Forehead and crown purplish crimson.   Throat and an area in front of and above frontal part of eye white.   Face, ventral parts of sides of neck and entire breast and lower breast pale bluish grey.   Many of the feathers of the lower breast are tipped with creamy white, especially along the lower edge of the grey breast shield where they usually form a whitish border.   Immediately below this is a broad band of dark reddish purple with an orange patch behind it.   Flanks green and yellow.   Belly yellow.   Tibial feathers green tipped yellow.   Under tail coverts orange.   Upperparts rich, rather dark green slightly tinged with golden bronze on mantle and rump and with blue on wings.   Narrow pale yellow fringes to secondaries and inner primaries.   Underwing and undersides of tail grey.   Irides orange or orange-yellow, paler round pupil ;

orbital skin yellowish.   Bill greenish yellow or yellow, usually darker at base.   Legs and feet purplish red or purplish pink; one specimen's feet said to have been olive.   Sexes alike but purple and orange on belly of female less extensive.   Juvenile duller without crimson on cap and with only suggestion of the purple and orange belly patch.

DISTRIBUTION AND HABITAT: New Guinea and the western Papuan Islands.   Inhabits lowland forest.

FEEDING AND GENERAL HABITS: Known to feed on small fruits and berries taken from the branches. Rand found it usually feeding or resting singly and not much afraid of man.   Grant (in Ogilvie-Grant, 1915) found it usually in pairs and quite tame.   Flight swift and direct.

NESTING: Usual pigeon nest in tree or shrub.   One white egg.   Rand (1942) records that birds flushed from nests containing an egg or young one flew with 'a slow fluttering flight, very different from their usual' (flight).

VOICE: Grant (in Ogilvie-Grant, 1915) says it has 'a low call'.

DISPLAY: No information.

OTHER NAMES: Rose-fronted Pigeon; Beautiful Fruit Dove; Grey-breasted Fruit Dove.

REFERENCES

MAYR, E. 1941. *List of New Guinea Birds* (published by the Amer. Mus. Nat. Hist.).
OGILVIE-GRANT, W. R. 1915. Report on the Birds collected by the British Ornithologists' Union Expedition and the Wollaston Expedition in Dutch New Guinea. *Ibis*, Jubilee Suppl No. **2**: 292–293.
RAND, A. L. 1942. Results of the Archbold Expeditions No. 42. *Bull. Amer. Mus. Nat. Hist.*, Vol. LXXIX, Art. 4: 289–366.

BLUE-CAPPED FRUIT DOVE   *Ptilinopus monacha*

Columba monacha 'Reinw.' Temminck, pl. col., Livr. 43, 1824, pl. 253.

DESCRIPTION: Between Diamond Dove and Barbary Dove in size but compact in shape with short tail. Outermost primary attenuated.   Forehead and crown greyish blue bordered by a bright yellow stripe that runs from in front of and over eye.   Malar patches and patch on breast also greyish blue.   Throat stripe, ventral areas and under tail coverts pale bright yellow.   Rest of plumage rich green with a golden bronze tinge when new.   Outer tail feathers blackish green with paler terminal band.   Underside of wings and tail grey.   Irides 'dark' or orange (one specimen only).   Bill greenish.   Feet red.   These soft part colours are based on only a few specimens and further information is needed.   Female has the blue head markings only slightly 'suggested' and lacks the blue breast patch.   I have not seen a juvenile specimen.

DISTRIBUTION AND HABITAT: The northern Moluccas: Halmahera, Ternate, Batjan.   Presumably inhabits forest but I can find no detailed information.

FEEDING AND GENERAL HABITS: No information.

NESTING: No information.

VOICE : No information.

DISPLAY : No information.

OTHER NAME : Blue-crowned Fruit Dove.

WHITE-BIBBED FRUIT DOVE   *Ptilinopus rivoli*

Columba rivoli Prevost, in Knip, Les Pigeons, Ed. 2, 2, 1843, p. 107, pl. 57.

DESCRIPTION : Rather smaller than a Barbary Dove but plumper and more heavily built with short, rather rounded tail. Predominantly dark rich green with a slight golden tinge. Forehead and fore-crown dark bright purple or purplish red. A large white or yellowish white half-moon shaped patch on the breast (see sketch). Oval or longitudinal purple patch on belly. Ventral regions and under tail coverts bright yellow. Dark blue spots on scapulars formed by dark centres to feathers. Underwing and inner webs of primaries dark grey. Irides yellowish, orange, pinkish or with orange outer ring and yellow or buff inner ring. Orbital skin probably as the race *bellus* (q.v.) but apparently not recorded. Bill greenish yellow or yellow. Feet red or purplish red.

Female differs strikingly from the male in lacking the white, purple and blue markings and is green all over except for the yellow ventral regions and under tail coverts. Her forehead and crown are somewhat darker green and tinged with blue. Juvenile female like adult but paler and with yellow fringes to feathers of wings, breast and underparts. Juvenile male similar but with traces of the adult male's bright markings.

The above description applies to the nominate form of the species and some other races that do not significantly differ from it. The form from the Louisiade Archipelago and the Egum atoll in the Trobriand Group, *P. rivoli strophium* and that from the islands of Jobi (Japen) and Miosnum in Geelvink Bay lack the purple belly patch. The form from the mountains of New Guinea, *P. rivoli bellus*, is larger, being larger than a Barbary Dove, and has the frontal part of the breast patch bright yellow so that the effect is that of a yellow half-moon bordered by a white crescent. It otherwise resembles the typical race in colour and sexual dimorphism. Its orbital skin (recorded for several specimens) is dark olive in the male and purplish grey to dark purple in the female. The skin between the bill and front of the eye is bright yellow in the male and pale yellow to yellowish green in the female.

DISTRIBUTION AND HABITAT : The Moluccas, Sudest Islands, Kei Islands, Western Papuan Islands, islands in Geelvink Bay, Numfor, Traitors Island, Mios Korwar, the Bismark Archipelago, Louisade

Archipelago, East and Hastings Islands, Woodlark Islands (Egum and Alcester), Goodenough Islands, and the mountains of New Guinea. The island forms inhabit coral islands, coastal woods of larger islands and lowland forest. The yellow-breasted New Guinea form (*P. r. bellus*), inhabits mountain and hill forest.

FEEDING AND GENERAL HABITS: Recorded feeding on fruits in large trees. Grant (in Ogilvie-Grant, 1915) found it (in New Guinea) usually in pairs.

NESTING: No information.

VOICE: Grant records a 'sweet, low coo'.

DISPLAY: No information.

OTHER NAMES: Beautiful Fruit Dove; Moon-breasted Fruit Dove; White-breasted Fruit Dove.

REFERENCES

MAYR, E. 1941. List of New Guinea Birds. Amer. Mus. Nat. Hist.
OGILVIE-GRANT, W. R. 1915. *Ibis*, Jubilee Suppl. No. 2.

YELLOW-BIBBED FRUIT DOVE   *Ptilinopus solomonensis*

Ptilonopus solomonensis G. R. Gray, Ann. M   Nat. Hist. (4), 5, 1870, p. 382.

DESCRIPTION: This species is closely related to the White-bibbed Fruit Dove which it much resembles in colour-pattern. It is slightly smaller than *P. rivoli* but of similar plump, short-tailed shape. General plumage colour rich green with a slight golden tinge. Forehead and front of crown bright mauve, this colour extends further at either side, over the eyes, than it does in mid-crown. There is a large patch of slightly paler mauve on the belly. A broad crescent-shaped band across the breast, the ventral regions and under tail coverts are bright yellow. Dark blue spots on scapulars less prominent than those of *rivoli*. Outer tail feathers with blackish bases and grey terminal bands, green suffusion largely masking this pattern on the outer webs. Outer primaries and underwing dark grey. Irides pinkish yellow, orange yellow or dull orange with pale green inner ring. Orbital skin pale green, greenish blue or blue. Bill sage green, sometimes tinged grey or blue. Feet dull mauve, exposed part of legs reddish purple.

The female lacks the bright markings and is green with yellow on the ventral areas and under tail coverts. Juvenile female like adult but with conspicuous yellow fringes to most feathers. Juvenile male similar but with some purple on forehead.

The above description is of the nominate form, *P. s. solomonensis*, which inhabits Ugi and San Cristobal in the Solomon Islands. *P. s. neumanni* from Nissan Island; *P. s. meyeri* from New Britain, Uatom Island, Witu Islands and Rook Island; *P. s. johannis* from Manus, St. Matthias Island, Squally Island, New

Hanover and Nusa Island; and *P. s. vulcanorum* from the central Solomon Islands are all very similar but have the mauve on the head more extensive and not divided by green on the centre.

P. s. ocularis of Guadalcanar Island differs strikingly in having the purple on the head darker in colour and restricted to a large spot above and in front of each eye. Its irides are sage green. *P. s. ambiguus* of Malaita Island and *P. s. bistictus* of Bougainville are intermediate in head pattern between the nominate form and *ocularis*. Most distinct is *P. s. speciosus* from the Geelvink Bay islands of Numfor, Biak and Traitors Island. In this the only purple on the head is a spot in front of the eye. The mauve belly patch is very bright and extensive and the yellow crescent on the breast is broadly bordered with white.

DISTRIBUTION AND HABITAT: Solomon Islands, Bismark Archipelago and some islands in Geelvink Bay. In most of its range inhabits lowland forest. Cain and Galbraith (1956) found it on San Cristobal and Ugi in coastal, lowland and ridge forest, often in second growth and substage forest. In Guadalcanar however, the form *ocularis* was found in unbroken hill and mist forest and was the only fruit dove seen in the mist forest.

FEEDING AND GENERAL HABITS: Known to feed on berries and fruits taken from the branches. Cain & Galbraith (1956) found it usually singly or in pairs and noted that it did not come to large isolated fruiting trees as some other fruit doves did.

NESTING: Usual pigeon nest in tree or shrub. In New Britain (and elsewhere?) breeds throughout the year (Meyer, 1930). One white egg.

VOICE: Cain & Galbraith record 'a rapid accelerating' tu-tu-tu-tu-tu-tu-to tututututututu ... becoming louder and shriller and then dying away.

DISPLAY: No information.

OTHER NAMES: Yellow-breasted Fruit Dove.

REFERENCES

CAIN, A. J. & GALBRAITH, I. C. J. 1956. Field notes on the Birds of the eastern Solomon Islands. *Ibis* 98:100–134. :
MEYER, P. O. 1930. Uebersicht über die Brutzeiten der Vögel auf der Insel Vuatom (New Britain). *Journ. f. Orn.* 77
19–38.

RED-BIBBED FRUIT DOVE   *Ptilinopus viridis*
Columba viridis Linnaeus, Syst. Nat., ed. 12, 1, 1755, p. 283.

DESCRIPTION: Rather smaller than a Barbary Dove; plump and compact in shape with short tail. General colour rich deep green with a faint coppery or golden tinge. Chin, face, forehead and forecrown bluish grey. Lower part of throat and upper breast dark purplish crimson very sharply demarcated from the green of the lower breast. Small silver grey patch on shoulder of wing, silver grey centres to some inner secondaries form spots on inner edge of wing. Greater wing coverts and outer secondaries narrowly, and feathers of ventral area broadly edged yellow. Under tail coverts broadly edged with yellow or whitish yellow, giving spotted effect. Pale tips and dark bases to outer tail feathers which are edged yellow. Underwing and parts of primaries not visible when wing is folded dark grey. Irides yellow, orange or red, sometimes (or usually?) with a paler and duller inner ring. Orbital skin yellow or greenish yellow. Bill yellowish green, yellow or orange with red or deep orange base. Feet purplish or purplish red.

The female resembles the male but has a less extensive crimson area on the breast and sometimes, perhaps normally, grey or bluish irides. Juvenile like adult but with yellow edgings to most wing coverts and the grey and red areas on head and breast much duller and less extensive.

The above description is of the nominate form, *P. v. viridis* from the southern Moluccas. *P. viridis lewisii* from the Solomon Islands of Guadalcanar and Malaita and the Lihir Islands is similar but has a narrow dark purplish edging to the crimson breast, and the silver grey markings on its wings are paler and more conspicuous. It has a yellow or orange bill and the irides of both sexes are yellow or orange; red in one female specimen. The forms from the islands of Geelvink Bay, *P. viridis geelvinkiana* and *P. v.*

pseudogeelvinkiana, are similar to the nominate form but have the red breast paler and slightly less extensive and tend to be a little larger. The form from the Trobriand and D'Entrecasteaux Islands, *P. viridis vicinus*, has the purplish crimson area much reduced in size, expecially in the female. This reduction in the red area has been carried a stage further in *P. viridis salvadorii* from Japen (Jobi) Island and northern New Guinea whose male has a large and the female a small crescentic red mark on the breast. In the form from the Western Papuan Islands of Gebe, Waigeu, Gagi, Kofiau and Misol and north-western New Guinea east to Geelvink Bay and Triton Bay, *P. viridis pectoralis*, reduction of the red breast has progressed even further. In this form the male alone shows a small red patch on the breast; the female's breast is entirely green.

DISTRIBUTION AND HABITAT: Southern Moluccas, western Papuan Islands, north-west New Guinea, islands in Geelvink Bay, some islands off south-eastern New Guinea, Solomon Islands. Inhabits lowland forest up to 600 metres in New Guinea. In the Solomons (Guadalcanar and Ulawa) in lowland, hill and ridge forest.

FEEDING AND GENERAL HABITS: Known to feed on fruits and berries taken from the branches. Cain & Galbraith (1956) found it usually in parties in the canopy of tall fruiting trees, often in isolated trees or groves in open areas. They noted that when feeding it was aggressive and successfully drove away Superb Fruit Doves and glossy starlings, *Aplonis*, from feeding perches though itself giving way to the large starling *Mino dumonti*.

NESTING: No information.

VOICE: Cain & Galbraith record a 'repeated soft' cooroo coo, cooroo coo . . . 'A call of the form *P. v. lewisii* is described by Sibley (1951) as "a series of mellow coos" . . ."coo-óo-coo-whó – coo-whó – coo-whó" the first notes are slurred as "coo-oo" lacking the aspirated "w" sound of the subsequent notes'.

DISPLAY: Apparent driving (males chasing and pecking females) seen from birds feeding in company (Sibley, 1951).

OTHER NAMES: Red-breasted Fruit Dove, Red-throated Fruit Dove.

REFERENCES

CAIN, A. J. & GALBRAITH, I. C. J. 1956. Field notes on Birds of the eastern Solomon Islands. *Ibis* **98**: 100–134.
SIBLEY, C. G. 1951. Notes on the Birds of New Georgia, central Solomon Islands. *Condor* **53**: 81–92.

WHITE-HEADED FRUIT DOVE

Ptilinopus eugeniae

Iotreron eugeniae Gould, Proc. Zool. Soc. London, 1856, p. 137.

This is a very close relative of the Red-bibbed Fruit Dove and may be conspecific with it, but for reasons discussed elsewhere (see p. 330) is treated separately here.

DESCRIPTION: Size, shape, colour pattern and general plumage coloration very similar to the Guadalcanar form of the Red-bibbed Fruit Dove, *P. viridis lewisii* (q.v.), but differing strikingly from it in having the entire head, inclusive of face and upper part of throat, white more or less tinged with yellow. It also has the dark purple border to the purplish crimson breast more extensive at the sides and the green of the underparts duller and often with grey or bluish tinge. Irides tawny orange, orange, or red usually with a pale yellowish or greenish inner ring. Orbital skin bluish grey. Bill yellow, greenish, or golden at tip, dull maroon at base. Feet purplish red or purple. Sexes alike. The only juveniles I have seen have begun to moult but from them it seems probable that the juvenile is at first green with yellow fringes to most feathers, white only around the base of the bill and upper throat and with little or no red on the breast.

DISTRIBUTION AND HABITAT: The Solomon Islands of San Cristobal and Ugi. Inhabits lowland, hill and ridge forest.

FEEDING AND GENERAL HABITS: Cain & Galbraith (who treat them as conspecific) record no differences between this and *P. viridis* (q.v.).

NESTING: No information.

VOICE: As *P. viridis* (*fide* Cain & Galbraith, 1956).

DISPLAY: No information.

OTHER NAMES: Eugene's Fruit Dove; Eugene's Fruit Pigeon.

ORANGE-BELLIED FRUIT DOVE

Ptilinopus iozonus

Ptilonopus iozonus G. R. Gray, Proc. Zool. Soc. London, 1858, p. 186.

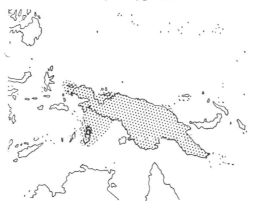

DESCRIPTION: Slightly smaller than a Barbary Dove but plumper and more compact in shape with short tail. Outer primary attenuated but not to an extreme degree. General colour rich green, usually with a yellow or golden-bronze tinge. A large bright orange patch on belly. Ventral area and under tail coverts yellowish, marked with green. A small greyish-mauve patch on carpal area of wing. Secondaries and greater coverts narrowly edged yellow. Primaries dark iridescent green or bronze-green, blackish on the portions concealed when wing folded. Grey-blue centres to scapulars and some inner wing coverts give a spotted effect to upperpart of folded wing. Tail blackish green, central feathers with grey green-edged terminal band, outer ones same but with a large white spot on the otherwise grey part of inner web. Underwing bluish grey. Irides greyish with red tinge, white or yellowish. Bill greyish black with cream coloured tip. Orbital skin bluish green. Feet bright purple. Sexes alike, but female tends to have less yellow or bronzy tinge to her green parts and more pronounced grey tinge on chin.

The above is a composite description of the forms found in the Aru Islands and south-eastern New Guinea, *P. i. iozonus* and *P. iozonus finschii*, which are very alike. I have not seen a juvenile of these forms.

The forms from the western Papuan Islands, north-western New Guinea and south New Guinea east to the Noord River and the Upper Fly River and northern New Guinea, *P. i. humeralis*, *P. i. pseudohumeralis* and *P. i. jobiensis*, differ in having the mauve-grey feathers on the carpal patch broadly tipped with dark purple. The juvenile lacks the grey, purple and orange markings and has narrow yellow edges to most cover feathers and broad yellow edges to those on the 'belly patch' area.

DISTRIBUTION AND HABITAT: New Guinea and adjacent islands of Salawati, Waigeu, Aru, Japen (Jobi), Manam and Tarawai. Inhabits lowland forest and open woodlands. Freely comes into gardens and cultivated areas where there are trees.

FEEDING AND GENERAL HABITS: Little recorded. Known to take fruits and berries from the branches. Rand (1942) found it usually high up in trees, feeding and flying in flocks of up to about twelve individuals.

NESTING: No information.

VOICE: One call has been described as 'a penetrating distinctive call, almost like a person in pain'. (Watson *et al.*, 1962) and another (? the advertising coo) as five or six melodious, quickly repeated 'coos' (Grant, in Ogilvie-Grant, 1915).

DISPLAY: No information.

REFERENCES

MAYR, E. 1941. List of New Guinea Birds. Amer. Mus. Nat. Hist.
OGILVIE-GRANT, W. R. 1915. *Ibis*, Jubilee Suppl. No. 2 : 294–295.
RAND, A. L. 1942. Results of the Archbold Expeditions No. 42. *Bull. Amer. Mus. Nat. Hist.* **79** : Art 4 : 289–366.
WATSON, J. D., WHEELER, W. R. & WHITBOURN, E. 1962. With the R.A.O.U. in Papua, New Guinea. *Emu* **62** : 31–50.

KNOB-BILLED FRUIT DOVE   *Ptilinopus insolitus*

Ptilinopus insolitus Schlegel, Nederl Tijdschr. Dierk, 1, 1863, p. 61, Vögels, pl. 3, f. 3.

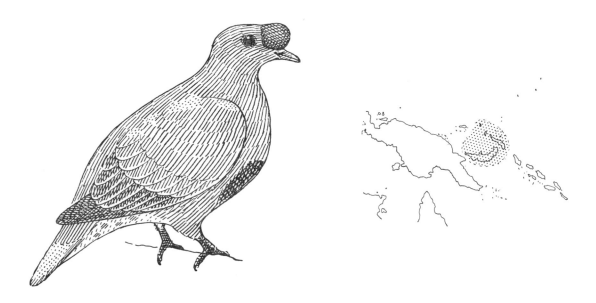

DESCRIPTION: Resembles the Orange-bellied Fruit Dove, to which it is very closely related, except in the following points: The cere is enormously enlarged, forming a big red fruit-like protuberance on the front of the head.   The outer primary less attenuated.   The spots on the inner edge of the wing and the terminal tail-band are a pale silver grey and more extensive than in *iozonus*.   The shoulder patch is of the same colour and extends into a narrow line of grey along the upper inner edge of the folded wing. The sexes are alike although probably in life the female's cere averages smaller.   The form of this species from St. Mathias' Island, *P. insolitus inferior*, is smaller than the nominate form.

DISTRIBUTION AND HABITAT: New Ireland, New Britain, Duke of York Island, Lihir Islands and St. Mathias Island.   In woodland.

FEEDING AND GENERAL HABITS: No information.

NESTING: Usual pigeon nest in tree or shrub.   In New Britain Meyer (1933) recorded it as usually nesting in thickly foliaged trees.   One white egg.   Incubation period nineteen days.   Young flew when fourteen days old (data on one nest only).   Probably breeds throughout the year (Meyer, 1930).

VOICE: Two short hard cooing notes followed by a rolling 'rrrr' sound (Meyer, 1930).

DISPLAY: No information.

OTHER NAMES: Knob-billed Orange-bellied Fruit Dove; Red-knobbed Fruit Dove; Knob-billed Fruit Pigeon.

REFERENCES

MEYER, P. O.   1930.   Uebersicht über Die Brutzeiten Der Vögel Auf der Insel Vuatom (New Britain).   *Journ. f. Orn.* 77: 19–38.
—— 1933.   Vogeleier Und Nester Aus Neubritannien, Südsee.   *Beitr. z. Fortpfl. d. Vög.* 9: 122–136.

GREY-HEADED FRUIT DOVE *Ptilinopus hyogastra*

Columba hyogastra 'Reinw'. Temminck, pl. col. livr. 43, 1824, pl. 252.

DESCRIPTION: About size of Barbary Dove but more compact in shape and with short tail. Colour generally rich green with (in new plumage) a golden bronze tinge except for the pale bluish grey head, two pale bluish grey bands on the shoulder and across the wing, a large dark purple patch on the belly and bright yellow ventral regions and under tail coverts. Irides brown. Bill greyish blue or whitish blue at base, yellow at tip. Legs and feet dark grey or greyish purple. Sexes alike. I have not seen a juvenile of this species.

DISTRIBUTION AND HABITAT: Northern Moluccan islands of Halmahera and Batjan. Presumably inhabits woodland.

FEEDING AND GENERAL HABITS: No information.

NESTING: No information.

VOICE: No information.

DISPLAY: No information.

OTHER NAMES: Purple-bellied Fruit Dove.

CARUNCULATED FRUIT DOVE *Ptilinopus granulifrons*

Ptilinopus granulifrons Hartert, Bull. Brit. Orn. Cl. 7, 1898, p. 35.

DESCRIPTION: Except for its cere very similar to the Grey-headed Fruit Dove with which it forms a superspecies. Head and patches on scapulars and inner wing coverts silver grey. Patch on belly deep purple edged posteriorly with deep yellow which shades to pale yellow on ventral area and under tail coverts. Primaries blackish green. Underwing slate grey. Outer tail feathers dark green with ill-defined greyish white terminal bar. Rest of plumage rich green strongly tinged with golden yellow, especially on neck and breast. Base of cere developed into a mass of protuberant fleshy knobs. Irides crimson. Bill yellow, olivaceous at tip and crimson on flat part of cere, protuberant part of cere buffish orange. Sexes alike in plumage but female has more greenish tinged bill and buffish orange irides.

DISTRIBUTION AND HABITAT: The island of Obi Major in the central Moluccas.   Inhabits forest.

FEEDING AND GENERAL HABITS: I can find nothing recorded.

NESTING: No information.

VOICE: No information.

DISPLAY: No information.

OTHER NAMES: Obi Fruit Dove; Wattled Fruit Dove.

REFERENCE

HARTERT, E. 1903.   The Birds of the Obi Group, central Moluccas.   *Novit. Zool.* **10** : 1–17.

BLACK-NAPED FRUIT DOVE   *Ptilinopus melanospila*

Jotreron melanospila Salvadori, Ann. Mus. Civ. Genova, 7, 1875, p. 670.

DESCRIPTION: From slightly smaller than a Barbary Dove to about midway between Barbary Dove and Feral Pigeon in size, but plumper and more compact in build, with shortish tail, outer primary slightly attenuated. Head pale silver grey with yellow or golden median stripe from beneath lower mandible to front of neck and a large black patch on hind crown and nape. Ventral area yellow, golden or orange. The long tail coverts bright purplish red, the shorter ones yellow or orange with red tips. Underwing and underside of tail grey. Rest of plumage a rich deep green, usually with a strong tinge of golden bronze but sometimes, especially in old and worn feathers, with a bluish green tinge. Irides yellow, buff, or with yellow outer ring, dark grey median ring and pale grey inner ring. Eyelids yellow. Orbital skin greyish or greenish. Bill yellow, greenish yellow, or blackish with yellowish or pale greenish tip. Feet dark red or purplish red.

The female lacks the contrasting head markings and is entirely green except for usually having some purplish red on the under tail coverts and narrow yellow fringes to her outer wing coverts and secondaries and yellow edges to the feathers of her belly and ventral regions. Juvenile like female but with more conspicuous yellow edges to most feathers. The feathers that grow at base of the juvenile bill at the time it becomes independent (probably when about four weeks old) are pale grey in the young male. Several races of this species, differing a little in size and a very little in colour, have been described but the above description covers them all.

DISTRIBUTION AND HABITAT: The Philippine Islands of Palawan, Cagayan Sulu, Mindanao, Basilan, Sulu and nearby islets, the North Bornean Islands of Bangueay and Balambangan, Talaut and Sangir Islands, Celebes and Togian Islands, Tukang Besi, Peling and Banggai Islands, Sula Island and Ceram, Kalao Tua and Madu Islands, Pulo Mata Siri, Java, the Lesser Sunda Islands from Bali to Alor; Kalao, Saleyer and Kangean Islands. Inhabits woodland. In the Celebes (and probably elsewhere) commonly in forest edge and patches of scrub or forest in open country. Will visit isolated trees for feeding purposes.

FEEDING AND GENERAL HABITS: Little apparently recorded in spite of its being common over a large area and very frequently collected. Known to take berries and fruits from the branches. A completely tame captive bird that I was able to observe took strong sudden leaps from its perch to another higher and several feet away without using its wings. When it flew, its flight was swift (in a large aviary) and with a loud whirring. It fought my hands with pecks and wing blows in the usual manner of male pigeons that are reacting socially to man.

NESTING: I can find nothing recorded.

VOICE: The advertising coo of the tame captive male bird mentioned above was a single 'coo' repeated many times but not run together. It was, when given at full intensity, quite loud but with the same sad, 'haunting' tone that one finds in the cooing of the Mountain Witch (*Geotrygon cristata*), and some other species. When I was standing near to it, after it had been attacking me, it gave the same coos more softly and interspersed its cooing with nodding (q.v.).

DISPLAY: The tame captive bird had a display that appeared to represent the nodding of *Columba* species. In this it lowered its head till the bill was at an angle of about 90 degrees, and the black nuchal patch shown frontally constrasting with the green mantle and silver crown. At the lowest point of the nod it made a quick movement with its mandibles.

OTHER NAMES: Black-headed Fruit Dove; Black-naped Fruit Pigeon.

REFERENCE

STRESEMANN, E. 1941. Die Vögel von Celebes. *Journ. f. Orn.* **89**: 1–102.

DWARF FRUIT DOVE   *Ptilonopus naina*

Columba naina Temminck, pl. col., livr., 95, 1835, pl. 565.

DESCRIPTION: The smallest of all the fruit doves. A little larger than a Diamond Dove. Plump and compact in shape. General colour rich green with a golden tinge. Wing coverts a slightly darker and more shining green; inner wing coverts and inner secondaries tending to a shining bluish green, this bluish colour being more pronounced on the scapulars. Primaries and tail feathers with mainly blackish inner webs. Median and greater coverts and outer secondaries edged narrowly and inner secondaries and scapulars more broadly with yellow, forming bright yellow markings across the folded wing. Underwing, a small patch at sides of breast and underside of tail light bluish grey. Dark purple patch on belly. Ventral regions and under tail coverts bright yellow. Irides inner ring pale grey, outer ring darker grey. Orbital skin blue grey. Bill yellowish green. Feet purplish red.

The female lacks the purple belly patch and the grey patches at sides of breast. Her irides are paler and her feet and bill darker and duller than the male's. Juvenile (only one specimen seen) like female but with yellow fringes to most of the feathers.

DISTRIBUTION AND HABITAT: Southern and south-eastern New Guinea and the Western Papuan Islands of Waigeu, Salawati and, probably, Misol. Inhabits lowland forest.

FEEDING AND GENERAL HABITS: Apparently little recorded. Presumably feeds on berries and small fruits taken from the branches.

NESTING: No information.

VOICE: No information.

DISPLAY: No information.

OTHER NAMES: Little Fruit Dove; Small Fruit Dove.

RIPLEY'S FRUIT DOVE   *Ptilinopus arcanus*

Ptilinopus arcanus Ripley and Rabor. Postilla 21, Feb. 28th, 1955.

DESCRIPTION: Known only from the female type specimen. A fruit dove with vivid green plumage, yellow under tail coverts and extensive bare orbital skin.

DISTRIBUTION AND HABITAT: Known only from the slopes of Mount Canlaon, north-central Negros Island, Philippines where two were seen in a large fruiting tree in a clearing at 3600 ft., and a female shot.

FEEDING AND GENERAL HABITS: No information.

NESTING: No information.

VOICE: No information.

DISPLAY: No information.

ORANGE DOVE
Ptilinopus victor

Chrysoena victor Gould, Proc. Zool. Soc. London, 1871 (1872), p. 642.

DESCRIPTION: Rather smaller than a Barbary Dove and much more compact in shape, with a short tail which is more or less completely covered (when folded) by the long upper tail coverts. Head dark greenish yellow, paler on the throat and narrowly edged paler greenish yellow except on the nape. Primaries, primary coverts and outer secondaries orange yellow or pinkish yellow, strongly suffused with greyish olive except at feather edges, and with blackish shafts. Tail orange-yellow with ill-defined olivaceous central bar. Rest of plumage a vivid fire orange, slightly darker on the mantle and back, except in the population on Ngamea, and with the exposed (i.e. the orange-coloured) parts of the feathers having a peculiar loose hairy appearance and texture. Underwing light orange. Bill, cere, legs and orbital skin green. Irides yellowish buff.

The female is dark green where the male is orange, and blackish where he is olivaceous except that her underwing is dusky with golden yellow edges to the feathers and her tail coverts are golden orange with olivaceous centres to the feathers. The feathers of her underparts, except the breast, are more or less fringed with buffish yellow. Her head is more or less suffused with greenish yellow and the median line of her throat is light yellowish. The juveniles are green with yellow edges to most feathers. The young male moults first into a subadult plumage in which he resembles the adult female but has more orange on the under tail coverts and a brighter yellow tinge to the head. The cover feathers of the female and young show only a hint of the loose hairy texture of the adult male.

DISTRIBUTION AND HABITAT: The Fiji Islands: Vanua Levu, Taiviuni, Kio Rambi, Ngamea, Luathala. Inhabits forest areas but I have been able to find little recorded of its ecology and habits other than Layard's observations made nearly a century ago.

FEEDING AND GENERAL HABITS: Layard recorded it as taking many sorts of berries and fruits.

NESTING: According to Layard this species nests in November and December, building the usual type of nest and laying two eggs. If this statement as to clutch-size is correct the Orange Dove differs in this from other species of *Ptilinopus* whose clutch-size is known, but agrees with *Drepanoptila*.

VOICE: Layard records 'an odd chuckling sound like a coachman starting his horses' which he heard only from adult males, never from females or young.

OTHER NAME: Flame Dove.

REFERENCE

LAYARD, E. L. 1876. Notes on some little-known Birds of the new Colony of the Fiji Islands. *Ibis* 6: Third Series, 137–139 and 151–152.

GOLDEN DOVE   *Ptilinopus luteovirens*

Columba luteovirens Hombron and Jacquinot, Ann. Sci. Nat., Zool. (2), 16, 1841, p. 315.

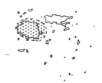

DESCRIPTION: Slightly smaller than the Orange Dove (q.v.), but similar in shape. Head dark greenish yellow, narrowly edged lemon yellow except at nape. Outer and median wing coverts green with bright golden edges. Primaries olivaceous with golden yellow edges and black shafts. Rest of cover feathers elongated and strap-shaped (most areas) or accuminate (lesser and median wing coverts), some of those on mantle and breast showing varying degrees of bifurcation. These feathers are yellowish green or greenish gold (some individual variation), each being dark at the base and having a narrow edging of dark greenish edged with golden yellow. These dark yellow-edged fringes are (unlike the rest of the feather) of a loose hairy texture. On the lower breast, belly and flanks the feathers are less modified and their fringes are much broader and entirely golden yellow. Under tail coverts and underwing golden yellow. Irides buff or yellow. Orbital skin bright green. Bill and feet emerald green. (See Pl. 2).

The female resembles the female of the Orange Dove (q.v.) except for being a slightly brighter green. It is of interest that in this species the body fat shows the same sexual difference as the plumage, the male's being golden yellow and the female's green. I have not seen a juvenile.

FIELD CHARACTERS: Appears distinctly streaked lime yellow and dark on head and back (Morris).

DISTRIBUTION AND HABITAT: Fiji Islands, Viti Levu and nearby islands. In woodland. Morris (1964, pers. comm.) found it, near Suva, fairly common in dense jungle with tall trees with a thick little-broken canopy and relatively scanty undergrowth.

FEEDING AND GENERAL HABITS: Known to feed on small fruits and berries plucked from the branches. A captive male ate fruit, cake, rice and canary seed, apparently without ill-effects (Wood, 1924). Morris (1964) found it usually in the top of tall trees but once came on a male creeping about in a tangled thicket about 3 feet from the ground.

VOICE: What is, probably, the equivalent of the advertising coo is a dog-like barking call 'exactly like a yelping puppy'. Two captive males uttered a growling cry when threatening other birds (Wood, 1924).

DISPLAY: No information.

OTHER NAMES: Lemon Dove; Yellow Dove.

REFERENCES

BAHR, P. H. 1912. Notes on the Avifauna of the Fiji Islands. *Ibis* 6: Ninth Series, 282–314.
MORRIS, R. O. 1964. A note on the Birds observed in Fiji (unpublished MSS.) and pers. comm.
WOOD, C. A. 1924. The Golden Doves of Fiji. *Bird Lore* 26: 387–390.

YELLOW-HEADED DOVE   *Ptilinopus layardi*

Ptilopus layardi Elliot, 1878, Proc. Zool. Soc. London, p. 567.

DESCRIPTION: Size and shape as in the Golden Dove (q.v.). Head dark bright greenish yellow, narrowly ringed all round neck with lighter yellow. Ventral regions and the dense 'woolly' feathers on tibia and upper part of tarsus mainly grey. Under tail coverts bright golden yellow. Underwing mainly golden yellow. Outer primaries dusky green, edged bright golden yellow. Rest of plumage dark, bright green with shining golden fringes to the feathers of mantle, lower neck and upper breast, which are bifurcated. Cover feathers with a rather loose hairy texture approaching the condition found in the male Orange Dove (q.v.). Irides yellow or buff. Feet and bill green; at least this is the colour recorded on the labels of most collected specimens but one was recorded (? correctly) as having a blue-black bill and crimson feet. Female dark green with blackish, yellow fringed primaries and mainly pale yellow underwing and under tail coverts. Juvenile presumably much as young of *luteovirens* and *victor*.

DISTRIBUTION AND HABITAT: The Fijian islands of Kandavu and Ono. Presumably inhabits woodland.

FEEDING AND GENERAL HABITS: No information.

NESTING: No information.

VOICE: No information.

DISPLAY: No information.

OTHER NAMES: Green Dove; Kandavu Dove.

CLOVEN-FEATHERED DOVE   *Drepanoptila holosericea*

Columba Holosericea Temminck, in Knip. les Pigeons, 1810, les colombes, p. 73, pl. 32.

DESCRIPTION: Somewhat smaller than a smallish Feral Pigeon. Plump and compact in shape with short and very rounded wings with notched primaries and short broad tail. General colour a beautiful rich, pure green with a silvery tinge on the outer webs of the primaries and silvery-white subterminal areas on most of the greater wing coverts, secondaries, upper tail coverts and central rectrices. These pale markings form transverse bands across the bird when looked at from above. The effect is very unusual and difficult to describe, the silver bands on the green having an odd nebulous quality much like the similar markings of the Emerald Moth. Chin, median part of upper throat and the dense fluffy tibial feathers pure white. A narrow white band and a broader black one behind it divide the green of the breast from the deep greenish-yellow belly patch. Outer primaries (concealed when wing is folded) and underwing dark grey. The long under tail coverts are brilliant yellow. Irides red. Legs and feet dull red. Bill dark greenish. (See Pl. 1).

The female is appreciably smaller than the male, the green of her plumage is tinged with yellow and her markings are less clearly defined.

DISTRIBUTION AND HABITAT: New Caledonia and the Isle of Pines. Confined to forest.

FEEDING AND GENERAL HABITS: Feeds on berries and fruits. Keeps to woodland and is very quiet when feeding.

NESTING: Usual pigeon nest in tree or shrub. It is said by Layard, to whom is owed what little has been recorded about the species in life, to lay two eggs. This is interesting in view of the fact that most other fruit pigeons lay only one egg to a clutch. Breeds from August to November.

VOICE: Layard says that the male utters 'a loud booming call'. Presumably this is its advertising coo.

DISPLAY: No information.

REFERENCES

LAYARD, E. L.   1880.   Notes on the Avifauna of New Caledonia and the Loyalty Islands.   *Ibis* **4**: Fourth Series, 336–339.
LAYARD, E. L. & E. L. C.   1882.   Avifauna of New Caledonia.   *Ibis* **6**: Fourth Series, 493–546.

THE BLUE FRUIT DOVES

The blue fruit doves or blue pigeons of the genus *Alectroenas* are found only in Madagascar and other islands in the Indian Ocean. They are striking birds, somewhat larger than a Barbary Dove and with usual heavier build characteristic of most fruit pigeons. They have a 'scooped-out' indentation on the inner web of the outermost primary which is most pronounced in *madagascariensis* and least in *pulcherrima*. They are, or rather were – for one of them, the famous Pigeon hollandais of Mauritius, is now extinct–predominantly a rich dark blue in colour marked with silver and/or purplish red. Their colour patterns, the colours of the juvenile plumage, their anatomy and what is known of their habits all indicate that they are very closely allied to the fruit doves and imperial pigeons. They appear to represent a westward extension of the *Ducula-Ptilinopus* group.

All four blue fruit doves are allopatric and very closely related to each other. They have, however reached a considerable degree of differentiation and it is better, in my opinion, to regard them as members of a superspecies rather than as races of a single species. It is interesting that although these blue fruit doves coexist with green pigeons of the genus *Treron* they have not succeeded in establishing themselves on the African continent.

The blue fruit doves show a surprising similarity to the African Speckled Pigeon, *Columba guinea*, in also having long deeply bifurcated neck feathers and an extensive area of bare red orbital skin. This must, however, be due to convergence since in no other point do they resemble each other.

MADAGASCAR BLUE PIGEON   *Alectroenas madagascariensis*

Columba madagascariensis Linnaeus, Syst. Nat., ed. 12, 1, 1766, p. 283.

DESCRIPTION: About size of a Barbary Dove but heavier built and proportionately shorter tail and bill. Throat and neck silvery grey but not so pale as in the other blue pigeons. Two outermost tail feathers blackish blue with a red patch near the tip. Other tail feathers and upper tail coverts mostly rich purplish crimson. Under tail coverts white with dark olive or reddish tips. Rest of plumage blackish blue with silvery wash on mantle and primaries. Irides greenish yellow with red outer ring. Orbital skin bright red. Bill greenish with yellow tip. Feet dull red.

The juvenile is predominantly dark bluish green and greyish green with narrow pale fringes to many of the feathers. It has, however, red on the tail and coverts similar to the adult.

DISTRIBUTION AND HABITAT: Madagascar. Inhabits evergreen forests, locally migratory.

FEEDING AND GENERAL HABITS: Arboreal. Only known to feed on fruits. Keeps to the tree tops. Usually in parties of three to twelve or more. Often perches on some dead tree projecting above the canopy or on the forest edge (Rand, 1936).

NESTING: Dates at which breeding birds and juveniles have been collected suggest a prolonged breeding season, at least from July to March.

VOICE: No information.

DISPLAY: No information.

OTHER NAMES: Red-tailed Blue Pigeon; Madagascar Blue Fruit Dove.

REFERENCE

RAND, A. L. 1936. *Bull. Amer. Mus. Nat. Hist.* Vol. LXXII, Art. 5; 143-499 (373).

COMORO BLUE PIGEON *Alectroenas sganzini*

Funingus sganzini 'O. Des Murs d'apres Verreaux' Bonaparte, Compt. Rend. Acad. Sci. Paris, 39, 1854, p. 880.

DESCRIPTION: Between Barbary Dove and Feral Pigeon size but proportionately shorter wings and tail. Outer primary recurved at tip and deeply indented on inner web. Neck feathers very long and deeply bifurcated. Head, neck and upper breast pale silvery grey. Rest of plumage blackish-blue with silvery wash on mantle and wing quills. Some specimens from Mayotte and Moheli have a purple tinge on the tail feathers and two from Mayotte have one partly red tail feather. Irides red with yellow inner ring. Orbital skin purplish-red. Bill olive green, paler at tip. Legs and feet greyish blue. Sexes nearly alike, female averages slightly duller and darker silver grey on neck and breast.

The juvenile is a general dull bronzy olive-green where the adult is blue, with narrow pale yellowish fringes to many feathers and greenish grey where the adult is silver grey. Its eyes and orbital skin are dull at first.

DISTRIBUTION AND HABITAT: The nominate form *Alectroenas s. sganzini* is found in the Comoro Islands. A slightly smaller race *A. sganzini minor* inhabits Aldabra Island. Inhabits evergreen forest.

FEEDING AND GENERAL HABITS: So far as is known entirely arboreal, feeding only on fruits and berries.   Like many pigeons it is fond of perching on a bare branch or tree top above the level of the surrounding canopy.   Mr. C. W. Benson found it, in 1959, still tame, confiding and common in spite of persecution.   As it is being shot in ever-increasing numbers it is to be feared that it will, in view of the inevitable increase of shotgun-carrying sportsmen, soon join its Mauritius relative in extinction.

NESTING: On Aldabra nests with eggs have been found in January and one with a nestling in February. Nests were of usual type, in mangroves 3 to 20 feet high.   One white egg per clutch.   Down of nestling (1), greenish grey (Benson & Penny).

VOICE: What is probably the advertising coo is described (by Benson) as a series of five coos, harsher and more rapid than those of the Madagascar Turtledove.

DISPLAY: Gaymer (1967) describes display in which the male 'hops through the canopy of a tree, cooing, bowing, and raising the plume feathers of head and neck'.   Benson (pers. comm.) saw a display flight similar to that of *A. pulcherrima* (q.v.).

OTHER NAMES: Comoro Blue Fruit Dove.

REFERENCES

BENSON, C. W.   1960.   The Birds of the Comoro Islands.   *Ibis* **103B**: 5–106.
BENSON, C. W. & PENNY, M. J.   The land birds of Aldabra.   In Press.
GAYMER, R.   1967.   Observations on the birds of Aldabra in 1964 and 1965.   *Atoll Research Bull.* **118**: 113–125.
NICHOLL, M. J.   1908.   *Three Voyages of a Naturalist*.   London.

MAURITIUS BLUE PIGEON   *Alectroenas nitidissima*

Columba nitidissima Scopoli, Del. Flor. et Faun. Insubr., fasc. 2, 1786, p. 93.

DESCRIPTION: Much like the Comoro Blue Pigeon (q.v.) but with tail and upper tail coverts red.

DISTRIBUTION AND HABITAT: Mauritius, now extinct.   Desjardins, the only eye-witness whose accounts have come down to us, said it lived near river banks.   Probably it was a bird of the forest canopy but more easily observed at watering places or openings in the forest.

FEEDING AND GENERAL HABITS: Desjardins said it ate fruits and molluscs. The latter statement has been questioned by most writers but in view of the number of pigeons (one, *Columba leucocephala*, also mainly a fruit eater) known to eat molluscs, I see no reason to doubt it.

NESTING: No information.

VOICE: No information.

DISPLAY: No information.

OTHER NAMES: Pigeon hollandais.

REFERENCE

GREENWAY, J. C. Jnr. 1958. *Extinct and Vanishing Birds of the World*. Special Publication No. 13 of the American Committee for International Wild Life Protection. New York.

SEYCHELLES BLUE PIGEON   *Alectroenas pulcherrima*

Columba pulcherrima Scopoli, Del. Flor. et Faun. Insubr., fasc. 2, 1786, p. 94.

DESCRIPTION: About the size of a Barbary Dove but much more heavily built and compact. Throat, sides of face and nape light grey shading into pale silvery-grey on neck and breast. Neck feathers attenuated and bifurcated. Forehead and crown crimson. Rest of plumage dark blackish-blue with a silvery tinge on the primaries.   Bare orbital skin extending to gape and with wart-like caruncles on the enlarged cere and at base of lower mandible.   Irides yellowish.   Orbital skin and caruncles bright red. Legs and feet grey.

The juvenile is predominantly a bronzy olive-green, paler on the parts that are grey in the adult, with yellow edgings to the feathers and brownish orbital skin.   (See Pl. 3).

DISTRIBUTION AND HABITAT: The Seychelles.   Probably at least originally a bird of evergreen forest, but Vesey-Fitzgerald (1940) found it abundant on all the larger islands from sea-level to the mountain tops and 'invariably to be found wherever a *Ficus* tree, of native or introduced species, is in fruit'.   By 1965, however, it was only found with certainty on Praslin, Mahé, and Silhouette; and only in small numbers on those islands (Gaymer, *et al.* 1969).   Shooting for sport (*sic*) and food is almost certainly the cause of this decline.

FEEDING AND GENERAL HABITS: Arboreal, feeding on fruits of *Ficus* and other trees.   In captivity Delacour (1929) found it extremely aggressive when in breeding condition.

NESTING: Usual pigeon nest in tree or shrub.   One white egg.   Recorded nesting in October and November in the wild.   A captive pair in France laid in June and again in August.   Loustau-Lalayne (1962) says 2 eggs are laid and that during incubation the male roosts near the nest.   I suspect this is based on some unusual occurrence such as two hens pairing together or, at least, laying in same nest.

VOICE: No information.

DISPLAY: Fitzgerald described a display flight in which the bird takes a 'short upward flapping flight followed by a downward glide in which the wings are depressed'.   'This performance is repeated several times as the bird describes a wide circle in the air'.   In what is, apparently, the equivalent of the bowing display the male described (Loustau-Lalanne 1962) as swaying his body slowly from side to side with throat bulging and (neck?) feathers erected.   Copulation is preceded by billing.

OTHER NAMES: Seychelles Blue Fruit Dove; Red-crowned Wart Pigeon; Red-crowned Blue Pigeon; Warty-faced Blue Pigeon.

REFERENCES

DELACOUR, J.   1929.   The Red-crowned Wart Pigeon.   *Avicult. Mag.*, Fourth Series: 7: 105–107.
GAYMER, R. *et al.* 1969.   The endemic birds of Seychelles.   *Ibis* 111: 159–160.
VESEY-FITZGERALD, D.   1940.   The Birds of the Seychelles.   *Ibis* 4: Fourteenth Series, 485.

THE LARGER FRUIT PIGEONS OR IMPERIAL PIGEONS

The large species of fruit pigeons are often termed the imperial pigeons presumably because of their impressive and majestic-looking if somewhat ponderous appearance.   They are big heavy birds ranging in size from about as large as a smallish Feral Pigeon to twice the size of a Wood Pigeon.   Most of them are clad in soft greys and pinks with iridescent green on the upperparts but some are very dull and others are strikingly marked with patterns of contrasting colours.   Most distinct are the pied imperial pigeons which are white, silver or cream coloured with black on the tail and wings.

These large fruit pigeons inhabit southern Asia, Australasia and some of the Pacific Islands.   They are fruit eaters and digest only the pulp of the fruits they eat, voiding the stones intact.   They have distensible gapes and can swallow surprisingly large fruits whole.   Some of them are known to eke out their fruit diet with young foliage.   They are arboreal but some (probably all) come to the ground to obtain mineral matter, often coming regulary to eat the earth at 'salt licks'.   They are highly edible to man and consequently suffer heavy predation by him.   They lay only one egg to a clutch.

They are very closely related to the fruit doves *Ptilinopus*, and are treated here under a separate heading mainly for reasons of convenience. They were formerly placed in several genera (see Salvadori, 1893) but I agree with Peters (1937) in thinking that most of those are best included in *Ducula* (Goodwin, 1959).

The Philippine Zone-tailed Pigeon *Ducula poliocephala*, the Green and White Zone-tailed Pigeon *D. forsteni*, the Mindoro Zone-tailed Pigeon *D. mindorensis* and the Grey-headed Zone-tailed Pigeon *Ducula radiata* are a group which form a link between the genera *Ducula* and *Ptilinopus* but on the whole are closest to other species of *Ducula* and best included in that genus. *D. poliocephala* and *D. forsteni* are closely allied and allopatric, they are treated here as members of a superspecies. *D. mindorensis* and *D. radiata* appear to be more closely related to one another than either is to any other species. They differ in size but agree closely in colour pattern, are allopatric and are most probably geographical representatives.

The Grey-necked Fruit Pigeon *Ducula carola* is a very distinct species whose nearest affinities are uncertain. It seems most likely to be a rather aberrant offshoot from some form ancestral to both it and the *poliocephala* group to whose members it bears some resemblance in colour and which have a similar distribution.

The *aenea* species-group consists of numerous apparently fairly closely-related forms of medium to large size with predominantly green and iridescent upper parts and greyish or pinkish head and neck. The Green Imperial Pigeon *Ducula aenea*, the White-eyed Imperial Pigeon *D. perspicillata* and the Blue-tailed Imperial Pigeon *D. concinna* appear to be closely allied. *D. aenea* and *D. perspicillata* are completely allopatric. The range of *D. concinna* is adjacent to that of both *aenea* and *perspicillata* but it is confined to small islands and the only evidence of overlap (with *perspicillata*) is that of a single specimen of *concinna* taken on Buru (Van Bemmel, 1948). The three forms are very probably geographic representatives and may represent a superspecies but information on behaviour and ecology will be needed before this can be taken as certain in view of the existence of other fairly similar forms. For example, *perspicillata* shows some approach to the *rosacea* species group in the colour pattern of its upper parts, the grey tinge on its wing quills and its conspicuous white orbital ring; *concinna*, on the other hand, resembles *myristicivora* quite as much as it does *aenea*, except for not having the enlarged cere of the former.

Of the forms with an enlarged cere the Pacific Pigeon *Ducula pacifica*, the Micronesian Pigeon *D. oceanica*, the Society Islands Pigeon *D. aurorae* and the Marquesas Pigeon *D. galaeata* are representatives of one superspecies; the Black-knobbed Pigeon *D. myristicivora* and the Red-knobbed Pigeon *D. rubricera* of another. The enlarged cere, although a taxonomically convenient character, is probably not a very important one phylogenetically and may have arisen independently in the two superspecies. All the large-cered forms are allopatric except for *rubricera* and *pacifica* which both occur on the Three Sisters Islands in the Solomons (Cain & Galbraith, 1956). It is likely that the enlarged red cere of *rubricera* has evolved as an isolating mechanism in reference to *pacifica* which has a similarly large but black cere or to the normal-cered *D. finschii* which overlaps widely with *rubricera* in the Solomons.

The rufous-bellied fruit pigeons *Ducula rufigaster*, *D. basilica*, *D. finschii*, and *D. chalconota* are very closely allied. Both *rufigaster* and *chalconota* occur in New Guinea where they are, so far as is known, ecologically isolated (Mayr, 1941), *rufigaster* being an inhabitant of lowland forest and *chalconota* of mountain forest. Since *chalconota* and *rufigaster* are specifically distinct and it is impossible to say, on present evidence, to which of them *basilica* and *finschii* are more closely related I treat all four as members of a superspecies. This might be questioned in regard to *chalconota* and *rufigaster* on the grounds that they are only separated altitudinally and could be regarded as at least potentially in contact. I think, however, that such treatment is justified because it emphasises their obviously close relationship both with each other and with *basilica* and *finschii*.

The fourth subgroup of the *aenea* species group is composed of the Pink-headed Imperial Pigeon *Ducula rosacea*, the Christmas Island Imperial Pigeon *D. whartoni*, the Island Imperial Pigeon, *D. pistrinaria* and the Grey Imperial Pigeon, *D. pickeringii*. These four are representatives of a single superspecies.

Chasens' (1933) arguments for considering *whartoni* to be related to *rosacea* rather than to *aenea* are quite valid. All four have rather dull plumage, markedly rounded nostrils and inhabit small islands where they seem to be isolated from other *Ducula* species except (sometimes) the very differently coloured pied imperial pigeons. It is true that *pistrinaria* also inhabits some quite large islands but this may represent a recent trend. In the eastern Solomons it appears to be confined to the coastal regions (Cain & Galbraith, 1956) as it probably is elsewhere.

Another group of related species is composed of the Chestnut-bellied Pigeon, *Ducula brenchleyi*, Baker's Pigeon, *D. bakeri*, Peale's Pigeon, *D. latrans* and the New Caledonian Pigeon, *D. goliath*, the Pinon Imperial Pigeon, *D. pinon*, the Black-collared Fruit Pigeon, *D. mullerii* and the Black Imperial Pigeon, *melanochroa*. The species *bakeri*, *brenchleyi*, *goliath* and *latrans* are geographical representatives as was pointed out by Amadon (1943). Amadon thought that the relatively dull and unspecialised plumage of these might indicate relationship to *rosacea* and its allies. I think, however, such resemblances are due to the tendency to acquire dull plumage when there is no premium on the possession of distinctive signal markings and that these forms are most closely related to *pinon*, *mullerii* and *melanochroa*.

The differences of size, bill, wing and tail proportions between *pinon* and *mullerii* probably indicate adaptation to different ecological niches. Their colours and colour patterns are rather similar, that of *mullerii* suggesting an elaboration of the *pinon* pattern with a vinous-pink instead of grey crown. The two features which make them so strikingly unlike, especially when viewed head-on, the black collar of *mullerii* and the large bare orbital patch of *pinon*, are most likely isolating mechanisms that have developed in reference to each other. *D. melanochroa* resembles *mullerii* in size and shape of bill and in lacking an extensive bare orbital patch although the pale, lace-like pattern on its wing coverts is very suggestive of that of the darker races of *pinon*. Possibly *melanochroa* is representative of an ancestral form which in New Guinea has given rise to both *mullerii* and *pinon*.

The Banded Imperial Pigeon *Ducula zoeae* is very distinct from all others but the unique features of its colour pattern are probably characters that function as isolating mechanisms and so do not imply any great phylogenetic gap between it and other *Ducula* species. It has an attenuated first primary similar to that of *mullerii* and if this indicates relationship between them then *zoeae* would be a connecting link between the *aenea* species-group and the *brenchleyi* species-group.

The Mountain Imperial Pigeon *Ducula badia* and the Dark-backed Imperial Pigeon, *D. lacernulata* are here treated as members of a superspecies. They may possibly overlap in western Java where both have been obtained but where *badia* is either a casual visitor or else inhabits only a restricted area (Chasen, 1935). The Timor Imperial Pigeon, *D. cineracea* appears to be a geographical representative of this group. It agrees very closely with them in colour pattern but lacks the pale tail band. The loss of this signal marking is probably a consequence of its having been long isolated from congenors on the mountains of Timor and Wetar.

The pied imperial pigeons *D. bicolor*, *D. luctuosa* and *D. spilorrhoa* form a very discrete group differing from all other *Ducula* species in colour and, at least from those others in which the point has been investigated, in the development and specialisation of the alimentary tract (Cadow, 1931). So far as is known they are allopatric when breeding (Siebers, 1930) although *bicolor*, a form which inhabits small islands and wanders a great deal in search of food, has sometimes been found within the ranges of *luctuosa* and *spilorrhoa*. The three forms are here treated as members of a superspecies.

Besides the differences mentioned above the flight of the pied imperial pigeons apparently differs from that of other large fruit pigeons. It has been suggested that they should be separated generically from *Ducula* but I do not think this would be advisable in our present state of knowledge. Specimens of *bicolor* that I have watched in captivity struck me as being more like *aenea* in everything but colour, than is, for example, *Streptopelia chinensis* like *S. tranquebarica*.

The Topknot Pigeon *Lopholaimus antarcticus* of eastern Australia and the New Zealand Pigeon *Hemiphaga novaeseelandiae* may be more closely related to one another than either is to any *Ducula* species in spite of their great differences of colour and bill shape. Both agree in having only twelve tail feathers

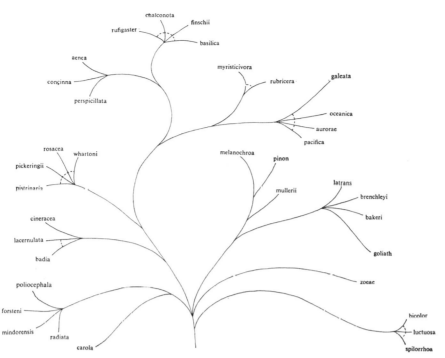

FIG. D.14: Presumed relationships of species in the genus *Ducula*.

and the top of the cere feathered. The Topknot Pigeon's peculiar double crest and bright-coloured, laterally compressed bill are such striking specific characters that I am inclined to think they may have evolved in reference to formerly existing related species which became extinct prior to the discovery of Australia by Europeans. The New Zealand Pigeon appears at first surprisingly brightly coloured when compared to similarly isolated forms of *Ducula*. This brightness is probably more apparent to a human than an avian eye as *Hemiphaga* lacks signal markings on wings or tail or any well differentiated display plumage. I think its colour pattern is most likely a relatively simplified version of that of some ancestral form that may have had some such colours and patterns as those possessed now, by, for example, *D. poliocephala*. No existing species appears to be very closely related to *Hemiphaga* and it is, I think, likely that its immediate ancestor was some form, possibly Australian, which became extinct.

The affinities of the Celebes Dusky Pigeon *Cryptophaps poecilorrhoa* are uncertain. Little has been recorded of its habits and anatomy. In appearance, so far as one can judge from skins, it does not appear to be very closely related to any other species.

REFERENCES

AMADON, D. 1943. *Amer. Mus. Novit.* **1237**: 8–13.
CADOW, G. 1933. Magen und Darm der Fruchttauben. *J. Orn.* **81**: 236–252.
CAIN, A. J. & GALBRAITH, J. 1956. Field notes on the birds of the eastern Solomon Islands. *Ibis* **98**: 100–134
CHASEN, F. N. 1933. Notes on the birds of Christmas Island, Indian Ocean. *Bull. Raffles Mus.* **8**: 58–61.
CHASEN, F. N. 1935. A handlist of Malaysian birds. *Bull. Raffles Mus.* **11**: 19.
HACHISUKA, M. 1931. *The Birds of the Philippine Islands*, **1**: 194. London.
HARTERT, E. 1925. A collection of birds from New Ireland. *Novit. Zool.* **32**: 115–136.
LAYARD, E. L. & E. L. C. 1882. Notes on the avifauna of New Caledonia. *Ibis* (4) **6**: 527–528
MAYR, E. 1941. *List of New Guinea Birds*. New York.
PETERS, J. L. 1937. *Check-list of Birds of the World.* **3**: 42–56. Harvard.
SALVADORI, T. 1893. *Cat. Birds Brit. Mus.* **21**: 171–239. London.
SIEBERS, H. C. 1930. Fauna Buruana. *Treubia* **7** (Suppl. 5): 181–187.
VAN BEMMEL, A. C. 1948. A faunal list of the birds of the Moluccan Islands. *Treubia* **19**: 323–402.

PHILIPPINE ZONE-TAILED PIGEON   *Ducula poliocephala*

Carpophaga poliocephala G. R. Gray, Gen. Birds, 2, 1844, p. 469, pl. 119.

DESCRIPTION: Slightly larger than a Wood Pigeon. Chin and throat chestnut with a narrow white border between the chestnut area and the green of the breast. Face and forehead greyish white shading to purplish-grey on crown and purple on nape. Belly very pale vinous pink or salmon pink. Flanks and under tail coverts chestnut. Rest of plumage rich emerald green, bronze-green or golden-green often in some lights shot with coppery red. The hind neck, sides of neck and upper mantle appear more or less reddish purple in most lights. A very conspicuous greyish-white band across centre of tail Underwing dark green and blackish. Underside of tail blackish with greyish white band. Irides yellow with red outer ring. Orbital skin crimson. Legs and feet red. Bill greyish black.

Female as male but with greenish tinge on crown, less well defined chestnut patch on throat and sometimes rufous fringes to pink belly feathers. Juvenile as female but less brilliant and pronounced rufous fringes to belly feathers.

DISTRIBUTION AND HABITAT: The Philippine Islands: Luzon, Mindoro, Sibuyan, Masbate, Samar, Leyte, Cebu, Negros, Panay, Dinagat, Mindanao, Basilan and Tawi Tawi. Usually in high trees but sometimes comes into lower trees and shrubs.

FEEDING AND GENERAL HABITS: No information.

NESTING: No information.

VOICE: A loud, deep booming note, suggestive of the hooting of a large owl is the only call that appears to be recorded.

DISPLAY: No information.

OTHER NAMES: Pink-bellied Imperial Pigeon.

REFERENCES

DELACOUR, J. & MAYR, E. 1946. *Birds of the Philippines*. New York.
HACHISUKA, M. 1932. *The Birds of the Philippine Islands* 1: 199–200. London

GREEN & WHITE ZONE-TAILED PIGEON   *Ducula forsteni*

Hemiphaga forsteni 'Temminck', Bonaparte, Compt. Rend. Acad. Sci. Paris, 39, 1854, p. 1077.

DESCRIPTION: A little larger than a Wood Pigeon.   Head pale grey shading to white on forehead and throat.   Lower breast and belly white tinged with cream or pinkish.   Under tail coverts chestnut.   A broad pale grey band narrowly edged with blackish across centre of tail.   Parts of wings and tail not visible when folded, blackish green.   Rest of plumage rich emerald green, golden green or bronze green. In most lights centre of mantle looks purplish and there is a strong coppery tinge on hind neck.   Irides orange or yellow with darker orange or red outer ring.   Bill black.   Legs and feet purplish.

Female has grey parts of plumage slightly darker.   I have not seen a juvenile.

DISTRIBUTION AND HABITAT: Celebes.   Inhabits mountainous areas at between 300 and 1,500 metres elevation.   Prefers dense primeval forest but also found in quite small patches of hill forest.

FEEDING AND GENERAL HABITS: Little appears to be recorded.   Said to coo mostly before dawn and after mid-day (Heinrich, in Stresemann, 1941).

NESTING: No information.

VOICE: A deep monosyllabic cooing, very deep and loud and suggestive of the booming of a Bittern (*Botaurus stellaris*) is the only call recorded.

DISPLAY: No information.

OTHER NAMES: Large Celebes Zone-tailed Pigeon; Celebes Zone-tailed Imperial Pigeon.

REFERENCE
STRESEMANN, E.   1941.   Die Vögel von Celebes.   *Journ. f. Orn.*: **89**: 1–102.

MINDORO ZONE-TAILED PIGEON   *Ducula mindorensis*

Carpophaga mindorensis Whitehead, Ann. and Mag. Nat. Hist. (6), 18, 1896, p. 189.

DESCRIPTION: About a quarter larger than a Wood Pigeon and longer tailed and shorter winged in proportion.   Very similar in colour pattern to the Grey-headed Zone-tailed Pigeon and probably most closely related to it although in the degree of 'scooping' of the inner webs of its outer primaries it resembles the two equally large zone-tailed species, *D. poliocephala* and *D. forsteni*.   Area around base of bill, throat and face (below eye) pale salmon pink.   Forehead pale silver grey, sometimes tinged pink.

Head, neck, breast and underparts light bluish grey tinged with rufous on ventral areas and under tail coverts.   A dark greyish-black ring around the orbit culminates in a short post-ocular stripe.   Hind neck dark grey shading to blackish purple on upper part of mantle.   Upperparts iridescent, mantle and inner wing coverts predominantly purple and bronzy-red.   Back, wings, and upper tail coverts predominantly emerald green.   Primaries and tail greenish black, tail crossed with a dark grey central band. Underwing blackish grey.   Underside of tail blackish with pale grey central band.   Irides bright yellow with red outer ring.   Orbital skin dark red.   Bill black.   Legs and feet reddish pink.   The female, of which I have not seen a specimen, is said to differ in having a yellow and brown iris and orange-yellow orbital skin.   I have not seen a juvenile nor been able to find a description of one.

DISTRIBUTION AND HABITAT: The Island of Mindoro in the Philippines.   So far as is known only found in the highlands of Mindoro.   In woodland, but apparently nowhere numerous.

FEEDING AND GENERAL HABITS: Has been recorded feeding on 'large purple fruits as big as a pigeon's egg'.

NESTING: No information.

VOICE: What is, probably, the advertising coo has been described as 'a penetrating booming note'.

DISPLAY: No information.

OTHER NAMES: Great Mindoro Fruit Pigeon; Pink-throated Imperial Pigeon.

REFERENCE

DELACOUR, J. & MAYR, E.   1946.   *Birds of the Philippines*.   New York.

GREY-HEADED ZONE-TAILED PIGEON   *Ducula radiata*

Columba radiata Quoy and Gaimard, Voy. 'Astrolabe' Zool., 1, 1830, p. 244.

DESCRIPTION: About the size of a smallish Feral Pigeon but with proportionately rather shorter wings and longer tail and, of course, the usual shorter legs as with all fruit pigeons. Head, sides of neck, breast, and underparts pale grey becoming mixed with dull chestnut on flanks and belly. Under tail coverts chestnut. A blackish purple area on hind neck. Mantle, back, wings and tail richly iridescent. This iridescence usually appears predominantly reddish purple on the mantle, scapulars and inner secondaries, and bronze green shot or intermixed with coppery red elsewhere. In some lights, however, the upperparts appear emerald green with no trace of red. The tail is crossed centrally by a grey band with narrow blackish edges. Underwing dark greyish, under side of tail feathers blackish with grey central band. Irides orange or orange with red outer ring. Bill black with dark grey cere. Legs and feet purple or purplish red.

The female has the grey areas slightly darker and except on the upper parts of the mantle, shows, in most lights, little or no purple or red sheen. Her back and wings usually appear emerald green intermixed with bluish green and bronzy green. I have not seen a juvenile of the species.

DISTRIBUTION AND HABITAT: Celebes, inhabits mountain forest and is said to be nowhere common. Only rarely seen at low altitudes.

FEEDING AND GENERAL HABITS: No information.

NESTING: Sometimes, perhaps usually, nests in hollows and on sheltered ledges in rock faces and rocky outcrops in mountain forest One egg. Nests with eggs were found in December, but probably has a prolonged breeding season like most pigeons.

VOICE: A monosyllabic rather quiet 'coo' is the only call that appears to have been recorded.

DISPLAY: No information.

OTHER NAMES: Celebes Zone-tailed Imperial Pigeon; Celebes Band-tailed Fruit Pigeon; Grey-banded Imperial Pigeon.

REFERENCE

STRESEMANN, E. 1941. Die Vögel von Celebes. *Journ. f. Orn.* **89**: 1–102.

GREY-NECKED FRUIT PIGEON   *Ducula carola*

Ptilocolpa carola Bonaparte, Compt. Rend. Acad. Sci. Paris. 39, 1854, p. 1075.

DESCRIPTION: About size of Feral Pigeon. Outermost primary attenuated and with a scooped indentation on inner web. Inner primaries obliquely cut at tips and sinuous in outline with outer web extending beyond the shaft. Head, neck and breast silver grey to light bluish grey with a crescent-shaped white band across the breast. Mantle, back and wing coverts silver grey or mauvish grey spotted and smudged with black. Outer greater coverts, secondaries and rump greyish mauve intermixed with iridescent green. Primaries, secondaries and tail greenish black; longer upper tail coverts iridescent green, others as rump. Underparts below breast dark chestnut, divided from the grey breast by a narrow black band. Flanks and underwing greyish. Irides white, mottled with pink or with white inner ring and pink outer ring. Eye rims whitish; orbital skin bluish grey. Bill pink or pinkish red, white at extreme tip. Legs and feet pink or pinkish red. (These soft part colours are based on only a few specimens and on the published works of Macgregor and Hachisuka.)

The female differs markedly from the male. Her head and neck are a darker less silvery grey and she lacks the white crescent on the breast. Her underparts, except for the chestnut under tail coverts, are greyish mauve tinged with rufous. Her upperparts are purplish and iridescent green, more or less intermixed and brightest on the rump. The only juvenile specimen I have seen, probably a male although it was not sexed by the collector, is much like the adult female but greener on back and wings and more rufous on the underparts.

The above description is of nominate *D. c. carola* from Luzon and Mindoro. The form from Mindanao, *D. carola mindanensis*, has the breast below the white band greyish black; that from Negros, *D. carola nigrorum*, is similar to *mindanensis* but darker.

DISTRIBUTION AND HABITAT: The Philippine Islands of Luzon, Mindoro, Negros and Mindanao. Inhabits forest, in Mindoro (and elsewhere?) from sea level to over 6,500 feet in mountains.

FEEDING AND GENERAL HABITS: Known to take fruits from the branches. Often gather in large numbers at fruiting trees. Also said to eat seeds and nuts (McGregor, 1909) but this probably means that, as with other *Ducula* species, these are swallowed together with their surrounding fruit and later passed through undigested. Said to fly in flocks at regular times over the mountains (Delacour and Mayr, 1946).

NESTING: Ripley and Rabor (1958) record a nest in a small hollow in the side of a perpendicular cliff about 12 feet high. It was usual type of twig nest with one white egg. It was found at 5,500 feet.

VOICE: No information.

DISPLAY: No information.

OTHER NAMES: Grey-breasted Fruit Pigeon; Spotted Imperial Pigeon.

REFERENCES

DELACOUR, J. & MAYR, E. 1946. *Birds of the Philippines*. New York.
HACHISUKA, M. 1932. *The Birds of the Philippine Islands*. Vol. 1. London.
McGREGOR, R. C. 1909. *A Manual of Philippine Birds*. Pt. 1. Manila.
RIPLEY, S. D. & RABOR, D. S. 1958. Notes on a collection of Birds from Mindoro Island, Philippines. *Peabody Museum of Yale University, Bull.* 13.

GREEN IMPERIAL PIGEON   *Ducula aenea*

Columba aenea Linnaeus, Syst. Nat. ed. 12, 1, 1766, p. 283.

DESCRIPTION: Rather larger than a Wood Pigeon and more heavily built with larger, longer head. Head, neck, upper mantle, breast and belly a delicate pale greyish-pink, except for some white or cream feathers at base of bill and around eye. Upperparts iridescent green, bluish green, or bronze green. Worn feathers often more bronze-red than green so moulting birds may appear mottled green and copper. Visible parts of wing and tail quills mainly powdery grey with only slight green, or blackish green iridescence. Under tail coverts dark chestnut. Sexes alike or nearly so but females tending to be, on average, a little less bright than males. Irides and (narrow) orbital skin red. Bill bluish grey, purplish at base. Feet carmine red. Juvenile only slightly duller than adult and with the pink tinge of head and underparts less pronounced.

The above description applies to the nominate form, *Ducula a. aenea*, of most of the Philippines; the forms from India and the Indo-Malayan regions are very similar. The most strongly differentiated races of this species are *D. aenea nuchalis* of north-eastern Luzon which has a purplish maroon patch on the nape; *D. aenea paulina* from Celebes and the Talaut Islands which has a large rust-red patch on the nape, very richly green upperparts and dark greenish blue wing and tail quills; *D. aenea nicobarica* from the Nicobar Islands which has very dark, almost blackish upperparts and the head, neck and underparts grey without any pink tinge; and *D. aenea aenothorax* from Engano Island, off the western coast of Sumatra, which is very brightly iridescent above, has a grey head and neck with pinkish breast and greenish, instead of chestnut, under tail coverts.

DISTRIBUTION AND HABITAT: India and Ceylon, east and south-east through the Indo-Malayan regions to Indo-China, the Philippines, Celebes and Sula Islands. Inhabits forest, especially evergreen forest at low elevation, but also mangrove swamps and open country with small woods or groups of trees.

FEEDING AND GENERAL HABITS: Feeds on fruits and berries plucked from the branches. Many different kinds of fruit have been recorded, including wild nutmegs and other large species. Has been seen eating the saline earth at 'salt licks' on the ground. Usually in pairs or small parties, but large numbers may gather at a food source such as a fruiting wild fig tree. Flight often appears leisurely with slow flaps of widespread (and hence more rounded) wings, but when alarmed or when returning to roost uses a quicker wing-beat with less widely spread (hence more 'pointed') wing. Keeps to the same flight lines to and from roosting places in spite of constant persecution by sportsmen.

NESTING: Usual pigeon nest in tree or shrub. Very often (as with other woodland birds) the tree selected is one at the forest edge or adjacent to a small clearing, stream or other break in the canopy. In India (and probably elsewhere) nests more often in young than in mature trees and at no great height. One white egg.

VOICE: From captive birds of the Indian form I have heard a deep, loud single ōōm uttered with head lowered; a grunting 'grŏŏ', a half-grunting, half cooing 'grŏŏ-grōō' uttered with head erect and lower half of neck (crop area) swelling markedly as the bird called. From a captive bird – race uncertain – I heard what was probably a more intense version of the last, 'wŏŏf-wŏŏf-wŏŏf,-wōōrh-wōōrh', starting very gruffly but ending in a 'coo'. Most written descriptions I have seen of the Indian form's calls suggest that they are alternative renderings of those described here but Ali (1949) describes the series of cooing notes as ending in a 'peculiar prolonged rolling'. Hachisuka (1932) describes calls of *D. a. palawanensis* as a 'deep "ah-hoo-oo" and (a) guttural "kr'r-r-r-r, kr'-r-r-r-r, kr'-r-r-r-r" '. One call of the very distinct Celebes form is described (Stresemann, 1941) as a loud, energetic 'kurrekurrekurre'.

DISPLAY: When giving the 'oom' call the head is lowered deeply, the bill lying against the breast at the lowest point of the movement. Probably the species' bowing display consists mainly – or entirely – of this movement as is suggested by Banks, who says that captive birds (kept as decoys by Bornean natives) would occasionally 'perform, cooing deeply moving the head up and down like a domestic pigeon'.

Banks describes a spectacular display flight in which the bird, from normal flight, gives two or three strong wing-beats, shoots vertically up for one or two yards, hangs poised a moment with upstretched neck, and tail vertically downwards, then flattens out and rushes downwards to resume normal flight.

OTHER NAMES: Chestnut-naped Imperial Pigeon (the Celebes form).

REFERENCES

BAKER, E. C. S. 1913. *Indian Pigeons and Doves*. London.
BANKS, E. 1935. Notes on the Birds of Sarawak with a List of Native Names. *Sarawak Museum Journal* 4 (Pt. 3), No. **14**: 280–281.
HACHISUKA, M. 1932. *The Birds of the Philippine Islands*, 2. London.
STRESEMANN, E. 1941. Die Vögel von Celebes. *Journ. f. Orn.* **89**: 56–57.

WHITE-EYED IMPERIAL PIGEON   *Ducula perspicillata*

Columba perspicillata Temminck, pl. col. livr., 42, 1824, pl. 246

DESCRIPTION: Very similar in size and general appearance to the Blue-tailed Imperial Pigeon, with which and the Green Imperial Pigeon, it forms a superspecies. Head dark bluish grey with conspicuous white ring round eye and white band round base of bill. Dark grey of head shades on underparts to pale grey on breast and very pale pinkish grey on belly and above through dark grey more or less suffused with green and bronze on nape to iridescent green, blue-green or bronze green on hind neck, mantle, back and wing coverts. Outer secondaries and primaries dark greenish blue or blue, with some silvery grey bloom. Tail dark greenish blue, blue or purplish blue, when old and worn tail feathers are mainly or entirely dull black. Under tail coverts pale greyish rufous or pinkish grey. Irides dark brown. Bill greyish blue or purplish blue, with purplish red or purple base. Legs and feet red or purple. The sexes are alike and the juvenile only slightly less brilliant.

The above description is of the nominate form *D. p. perspicillata* from the Moluccas. *D. p. neglecta* from Ceram, Amboina, Saparua and Buano is paler in colour. Its head is light grey, the iridescent upperparts usually of a more golden green and the silver-grey bloom on its wing quills is more prominent.

DISTRIBUTION AND HABITAT: The Moluccan Islands of Morotai, Halmahera, Weda, Batjan, Obi and Buru and the islands of Ceram, Amboina, Saparua and Buano. Inhabits forest.

FEEDING AND GENERAL HABITS: Recorded feeding on fruits, some as large as plums, taken from the branches (Stresemann, 1914). Heinroth (1903) found that captive individuals eagerly took and swallowed hard boiled egg yolks dipped in cream and throve better after being given these as well as fruit.

NESTING: No information.

VOICE: Heinroth recalls a deep single note, rather like the distress call of the Domestic Pigeon which was given by a captive bird eager to be fed.

DISPLAY: No information.

OTHER NAMES: Spectacled Imperial Pigeon.

REFERENCES

HEINROTH, O. 1903. Ornithologische Ergebnisse der '1 Deutschen Sudsee Exped. von Br. Mencke'. *Journ. f. Orn.* **5**: 65–125.
STRESEMANN, E. 1914. Die Vögel von Seran (Ceram). *Nov. Zool.* **21**: 25–153 (47–48).

BLUE-TAILED IMPERIAL PIGEON   *Ducula concinna*

Carpophaga concinna Wallace, Ibis, 1865, 1, new series, p. 383.

DESCRIPTION: Slightly larger than the Green Imperial Pigeon (q.v.), with wings and tail proportionately a little longer than that species, and a similar colour-pattern.   White feathers at base of bill forming a narrow but, in life conspicuous, white ring dividing the blackish bill from the grey of the face.   Forehead, face, including a band over eye, neck and breast very pale silvery grey.   Crown and nape a very pale delicate salmon-pink or mauve-pink.   Hind neck, upper mantle and rest of underparts pale silvery grey tinged with pink to a greater or lesser (usually lesser) degree.   Under tail coverts chestnut.   Upperparts a beautiful shining green, sometimes shot with golden bronze or intermixed with blue, shading to dark purplish blue on visible parts of wing and tail quills.   Underwing coverts blackish green with faint iridescence.   Irides golden or yellow, red recorded for one specimen.   Bill blue-grey, grey or blackish with lighter tip.   Legs and feet red.   Female with the grey and pink parts slightly less clear and pale, otherwise sexes alike.   Juvenile almost as bright as adults.

DISTRIBUTION AND HABITAT: Talaut Islands; smaller islands north and south of Celebes; Sangir, Siao, Tejore, Djampea and Kalao tua; islands of Teun and Nila near Babar; small islands between Ceram and the Kei Islands.   Goram, Manawoka, Watubela; Banda Island; the Aru Islands.

Apparently found only on small islands throughout its range.

FEEDING AND GENERAL HABITS: Meise (1930) found it usually in large flocks on Kalao tua, where it was abundant.

NESTING: No information.

VOICE: A captive bird in the New York Zoo uttered a loud guttural, almost barking, 'Ur-aow', opening its bill widely as it did so.   Once it uttered a series of such calls in succession.   The call appeared to be homologous to the 'grŏŏ-grōō of *aenea* and was given in a similar posture, but was much louder and harsher.

DISPLAY: 'Behind the wing' displacement-preening was seen from the captive mentioned above. Display coo 'hoo-hoo-hoo' becoming faster and faster (Newman, in Goodchild).   Bowing display in which bird lowers head and bows repeatedly and jumps up and down on perch, both feet leaving perch at once (Newman, in Goodchild 1905).

OTHER NAMES: Gold-eyed Imperial Pigeon; Yellow-eyed Imperial Pigeon.

REFERENCES

MEISE, W.   1930.   Die Vôgel von Djampea.   *Journ. f. Orn.* **78**: 180–214.
GOODCHILD, H.   1905.   The Blue-tailed Fruit Pigeon.   *Bird Notes* **4**: 107–109.

PACIFIC PIGEON

Ducula pacifica

Columba pacifica Gmelin, Syst. Nat., 1, pt. 2, 1789, p. 777.

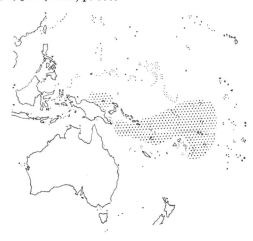

DESCRIPTION: Slightly larger than the average Feral Pigeon, with rather longer, square-ended tail. Narrow white band round base of bill. Head, nape and hind neck light grey or pinkish grey. Underparts greyish pink shading to deep dull rufous pink on ventral regions, grey on flanks and tibial feathers. Under tail coverts chestnut. Upperparts dark iridescent green, more or less intermixed with purple bronze or blue. Underwing dark slate. Irides red. Bill and enlarged cere black. Feet and legs red. Sexes are alike but female tends to be slightly duller and in life probably has smaller cere than males in same condition. Juvenile as adult but slightly duller and less pinkish on breast.

DISTRIBUTION AND HABITAT: Widespread on islands in the Pacific. Islands off the northern coast of New Guinea, Louisiade Archipelago, Gower Island, Rennell Island, Stewart Island, Santa Cruz group, New Hebrides, Ellui, Phoenix and Tonga Islands, Fiji and Samoan islands. Usually inhabits only small islands and atolls.

FEEDING AND GENERAL HABITS: Feeds on fruits and berries taken from the branches. The fruits of *Cananga odorata*, *Dysoxylon* sp., *Rhus taitense*, *Faradaya powelli* and *Myristica* sp. appear to be important foods. Often in large flocks which migrate or wander from island to island.

NESTING: No information.

VOICE: A loud barking call a 'deep cooing "Prr-rr-oo" ' followed by deep 'Oooo', have been described. Probably these represent at least two different calls.

DISPLAY: No information.

REFERENCES

WHITMEE, S. J. 1875. List of Samoan Birds with Notes on their Habits. *This* 5: Third Series, 436–447.
YALDWIN, J. C. 1952. Notes on the Present Status of Samoan Birds. *Notornis* 5: 28–30.

MICRONESIAN PIGEON

Ducula oceanica

Columba oceanica Lesson and Garnot, Dict. Sci. Nat., ed. Levrault, 40, 1826, p. 316.

DESCRIPTION: Very similar to the previous species *D. pacifica* (q.v.) but slightly smaller, with more rounded wings and chestnut of under tail coverts extending onto the belly. Several races have been recognised (see Amadon, 1943) which differ chiefly in colour of crown and hind neck which is pale grey in *D. o. monacha* from Palau (Pelew) and Yap and *D. m. teraokai* from Truk and dusky grey in *D. o.*

oceanica from Kusaie, Carolines, Jaluit, Elmore, Marshall and (probably) Gilbert Islands and *D. o. ratakensis* of Arno and Wotje.

DISTRIBUTION AND HABITAT: Caroline, Pelew (Palau) and Marshall Islands; Yap, Babelthuap, Koror, Angaur, Current, Ruk (Truk), Ponape, Kusaie, Jaluit, Elmore, Wotje and Arno islands. Inhabits woodland, particularly along the crests of wooded ridges.

FEEDING AND GENERAL HABITS: Feeds on fruits and berries taken from the branches, freely swallowing fruits with stones 23 mm. in diameter. Usually feeds on the periphery of the tree, often hangs upside down when feeding. Marshall (1949), from whose paper the notes on behaviour and ecology given here are taken, found that immature birds were much less afraid of humans than were the adults.

NESTING: No information.

VOICE: What is probably the advertising coo is described by Marshall as 'resembling the barking of sea-lions, . . . a rasping, deep-throated Arrooo, arrooo, aroo, aroo, aroo, consisting of three to seven notes each lower in pitch, shorter and of less intensity than the preceding. At close range a super-imposed tone of rising inflection can be heard accompanying each bark'; he also describes 'another song heard less frequently' (alternative advertising coo? nest call? display coo?) as 'a series of mellow hoots all on the same pitch and in tempo identical with the barking song'.

DISPLAY: No information.

REFERENCES

AMADON, D. 1943. Birds collected during the Whitney South Sea Expedition 52. *Amer. Mus. Novit.* **1237**: 11–12.
MARSHALL, Jnr. T. J. 1949. The Endemic Avifauna of Saipan, Tinian, Guam and Palau. *Condor* **51**: 200–221.

SOCIETY ISLANDS PIGEON   *Ducula aurorae*

Carpophaga aurorae Peale, U.S. Expl. Exped. 8, 1848, p. 201.

DESCRIPTION: Rather larger than the average Feral Pigeon, with enlarged cere and with a longer tail which is square ended and may show slight suggestion of a fork. Narrow creamy white band around base of bill. Head, neck, upperparts of mantle and underparts pale silvery grey shading into dull grey on the belly and greyish green, sometimes tinged with rufous, on the under tail coverts. Upperparts dark iridescent green usually intermixed with blue or purplish blue. Primaries nearly black with only slight green or blue green. Underwing dull black. Irides red. Bill and cere black. Legs and feet bright red. Sexes are alike but female averages smaller in size. Juvenile: I have seen only one specimen partially in this plumage. From this it appears to be of a general dark greyish brown with ill-defined dull fawn tips and bands. From this juvenile plumage the bird moults into an intermediate plumage which differs from that of the adult in having the head and neck dark greyish green and the underparts dark grey.

DISTRIBUTION AND HABITAT: The islands of Makatea (Aurora Island) and Tahiti in the Society group. Probably now extinct in Tahiti where it was rare and much persecuted by man as early as 1904. At that time it was, in Tahiti, confined to wooded regions in the interior of the island.

FEEDING AND GENERAL HABITS: Recorded feeding on the seeds of a vine, *Freycinetia arborea*, seeds of wild figs and wild plantains. Most probably it is the fruits of all these plants that are taken, their pulp digested and their seeds passing undigested through the bird as with other *Ducula* species.

NESTING: No information.

VOICE: No information.

DISPLAY: No information.

OTHER NAMES: Tahitian Pigeon.

REFERENCES

GREENWAY, J. C. 1958. *Extinct and Vanishing Birds of the World*. New York.
WILSON, S. B. 1907. Notes on Birds of Tahiti and the Society Group. *Ibis* **3**: Ninth Series, 373–379.

MARQUESAS PIGEON   *Ducula galeata*

Serresius galeatus Bonaparte, Compt. Rend. Acad. Sci. Paris, 41, 1855, p. 1110.

DESCRIPTION: About twice the size of a Feral Pigeon, with large, long head and long tail. Feathers at base of bill above the cere, which in this species forms a deep U-shaped structure surrounding these short feathers, creamy white shading to light grey on forehead and darker grey on crown and hind neck. Feathers on hind neck loose, long and rather hairy (although soft) in texture. Underparts light medium grey, darker grey on ventral regions. Under tail coverts chestnut. Mantle, back, rump and wing coverts dark green shot with purple and blue. Wing and tail quills greenish black.

Irides white or cream-coloured. Bill and cere blackish. Legs and feet dark red. Female very slightly smaller and duller than male. Juvenile much duller greenish above. Feathers of neck and underparts brownish grey tinged with rufous and of a very loose 'woolly' texture. This plumage is soon moulted and the sub-adult dress assumed. In this second plumage the grey areas are darker and duller than in the adult.

DISTRIBUTION: The Island of Nukuhiva, in the Marquesas Islands.

FEEDING AND GENERAL HABITS: No information.

NESTING: No information.

VOICE No information.

DISPLAY: No information.

RED-KNOBBED PIGEON
Ducula rubricera

Globicera rubricera Bonaparte, ex G. R. Gray MS, Compt. Rend. Acad. Sci. Paris, 39, 1854, p. 1073.

DESCRIPTION: Slightly larger and more heavily built than a Wood Pigeon and with enlarged cere. Narrow creamy white band around base of bill and around eye. Head, nape and upper breast a beautiful pale vinous pink or creamy salmon-pink shading through darker vinous pink on the lower breast to chestnut on belly, flanks and under tail coverts: hind neck pale silver grey. Mantle, rump and wing coverts a brilliant iridescent emerald green, bronze green or golden green; in some individuals (usually males) these parts appear largely coppery red in some lights. Secondaries and tail feathers dark glossy green and blackish blue. Primaries blackish blue, tinged green. Underwing dull grey. Irides dark red, red or orange. Orbital skin greyish. Bill dark grey or grey and black. Cere cherry red. Feet and legs purplish red or red.   Sexes are alike but females seldom have pronounced bronze-red gloss on mantle.   Juvenile as adult.

The above description is of the nominate form *D. r. rubricera* from the Bismarck Archipelago.   The form found in the Solomons, *D. rubricera rufigula,* has the pink on the head confined to the cheeks and throat, its crown, neck and breast are pale grey.   Its lower breast is darker pink and its underparts a darker chestnut.

DISTRIBUTION AND HABITAT :   The Lihir Islands of the Bismarck Archipelago and the Solomon Islands. Found in both lowland and hill forest, locally also in open or broken country with trees.

FEEDING AND GENERAL HABITS :   Feeds on fruits and berries taken from the branches.   In the Solomons, Cain and Galbraith (1956) found it usually single (? breeding birds whose mates were incubating or brooding) or in pairs. Sometimes gathers in large numbers in fruiting trees.

NESTING :   In the central Solomons Sibley (1951) found large numbers nesting in low shrubs on a small islet on the north side of Simbo Island.   One of the nests contained a well grown nestling on February 9th.

VOICE :   Cain & Galbraith (1956) describe a loud barking 'ku-wau . . . ku-wau' and a variety of deep throaty coos.   Also a loud 'cherroor' uttered with bill closed and throat inflating.   Meyer (1934) states that 'kuakuakua' is the 'full call' of the male which is uttered as he 'nods and shakes'.

DISPLAY :   No information.

OTHER NAMES :   Red-knobbed Imperial Pigeon.

REFERENCES

CAIN, A. J. & GALBRAITH, I. C. J.   1956.   Field Notes on Birds of the eastern Solomon Islands.   *Ibis* **98** :   100–134.
MEYER, O.   1934.   Die Vogelwelt der Inselgruppe Lihir.   *Journ. f. Orn.* **82** :   294–308.
SIBLEY, C. G.   1951.   Notes on the Birds of New Georgia, central Solomon Islands.   *Condor* **53** :   81–92.

BLACK-KNOBBED PIGEON   *Ducula myristicivora*

Columba myristicivora Scopoli, 1786, Del. Flor. et Faun. Insubr., Fasc. 2, p. 94.

DESCRIPTION :   In size and general appearance very similar to the Red-knobbed Pigeon with which it forms a superspecies but differs in its black cere and minor details of plumage colour.   Head, neck and breast a pale silvery grey sometimes tinged with pink, except for a creamy white band at base of bill (behind cere) and the hind crown and nape which are pale mauve pink or silvery pink. Lower breast and belly pale mauve pink or greyish pink, not sharply demarcated from silver grey of upper breast, darkening to a more dusky pinkish grey on flanks and tibial feathers. Under tail coverts chestnut. Mantle, back, rump and wing coverts a brilliant iridescent emerald green, blue-green or bronze-green. Secondaries and tail feathers dark glossy green and blackish blue. Primaries blackish blue tinged green. Underwing dull grey. Irides brown. Bill and cere black. Legs and feet deep red. These soft part colours are based on only two adult females so are not comprehensive. Sexes alike. I have not seen a juvenile, it almost certainly resembles the adult, but at first lacks the enlarged cere, as with *D. rubricera*.

The above description is of nominate *D. m. myristicivora* from most of the species' range. *D. myristicivora geelvinkiana* from the islands in Geelvink Bay has the pink and grey parts of the plumage slightly darker and has no pink on its crown and nape which are the same grey as the rest of the head.

DISTRIBUTION AND HABITAT: The Western Papuan Islands (Gebe, Gagi, Gemien, Waigeu, Batanta, Sorong, Salawati, Schildpad and Misol), the small islands off the coast of Halmahera and the islands in Geelvink Bay. Inhabits wooded areas.

FEEDING AND GENERAL HABITS: No information.

NESTING: No information.

VOICE: No information.

DISPLAY: No information.

OTHER NAMES: Nutmeg-eating Fruit Pigeon; Black-knobbed Imperial Pigeon.

RUFOUS-BELLIED FRUIT PIGEON   *Ducula rufigaster*

Columba rufigaster Quoy and Gaimard, Voy. 'Astrolabe', Zool., 1, 1830, p. 245.

DESCRIPTION: About the size of a largish Feral Pigeon but much plumper in shape with proportionately shorter wings and tail. Head, face and throat mauve-pink shading into a rich golden-rufous on breast and flanks which pales into buffish on the ventral region and under tail coverts. Hind neck and upper part of mantle bluish grey. Upper parts richly iridescent. In most lights rich red purple on mantle, back and rump shading through green and purple on the inner wing coverts and secondaries to golden-green or emerald green on outer part of the (closed) wing. Primaries blackish green. Lower part of rump and upper tail coverts dark bluish purple. In some lights, especially if bird is between observer and the source of light, the upperparts may appear emerald green except on the upper tail coverts which then appear bronzy-red. The tail, which is half covered by the upper tail coverts when closed, dark purplish with a broad grey terminal band. Underside of tail drab grey and pale grey. Under wing coverts and axillaries chestnut.   Underside of primaries grey.   Irides red or dark red.   Orbital skin dark red.   Bill black or dark brown.   Feet and legs purplish red.   Female averages a little darker pink on the head and often shows more green and less red iridescence on upperparts.   Juvenile like adult in colour but less brilliant.

The above description is of the nominate form, *D. r. rufigaster*, of western and southern New Guinea. The form from northern New Guinea, *D. r. uropygialis*, has the pink, grey and rufous areas slightly darker in shade.   Southern New Guinea birds from the Noord River, which are rather pale in colour, have been racially separated as *D. r. pallida*.

DISTRIBUTION AND HABITAT: New Guinea and the adjacent Western Papuan islands and Jobi (Japen) Island.   Found in lowland forest and some savannah edge near forest.

FEEDING AND GENERAL HABITS: Known to take fruits from the branches.

NESTING: No information.

VOICE: A 'deep melodious coo' has been recorded (Grant, in Ogilvie-Grant, 1915).

DISPLAY: No information.

OTHER NAMES: Rufous-breasted Imperial Pigeon; Red-breasted Fruit Pigeon.

REFERENCE

OGILVIE-GRANT, W. R.   1915.   Report on the Birds collected by the British Ornithologists' Union Expedition and the Wollaston Expedition in Dutch New Guinea.   *Ibis*, Jubilee Supplement, No. 2.

MOLUCCAN RUFOUS-BELLIED FRUIT PIGEON   *Ducula basilica*

Ducula basilica Bonaparte, Compt. Rend. Acad. Sci. Paris, 39, 1834.

DESCRIPTION: Very similar to the previous species, to which it is very closely related.   Head, sides of neck and breast a beautiful pale, delicate pink or creamy-pink.   Rest of underparts light golden-rufous.   Hind neck pale bluish-grey.   Mantle, back, rump, upper tail coverts, wing coverts and second-aries predominantly emerald green, golden-green or blue-green with only a little bronzy-red on upper mantle and rump in some lights.   Primaries blackish blue.   Tail blackish blue with broad grey terminal band.   Some tail feathers show narrow dark iridescent tips.   Differences of age and sex as in *D. rufigaster*. The above description is of the northern Moluccan form, *D. b. basilica*.   The form found in Obi, *D. b. obiensis*, in the central Moluccas is darker and has golden-rufous on the nape and sides of neck.

DISTRIBUTION AND HABITAT: The northern Moluccan islands of Morotai, Halmaheira, Ternate and Batjan, and Obi island in the central Moluccas.   Inhabits dense montane forest.

FEEDING AND GENERAL HABITS: No information.

NESTING: No information.

VOICE: Soft deep muffled 'drumming' coo (Heinrich 1956).

DISPLAY: No information.

OTHER NAMES: Rufous-bellied Imperial Pigeon ; Pink-headed Fruit Pigeon.

REFERENCE

HEINRICH, G. 1956. Biologische Aufzeichnungen über Vögel von Halmahera und Batjan. *J. Orn.* **97**: 31–40.

FINSCH'S RUFOUS-BELLIED FRUIT PIGEON   *Ducula finschii*

Carpophaga Finschii Ramsay, Journ. Linn. Soc. London, Zool., 16, 1882, p. 129.

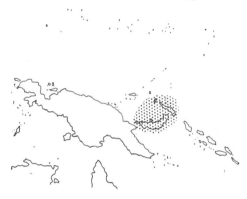

DESCRIPTION: Very similar to the last species to which it is very closely related. It differs in having the top of the head and sides of neck as well as the hind neck and nape very pale bluish grey and a broad iridescent green bar at the end of the tail so that the grey area forms a central, not a terminal band. The female has the grey on the head and tail darker and her breast is suffused with grey.

DISTRIBUTION AND HABITAT: The Bismarck Archipelago. Presumably in forest but little recorded.

FEEDING AND GENERAL HABITS: No information.

NESTING: No information.

VOICE: No information.

DISPLAY: No information.

MOUNTAIN RUFOUS-BELLIED FRUIT PIGEON   *Ducula chalconota*

Carpophaga chalconota Salvadori, Ann. Mus. Civ. Genova, 6, 1874, p. 87.

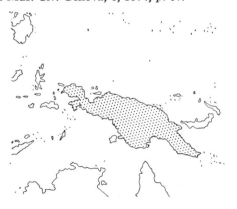

DESCRIPTION: Very similar to the Rufous-bellied Fruit Pigeon but larger and differing a little in colour pattern also. Head and neck medium to darkish blue-grey. Throat and median line of foreneck light pinkish brown. Front of breast dark pinkish-brown shading to deep chestnut on belly and flanks and then to pale chestnut on the under tail coverts. Upperparts iridescent bronze-green or emerald green with, in some lights, a coppery-red tinge on mantle, back and rump. Outer secondaries blackish green, primaries bluish black. Tail bluish black with dark grey terminal band. Underside of tail dark and light grey. Underwing coverts and axillaries chestnut. Female as male but usually shows little or no coppery red tinge on the green upperparts which, in most lights, look emerald green or blue-green. Irides and eyelids red or dark red. Orbital skin grey. Bill blackish, dark red at base. Legs and feet purplish red. Juvenile like adult but less brilliant.

The above description is of the form, *D. chalconota smaragdina*, which is widely distributed in New Guinea. The nominate race, *D. c. chalconota*, which is found in the Arfak Mountains, is slightly smaller and shows, in most lights, a considerable amount of reddish purple or coppery red on the mantle, back and rump.

DISTRIBUTION AND HABIT: The mountains of New Guinea. Inhabits forest at high altitudes.

FEEDING AND GENERAL HABITS: No information.

NESTING: No information.

VOICE: No information.

DISPLAY: No information.

OTHER NAMES: Shining Fruit Pigeon; Grey-hooded Fruit Pigeon.

ISLAND IMPERIAL PIGEON   *Ducula pistrinaria*

Ducula pistrinaria Bonaparte, Consp. Av., 2, 1855, p. 34.

DESCRIPTION: About the size of a Wood Pigeon but rather more heavily built with relatively large head and sloping forehead as in most Imperial Pigeons. Nostrils markedly rounded. Top of head and neck pale bluish grey with creamy white band at base of bill and ring of same colour round eyes. Throat and face vinous pink shading to greyish pink on breast and then to pale silvery grey on flanks and tibial feathers. Mantle, back, rump, wing coverts and inner secondaries a dull iridescent bronze-green or green, washed and clouded with silver grey. Primaries and outer secondaries blackish with strong silver grey wash. Upper tail coverts iridescent green, darker and brighter than rump. Tail feathers dark blackish green sometimes glossed purplish or blue. Under tail coverts dark chestnut. Underwing silver grey. Irides dark red, red, reddish brown or dark brown, eyelids red. Bill greyish blue, cere red. Legs and feet purplish red or dark red.

The sexes are alike. The juvenile is duller and slightly paler and has narrow buff fringes to the wing feathers and those of the underparts.

The above description is of the nominate form *D. p. pistrinaria* from the Solomon Islands of Feni and Nissan and the Lihir Islands. *D. pistrinaria vanwyckii* from the Bismarck Archipelago has the face tinged with silver grey and the breast and underparts silver grey only slightly tinged with vinous pink. Its upperparts are slightly darker and more iridescent. *D. p. rhodinolaema* from the Admiralty Islands, New Hanover, Rook Island, Manam, Karkar and islands in Astrolabe Bay is very slightly larger in size. Its face and throat are pink but it is otherwise like *vanwyckii* or even slightly brighter above. *D. p. postrema* from the islands east of New Guinea closely resembles *rhodinolaema* but is slightly smaller.

DISTRIBUTION AND HABITAT: The Soloman Islands of Feni and Nissan, the Lihir Islands; Deboyne Island, Amphlett Group, Woodlark, Egum, Alcester, Bramble Haven and Misima islands off eastern New Guinea; the small off-coastal islands in Astrolabe Bay; New Britain, New Ireland, Duke of York Group, Credner Islands and Nusa Island in the Bismarck Archipelago; the Admiralty Islands, New Hanover, Rook Island, Manam and Karkar Island. Inhabits small islands and coastal forest on larger islands.

FEEDING AND GENERAL HABITS: In the Solomons, Cain & Galbraith (1956) found it common in the canopy of coastal forest, especially in large isolated fruiting trees. Known to feed on fruit taken from the branches.

NESTING: No information.

VOICE: Cain and Galbraith describe one call as a 'high "Ahu-ahu-ahu-ahu-ahu", falling in pitch and volume'.

DISPLAY: No information.

OTHER NAMES: Grey Pigeon; Grey Imperial Pigeon.

REFERENCE

CAIN, A. G. & GALBRAITH, I. C. J. 1956. Field Notes on Birds of the eastern Solomon Islands. *Ibis* **98**: 100–134.

PINK-HEADED IMPERIAL PIGEON   *Ducula rosacea*

Columba rosacea Temminck, pl. col., livr., 98, 1835, pl. 578.

DESCRIPTION: Very similar to the previous species, *D. pistrinaria*, together with which, *D. whartoni* and *D. pickeringi*, it forms a superspecies. Head, including extreme upperpart of throat but not lower throat, pale mauve-pink or salmon pink with a mauve tinge. Whitish ring round eye and white band at base of bill less prominent than in *D. pistrinaria*. Most of throat and neck pale grey. Upper breast pinkish grey shading to pale mauve pink on lower breast and belly. Upperparts a not very bright iridescent bronze green and bluish green washed with silver grey. Primaries blackish but strongly washed silver grey when new. Tail blackish green. Under tail coverts chestnut. Irides dark brown, sometimes red or orange; eyelids scarlet. Bill blue grey, slate grey or blue with red or purple cere. Legs and feet crimson, purple or reddish purple.

Sexes alike. Juvenile similar to that of previous species *D. pistrinaria*. The above description is of the nominate form *D. r. rosacea*. *D. rosacea zamydra* from the islands of Arends and Solombo Besar in the Java Sea is said to be more brightly iridescent above. I have not seen specimens of this form.

DISTRIBUTION AND HABITAT: Duizend Islands, Satonda Island, Tukang Besi Islands, islands in Flores Sea, the entire chain of Lesser Sunda Islands from Flores to Babar; Tenimber Islands, Kei Islands, Sudest Islands, Arends Island and Solombo Besar Island. Straggler on Celebes. Inhabits only small islands with forest or, at least, fruit-bearing trees.

FEEDING AND GENERAL HABITS: No information.

NESTING: No information.

VOICE: Hoogerwerf (1967) records 'booming notes'.

DISPLAY: No information.

OTHER NAME: Island Imperial Pigeon.

REFERENCE

HOOGERWERF, A. 1966. Notes on the island of Bawean (Java Sea). *Nat. Hist. Bull. Siam. Soc.* **22**: 23.

CHRISTMAS ISLAND IMPERIAL PIGEON

Ducula whartoni

Carpophaga whartoni Sharpe, Proc. Zool. Soc. London, 1887, p. 515, pl. 43.

DESCRIPTION: Rather larger than a Wood Pigeon and heavier built with typical *Ducula* proportions. Legs almost completely feathered. Body feathering with a rather coarse, hairy texture. Small area immediately above base of bill greyish white, shading to medium or dark grey on forehead. Rest of head and neck dark blackish grey with slight green and bronzy-purple iridescence on hind neck. Breast and underparts dark, dull greyish purple. Under tail coverts dark chestnut. Mantle, back, wings and tail greenish black with a rather dull and 'oily looking' green, blue-green and bronzy purple iridescence. Irides bright yellow. Bill black or greyish black. Feet red or purplish red. Sexes alike. Juvenile duller, browner below with faint rufous fringes to feathers and buff tips to feathers along edge of wing.

DISTRIBUTION AND HABITAT: Christmas Island, in the Indian Ocean. Mainly inhabits the inland plateau.

FEEDING AND GENERAL HABITS: Known to feed on fruits, buds and young leaves taken from the branches. Among the fruits those of *Eugenia* have been certainly and those of *Sideroxylon* probably identified (Lister, 1888). Usually found high up in large forest trees. Feeds intensively just before dusk. Was (and still is) tame in spite of being shot and snared extensively.

NESTING: Usual pigeon nest high in tree. Said to lay two eggs to a clutch (Andrews, 1900) but the few records of eggs actually collected suggest that one is the normal clutch as in other imperial pigeons. Breeding season prolonged. Eggs or dependent young have been taken in January, April and August; juveniles still with grey feet seen in November and a pair seen building in December (Andrews, 1900).

VOICE: Lister (1888) records 'a long croo-croo-croo, rather low' and 'a deep sound, like the distant lowing of cattle, do-o-o-o-o-o, and sometimes dooooo – too-dooo – too – doo – too – doo'. Doubtless these are the same as the calls Andrews (1900) refers to as 'the ordinary cooing note' and 'a deep booming cry'.

DISPLAY: No information.

OTHER NAMES: Black Imperial Pigeon; Dusky Imperial Pigeon.

REFERENCES

ANDREWS, C. W. 1900. *A Monograph of Christmas Island* (*Indian Ocean*), pp. 38 published by British Museum (Natural History), London.
CHASEN, F. N. 1933. Notes on the Birds of Christmas Island. *Bull. Raffles Mus.*, No. 8, 58–61.
LISTER, J. J. 1888. On the Natural History of Christmas Island in the Indian Ocean. *Proc. Zool. Soc.* 1888: 512–564.

GREY IMPERIAL PIGEON · *Ducula pickeringii*

Carpophaga pickeringii Cassin, Proc. Acad. Nat. Sci. Philad. 7, 1854, p. 228.

DESCRIPTION: Very similar to previous species, *D. rosacea*, but slightly smaller and duller. Head light mauve pink or greyish pink with narrow creamy-white ring round eye and white band at base of bill. Neck, breast and underparts pale pinkish grey, usually pinkest on the breast and throat and greyest on the hind neck. Mantle, back, rump and wings greenish grey and/or purplish grey with slight iridescence; the new feathers being most green and the worn old ones more pinkish mauve. Tail blackish green, old feathers fading to dull grey. Under tail coverts greyish pink with faint rufous tinge. Irides red, purplish red or brownish red; eyelids purplish, orbital skin grey. Legs and feet purplish or purplish red. Bill bluish grey, darker grey at base.

The sexes are alike but females tend to be slightly less pink on head and breast.   The juvenile is similar to the adult but with faint pale rufous fringes to the feathers of the underparts.

The above description is of the nominate form *D. p. pickeringi*.   *D. pickeringi palmasensis* from Palmas Island in the Celebes Sea is said to be paler and less pinkish on the underparts;   *D. p. langhornei* from the east and west Bolod Islands and Loran Island, in the Philippines is said to be paler in colour and with a more conspicuous white ring round the eye.

DISTRIBUTION AND HABITAT: Small islands off the north and north-east coast of Borneo, islands in the Sula Sea, Sulu Archipelago, Talaut Islands, east and west Bolod Islands, Loran Island and Palmas Island.   Inhabits only small wooded islands.

FEEDING AND GENERAL HABITS: Has been recorded feeding on young leaves of trees (Hachisuka, 1932) but probably takes fruits when available.

NESTING: No information.

VOICE: No information.

DISPLAY: No information.

OTHER NAMES: Pickering's Imperial Pigeon; Grey Island Pigeon.

REFERENCE

HACHISUKA, M.   1932.   *The Birds of the Philippine Islands*.   1–2: 197.

PEALE'S PIGEON   *Ducula latrans*

Carpophaga latrans Peale, U.S. Expl. Exped., 8, 1848, p. 200.

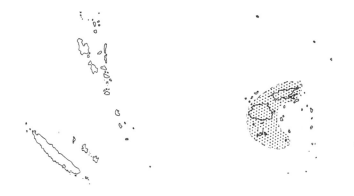

DESCRIPTION: About size of Wood Pigeon but with rather shorter wings and longer tail.   Throat pale pinkish grey and pinkish buff.   Head and neck light grey, strongly tinged with mauvish pink on nape shading into darker grey on hind neck, mantle, back and rump and dark brownish grey on wings. Primaries greyish black with silvery bloom on the outer webs.   Upper tail coverts and tail dark brownish rufous, inner webs of outer tail feathers brighter rufous; underside of tail light dull rufous.   Breast deep greyish pink or greyish mauve shading to dark pinkish buff on belly and light buff, slightly intermixed with grey on ventral regions.   Underwing chestnut.   Irides crimson red.   Bill black.   Legs and feet dark red.   Sexes nearly alike but female usually has less pronounced pink tinge on nape and underparts.   Juvenile very like adult but duller, buffish drab where adult is pinkish and with narrow, faint rufous-buff fringes to most feathers.

DISTRIBUTION AND HABITAT: The Fiji Islands: Vanua Levu, Viti Levu, Ovalau, Kandavu and Matuku.   Inhabits both lowland and mountain forest.   Recently, on Viti Levu, R. Morris (in litt.), found it only behind Suva and in the Rewa valley near Nandurululu. In both places it was in dense jungle of tall trees with a thick overhead canopy broken only in a few places and with little undergrowth. It was not common and usually seen singly.

FEEDING AND GENERAL HABITS: Known to feed on fruit taken from the branches.

NESTING: No information.

VOICE: The only call Morris heard was 'A single deep harsh bark'. A 'booming bark' described by another observer, probably refers to the same call.

DISPLAY: No information.

OTHER NAMES: Barking Pigeon; Fijian Imperial Pigeon.

REFERENCE

MORRIS, R. 1963. In litt.

CHESTNUT-BELLIED PIGEON
Ducula brenchleyi

Carpophaga Brenchleyi G. R. Gray, Ann. & Mag. Nat. Hist. (4) 5, 1870, p. 328.

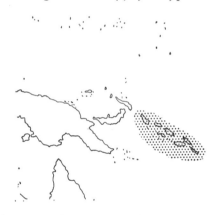

DESCRIPTION: Similar size and proportions to previous species, *D. latrans*, to which it is closely allied. Head silver grey, washed with pinkish rufous on throat and face, shading to dark blue grey on hind neck and blackish grey with a pronounced silvery bloom on back, rump, wings, and central tail feathers. Outer tail feathers dark chestnut with some black on tips and outer webs. Under wing coverts and underside of tail chestnut. Upper breast dark purplish pink shading to dark chestnut, with a slight purplish tint, on rest of underparts. Irides dark red. Bill blackish. Legs and feet dark red. The sexes are alike. Juvenile very like adult but lighter and duller with feathers of purplish areas of breast greyish with buffish rufous tips and centres and ill defined rufous bars, throat buffish.

DISTRIBUTION AND HABITAT: The Solomon Islands. Inhabits forest, especially mountain forest but, at least on San Cristoval, Ulawa, Ugi and the Three Sisters Islands, it is also common in coastal areas and often seen in isolated trees in fairly open country (Galbraith & Galbraith, 1962).

FEEDING AND GENERAL HABITS: Known to take fruit from the branches. Often feeds in same trees as *Ducula pistrinaria*.

NESTING: No information.

VOICE: No information.

DISPLAY: No information.

REFERENCES

GALBRAITH, I. C. J. & E. H. 1962. Land Birds of Guadalcanal and the San Cristoval Group, Eastern Solomon Islands. *Bull. Brit. Mus. (Nat. Hist.), Zool.* **9**: 1–86 (27).

BAKER'S PIGEON   *Ducula bakeri*

Muscadivora bakeri Kinnear, Bull. Brit. Orn. Cl., 48, 1928. p. 56.

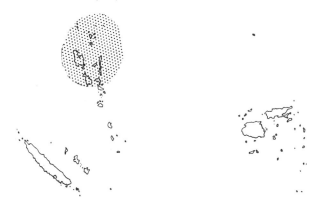

DESCRIPTION: About size of last species (Wood Pigeon size) but with shorter and more rounded wings. Feathers on neck and breast, and to a slight extent elsewhere, long and loose in texture. Often some bifurcated feathers on breast. Head dark bluish grey, paler on forehead and throat. Neck, including hind neck, and breast, a very dark reddish purple, almost blackish purple shading to dark purplish chestnut on lower breast and belly. Under tail coverts a bright and very much lighter chestnut. Mantle, back, wings and tail slaty black with a slight silvery bloom. Underwing predominantly chestnut. Sexes alike. Juvenile very like adult but duller with grey of head suffused brown and narrow rufous fringes to feathers of back and wings.

DISTRIBUTION AND HABITAT: The larger islands of the northern New Hebrides (Santo, Pentecost, Ambryn, Aurora) and Banks Islands (Vanua Lava, Gaua, Bligh). Inhabits mountain forest. Not known if it also occurs at low altitudes.

FEEDING AND GENERAL HABITS: No information.

NESTING: No information.

VOICE: Mayr (1945) describes a 'characteristic single-noted ascending call'.

DISPLAY: No information.

REFERENCE

MAYR, E. 1945. *Birds of the South-west Pacific*, p. 181, published by Macmillan Co., New York.

NEW CALEDONIAN PIGEON   *Ducula goliath*

Carpophaga (Phaenorhina) goliath G. R. Gray, Proc. Zool. Soc. London, 1859, p. 165, pl. 155.

DESCRIPTION: A big, large-tailed pigeon at least one and a half times the size of a Wood Pigeon. General colour dark slate grey with a slight silvery sheen on neck, breast and wings. Feathers on neck and breast long and bifurcated. Basal half of primaries silver grey, forming a large pale patch when the wing is spread. Belly chestnut shading to rufous cream on ventral regions and under tail coverts. Tail dark slate at base and tip with ill-defined dark chestnut central area. Underside of tail light chestnut with grey terminal band. Dull purple patch on inner wing coverts. Sexes alike. Irides orange and red. Feet red. Bill red with dull horn-coloured tip. Juvenile duller, and with rusty fringes to most wing coverts.

DISTRIBUTION AND HABITAT: New Caledonia and the Isle of Pines. Inhabits mountain forest.

FEEDING AND GENERAL HABITS: Little recorded, and that nearly a century ago by Layard. Feeds on fruits and berries and also the burning-hot pods of the introduced capsicum. Intensely persecuted by local sportsmen even at that early date.

NESTING: Nothing recorded.   Layard found that birds killed in September, October and November were in breeding condition.

VOICE: The Layards (1882) describe a 'deep booming note like the bellowing of a bull, which may be heard at a great distance'.

DISPLAY: No information.

OTHER NAMES: Goliath Pigeon; Giant Imperial Pigeon.

REFERENCE

LAYARD, E. L. & E. L. C. 1882. Notes on the Avifauna of New Caledonia. *Ibis* **4**: Fourth series, 493–546.

PINON IMPERIAL PIGEON   *Ducula pinon*

Columba pinon Quoy and Gaimard. Voy. de la 'Uranie' Zool., 1824, p. 118, Atalas, pl. 28.

DESCRIPTION: Rather larger than a Wood Pigeon and more heavily built with large head with sloping forehead and rather long, large bill; extensive area of bare orbital skin. Band of creamy white at base of bill and a narrow but conspicuous white ring bordering the orbital skin. Forehead and crown pale grey. Throat and face pale mauve pink or greyish pink shading to a rather darker shade of the same colour on sides of neck, hind neck and upper mantle. Lower mantle, back and rump light bluish or silvery grey. Upper tail coverts and wings a rather darker, more slaty grey with, in new feathers, a silvery sheen. Black and black tipped feathers on scapulars form a broad black 'V' on the back. Tail dark slate grey with a narrow white or greyish white central band. Breast a slightly darker mauve pink than sides of neck, shading into very dark reddish purple and purplish chestnut on lower breast and belly and chestnut on the under tail coverts. Irides blood red or crimson usually with a paler red or pink inner ring. Orbital skin blood red, crimson or purplish red. Bill dark grey or greyish olive with pale grey tip. Legs and feet purplish red, dark pink or dull red. Sexes alike. The juvenile is like the adult but somewhat paler and duller.

The above description is of nominate *D. p. pinon* from the Western Papuan islands of Misol, Salawati, Batanta and Waigeu, the Aru Islands; the Vogelkop peninsula of western New Guinea and southern New Guinea from the Mimika River to Hall Sound. *D. pinon jobiensis* from Japen (Jobi) Island, Manam and Karkar islands and northern New Guinea from the Memberano River to Huon Gulf has the pink and grey on head, breast, neck, mantle, back and rump paler and the wing coverts and upper tail coverts black, each feather fringed with silver grey giving a beautiful scaled or laced effect. Its irides are sometimes orange but usually as in *D. p. pinon*. Where the ranges of the above forms meet an intermediate form, which has been named *D. pinon rubiensis* occurs. It has the wing coverts patterned as in *jobiensis* but much less clearly and sharply, the individual feathers being slate rather than black and their fringes a less silvery grey. *D. pinon salvadorii* from Ferguson and Goodenough Islands in the D'Entrecasteaux Archipelago and Misima, Tagula and Rossel islands in the Louisade Archipelago differs from nominate *pinon* in having the entire head a very pale delicate pink, only slightly tinged with mauve, shading to a slightly darker tone of the same colour on the mantle and upper back which are entirely pink except for the black scapulars. The pink on the breast is slightly more greyish (but much brighter and paler than in other forms), and fairly abruptly demarcated from the purplish chestnut of the lower breast and belly. The upper tail coverts and tail are slaty black, except for the white tail bar.

DISTRIBUTION AND HABITAT: New Guinea and adjacent islands and archipelagoes. Inhabits lowland forest and the denser parts of savanna woodland.

FEEDING AND GENERAL HABITS: Known to feed on fruits and berries taken from the branches. Frequently perches on high bare trees. Sometimes (? when breeding) singly or in pairs at other times in small scattered flocks (Rand, 1942) (Tubb, 1945), Tubb records seeing mixed flocks of this species, *Ducula zooeae* and *D. spilorrhoa*.

NESTING: Rand (1942) found a nest, of usual pigeon type with one white egg, sixty feet high on a flat branch of a tall tree. He collected birds in breeding condition in May, July, September, October and December.

VOICE: Capt. C. H. B. Grant (in Ogilvie-Grant, 1915) records a cooing call 'very similar to that of the Common European Wood-pigeon'.

DISPLAY: No information.

OTHER NAMES: Pinon Fruit Pigeon; Bare-eyed Imperial Pigeon.

REFERENCES

OGILVIE-GRANT, W. R. 1915. On Birds collected in Dutch New Guinea. *Ibis*, Jubilee Supplement: 303–304.
RAND, A. L. 1942. Results of the Archbold Expeditions No. 41. *Bull. Amer. Mus. Nat. Hist.* Vol. 79 Art. 3: 197–288 (303–304).
TUBB, J. A. 1945. Field Notes on some New Guinea Birds. *Emu* 44: 249–273.

BLACK IMPERIAL PIGEON　　　　　　　　　　　　　　　*Ducula melanochroa*

Carphoga melanochroa Sclater, Proc. Zool. Soc. London, 1878, p. 672, pl. 42.

DESCRIPTION: Slightly larger than a Wood Pigeon and usual *Ducula* build. Bill much smaller than in previous species, to which it is probably closely related, and with no bare orbital patch. General colour slaty black with a powdery bluish silver 'bloom'. Narrow silver edgings to the wing coverts form a delicate scaled pattern on the closed wing. Ventral area and under tail coverts predominantly dark chestnut and a hint of same colour on underwing coverts. Underside of tail silver grey. Irides bright red or dark red. Bill greyish blue with black tip. Legs and feet dark purplish red. Sexes alike. I have not seen a juvenile but the juvenile plumage is said (Hartert, 1925) to be similar to that of the adult but with lighter chestnut under tail coverts.

DISTRIBUTION AND HABITAT: The Bismarck Archipelago; New Britain, New Ireland, Duke of York Group. Presumably in forest but I can find no definite information. In New Britain (? and elsewhere) said not to occur below 1,500 feet (Hartert, 1926).

FEEDING AND GENERAL HABITS: Known to eat wild figs.

NESTING: No information.

VOICE: No information.

DISPLAY: No information.

OTHER NAMES: Silver-laced Imperial Pigeon.

REFERENCES

HARTERT, E. 1925. A Collection of Birds from New Ireland (New Mecklenburg). *Nov. Zool.* 32: 115–136.
—— 1926. On the Birds of the District of Talasea in New Britain. *Nov. Zool.* 33: 122–145.

BLACK-COLLARED FRUIT PIGEON　　　　　　　　　　　　*Ducula mullerii*

Columba mullerii Temminck, pl. col. livr., 96, 1835, p. 566.

DESCRIPTION: About the size of a Wood Pigeon but proportionately more compact, broader across the shoulders and with tighter feathering. First primary attenuated. Top of head dull mauve-pink or greyish pink. Throat, head below eye and a narrow line dividing the pinkish cap from the black neck band silver grey.   A broad black collar completely encircles the neck.   Upper part of mantle and sides of upper breast dark shining wine-red; remainder of underparts dark mauve-pink.   Except on the median line of the neck the black collar is divided from the pink and wine-red areas by another (but incomplete) equally broad collar of silver-grey.   Rest of upperparts, including wings, dark slate grey; nearly black

on the tail which is crossed by a broad silver-grey central band.   Under tail coverts dark reddish chestnut. Irides light reddish brown or dark brown.   Feet and legs crimson or purplish red.   The bill and orbital skin are stated by some collectors to be 'raw sienna' by others 'plumbeous'.   From examination of museum skins it looks as if the bill is certainly greyish or dark and the orbital skin some shade of yellow, orange, or red in life.   Sexes alike except that the female's pink parts tend to be slightly suffused with brown.   I have not been able to examine, or find a description of, the juvenile.

DISTRIBUTION AND HABITAT: New Guinea and the Aru Islands.   Inhabits low-lying wooded areas, especially tree-fringed rivers and lakes.

FEEDING AND GENERAL HABITS: Known to feed on fruits gathered in the branches, like other imperial pigeons.   Flight, except when displaying, swift and direct.

NESTING: The many nests found by Rand were all on flat, leafy branches of trees adjacent to lakes or rivers.   Nest of usual pigeon type.   One egg.

VOICE: Unrecorded.

DISPLAY: Display flight (described by Rand) 'an upward glide on stiff downward extended wings; a downward swoop following a raising of its wings'.

OTHER NAMES: Muller's Fruit Pigeon; Black-collared Imperial Pigeon; Pink-capped Imperial Pigeon.

REFERENCE
RAND, A. L. 1942.   Results of the Archbold Expeditions No. 42.   *Bull. Amer. Mus. Nat. Hist.* **79**: Art. 4: 289-366.

BANDED IMPERIAL PIGEON

Ducula zoeae

Columba Zoeae Lesson, Dict. Sci. Nat. Ed. Levrault, 40, 1826, p. 314.

DESCRIPTION: About size of Wood Pigeon.   Heavy build, rather hard, 'close' plumage (for a pigeon). First primary somewhat attenuated.   Head light bluish grey shading to greyish white on throat.   Neck, breast and upper part of mantle a delicate mauve pink with a silvery tinge. A very narrow line of iridescent green (green tips to pink feathers) divides the pink of the upper mantle from the dark reddish purple or purplish chestnut of the rest of the mantle, scapulars and wing coverts. Lower back, rump, tail and secondaries iridescent green, bronze-green or blue-green, least brilliant on outer secondaries.

Inner webs of outer tail feathers and primaries blackish green or blackish. Underside of tail chestnut. Underwing black. Lower breast, belly and sides silver grey, sharply divided from the pink breast by a narrow black band. Tibial feathers, ventral region and under tail coverts spotted purplish chestnut and dull white (white tips to chestnut feathers). Irides white, buff or greyish white, often (or usually)? with a ragged or ill-defined black outer ring; reddish brown irides have twice been recorded. Orbital skin dark red or purplish red, eye-rim black. Bill dark grey or black. Legs and feet dark red or purplish red. Sexes alike. I have not seen a juvenile of this species.

DISTRIBUTION AND HABITAT: New Guinea and the Salawati, Japen (Jobi), Fergusson, St. Aignan and Aru Islands. Inhabits lowland forest and hill forest up to about 1,250 metres.

FEEDING AND GENERAL HABITS: Beyond statements to the effect that it is commonly found perching in the tops of high trees and apparently prefers to perch among foliage to perching on a bare bough I can find nothing recorded.

NESTING: No information.

VOICE: No information.

DISPLAY: No information.

OTHER NAMES: Zoe's Fruit Pigeon; Banded Fruit Pigeon; Bar-breasted Fruit Pigeon.

MOUNTAIN IMPERIAL PIGEON   *Ducula badia*

Columba badia Raffles, Trans. Linn. Soc. London, 13, pt. 2, 1822, p. 317.

DESCRIPTION: About the size of a Wood Pigeon or slightly larger. Head, neck and underparts vinous pink, brightest on the hind neck and more or less suffused with silvery grey elsewhere. Crown and sides of face sometimes entirely pale grey. Chin and throat white. Mantle, lesser and median wing coverts dark reddish purple. Back, rump, greater wing coverts dark greyish-brown with purple edgings.

The purple fades to chestnut in worn plumage. Primaries and secondaries blackish brown. Tail blackish brown with broad light grey terminal band. Underside of tail medium grey with silver grey terminal band. Ventral regions and under tail coverts creamy buff. Sexes alike. Irides white or greyish-white.

Orbital skin crimson or dark red. Feet dark pink or maroon red with pale claws. Bill dark pink or red with white or pale yellowish tip. Juvenile duller and rusty brown in most areas where adult is purple. The above description is of the nominate race, *D. b. badia*, which inhabits southern Tenasserim, the Malay Peninsula, Sumatra, Borneo and nearby islands. The form inhabiting Burma, Siam and Indo-China, *D. badia griseicapilla*, differs in having less extensive purple areas on the upperparts, a grey tinge on the rump, a pale grey crown and face which contrasts strongly with the pink hind neck, pale creamy grey underparts, pale cream under tail coverts and a greyish or pale fawn bill tip. The form found in the Himalayan foothills of Nepal, Sikkim and Bhutan, *D. badia insignis*, is like *griseicapilla* but has an entirely pink head. The form from south-western India, *D. b. cupreus*, is like *insignis* but has no purple on the upperparts, the wings and mantle being dark brown.

DISTRIBUTION AND HABITAT: South-western India, northern India from western Nepal eastwards, Burma, Indo-China, Malaya, Borneo, Sumatra and western Java.

Inhabits forested hills and mountain ranges, in some areas regularly visiting adjacent low-lying areas.

FEEDING AND GENERAL HABITS: Feeds on fruits, berries, buds and young leaves. Also takes salt-impregnated earth. Commonly seen in pairs or small parties. Flies often at considerable height above the forest canopy with leisurely deliberate wing beats.

NESTING: Usual pigeon nest in tree or shrub, often at no great height. One white egg. Breeding season apparently prolonged and varying locally.

VOICE: What is probably the advertising call is described by different writers as a clicking or clucking sound followed by two booming coos. These latter strike some people as sad, others as melodious in tone. I heard a captive *D. b. cupreus* at a zoo give a very deep but not gruff 'oo-oo-oo (ōō)'; the middle note somewhat upward-inflected, the bracketed final 'oo' much less loud.

DISPLAYS: Salim Ali (1953) describes a display flight in which the bird launches itself into the air from a high tree and flies in a series of wave crests and nose-diving.

OTHER NAMES: Hodgson's Imperial Pigeon; Jerdon's Imperial Pigeon; Bronze-backed Imperial Pigeon; Grey-headed Imperial Pigeon; Band-tailed Imperial Pigeon.

REFERENCES

ALI, S. 1953. *The Birds of Travancore and Cochin.* Oxford.
JERDON, T. C. 1862. *The Birds of India* **2**: 457–459. Calcutta.
ROBINSON, H. C. & CHASEN, F. N. 1928. *The Birds of the Malay Peninsula* **2**: 16–18. London.
SMYTHIES, B. E. 1954. *The Birds of Burma.* London.

DARK-BACKED IMPERIAL PIGEON   *Ducula lacernulata*

Columba lacernulata Temminck, pl. col. livr., 28, 1823, pl. 164.

DESCRIPTION: Very similar to the previous species, *D. badia*, with which it forms a superspecies. Forehead, face and crown light bluish grey. Throat, neck and breast mauve pink with a silvery grey wash, shading to buffy grey on the belly. Upperparts dark brownish grey with a subdued but pervasive bronzy green sheen which is most intense on the wings and almost or quite absent on the rump and upper tail coverts which are a more bluish grey. The mauve pink of the hind neck shades into the brownish grey of the mantle. Tail feathers greyish black with broad grey terminal band. Underside of tail feathers dark grey with silver-grey terminal band. Under tail coverts chestnut. Irides dark red or dark reddish brown. Legs and feet red, purplish red or dark pink. Bill blackish, dark grey or bluish grey. I have not seen a juvenile, it is almost certainly similar to that of the previous species *D. badia*.

The above description is of nominate *D. l. lacernulata* from western and central Java. *D. lacernulata williami* from eastern Java and Bali has no grey on its head which is entirely of a less greyish pink than neck and underparts. Except in head colour it is like the nominate form. *D. lacernulata sasakensis* from Lombok and Flores has the grey on the head restricted to forehead and crown, the sides of the face and ear coverts being pink. Its breast is a slightly paler and brighter pink than in the nominate form shading to a deep brownish pink on the lower belly. The under tail coverts are also brownish pink, not chestnut. Its mantle and wings are darker than in the nominate form being greenish black with a more pronounced green lustre.

DISTRIBUTION AND HABITAT: Java, Bali, Lombok and Flores. Inhabits wooded mountains and hilly country.

FEEDING AND GENERAL HABITS: No information.

NESTING: No information.

VOICE: No information.

DISPLAY: No information.

OTHER NAMES: Javanese Imperial Pigeon; Javanese Mountain Pigeon; Black-backed Imperial Pigeon.

TIMOR IMPERIAL PIGEON   *Ducula cineracea*

Columba cineracea Temminck, pl. col. livr., 95, 1835, pl. 563.

DESCRIPTION: Very similar to the previous species, *D. lacernulata*. It is probably a geographical representative of *D. lacernulata* and *D. badia* and closely allied to them although it differs in its duller colouring and unmarked tail. Head and neck dull bluish grey shading to a rather darker slaty grey on upperparts. The wings and tail show in some lights a very faint greenish gloss on new feathers. Primaries with narrow buff fringes to outer webs. Median line of throat and breast dull mauve pink shading to buff on the belly and under tail coverts. Irides dark, bill black. Feet purplish black. Sexes alike. I have not seen a specimen in entire juvenile plumage. One which has moulted into adult dress except for parts of wings and tail has its juvenile primaries and primary coverts with broad reddish buff fringes, the remaining juvenile wing coverts are a browner grey than the adult's and the tail feathers have broad but ill-defined rufous tips.

The above description is of nominate *D. c. cineracea* from Timor. *D. cineracea schistacea* from Wetar Island was described by Mayr (1944) as having the underparts strongly washed with grey.

DISTRIBUTION AND HABITAT: Timor and Wetar Islands. Inhabits mountain forest.

FEEDING AND GENERAL HABITS: I can find nothing recorded.

NESTING: No information.

VOICE: No information.

DISPLAY: No information.

OTHER NAMES: Ashy Imperial Pigeon.

REFERENCE
MAYR, E. 1944. The Birds of Timor and Sumba. *Bull. Amer. Mus. Nat. Hist.* **83**: Art. 2.

PIED IMPERIAL PIGEON   *Ducula bicolor*

Columba bicolor Scopoli, Del/Flor. et Faun. Insubr., fasc. 2, 1786, p. 94.

DESCRIPTION: Rather larger than a Wood Pigeon with proportionately larger head and shorter tail. Pure white more or less suffused with yellow. Often stained, especially about the head, with fruit juices. Primaries, primary coverts, outer secondaries, and much of tail black with a slight silvery grey lustre. Irides dark brown. Bill grey or bluish cream with darker tip. Legs and feet greyish blue.

Juvenile has the white parts suffused with grey and broad yellow-buff edges to most feathers. The above description is of nominate *D. b. bicolor*, the Moluccan form *D. b. melanura* always has some black on the under tail coverts and more extensive black markings on the tail.

DISTRIBUTION AND HABITAT: From the Andamans and Nicobars eastwards to the Philippines, Moluccas and islands west of New Guinea. Normally roosts and breeds only on small islands and islets but often visits the coastal regions of larger islands and archipelagoes to feed there. Inhabits woods, mangrove swamps and coconut groves.

FEEDING AND GENERAL HABITS: Known to feed on various fruits and berries including wild figs and wild nutmegs. Most – perhaps all – food taken from the branches. Usually in flocks or small parties, especially when flying over the sea to and from its feeding place. It is said to have an 'easy almost idling' flight, several wing beats being often followed by a swoop or bank. It 'lunges and plunges through the air . . . quite unlike any other wild pigeon'. (Harrison, in Smythies, 1960.)

NESTING: Many pairs usually nest in the same area but the nests are well spaced out. Usual pigeon nest in a tree, palm or shrub. One white egg. In the Andamans and Nicobars breeds from December to March.

VOICE: Baker (1913) describes a 'chuckling hu-hu-hu'. I have heard a loud, sharp 'check!', suggestive of the cry of some large passerine bird, uttered by a captive bird when hopping aggressively towards another pigeon and a slightly less loud and strident 'kuck' when defending itself from attack.

DISPLAY: No information.

OTHER NAMES: Nutmeg Pigeon; White Fruit Pigeon; White Imperial Pigeon.

REFERENCES

BAKER, E. C. S. 1913. *Indian Pigeons and Doves*. London.
SMYTHIES, B. E. 1960. *The Birds of Borneo*. London.

CELEBES PIED IMPERIAL PIGEON   *Ducula luctuosa*

Columba luctuosa 'Reinw' Temminck, pl. col., livr., 42, 1825, pl. 247.

DESCRIPTION: As *bicolor*, but dark wing feathers are silver-grey edged with black, and many feathers of tibial and ventral regions are largely black, giving a smudged or spotted effect.

DISTRIBUTION AND HABITAT: Celebes, Sula Islands, Peling and Banggai Islands. In the Celebes (and probably elsewhere) inhabits low-lying areas where it is found in open country with trees, at the forest edge, and in cultivated country.

FEEDING AND GENERAL HABITS: Much as *bicolor*, but little seems to have been recorded. In the Celebes seen both in pairs and in large flocks.

NESTING: No information.

VOICE: Heinrich in Stresemann (1941) describes the voice as 'a deep and loud BOOH'. Probably has other calls.

DISPLAY: No information.

OTHER NAMES: Nutmeg Pigeon; White Fruit Pigeon.

REFERENCE
STRESEMANN, E. 1941. Die Vögel von Celebes. *Journ. f. Orn.* **89**: 1–102.

AUSTRALIAN PIED IMPERIAL PIGEON   *Ducula spilorrhoa*

Carpophaga spilorrhoa G. R. Gray, Proc. Zool. Soc. London, 1858, p. 196.

DESCRIPTION: As *bicolor* but dark parts of wings more strongly tinged with grey and with black subterminal spots or bands on the feathers of the tibial regions and under tail coverts. Some forms of this species have the head more or less tinged with pale grey, and one from south-east New Guinea, *D. spilorrhoa tarara*, has the 'white' areas silver grey. Soft parts much as *bicolor* but bill yellow with greyish base.

DISTRIBUTION AND HABITAT: New Guinea, north-eastern and eastern Australia and adjacent and intervening islands and archipelagoes. Typically roosts and breeds on small islands, flying over the sea, often long distances, to feed on larger islands and the mainland. The silver-grey form, *D. s. tarara*, is, however, habitually found inland from the coast. Inhabits woodlands, mangrove swamps, savanna country and forest edge. Locally also in gardens and cultivated areas.

FEEDING AND GENERAL HABITS: Feeds on fruits and berries, especially wild nutmegs. Commonly flies daily from small islands where it roosts and breeds over the sea to large islands or coastal areas of the mainland to feed. Warham found that those breeding on islands in the Barrier Reef of Australia flew high when leaving for the mainland feeding place but coming back flew very low, skimming over the waves.

NESTING: Usual pigeon nest in a tree or shrub. One white egg. Large numbers commonly nest on the same islet or group of islets. Has been found with eggs and young on the Barrier Reef islands in October and November and in September and January in southern New Guinea.

VOICE: Warham (1962) describes the (presumed) advertising coo as 'a low moaning "up-oooo"'. The display coo as a 'low oom-oom-oom', and a call 'like a honeyeater's' given when bird dropped to a lower perch. Campbell (1901) records both 'cooing' and 'a curious chuckling sound', the latter he thought was uttered by males only.

DISPLAY: Bowing display in which the bird 'swings its head up and down' (Warham, 1962). A display flight in which one of two flying birds shoots sharply upwards, then glides down again was recorded by Rand for the New Guinea form. A similar display flight was seen by Frith (pers. obs.) who noted that the wings were closed at the start of the downward glide.

OTHER NAMES: Torres Strait Pigeon; Nutmeg Pigeon; White Fruit Pigeon; Silver-grey Fruit Pigeon.

REFERENCES

CAMPBELL, A. J. 1901. *Nests and Eggs of Australian Birds*. Pt. 2. Sheffield.
RAND, A. L. 1942. *Bull. Amer. Mus. Nat. Hist.* **79**, Art. 4: 289–366.
WARHAM, J. 1962. Bird Islands within the Barrier Reef. *Emu* **62**: 99–111.

TOPKNOT PIGEON   *Lopholaimus antarcticus*

Columba Antarctica Shaw, Zool. New Holland, 1, 1794, p. 15, pl. 5.

DESCRIPTION: About the size of a Wood Pigeon, with rather long tail; thick laterally compressed bill, and elongated head feathers that form a peculiar double crest which is grey on the forehead and chestnut, broadly bordered with black, on crown and nape. Feathers of the neck are silver grey with darker bases. They are somewhat stiffened and elongated. Rest of plumage mainly bluish grey, darkest on the wings and palest on underparts and rump. Primaries and outer secondaries black. Tail pale grey at base then a band of black followed by a narrower band of silver grey and a broad black terminal band. Irides orange. Orbital skin pink or red. Bill pink or rose red, paler and greyish at tip, the fleshy cere at base of bill and the similar fleshy area at base of lower mandible greyish green. Feet and legs purplish red or pink. Sexes alike. Juvenile slightly paler and duller with neck feathers normally shaped.

DISTRIBUTION AND HABITAT: Eastern Australia from Cape York to north-eastern Victoria. Inhabits rain forest and adjacent ridges or eucalyptus forest. Will traverse open country in search of suitable patches of forest to feed in.

FEEDING AND GENERAL HABITS: Feeds on fruits and berries taken from the branches. Frith (1952) records fruits of wild figs, *Ficus* sp., bangalow palms, *Archontophoenix cunninghami*, *Cryptocarya* sp., corkwood, *Endiandra sieberi*, native mulberry, *Hedycarya angustifolia*, white cedar, *Melia azederach*, tulipwood, *Hemicyclia australasica*, and various unidentified shrubs as its food in the Richmond River area of New South Wales.

Nomadic, ranges widely in search of food. Commonly in small or large flocks and very large numbers may gather in suitable feeding areas. Frith found that the birds he studied roosted on taller trees on high ridges, descending into the rain forest in the gorge to feed only after the sun was well up. This behaviour very closely parallels that of the Olive Pigeon in Africa.

NESTING: Usual pigeon nest; most or all the nests found appear to have been high up in tall trees. One white egg. Gilbert (1936) implies that only the female incubates and said that the male fed the female at the nest. Confirmation of such unusual behaviour is desirable.

VOICE: Gilbert records 'a clear measured and low-toned "wir-hig-a" . . . heard as the pigeon quietly searched for food'.

DISPLAY: No information.

OTHER NAMES: Flock Fruit Pigeon; Crested Fruit Pigeon.

REFERENCES

FRITH, H. J. 1957. Food Habits of the Topknot Pigeon. *Emu* **57**: 341–345.
GILBERT, P. A. 1936. The Topknot Pigeon. *Emu* **35**: 301–312.

NEW ZEALAND PIGEON   *Hemiphaga novaeseelandiae*

Columba novaeseelandiae Gmelin, Syst. Nat., 1, pt. 2, 1789, p. 773.

DESCRIPTION: Rather larger and more heavily built and longer tailed than a Wood Pigeon, with a proportionately small head with flattish forehead. Most of head, sides and front of neck and breast iridescent green, bronze-green or golden-green. Nape, hind neck, mantle and innermost wing coverts dark reddish purple. Rest of upperparts iridescent green washed with silvery grey on outer part of wings and rump. Outer webs of the secondaries and basal areas of primaries are mainly silvery grey but bordered with green so that the grey is not very noticeable till the wing is opened. Ends of primaries dark greenish black or bluish black. Tail dull black with narrow ill-defined pale terminal bar. Underparts below breast snow white. Underwing coverts pale grey. Irides brownish red or purplish red. Eyelids pale red. Bill brownish red or purplish at base, yellowish at tip. Legs and feet dull red or purplish red. Sexes nearly alike but female often, or perhaps usually, with the purplish of the mantle area less extensive.   Both sexes show minor variations in intensity and tone of iridescence, amount of grey wash, etc., and often have upper part of throat greyish.   I have not seen a juvenile of this species. It is said the be duller than the adult, with buffish fringes to the breast feathers and buff-tinted underparts.

The above description is of nominate *H. n. novaeseelandiae* from New Zealand.   *H. n. spadicea* from Norfolk Island (now extinct) was slightly larger and duller with greyish rump.   *H. n. chathamensis* from the Chatham Islands is considerably larger, has a larger and stronger bill and the dark parts of the plumage less bright and more strongly suffused with grey.   Its wings are predominantly silver grey with greenish edges to the feathers and the lower back and rump silver grey only faintly tinged with green.

DISTRIBUTION AND HABITAT: New Zealand; North Island, South Island, Little and Great Barrier Islands, Hen and Chickens, Mayer Island, Kapita Island, and Stewart Island.   Also Chatham Islands and (formerly) Norfolk Island.   Inhabits forest; locally in gardens or cultivated country adjacent to or interspersed with patches of forest.

FEEDING AND GENERAL HABITS: Feeds on fruits, berries, buds, flowers and young leaves taken from the branches; sometimes comes to the ground to feed on low-growing plants.   Has been recorded feeding on the fruits or foliage of a great many trees and shrubs, including some introduced species (McLean, 1911; Wilkinson, 1952; Oliver, 1955).   Shows little fear of man in spite of having been much persecuted by him.

NESTING: Usual pigeon nest in tree or shrub.   One white egg.   Data for a single nest (Wilkinson, 1952) suggest an incubation period of about 28 days and fledging period of about 36 days.   If normal these periods are remarkably long even for so large a pigeon.   However, the relative lack of predators, before man became abundant in New Zealand, and the possibly rather poor quality foods available, may have favoured slow development in contrast to the situation with most other pigeon species.

VOICE: Wilkinson (1952) describes 'a low coo, sometimes drawn out into almost a wail, but generally given in short and enquiring tone', and 'a harsh, growling cry', given by an incubating bird striking at a human intruder.   Besides the above, Guthrie-Smith (in Oliver, 1955) describes a short 'du' uttered 'to express caution or alarm' (evidently the distress call), a 'moan' and a 'sibilant whistle'.

DISPLAY: In display flight flies upwards to a considerable height and then glides down with wings and tail outspread (Porter, 1933).

OTHER NAMES: Wood Pigeon; New Zealand Fruit Pigeon.

REFERENCES

McLEAN, J. C. 1911. 'Bush Birds of New Zealand.' *Emu* **11**: 1–17.
OLIVER, W. R. B. 1955. *New Zealand Birds*, Second Edition, pp. 440–444. Wellington.
PORTER, S. 1933. Notes on New Zealand Birds. *Avicult. Mag.* Fourth Series, **11**: 403–412.
WILKINSON, A. S. & A. 1952. *Kapiti Bird Sanctuary*. pp. 36–41. Masterton.

CELEBES DUSKY PIGEON *Cryptophaps poecilorrhoa*

Carpophaga poecilorrhoa Bruggemann, Abh. naturwiss. Ver. Bremen, 5, 1876, p. 84.

DESCRIPTION: About the size of a Wood Pigeon but longer bodied and with a longer tail. Head, neck and breast grey, palest on the forehead and lower breast and darkening towards the mantle. Some individuals, especially from northern Celebes, have a strong purplish tinge in the grey areas. Belly more suffused brownish, flanks dark brownish with broad rusty buff edgings to feathers, giving a mottled effect. Under tail coverts blackish with broad creamy buff edges. Mantle, back, rump, upper tail coverts and wings blackish-olive with a faint bronze-green gloss and buff edgings to some feathers when new. Underwing with a central chestnut patch, otherwise blackish. Tail dull black, tipped narrowly with buffish white. Bill bluish grey, purplish at base. Irides blood red or dark red. Legs and feet red or purplish red.

The female has the grey areas suffused with dull wine pink, some females also have brownish fringes to the breast feathers. I have not been able to examine a juvenile or find a description of one.

DISTRIBUTION AND HABITAT: Northern and south-eastern Celebes. Found in primeval mountain forest.

FEEDING AND GENERAL HABITS: Heinrich (in Stresemann, 1941) found it always singly (? breeding birds whose mates are on the nest) and noted that it had a heavy flight and little fear of man. He found that all the specimens he shot had been feeding on a hard fruit with a scaled pinecone-like outer surface. Another collector killed one that had been eating palm fruit.

NESTING: No information.

VOICE: No information.

DISPLAY: No information.

OTHER NAMES: Rusty-bellied Fruit Pigeon; Celebes Fruit Pigeon; Long-tailed Imperial Pigeon.

REFERENCE

STRESEMANN, E.   1941.   Die Vögel von Celebes.   *Journ. f. Orn.* **89** : 1–102.

MOUNTAIN PIGEONS

The Mountain Pigeons of the genus *Gymnophaps* are well named as they all inhabit forested hills or mountain slopes though they are not, of course, the only pigeons found in such places.   Little is known in any detail of their behaviour and ecology.   They have usually been considered most closely related to the genus *Columba*, some authorities having, indeed, placed them in that genus.   They agree with *Columba* species in having twelve tail-feathers and, in life, their swift flight much resembles that of some species of *Columba*.

I think, however, that they are more closely related to the fruit pigeons (*Ducula, Ptilinopus, Lopholaimus* et al.) than to any others.   Their alimentary system is very similar to that of many species of *Ptilonopus* and *Ducula* and unlike that of *Columba*.   The little that is known about their feeding habits suggests that they are primarily fruit eaters.   In colours and colour-patterns they show more resemblance to some species of *Ducula* than they do to any species of *Columba*.

On present evidence they therefore seem most likely to be an offshoot of the fruit pigeons.   They are, however, one of the many groups of pigeons about which little is known and which would prove most rewarding to anyone able to undertake a study of them either in the wild or in captivity.

The three forms *G. albertisii*, *G. mada* and *G. solomonensis* replace one another geographically and are, I think, best treated as members of a superspecies.

BARE-EYED MOUNTAIN PIGEON   *Gymnophaps albertisii*

Gymnophaps albertisii Salvadori, Ann. Mus. Civ. Genova, 6, 1874, p. 86.

DESCRIPTION: About the size of an average Feral Pigeon but with proportionately longer and narrower tail. Outermost primary, and to some extent the next also, with a 'scooped' indentation on inner web. Head and sides of neck dark grey. Upperparts dark greenish black with a slight silvery sheen. Narrow blackish feather edges form a scale-like pattern on back and wing coverts. Tail with a narrow grey terminal band. Ear coverts, throat and belly dark purplish chestnut. Breast pinkish cream. Tibial feathers and under tail coverts grey. Irides red with orange, yellow or greenish inner ring. The extensive orbital skin bright red. Bill parti-coloured, usually with pinkish tip, grey or whitish central part and red cere. Feet and legs red, purplish red or dark pink.

Females often have some grey suffusion on the breast and a broader grey edging to the chestnut throat. Juvenile duller, with dull brown breast, pale creamy rufous underparts, chestnut forehead and broad chestnut edgings to innermost secondaries.

The above description applies to the nominate race, *G. a. albertisii*, of New Guinea and nearby areas. The form found in Batjan in the Moluccas, *G. albertisii exul*, is a little larger and darker.

DISTRIBUTION AND HABITAT: New Guinea and adjacent islands; Bismarck Archipelago; New Ireland and New Britain, the island of Batjan in the Moluccas. Found in mountain forests.

FEEDING AND GENERAL HABITS: Known to feed on fruits taken from the trees. Does not appear to have been recorded feeding on the ground. Commonly seen in small flocks. Flight very fast with noisy wing-beats. Sometimes, perhaps usually, roosts at higher elevations than it feeds during the day.

NESTING: No information.

VOICE: Gyldenstolpe (1954) records 'loud booming calls' – presumably this is the advertising coo.

DISPLAY: The display flight or what, from descriptions, appears to be such, consists of a steep upward climb with swift wing-beats till the bird is some distance above the forest when it pauses, turns and plunges down in an arc on half-closed wings.

OTHER NAMES: D'Albertis' Mountain Pigeon; Bare-eyed Pigeon.

REFERENCES

GYLDENSTOLPE, N. 1954. Arkiv. för zoologi band 8, nr. 1, p. 41.
MAYR, E. & RAND, A. L. 1937. *Bull Amer. Mus. Nat. Hist.* **73**: Art. 1: 1–248 (37).
WATSON, J. D., WHEELER, W. R. & WHITBOURN, E. 1962. With the R.A.O.U. in Papua, New Guinea. *Emu* **62**: 31–50.

LONG-TAILED MOUNTAIN PIGEON   *Gymnophaps mada*

Columba mada Hartert, Bull, Brit. Orn. Cl., 8, 1899, p. 33.

DESCRIPTION: Slightly larger than the previous species with proportionately longer tail and more rounded wings; softer and thicker plumage. Crown, nape and hind neck light bluish grey shading into darker grey on mantle. Upperparts dark slaty green with a slight gloss. The feathers of mantle, back and rump have very narrow blackish subterminal borders and broader silver grey fringes. On the wing coverts the grey fringes are very narrow and soon wear off. Wing and tail quills greenish black, very narrow pale fringes to outer sides of primaries and ends of tail feathers in unworn plumage. Face, throat and upper breast creamy white to pale buffish pink, shading into a deep buffy vinous-pink on the belly. Tibial feathers creamy buff. Irides orange or red, usually with an inner circle of grey, pale brown or yellow. Orbital skin bright red. Feet and legs purplish red, purple or brownish red.

Female, as male, but orbital skin and cere a dull blackish red. Juvenile is duller than adult with dusky greyish breast and pale rufous underparts.

The above description is of the nominate form which occurs on the island of Buru. The form found on Ceram, *Gymnophaps mada stalkeri*, differs in having the face and breast a deep buffish pink shading to a darker vinous pink on the underparts, grey tibial feathers and deeper chestnut under tail coverts. Its irides differ in usually having a red inner ring and the oribital skin is purple or purplish red.

DISTRIBUTION AND HABITAT: The island of Buru and the island of Ceram. Inhabits mountain forest.

FEEDING AND GENERAL HABITS: Little recorded, probably feeds largely on berries and fruits taken from the trees. On Ceram about half a century ago Professor Stresemann found it fairly common between 5,000 and 6,000 metres, but only rarely as low as 2,000 metres. It was usually seen in small flocks.

NESTING: No information.

VOICE: No information.

DISPLAY: No information.

REFERENCE

STRESEMANN, E. 1914. Die Vögel von Seran (Ceram). *Novit. Zool.* **21**: 25–153 (49).

PALE MOUNTAIN PIGEON   *Gymnophaps solomonensis*

Gymnophaps solomonensis Mayr, Am. Mus. Novit., No. 504, 1931, p. 11.

DESCRIPTION: Similar in size and shape to the last species but wing less rounded though not so sharply pointed as that of *albertisii*. Head and neck whitish grey, nearly clear white on throat and upper breast. Lower breast and belly pale salmon pink. Ventral regions and under tail coverts pale grey. Mantle, back and wing coverts silver grey with a greenish tinge, each feather edged with black. Primaries and secondaries blackish but with a silvery green tinge on the parts exposed when wing is closed. Bill yellowish or pale brown at tip, yellow at base, tinged purplish pink around nostrils and edge of mandibles. Irides orange or reddish. Orbital skin red or purplish and less extensive than in its relatives. Feet and legs purplish.

DISTRIBUTION AND HABITAT: The Solomon Islands. Inhabits hill forest.

FEEDING AND GENERAL HABITS: Little recorded. Known to eat fruit. Commonly seen in small flocks.

NESTING: No information.

VOICE: No information.

DISPLAY: No information.

REFERENCE

CAIN, A. J. & GALBRAITH, I. C. J. 1955. Field notes on birds of the eastern Solomon Islands. *Ibis* **98**: 101–134.

INDEX OF ENGLISH NAMES

INDEX OF SCIENTIFIC NAMES

AU